CLOUD COMPUTING

CLOUD COMPUTING
Principles and Paradigms

Edited by

Rajkumar Buyya
The University of Melbourne and Manjrasoft Pty Ltd., Australia

James Broberg
The University of Melbourne, Australia

Andrzej Goscinski
Deakin University, Australia

A JOHN WILEY & SONS, INC., PUBLICATION

Library of Congress Cataloging-in-Publication Data:

Cloud computing : principles and paradigms / edited by Rajkumar Buyya, James Broberg, Andrzej Goscinski.
    p.   ; cm.
Includes bibliographical references and index.
ISBN 978-0-470-88799-8 (hardback)
1. Cloud computing.   I. Buyya, Rajkumar, 1970–   II. Broberg, James.   III. Goscinski, Andrzej.
QA76.585.C58 2011
004.67′8—dc22

                                                                        2010046367

Printed in the United States of America

10 9 8 7 6 5 4 3 2 1

CONTENTS

6   On the Management of Virtual Machines for Cloud Infrastructures   157

Ignacio M. Llorente, Rubén S. Montero, Borja Sotomayor, David Breitgand, Alessandro Maraschini, Eliezer Levy, and Benny Rochwerger

7   Enhancing Cloud Computing Environments Using a Cluster as a Service   193

Michael Brock and Andrzej Goscinski

8   Secure Distributed Data Storage in Cloud Computing   221

Yu Chen, Wei-Shinn Ku, Jun Feng, Pu Liu, and Zhou Su

PART III PLATFORM AND SOFTWARE AS A SERVICE (PaaS/IaaS)   249

9 Aneka—Integration of Private and Public Clouds   251

Christian Vecchiola, Xingchen Chu, Michael Mattess, and Rajkumar Buyya

10 CometCloud: An Autonomic Cloud Engine   275

Hyunjoo Kim and Manish Parashar

11 T-Systems' Cloud-Based Solutions for Business Applications   299

Michael Pauly

PART IV   MONITORING AND MANAGEMENT   391

PART V APPLICATIONS 457

PREFACE

Cloud computing has recently emerged as one of the buzzwords in the ICT industry. Numerous IT vendors are promising to offer computation, storage, and application hosting services and to provide coverage in several continents, offering service-level agreements (SLA)-backed performance and uptime promises for their services. While these "clouds" are the natural evolution of traditional data centers, they are distinguished by exposing resources (computation, data/storage, and applications) as standards-based Web services and following a "utility" pricing model where customers are charged based on their utilization of computational resources, storage, and transfer of data. They offer subscription-based access to infrastructure, platforms, and applications that are popularly referred to as IaaS (Infrastructure as a Service), PaaS (Platform as a Service), and SaaS (Software as a Service). While these emerging services have increased interoperability and usability and reduced the cost of computation, application hosting, and content storage and delivery by several orders of magnitude, there is significant complexity involved in ensuring that applications and services can scale as needed to achieve consistent and reliable operation under peak loads.

Currently, expert developers are required to implement cloud services. Cloud vendors, researchers, and practitioners alike are working to ensure that potential users are educated about the benefits of cloud computing and the best way to harness the full potential of the cloud. However, being a new and popular paradigm, the very definition of cloud computing depends on which computing expert is asked. So, while the realization of true utility computing appears closer than ever, its acceptance is currently restricted to cloud experts due to the perceived complexities of interacting with cloud computing providers.

This book illuminates these issues by introducing the reader with the cloud computing paradigm. The book provides case studies of numerous existing compute, storage, and application cloud services and illustrates capabilities and limitations of current providers of cloud computing services. This allows the reader to understand the mechanisms needed to harness cloud computing in their own respective endeavors. Finally, many open research problems that have arisen from the rapid uptake of cloud computing are detailed. We hope that this motivates the reader to address these in their own future research and development. We believe the book to serve as a reference for larger audience such as systems architects, practitioners, developers, new researchers, and graduate-level students. This book also comes with an associated Web site (hosted at http://www.manjrasoft.com/CloudBook/) containing pointers to advanced on-line resources.

ORGANIZATION OF THE BOOK

This book contains chapters authored by several leading experts in the field of cloud computing. The book is presented in a coordinated and integrated manner starting with the fundamentals and followed by the technologies that implement them.

The content of the book is organized into six parts:

    I. Foundations
   II. Infrastructure as a Service (IaaS)
 III. Platform and Software as a Service (PaaS/SaaS)
 IV. Monitoring and Management
   V. Applications
 VI. Governance and Case Studies

Part I presents fundamental concepts of cloud computing, charting their evolution from mainframe, cluster, grid, and utility computing. Delivery models such as Infrastructure as a Service, Platform as a Service, and Software as a Service are detailed, as well as deployment models such as Public, Private, and Hybrid Clouds. It also presents models for migrating applications to cloud environments.

Part II covers Infrastructure as a Service (IaaS), from enabling technologies such as virtual machines and virtualized storage, to sophisticated mechanisms for securely storing data in the cloud and managing virtual clusters.

Part III introduces Platform and Software as a Service (PaaS/IaaS), detailing the delivery of cloud hosted software and applications. The design and operation of sophisticated, auto-scaling applications and environments are explored.

Part IV presents monitoring and management mechanisms for cloud computing, which becomes critical as cloud environments become more complex and interoperable. Architectures for federating cloud computing resources are explored, as well as service level agreement (SLA) management and performance prediction.

Part V details some novel applications that have been made possible by the rapid emergence of cloud computing resources. Best practices for architecting cloud applications are covered, describing how to harness the power of loosely coupled cloud resources. The design and execution of applications that leverage cloud resources such as massively multiplayer online game hosting, content delivery and mashups are explored.

Part VI outlines the organizational, structural, regulatory and legal issues that are commonly encountered in cloud computing environments. Details on how companies can successfully prepare and transition to cloud environments are explored, as well as achieving production readiness once such a transition is completed. Data security and legal concerns are explored in detail, as users reconcile moving their sensitive data and computation to cloud computing providers.

Rajkumar Buyya
The University of Melbourne and Manjrasoft Pty Ltd., Australia

James Broberg
The University of Melbourne, Australia

Andrzej Goscinski
Deakin University, Australia

ACKNOWLEDGMENTS

First and foremost, we are grateful to all the contributing authors for their time, effort, and understanding during the preparation of the book.

We thank Professor Albert Zomaya, editor of the Wiley book series on parallel and distributed computing, for his enthusiastic support and guidance during the preparation of book and enabling us to easily navigate through Wiley's publication process.

We would like to thank members of the book Editorial Advisory Board for their guidance during the preparation of the book. The board members are: Dr. Geng Lin (CISCO Systems, USA), Prof. Manish Parashar (Rutgers: The State University of New Jersey, USA), Dr. Wolfgang Gentzsch (Max-Planck-Gesellschaft, München, Germany), Prof. Omer Rana (Cardiff University, UK), Prof. Hai Jin (Huazhong University of Science and Technology, China), Dr. Simon See (Sun Microsystems, Singapore), Dr. Greg Pfister (IBM, USA (retired)), Prof. Ignacio M. Llorente (Universidad Complutense de Madrid, Spain), Prof. Geoffrey Fox (Indiana University, USA), and Dr. Walfredo Cirne (Google, USA).

All chapters were reviewed and authors have updated their chapters to address review comments. We thank members of the Melbourne CLOUDS Lab for their time and effort in peer reviewing of chapters.

Raj would like to thank his family members, especially Smrithi, Soumya, and Radha Buyya, for their love, understanding, and support during the preparation of the book. James would like to thank his wife, Amy, for her love and support. Andrzej would like to thank his wife, Teresa, for her love and support.

Finally, we would like to thank the staff at Wiley, particularly, Simone Taylor (Senior Editor, Wiley), Michael Christian (Editorial Assistant, Wiley), and S. Nalini (MPS Limited, a Macmillan Company, Chennai, India). They were wonderful to work with!

R.B.

J.B.

A.G.

CONTRIBUTORS

MATTHIAS ASSEL, High Performance Computing Center Stuttgart (HLRS), University of Stuttgart, 70550 Stuttgart, Germany

ROCCO AVERSA, Department of Information Engineering, Second University of Naples, 81031 Aversa (CE), Italy

SUMIT BOSE, Unisys Research Center, Bangalore, India - 560025

JANINE ANTHONY BOWEN, ESQ., McKenna Long & Aldridge LLP, Atlanta, GA 30308, USA

DAVID BREITGAND, IBM Haifa Research Lab, Haifa University Campus, 31095, Haifa, Israel

JAMES BROBERG, Department of Computer Science and Software Engineering, The University of Melbourne, Parkville, Melbourne, VIC 3010, Australia

MICHAEL BROCK, School of Information Technology, Deakin University, Geelong, Victoria 3217, Australia

RAJKUMAR BUYYA, Department of Computer Science and Software Engineering, The University of Melbourne, Parkville, Melbourne, VIC 3010, Australia

HAIJUN CAO, School of Computer Science and Technology, Huazhong University of Science and Technology, Wuhan, 430074, China

WAI-KIT CHEAH, Advanced Customer Services, Oracle Corporation (S) Pte Ltd., Singapore 038986

YU CHEN, Department of Electrical and Computer Engineering, State University of New York—Binghamton, Binghamton, NY 13902

XINGCHEN CHU, Department of Computer Science and Software Engineering, The University of Melbourne, Parkville, Melbourne, VIC 3010, Australia

BENIAMINO DI MARTINO, Department of Information Engineering, Second University of Naples, 81031 Aversa (CE), Italy

TARIQ ELLAHI, SAP Research Belfast, BT3 9DT, Belfast, United Kingdom

MOHAMED A. EL-REFAEY, Arab Academy for Science, Technology and Maritime Transport, College of Computing and Information Technology, Cairo, Egypt

JUN FENG, Department of Electrical and Computer Engineering, State University of New York—Binghamton, Binghamton, NY 13902

FERMÍN GALÁN, Telefónica I + D, Emilio Vargas, 6. 28043 Madrid, Spain

ALEX GALIS, University College London, Department of Electronic and Electrical Engineering, Torrington Place, London WC1E 7JE, United Kingdom

ANDRZEJ GOSCINSKI, School of Information Technology, Deakin University, Geelong, Victoria 3217, Australia

DAVID HADAS, IBM Haifa Research Lab, Haifa University Campus, 31095, Haifa, Israel

BENOIT HUDZIA, SAP Research Belfast, BT3 9DT, Belfast, United Kingdom

SHADI IBRAHIM, School of Computer Science and Technology, Huazhong University of Science and Technology, Wuhan, 430074, China

ALEXANDRU IOSUP, Electrical Engineering, Mathematics and Computer Science Department, Delft University of Technology, 2628 CD, Delft, The Netherlands

SHANTENU JHA, Center for Computation and Technology and Department of Computer Science, Louisiana State University, Baton Rouge, LA 70803

HAI JIN, School of Computer Science and Technology, Huazhong University of Science and Technology, Wuhan, 430074, China

DILEBAN KARUNAMOORTHY, Department of Computer Science and Software Engineering, The University of Melbourne, Parkville, Melbourne, VIC 3010, Australia

HENRY KASIM, HPC and Cloud Computing Center, Oracle Corporation (S) Pte Ltd, #18-01 Suntec Tower Four, Singapore 038986

DANIEL S. KATZ, Computation Institute, University of Chicago, Chicago, Illinois 60637

HYUNJOO KIM, Department of Electrical and Computer Engineering, Rutgers, The State University of New Jersey, New Brunswick, NJ

ALEXANDER KIPP, High Performance Computing Center Stuttgart (HLRS), University of Stuttgart, 70550 Stuttgart, Germany

WEI-SHINN KU, Department of Computer Science and Software Engineering, Auburn University, AL 36849

ROBERT LAM, School of Information and Communication Technologies SAIT Polytechnic, Calgary, Canada T2M 0L4

LARS LARSSON, Department of Computing Science, University Umea, Sweden

ELIEZER LEVY, SAP Research SRC Ra'anana, Ra'anana 43665; Israel

HUI LI, SAP Research Karlsruhe, Vincenz-Priessnitz-Strasse, 176131 Karlsruhe, Germany

MAIK A. LINDNER, SAP Research Belfast, BT3 9DT, Belfast, United Kingdom

PU LIU, IBM Endicott Center, New York, NY

IGNACIO M. LLORENTE, Distributed Systems Architecture Research Group, Departmento de Arquitectura de Computadores y Automática, Facultad de Informática, Universidad Complutense de Madrid, 28040 Madrid, Spain

ANDRE LUCKOW, Center for Computation and Technology, Louisiana State University, Baton Rouge, LA, 70803

GANESAN MALAIYANDISAMY, SETLabs, Infosys Technologies Limited, Electronics City, Bangalore, India, 560100

ALESSANDRO MARASCHINI, ElsagDatamat spa, Rome, Italy

PHILIPPE MASSONET, CETIC, B-6041 Charleroi, Belgium

MICHAEL MATTESS, Department of Computer Science and Software Engineering, The University of Melbourne, Parkville, Melbourne, VIC 3010, Australia

ANDRE MERZKY, Center for Computation and Technology, Louisiana State University, Baton Rouge, LA, 70803

T. S. MOHAN, Infosys Technologies Limited, Electronics City, Bangalore, India, 560100

RUBÉN S. MONTERO, Distributed Systems Architecture Research Group, Departmento de Arquitectura de Computadores, y Automática, Facultad de Informatica, Universidad Complutense de Madrid, 28040 Madrid, Spain

SUSAN MORROW, Avoco Secure, London W1S 2LQ, United Kingdom

SRIDHAR MURTHY, Infosys Technologies Limited, Electronics City, Bangalore, India, 560100

VLAD NAE, Institute of Computer Science, University of Innsbruck, Technikerstraße 21a, A-6020 Innsbruck, Austria

KENNETH NAGIN, IBM Haifa Research Lab, Haifa University Campus, 31095, Haifa, Israel

Suraj Pandey, Department of Computer Science and Software Engineering, The University of Melbourne, Parkville, Melbourne, VIC 3010, Australia

Manish Parashar, Department of Electrical and Computer Engineering, Rutgers, The State University of New Jersey, New Jersey, USA.

Anjaneyulu Pasala, SETLabs, Infosys Technologies Limited, Electronics City, Bangalore, India, 560100

Michael Pauly, T-Systems, Aachen, Germany

Radu Prodan, Institute of Computer Science, University of Innsbruck, A-6020 Innsbruck, Austria

Li Qi, School of Computer Science and Technology, Huazhong University of Science and Technology, Wuhan, 430074, China

Dheepak R A, SETLabs, Infosys Technologies Limited, Electronics City, Bangalore, India, 560100

Pethuru Raj, Robert Bosch India, Bangalore 560068, India

Massimiliano Rak, Department of Information Engineering, Second University of Naples, 81031 Aversa (CE), Italy

Philip Robinson, SAP Research Belfast, BT3 9DT, Belfast, United Kingdom

Benny Rochwerger, IBM Haifa Research Lab, Haifa University Campus, 31095, Haifa, Israel

Lutz Schubert, High Performance Computing Center Stuttgart (HLRS), University of Stuttgart, 70550 Stuttgart, Germany

Xuanhua Shi, School of Computer Science and Technology, Huazhong University of Science and Technology, Wuhan, 430074, China

Borja Sotomayor, Department of Computer Science, University of Chicago, Chicago, IL

Katerina Stamou, Department of Computer Science, Louisiana State University, Baton Rouge, LA, 70803

Zhou Su, Department of Computer Science, Graduate School of Science and Engineering, Waseda University, Japan

Jinesh Varia, Amazon Web Services, Seattle, WA 98109

Constantino Vázquez, Facultad de Informática, Universidad Complutense de Madrid, 28040 Madrid, Spain

Christian Vecchiola, Department of Computer Science and Software Engineering, The University of Melbourne, Parkville, Melbourne, VIC 3010, Australia

SALVATORE VENTICINQUE, Department of Information Engineering, Second University of Naples, 81031 Aversa (CE), Italy

UMBERTO VILLANO, Department of Engineering, University of Sannio, 82100 Benevento, Italy

MASSIMO VILLARI, Department. of Mathematics Faculty of Engineering, University of Messina, 98166 Messina, Italy

WILLIAM VOORSLUYS, Department of Computer Science and Software Engineering, The University of Melbourne, Parkville, Melbourne, VIC 3010, Australia

STEFAN WESNER, High Performance Computing Center Stuttgart (HLRS), University of Stuttgart, 70550 Stuttgart, Germany

YARON WOLFSTHAL, IBM Haifa Research Lab, Haifa University Campus, 31095, Haifa, Israel

SONG WU, School of Computer Science and Technology, Huazhong University of Science and Technology, Wuhan, 430074, China

PART I

FOUNDATIONS

CHAPTER 1

INTRODUCTION TO CLOUD COMPUTING

WILLIAM VOORSLUYS, JAMES BROBERG, and RAJKUMAR BUYYA

1.1 CLOUD COMPUTING IN A NUTSHELL

When plugging an electric appliance into an outlet, we care neither how electric power is generated nor how it gets to that outlet. This is possible because electricity is virtualized; that is, it is readily available from a wall socket that hides power generation stations and a huge distribution grid. When extended to information technologies, this concept means delivering useful functions while hiding how their internals work. Computing itself, to be considered fully virtualized, must allow computers to be built from distributed components such as processing, storage, data, and software resources [1].

Technologies such as *cluster*, *grid*, and now, *cloud* computing, have all aimed at allowing access to large amounts of computing power in a fully virtualized manner, by aggregating resources and offering a single system view. In addition, an important aim of these technologies has been delivering computing as a utility. Utility computing describes a business model for on-demand delivery of computing power; consumers pay providers based on usage ("pay-as-you-go"), similar to the way in which we currently obtain services from traditional public utility services such as water, electricity, gas, and telephony.

Cloud computing has been coined as an umbrella term to describe a category of sophisticated on-demand computing services initially offered by commercial providers, such as Amazon, Google, and Microsoft. It denotes a model on which a computing infrastructure is viewed as a "cloud," from which businesses and individuals access applications from anywhere in the world on demand [2]. The main principle behind this model is offering computing, storage, and software "as a service."

Cloud Computing: Principles and Paradigms, Edited by Rajkumar Buyya, James Broberg and Andrzej Goscinski Copyright © 2011 John Wiley & Sons, Inc.

Many practitioners in the commercial and academic spheres have attempted to define exactly what "cloud computing" is and what unique characteristics it presents. Buyya et al. [2] have defined it as follows: "Cloud is a parallel and distributed computing system consisting of a collection of inter-connected and virtualised computers that are dynamically provisioned and presented as one or more unified computing resources based on service-level agreements (SLA) established through negotiation between the service provider and consumers."

Vaquero et al. [3] have stated "clouds are a large pool of easily usable and accessible virtualized resources (such as hardware, development platforms and/or services). These resources can be dynamically reconfigured to adjust to a variable load (scale), allowing also for an optimum resource utilization. This pool of resources is typically exploited by a pay-per-use model in which guarantees are offered by the Infrastructure Provider by means of customized Service Level Agreements."

A recent McKinsey and Co. report [4] claims that "Clouds are hardware-based services offering compute, network, and storage capacity where: Hardware management is highly abstracted from the buyer, buyers incur infrastructure costs as variable OPEX, and infrastructure capacity is highly elastic."

A report from the University of California Berkeley [5] summarized the key characteristics of cloud computing as: "(1) the illusion of infinite computing resources; (2) the elimination of an up-front commitment by cloud users; and (3) the ability to pay for use ... as needed ..."

The National Institute of Standards and Technology (NIST) [6] characterizes cloud computing as "... a pay-per-use model for enabling available, convenient, on-demand network access to a shared pool of configurable computing resources (e.g. networks, servers, storage, applications, services) that can be rapidly provisioned and released with minimal management effort or service provider interaction."

In a more generic definition, Armbrust et al. [5] define cloud as the "data center hardware and software that provide services." Similarly, Sotomayor et al. [7] point out that "cloud" is more often used to refer to the IT infrastructure deployed on an Infrastructure as a Service provider data center.

While there are countless other definitions, there seems to be common characteristics between the most notable ones listed above, which a cloud should have: (i) pay-per-use (no ongoing commitment, utility prices); (ii) elastic capacity and the illusion of infinite resources; (iii) self-service interface; and (iv) resources that are abstracted or virtualised.

In addition to raw computing and storage, cloud computing providers usually offer a broad range of software services. They also include APIs and development tools that allow developers to build seamlessly scalable applications upon their services. The ultimate goal is allowing customers to run their everyday IT infrastructure "in the cloud."

A lot of hype has surrounded the cloud computing area in its infancy, often considered the most significant switch in the IT world since the advent of the

Internet [8]. In midst of such hype, a great deal of confusion arises when trying to define what cloud computing is and which computing infrastructures can be termed as "clouds."

Indeed, the long-held dream of delivering computing as a utility has been realized with the advent of cloud computing [5]. However, over the years, several technologies have matured and significantly contributed to make cloud computing viable. In this direction, this introduction tracks the roots of cloud computing by surveying the main technological advancements that significantly contributed to the advent of this emerging field. It also explains concepts and developments by categorizing and comparing the most relevant R&D efforts in cloud computing, especially public clouds, management tools, and development frameworks. The most significant practical cloud computing realizations are listed, with special focus on architectural aspects and innovative technical features.

1.2 ROOTS OF CLOUD COMPUTING

We can track the roots of clouds computing by observing the advancement of several technologies, especially in hardware (virtualization, multi-core chips), Internet technologies (Web services, service-oriented architectures, Web 2.0), distributed computing (clusters, grids), and systems management (autonomic computing, data center automation). Figure 1.1 shows the convergence of technology fields that significantly advanced and contributed to the advent of cloud computing.

Some of these technologies have been tagged as hype in their early stages of development; however, they later received significant attention from academia and were sanctioned by major industry players. Consequently, a specification and standardization process followed, leading to maturity and wide adoption. The emergence of cloud computing itself is closely linked to the maturity of such technologies. We present a closer look at the technologies that form the base of cloud computing, with the aim of providing a clearer picture of the cloud ecosystem as a whole.

1.2.1 From Mainframes to Clouds

We are currently experiencing a switch in the IT world, from in-house generated computing power into utility-supplied computing resources delivered over the Internet as Web services. This trend is similar to what occurred about a century ago when factories, which used to generate their own electric power, realized that it is was cheaper just plugging their machines into the newly formed electric power grid [8].

Computing delivered as a utility can be defined as "on demand delivery of infrastructure, applications, and business processes in a security-rich, shared, scalable, and based computer environment over the Internet for a fee" [9].

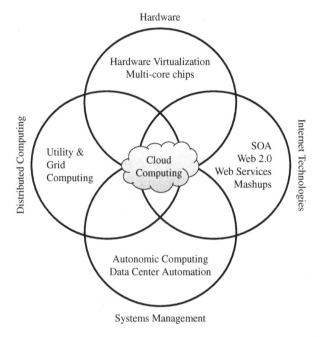

FIGURE 1.1. Convergence of various advances leading to the advent of cloud computing.

This model brings benefits to both consumers and providers of IT services. Consumers can attain reduction on IT-related costs by choosing to obtain cheaper services from external providers as opposed to heavily investing on IT infrastructure and personnel hiring. The "on-demand" component of this model allows consumers to adapt their IT usage to rapidly increasing or unpredictable computing needs.

Providers of IT services achieve better operational costs; hardware and software infrastructures are built to provide multiple solutions and serve many users, thus increasing efficiency and ultimately leading to faster return on investment (ROI) as well as lower total cost of ownership (TCO) [10].

Several technologies have in some way aimed at turning the utility computing concept into reality. In the 1970s, companies who offered common data processing tasks, such as payroll automation, operated time-shared mainframes as utilities, which could serve dozens of applications and often operated close to 100% of their capacity. In fact, mainframes had to operate at very high utilization rates simply because they were very expensive and costs should be justified by efficient usage [8].

The mainframe era collapsed with the advent of fast and inexpensive microprocessors and IT data centers moved to collections of commodity servers. Apart from its clear advantages, this new model inevitably led to isolation of workload into dedicated servers, mainly due to incompatibilities between software stacks and operating systems [11]. In addition, the unavail-ability of efficient computer networks meant that IT infrastructure should be hosted in proximity to where it would be consumed. Altogether, these facts have prevented the utility computing reality of taking place on modern computer systems.

Similar to old electricity generation stations, which used to power individual factories, computing servers and desktop computers in a modern organization are often underutilized, since IT infrastructure is configured to handle theore-tical demand peaks. In addition, in the early stages of electricity generation, electric current could not travel long distances without significant voltage losses. However, new paradigms emerged culminating on transmission systems able to make electricity available hundreds of kilometers far off from where it is generated. Likewise, the advent of increasingly fast fiber-optics networks has relit the fire, and new technologies for enabling sharing of computing power over great distances have appeared.

These facts reveal the potential of delivering computing services with the speed and reliability that businesses enjoy with their local machines. The benefits of economies of scale and high utilization allow providers to offer computing services for a fraction of what it costs for a typical company that generates its own computing power [8].

1.2.2 SOA, Web Services, Web 2.0, and Mashups

The emergence of Web services (WS) open standards has significantly con-tributed to advances in the domain of software integration [12]. Web services can glue together applications running on different messaging product plat-forms, enabling information from one application to be made available to others, and enabling internal applications to be made available over the Internet.

Over the years a rich WS software stack has been specified and standardized, resulting in a multitude of technologies to describe, compose, and orchestrate services, package and transport messages between services, publish and dis-cover services, represent quality of service (QoS) parameters, and ensure security in service access [13].

WS standards have been created on top of existing ubiquitous technologies such as HTTP and XML, thus providing a common mechanism for delivering services, making them ideal for implementing a service-oriented architecture (SOA). The purpose of a SOA is to address requirements of loosely coupled, standards-based, and protocol-independent distributed computing. In a SOA, software resources are packaged as "services," which are well-defined, self-contained modules that provide standard business functionality and are independent of the state or context of other services. Services are described in a standard definition language and have a published interface [12].

The maturity of WS has enabled the creation of powerful services that can be accessed on-demand, in a uniform way. While some WS are published with the intent of serving end-user applications, their true power resides in its interface being accessible by other services. An enterprise application that follows the SOA paradigm is a collection of services that together perform complex business logic [12].

This concept of gluing services initially focused on the enterprise Web, but gained space in the consumer realm as well, especially with the advent of Web 2.0. In the consumer Web, information and services may be programmatically aggregated, acting as building blocks of complex compositions, called *service mashups*. Many service providers, such as Amazon, del.icio.us, Facebook, and Google, make their service APIs publicly accessible using standard protocols such as SOAP and REST [14]. Consequently, one can put an idea of a fully functional Web application into practice just by gluing pieces with few lines of code.

In the Software as a Service (SaaS) domain, cloud applications can be built as compositions of other services from the same or different providers. Services such user authentication, e-mail, payroll management, and calendars are examples of building blocks that can be reused and combined in a business solution in case a single, ready-made system does not provide all those features. Many building blocks and solutions are now available in public marketplaces. For example, Programmable Web[1] is a public repository of service APIs and mashups currently listing thousands of APIs and mashups. Popular APIs such as Google Maps, Flickr, YouTube, Amazon eCommerce, and Twitter, when combined, produce a variety of interesting solutions, from finding video game retailers to weather maps. Similarly, Salesforce.com's offers AppExchange,[2] which enables the sharing of solutions developed by third-party developers on top of Salesforce.com components.

1.2.3 Grid Computing

Grid computing enables aggregation of distributed resources and transparently access to them. Most production grids such as TeraGrid [15] and EGEE [16] seek to share compute and storage resources distributed across different administrative domains, with their main focus being speeding up a broad range of scientific applications, such as climate modeling, drug design, and protein analysis.

A key aspect of the grid vision realization has been building standard Web services-based protocols that allow distributed resources to be "discovered, accessed, allocated, monitored, accounted for, and billed for, etc., and in general managed as a single virtual system." The Open Grid Services Architecture (OGSA) addresses this need for standardization by defining a set of core capabilities and behaviors that address key concerns in grid systems.

---

[1] http://www.programmableweb.com

[2] http://sites.force.com/appexchange

Globus Toolkit [18] is a middleware that implements several standard Grid services and over the years has aided the deployment of several service-oriented Grid infrastructures and applications. An ecosystem of tools is available to interact with service grids, including grid brokers, which facilitate user interaction with multiple middleware and implement policies to meet QoS needs.

The development of standardized protocols for several grid computing activities has contributed—theoretically—to allow delivery of on-demand computing services over the Internet. However, ensuring QoS in grids has been perceived as a difficult endeavor [19]. Lack of performance isolation has prevented grids adoption in a variety of scenarios, especially on environments where resources are oversubscribed or users are uncooperative. Activities associated with one user or virtual organization (VO) can influence, in an uncontrollable way, the performance perceived by other users using the same platform. Therefore, the impossibility of enforcing QoS and guaranteeing execution time became a problem, especially for time-critical applications [20].

Another issue that has lead to frustration when using grids is the availability of resources with diverse software configurations, including disparate operating systems, libraries, compilers, runtime environments, and so forth. At the same time, user applications would often run only on specially customized environments. Consequently, a portability barrier has often been present on most grid infrastructures, inhibiting users of adopting grids as utility computing environments [20].

Virtualization technology has been identified as the perfect fit to issues that have caused frustration when using grids, such as hosting many dissimilar software applications on a single physical platform. In this direction, some research projects (e.g., Globus Virtual Workspaces [20]) aimed at evolving grids to support an additional layer to virtualize computation, storage, and network resources.

1.2.4 Utility Computing

With increasing popularity and usage, large grid installations have faced new problems, such as excessive spikes in demand for resources coupled with strategic and adversarial behavior by users. Initially, grid resource management techniques did not ensure fair and equitable access to resources in many systems. Traditional metrics (throughput, waiting time, and slowdown) failed to capture the more subtle requirements of users. There were no real incentives for users to be flexible about resource requirements or job deadlines, nor provisions to accommodate users with urgent work.

In utility computing environments, users assign a "utility" value to their jobs, where utility is a fixed or time-varying valuation that captures various QoS constraints (deadline, importance, satisfaction). The valuation is the amount they are willing to pay a service provider to satisfy their demands. The service providers then attempt to maximize their own utility, where said utility may directly correlate with their profit. Providers can choose to prioritize high yield (i.e., profit per unit of resource) user jobs, leading to a scenario where shared systems are viewed as a marketplace, where users compete for resources based on the perceived utility or value of their jobs. Further information and comparison of these utility computing environments are available in an extensive survey of these platforms [17].

1.2.5 Hardware Virtualization

Cloud computing services are usually backed by large-scale data centers composed of thousands of computers. Such data centers are built to serve many users and host many disparate applications. For this purpose, hardware virtualization can be considered as a perfect fit to overcome most operational issues of data center building and maintenance.

The idea of virtualizing a computer system's resources, including processors, memory, and I/O devices, has been well established for decades, aiming at improving sharing and utilization of computer systems [21]. Hardware virtualization allows running multiple operating systems and software stacks on a single physical platform. As depicted in Figure 1.2, a software layer, the virtual machine monitor (VMM), also called a hypervisor, mediates access to the physical hardware presenting to each guest operating system a virtual machine (VM), which is a set of virtual platform interfaces [22].

The advent of several innovative technologies—multi-core chips, paravirtualization, hardware-assisted virtualization, and live migration of VMs—has contributed to an increasing adoption of virtualization on server systems. Traditionally, perceived benefits were improvements on sharing and utilization, better manageability, and higher reliability. More recently, with the adoption of virtualization on a broad range of server and client systems, researchers and practitioners have been emphasizing three basic capabilities regarding

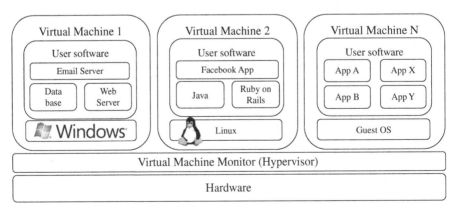

FIGURE 1.2. A hardware virtualized server hosting three virtual machines, each one running distinct operating system and user level software stack.

management of workload in a virtualized system, namely isolation, consolidation, and migration [23].

Workload isolation is achieved since all program instructions are fully confined inside a VM, which leads to improvements in security. Better reliability is also achieved because software failures inside one VM do not affect others [22]. Moreover, better performance control is attained since execution of one VM should not affect the performance of another VM [23].

The consolidation of several individual and heterogeneous workloads onto a single physical platform leads to better system utilization. This practice is also employed for overcoming potential software and hardware incompatibilities in case of upgrades, given that it is possible to run legacy and new operation systems concurrently [22].

Workload migration, also referred to as application mobility [23], targets at facilitating hardware maintenance, load balancing, and disaster recovery. It is done by encapsulating a guest OS state within a VM and allowing it to be suspended, fully serialized, migrated to a different platform, and resumed immediately or preserved to be restored at a later date [22]. A VM's state includes a full disk or partition image, configuration files, and an image of its RAM [20].

A number of VMM platforms exist that are the basis of many utility or cloud computing environments. The most notable ones, VMWare, Xen, and KVM, are outlined in the following sections.

VMWare ESXi. VMware is a pioneer in the virtualization market. Its ecosystem of tools ranges from server and desktop virtualization to high-level management tools [24]. ESXi is a VMM from VMWare. It is a bare-metal hypervisor, meaning that it installs directly on the physical server, whereas others may require a host operating system. It provides advanced virtualization techniques of processor, memory, and I/O. Especially, through memory ballooning and page sharing, it can overcommit memory, thus increasing the density of VMs inside a single physical server.

Xen. The Xen hypervisor started as an open-source project and has served as a base to other virtualization products, both commercial and open-source. It has pioneered the para-virtualization concept, on which the guest operating system, by means of a specialized kernel, can interact with the hypervisor, thus significantly improving performance. In addition to an open-source distribution [25], Xen currently forms the base of commercial hypervisors of a number of vendors, most notably Citrix XenServer [26] and Oracle VM [27].

KVM. The kernel-based virtual machine (KVM) is a Linux virtualization subsystem. Is has been part of the mainline Linux kernel since version 2.6.20, thus being natively supported by several distributions. In addition, activities such as memory management and scheduling are carried out by existing kernel features, thus making KVM simpler and smaller than hypervisors that take control of the entire machine [28].

KVM leverages hardware-assisted virtualization, which improves performance and allows it to support unmodified guest operating systems [29]; currently, it supports several versions of Windows, Linux, and UNIX [28].

1.2.6 Virtual Appliances and the Open Virtualization Format

An application combined with the environment needed to run it (operating system, libraries, compilers, databases, application containers, and so forth) is referred to as a "virtual appliance." Packaging application environments in the shape of virtual appliances eases software customization, configuration, and patching and improves portability. Most commonly, an appliance is shaped as a VM disk image associated with hardware requirements, and it can be readily deployed in a hypervisor.

On-line marketplaces have been set up to allow the exchange of ready-made appliances containing popular operating systems and useful software combinations, both commercial and open-source. Most notably, the VMWare virtual appliance marketplace allows users to deploy appliances on VMWare hypervisors or on partners public clouds [30], and Amazon allows developers to share specialized Amazon Machine Images (AMI) and monetize their usage on Amazon EC2 [31].

In a multitude of hypervisors, where each one supports a different VM image format and the formats are incompatible with one another, a great deal of interoperability issues arises. For instance, Amazon has its Amazon machine image (AMI) format, made popular on the Amazon EC2 public cloud. Other formats are used by Citrix XenServer, several Linux distributions that ship with KVM, Microsoft Hyper-V, and VMware ESX.

In order to facilitate packing and distribution of software to be run on VMs several vendors, including VMware, IBM, Citrix, Cisco, Microsoft, Dell, and HP, have devised the Open Virtualization Format (OVF). It aims at being "open, secure, portable, efficient and extensible" [32]. An OVF package consists of a file, or set of files, describing the VM hardware characteristics (e.g., memory, network cards, and disks), operating system details, startup, and shutdown actions, the virtual disks themselves, and other metadata containing product and licensing information. OVF also supports complex packages composed of multiple VMs (e.g., multi-tier applications) [32].

OVF's extensibility has encouraged additions relevant to management of data centers and clouds. Mathews et al. [33] have devised virtual machine contracts (VMC) as an extension to OVF. A VMC aids in communicating and managing the complex expectations that VMs have of their runtime environment and vice versa. A simple example of a VMC is when a cloud consumer wants to specify minimum and maximum amounts of a resource that a VM needs to function; similarly the cloud provider could express resource limits as a way to bound resource consumption and costs.

1.2.7 Autonomic Computing

The increasing complexity of computing systems has motivated research on autonomic computing, which seeks to improve systems by decreasing human involvement in their operation. In other words, systems should manage themselves, with high-level guidance from humans [34].

Autonomic, or self-managing, systems rely on monitoring probes and gauges (sensors), on an adaptation engine (autonomic manager) for computing optimizations based on monitoring data, and on effectors to carry out changes on the system. IBM's Autonomic Computing Initiative has contributed to define the four properties of autonomic systems: self-configuration, self-optimization, self-healing, and self-protection. IBM has also suggested a reference model for autonomic control loops of autonomic managers, called MAPE-K (Monitor Analyze Plan Execute—Knowledge) [34, 35].

The large data centers of cloud computing providers must be managed in an efficient way. In this sense, the concepts of autonomic computing inspire software technologies for data center automation, which may perform tasks such as: management of service levels of running applications; management of data center capacity; proactive disaster recovery; and automation of VM provisioning [36].

1.3 LAYERS AND TYPES OF CLOUDS

Cloud computing services are divided into three classes, according to the abstraction level of the capability provided and the service model of providers, namely: (1) Infrastructure as a Service, (2) Platform as a Service, and (3) Software as a Service [6]. Figure 1.3 depicts the layered organization of the cloud stack from physical infrastructure to applications.

These abstraction levels can also be viewed as a layered architecture where services of a higher layer can be composed from services of the underlying layer [37]. The reference model of Buyya et al. [38] explains the role of each layer in an integrated architecture. A core middleware manages physical resources and the VMs deployed on top of them; in addition, it provides the required features (e.g., accounting and billing) to offer multi-tenant pay-as-you-go services. Cloud development environments are built on top of infrastructure services to offer application development and deployment capabilities; in this level, various programming models, libraries, APIs, and mashup editors enable the creation of a range of business, Web, and scientific applications. Once deployed in the cloud, these applications can be consumed by end users.

1.3.1 Infrastructure as a Service

Offering virtualized resources (computation, storage, and communication) on demand is known as Infrastructure as a Service (IaaS) [7]. A *cloud infrastructure*

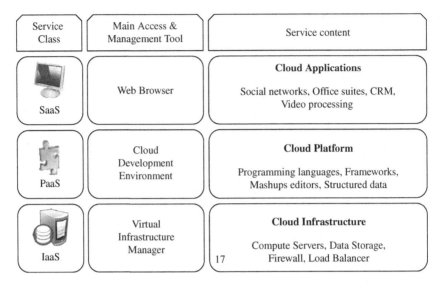

Service Class	Main Access & Management Tool	Service content
SaaS	Web Browser	**Cloud Applications** Social networks, Office suites, CRM, Video processing
PaaS	Cloud Development Environment	**Cloud Platform** Programming languages, Frameworks, Mashups editors, Structured data
IaaS	Virtual Infrastructure Manager	**Cloud Infrastructure** Compute Servers, Data Storage, Firewall, Load Balancer

FIGURE 1.3. The cloud computing stack.

enables on-demand provisioning of servers running several choices of operating systems and a customized software stack. Infrastructure services are considered to be the bottom layer of cloud computing systems [39].

Amazon Web Services mainly offers IaaS, which in the case of its EC2 service means offering VMs with a software stack that can be customized similar to how an ordinary physical server would be customized. Users are given privileges to perform numerous activities to the server, such as: starting and stopping it, customizing it by installing software packages, attaching virtual disks to it, and configuring access permissions and firewalls rules.

1.3.2 Platform as a Service

In addition to infrastructure-oriented clouds that provide raw computing and storage services, another approach is to offer a higher level of abstraction to make a cloud easily programmable, known as Platform as a Service (PaaS). A *cloud platform* offers an environment on which developers create and deploy applications and do not necessarily need to know how many processors or how much memory that applications will be using. In addition, multiple programming models and specialized services (e.g., data access, authentication, and payments) are offered as building blocks to new applications [40].

Google AppEngine, an example of Platform as a Service, offers a scalable environment for developing and hosting Web applications, which should be written in specific programming languages such as Python or Java, and use the services' own proprietary structured object data store. Building blocks include an in-memory object cache (memcache), mail service, instant messaging service (XMPP), an image manipulation service, and integration with Google Accounts authentication service.

1.3.3 Software as a Service

Applications reside on the top of the cloud stack. Services provided by this layer can be accessed by end users through Web portals. Therefore, consumers are increasingly shifting from locally installed computer programs to on-line software services that offer the same functionally. Traditional desktop applications such as word processing and spreadsheet can now be accessed as a service in the Web. This model of delivering applications, known as Software as a Service (SaaS), alleviates the burden of software maintenance for customers and simplifies development and testing for providers [37, 41].

Salesforce.com, which relies on the SaaS model, offers business productivity applications (CRM) that reside completely on their servers, allowing costumers to customize and access applications on demand.

1.3.4 Deployment Models

Although cloud computing has emerged mainly from the appearance of public computing utilities, other deployment models, with variations in physical location and distribution, have been adopted. In this sense, regardless of its service class, a cloud can be classified as public, private, community, or hybrid [6] based on model of deployment as shown in Figure 1.4.

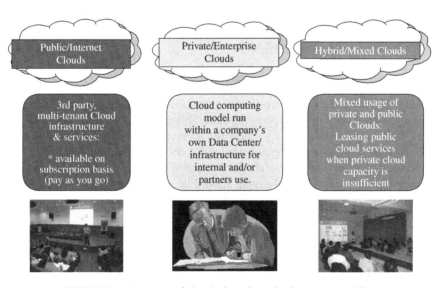

FIGURE 1.4. Types of clouds based on deployment models.

Armbrust et al. [5] propose definitions for *public cloud* as a "cloud made available in a pay-as-you-go manner to the general public" and *private cloud* as "internal data center of a business or other organization, not made available to the general public."

In most cases, establishing a private cloud means restructuring an existing infrastructure by adding virtualization and cloud-like interfaces. This allows users to interact with the local data center while experiencing the same advantages of public clouds, most notably self-service interface, privileged access to virtual servers, and per-usage metering and billing.

A *community cloud* is "shared by several organizations and supports a specific community that has shared concerns (e.g., mission, security require-ments, policy, and compliance considerations) [6]."

A *hybrid cloud* takes shape when a private cloud is supplemented with computing capacity from public clouds [7]. The approach of temporarily renting capacity to handle spikes in load is known as "cloud-bursting" [42].

1.4   DESIRED FEATURES OF A CLOUD

Certain features of a cloud are essential to enable services that truly represent the cloud computing model and satisfy expectations of consumers, and cloud offerings must be (i) self-service, (ii) per-usage metered and billed, (iii) elastic, and (iv) customizable.

1.4.1   Self-Service

Consumers of cloud computing services expect on-demand, nearly instant access to resources. To support this expectation, clouds must allow self-service access so that customers can request, customize, pay, and use services without intervention of human operators [6].

1.4.2   Per-Usage Metering and Billing

Cloud computing eliminates up-front commitment by users, allowing them to request and use only the necessary amount. Services must be priced on a short-term basis (e.g., by the hour), allowing users to release (and not pay for) resources as soon as they are not needed [5]. For these reasons, clouds must implement features to allow efficient trading of service such as pricing, accounting, and billing [2]. Metering should be done accordingly for different types of service (e.g., storage, processing, and bandwidth) and usage promptly reported, thus providing greater transparency [6].

1.4.3   Elasticity

Cloud computing gives the illusion of infinite computing resources available on demand [5]. Therefore users expect clouds to rapidly provide resources in any quantity at any time. In particular, it is expected that the additional resources can be (a) provisioned, possibly automatically, when an application load increases and (b) released when load decreases (scale up and down) [6].

1.4.4 Customization

In a multi-tenant cloud a great disparity between user needs is often the case. Thus, resources rented from the cloud must be highly customizable. In the case of infrastructure services, customization means allowing users to deploy specialized virtual appliances and to be given privileged (root) access to the virtual servers. Other service classes (PaaS and SaaS) offer less flexibility and are not suitable for general-purpose computing [5], but still are expected to provide a certain level of customization.

1.5 CLOUD INFRASTRUCTURE MANAGEMENT

A key challenge IaaS providers face when building a cloud infrastructure is managing physical and virtual resources, namely servers, storage, and networks, in a holistic fashion [43]. The orchestration of resources must be performed in a way to rapidly and dynamically provision resources to applications [7].

The software toolkit responsible for this orchestration is called a virtual infrastructure manager (VIM) [7]. This type of software resembles a traditional operating system—but instead of dealing with a single computer, it aggregates resources from multiple computers, presenting a uniform view to user and applications. The term "cloud operating system" is also used to refer to it [43]. Other terms include "infrastructure sharing software [44]" and "virtual infrastructure engine [45]."

Sotomayor et al. [7], in their description of the cloud ecosystem of software tools, propose a differentiation between two categories of tools used to manage clouds. The first category—cloud toolkits—includes those that "expose a remote and secure interface for creating, controlling and monitoring virtualize resources," but do not specialize in VI management. Tools in the second category—the virtual infrastructure managers—provide advanced features such as automatic load balancing and server consolidation, but do not expose remote cloud-like interfaces. However, the authors point out that there is a superposition between the categories; cloud toolkits can also manage virtual infrastructures, although they usually provide less sophisticated features than specialized VI managers do.

The availability of a remote cloud-like interface and the ability of managing many users and their permissions are the primary features that would distinguish "cloud toolkits" from "VIMs." However, in this chapter, we place both categories of tools under the same group (of the VIMs) and, when applicable, we highlight the availability of a remote interface as a feature.

Virtually all VIMs we investigated present a set of basic features related to managing the life cycle of VMs, including networking groups of VMs together and setting up virtual disks for VMs. These basic features pretty much define whether a tool can be used in practical cloud deployments or not. On the other hand, only a handful of software present advanced features (e.g., high availability) which allow them to be used in large-scale production clouds.

1.5.1 Features

We now present a list of both basic and advanced features that are usually available in VIMs.

Virtualization Support. The multi-tenancy aspect of clouds requires multiple customers with disparate requirements to be served by a single hardware infrastructure. Virtualized resources (CPUs, memory, etc.) can be sized and resized with certain flexibility. These features make hardware virtualization, the ideal technology to create a virtual infrastructure that partitions a data center among multiple tenants.

Self-Service, On-Demand Resource Provisioning. Self-service access to resources has been perceived as one the most attractive features of clouds. This feature enables users to directly obtain services from clouds, such as spawning the creation of a server and tailoring its software, configurations, and security policies, without interacting with a human system administrator. This capability "eliminates the need for more time-consuming, labor-intensive, human-driven procurement processes familiar to many in IT" [46]. Therefore, exposing a self-service interface, through which users can easily interact with the system, is a highly desirable feature of a VI manager.

Multiple Backend Hypervisors. Different virtualization models and tools offer different benefits, drawbacks, and limitations. Thus, some VI managers provide a uniform management layer regardless of the virtualization technology used. This characteristic is more visible in open-source VI managers, which usually provide pluggable drivers to interact with multiple hypervisors [7]. In this direction, the aim of libvirt [47] is to provide a uniform API that VI managers can use to manage domains (a VM or container running an instance of an operating system) in virtualized nodes using standard operations that abstract hypervisor specific calls.

Storage Virtualization. Virtualizing storage means abstracting logical storage from physical storage. By consolidating all available storage devices in a data center, it allows creating virtual disks independent from device and location. Storage devices are commonly organized in a storage area network (SAN) and attached to servers via protocols such as Fibre Channel, iSCSI, and

NFS; a storage controller provides the layer of abstraction between virtual and physical storage [48].

In the VI management sphere, storage virtualization support is often restricted to commercial products of companies such as VMWare and Citrix. Other products feature ways of pooling and managing storage devices, but administrators are still aware of each individual device.

Interface to Public Clouds. Researchers have perceived that extending the capacity of a local in-house computing infrastructure by borrowing resources from public clouds is advantageous. In this fashion, institutions can make good use of their available resources and, in case of spikes in demand, extra load can be offloaded to rented resources [45].

A VI manager can be used in a hybrid cloud setup if it offers a driver to manage the life cycle of virtualized resources obtained from external cloud providers. To the applications, the use of leased resources must ideally be transparent.

Virtual Networking. Virtual networks allow creating an isolated network on top of a physical infrastructure independently from physical topology and locations [49]. A virtual LAN (VLAN) allows isolating traffic that shares a switched network, allowing VMs to be grouped into the same broadcast domain. Additionally, a VLAN can be configured to block traffic originated from VMs from other networks. Similarly, the VPN (virtual private network) concept is used to describe a secure and private overlay network on top of a public network (most commonly the public Internet) [50].

Support for creating and configuring virtual networks to group VMs placed throughout a data center is provided by most VI managers. Additionally, VI managers that interface with public clouds often support secure VPNs connecting local and remote VMs.

Dynamic Resource Allocation. Increased awareness of energy consumption in data centers has encouraged the practice of dynamic consolidating VMs in a fewer number of servers. In cloud infrastructures, where applications have variable and dynamic needs, capacity management and demand prediction are especially complicated. This fact triggers the need for dynamic resource allocation aiming at obtaining a timely match of supply and demand [51].

Energy consumption reduction and better management of SLAs can be achieved by dynamically remapping VMs to physical machines at regular intervals. Machines that are not assigned any VM can be turned off or put on a low power state. In the same fashion, overheating can be avoided by moving load away from hotspots [52].

A number of VI managers include a dynamic resource allocation feature that continuously monitors utilization across resource pools and reallocates available resources among VMs according to application needs.

Virtual Clusters. Several VI managers can holistically manage groups of VMs. This feature is useful for provisioning computing *virtual clusters on demand*, and interconnected VMs for multi-tier Internet applications [53].

Reservation and Negotiation Mechanism. When users request computational resources to available at a specific time, requests are termed advance reservations (AR), in contrast to best-effort requests, when users request resources whenever available [54]. To support complex requests, such as AR, a VI manager must allow users to "lease" resources expressing more complex terms (e.g., the period of time of a reservation). This is especially useful in clouds on which resources are scarce; since not all requests may be satisfied immediately, they can benefit of VM placement strategies that support queues, priorities, and advance reservations [55].

Additionally, leases may be negotiated and renegotiated, allowing provider and consumer to modify a lease or present counter proposals until an agreement is reached. This feature is illustrated by the case in which an AR request for a given slot cannot be satisfied, but the provider can offer a distinct slot that is still satisfactory to the user. This problem has been addressed in OpenPEX, which incorporates a bilateral negotiation protocol that allows users and providers to come to an alternative agreement by exchanging offers and counter offers [56].

High Availability and Data Recovery. The high availability (HA) feature of VI managers aims at minimizing application downtime and preventing business disruption. A few VI managers accomplish this by providing a failover mechanism, which detects failure of both physical and virtual servers and restarts VMs on healthy physical servers. This style of HA protects from host, but not VM, failures [57, 58].

For mission critical applications, when a failover solution involving restarting VMs does not suffice, additional levels of fault tolerance that rely on redundancy of VMs are implemented. In this style, redundant and synchronized VMs (running or in standby) are kept in a secondary physical server. The HA solution monitors failures of system components such as servers, VMs, disks, and network and ensures that a duplicate VM serves the application in case of failures [58].

Data backup in clouds should take into account the high data volume involved in VM management. Frequent backup of a large number of VMs, each one with multiple virtual disks attached, should be done with minimal interference in the systems performance. In this sense, some VI managers offer data protection mechanisms that perform incremental backups of VM images. The backup workload is often assigned to proxies, thus offloading production server and reducing network overhead [59].

1.5.2 Case Studies

In this section, we describe the main features of the most popular VI managers available. Only the most prominent and distinguishing features of each tool are discussed in detail. A detailed side-by-side feature comparison of VI managers is presented in Table 1.1.

Apache VCL. The Virtual Computing Lab [60, 61] project has been incepted in 2004 by researchers at the North Carolina State University as a way to provide customized environments to computer lab users. The software components that support NCSU's initiative have been released as open-source and incorporated by the Apache Foundation.

Since its inception, the main objective of VCL has been providing desktop (virtual lab) and HPC computing environments anytime, in a flexible cost-effective way and with minimal intervention of IT staff. In this sense, VCL was one of the first projects to create a tool with features such as: self-service Web portal, to reduce administrative burden; advance reservation of capacity, to provide resources during classes; and deployment of customized machine images on multiple computers, to provide clusters on demand.

In summary, Apache VCL provides the following features: (i) multi-platform controller, based on Apache/PHP; (ii) Web portal and XML-RPC interfaces; (iii) support for VMware hypervisors (ESX, ESXi, and Server); (iv) virtual networks; (v) virtual clusters; and (vi) advance reservation of capacity.

AppLogic. AppLogic [62] is a commercial VI manager, the flagship product of 3tera Inc. from California, USA. The company has labeled this product as a Grid Operating System.

AppLogic provides a fabric to manage clusters of virtualized servers, focusing on managing multi-tier Web applications. It views an entire application as a collection of components that must be managed as a single entity. Several components such as firewalls, load balancers, Web servers, application servers, and database servers can be set up and linked together. Whenever the application is started, the system manufactures and assembles the virtual infrastructure required to run it. Once the application is stopped, AppLogic tears down the infrastructure built for it [63].

AppLogic offers dynamic appliances to add functionality such as Disaster Recovery and Power optimization to applications [62]. The key differential of this approach is that additional functionalities are implemented as another pluggable appliance instead of being added as a core functionality of the VI manager.

In summary, 3tera AppLogic provides the following features: Linux-based controller; CLI and GUI interfaces; Xen backend; Global Volume Store (GVS) storage virtualization; virtual networks; virtual clusters; dynamic resource allocation; high availability; and data protection.

TABLE 1.1. Feature Comparison of Virtual Infrastructure Managers

	License	Installation Platform of Controller	Client UI, API, Language Bindings	Backend Hypervisor(s)	Storage Virtualization	Interface to Public Cloud	Virtual Networks	Dynamic Resource Allocation	Advance Reservation of Capacity	High Availability	Data Protection
Apache VCL	Apache v2	Multiplatform (Apache/PHP)	Portal, XML-RPC	VMware ESX, ESXi, Server	No	No	Yes	No	Yes	No	No
AppLogic	Proprietary	Linux	GUI, CLI	Xen	Global Volume Store (GVS)	No	Yes	Yes	No	Yes	Yes
Citrix Essentials	Proprietary	Windows	GUI, CLI, Portal, XML-RPC	XenServer, Hyper-V	Citrix Storage Link	No	Yes	Yes	No	Yes	Yes
Enomaly ECP	GPL v3	Linux	Portal, WS	Xen	No	Amazon EC2	Yes	No	No	No	No
Eucalyptus	BSD	Linux	EC2 WS, CLI	Xen, KVM	No	EC2	Yes	No	No	No	No
Nimbus	Apache v2	Linux	EC2 WS, WSRF, CLI	Xen, KVM	No	EC2	Yes	Via integration with OpenNebula	Yes (via integration with OpenNebula)	No	No
OpenNEbula	Apache v2	Linux	XML-RPC, CLI, Java	Xen, KVM	No	Amazon EC2, Elastic Hosts	Yes	Yes	Yes (via Haizea)	No	No
OpenPEX	GPL v2	Multiplatform (Java)	Portal, WS	XenServer	No	No	No	No	Yes	No	No
oVirt	GPL v2	Fedora Linux	Portal	KVM	No	No	No	No	No	No	No
Platform ISF	Proprietary	Linux	Portal	Hyper-V XenServer, VMWare ESX	No	EC2, IBM CoD, HP Enterprise Services	Yes	Yes	Yes	Unclear	Unclear
Platform VMO	Proprietary	Linux, Windows	Portal	XenServer	No	No	Yes	Yes	No	Yes	No
VMware vSphere	Proprietary	Linux, Windows	CLI, GUI, Portal, WS	VMware ESX, ESXi	VMware vStorage VMFS	VMware vCloud partners	Yes	VMware DRM	No	Yes	Yes

Citrix Essentials. The Citrix Essentials suite is one the most feature complete VI management software available, focusing on management and automation of data centers. It is essentially a hypervisor-agnostic solution, currently supporting Citrix XenServer and Microsoft Hyper-V [64].

By providing several access interfaces, it facilitates both human and programmatic interaction with the controller. Automation of tasks is also aided by a workflow orchestration mechanism.

In summary, Citrix Essentials provides the following features: Windows-based controller; GUI, CLI, Web portal, and XML-RPC interfaces; support for XenServer and Hyper-V hypervisors; Citrix Storage Link storage virtualization; virtual networks; dynamic resource allocation; three-level high availability (i.e., recovery by VM restart, recovery by activating paused duplicate VM, and running duplicate VM continuously) [58]; data protection with Citrix Consolidated Backup.

Enomaly ECP. The Enomaly Elastic Computing Platform, in its most complete edition, offers most features a service provider needs to build an IaaS cloud.

Most notably, ECP Service Provider Edition offers a Web-based customer dashboard that allows users to fully control the life cycle of VMs. Usage accounting is performed in real time and can be viewed by users. Similar to the functionality of virtual appliance marketplaces, ECP allows providers and users to package and exchange applications.

In summary, Enomaly ECP provides the following features: Linux-based controller; Web portal and Web services (REST) interfaces; Xen back-end; interface to the Amazon EC2 public cloud; virtual networks; virtual clusters (ElasticValet).

Eucalyptus. The Eucalyptus [39] framework was one of the first open-source projects to focus on building IaaS clouds. It has been developed with the intent of providing an open-source implementation nearly identical in functionality to Amazon Web Services APIs. Therefore, users can interact with a Eucalyptus cloud using the same tools they use to access Amazon EC2. It also distinguishes itself from other tools because it provides a storage cloud API—emulating the Amazon S3 API—for storing general user data and VM images.

In summary, Eucalyptus provides the following features: Linux-based controller with administration Web portal; EC2-compatible (SOAP, Query) and S3-compatible (SOAP, REST) CLI and Web portal interfaces; Xen, KVM, and VMWare backends; Amazon EBS-compatible virtual storage devices; interface to the Amazon EC2 public cloud; virtual networks.

Nimbus3. The Nimbus toolkit [20] is built on top of the Globus framework. Nimbus provides most features in common with other open-source VI managers, such as an EC2-compatible front-end API, support to Xen, and a backend interface to Amazon EC2. However, it distinguishes from others by providing a Globus Web Services Resource Framework (WSRF) interface. It also provides a backend service, named Pilot, which spawns VMs on clusters managed by a local resource manager (LRM) such as PBS and SGE.

Nimbus' core was engineered around the Spring framework to be easily extensible, thus allowing several internal components to be replaced and also eases the integration with other systems.

In summary, Nimbus provides the following features: Linux-based controller; EC2-compatible (SOAP) and WSRF interfaces; Xen and KVM backend and a Pilot program to spawn VMs through an LRM; interface to the Amazon EC2 public cloud; virtual networks; one-click virtual clusters.

OpenNebula. OpenNebula is one of the most feature-rich open-source VI managers. It was initially conceived to manage local virtual infrastructure, but has also included remote interfaces that make it viable to build public clouds. Altogether, four programming APIs are available: XML-RPC and libvirt [47] for local interaction; a subset of EC2 (Query) APIs and the OpenNebula Cloud API (OCA) for public access [7, 65].

Its architecture is modular, encompassing several specialized pluggable components. The *Core* module orchestrates physical servers and their hypervisors, storage nodes, and network fabric. Management operations are performed through pluggable *Drivers*, which interact with APIs of hypervisors, storage and network technologies, and public clouds. The *Scheduler* module, which is in charge of assigning pending VM requests to physical hosts, offers dynamic resource allocation features. Administrators can choose between different scheduling objectives such as packing VMs in fewer hosts or keeping the load balanced. Via integration with the Haizea lease scheduler [66], OpenNebula also supports advance reservation of capacity and queuing of best-effort leases [7].

In summary, OpenNebula provides the following features: Linux-based controller; CLI, XML-RPC, EC2-compatible Query and OCA interfaces; Xen, KVM, and VMware backend; interface to public clouds (Amazon EC2, ElasticHosts); virtual networks; dynamic resource allocation; advance reservation of capacity.

OpenPEX. OpenPEX (Open Provisioning and EXecution Environment) was constructed around the notion of using advance reservations as the primary method for allocating VM instances. It distinguishes from other VI managers by its leases negotiation mechanism, which incorporates a bilateral negotiation protocol that allows users and providers to come to an agreement by exchanging offers and counter offers when their original requests cannot be satisfied.

In summary, OpenPEX provides the following features: multi-platform (Java) controller; Web portal and Web services (REST) interfaces; Citrix XenServer backend; advance reservation of capacity with negotiation [56].

oVirt. oVirt is an open-source VI manager, sponsored by Red Hat's Emergent Technology group. It provides most of the basic features of other VI managers, including support for managing physical server pools, storage pools, user accounts, and VMs. All features are accessible through a Web interface [67].

The oVirt admin node, which is also a VM, provides a Web server, secure authentication services based on freeIPA, and provisioning services to manage VM image and their transfer to the managed nodes. Each managed node libvirt, which interfaces with the hypervisor.

In summary, oVirt provides the following features: Fedora Linux-based controller packaged as a virtual appliance; Web portal interface; KVM backend.

Platform ISF. Infrastructure Sharing Facility (ISF) is the VI manager offering from Platform Computing [68]. The company, mainly through its LSF family of products, has been serving the HPC market for several years.

ISF's architecture is divided into three layers. The top most *Service Delivery* layer includes the user interfaces (i.e., self-service portal and APIs); the *Allocation Engine* provides reservation and allocation policies; and the bottom layer—*Resource Integrations*—provides adapters to interact with hypervisors, provisioning tools, and other systems (i.e., external public clouds). The Allocation Engine also provides policies to address several objectives, such as minimizing energy consumption, reducing impact of failures, and maximizing application performance [44].

ISF is built upon Platform's VM Orchestrator, which, as a standalone product, aims at speeding up delivery of VMs to end users. It also provides high availability by restarting VMs when hosts fail and duplicating the VM that hosts the VMO controller [69].

In summary, ISF provides the following features: Linux-based controller packaged as a virtual appliance; Web portal interface; dynamic resource allocation; advance reservation of capacity; high availability.

VMWare vSphere and vCloud. vSphere is VMware's suite of tools aimed at transforming IT infrastructures into private clouds [36, 43]. It distinguishes from other VI managers as one of the most feature-rich, due to the company's several offerings in all levels the architecture.

In the vSphere architecture, servers run on the ESXi platform. A separate server runs vCenter Server, which centralizes control over the entire virtual infrastructure. Through the vSphere Client software, administrators connect to vCenter Server to perform various tasks.

The Distributed Resource Scheduler (DRS) makes allocation decisions based on predefined rules and policies. It continuously monitors the amount of resources available to VMs and, if necessary, makes allocation changes to meet VM requirements. In the storage virtualization realm, vStorage VMFS is a cluster file system to provide aggregate several disks in a single volume. VMFS is especially optimized to store VM images and virtual disks. It supports storage equipment that use Fibre Channel or iSCSI SAN.

In its basic setup, vSphere is essentially a private administration suite. Self-service VM provisioning to end users is provided via the vCloud API, which interfaces with vCenter Server. In this configuration, vSphere can be used by service providers to build public clouds. In terms of interfacing with public clouds, vSphere interfaces with the vCloud API, thus enabling cloud-bursting into external clouds.

In summary, vSphere provides the following features: Windows-based controller (vCenter Server); CLI, GUI, Web portal, and Web services interfaces; VMware ESX, ESXi backend; VMware vStorage VMFS storage virtualization; interface to external clouds (VMware vCloud partners); virtual networks (VMWare Distributed Switch); dynamic resource allocation (VMware DRM); high availability; data protection (VMWare Consolidated Backup).

1.6 INFRASTRUCTURE AS A SERVICE PROVIDERS

Public Infrastructure as a Service providers commonly offer virtual servers containing one or more CPUs, running several choices of operating systems and a customized software stack. In addition, storage space and communication facilities are often provided.

1.6.1 Features

In spite of being based on a common set of features, IaaS offerings can be distinguished by the availability of specialized features that influence the cost−benefit ratio to be experienced by user applications when moved to the cloud. The most relevant features are: (i) geographic distribution of data centers; (ii) variety of user interfaces and APIs to access the system; (iii) specialized components and services that aid particular applications (e.g., load-balancers, firewalls); (iv) choice of virtualization platform and operating systems; and (v) different billing methods and period (e.g., prepaid vs. post-paid, hourly vs. monthly).

Geographic Presence. To improve availability and responsiveness, a provider of worldwide services would typically build several data centers distributed around the world. For example, Amazon Web Services presents the concept of "availability zones" and "regions" for its EC2 service. Availability zones are "distinct locations that are engineered to be insulated from failures in other availability zones and provide inexpensive, low-latency network connectivity to other availability zones in the same region." Regions, in turn, "are geographically dispersed and will be in separate geographic areas or countries [70]."

User Interfaces and Access to Servers. Ideally, a public IaaS provider must provide multiple access means to its cloud, thus catering for various users and their preferences. Different types of user interfaces (UI) provide different levels of abstraction, the most common being graphical user interfaces (GUI), command-line tools (CLI), and Web service (WS) APIs.

GUIs are preferred by end users who need to launch, customize, and monitor a few virtual servers and do not necessary need to repeat the process several times. On the other hand, CLIs offer more flexibility and the possibility of automating repetitive tasks via scripts (e.g., start and shutdown a number of virtual servers at regular intervals). WS APIs offer programmatic access to a cloud using standard HTTP requests, thus allowing complex services to be built on top of IaaS clouds.

Advance Reservation of Capacity. Advance reservations allow users to request for an IaaS provider to reserve resources for a specific time frame in the future, thus ensuring that cloud resources will be available at that time. However, most clouds only support best-effort requests; that is, users requests are server whenever resources are available [54].

Amazon Reserved Instances is a form of advance reservation of capacity, allowing users to pay a fixed amount of money in advance to guarantee resource availability at anytime during an agreed period and then paying a discounted hourly rate when resources are in use. However, only long periods of 1 to 3 years are offered; therefore, users cannot express their reservations in finer granularities—for example, hours or days.

Automatic Scaling and Load Balancing. As mentioned earlier in this chapter, elasticity is a key characteristic of the cloud computing model. Applications often need to scale up and down to meet varying load conditions. Automatic scaling is a highly desirable feature of IaaS clouds. It allow users to set conditions for when they want their applications to scale up and down, based on application-specific metrics such as transactions per second, number of simultaneous users, request latency, and so forth.

When the number of virtual servers is increased by automatic scaling, incoming traffic must be automatically distributed among the available servers. This activity enables applications to promptly respond to traffic increase while also achieving greater fault tolerance.

Service-Level Agreement. Service-level agreements (SLAs) are offered by IaaS providers to express their commitment to delivery of a certain QoS. To customers it serves as a warranty. An SLA usually include availability and performance guarantees. Additionally, metrics must be agreed upon by all parties as well as penalties for violating these expectations.

Most IaaS providers focus their SLA terms on availability guarantees, specifying the minimum percentage of time the system will be available during a certain period. For instance, Amazon EC2 states that "if the annual uptime Percentage for a customer drops below 99.95% for the service year, that customer is eligible to receive a service credit equal to 10% of their bill.[3]"

---

[3] http://aws.amazon.com/ec2-sla

Hypervisor and Operating System Choice. Traditionally, IaaS offerings have been based on heavily customized open-source Xen deployments. IaaS providers needed expertise in Linux, networking, virtualization, metering, resource management, and many other low-level aspects to successfully deploy and maintain their cloud offerings. More recently, there has been an emergence of turnkey IaaS platforms such as VMWare vCloud and Citrix Cloud Center (C3) which have lowered the barrier of entry for IaaS competitors, leading to a rapid expansion in the IaaS marketplace.

1.6.2 Case Studies

In this section, we describe the main features of the most popular public IaaS clouds. Only the most prominent and distinguishing features of each one are discussed in detail. A detailed side-by-side feature comparison of IaaS offerings is presented in Table 1.2.

Amazon Web Services. Amazon WS[4] (AWS) is one of the major players in the cloud computing market. It pioneered the introduction of IaaS clouds in 2006. It offers a variety cloud services, most notably: S3 (storage), EC2 (virtual servers), Cloudfront (content delivery), Cloudfront Streaming (video streaming), SimpleDB (structured datastore), RDS (Relational Database), SQS (reliable messaging), and Elastic MapReduce (data processing).

The Elastic Compute Cloud (EC2) offers Xen-based virtual servers (instances) that can be instantiated from Amazon Machine Images (AMIs). Instances are available in a variety of sizes, operating systems, architectures, and price. CPU capacity of instances is measured in Amazon Compute Units and, although fixed for each instance, vary among instance types from 1 (small instance) to 20 (high CPU instance). Each instance provides a certain amount of nonpersistent disk space; a persistence disk service (Elastic Block Storage) allows attaching virtual disks to instances with space up to 1TB.

Elasticity can be achieved by combining the CloudWatch, Auto Scaling, and Elastic Load Balancing features, which allow the number of instances to scale up and down automatically based on a set of customizable rules, and traffic to be distributed across available instances. Fixed IP address (Elastic IPs) are not available by default, but can be obtained at an additional cost.

In summary, Amazon EC2 provides the following features: multiple data centers available in the United States (East and West) and Europe; CLI, Web services (SOAP and Query), Web-based console user interfaces; access to instance mainly via SSH (Linux) and Remote Desktop (Windows); advanced reservation of capacity (aka reserved instances) that guarantees availability for periods of 1 and 3 years; 99.5% availability SLA; per hour pricing; Linux and Windows operating systems; automatic scaling; load balancing.

---

[4] http://aws.amazon.com

TABLE 1.2. Feature Comparison Public Cloud Offerings (Infrastructure as a Service)

	Geographic Presence	Client UI API Language Bindings	Primary Access to Server	Advance Reservation of Capacity	SLA Uptime	Smallest Billing Unit	Hypervisor	Guest Operating Systems	Automated Horizontal Scaling	Load Balancing	Runtime Server Resizing/ Vertical Scaling	Instance Hardware Capacity		
												Processor	Memory	Storage
Amazon EC2	US East, Europe	CLI, WS, Portal	SSH (Linux), Remote Desktop (Windows)	Amazon reserved instances (Available in 1 or 3 years terms, starting from reservation time)	99.95%	Hour	Xen	Linux, Windows	Available with Amazon CloudWatch	Elastic Load Balancing	No	1–20 EC2 compute units	1.7–15 GB	160–1690 GB 1 GB–1 TB (per EBS volume)
Flexiscale	UK	Web Console	SSH	No	100%	Hour	Xen	Linux, Windows	No	Zeus software loadbalancing	Processors, memory (requires reboot)	1–4 CPUs	0.5–16 GB	20–270 GB
GoGrid		REST, Java, PHP, Python, Ruby	SSH	No	100%	Hour	Xen	Linux, Windows	No	Hardware (F5)	No	1–6 CPUs	0.5–8 GB	30–480 GB
Joyent Cloud	US (Emery-ville, CA; San Diego, CA; Andover, MA; Dallas, TX)		SSH, VirtualMin (Web-based system administration)	No	100%	Month	OS Level (Solaris Containers)	OpenSolaris	No	Both hardware (F5 networks) and software (Zeus)	Automatic CPU bursting (up to 8 CPUs)	1/16–8 CPUs	0.25–32 GB	5–100 GB
Rackspace Cloud Servers	US (Dallas, TX)	Portal, REST, Python, PHP, Java, C#/. NET	SSH	No	100%	Hour	Xen	Linux	No	No	Memory, disk (requires reboot) Automatic CPU bursting (up to 100% of available CPU power of physical host)	Quad-core CPU (CPU power is weighed proportionally to memory size)	0.25–16 GB	10–620 GB

Flexiscale. Flexiscale is a UK-based provider offering services similar in nature to Amazon Web Services. However, its virtual servers offer some distinct features, most notably: persistent storage by default, fixed IP addresses, dedicated VLAN, a wider range of server sizes, and runtime adjustment of CPU capacity (aka CPU bursting/vertical scaling). Similar to the clouds, this service is also priced by the hour.

In summary, the Flexiscale cloud provides the following features: available in UK; Web services (SOAP), Web-based user interfaces; access to virtual server mainly via SSH (Linux) and Remote Desktop (Windows); 100% availability SLA with automatic recovery of VMs in case of hardware failure; per hour pricing; Linux and Windows operating systems; automatic scaling (horizontal/vertical).

Joyent. Joyent's Public Cloud offers servers based on Solaris containers virtualization technology. These servers, dubbed accelerators, allow deploying various specialized software-stack based on a customized version of Open-Solaris operating system, which include by default a Web-based configuration tool and several pre-installed software, such as Apache, MySQL, PHP, Ruby on Rails, and Java. Software load balancing is available as an accelerator in addition to hardware load balancers.

A notable feature of Joyent's virtual servers is automatic vertical scaling of CPU cores, which means a virtual server can make use of additional CPUs automatically up to the maximum number of cores available in the physical host.

In summary, the Joyent public cloud offers the following features: multiple geographic locations in the United States; Web-based user interface; access to virtual server via SSH and Web-based administration tool; 100% availability SLA; per month pricing; OS-level virtualization Solaris containers; Open-Solaris operating systems; automatic scaling (vertical).

GoGrid. GoGrid, like many other IaaS providers, allows its customers to utilize a range of pre-made Windows and Linux images, in a range of fixed instance sizes. GoGrid also offers "value-added" stacks on top for applications such as high-volume Web serving, e-Commerce, and database stores.

It offers some notable features, such as a "hybrid hosting" facility, which combines traditional dedicated hosts with auto-scaling cloud server infrastructure. In this approach, users can take advantage of dedicated hosting (which may be required due to specific performance, security or legal compliance reasons) and combine it with on-demand cloud infrastructure as appropriate, taking the benefits of each style of computing.

As part of its core IaaS offerings, GoGrid also provides free hardware load balancing, auto-scaling capabilities, and persistent storage, features that typically add an additional cost for most other IaaS providers.

Rackspace Cloud Servers. Rackspace Cloud Servers is an IaaS solution that provides fixed size instances in the cloud. Cloud Servers offers a range of Linux-based pre-made images. A user can request different-sized images, where the size is measured by requested RAM, not CPU.

Like GoGrid, Cloud Servers also offers hybrid approach where dedicated and cloud server infrastructures can be combined to take the best aspects of both styles of hosting as required. Cloud Servers, as part of its default offering, enables fixed (static) IP addresses, persistent storage, and load balancing (via A-DNS) at no additional cost.

1.7 PLATFORM AS A SERVICE PROVIDERS

Public Platform as a Service providers commonly offer a development and deployment environment that allow users to create and run their applications with little or no concern to low-level details of the platform. In addition, specific programming languages and frameworks are made available in the platform, as well as other services such as persistent data storage and in-memory caches.

1.7.1 Features

Programming Models, Languages, and Frameworks. Programming models made available by IaaS providers define how users can express their applications using higher levels of abstraction and efficiently run them on the cloud platform. Each model aims at efficiently solving a particular problem. In the cloud computing domain, the most common activities that require specialized models are: processing of large dataset in clusters of computers (MapReduce model), development of request-based Web services and applications; definition and orchestration of business processes in the form of workflows (Workflow model); and high-performance distributed execution of various computational tasks.

For user convenience, PaaS providers usually support multiple programming languages. Most commonly used languages in platforms include Python and Java (e.g., Google AppEngine), .NET languages (e.g., Microsoft Azure), and Ruby (e.g., Heroku). Force.com has devised its own programming language (Apex) and an Excel-like query language, which provide higher levels of abstraction to key platform functionalities.

A variety of software frameworks are usually made available to PaaS developers, depending on application focus. Providers that focus on Web and enterprise application hosting offer popular frameworks such as Ruby on Rails, Spring, Java EE, and .NET.

Persistence Options. A persistence layer is essential to allow applications to record their state and recover it in case of crashes, as well as to store user data.

Traditionally, Web and enterprise application developers have chosen relational databases as the preferred persistence method. These databases offer fast and reliable structured data storage and transaction processing, but may lack scalability to handle several petabytes of data stored in commodity computers [71].

In the cloud computing domain, distributed storage technologies have emerged, which seek to be robust and highly scalable, at the expense of relational structure and convenient query languages. For example, Amazon SimpleDB and Google AppEngine datastore offer schema-less, automatically indexed database services [70]. Data queries can be performed only on individual tables; that is, join operations are unsupported for the sake of scalability.

1.7.2   Case Studies

In this section, we describe the main features of some Platform as Service (PaaS) offerings. A more detailed side-by-side feature comparison of VI managers is presented in Table 1.3.

Aneka. Aneka [72] is a .NET-based service-oriented resource management and development platform. Each server in an Aneka deployment (dubbed Aneka cloud node) hosts the Aneka container, which provides the base infrastructure that consists of services for persistence, security (authorization, authentication and auditing), and communication (message handling and dispatching). Cloud nodes can be either physical server, virtual machines (XenServer and VMware are supported), and instances rented from Amazon EC2.

The Aneka container can also host any number of optional services that can be added by developers to augment the capabilities of an Aneka Cloud node, thus providing a single, extensible framework for orchestrating various application models.

Several programming models are supported by such task models to enable execution of legacy HPC applications and MapReduce, which enables a variety of data-mining and search applications.

Users request resources via a client to a reservation services manager of the Aneka master node, which manages all cloud nodes and contains scheduling service to distribute request to cloud nodes.

App Engine. Google App Engine lets you run your Python and Java Web applications on elastic infrastructure supplied by Google. App Engine allows your applications to scale dynamically as your traffic and data storage requirements increase or decrease. It gives developers a choice between a Python stack and Java. The App Engine serving architecture is notable in that it allows real-time auto-scaling without virtualization for many common types of Web applications. However, such auto-scaling is dependent on the

TABLE 1.3. Feature Comparison of Platform-as-a-Service Cloud Offerings

	Target Use	Programming Language, Frameworks	Developer Tools	Programming Models	Persistence Options	Automatic Scaling	Backend Infrastructure Providers
Aneka	.Net enterprise applications, HPC	.NET	Standalone SDK	Threads, Task, MapReduce	Flat files, RDBMS, HDFS	No	Amazon EC2
AppEngine	Web applications	Python, Java	Eclipse-based IDE	Request-based Web programming	BigTable	Yes	Own data centers
Force.com	Enterprise applications (esp. CRM)	Apex	Eclipse-based IDE, Web-based wizard	Workflow, Excel-like formula language, Request-based web programming	Own object database	Unclear	Own data centers
Microsoft Windows Azure	Enterprise and Web applications	.NET	Azure tools for Microsoft Visual Studio	Unrestricted	Table/BLOB/queue storage, SQL services	Yes	Own data centers
Heroku	Web applications	Ruby on Rails	Command-line tools	Request-based web programming	PostgreSQL, Amazon RDS	Yes	Amazon EC2
Amazon Elastic MapReduce	Data processing	Hive and Pig, Cascading, Java, Ruby, Perl, Python, PHP, R, C++	Karmasphere Studio for Hadoop (NetBeans-based)	MapReduce	Amazon S3	No	Amazon EC2

application developer using a limited subset of the native APIs on each platform, and in some instances you need to use specific Google APIs such as URLFetch, Datastore, and memcache in place of certain native API calls. For example, a deployed App Engine application cannot write to the file system directly (you must use the Google Datastore) or open a socket or access another host directly (you must use Google URL fetch service). A Java application cannot create a new Thread either.

Microsoft Azure. Microsoft Azure Cloud Services offers developers a hosted . NET Stack (C#, VB.Net, ASP.NET). In addition, a Java & Ruby SDK for .NET Services is also available. The Azure system consists of a number of elements. The Windows Azure Fabric Controller provides auto-scaling and reliability, and it manages memory resources and load balancing. The .NET Service Bus registers and connects applications together. The .NET Access Control identity providers include enterprise directories and Windows LiveID. Finally, the .NET Workflow allows construction and execution of workflow instances.

Force.com. In conjunction with the Salesforce.com service, the Force.com PaaS allows developers to create add-on functionality that integrates into main Salesforce CRM SaaS application.

Force.com offers developers two approaches to create applications that can be deployed on its SaaS plaform: a hosted Apex or Visualforce application. Apex is a proprietary Java-like language that can be used to create Salesforce applications. Visualforce is an XML-like syntax for building UIs in HTML, AJAX, or Flex to overlay over the Salesforce hosted CRM system. An application store called AppExchange is also provided, which offers a paid & free application directory.

Heroku. Heroku is a platform for instant deployment of Ruby on Rails Web applications. In the Heroku system, servers are invisibly managed by the platform and are never exposed to users. Applications are automatically dispersed across different CPU cores and servers, maximizing performance and minimizing contention. Heroku has an advanced logic layer than can automatically route around failures, ensuring seamless and uninterrupted service at all times.

1.8 CHALLENGES AND RISKS

Despite the initial success and popularity of the cloud computing paradigm and the extensive availability of providers and tools, a significant number of challenges and risks are inherent to this new model of computing. Providers, developers, and end users must consider these challenges and risks to take good advantage of cloud computing. Issues to be faced include user privacy, data security, data lock-in, availability of service, disaster recovery, performance, scalability, energy-efficiency, and programmability.

1.8.1 Security, Privacy, and Trust

Ambrust et al. [5] cite information security as a main issue: "current cloud offerings are essentially public...exposing the system to more attacks." For this reason there are potentially additional challenges to make cloud computing environments as secure as in-house IT systems. At the same time, existing, well-understood technologies can be leveraged, such as data encryption, VLANs, and firewalls.

Security and privacy affect the entire cloud computing stack, since there is a massive use of third-party services and infrastructures that are used to host important data or to perform critical operations. In this scenario, the trust toward providers is fundamental to ensure the desired level of privacy for applications hosted in the cloud [38].

Legal and regulatory issues also need attention. When data are moved into the Cloud, providers may choose to locate them anywhere on the planet. The physical location of data centers determines the set of laws that can be applied to the management of data. For example, specific cryptography techniques could not be used because they are not allowed in some countries. Similarly, country laws can impose that sensitive data, such as patient health records, are to be stored within national borders.

1.8.2 Data Lock-In and Standardization

A major concern of cloud computing users is about having their data locked-in by a certain provider. Users may want to move data and applications out from a provider that does not meet their requirements. However, in their current form, cloud computing infrastructures and platforms do not employ standard methods of storing user data and applications. Consequently, they do not interoperate and user data are not portable.

The answer to this concern is standardization. In this direction, there are efforts to create open standards for cloud computing.

The Cloud Computing Interoperability Forum (CCIF) was formed by organizations such as Intel, Sun, and Cisco in order to "enable a global cloud computing ecosystem whereby organizations are able to seamlessly work together for the purposes for wider industry adoption of cloud computing technology." The development of the Unified Cloud Interface (UCI) by CCIF aims at creating a standard programmatic point of access to an entire cloud infrastructure.

In the hardware virtualization sphere, the Open Virtual Format (OVF) aims at facilitating packing and distribution of software to be run on VMs so that virtual appliances can be made portable—that is, seamlessly run on hypervisor of different vendors.

1.8.3 Availability, Fault-Tolerance, and Disaster Recovery

It is expected that users will have certain expectations about the service level to be provided once their applications are moved to the cloud. These expectations include availability of the service, its overall performance, and what measures are to be taken when something goes wrong in the system or its components. In summary, users seek for a warranty before they can comfortably move their business to the cloud.

SLAs, which include QoS requirements, must be ideally set up between customers and cloud computing providers to act as warranty. An SLA specifies the details of the service to be provided, including availability and performance guarantees. Additionally, metrics must be agreed upon by all parties, and penalties for violating the expectations must also be approved.

1.8.4 Resource Management and Energy-Efficiency

One important challenge faced by providers of cloud computing services is the efficient management of virtualized resource pools. Physical resources such as CPU cores, disk space, and network bandwidth must be sliced and shared among virtual machines running potentially heterogeneous workloads.

The multi-dimensional nature of virtual machines complicates the activity of finding a good mapping of VMs onto available physical hosts while maximizing user utility. Dimensions to be considered include: number of CPUs, amount of memory, size of virtual disks, and network bandwidth. Dynamic VM mapping policies may leverage the ability to suspend, migrate, and resume VMs as an easy way of preempting low-priority allocations in favor of higher-priority ones. Migration of VMs also brings additional challenges such as detecting when to initiate a migration, which VM to migrate, and where to migrate. In addition, policies may take advantage of live migration of virtual machines to relocate data center load without significantly disrupting running services. In this case, an additional concern is the trade-off between the negative impact of a live migration on the performance and stability of a service and the benefits to be achieved with that migration [73].

Another challenge concerns the outstanding amount of data to be managed in various VM management activities. Such data amount is a result of particular abilities of virtual machines, including the ability of traveling through space (i.e., migration) and time (i.e., checkpointing and rewinding) [74], operations that may be required in load balancing, backup, and recovery scenarios. In addition, dynamic provisioning of new VMs and replicating existing VMs require efficient mechanisms to make VM block storage devices (e.g., image files) quickly available at selected hosts.

Data centers consumer large amounts of electricity. According to a data published by HP [4], 100 server racks can consume 1.3 MW of power and another 1.3 MW are required by the cooling system, thus costing USD 2.6 million per year. Besides the monetary cost, data centers significantly impact the environment in terms of CO_2 emissions from the cooling systems [52].

In addition to optimize application performance, dynamic resource management can also improve utilization and consequently minimize energy consumption in data centers. This can be done by judiciously consolidating workload onto smaller number of servers and turning off idle resources.

1.9 SUMMARY

Cloud computing is a new computing paradigm that offers a huge amount of compute and storage resources to the masses. Individuals (e.g., scientists) and enterprises (e.g., startup companies) can have access to these resources by paying a small amount of money just for what is really needed.

This introductory chapter has surveyed many technologies that have led to the advent of cloud computing, concluding that this new paradigm has been a result of an evolution rather than a revolution.

In their various shapes and flavors, clouds aim at offering compute, storage, network, software, or a combination of those "as a service." Infrastructure-, Platform-, and Software-as-a-service are the three most common nomenclatures for the levels of abstraction of cloud computing services, ranging from "raw" virtual servers to elaborate hosted applications.

A great popularity and apparent success have been visible in this area. However, as discussed in this chapter, significant challenges and risks need to be tackled by industry and academia in order to guarantee the long-term success of cloud computing. Visible trends in this sphere include the emergence of standards; the creation of value-added services by augmenting, combining, and brokering existing compute, storage, and software services; and the availability of more providers in all levels, thus increasing competiveness and innovation. In this sense, numerous opportunities exist for practitioners seeking to create solutions for cloud computing.

REFERENCES

1. I. Foster, The grid: Computing without bounds, *Scientific American*, vol. 288, No. 4, (April 2003), pp. 78–85.

2. R. Buyya, C. S. Yeo, S. Venugopal, J. Broberg, and I. Brandic, Cloud computing and emerging IT platforms: Vision, hype, and reality for delivering computing as the 5th utility, *Future Generation Computer Systems*, **25**:599–616, 2009.

3. L. M. Vaquero, L. Rodero-Merino, J. Caceres, and M. Lindner, A break in the clouds: Towards a cloud definition, *SIGCOMM Computer Communications Review*, **39**:50–55, 2009.

4. McKinsey & Co., Clearing the Air on Cloud Computing, *Technical Report*, 2009.

5. M. Armbrust, A. Fox, R. Griffith, A. D. Joseph, and R. Katz, Above the Clouds: A Berkeley View of Cloud Computing, *UC Berkeley Reliable Adaptive Distributed Systems Laboratory White Paper*, 2009.

6. P. Mell and T. Grance, The NIST Definition of Cloud Computing, National Institute of Standards and Technology, Information Technology Laboratory, *Technical Report Version 15*, 2009.

7. B. Sotomayor, R. S. Montero, I. M. Llorente, and I. Foster, Virtual infrastructure management in private and hybrid clouds, *IEEE Internet Computing*, **13**(5):14–22, September/October, 2009.

8. N. Carr, *The Big Switch: Rewiring the World*, from Edison to Google.W. W. Norton & Co., New York, 2008.

9. M. A. Rappa, The utility business model and the future of computing systems, *IBM Systems Journal*, **43**(1):32–42, 2004.

10. C. S. Yeo et al., Utility computing on global grids, Chapter 143, Hossein Bidgoli (ed.), *The Handbook of Computer Networks*, ISBN: 978-0-471-78461-6, John Wiley & Sons, New York, USA, 2007.

11. I. Foster and S. Tuecke, Describing the elephant: The different faces of IT as service, *ACM Queue*, **3**(6):26–29, 2005.

12. M. P. Papazoglou and W.-J. van den Heuvel, Service oriented architectures: Approaches, technologies and research issues, *The VLDB Journal*, **16**:389–415, 2007.

13. H. Kreger, Fulfilling the Web services promise, *Communications of the ACM*, **46**(6):29, 2003.

14. B. Blau, D. Neumann, C. Weinhardt, and S. Lamparter, Planning and pricing of service mashups, in *Proceedings of the 2008 10th IEEE Conference on E-Commerce Technology and the Fifth IEEE Conference on Enterprise Computing, E-Commerce and E-Services*, Crystal City, Washington, DC, 2008, pp.19–26.

15. C. Catlett, The philosophy of TeraGrid: Building an open, extensible, distributed TeraScale facility, in *Proceedings of 2nd IEEE/ACM International Symposium on Cluster Computing and the Grid*, Berlin, Germany, 2002, p. 8.

16. F. Gagliardi, B. Jones, F. Grey, M. E. Begin, and M. Heikkurinen, Building an infrastructure for scientific grid computing: Status and goals of the EGEE project, *Philosophical Transactions of the Royal Society A: Mathematical, Physical and Engineering Sciences*, **363**(1833):1729, 2005.

17. J. Broberg, S. Venugopal, and R. Buyya, Market-oriented Grid and utility computing: The state-of-the-art and future directions, *Journal of Grid Computing*, **6**:255–276, 2008.

18. I. Foster, Globus toolkit version 4: Software for service-oriented systems, *Journal of Computer Science and Technology*, **21**(513–520), 2006.

19. R. Buyya and S. Venugopal, *Market oriented computing and global Grids: An introduction*, in *Market Oriented Grid and Utility Computing*, R. Buyya and K. Bubendorfer (eds.), John Wiley & Sons, Hoboken, NJ, 2009, pp. 24–44.

20. K. Keahey, I. Foster, T. Freeman, and X. Zhang, Virtual workspaces: Achieving quality of service and quality of life in the grid, *Scientific Programming*, **13**(4):265–275, 2005.

21. R. P. Goldberg, Survey of virtual machine research, *IEEE Computer*, **7**(6):34–45, 1974.

22. R. Uhlig et al., Intel virtualization technology, *IEEE Computer*, **38**(5):48–56, 2005.

23. P. Barham et al., Xen and the art of virtualization, in *Proceedings of 19th ACM Symposium on Operation Systems Principles*, New York, 2003, pp. 164–177.

24. VMWare Inc., VMWare, *http://www.vmware.com*, 22/4/2010.

25. Xen.org Community, *http://www.xen.org*, 22/4/2010.

26. Citrix Systems Inc., XenServer, *http://www.citrix.com/XenServer*, 22/4/2010.

27. Oracle Corp., Oracle VM, *http://www.oracle.com/technology/products/vm*, 24/4/2010.

28. KVM Project, Kernel based virtual machine, *http://www.linux-kvm.org*, 22/4/2010.

29. A. Kivity, Y. Kamay, D. Laor, U. Lublin, and A. Liguori, KVM: The Linux virtual machine monitor, in *Proceedings of the Linux Symposium*, Ottawa, Canada, 2007, p. 225.

30. VMWare Inc., VMWare Virtual Appliance Marketplace, *http://www.vmware.com/appliances*, 22/4/2010.

31. Amazon Web Services Developer Community, Amazon Machine Images, *http://developer.amazonwebservices.com/connect/kbcategory.jspa?categoryID = 171*, 22/4/2010.

32. Distributed Management Task Force Inc, Open Virtualization Format, *Specification DSP0243 Version 1.0.0*, 2009.

33. J. Matthews, T. Garfinkel, C. Hoff, and J. Wheeler, Virtual machine contracts for datacenter and cloud computing environments, in *Proceedings of the 1st Workshop on Automated Control for Datacenters and Clouds*, 2009, pp. 25–30.

34. International Business Machines Corp., An architectural blueprint for autonomic computing, *White Paper Fourth Edition*, 2006.

35. M. C. Huebscher and J. A. McCann, A survey of autonomic computing—degrees, models, and applications, *ACM Computing Surveys*, **40**:1–28, 2008.

36. VMWare Inc., VMware vSphere, *http://www.vmware.com/products/vsphere/*, 22/4/2010.

37. L. Youseff, M. Butrico, and D. Da Silva, Toward a unified ontology of cloud computing, in *Proceedings of the 2008 Grid Computing Environments Workshop*, 2008, pp. 1–10.

38. R. Buyya, S. Pandey, and C. Vecchiola, Cloudbus toolkit for market-oriented cloud computing, in *Proceedings 1st International Conference on Cloud Computing (CloudCom 09)*, Beijing, 2009, pp. 3–27.

39. D. Nurmi, R. Wolski, C. Grzegorczyk, G. Obertelli, S. Soman, L. Youseff, and D. Zagorodnov, The Eucalyptus open-source cloud-computing system, in *Proceedings of IEEE/ACM International Symposium on Cluster Computing and the Grid (CCGrid 2009)*, Shanghai, China, pp. 124–131, University of California, Santa Barbara. (2009, Sep.) Eucalyptus [online]. http://open.eucalyptus.com.

40. Appistry Inc., Cloud Platforms vs. Cloud Infrastructure, *White Paper*, 2009.

41. B. Hayes, Cloud computing, *Communications of the ACM*, **51**:9–11, 2008.

42. P. T. Jaeger, J. Lin, J. M. Grimes, and S. N. Simmons, Where is the cloud? Geography, economics, environment, and jurisdiction in cloud computing, *First Monday*, **14**(4–5): 2009.

43. VMWare Inc., VMware vSphere, the First Cloud Operating, *White Paper*, 2009.

44. Platform Computing, Platform ISF Datasheet, *White Paper*, 2009.

45. M. D. de Assuncao, A. di Costanzo, and R. Buyya, Evaluating the cost–benefit of using cloud computing to extend the capacity of clusters, in *Proceedings of the 18th ACM International Symposium on High Performance Distributed Computing (HPDC 2009)*, Munich, Germany, 2009, pp. 141–150.

46. D. Amrhein, Websphere Journal, *http://websphere.sys-con.com/node/1029500*, 22/4/2010.

47. Libvirt: The Virtualization API, Terminology and Goals, *http://libvirt.org/goals.html*, 22/4/2010.

48. A. Singh, M. Korupolu, and D. Mohapatra, Server-storage virtualization: Integration and load balancing in data centers, in *Proceedings of the 2008 ACM/IEEE Conference on Supercomputing*, 2008, pp. 1–12.

49. R. Perlman, *Interconnections: Bridges, Routers, Switches, and Internetworking Protocols*, Addison-Wesley Longman, Boston, MA, 1999.

50. A. S. Tanenbaum, *Computer Networks*, Prentice-Hall, Upper Saddle River, NJ, 2002.

51. D. Gmach, J. Rolia, L. Cherkasova, and A. Kemper, Capacity management and demand prediction for next generation data centers, in *Proceedings of IEEE International Conference on Web Services*, 2007, pp. 43—50.

52. A. Verma, P. Ahuja, and A. Neogi, pMapper: Power and migration cost aware application placement in virtualized systems, in *Proceedings of the 9th ACM/IFIP/USENIX International Conference on Middleware*, 2008, pp. 243—264.

53. K. Keahey and T. Freeman, Contextualization: Providing one-click virtual clusters, in *Proceedings of IEEE Fourth International Conference on eScience*, 2008, pp. 301—308.

54. B. Sotomayor, K. Keahey, and I. Foster, Combining batch execution and leasing using virtual machines, in *Proceedings of the 17th International Symposium on High Performance Distributed Computing*, 2008, pp. 87—96.

55. B. Sotomayor, R. Montero, I. M. Llorente, and I. Foster, Capacity leasing in cloud systems using the opennebula engine, *Cloud Computing and Applications*, 2008.

56. S. Venugopal, J. Broberg, and R. Buyya, OpenPEX: An open provisioning and EXecution system for virtual machines, in *Proceedings of the 17th International Conference on Advanced Computing and Communications (ADCOM 2009)*, Bengaluru, India, 2009.

57. VMWare Inc., VMware High Availability (HA), *http://www.vmware.com/products/high-availability/index.html*, 22/4/2010.

58. Citrix Systems Inc., The three levels of high availability—Balancing priorities and cost, *White Paper*, 2008.

59. VMWare Inc., VMWare vStorage APIs for Data Protection, *http://www.vmware.com/products/vstorage-apis-for-data-protection*, 22/4/2010.

60. H. E. Schaffer et al., NCSUs Virtual Computing Lab: A cloud computing solution, *Computer*, **42**:94–97, 2009.

61. North Carolina State University, Virtual Computing Lab (VCL), *http://vcl.ncsu.edu*, 22/4/2010.

62. 3tera Inc., AppLogic—Grid Operating System for Web Applications, *http://www.3tera.com/AppLogic*, 22/4/2010.

63. 3Tera Inc., The AppLogic Grid Operating System, *White Paper*, 2006.

64. Citrix Systems Inc., Citrix essentials for Hyper-V, *http://www.citrix.com/ehv*, 22/4/2010.

65. Distributed Systems Architecture Group, OpenNebula: The open source toolkit for cloud computing, *http://www.opennebula.org*, 22/4/2010.

66. University of Chicago, Haizea—An open source VM-based lease manager, *http://haizea.cs.uchicago.edu*, 22/4/2010.

67. Red Hat's Emerging Technology group, oVirt, *http://ovirt.org*, 22/4/2010.

68. Platform Computing Corporation, Platform ISF. *http://www.platform.com/Products/platform-isf*, 22/4/2010.

69. Platform Computing, Platform VM Orchestrator, *http://www.platform.com/Products/platform-vm-orchestrator*, 22/4/2010.

70. Amazon Inc., Amazon Web Services, *http://www.amazon.com*, 22/4/2010.

71. F. Chang et al., Bigtable: A distributed storage system for structured data, in *Proceedings of the 7th USENIX Symposium on Operating Systems Design and Implementation (OSDI'06)*, 2006, pp. 205–218.

72. C. Vecchiola, X. Chu, and R. Buyya, Aneka: A software platform for .NET-based cloud computing, in *High Speed and Large Scale Scientific Computing*, W. Gentzsch, L. Grandinetti, and G. Joubert (eds.), IOS Press, Amsterdam, Netherlands, 2009, pp. 267–295.

73. W. Voorsluys, J. Broberg, S. Venugopal, and R. Buyya, Cost of virtual machine live migration in clouds: A performance evaluation, in *Proceedings 1st International Conference on Cloud Computing*, Beijing, 2009, pp. 254–265.

74. D. T. Meyer et al., Parallax: Virtual disks for virtual machines, in *Proceedings of the 3rd ACM SIGOPS/EuroSys European Conference on Computer Systems*, 2008, pp. 41–54.

CHAPTER 2

MIGRATING INTO A CLOUD

T. S. MOHAN

2.1 INTRODUCTION

The promise of cloud computing has raised the IT expectations of small and medium enterprises beyond measure. Large companies are deeply debating it. Cloud computing is a disruptive model of IT whose innovation is part technology and part business model—in short a "disruptive techno-commercial model" of IT. This tutorial chapter focuses on the key issues and associated dilemmas faced by decision makers, architects, and systems managers in trying to understand and leverage cloud computing for their IT needs. Questions asked and discussed in this chapter include: when and how to migrate one's application into a cloud; what part or component of the IT application to migrate into a cloud and what not to migrate into a cloud; what kind of customers really benefit from migrating their IT into the cloud; and so on. We describe the key factors underlying each of the above questions and share a Seven-Step Model of Migration into the Cloud.

Cloud computing has been a hotly debated and discussed topic amongst IT professionals and researchers both in the industry and in academia. There are intense discussions on several blogs, in Web sites, and in several research efforts [1−4]. This also resulted in several entrepreneurial efforts to help leverage and migrate into the cloud given the myriad issues, challenges, benefits, and limitations and lack of comprehensive understanding of what cloud computing can do. On the one hand, there were these large cloud computing IT vendors like Google, Amazon, and Microsoft, who had started offering cloud computing services on what seemed like a demonstration and trial basis though not explicitly mentioned. They were charging users fees that in certain contexts demonstrated very attractive pricing models. It demonstrated that cloud computing *per se* was for real and that the "techno-commerical disruptive

Cloud Computing: Principles and Paradigms, Edited by Rajkumar Buyya, James Broberg and Andrzej Goscinski Copyright © 2011 John Wiley & Sons, Inc.

business model" was indeed giving a greater return on investment (ROI) than traditional IT investment for a business. On the other hand, these initial cloud computing offerings were premature. The cloud computing service vendors were grappling real issues of distributed systems as well as business models and had a number open engineering and research problems [2] that indicated in multiple ways that the cloud computing services were yet to mature fully.

Several efforts have been made in the recent past to define the term "cloud computing" and many have not been able to provide a comprehensive one [2, 5, 6]. This has been more challenging given the scorching pace of the technological advances as well as the newer business model formulations for the cloud services being offered. We propose the following definition of cloud computing: "*It is a techno-business disruptive model of using distributed large-scale data centers either private or public or hybrid offering customers a scalable virtualized infrastructure or an abstracted set of services qualified by service-level agreements (SLAs) and charged only by the abstracted IT resources consumed.*" Most enterprises today are powered by captive data centers. In most large or small enterprises today, IT is the backbone of their operations. Invariably for these large enterprises, their data centers are distributed across various geographies. They comprise systems and software that span several generations of products sold by a variety of IT vendors. In order to meet varying loads, most of these data centers are provisioned with capacity beyond the peak loads experienced. If the enterprise is in a seasonal or cyclical business, then the load variation would be significant. Thus what is observed generally is that the provisioned capacity of IT resources is several times the average demand. This is indicative of significant degree of idle capacity. Many data center management teams have been continuously innovating their management practices and technologies deployed to possibly squeeze out the last possible usable computing resource cycle through appropriate programming, systems configurations, SLAs, and systems management. Cloud computing turned attractive to them because they could pass on the additional demand from their IT setups onto the cloud while paying only for the usage and being unencumbered by the load of operations and management.

2.1.1 The Promise of the Cloud

Most users of cloud computing services offered by some of the large-scale data centers are least bothered about the complexities of the underlying systems or their functioning. More so given the heterogeneity of either the systems or the software running on them. They were most impressed by the simplicity, uniformity, and ease of use of the Cloud Computing Service abstractions. In small and medium enterprises, cloud computing usage for all additional cyclical IT needs has yielded substantial and significant economic savings. Many such success stories have been documented and discussed on the Internet. This economics and the associated trade-offs, of leveraging the cloud computing services, now popularly called "cloudonomics," for satisfying enterprise's

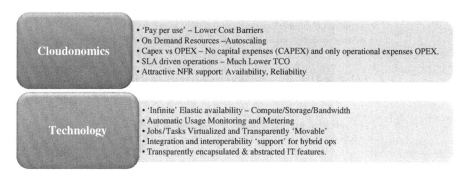

Cloudonomics
- 'Pay per use' – Lower Cost Barriers
- On Demand Resources –Autoscaling
- Capex vs OPEX – No capital expenses (CAPEX) and only operational expenses OPEX.
- SLA driven operations – Much Lower TCO
- Attractive NFR support: Availability, Reliability

Technology
- 'Infinite' Elastic availability – Compute/Storage/Bandwidth
- Automatic Usage Monitoring and Metering
- Jobs/Tasks Virtualized and Transparently 'Movable'
- Integration and interoperability 'support' for hybrid ops
- Transparently encapsulated & abstracted IT features.

FIGURE 2.1. The promise of the cloud computing services.

seasonal IT loads has become a topic of deep interest amongst IT managers and technology architects.

As shown in Figure 2.1, the promise of the cloud both on the business front (the attractive cloudonomics) and the technology front widely aided the CxOs to spawn out several non-mission critical IT needs from the ambit of their captive traditional data centers to the appropriate cloud service. Invariably, these IT needs had some common features: They were typically Web-oriented; they represented seasonal IT demands; they were amenable to parallel batch processing; they were non-mission critical and therefore did not have high security demands. They included scientific applications too [7]. Several small and medium business enterprises, however, leveraged the cloud much beyond the cautious user. Many startups opened their IT departments exclusively using cloud services—very successfully and with high ROI. Having observed these successes, several large enterprises have started successfully running pilots for leveraging the cloud. Many large enterprises run SAP to manage their operations. SAP itself is experimenting with running its suite of products: SAP Business One as well as SAP Netweaver on Amazon cloud offerings. Gartner, Forrester, and other industry research analysts predict that a substantially significant percentage of the top enterprises in the world would have migrated a majority of their IT needs to the cloud offerings by 2012, thereby demonstrating the widespread impact and benefits from cloud computing. Indeed the promise of the cloud has been significant in its impact.

2.1.2 The Cloud Service Offerings and Deployment Models

Cloud computing has been an attractive proposition both for the CFO and the CTO of an enterprise primarily due its ease of usage. This has been achieved by large data center service vendors or now better known as cloud service vendors again primarily due to their scale of operations. Google,[1] Amazon,[2]

[1] http://appengine.google.com

[2] http://aws.amazon.com

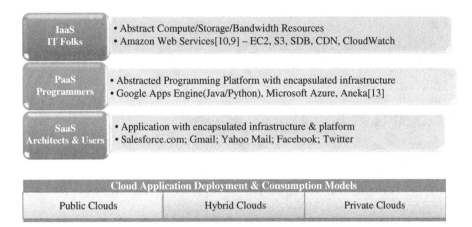

Cloud Application Deployment & Consumption Models		
Public Clouds	Hybrid Clouds	Private Clouds

FIGURE 2.2. The cloud computing service offering and deployment models.

Microsoft,[3] and a few others have been the key players apart from open source Hadoop[4] built around the Apache ecosystem. As shown in Figure 2.2, the cloud service offerings from these vendors can broadly be classified into three major streams: the *Infrastructure as a Service* (IaaS), the *Platform as a Service* (PaaS), and the *Software as a Service* (SaaS). While IT managers and system administrators preferred IaaS as offered by Amazon for many of their virtualized IT needs, the programmers preferred PaaS offerings like Google AppEngine (Java/Python programming) or Microsoft Azure (.Net programming). Users of large-scale enterprise software invariably found that if they had been using the cloud, it was because their usage of the specific software package was available as a service—it was, in essence, a SaaS offering. Salesforce.com was an exemplary SaaS offering on the Internet.

From a technology viewpoint, as of today, the IaaS type of cloud offerings have been the most successful and widespread in usage. However, the potential of PaaS has been high: All new cloud-oriented application development initiatives are based on the PaaS model. The significant impact of enterprises leveraging IaaS and PaaS has been in the form of services whose usage is representative of SaaS on the Cloud. Be it search (Google/Yahoo/Bing, etc.) or email (Gmail/Yahoomail/Hotmail, etc.) or social networking (Facebook/Twitter/Orkut, etc.), most users are unaware that much of their on-line activities has been supported in one form or the other by the cloud.

The cloud application deployment and consumption was modeled at three levels: the public cloud offerings from cloud vendors; the private cloud initiatives within large enterprises; and the hybrid cloud initiatives that leverage both the public cloud and the private cloud or managed services data centers.

[3] http://azure.microsoft.com
[4] http://hadoop.apache.org

The IaaS–oriented services offered abstracted (or virtualized and scalable) hardware—like compute power or storage or bandwidth. For example, as seen from its pricing tariffs webpage for 2009, Amazon[5] offered six levels of abstracted *elastic cloud compute* (EC2) server power: the "small-instance," "large-instance," "extra-large instance," "high-cpu instance," "high-cpu medium instance," or "high-cpu extra-large instance." Each of these are accompanied by appropriate RAM, storage, performance guarantees, and bandwidth support. The PaaS offerings are focused on supporting programming platforms whose runtime implicitly use's cloud services offered by their respective vendors. As of today, these highly vendor-locked PaaS technologies have been leveraged to develop new applications by many startups. Compared to IaaS offerings, applications riding on PaaS deliver better performance due to the intrinsic cloud support for the programming platform. The SaaS on Cloud offerings are focused on supporting large software package usage leveraging cloud benefits. Most users of these packages are invariably ignorant of the underlying cloud support—in fact most, if not all, do not care. Indeed, a significant degree of the features of the software package invariably reflect the support of the cloud computing platform under the hood. For example, in gmail, users hardly bother about either the storage space taken up or whether an email needs to be deleted or its storage location. Invariably these reflect the cloud underneath, where storage (most do not know on which system it is) is easily scalable or for that matter where it is stored or located.

2.1.3 Challenges in the Cloud

While the cloud service offerings present a simplistic view of IT in case of IaaS or a simplistic view of programming in case PaaS or a simplistic view of resources usage in case of SaaS, the underlying systems level support challenges are huge and highly complex. These stem from the need to offer a uniformly consistent and robustly simplistic view of computing while the underlying systems are highly failure-prone, heterogeneous, resource hogging, and exhibiting serious security shortcomings. As observed in Figure 2.3, the promise of the cloud seems very similar to the typical distributed systems properties that most would prefer to have. Invariably either in the IaaS or PaaS or SaaS cloud services, one is proffered features that smack of full network reliability; or having "instant" or "zero" network latency; or perhaps supporting "infinite" bandwidth; and so on. But then robust distributed systems are built while keeping mind that are these fallacies[6] that must be studiously avoided at design time as well as during implementations and deployments. Cloud computing has the ironical role of projecting this idealized view of its services while ensuring that the underlying systems are managed realistically. In fact the challenges in implementing cloud computing services are plenty: Many

---

[5] http://aws.amazon.com/ec2
[6] http://blogs.sun.com/jag/resource/Fallacies.html

FIGURE 2.3. 'Under the hood' challenges of the cloud computing services implementations.

of them are listed in Figure 2.3. Prime amongst these are the challenges of security. The Cloud Security Alliance seeks to address many of these issues [8].

2.2 BROAD APPROACHES TO MIGRATING INTO THE CLOUD

Given that cloud computing is a "techno-business disruptive model" and is on the top of the top 10 strategic technologies to watch for 2010 according to Gartner,[7] migrating into the cloud is poised to become a large-scale effort in leveraging the cloud in several enterprises. "Cloudonomics" deals with the economic rationale for leveraging the cloud and is central to the success of cloud-based enterprise usage. At what IT costs—both short term and long term—would one want to migrate into the cloud? While all capital expenses are eliminated and only operational expenses incurred by leveraging the cloud, does this satisfy all strategic parameters for enterprise IT? Does the total cost of ownership (TCO) become significantly less as compared to that incurred when running one's own private data center? Decision-makers, IT managers, and software architects are faced with several dilemmas when planning for new Enterprise IT initiatives.

2.2.1 Why Migrate?

There are economic and business reasons why an enterprise application can be migrated into the cloud, and there are also a number of technological reasons. Many of these efforts come up as initiatives in adoption of cloud technologies in the enterprise, resulting in integration of enterprise applications running off the captive data centers with the new ones that have been developed on the cloud. Adoption of or integration with cloud computing services is a use case of migration.

[7] http://www.gartner.com/it/page.jsp?id=1210613

At the core, migration of an application into the cloud can happen in one of several ways: Either the application is clean and independent, so it runs as is; or perhaps some degree of code needs to be modified and adapted; or the design (and therefore the code) needs to be first migrated into the cloud computing service environment; or finally perhaps the migration results in the core architecture being migrated for a cloud computing service setting, this resulting in a new architecture being developed, along with the accompanying design and code implementation. Or perhaps while the application is migrated as is, it is the usage of the application that needs to be migrated and therefore adapted and modified. In brief, migration can happen at one of the five levels of application, code, design, architecture, and usage.

With due simplification, the migration of an enterprise application is best captured by the following:

$$P \rightarrow P'_C + P'_l \rightarrow P'_{OFC} + P'_l$$

where P is the application before migration running in captive data center, P'_C is the application part after migration either into a (hybrid) cloud, P'_l is the part of application being run in the captive local data center, and P'_{OFC} is the application part *optimized for cloud.* If an enterprise application cannot be migrated fully, it could result in some parts being run on the captive local data center while the rest are being migrated into the cloud—essentially a case of a hybrid cloud usage. However, when the entire application is migrated onto the cloud, then P'_l is null. Indeed, the migration of the enterprise application P can happen at the five levels of application, code, design, architecture, and usage. It can be that the P'_C migration happens at any of the five levels without any P'_l component. Compound this with the kind of cloud computing service offering being applied—the IaaS model or PaaS or SaaS model—and we have a variety of migration use cases that need to be thought through thoroughly by the migration architects. To capture this situation succinctly, on enumeration, we have the following migration scenario use-case numbers: For migrating into an IaaS offering, there are 30 use-case scenarios. For migrating into a PaaS offering, there are 20 use-case scenarios. For migrating into a SaaS offering, it is purely a case of migration of usage, with no accompanying enterprise application migration—like the case of migrating from an existing local ERP system to SAP already being offered on a cloud. Of course, for each of these migration use-case scenarios, detailed approaches exist while for many commonly applicable scenarios, enterprises have consolidated their migration strategy best practices. In fact, the migration industry thrives on these custom and proprietary best practices. Many of these best practices are specialized at the level of the components of an enterprise application—like migrating application servers or the enterprise databases.

Cloudonomics. Invariably, migrating into the cloud is driven by economic reasons of cost cutting in both the IT capital expenses (Capex) as well as

operational expenses (Opex). There are both the short-term benefits of opportunistic migration to offset seasonal and highly variable IT loads as well as the
long-term benefits to leverage the cloud. For the long-term sustained usage, as of
2009, several impediments and shortcomings of the cloud computing services
need to be addressed.

At the core of the cloudonomics, as articulated in Ambrust et al. [2], is the
expression of when a migration can be economically feasible or tenable. If
the average costs of using an enterprise application on a cloud is substantially
lower than the costs of using it in one's captive data center and if the cost of
migration does not add to the burden on ROI, then the case for migration into
the cloud is strong.

Apart from these costs, other factors that play a major role in the cloudonomics of migration are the licensing issues (for perhaps parts of the enterprise
application), the SLA compliances, and the pricing of the cloud service offerings.
Most cloud service vendors, at a broad level, have tariffs for the kind of elastic
compute, the elastic storage, or the elastic bandwidth. Of course these pricing
tariffs can be variable too, and therefore the cloudonomics of migration should
be soundly meaningful accommodating the pricing variability.

2.2.2 Deciding on the Cloud Migration

In fact, several proof of concepts and prototypes of the enterprise application
are experimented on the cloud to take help in making a sound decision on
migrating into the cloud. Post migration, the ROI on the migration should be
positive for a broad range of pricing variability. Arriving at a decision for
undertaking migration demands that either the compelling factors be clearly
understood or the pragmatic approach of consulting a group of experts be
constituted. In the latter case, much like software estimation, one applies Wide-
Band Delphi Techniques [9] to make decisions. We use the following technique:
A questionnaire with several classes of key questions that impact the IT due to
the migration of the enterprise application is posed to a select audience chosen
for their technology and business expertise. Assume that there are M such
classes. Each class of questions is assigned a certain relative weightage B_i in the
context of the entire questionnaire. Assume that in the M classes of questions,
there was a class with a maximum of N questions. We can then model the
weightage-based decision making as $M \times N$ weightage matrix as follows:

$$C_l \leq \sum_{i=1}^{M} B_i \left(\sum_{j=1}^{N} A_{ij} X_{ij} \right) \leq C_h$$

where C_l is the lower weightage threshold and C_h is the higher weightage
threshold while A_{ij} is the specific constant assigned for a question and X_{ij} is the
fraction between 0 and 1 that represents the degree to which that answer to
the question is relevant and applicable. Since all except one class of questions
do not have all N questions, the corresponding has a null value. The lower

and higher thresholds are defined to rule out trivial cases of migration. A simplified variant of this method can be presented as a balanced scorecard-oriented decision making. An example of that approach to the adoption of cloud is found in Dargha [10].

2.3 THE SEVEN-STEP MODEL OF MIGRATION INTO A CLOUD

Typically migration initiatives into the cloud are implemented in phases or in stages. A structured and process-oriented approach to migration into a cloud has several advantages of capturing within itself the best practices of many migration projects. While migration has been a difficult and vague subject—of not much interest to the academics and left to the industry practitioners—not many efforts across the industry have been put in to consolidate what has been found to be both a top revenue earner and a long standing customer pain. After due study and practice, we share the *Seven-Step Model of Migration into the Cloud* as part of our efforts in understanding and leveraging the cloud computing service offerings in the enterprise context. In a succinct way, Figure 2.4 captures the essence of the steps in the model of migration into the cloud, while Figure 2.5 captures the iterative process of the seven-step migration into the cloud.

Cloud migration assessments comprise assessments to understand the issues involved in the specific case of migration at the application level or the code, the design, the architecture, or usage levels. In addition, migration assessments are done for the tools being used, the test cases as well as configurations, functionalities, and NFRs of the enterprise application. This results in a meaningful formulation of a comprehensive migration strategy. The first step of the iterative process of the seven-step model of migration is basically at the assessment level. Proof of concepts or prototypes for various approaches to the migration along with the leveraging of pricing parameters enables one to make appropriate assessments.

These assessments are about the cost of migration as well as about the ROI that can be achieved in the case of production version. The next process step is in isolating all systemic and environmental dependencies of the enterprise

1. Conduct Cloud Migration Assessments

2. Isolate the Dependencies

3. Map the Messaging & Environment

4. Re-architect & Implement the lost Functionalities

5. Leverage Cloud Functionalities & Features

6. Test the Migration

7. Iterate and Optimize

FIGURE 2.4. The Seven-Step Model of Migration into the Cloud. (*Source:* Infosys Research.)

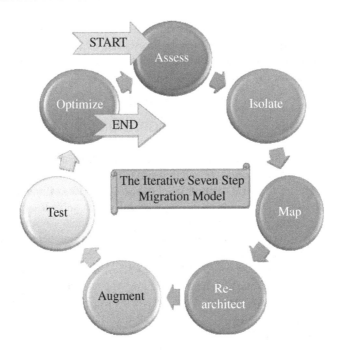

FIGURE 2.5. The iterative Seven-step Model of Migration into the Cloud. (*Source:* Infosys Research.)

application components within the captive data center. This, in turn, yields a picture of the level of complexity of the migration. After isolation is complete, one then goes about generating the mapping constructs between what shall possibly remain in the local captive data center and what goes onto the cloud. Perhaps a substantial part of the enterprise application needs to be re-architected, redesigned, and reimplemented on the cloud. This gets in just about the functionality of the original enterprise application. Due to this migration, it is possible perhaps that some functionality is lost. In the next process step we leverage the intrinsic features of the cloud computing service to augment our enterprise application in its own small ways. Having done the augmentation, we validate and test the new form of the enterprise application with an extensive test suite that comprises testing the components of the enterprise application on the cloud as well. These test results could be positive or mixed. In the latter case, we iterate and optimize as appropriate. After several such optimizing iterations, the migration is deemed successful. Our best practices indicate that it is best to iterate through this Seven-Step Model process for optimizing and ensuring that the migration into the cloud is both robust and comprehensive. Figure 2.6 captures the typical components of the best practices accumulated in the practice of the Seven-Step Model of Migration into the Cloud. Though not comprehensive in enumeration, it is representative.

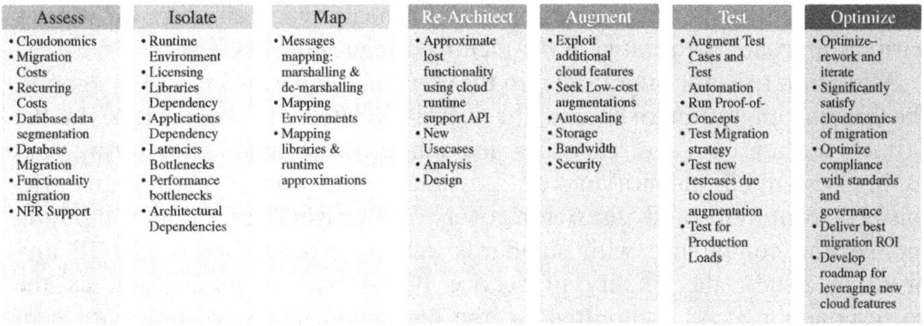

Assess	Isolate	Map	Re-Architect	Augment	Test	Optimize
• Cloudonomics • Migration Costs • Recurring Costs • Database data segmentation • Database Migration • Functionality migration • NFR Support	• Runtime Environment • Licensing • Libraries Dependency • Applications Dependency • Latencies Bottlenecks • Performance bottlenecks • Architectural Dependencies	• Messages mapping: marshalling & de-marshalling • Mapping Environments • Mapping libraries & runtime approximations	• Approximate lost functionality using cloud runtime support API • New Usecases • Analysis • Design	• Exploit additional cloud features • Seek Low-cost augmentations • Autoscaling • Storage • Bandwidth • Security	• Augment Test Cases and Test Automation • Run Proof-of-Concepts • Test Migration strategy • Test new testcases due to cloud augmentation • Test for Production Loads	• Optimize–rework and iterate • Significantly satisfy cloudonomics of migration • Optimize compliance with standards and governance • Deliver best migration ROI • Develop roadmap for leveraging new cloud features

FIGURE 2.6. Some details of the iterative Seven-Step Model of Migration into the Cloud.

Compared with the typical approach[8] to migration into the Amazon AWS, our Seven-step model is more generic, versatile, and comprehensive. The typical migration into the Amazon AWS is a phased over several steps. It is about six steps as discussed in several white papers in the Amazon website and is as follows: The first phase is the cloud migration assessment phase wherein dependencies are isolated and strategies worked out to handle these dependencies. The next phase is in trying out proof of concepts to build a reference migration architecture. The third phase is the data migration phase wherein database data segmentation and cleansing is completed. This phase also tries to leverage the various cloud storage options as best suited. The fourth phase comprises the application migration wherein either a "forklift strategy" of migrating the key enterprise application along with its dependencies (other applications) into the cloud is pursued. Or perhaps using the "hybrid migration strategy," the critical parts of the enterprise application are retained in the local captive data center while noncritical parts are moved into the cloud. The fifth phase comprises leveraging the various Amazon AWS features like elasticity, autoscaling, cloud storage, and so on. Finally in the sixth phase, the migration is optimized for the cloud. These phases are representative of how typical IT staff would like to migrate an enterprise application without touching its innards but only perhaps at the level of configurations—this perfectly matches with the typical IaaS cloud computing offerings. However, this is just a subset of our Seven-step Migration Model and is very specific and proprietary to Amazon cloud offering.

2.3.1 Migration Risks and Mitigation

The biggest challenge to any cloud migration project is how effectively the migration risks are identified and mitigated. In the Seven-Step Model of Migration into the Cloud, the process step of testing and validating includes

---

[8] http://aws.amazon.com

efforts to identify the key migration risks. In the optimization step, we address various approaches to mitigate the identified migration risks.

Migration risks for migrating into the cloud fall under two broad categories: the general migration risks and the security-related migration risks. In the former we address several issues including performance monitoring and tuning—essentially identifying all possible production level deviants; the business continuity and disaster recovery in the world of cloud computing service; the compliance with standards and governance issues; the IP and licensing issues; the quality of service (QoS) parameters as well as the corresponding SLAs committed to; the ownership, transfer, and storage of data in the application; the portability and interoperability issues which could help mitigate potential vendor lock-ins; the issues that result in trivializing and noncomprehending the complexities of migration that results in migration failure and loss of senior management's business confidence in these efforts.

On the security front, the cloud migration risks are plenty—as addressed in the guideline document published by the Cloud Security Alliance [8]. Issues include security at various levels of the enterprise application as applicable on the cloud in addition to issues of trust and issues of privacy. There are several legal compliances that a migration strategy and implementation has to fulfill, including obtaining the right execution logs as well as retaining the rights to all audit trails at a detailed level—which currently may not be fully available. On matters of governance, there are several shortcomings in the current cloud computing service vendors. Matters of multi-tenancy and the impact of IT data leakage in the cloud computing environments is acknowledged; however, the robustness of the solutions to prevent it is not fully validated. Key aspects of vulnerability management and incident responses quality are yet to be supported in a substantial way by the cloud service vendors. Finally there are issues of consistent identity management as well. These and several of the issues are discussed in Section 2.1. Issues and challenges listed in Figure 2.3 continue to be the persistent research and engineering challenges in coming up with appropriate cloud computing implementations.

2.4 CONCLUSIONS

While migrating into a cloud has a lot of challenges, many migration projects fail to fully comprehend the issues at stake—with the key sponsors and management either trivializing it or committing to migrating a piece of code and/or data into the cloud. There are significant opportunities and success factors for a well-designed cloud migration strategy leveraging the Seven-Step Model of Migration into the Cloud. Primary amongst them is a comprehensive understanding of the cloudonomics of the migration as well as the underlying technical challenges.

Developing the best practices in migrating to the cloud is unique to every class of enterprise applications and unique to every corporate practice group. Some of the key best practices include designing the migration as well as the new application architecture or design or code for failures when in reality most assume that cloud computing service environments are failsafe. In fact most cloud computing data centers use commodity hardware and are routinely prone to failure. Approaches not reflecting this reality results in several performance penalties. Another best practice is the application and enforcement of loose-coupling between various parts of the target enterprise application. A key best practice has to been to build security at every level and layer of the migration. Finally the most important of the best practices has been to fully leverage the cloud computing service features while not being constrained by the baggage carried by the enterprise application in its traditional deployment in the captive data centers. Migrating into a cloud is a nontrivial activity. It is challenging given the complexity of comprehending the various factors involved for a successful migration. The proposed Seven-Step Model of Migration into the cloud helps structure and organize one's efforts in putting together a plan of action and process to successful complete the migration without problems. Of course best practices are accumulated through migration project executions, and the seven-step model of migration is reflective of this.

ACKNOWLEDGMENTS

The author sincerely thanks S. V. Subrahmanya as well as the members of E-Com Research Labs, E&R, and Infosys for all the help and support.

REFERENCES

1. J. Broberg, S. Venugopal, and R. Buyya, Market-oriented Grids and utility computing: The state-of-the-art and future directions, *Journal of Grid Computing*, **6**(3):255–276, 2008.

2. M. Ambrust, A. Fox, R. Griffith, A. D. Joseph, R. Katz, A. Konwinski, G. Lee, D. Patterson, A. Rabkin, I. Stoica, and M. Zaharia, Above the Clouds: A Berkeley View of Cloud Computing, *UC Berkeley RAD Systems Labs*, Feb 2009.

3. G. Reese, *Cloud Application Architectures: Building Applications and Infrastructure in the Cloud*, O'Reilly, April 2007.

4. R. Buyya, C. S. Yeo, and S. Venugopal, Market-oriented cloud computing: Vision, hype, and reality for delivering IT Services as Computing Utilities, in *Proceedings of the 10th IEEE International Conference on High Performance Computing and Communications*, September 25–27, 2008, pp. 5–13 Dalian, China.

5. Cloud Definitions: NIST, Gartner, Forrester in Cloud enterprise, August 2009. (Also available at: http://cloudenterprise.info/2009/08/04/cloud-definitions-nist-gartner-forrester/)

6. T. Velte, A. Velte, and R. Elsenpeter, *Cloud Computing, A Practical Approach*, McGraw-Hill Computing, New York, 2009.

7. C. Vecchiola, S. Pandey, and R. Buyya, High-performance cloud computing: A view of scientific applications, in *Proceedings of the 10th International Symposium on Pervasive Systems, Algorithms and Networks (I-SPAN 2009, IEEE CS Press, USA)*, Kaohsiung, Taiwan, December 14–16, 2009.

8. Security Guidance for Critical Areas of Focus in Cloud Computing, The Cloud Security Alliance April/November 2009. (Also available at: http://www.cloudsecurityalliance.org/csaguide.pdf)

9. A. Stellman and J. Greene, *Applied Software Project Management*, O'Reilly Media.

10. R. Dargha, Cloud Computing—Key Considerations for Adoption, *Infosys Technologies Whitepaper*. 2009. (Also available at http://www.infosys.com/cloud-computing/white-papers/cloud-computing.pdf)

11. C. Keene, I. Poddar, J. Nicke, and U. Budink, Cloud Quick Start—A Roadmap for Adopting Cloud Computing—IBM, WaveMaker and Rightscale, *WaveMaker Software Inc. Whitepaper*, November 2009. (Also available at: http://www.wavemaker.com/ibm-quickstart.pdf)

12. A. Dubey, J. Mohiuddin, and A. Baijal, The Emerging Platform Wars in Enterprise Software, *A McKinsey & Company Whitepaper*, April 2008. (Available at http://www.mckinsey.com/clientservice/hightech/pdfs/Emerging_Platform_Wars.pdf)

13. C. Vecchiola, X. Chu, and R. Buyya, Aneka: A software platform for .NET-based Cloud computing, *High Performance & Large Scale Computing, Advances in Parallel Computing*, W. Gentzsch, L. Grandinetti, and G. Joubert (eds.), IOS Press, 2009.

14. SMART—The Service Oriented Migration and Reuse Technique. *Software Engineering Institute Tech Report*: CMU/SEI-2005-TN-029.

CHAPTER 3

ENRICHING THE 'INTEGRATION AS A SERVICE' PARADIGM FOR THE CLOUD ERA

PETHURU RAJ

3.1 AN INTRODUCTION

The trend-setting cloud paradigm actually represents the cool conglomeration of a number of proven and promising Web and enterprise technologies. Though the cloud idea is not conceptually new, practically it has brought in myriad tectonic shifts for the whole information and communication technology (ICT) industry. The cloud concepts have progressively and perceptibly impacted the IT and business domains on several critical aspects. The cloud computing has brought in series of novelty-packed deployment, delivery, consumption and pricing models whereas the service orientation prescribes a much simpler application design mechanism. The noteworthy contribution of the much-discoursed and deliberated cloud computing is the faster realization and proliferation of dynamic, converged, adaptive, on-demand, and online compute infrastructures, which are the key requirement for the future IT. The delightful distinctions here are that clouds guarantee most of the non-function requirements (Quality of Service (QoS) attributes) such as availability, high performance, on-demand scalability/elasticity, affordability, global-scale accessibility and usability, energy efficiency etc.

Having understood the exceptional properties of cloud infrastructures (hereafter will be described as just clouds), most of the global enterprises (small, medium and even large) are steadily moving their IT offerings such as business services and applications to clouds. This transition will facilitate a

Cloud Computing: Principles and Paradigms, Edited by Rajkumar Buyya, James Broberg and Andrzej Goscinski Copyright © 2011 John Wiley & Sons, Inc.

higher and deeper reach and richness in application delivery and consumability. Product vendors having found that the cloud style is a unique proposition are moving their platforms, databases, and middleware to clouds. Cloud Infrastructure providers are establishing cloud centers to host a variety of ICT services and platforms of worldwide individuals, innovators, and institutions. Cloud service providers (CSPs) are very aggressive in experimenting and embracing the cool cloud ideas and today every business and technical services are being hosted in clouds to be delivered to global customers, clients and consumers over the Internet communication infrastructure. For example, security as a service (SaaS) is a prominent cloud-hosted security service that can be subscribed by a spectrum of users of any connected device and the users just pay for the exact amount or time of usage. In a nutshell, on-premise and local applications are becoming online, remote, hosted, on-demand and off-premise applications. With the unprecedented advertisement, articulation and adoption of cloud concepts, the cloud movement is picking up fast as per leading market research reports. Besides the modernization of legacy applications and positing the updated and upgraded in clouds, fresh applications are being implemented and deployed on clouds to be delivered to millions of global users simultaneously affordably. It is hence clear that a number of strategic and significant movements happen silently in the hot field of cloud computing.

All these portend and predict that there is a new dimension to the integration scenario. Hitherto enterprise data and applications are being linked up via one or more standards-compliant integration platforms, brokers, engines, and containers within the corporate intranet. Business-to-business (B2B) integration is being attended via special data formats, message templates, and networks and even via the Internet. Enterprises consistently expand their operations to several parts of the world as they establish special partnerships with their partners or buy other companies in different geographies for enhancing the product and service portfolios. Business applications are finding their new residence in clouds. However most of the confidential and corporate data are still being maintained in enterprise servers for security reasons. The integration task gets just bigger with the addition of the cloud space and the integration complexity is getting murkier. Hence it is logical to take the integration middleware to clouds to simplify and streamline the enterprise-to-enterprise (E2E), enterprise-to-cloud (E2C) and cloud-to-cloud (C2C) integration.

In this chapter, we want you to walk through how cloud paradigm impacts the integration scene. That is, how cloud applications are being integrated with both enterprise as well as other cloud applications. Similarly how applications hosted in distributed clouds can find on another and share their functionality is also being given its share of attention. We have visualised and written about a few important integration scenarios wherein cloud-based middleware exceptionally contributes for simplifying and streamlining the increasingly complex integration goal. It is all about how integration becomes a cloud service.

3.2 THE ONSET OF KNOWLEDGE ERA

Having started its innings as the greatest business-enabler, today IT is tending towards the significant factor and the facilitator of every aspect of human lives. Path-breaking and people-centric technologies (miniaturization, virtualization, federation, composition, collaboration, etc.) are emerging and are being experimented, expounded, and established in order to empower the professional and the personal IT to be smart, simple, supple and sensitive towards users' situational needs and to significantly enhance peoples' comfort, care, convenience and choice. Novel computing paradigms (grid, on-demand, service, cloud, etc.) erupt and evolve relentlessly to be greatly and gracefully impactful and insightful. In the monolithic mainframe era, one centralized and large system performed millions of operations to respond to thousands of users (one-to-many), today everyone has his own compute machine (one-to-one), and tomorrow a multitude of smart objects and electronic devices (nomadic, wearable, portable, implantable etc.) will seamlessly and spontaneously co-exist, corroborate, correlate, and coordinate with one another dynamically with dexterity to understand one or more users' needs, conceive, construct, and deliver them at right time at right place (many-to-one). Anytime anywhere computing tends towards everywhere, every time and everything computing.

Ambient intelligence (AmI) is the newest buzzword today with ambient sensing, networking, perception, decision-making and actuation technologies. Multimedia and multimodal technologies are flourishing in order to be make human interaction more friendly and fruitful. Dynamic, virtualized and autonomic infrastructures, flexible, integrated and lean processes, constructive and contributive building-blocks (service, model, composite, agent, aspect etc.), slim and sleek devices and appliances, smart objects empowered by invisible tags and stickers, natural interfaces, ad-hoc and situational networking capabilities all combine adaptively together to accomplish the grandiose goals of the forthcoming ambient intelligence days and decades. In short, IT-sponsored and splurged smartness in every facet of our living in this world is the vision. Software engineering is on the right track with the maturity of service orientation concepts and software as a service (SaaS) model. Clouds chip in mightily in realizing the much-acclaimed knowledge era. Technologies form a dynamic cluster in real-time in order to contribute immensely and immeasurably for all the existing, evolving and exotic expectations of people.

3.3 THE EVOLUTION OF SaaS

SaaS paradigm is on fast track due to its innate powers and potentials. Executives, entrepreneurs, and end-users are ecstatic about the tactic as well as strategic success of the emerging and evolving SaaS paradigm. A number of positive and progressive developments started to grip this model. Newer resources and activities are being consistently readied to be delivered as a service. Experts and evangelists are in unison that cloud is to rock the total IT community as the best possible infrastructural solution for effective service delivery. There are several ways clouds can be leveraged inspiringly and incredibly for diverse IT problems. Today there is a small list of services being delivered via the clouds and in future, many more critical applications will be deployed and consumed. In short, clouds are set to decimate all kinds of IT inflexibility and dawn a growing array of innovations to prepare the present day IT for sustainable prosperity.

IT as a Service (ITaaS) is the most recent and efficient delivery method in the decisive IT landscape. With the meteoric and mesmerizing rise of the service orientation principles, every single IT resource, activity and infrastructure is being viewed and visualized as a service that sets the tone for the grand unfolding of the dreamt service era. These days, systems are designed and engineered as elegant collections of enterprising and evolving services. Infrastructures are service-enabled to be actively participative and collaborative. In the same tenor, the much-maligned delivery aspect too has gone through several transformations and today the whole world has solidly settled for the green paradigm 'IT as a service (ITaaS)'. This is accentuated due to the pervasive Internet. Also we are bombarded with innumerable implementation technologies and methodologies. Clouds, as indicated above, is the most visible and viable infrastructure for realizing ITaaS. Another influential and impressive factor is the maturity obtained in the consumption-based metering and billing capability. HP even proclaims this evolving trend as 'everything as a service'.

Integration as a service (IaaS) is the budding and distinctive capability of clouds in fulfilling the business integration requirements. Increasingly business applications are deployed in clouds to reap the business and technical benefits. On the other hand, there are still innumerable applications and data sources locally stationed and sustained primarily due to the security reason. The question here is how to create a seamless connectivity between those hosted and on-premise applications to empower them to work together. IaaS overcomes these challenges by smartly utilizing the time-tested business-to-business (B2B) integration technology as the value-added bridge between SaaS solutions and in-house business applications.

B2B systems are capable of driving this new on-demand integration model because they are traditionally employed to automate business processes between manufacturers and their trading partners. That means they provide application-to-application connectivity along with the functionality that is very crucial for linking internal and external software securely. Unlike the conventional EAI solutions designed only for internal data sharing, B2B platforms have the ability to encrypt files for safe passage across the public network, manage large data volumes, transfer batch files, convert disparate file formats, and guarantee data delivery across multiple enterprises. IaaS just imitates this established communication and collaboration model to create reliable and durable linkage for ensuring smooth data passage between traditional and cloud systems over the Web infrastructure.

The use of hub & spoke (H&S) architecture further simplifies the implementation and avoids placing an excessive processing burden on the customer sides. The hub is installed at the SaaS provider's cloud center to do the heavy lifting such as reformatting files. A spoke unit at each user site typically acts as basic data transfer utility. With these pieces in place, SaaS providers can offer integration services under the same subscription / usage-based pricing model as their core offerings. This trend of moving all kinds of common and centralised services to clouds is gaining momentum these days. As resources are getting distributed and decentralised, linking and leveraging them for multiple purposes need a multifaceted infrastructure. Clouds, being the Web-based infrastructures are the best fit for hosting scores of unified and utility-like platforms to take care of all sorts of brokering needs among connected and distributed ICT systems.

1. The Web is the largest **digital information superhighway**
2. The Web is the largest repository of all kinds of resources such as **web pages, applications comprising enterprise components, business services, beans, POJOs, blogs, corporate data**, etc.
3. The Web is turning out to be the open, cost-effective and generic **business execution platform** (E-commerce, business, auction, etc. happen in the web for global users) comprising a wider variety of containers, adaptors, drivers, connectors, etc.
4. The Web is the global-scale **communication infrastructure (VoIP, Video conferencing, IP TV etc,)**
5. The Web is the next-generation **discovery, Connectivity, and integration middleware**

Thus the unprecedented absorption and adoption of the Internet is the key driver for the continued success of the cloud computing.

3.4 THE CHALLENGES OF SaaS PARADIGM

As with any new technology, SaaS and cloud concepts too suffer a number of limitations. These technologies are being diligently examined for specific situations and scenarios. The prickling and tricky issues in different layers and levels are being looked into. The overall views are listed out below. Loss or lack of the following features deters the massive adoption of clouds

1. Controllability
2. Visibility & flexibility
3. Security and Privacy
4. High Performance and Availability
5. Integration and Composition
6. Standards

A number of approaches are being investigated for resolving the identified issues and flaws. Private cloud, hybrid and the latest community cloud are being prescribed as the solution for most of these inefficiencies and deficiencies. As rightly pointed out by someone in his weblogs, still there are miles to go. There are several companies focusing on this issue. Boomi (http://www.dell .com/) is one among them. This company has published several well-written white papers elaborating the issues confronting those enterprises thinking and trying to embrace the third-party public clouds for hosting their services and applications.

Integration Conundrum. While SaaS applications offer outstanding value in terms of features and functionalities relative to cost, they have introduced several challenges specific to integration. The first issue is that the majority of SaaS applications are point solutions and service one line of business. As a result, companies without a method of synchronizing data between multiple lines of businesses are at a serious disadvantage in terms of maintaining accurate data, forecasting, and automating key business processes. Real-time data and functionality sharing is an essential ingredient for clouds.

APIs are Insufficient. Many SaaS providers have responded to the integration challenge by developing application programming interfaces (APIs). Unfortunately, accessing and managing data via an API requires a significant amount of coding as well as maintenance due to frequent API modifications and updates. Furthermore, despite the advent of web services, there is little to no standardization or consensus on the structure or format of SaaS APIs. As a result, the IT department expends an excess amount of time and resources developing and maintaining a unique method of communication for the API of each SaaS application deployed within the organization.

Data Transmission Security. SaaS providers go to great length to ensure that customer data is secure within the hosted environment. However, the need to transfer data from on-premise systems or applications behind the firewall with SaaS applications hosted outside of the client's data center poses new challenges that need to be addressed by the integration solution of choice. It is critical that the integration solution is able to synchronize data bi-directionally from SaaS to on-premise without opening the firewall. Best-of-breed integration providers can offer the ability to do so by utilizing the same security as when a user is manually typing data into a web browser behind the firewall.

For any relocated application to provide the promised value for businesses and users, the minimum requirement is the interoperability between SaaS applications and on-premise enterprise packages. As SaaS applications were not initially designed keeping the interoperability requirement in mind, the integration process has become a little tougher assignment. There are other obstructions and barriers that come in the way of routing messages between on-demand applications and on-premise resources. Message, data and protocol translations have to happen at end-points or at the middleware layer in order to decimate the blockade that is prohibiting the spontaneous sharing and purposeful collaboration among the participants. As applications and data are diverse, distributed and decentralized, versatile integration technologies and methods are very essential to smoothen the integration problem. Reflective middleware is an important necessity for enterprise-wide, real-time and synchronized view of information to benefit executives, decision-makers as well as users tactically as well as strategically. Data integrity, confidentiality, quality and value have to be preserved as services and applications are interlinked and saddled to work together.

The Impacts of Clouds [1, 2]. On the infrastructural front, in the recent past, the clouds have arrived onto the scene powerfully and have extended the horizon and the boundary of business applications, events and data. That is, business applications, development platforms etc. are getting moved to elastic, online and on-demand cloud infrastructures. Precisely speaking, increasingly for business, technical, financial and green reasons, applications and services are being readied and relocated to highly scalable and available clouds. The immediate implication and impact is that integration methodologies and middleware solutions have to take clouds too into account for establishing extended and integrated processes and views. Thus there is a clarion call for adaptive integration engines that seamlessly and spontaneously connect enterprise applications with cloud applications. Integration is being stretched further to the level of the expanding Internet and this is really a litmus test for system architects and integrators.

The perpetual integration puzzle has to be solved meticulously for the originally visualised success of SaaS style. Interoperability between SaaS and non-SaaS solutions remains the lead demand as integration leads to business-aware and people-centric composite systems and services. Boundaryless flow of information is necessary for enterprises to strategize to achieve greater successes, value and for delivering on the elusive goal of customer delight. Integration has been a big challenge for growing business behemoths, fortune 500 companies, and system integrators. Now with the availability, affordability and suitability of the cloud-sponsored and the state-of-the-art infrastructures for application deployment and delivery, the integration's scope, size, and scale is expanding and this beneficial extension however have put integration architects, specialists and consultants in deeper trouble.

3.5 APPROACHING THE SaaS INTEGRATION ENIGMA

Integration as a Service (IaaS) is all about the migration of the functionality of a typical enterprise application integration (EAI) hub / enterprise service bus (ESB) into the cloud for providing for smooth data transport between any enterprise and SaaS applications. Users subscribe to IaaS as they would do for any other SaaS application. Cloud middleware is the next logical evolution of traditional middleware solutions. That is, cloud middleware will be made available as a service. Due to varying integration requirements and scenarios, there are a number of middleware technologies and products such as JMS-compliant message queues and integration backbones such as EAI, ESB, EII, EDB, CEP, etc. For performance sake, clusters, fabrics, grids, and federations of hubs, brokers, and buses are being leveraged.

For service integration, it is enterprise service bus (ESB) and for data integration, it is enterprise data bus (EDB). Besides there are message oriented middleware (MOM) and message brokers for integrating decoupled applications through message passing and pick up. Events are coming up fast and there are complex event processing (CEP) engines that receive a stream of diverse events from diverse sources, process them at real-time to extract and figure out the encapsulated knowledge, and accordingly select and activate one or more target applications thereby a kind of lighter connectivity and integration occurs between the initiating and the destination applications. Service orchestration and choreography enables process integration. Service interaction through ESB integrates loosely coupled systems whereas CEP connects decoupled systems. Besides data services, mashups perform and provide composite services, data and views. Thus at every layer or tier in the enterprise IT stack, there are competent integration modules and guidelines brewing for bringing up the much-anticipated dynamic integration.

With the unprecedented rise in cloud usage, all these integration software are bound to move to clouds. Amazon's Simple Queue Service (SQS) provides a straightforward way for applications to exchange messages via queues in the cloud. SQS is a classic example for understanding what happens when a familiar on-premise service is recast as a cloud service. However there are some problems with this. Because SQS replicates messages across multiple queues, an application reading from a queue is not guaranteed to see all messages from all queues on a particular read request. SQS also doesn't promise in-order and exactly-once delivery. These simplifications let Amazon make SQS more scalable, but they also mean that developers must use SQS differently from an on-premise message queuing technology.

Cloud infrastructure is not very useful without SaaS applications that run on top of them, and SaaS applications are not very valuable without access to the critical corporate data that is typically locked away in various corporate systems. So, for cloud applications to offer maximum value to their users, they need to provide a simple mechanism to import or load external data, export or replicate their data for reporting or analysis purposes, and finally keep their data synchronized with on-premise applications. That brings out the importance of SaaS integration subject.

As per one of the David Linthicum's white papers, approaching SaaS-to-enterprise integration is really a matter of making informed and intelligent choices. Choices are mainly around the integration approaches to leverage architectural patterns, the location of the integration engine, and, finally the enabling technology. The unprecedented growth of SaaS means that more and more software components are migrated and made to reside in off-premise SaaS platforms. Hence the need for integration between remote cloud platforms with on-premise enterprise platforms, wherein the customer and corporate data are stored for ensuring unbreakable, impeccable and impenetrable security, has caught the serious and sincere attention and imagination of product vendors and SaaS providers.

Why SaaS Integration is hard?. As indicated in the white paper, there is a mid-sized paper company that recently became a Salesforce.com CRM customer. The company currently leverages an on-premise custom system that uses an Oracle database to track inventory and sales. The use of the Salesforce.com system provides the company with a significant value in terms of customer and sales management. However, the information that persists within the Salesforce.com system is somewhat redundant with the information stored within the on-premise legacy system (e.g., customer data). Thus the "as is" state is in a fuzzy state and suffers from all kinds of costly inefficiencies including the need to enter and maintain data in two different locations, which ultimately costs more for the company. Another irritation is the loss of data quality which is endemic when considering this kind of dual operation. This includes data integrity issues, which are a natural phenomenon when data is being updated using different procedures, and there is no active synchronization between the SaaS and on-premise systems.

Having understood and defined the "to be" state, data synchronization technology is proposed as the best fit between the source, meaning Salesforce.com, and the target, meaning the existing legacy system that leverages Oracle. This technology is able to provide automatic mediation of the differences between the two systems, including application semantics, security, interfaces, protocols and native data formats. The end result is that information within the SaaS-delivered systems and the legacy systems are completely and compactly synchronized meaning that data entered into the CRM system would also exist in the legacy systems and vice versa, along with other operational data such as inventory, items sold, etc. The "to be" state thereby removes data quality and integrity issues fully. This directly and indirectly paves the way for saving thousands of dollars a month and producing a quick ROI from the integration technology that is studied and leveraged.

Integration has been the prominent subject of study and research by academic students and scholars for years as integration brings a sense of order to the chaos and mess created by heterogeneous systems, networks, and services. Integration technologies, tools, tips, best practices, guidelines, metrics, patterns, and platforms are varied and vast. Integration is not easier either to implement as successful untangling from the knotty situation is a big issue. The web of application and data silos really makes the integration task difficult and hence choosing a best-in class scheme for flexible and futuristic integration is insisted very frequently. First of all, we need to gain the insights about the special traits and tenets of SaaS applications in order to arrive at a suitable integration route. The constraining attributes of SaaS applications are

- Dynamic nature of the SaaS interfaces that constantly change
- Dynamic nature of the metadata native to a SaaS provider such as Salesforce.com
- Managing assets that exist outside of the firewall
- Massive amounts of information that need to move between SaaS and on-premise systems daily and the need to maintain data quality and integrity.

As SaaS are being deposited in cloud infrastructures vigorously, we need to ponder about the obstructions being imposed by clouds and prescribe proven solutions. If we face difficulty with local integration, then the cloud integration is bound to be more complicated. The most probable reasons are

- New integration scenarios
- Access to the cloud may be limited
- Dynamic resources
- Performance

Limited Access. Access to cloud resources (SaaS, PaaS, and the infrastructures) is more limited than local applications. Accessing local applications is quite simple and faster. Imbedding integration points in local as well as custom applications is easier. Even with the commercial applications, it is always possible to slip in database-triggers to raise events and provide hooks for integration access. Once applications move to the cloud, custom applications must be designed to support integration because there is no longer that low-level of access. Enterprises putting their applications in the cloud or those subscribers of cloud-based business services are dependent on the vendor to provide the integration hooks and APIs. For example, the SalesForce.com web services API does not support transactions against multiple records, which means integration code has to handle that logic. For PaaS, the platform might support integration for applications on the platform. However platform-to-platform integration is still an open question. There is an agreement that a limited set of APIs will improve the situation to an extent. But those APIs must be able to handle the integration required. Applications and data can be moved to public clouds but the application providers and data owners lose the much-needed controllability and flexibility, Most of the third-party cloud providers do not submit their infrastructures for third-party audit. Visibility is another vital factor lost out due to this transition.

Dynamic Resources. Cloud resources are virtualized and service-oriented. That is, everything is expressed and exposed as a service. Due to the dynamism factor that is sweeping the whole could ecosystem, application versioning and infrastructural changes are liable for dynamic changes. These would clearly impact the integration model. That is, the tightly coupled integration fails and falters at cloud. It is clear that the low-level interfaces ought to follow the Representational State Transfer (REST) route, which is a simple architectural style and subscribes to the standard methods of the Http protocol.

Performance. Clouds support application scalability and resource elasticity. However the network distances between elements in the cloud are no longer under our control. Bandwidth is not the limiting factor in most integration scenarios but the round trip latency is an issue not to be sidestepped. Because of the latency aggravation, the cloud integration performance is bound to slow down.

3.6 NEW INTEGRATION SCENARIOS

Before the cloud model, we had to stitch and tie local systems together. With the shift to a cloud model is on the anvil, we now have to connect local applications to the cloud, and we also have to connect cloud applications to each other, which add new permutations to the complex integration channel matrix. It is unlikely that everything will move to a cloud model all at once, so even the simplest scenarios require some form of local / remote integration. It is also likely that we will have applications that *never* leave the building, due to regulatory constraints like HIPPA, GLBA, and general security issues. All of this means integration must criss-cross firewalls somewhere.

Cloud Integration Scenarios. We have identified three major integration scenarios as discussed below.

Within a Public Cloud (figure 3.1). Two different applications are hosted in a cloud. The role of the cloud integration middleware (say cloud-based ESB or internet service bus (ISB)) is to seamlessly enable these applications to talk to each other. The possible sub-scenarios include these applications can be owned

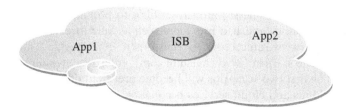

FIGURE 3.1. Within a Public Cloud.

FIGURE 3.2.   Across Homogeneous Clouds.

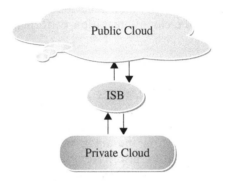

FIGURE 3.3.   Across Heterogeneous Clouds.

by two different companies. They may live in a single physical server but run on different virtual machines.

Homogeneous Clouds (figure 3.2). The applications to be integrated are posited in two geographically separated cloud infrastructures. The integration middleware can be in cloud 1 or 2 or in a separate cloud.

There is a need for data and protocol transformation and they get done by the ISB. The approach is more or less compatible to enterprise application integration procedure.

Heterogeneous Clouds (figure 3.3). One application is in public cloud and the other application is private cloud.

As described above, this is the currently dominating scene for cloud integration. That is, businesses are subscribing to popular on-demand enterprise packages from established providers such as Salesforce.com and Ramco Systems (http://www.ramco.com/)'s customer relationship management (CRM), NetSuite's (http://www.netsuite.com) enterprise resource planning (ERP), etc. The first two scenarios will become prevalent once there are several commercial clouds and cloud services become pervasive. Then service integration and composition domains will become an important and incredible factor for global computing.

3.7 THE INTEGRATION METHODOLOGIES

Excluding the custom integration through hand-coding, there are three types for cloud integration

1. **Traditional Enterprise Integration Tools can be empowered with special connectors to access Cloud-located Applications**—This is the most likely approach for IT organizations, which have already invested a lot in integration suite for their application integration needs. With a persistent rise in the necessity towards accessing and integrating cloud applications, special drivers, connectors and adapters are being built and incorporated on the existing integration platforms to enable bidirectional connectivity with the participating cloud services. As indicated earlier, there are several popular and pioneering enterprise integration methods and platforms such as EAI/ESB, which are accordingly empowered, configured and customized in order to access and leverage the growing array of cloud applications too. For attaining an enhanced performance, integration appliances are very hot in the market.

2. **Traditional Enterprise Integration Tools are hosted in the Cloud**—This approach is similar to the first option except that the integration software suite is now hosted in any third-party cloud infrastructures so that the enterprise does not worry about procuring and managing the hardware or installing the integration software. This is a good fit for IT organizations that outsource the integration projects to IT service organizations and systems integrators, who have the skills and resources to create and deliver integrated systems. The IT divisions of business enterprises need not worry about the upfront investment of high-end computer machines, integration packages, and their maintenance with this approach. Similarly system integrators can just focus on their core competencies of designing, developing, testing, and deploying integrated systems. It is a good fit for cloud-to-cloud (C2C) integration, but requires a secure VPN tunnel to access on-premise corporate data. An example of a hosted integration technology is Informatica PowerCenter Cloud Edition on Amazon EC2.

3. **Integration-as-a-Service (IaaS) or On-Demand Integration Offerings**— These are SaaS applications that are designed to deliver the integration service securely over the Internet and are able to integrate cloud applications with the on-premise systems, cloud-to-cloud applications. Even on-premise systems can be integrated with other on-premise applications via this integration service. This approach is a good fit for companies who insist about the ease of use, ease of maintenance, time to deployment, and are on a tight budget. It is appealing to small and mid-sized companies, as well as large enterprises with departmental application deployments. It is also a good fit for companies who plan to use their

SaaS administrator or business analyst as the primary resource for managing and maintaining their integration work. A good example is **Informatica On-Demand Integration Services**.

In a nutshell, the integration requirements can be realised using any one of the following methods and middleware products.

1. Hosted and extended ESB (Internet service bus / cloud integration bus)
2. Online Message Queues, Brokers and Hubs
3. Wizard and configuration-based integration platforms (Niche integration solutions)
4. Integration Service Portfolio Approach
5. Appliance-based Integration (Standalone or Hosted)

With the emergence of the cloud space, the integration scope grows further and hence people are looking out for robust and resilient solutions and services that would speed up and simplify the whole process of integration.

Characteristics of Integration Solutions and Products. The key attributes of integration platforms and backbones gleaned and gained from integration projects experience are connectivity, semantic mediation, Data mediation, integrity, security, governance etc

- **Connectivity** refers to the ability of the integration engine to engage with both the source and target systems using available native interfaces. This means leveraging the interface that each provides, which could vary from standards-based interfaces, such as Web services, to older and proprietary interfaces. Systems that are getting connected are very much responsible for the externalization of the correct information and the internalization of information once processed by the integration engine.
- **Semantic Mediation** refers to the ability to account for the differences between application semantics between two or more systems. Semantics means how information gets understood, interpreted and represented within information systems. When two different and distributed systems are linked, the differences between their own yet distinct semantics have to be covered.
- **Data Mediation** converts data from a source data format into destination data format. Coupled with semantic mediation, data mediation or data transformation is the process of converting data from one native format on the source system, to another data format for the target system.
- **Data Migration** is the process of transferring data between storage types, formats, or systems. Data migration means that the data in the old system is mapped to the new systems, typically leveraging data extraction and data loading technologies.

- **Data Security** means the ability to insure that information extracted from the source systems has to securely be placed into target systems. The integration method must leverage the native security systems of the source and target systems, mediate the differences, and provide the ability to transport the information safely between the connected systems.
- **Data Integrity** means data is complete and consistent. Thus, integrity has to be guaranteed when data is getting mapped and maintained during integration operations, such as data synchronization between on-premise and SaaS-based systems.
- **Governance** refers to the processes and technologies that surround a system or systems, which control how those systems are accessed and leveraged. Within the integration perspective, governance is about managing changes to core information resources, including data semantics, structure, and interfaces.

These are the prominent qualities carefully and critically analyzed for when deciding the cloud / SaaS integration providers.

Data Integration Engineering Lifecycle. As business data are still stored and sustained in local and on-premise server and storage machines, it is imperative for a lean data integration lifecycle. The pivotal phases, as per Mr. David Linthicum, a world-renowned integration expert, are understanding, definition, design, implementation, and testing.

1. **Understanding** the existing problem domain means defining the metadata that is native within the source system (say Salesforce.com) and the target system (say an on-premise inventory system). By doing this, there is a complete semantic understanding of both source and target systems. If there are more systems for integration, the same practice has to be enacted.

2. **Definition** refers to the process of taking the information culled during the previous step and defining it at a high level including what the information represents, ownership, and physical attributes. This contributes a better perceptive of the data being dealt with beyond the simple metadata. This insures that the integration process proceeds in the right direction.

3. **Design** the integration solution around the movement of data from one point to another accounting for the differences in the semantics using the underlying data transformation and mediation layer by mapping one schema from the source to the schema of the target. This defines how the data is to be extracted from one system or systems, transformed so it appears to be native, and then updated in the target system or systems. This is increasingly done using visual-mapping technology. In addition,

there is a need to consider both security and governance and also consider these concepts within the design of the data integration solution.

4. **Implementation** refers to actually implementing the data integration solution within the selected technology. This means connecting the source and the target systems, implementing the integration flows as designed in the previous step, and then other steps required getting the data integration solution up-and-running

5. **Testing** refers to assuring that the integration is properly designed and implemented and that the data synchronizes properly between the involved systems. This means looking at known test data within the source system and monitoring how the information flows to the target system. We need to insure that the data mediation mechanisms function correctly as well as review the overall performance, durability, security, modifiability and sustainability of the integrated systems.

3.8   SaaS INTEGRATION PRODUCTS AND PLATFORMS

Cloud-centric integration solutions are being developed and demonstrated for showcasing their capabilities for integrating enterprise and cloud applications. The integration puzzle has been the toughest assignment for long due to heterogeneity and multiplicity-induced complexity. Now with the arrival and adoption of the transformative and disruptive paradigm of cloud computing, every ICT products are being converted into a collection of services to be delivered via the open Internet. In that line, the standards-compliant integration suites are being transitioned into services so that any integration need of any one from any part of the world can be easily, cheaply and rapidly met. At this point of time, primarily data integration products are highly visible as their need is greater compared to service or message-based integration of applications. But as the days go by, there will be a huge market for application and service integration. Interoperability will become the most fundamental thing. Composition and collaboration will become critical and crucial for the mass adoption of clouds, which are prescribed and proclaimed as the next-generation infrastructure for creating, deploying and delivering hordes of ambient, artistic, adaptive, and agile services. Cloud interoperability is the prime demand and the figure 3.4 for creating cloud peers, clusters, fabrics, and grids.

3.8.1   Jitterbit [4]

Force.com is a Platform as a Service (PaaS), enabling developers to create and deliver any kind of on-demand business application. However, in order to take advantage of this breakthrough cloud technology, there is a need for a flexible and robust integration solution to synchronize force.com with any on-demand or on-premise enterprise applications, databases, and legacy systems.

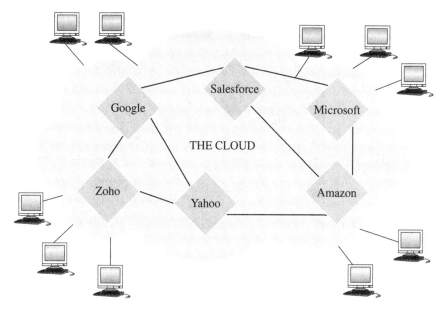

FIGURE 3.4. The Smooth and Spontaneous Cloud Interaction via Open Clouds.

Until now, integrating force.com applications with other on-demand applications and systems within an enterprise has seemed like a daunting and doughty task that required too much time, money, and expertise.

Jitterbit is a fully graphical integration solution that provides users a versatile platform and a suite of productivity tools to reduce the integration efforts sharply. Jitterbit can be used standalone or with existing EAI infrastructures, enabling users to create new projects or consume and modify existing ones offered by the open source community or service provider. The Jitterbit solution enables the cool integration among confidential and corporate data, enterprise applications, web services, XML data sources, legacy systems, simple and complex flat files. Apart from a scalable and secure server, Jitterbit provides a powerful graphical environment to help us quickly design, implement, test, deploy, and manage the integration projects. Jitterbit is comprised of two major components:

- **Jitterbit Integration Environment** An intuitive point-and-click graphical UI that enables to quickly configure, test, deploy and manage integration projects on the Jitterbit server.
- **Jitterbit Integration Server** A powerful and scalable run-time engine that processes all the integration operations, fully configurable and manageable from the Jitterbit application.

  Jitterbit is making integration easier, faster, and more affordable than ever before. Using Jitterbit, one can connect force.com with a wide variety

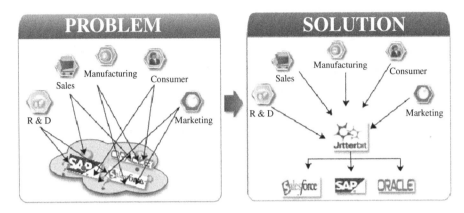

FIGURE 3.5. Linkage of On-Premise with Online and On-Demand Applications.

of on-premise systems including ERP, databases, flat files and custom applications. The figure 3.5 vividly illustrates how Jitterbit links a number of functional and vertical enterprise systems with on-demand applications

3.8.2 Boomi Software [5]

Has come out with an exciting and elegant SaaS integration product. It promises to fulfil the vision **"Integration on Demand"**. While the popularity of SaaS applications rises dramatically, the integration task has been the "Achilles heel" of the SaaS mechanism. The integration challenge is real and unanimously cited by industry analysts as the leading barrier to overwhelming SaaS adoption.

Boomi AtomSphere is an integration service that is completely on-demand and connects any combination of SaaS, PaaS, cloud, and on-premise applications without the burden of installing and maintaining software packages or appliances. Anyone can securely build, deploy and manage simple to complex integration processes using only a web browser. Whether connecting SaaS applications found in various lines of business or integrating across geographic boundaries, AtomSphere is being presented as a centralized platform that could deliver integration with all the benefits one would expect from a SaaS solution. As new applications are connected to the AtomSphere, they become instantly accessible to the entire community with no adapters to purchase or upgrade to install. Boomi offers the "pure SaaS" integration solution that enables to quickly develop and deploy connections between applications, regardless of the delivery model.

3.8.3 Bungee Connect [6]

For professional developers, Bungee Connect enables cloud computing by offering an application development and deployment platform that enables highly interactive applications integrating multiple data sources and facilitating instant deployment. Built specifically for cloud development, Bungee Connect reduces the efforts to integrate (mashup) multiple web services into a single application. Bungee automates the development of rich UI and eases the difficulty of deployment to multiple web browsers. Bungee Connect leverages the cloud development to bring an additional value to organizations committed to building applications for the cloud.

3.8.4 OpSource Connect [7]

Expands on the OpSource Services Bus (OSB) by providing the infrastructure for two-way web services interactions, allowing customers to consume and publish applications across a common web services infrastructure. OpSource Connect also addresses the problems of SaaS integration by unifying different SaaS applications in the "cloud" as well as legacy applications running behind a corporate firewall. By providing the platform to drive web services adoption and integration, OpSource helps its customers grow their SaaS application and increase customer retention.

The Platform Architecture. OpSource Connect is made up of key features including

- OpSource Services Bus
- OpSource Service Connectors
- OpSource Connect Certified Integrator Program
- OpSource Connect ServiceXchange
- OpSource Web Services Enablement Program

The OpSource Services Bus (OSB) is the foundation for OpSource's turnkey development and delivery environment for SaaS and web companies. Based on SOA, it allows applications running on the OpSource On-Demand platform to quickly and easily tap web services. There is no longer a need to write code for these business functions, as OpSource has already invested in the upfront development. It is all about leveraging the OSB to quickly gain business functions and accelerate time-to-market.

3.8.5 SnapLogic [8]

SnapLogic is a capable, clean, and uncluttered solution for data integration that can be deployed in enterprise as well as in cloud landscapes. The free community edition can be used for the most common point-to-point data integration tasks, giving a huge productivity boost beyond custom code. SnapLogic professional edition is a seamless upgrade that extends the power of this solution with production management, increased capacity, and multi-user features at a price that won't drain the budget, which is getting shrunk due to the economic slump across the globe. Even the much-expected "V" mode recovery did not happen; the craze for SaaS solutions is on the climb.

The web, SaaS applications, mobile devices, and cloud platforms have profoundly changed the requirements imposed on data integration technology. SnapLogic is a data integration platform designed for the changing landscape of data and applications. SnapLogic offers a solution that provides flexibility for today's data integration challenges.

- **Changing data sources.** SaaS and on-premise applications, Web APIs, and RSS feeds
- **Changing deployment options.** On-premise, hosted, private and public cloud platforms
- **Changing delivery needs.** Databases, files, and data services

Using a unique hybrid approach, SnapLogic delivers transparency and extensibility to adapt to new integration demands by combining the web principles and open source software with the traditional data integration capabilities.

Transformation Engine and Repository. SnapLogic is a single data integration platform designed to meet data integration needs. The SnapLogic server is built on a core of connectivity and transformation components, which can be used to solve even the most complex data integration scenarios. The SnapLogic designer runs in any web browser and provides an efficient and productive environment for developing transformation logic. The entire system is repository based, with a single metadata store for all the definitions and transformation logic.

The SnapLogic designer provides an initial hint of the web principles at work behind the scenes. The SnapLogic server is based on the web architecture and exposes all its capabilities through web interfaces to outside world. Runtime control and monitoring, metadata access, and transformation logic are all available through web interfaces using a security model just like the web. The SnapLogic web architecture also provides the ultimate flexibility in functionality and deployment. Data transformations are not restricted to a fixed source or target like traditional ETL engines. The ability to read or write a web interface comes naturally to SnapLogic, allowing the creation of on-demand data services using the same logic as fixed transformations. For deployment, the web architecture means one can choose to run SnapLogic on-premise or hosted in the cloud.

3.8.6   The Pervasive DataCloud [9]

Platform (figure 3.6) is unique multi-tenant platform. It provides dynamic "compute capacity in the sky" for deploying on-demand integration and other

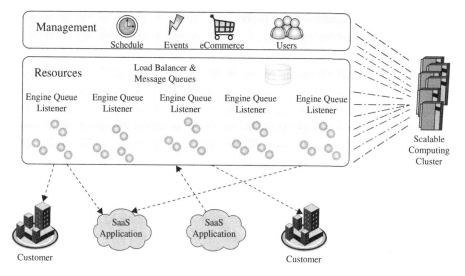

FIGURE 3.6. Pervasive Integrator Connects Different Resources.

data-centric applications. Pervasive DataCloud is the first multi-tenant platform for delivering the following.

1. Integration as a Service (IaaS) for both hosted and on-premises applications and data sources
2. Packaged turnkey integration
3. Integration that supports every integration scenario
4. Connectivity to hundreds of different applications and data sources

Pervasive DataCloud hosts Pervasive and its partners' data-centric applications. **Pervasive** uses Pervasive DataCloud as a platform for deploying on-demand integration via

- The **Pervasive DataSynch** family of packaged integrations. These are highly affordable, subscription-based, and packaged integration solutions. They bring a rapid, seamless, turnkey approach to cloud-based integration for popular applications such as Salesforce, QuickBooks and Microsoft Dynamics
- **Pervasive Data Integrator.** This runs on the Cloud or on-premises and is a design-once and deploy anywhere solution to support every integration scenario
  - Data migration, consolidation and conversion
  - ETL / Data warehouse
  - B2B / EDI integration

- Application integration (EAI)
- SaaS /Cloud integration
- SOA / ESB / Web Services
- Data Quality/Governance
- Hubs

Pervasive DataCloud provides multi-tenant, multi-application and multi-customer deployment. Pervasive DataCloud is a platform to deploy applications that are

- **Scalable**—Its multi-tenant architecture can support multiple users and applications for delivery of diverse data-centric solutions such as data integration. The applications themselves scale to handle fluctuating data volumes.
- **Flexible**—Pervasive DataCloud supports SaaS-to-SaaS, SaaS-to-on premise or on-premise to on-premise integration.
- **Easy to Access and Configure**—Customers can access, configure and run Pervasive DataCloud-based integration solutions via a browser.
- **Robust**—Provides automatic delivery of updates as well as monitoring activity by account, application or user, allowing effortless result tracking.
- **Secure**—Uses the best technologies in the market coupled with the best data centers and hosting services to ensure that the service remains secure and available.
- **Affordable**—The platform enables delivery of packaged solutions in a SaaS-friendly pay-as-you-go model.

3.8.7   Bluewolf [10]

Has announced its expanded "Integration-as-a-Service" solution, the first to offer ongoing support of integration projects guaranteeing successful integration between diverse SaaS solutions, such as salesforce.com, BigMachines, eAutomate, OpenAir and back office systems (e.g. Oracle, SAP, Great Plains, SQL Service and MySQL). Called the Integrator, the solution is the only one to include proactive monitoring and consulting services to ensure integration success. With remote monitoring of integration jobs via a dashboard included as part of the Integrator solution, Bluewolf proactively alerts its customers of any issues with integration and helps to solves them quickly. For administrative ease, the Bluewolf Integrator is designed with user-friendly administration rules that enable the administrator to manage the flow of data between front and back office systems with little or no IT support. With a Wizard-based approach, the Integrator prompts are presented in simple and non-technical terms. The Bluewolf Integrator integrates with Salesforce, BigMachines,

Oracle, SAP, Microsoft SQL server, MySQL, and supports flat files, such as CSV, XHTML and many more.

3.8.8 Online MQ

Online MQ is an Internet-based queuing system. It is a complete and secure online messaging solution for sending and receiving messages over any network. It is a cloud messaging queuing service. In the integration space, messaging middleware as a service is the emerging trend. Here are some of the advantages for using Online MQ.

- **Ease of Use**. It is an easy way for programs that may each be running on different platforms, in different systems and different networks, to communicate with each other without having to write any low-level communication code.
- **No Maintenance**. No need to install any queuing software/server and no need to be concerned with MQ server uptime, upgrades and maintenance.
- **Load Balancing and High Availability**. Load balancing can be achieved on a busy system by arranging for more than one program instance to service a queue. The performance and availability features are being met through clustering. That is, if one system fails, then the second system can take care of users' requests without any delay.
- **Easy Integration**. Online MQ can be used as a web-service (SOAP) and as a REST service. It is fully JMS-compatible and can hence integrate easily with any Java EE application servers. Online MQ is not limited to any specific platform, programming language or communication protocol.

3.8.9 CloudMQ [15]

This leverages the power of Amazon Cloud to provide enterprise-grade message queuing capabilities on demand. Messaging allows us to reliably break up a single process into several parts which can then be executed asynchronously. They can be executed within different threads, or even on different machines. The parts communicate by exchanging messages. The messaging framework guarantees that messages get delivered to the right recipient and wake up the appropriate thread when a message arrives. CloudMQ is the easiest way to start exploring integration of messaging into applications since no installation or configuration is necessary.

3.8.10 Linxter

Linxter [14] is a cloud messaging framework for connecting all kinds of applications, devices, and systems. Linxter is a behind-the-scenes, message-oriented and cloud-based middleware technology and smoothly automates the complex tasks that developers face when creating communication-based products and services. With everything becoming Internet-enabled (iPods, clothing, toasters . . . anything), Linxter's solution securely, easily, and dynamically connects all these things. Anything that is connected to the Internet can connect to each other through the Linxter's dynamic communication channels. These channels move data between any number of endpoints and the data can be reconfigured on the fly, simplifying the creation of communication-based products and services.

Online MQ, CloudMQ and Linxter are all accomplishing message-based application and service integration. As these suites are being hosted in clouds, messaging is being provided as a service to hundreds of distributed and enterprise applications using the much-maligned multi-tenancy property. "Messaging middleware as a service (MMaaS)" is the grand derivative of the SaaS paradigm. Thus integration as a service (IaaS) is being accomplished through this messaging service. As seen above, there are data mapping tools come handy in linking up different applications and databases that are separated by syntactic, structural, schematic and semantic deviations. Templates are another powerful mechanism being given serious thought these days to minimize the integration complexity. Scores of adaptors for automating the connectivity and subsequently the integration needs are taking off the ground successfully. The integration conundrum has acquired such a big proportion as the SaaS solutions were designed, developed, and deployed without visualizing the need for integration with the resources at the local and corporate servers.

3.9 SaaS INTEGRATION SERVICES

We have seen the state-of-the-art cloud-based data integration platforms for real-time data sharing among enterprise information systems and cloud applications. Another fast-emerging option is to link enterprise and cloud systems via messaging. This has forced vendors and service organizations to take message oriented middleware (MoM) to the all-powerful cloud infrastructures. Going forward, there are coordinated and calculated efforts for taking the standards-compatible enterprise service bus (ESB) to clouds in order to guarantee message enrichment, mediation, content and context-based message routing. Thus both loosely or lightly coupled and decoupled cloud services and applications will become a reality soon with the maturity and durability of message-centric and cloud-based service bus suites. We can still visualise the deployment of complex event processing (CEP) engines in clouds in order to capture and capitalise streams of events from diverse sources in different formats and forms in order to infer the existing and emerging situation precisely and concisely. Further on, all kinds of risks, threats, vulnerabilities, opportunities, trends, tips, associations, patterns, and other tactical as well as strategic insights and actionable insights can be deduced to act upon confidently and at real time.

In a highly interoperable environment, seamless and spontaneous composition and collaboration would happen in order to create sophisticated services dynamically. Context-aware applications covering all kinds of constituents and participants (self, surroundings and situation-aware devices, sensors, robots, instruments, media players, utensils, consumer electronics, information appliances, etc.), in a particular environment (home, hotel, hospital, office, station, stadium etc.), enterprise systems, integration middleware, cloud services and knowledge engines can be built and sustained. There are fresh endeavours in order to achieve service composition in cloud ecosystem. Existing frameworks such as service component architecture (SCA) are being revitalised for making it fit for cloud environments. Composite applications, services, data, views and processes will be become cloud-centric and hosted in order to support spatially separated and heterogeneous systems.

3.9.1 Informatica On-Demand [11]

Informatica offers a set of innovative on-demand data integration solutions called Informatica On-Demand Services. This is a cluster of easy-to-use SaaS offerings, which facilitate integrating data in SaaS applications, seamlessly and securely across the Internet with data in on-premise applications. The Informatica on-demand service is a subscription-based integration service that provides all the relevant features and functions, using an on-demand or an as-a-service delivery model. This means the integration service is remotely hosted, and thus provides the benefit of not having to purchase or host software. There are a few key benefits to leveraging this maturing technology.

- Rapid development and deployment with zero maintenance of the integration technology.
- Automatically upgraded and continuously enhanced by vendor.
- Proven SaaS integration solutions, such as integration with Salesforce .com, meaning that the connections and the metadata understanding are provided.
- Proven data transfer and translation technology, meaning that core integration services such as connectivity and semantic mediation are built into the technology.

Informatica On-Demand has taken the unique approach of moving its industry leading PowerCenter Data Integration Platform to the hosted model and then configuring it to be a true multi-tenant solution. That means that when developing new features or enhancements, they are immediately made available to all of their customers transparently. That means, no complex software upgrades required and no additional fee is demanded. Fixing, patching, versioning, etc are taken care of by the providers at no cost for the subscribers. Still the service and operation level agreements are being fully met. And the multi-tenant architecture means that bandwidth and scalability are shared resources so meeting different capacity demands becomes smoother and simpler.

3.9.2   Microsoft Internet Service Bus (ISB) [13]

Azure is an upcoming cloud operating system from Microsoft. This makes development, depositing and delivering Web and Windows application on cloud centers easier and cost-effective. Developers' productivity shoots up, customers' preferences are being provided, the enterprise goal of "more with less" gets achieved, etc. Azure is being projected as the comprehensive yet compact cloud framework that comprises a wider variety of enabling tools for a slew of tasks and a growing service portfolio. The primary components are explained below.

Microsoft .NET Services. is a set of Microsoft-built and hosted cloud infrastructure services for building Internet-enabled applications and the ISB acts as the cloud middleware providing diverse applications with a common infrastructure to name, discover, expose, secure and orchestrate web services. The following are the three broad areas.

.NET Service Bus. The .NET Service Bus (figure 3.7) provides a hosted, secure, and broadly accessible infrastructure for pervasive communication,

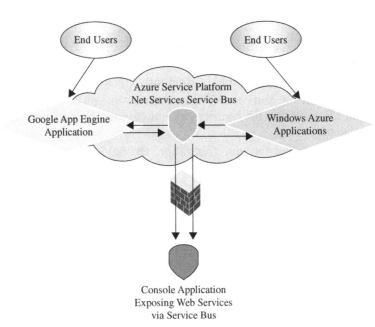

FIGURE 3.7.   .NET Service Bus.

large-scale event distribution, naming, and service publishing. Services can be exposed through the Service Bus Relay, providing connectivity options for service endpoints that would otherwise be difficult or impossible to reach. Endpoints can be located behind network address translation (NAT) boundaries or bound to frequently changing, dynamically assigned IP addresses, or both.

.NET Access Control Service. The .NET Access Control Service is a hosted, secure, standards-based infrastructure for multiparty, federated authentication, rules-driven, and claims-based authorization. The Access Control Service's capabilities range from simple, one-step, user name/password-based authentication and authorization with Web-style HTTP requests to sophisticated WS-Federation scenarios that employ two or more collaborating WS-Trust Security Token Services. The Access Control Service allows applications to rely on .NET Services solution credentials for simple scenarios or on on-premise enterprise accounts managed in Microsoft Active Directory and federated with the Access Control Service via next-generation Microsoft Active Directory Federation Services.

.NET Workflow Service. The .NET Workflow Service provide a hosted environment for service orchestration based on the familiar Windows Workflow Foundation (WWF) development experience. The Workflow services will provide a set of specialized activities for rules-based control flow, service invocation, as well as message processing and correlation that can be executed on demand, on schedule, and at scale inside the .NET Services environment.

The most important part of the Azure is actually the service bus represented as a WCF architecture. The key capabilities of the Service Bus are

- A **federated namespace** model that provides a shared, hierarchical namespace into which services can be mapped. This allows providing any endpoint with a stable, Internet-accessible URI, regardless of the location.
- A **service registry** service that provides an opt-in model for publishing service endpoints into a lightweight, hierarchical, and RSS-based discovery mechanism.
- A lightweight and scalable **publish/subscribe event bus**.
- A **relay** and **connectivity** service with advanced NAT traversal and pull-mode message delivery capabilities acting as a "perimeter network (also known as DMZ, demilitarized zone, and screened subnet) in the sky" for services that would otherwise be unreachable due to NAT/Firewall restrictions or frequently changing dynamic IP addresses, or that do not allow any incoming connections due to other technical limitations.

Relay Services. Often when we connect a service, it is located behind the firewall and behind the load balancer. Its address is dynamic and can be

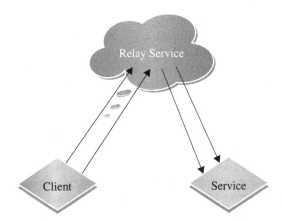

FIGURE 3.8. The .NET Relay Service.

resolved only on local network. When we are having the service call-backs to the client, the connectivity challenges lead to scalability, availability and security issues. The solution to Internet connectivity challenges is instead of connecting client directly to the service we can use a relay service as pictorially represented in the relay service figure 3.8.

The Relay service is a service residing in the cloud whose job is to assist the connectivity and relaying the calls to the service. Relay Service solution require both the client and the service intranets to allow connections to the cloud.

3.10 BUSINESSES-TO-BUSINESS INTEGRATION (B2Bi) SERVICES

B2Bi has been a mainstream activity for connecting geographically distributed businesses for purposeful and beneficial cooperation. Products vendors have come out with competent B2B hubs and suites for enabling smooth data sharing in standards-compliant manner among the participating enterprises. Now with the surging popularity of clouds, there are serious and sincere efforts to posit these products in clouds in order to deliver B2Bi as a service with very lest investment and maintenance costs. The cloud ideas and ideals lay the strong and stimulating foundation for transitioning from the capital expenditure to operational expenditure and for sustaining the transformed.

There are several proven integration methods in the B2Bi space and they can be captured and capitalized for achieving quicker success and better return and value in the evolving IaaS landscape. B2Bi systems are good candidate for IaaS as they are traditionally employed to automate business processes between manufacturers and their external trading partners such as retail, warehouse, transport, and inventory systems. This means that they provide application-to-application (A2A) connectivity along with functionality that is crucial to linking internal and external software: i.e. secure data exchange across the corporate firewall. Unlike pure EAI solutions designed only for internal data sharing, B2Bi platforms have the ability to encrypt files for safe passage across the public network, manage large data volumes, transfer batch files, convert disparate file formats and guarantee data accuracy, integrity, confidentiality, and delivery. Just as these abilities ensure smooth communication between manufacturers and their external suppliers or customers, they also enable reliable interchange between hosted and installed applications.

The IaaS model also leverages the adapter libraries developed by B2Bi vendors to provide rapid integration with various business systems. Because the B2Bi partners have the expertise and experience ad can supply pre-built connectors for major ERP, CRM, SCM and other packaged business applications as well as legacy systems from AS400 to MVS and mainframe. The use of a hub-and-spoke centralised architecture further simplifies implementation and provides a good control and grip on the system management and finally this avoids placing an excessive processing burden on the customer side. The hub is installed at the SaaS provider's cloud center to do the heavy lifting such as reformatting files. A spoke unit, typically consisting of a small downloadable Java client, is then deployed at each user site to handle basic tasks such as data transfer. This also eliminates the need for an expensive server-based solution, data mapping and other tasks at the customer location. As the Internet is the principal communication infrastructure, enterprises can leverage the IaaS to sync up with their partners across the continents towards smart and systematic collaboration.

Cloud- based Enterprise Mashup Integration Services for B2B Scenarios [17]. There is a vast need for infrequent, situational and ad-hoc B2B applications desired by the mass of business end-users. Enterprise mashup and lightweight composition approaches and tools are promising methods to unleash the huge and untapped potential of empowering end-users to develop or assemble aligned and aware composite services in order to overcome the "long-tail" dilemma. Currently available solutions to support B2B collaborations focus on the automation of long-term business relationships and still lack to provide their users intuitive ways to modify or to extend them according to their ad-hoc or situational needs. Conventional proceeding in the development of such applications directs to an immense use of time and work due to long development cycles and a lack of required business knowledge.

Especially in the area of applications to support B2B collaborations, current offerings are characterized by a high richness but low reach, like B2B hubs that focus on many features enabling electronic collaboration, but lack availability for especially small organizations or even individuals. The other extreme solutions with a low reach but high richness such as web sites, portals and emails, lack standardization and formularization which makes them inappropriate for automated or special enterprises' needs. New development approaches are hence needed to overcome theses hurdles and hitches to involve non-technical business users into the development process in order to address this long tail syndrome, to realize cost-effectiveness and efficiency gains, and to overcome the traditional constrictions between IT department and business units.

Enterprise Mashups, a kind of new-generation Web-based applications, seem to adequately fulfill the individual and heterogeneous requirements of end-users and foster End User Development (EUD). To shorten the traditional and time-consuming development process, these new breed of applications are developed by non-professional programmers, often in a non-formal, iterative, and collaborative way by assembling existing building blocks.

SOA has been presented as a potent solution to organization's integration dilemmas. ESBs are used to integrate different services within a SOA-driven company. However, most ESBs are not designated for cross-organizational collaboration, and thus problems arise when articulating and aiming such an extended collaboration. SOA simplifies and streamlines the integration of new and third-party services but still it can be done by skilled and experienced developers. End-users usually are not able to realize the wanted integration scenarios. This leads, beneath high costs for integration projects, to the unwanted inflexibility, because integration projects last longer, although market competition demands a timely response to uprising requirements proactively.

Another challenge in B2B integration is the ownership of and responsibility for processes. In many inter-organizational settings, business processes are only sparsely structured and formalized, rather loosely coupled and/or based on ad-hoc cooperation. Inter-organizational collaborations tend to involve more and more participants and the growing number of participants also draws a huge amount of differing requirements. Also, the participants may act according to different roles, controls and priorities. Historically, the focus for collaboration was participation within teams which were managed according to one set of rules.

Now, in supporting supplier and partner co-innovation and customer co-creation, the focus is shifting to collaboration which has to embrace the participants, who are influenced yet restricted by multiple domains of control and disparate processes and practices. This represents the game-changing shift from static B2B approaches to new and dynamic B2B integration, which can adaptively act and react to any unexpected disruptions, can allow a rapid configuration and customization and can manage and moderate the rising complexity by the use of end-to-end business processes.

Both Electronic data interchange translators (EDI) and Managed file transfer (MFT) have a longer history, while B2B gateways only have emerged during the last decade. However, most of the available solutions aim at supporting medium to larger companies, resulting from their high costs and long implementation cycles and times, which make them unaffordable and unattractive to smaller organizations. Consequently, these offerings are not suitable for short-term collaborations, which need to be set up in an ad hoc manner.

Enterprise Mashup Platforms and Tools. Mashups are the adept combination of different and distributed resources including content, data or application functionality. Resources represent the core building blocks for mashups. Resources can be accessed through APIs, which encapsulate the resources and describe the interface through which they are made available. Widgets or gadgets primarily put a face on the underlying resources by providing a graphical representation for them and piping the data received from the resources. Piping can include operators like aggregation, merging or filtering. Mashup platform is a Web based tool that allows the creation of Mashups by piping resources into Gadgets and wiring Gadgets together.

Enterprise Mashups, which are enterprise-scale, aware and ready, are extremely advantages in B2B integration scenes. Mashups can resolve many of the disadvantages of B2B hubs such as low reach due to hard-wired connections. Mashups enable EUD and lightweight connections of systems. Mashups can help adding richness to existing lightweight solutions such as Websites or Portals by adding a certain level of formalization and standardization. Mashups facilitate the ease of mixing and transforming various sources of information internally and from business partners. Complexity in B2B operations is often linked with heterogeneous systems and platforms. The tedious integration process and requirements of various support and maintenance for the software is a major hindrance to today's dynamic B2B integration, especially for the small and medium enterprises.

The Mashup integration services are being implemented as a prototype in the FAST project. The layers of the prototype are illustrated in figure 3.9 illustrating the architecture, which describes how these services work together. The authors of this framework have given an outlook on the technical realization of the services using cloud infrastructures and services.

Prototype architecture shows the services and their relations to each other. The core services are shown within the box in the middle. The external services shown under the box are attached via APIs to allow the usage of third-party offerings to realize their functionality. Users access the services through a Mashup platform of their choice. The Mashup platforms are connected via APIs to the Mashup integration services.

To use the services, users have to identify themselves against the user-access control service. This service is connected to a user management service, which controls the users and their settings. The user management service is connected via an API to allow the usage of external services, e.g. a corporate user database. All data coming from the users go through a translation engine to unify the data objects and protocols, so that different Mashup platforms can be integrated. The translation engine has an interface which allows connecting other external translation engines to add support for additional protocol and data standards. The translated data is forwarded to the routing engine, which is the core of the Mashup integration services. The routing engine takes care of processing the inputs received from the Mashup platforms and forwarding them to the right recipient. The routing is based on rules, which can be configured through an API.

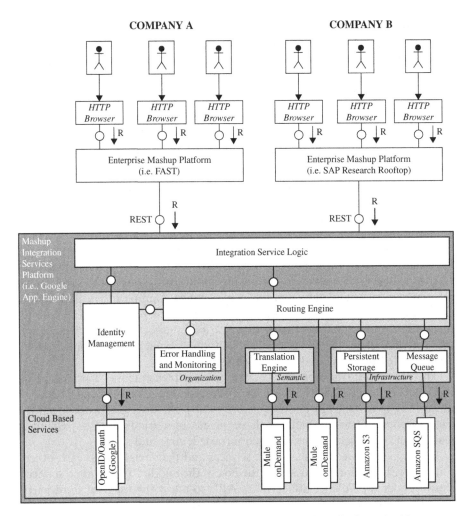

FIGURE 3.9. Cloud- based Enterprise Mashup Integration Platform Architecture.

To simplify this, a Gadget could be provided for the end-user. The routing engine is also connected to a message queue via an API. Thus, different message queue engines are attachable. The message queue is responsible for storing and forwarding the messages controlled by the routing engine. Beneath the message queue, a persistent storage, also connected via an API to allow exchangeability, is available to store large data. The error handling and monitoring service allows tracking the message-flow to detect errors and to collect statistical data. The Mashup integration service is hosted as a cloud-based service. Also, there are cloud-based services available which provide the functionality required by the integration service. In this way, the Mashup integration service can reuse and leverage the existing cloud services to speed up the implementation.

Message Queue. The message queue could be realized by using Amazon's Simple Queue Service (SQS). SQS is a web-service which provides a queue for messages and stores them until they can be processed. The Mashup integration services, especially the routing engine, can put messages into the queue and recall them when they are needed.

Persistent Storage. Amazon Simple Storage Service5 (S3) is also a web-service. The routing engine can use this service to store large files.

Translation Engine. This is primarily focused on translating between different protocols which the Mashup platforms it connects can understand, e.g. REST or SOAP web services. However, if the need of translation of the objects transferred arises, this could be attached to the translation engine. A company requiring such a service could on the one hand develop such a service and connect it to the Mashup integration services. Another possibility for this would be to connect existing translation services, e.g., the services by Mule on Demand, which is also a cloud-based offering.

Interaction between the Services. The diagram describes the process of a message being delivered and handled by the Mashup Integration Services Platform. The precondition for this process is that a user already established a route to a recipient. After having received a message from an Enterprise Mashup tool via an API, the Integration Services first check the access rights of the sender of the message against an external service. An incoming message is processed only if sender of the message is authorized, that is, he has the right to deliver the message to the recipient and to use the Mashup integration services. If he is not authorized, the processing stops, and an error message gets logged. The error log message is written into a log file, which could reside on Amazon's Simple Storage Service (S3). If the message has been accepted, it is put in the message queue in Amazon's SQS service. If required, the message is being translated into another format, which can also be done by an external, cloud-based service. After that, the services can begin trying delivering the message to a recipient. Evaluating the recipients of the message is based on the rules stored in the routing engine which have been configured by a user before. Finally, the successful delivery of the message can be logged, or an error if one occurred.

3.11   A FRAMEWORK OF SENSOR—CLOUD INTEGRATION [3]

In the past few years, wireless sensor networks (WSNs) have been gaining significant attention because of their potentials of enabling of novel and attractive solutions in areas such as industrial automation, environmental monitoring, transportation business, health-care etc. If we add this collection of sensor-derived data to various Web-based social networks or virtual communities, blogs etc., there will be fabulous transitions among and around us.

With the faster adoption of micro and nano technologies, everyday things are destined to become digitally empowered and smart in their operations and offerings. Thus the goal is to link smart materials, appliances, devices, federated messaging middleware, enterprise information systems and packages, ubiquitous services, handhelds, and sensors with one another smartly to build and sustain cool, charismatic and catalytic situation-aware applications. Clouds have emerged as the centralized, compact and capable infrastructure to deliver people-centric and context-aware services to users with all the qualities inherently. This long-term target demands that there has to be a cool connectivity and purposeful interactions between clouds and all these pervasive and minuscule systems. In this section, we explain about a robust and resilient a framework to enable this exploration by integrating sensor networks to clouds. But there are many challenges to enable this framework. The authors of this framework have proposed a pub-sub based model, which simplifies the integration of sensor networks with cloud based community-centric applications. Also there is a need for internetworking cloud providers in case of violation of service level agreement with users.

A virtual community consisting of team of researchers have come together to solve a complex problem and they need data storage, compute capability, security; and they need it all provided now. For example, this team is working on an outbreak of a new virus strain moving through a population. This requires more than a Wiki or other social organization tool. They deploy bio-sensors on patient body to monitor patient condition continuously and to use this data for large and multi-scale simulations to track the spread of infection as well as the virus mutation and possible cures. This may require computational resources and a platform for sharing data and results that are not immediately available to the team.

Traditional HPC approach like Sensor-Grid model can be used in this case, but setting up the infrastructure to deploy it so that it can scale out quickly is not easy in this environment. However, the cloud paradigm is an excellent move. But current cloud providers unfortunately did not address the issue of integrating sensor network with cloud applications and thus have no infrastructure to support this scenario. The virtual organization (VO) needs a place that can be rapidly deployed with social networking and collaboration tools, other specialized applications and tools that can compose sensor data and disseminate them to the VO users based on their subscriptions.

Here, the researchers need to register their interests to get various patients' state (blood pressure, temperature, pulse rate etc.) from bio-sensors for large-scale parallel analysis and to share this information with each other to find useful solution for the problem. So the sensor data needs to be aggregated, processed and disseminated based on subscriptions. On the other hand, as sensor data require huge computational power and storage, one cloud provider may not handle this requirement. This insists and induces for a dynamic collaboration with other cloud providers. The framework addresses the above issues and provides competent solutions.

To integrate sensor networks to cloud, the authors have proposed a content-based pub-sub model. A pub/sub system encapsulates sensor data into events and provides the services of event publications and subscriptions for asynchronous data exchange among the system entities. MQTT-S is an open topic-based pub-sub protocol that hides the topology of the sensor network and allows data to be delivered based on interests rather than individual device addresses. It allows a transparent data exchange between WSNs and traditional networks and even between different WSNs.

In this framework, like MQTT-S, all of the system complexities reside on the broker's side but it differs from MQTT-S in that it uses content-based pub-sub broker rather than topic-based which is suitable for the application scenarios considered. When an event is published, it is transmitted from a publisher to one or more subscribers without the publisher having to address the message to any specific subscriber. Matching is done by the pub-sub broker outside of the WSN environment. In content-based pub-sub system, sensor data has to be augmented with meta-data to identify the different data fields. For example, a meta-data of a sensor value (also event) can be body temperature, blood pressure etc.

To deliver published sensor data or events to subscribers, an efficient and scalable event matching algorithm is required by the pub-sub broker. This event matching algorithm targets a range predicate case suitable to the application scenarios and it is also efficient and scalable when the number of predicates increases sharply. The framework is shown in figure 3.10. In this framework, sensor data are coming through gateways to a pub/sub broker. Pub/sub broker is required in the system to deliver information to the consumers of SaaS applications as the entire network is very dynamic. On the WSN side, sensor or actuator (SA) devices may change their network addresses at any time. Wireless links are quite likely to fail. Furthermore, SA nodes could also fail at any time and rather than being repaired, it is expected that they will be replaced by new ones. Besides, different SaaS applications can be hosted and run on any machines anywhere on the cloud. In such situations, the conventional approach of using network address as communication means between the SA devices and the applications may be very problematic because of their dynamic and temporal nature.

Moreover, several SaaS applications may have an interest in the same sensor data but for different purposes. In this case, the SA nodes would need to manage and maintain communication means with multiple applications in parallel. This might exceed the limited capabilities of the simple and low-cost SA devices. So pub-sub broker is needed and it is located in the cloud side because of its higher performance in terms of bandwidth and capabilities. It has four components describes as follows:

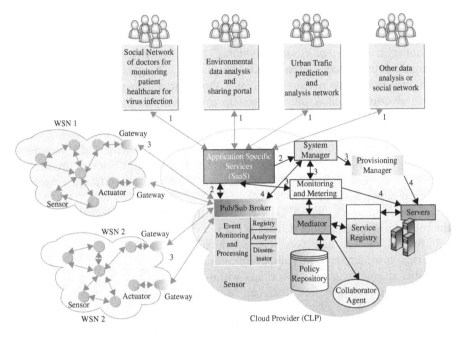

FIGURE 3.10.   The Framework Architecture of Sensor—Cloud Integration.

Stream monitoring and processing component (SMPC). The sensor stream comes in many different forms. In some cases, it is raw data that must be captured, filtered and analyzed on the fly and in other cases, it is stored or cached. The style of computation required depends on the nature of the streams. So the SMPC component running on the cloud monitors the event streams and invokes correct analysis method. Depending on the data rates and the amount of processing that is required, SMP manages parallel execution framework on cloud.

Registry component (RC). Different SaaS applications register to pub-sub broker for various sensor data required by the community user. For each application, registry component stores user subscriptions of that application and sensor data types (temperature, light, pressure etc.) the application is interested in. Also it sends all user subscriptions along with application id to the disseminator component for event delivery.

Analyzer component (AC). When sensor data or events come to the pub-sub broker, analyzer component determines which applications they are belongs to and whether they need periodic or emergency deliver. The events are then passed to the disseminator component to deliver to appropriate users through SaaS applications.

Disseminator component (DC). For each SaaS application, it disseminates sensor data or events to subscribed users using the event matching algorithm. It can utilize cloud's parallel execution framework for fast event delivery. The pub-sub components workflow in the framework is as follows:

Users register their information and subscriptions to various SaaS applications which then transfer all this information to pub/sub broker registry. When sensor data reaches to the system from gateways, event/stream monitoring and processing component (SMPC) in the pub/sub broker determines whether it needs processing or just store for periodic send or for immediate delivery. If sensor data needs periodic/ emergency delivery, the analyzer determines which SaaS applications the events belong to and then passes the events to the disseminator along with application ids. The disseminator, using the event matching algorithm, finds appropriate subscribers for each application and delivers the events for use.

Besides the pub-sub broker, the authors have proposed to include three other components: mediator, policy repository (PR) and collaborator agent (CA) along with system manager, provisioning manager, monitoring and metering and service registry in the sensor-cloud framework to enable VO based dynamic collaboration of primary cloud providers with other cloud providers in case of SLA violations for burst resource demand. These three components collectively act as a "gateway" for a given CLP in creation of a new VO. They are described as follows:

Mediator. The (resource) mediator is a policy-driven entity within a VO to ensure that the participating entities are able to adapt to changing circumstances and are able to achieve their objectives in a dynamic and uncertain environment. Once a VO is established, the mediator controls which resources to be used of the collaborating CLPs, how this decision is taken, and which policies are being used. When performing automated collaboration, the mediator will also direct any decision making during negotiations, policy management, and scheduling. A mediator holds the initial policies for VO creation and works in conjunction with its local Collaborating Agent (CA) to discover external resources and to negotiate with other CLPs.

Policy Repository (PR). The PR virtualizes all of the policies within the VO. It includes the mediator policies, VO creation policies along with any policies for resources delegated to the VO as a result of a collaborating arrangement. These policies form a set of rules to administer, manage, and control access to VO resources. They provide a way to manage the components in the face of complex technologies.

Collaborating Agent (CA). The CA is a policy-driven resource discovery module for VO creation and is used as a conduit by the mediator to exchange policy and resource information with other CLPs. It is used by a primary CLP to discover the collaborating CLPs' (external) resources, as well as to let them know about the local policies and service requirements prior to commencement of the actual negotiation by the mediator.

On concluding, to deliver published sensor data or events to appropriate users of cloud applications, an efficient and scalable event-matching algorithm called Statistical Group Index Matching (SGIM) is proposed and leveraged. The authors also have evaluated its performance and compared with existing algorithms in a cloud based ubiquitous health-care application scenario. The authors in the research paper have clearly described this algorithm that in sync with the framework enables sensor-cloud connectivity to utilize the ever-expanding sensor data for various next generation community-centric sensing applications on the cloud. It can be seen that the computational tools needed to launch this exploration is more appropriately built from the data center "cloud" computing model than the traditional HPC approaches or Grid approaches. The authors have embedded a content-based pub-sub model to enable this framework.

3.12 SaaS INTEGRATION APPLIANCES

Appliances are a good fit for high-performance requirements. Clouds too have gone in the same path and today there are cloud appliances (also termed as "cloud in a box"). In this section, we are to see an integration appliance.

Cast Iron Systems [12]. This is quite different from the above-mentioned schemes. Appliances with relevant software etched inside are being established as a high-performance and hardware-centric solution for several IT needs. Very frequently we read and hear about a variety of integration appliances considering the complexities of connectivity, transformation, routing, mediation and governance for streamlining and simplifying business integration. Even the total cloud infrastructure comprising the prefabricated software modules is being produced as an appliance (cloud in a box). This facilitates building private clouds quicker and easier. Further on, appliance solution is being taken to clouds in order to provide the appliance functionality and feature as a service. "Appliance as a service" is a major trend sweeping the cloud service provider (CSP) industry.

Cast Iron Systems (**www.ibm.com**) provides pre-configured solutions for each of today's leading enterprise and On-Demand applications. These solutions, built using the Cast Iron product offerings offer out-of-the-box connectivity to specific applications, and template integration processes (TIPs) for the most common integration scenarios. For example, the Cast Iron solution for salesforce.com comes with built-in AppExchange connectivity, and TIPs for customer master, product master and contact data integration. Cast Iron solutions enable customers to rapidly complete application-specific integrations using a "configuration, not coding" approach. By using a pre-configured template, rather than starting from scratch with complex software tools and writing lots of code, enterprises complete business-critical projects in days rather than months. Large and midsize companies in a variety of industries use Cast Iron solutions to solve their most common integration needs. From the image below, it is clear Cast Iron systems have readymade.

3.13 CONCLUSION

SaaS in sync with cloud computing has brought in strategic shifts for businesses as well as IT industries. Increasingly SaaS applications are being hosted in cloud infrastructures and the pervasive Internet is the primary communication infrastructure. These combinations of game-changing concepts and infrastructures have really come as a boon and blessing as the world is going through the economic slump and instability. The goal of "more with less" is being accomplished with the maturity of these freshly plucked and published ideas. Applications are studiously being moved to clouds, which are exposed as services, which are delivered via the Internet to user agents or humans and accessed through the ubiquitous web browsers. The unprecedented adoption is to instigate and instil a number of innovations as it has already created a lot of buzz on newer business, pricing, delivery and accessibility models. Ubiquity and utility will become common connotations. Value-added business transformation, augmentation, optimization along with on-demand IT will be the ultimate output. In the midst of all the enthusiasm and optimism, there are some restricting factors that need to be precisely factored out and resolved comprehensively in order to create an extended ecosystem for intelligent collaboration. Integration is one such issue and hence a number of approaches are being articulated by professionals. Product vendors, consulting and service organizations are eagerly coming out with integration platforms, patterns, processes, and best practices. There are generic as well as specific (niche) solutions. Pure SaaS middleware as well as standalone middleware solutions are being studied and prescribed based on "as-is" situation and to-be" aspiration. As the business and technical cases of cloud middleware suites are steadily evolving and enlarging, the realization of internet service bus (the internet-scale ESB) is being touted as the next big thing for the exotic cloud space. In this chapter, we have elaborated and expounded the need for a creative and futuristic ISB that streamlines and simplifies the integration among clouds (public, private, and hybrid).

REFERENCES

1. M. Armbrust, A. Fox, R. Griffith, A. Joseph, R. Katz, A. Konwinski, G. Lee, D. Patterson, A. Rabkin, I. Stoica, M. Zaharia. Above the Clouds: A Berkeley View of Cloud Computing. Technical Report No. UCB/EECS-2009-28, University of California at Berkley, USA, Feb. 10, 2009.

2. R. Buyya, C. S. Yeo, and S. Venugopal, *Market-Oriented Cloud Computing Vision, Hype, and Reality for Delivering IT Services as Computing Utilities*, Proceedings of the 10th IEEE International Conference on High Performance Computing and Communications, Sept. 25–27, 2008, Dalian, China.

3. Arista, "Cloud Networking: Design Patterns for 'Cloud Centric' Application Environments", January 2009.

4. http://www.jitterbit.com

5. http://www.dell.com

6. http://www.bungeeconnect.com/

7. http://www.opsource.net/

8. http://www.snaplogic.com

9. http://www.pervasiveintegration.com/

10. http://www.bluewolf.com

11. http://www.informaticaondemand.com

12. http://www.castiron.com/

13. http://www.microsoft.com/azure/servicebus.mspx

14. http://linxter.com/

15. http://www.cloudmq.com/

16. Mohammad Mehedi Hassan et al., "A framework of sensor-cloud integration opportunities and challenges", Proceedings of the Conference On Ubiquitous Information Management and Communication, Korea, 2009.

17. Robert G. Siebeck et al., "Cloudbased Enterprise Mashup Integration Services for B2B Scenarios", MEM2009 workshop, Spain, 2009.

CHAPTER 4

THE ENTERPRISE CLOUD COMPUTING PARADIGM

TARIQ ELLAHI, BENOIT HUDZIA, HUI LI, MAIK A. LINDNER, and PHILIP ROBINSON

4.1 INTRODUCTION

Cloud computing is still in its early stages and constantly undergoing changes as new vendors, offers, services appear in the cloud market. This evolution of the cloud computing model is driven by cloud providers bringing new services to the ecosystem or revamped and efficient exiting services primarily triggered by the ever changing requirements by the consumers. However, cloud computing is predominantly adopted by start-ups or SMEs so far, and wide-scale enterprise adoption of cloud computing model is still in its infancy. Enterprises are still carefully contemplating the various usage models where cloud computing can be employed to support their business operations. Enterprises will place stringent requirements on cloud providers to pave the way for more widespread adoption of cloud computing, leading to what is known as the enterprise cloud paradigm computing. Enterprise cloud computing is the alignment of a cloud computing model with an organization's business objectives (profit, return on investment, reduction of operations costs) and processes. This chapter explores this paradigm with respect to its motivations, objectives, strategies and methods.

Section 4.2 describes a selection of deployment models and strategies for enterprise cloud computing, while Section 4.3 discusses the issues of moving [traditional] enterprise applications to the cloud. Section 4.4 describes the technical and market evolution for enterprise cloud computing, describing some potential opportunities for multiple stakeholders in the provision of enterprise cloud computing.

Cloud Computing: Principles and Paradigms, Edited by Rajkumar Buyya, James Broberg and Andrzej Goscinski Copyright © 2011 John Wiley & Sons, Inc.

4.2 BACKGROUND

According to NIST [1], cloud computing is composed of five essential characteristics: on-demand self-service, broad network access, resource pooling, rapid elasticity, and measured service. The ways in which these characteristics are manifested in an enterprise context vary according to the deployment model employed.

4.2.1 Relevant Deployment Models for Enterprise Cloud Computing

There are some general cloud deployment models that are accepted by the majority of cloud stakeholders today, as suggested by the references [1] and [2] and discussed in the following:

- *Public clouds* are provided by a designated service provider for general public under a utility based pay-per-use consumption model. The cloud resources are hosted generally on the service provider's premises. Popular examples of public clouds are Amazon's AWS (EC2, S3 etc.), Rackspace Cloud Suite, and Microsoft's Azure Service Platform.
- *Private clouds* are built, operated, and managed by an organization for its internal use only to support its business operations exclusively. Public, private, and government organizations worldwide are adopting this model to exploit the cloud benefits like flexibility, cost reduction, agility and so on.
  - *Virtual private clouds* are a derivative of the private cloud deployment model but are further characterized by an isolated and secure segment of resources, created as an overlay on top of public cloud infrastructure using advanced network virtualization capabilities. Some of the public cloud vendors that offer this capability include Amazon Virtual Private Cloud [3], OpSource Cloud [4], and Skytap Virtual Lab [5].
- *Community clouds* are shared by several organizations and support a specific community that has shared concerns (e.g., mission, security requirements, policy, and compliance considerations). They may be managed by the organizations or a third party and may exist on premise or off premise [1]. One example of this is OpenCirrus [6] formed by HP, Intel, Yahoo, and others.
- *Managed clouds* arise when the physical infrastructure is owned by and/or physically located in the organization's data centers with an extension of management and security control plane controlled by the managed service provider [2]. This deployment model isn't widely agreed upon, however, some vendors like ENKI [7] and NaviSite's NaviCloud offers claim to be managed cloud offerings.
- *Hybrid clouds* are a composition of two or more clouds (private, community, or public) that remain unique entities but are bound together by standardized or proprietary technology that enables data and application

portability (e.g., cloud bursting for load-balancing between clouds) [1]. Recently some cloud vendors have started offering solutions which can be used to enable these hybrid cloud deployment models. Some examples of these offerings include Amazon Virtual Private Cloud [3], Skytap Virtual Lab [5], and CohesiveFT VPN-Cubed [8]. These solutions work by creating IPSec VPN tunneling capabilities to connect the public cloud infrastructure to the on-premise cloud resources.

The selection of a deployment model depends on the opportunities to increase earnings and reduce costs i.e. capital expenses (CAPEX) and operating expenses (OPEX). Such opportunities can also have an element of timeliness associated with it, in that decisions that lead to losses today could be done with a vision of increased earnings and cost reductions in a foreseeable future.

4.2.2 Adoption and Consumption Strategies

The selection of strategies for enterprise cloud computing is critical for IT capability as well as for the earnings and costs the organization experiences, motivating efforts toward convergence of business strategies and IT. Some critical questions toward this convergence in the enterprise cloud paradigm are as follows:

- Will an enterprise cloud strategy increase overall business value?
- Are the effort and risks associated with transitioning to an enterprise cloud strategy worth it?
- Which areas of business and IT capability should be considered for the enterprise cloud?
- Which cloud offerings are relevant for the purposes of an organization?
- How can the process of transitioning to an enterprise cloud strategy be piloted and systematically executed?

These questions are addressed from two strategic perspectives: (1) adoption and (2) consumption. Figure 4.1 illustrates a framework for enterprise cloud adoption strategies, where an organization makes a decision to adopt a cloud computing model based on fundamental drivers for cloud computing— scalability, availability, cost and convenience. The notion of a Cloud Data Center (CDC) is used, where the CDC could be an external, internal or federated provider of infrastructure, platform or software services.

An optimal adoption decision cannot be established for all cases because the types of resources (infrastructure, storage, software) obtained from a CDC depend on the size of the organisation understanding of IT impact on business, predictability of workloads, flexibility of existing IT landscape and available budget/resources for testing and piloting. The strategic decisions using these four basic drivers are described in following, stating objectives, conditions and actions.

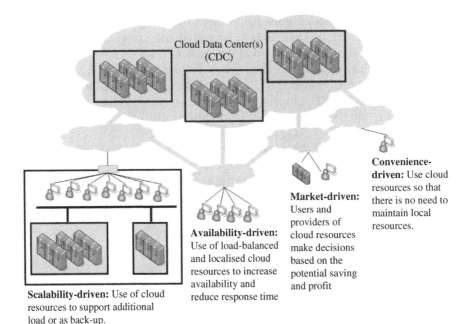

FIGURE 4.1. Enterprise cloud adoption strategies using fundamental cloud drivers.

1. **Scalability-Driven Strategy.** The objective is to support increasing work-loads of the organization without investment and expenses exceeding returns. The conditions are that the effort, costs (CAPEX and OPEX) and time involved in accessing and installing IT capability on a CDC are less than going through a standard hardware and software procurement and licensing process. Scalability will often make use of the IaaS delivery model because the fundamental need of the organization is to have compute power or storage capacity readily available.

2. **Availability-Driven Strategy.** Availability has close relations to scalability but is more concerned with the assurance that IT capabilities and functions are accessible, usable and acceptable by the standards of users. This is hence the objective of this basic enterprise cloud strategy. The conditions of this strategy are that there exist unpredictable usage peaks and locales, yet the risks (probability and impact) of not being able to satisfy demand outweigh the costs of acquiring the IT capability from a CDC.

3. **Market-Driven Strategy.** This strategy is more attractive and viable for small, agile organizations that do not have (or wish to have) massive investments in their IT infrastructure. The objective here is to identify and acquire the "best deals" for IT capabilities as demand and supply change, enabling ongoing reductions in OPEX and CAPEX. There is however always the need to support customer-driven service management based

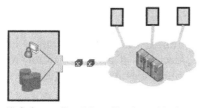

(1) Software Provision: Cloud provides instances of software but data is maintained within user's data center

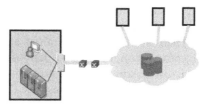

(2) Storage Provision: Cloud provides data management and software accesses data remotely from user's data center

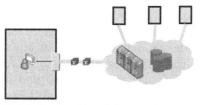

(3) Solution Provision: Software and storage are maintained in cloud and the user does not maintain a data center

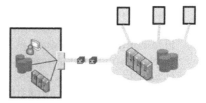

(4) Redundancy Services: Cloud is used as an alternative or extension of user's data center for software and storage

FIGURE 4.2. Enterprise cloud consumption strategies.

on their profiles and requests service requirements [9]. The conditions for this strategy would be the existence of standardized interfaces between and across CDCs, where the means by which customers access their resources on the CDC, deploy software/data and migrate software/data are uniformed. Ongoing efforts in the *Open Cloud Computing Interface (OCCI) Working Group* and the *Open Cloud Consortium (OCC)* are steps toward achieving these standards. Other features such as bidding, negotiation, service discovery and brokering would also be required at communal, regional or global scales.

4. **Convenience-Driven Strategy.** The objective is to reduce the load and need for dedicated system administrators and to make access to IT capabilities by users easier, regardless of their location and connectivity (e.g. over the Internet). The expectation is that the cost of obtaining IT capabilities from a CDC and making them accessible to users is significantly lower than the cost of having a dedicated administrator. However, it should be noted that, according to a recent Gartner study [10], the major reason for discontinuing with cloud-related strategies is the difficulty with integration, ahead of issues with the costs of services.

The consumption strategies make a distinction between data and application logic because there are questions of programming models used, data sensitivity, software licensing and expected response times that need to be considered. Figure 4.2 illustrates a set of enterprise cloud consumption strategies, where an organization makes decisions about how to best deploy its data and software using its internal resources and those of a selected CDC.

There are four consumptions strategies identified, where the differences in objectives, conditions and actions reflect the decision of an organization to trade-off hosting costs, controllability and resource elasticity of IT resources for software and data. These are discussed in the following.

1. **Software Provision.** This strategy is relevant when the elasticity requirement is high for software and low for data, the controllability concerns are low for software and high for data, and the cost reduction concerns for software are high, while cost reduction is not a priority for data, given the high controllability concerns for data, that is, data are highly sensitive. Implementing this strategy sees an organization requesting either software to be delivered as a service (SaaS) by the CDC or access to some portion of the CDC's compute infrastructure as a service (IaaS), such that it can deploy its application software on the provisioned resources. However, the organization chooses to maintain its data internally and hence needs to provide a means for the software running in the CDC to access data within its domain. This will entail changing some properties at the firewall or maintaining additional, supplementary software for secure access such as VPN, application-level proxy/gateway or wrapper software that could make the data base accessible via a remote messaging or service interface. According to a recent Gartner survey [10], the major hindrance to SaaS adoption is still the pricing and the lack of compelling indicators that the long-term investment in SaaS will be more cost-effective than traditional on-site maintenance of software.

2. **Storage Provision.** This strategy is relevant when the elasticity requirements is high for data and low for software, while the controllability of software is more critical than for data. This can be the case for data intensive applications, where the results from processing in the application are more critical and sensitive than the data itself. Furthermore, the cost reduction for data resources is a high concern, whereas cost for software, given its criticality, is not an issue for the organization within reasonable means. Other advantages of this strategy include the ease of sharing data between organizations, availability, fast provisioning, and management of storage utilization, because storage is a resource that is constantly in demand. Hasan, Yurcik and Myagmar [11] show in their study of storage service providers that reputation as storage vendors and the existence of established business relationships are major success and sustainability factors in this market.

3. **Solution Provision.** This strategy is relevant when the elasticity and cost reduction requirements are high for software and data, but the controllability requirements can be entrusted to the CDC. It is not the case that controllability is an insignificant requirement; it is rather the case that the

organization trusts the CDC sufficiently to manage access and usage control of its software and data. In some cases the organization might have greater trust in the CDC maintaining and securing its applications and data than it does in its own administrative capabilities. In other words, there are perceived gains in controllability for placing the entire IT solution (software and data) in the domain of the CDC. Solution provision also seemed like a more viable strategy than software or storage provision strategies, given the limitations of bandwidth between software and data that persists, especially for query-intensive solutions. Such a strategy is also attractive for testing systems, because these generally will not contain sensitive data (i.e., only test data) and are not the production-time versions of the software.

4. **Redundancy Services.** This strategy can be considered as a hybrid enterprise cloud strategy, where the organization switches between traditional, software, storage or solution management based on changes in its operational conditions and business demands. The trade-offs between controllability and cost reduction will therefore vary based on changes in load experienced by the organization. The strategy is referred to as the "redundancy strategy" because the CDC is used for situations such as disaster recovery, fail-over and load-balancing. Software, storage or solution services can be implemented using redundancy, such that users are redirected for the purpose of maintaining availability of functionality or performance/response times experienced by the user of the service. Business continuity is then the objective of this strategy, given that downtime and degradation of QoS can result in massive losses. There is however a cost for redundancy, because the subscription and access to redundant services needs to be maintained.

Even though an organization may find a strategy that appears to provide it significant benefits, this does not mean that immediate adoption of the strategy is advised or that the returns on investment will be observed immediately. There are still many issues to be considered when moving enterprise applications to the cloud paradigm.

4.3 ISSUES FOR ENTERPRISE APPLICATIONS ON THE CLOUD

Enterprise Resource Planning (ERP) is the most comprehensive definition of enterprise application today. The purpose of ERP solutions is to equip enterprises with a tool to optimize their underlying business processes with a seamless, integrated information flow from suppliers through to manufacturing and distribution [12] and the ability to effectively plan and control all resources [13], [14], necessary in the face of growing consumer demands, globalization and competition [15]. For these reasons, ERP solutions have emerged as the core of successful information management and the enterprise backbone of nearly any organization [16]. Organizations that have successfully implemented the ERP systems are reaping the benefits of having integrating working environment, standardized process and operational benefits to the organization [17]. However, as the market rapidly changes, organizations need new solutions for remaining competitive, such that they will constantly need to improve their business practices and procedures. For this reason the enterprise cloud computing paradigm is becoming attractive as a potential ERP execution environment. Nevertheless, such a transition will *require a balance of strategic and operational steps guided by socio-technical considerations, continuous evaluation, and tracking mechanisms* [18].

One of the first issues is that of infrastructure availability. Al-Mashari [19] and Yasser [20] argued that adequate IT infrastructure, hardware and networking are crucial for an ERP system's success. It is clear that ERP implementation involves a complex transition from legacy information systems and business processes to an integrated IT infrastructure and common business process throughout the organization. Hardware selection is driven by the organization's choice of an ERP software package. The ERP software vendor generally certifies which hardware (and hardware configurations) must be used to run the ERP system. This factor has always been considered critical [17]. The IaaS offerings hence bear promising, but also challenging future scenarios for the implementation of ERP systems.

One of the ongoing discussions concerning future scenarios considers varying infrastructure requirements and constraints given different workloads and development phases. Recent surveys among companies in North America and Europe with enterprise-wide IT systems showed that nearly all kinds of workloads are seen to be suitable to be transferred to IaaS offerings. Interest in use for production applications is nearly as high as for test and development use. One might think that companies will be much more comfortable with test and development workloads at an external service provider than with production workloads, where they must be more cautious. However, respondents in surveys said they were either just as comfortable, or only up to 8% less comfortable, deploying production workloads on "the cloud" as they were deploying test and development workloads. When the responses for all workload types are aggregated together, two-thirds or more of firms are willing to put at least one workload type into an IaaS offering at a service provider [21]. More technical issues for enterprise cloud computing adoption arise when considering the operational characteristics and behaviors of transactional and analytical applications [22], which extend and underlie the capabilities of ERP.

4.3.1 Considering Transactional and Analytical Capabilities

Transactional type of applications or so-called OLTP (On-line Transaction Processing) applications, refer to a class of systems that manage transaction-oriented applications, typically using relational databases. These applications rely on strong ACID (*atomicity, consistency, isolation, durability*) properties and are relatively write/update-intensive. Typical OLTP-type ERP components are sales and distributions (SD), banking and financials, customer relationship management (CRM) and supply chain management (SCM). These applications face major technical and non-technical challenges to deploy in cloud environments. For instance, they provide mission-critical functions and enterprises have clear security and privacy concerns. The classical transactional systems typically use a shared-everything architecture, while cloud platforms mostly consist of shared-nothing commodity hardware. ACID properties are also difficult to guarantee given the concurrent cloud-based data management and storage systems. Opportunities arise while the highly complex enterprise applications are decomposed into simpler functional components, which are characterized and engineered accordingly. For example, salesforce.com focuses on CRM-related applications and provides both a hosted software and development platform. Companies such as taleo.com offer on-demand Human Relationship (HR) applications and are gaining momentum in the SaaS market. A suite of core business applications as managed services can also be an attractive option, especially for small and medium companies. Despite the big engineering challenges, leading software providers are offering tailored business suite solutions as hosted services (e.g. SAP Business ByDesign).

Secondly, analytical types of applications or so-called OLAP (On-line Analytical Processing) applications, are used to efficiently answer multi-dimensional queries for analysis, reporting, and decision support. Typical OLAP applications are business reporting, marketing, budgeting and forecasting, to name a few, which belong to the larger Business Intelligence (BI) category [23]. These systems tend to be read-most or read-only, and ACID guarantees are typically not required. Because of its data-intensive and data-parallel nature, this type of applications can benefit greatly from the elastic compute and storage available in the cloud. Business Intelligence and analytical applications are relatively better suited to run in a cloud platform with a shared-nothing architecture and commodity hardware. Opportunities arise in the vision of Analytics as a Service, or Agile Analytics [24]. Data sources residing within private or public clouds, can be processed using elastic computing resources on-demand, accessible via APIs, web services, SQL, BI, and data mining tools. Of course security, data integrity, and other issues can not be overlooked, but a cloud way offers a direction with unmatched performance and TCO (total cost of ownership) benefits toward large-scale analytic processing. Leading providers have been offering on-demand BI and analytics services (e.g. BusinessObjects' ondemand.com and Cognos Now!). Startup companies and niche players (e.g. Brist, PivotLink, Oco) provide a range of SaaS BI products from reporting to ETL (Extract, Transform, Load).

One can conclude that analytical applications will benefit more than their transactional counterparts from the opportunities created by cloud computing, especially on compute elasticity and efficiency. The success of separate functional components such as CRM and HR offered as hosted services has been observed, such that predictions of an integrated suite of core enterprise functionalities emerging as on-demand solutions for small and medium enterprises can be made, given that the transition challenges can be overcome.

4.4 TRANSITION CHALLENGES

The very concept of cloud represents a leap from traditional approach for IT to deliver mission critical services. With any leap comes the gap of risk and challenges to overcome. These challenges can be classified in five different categories, which are the five aspects of the enterprise cloud stages: build, develop, migrate, run, and consume (Figure 4.3).

At the moment, the private and hybrid models (Section 4.2) appear as most relevant for comprehensive ERP transitioning and will hence be considered in this discussion of challenges. The first immediate challenge facing organizations, embarking on this transition, is the understanding of the state of their own IT assets and what is already, can, and cannot be *sublimed* (the process of transitioning from physical to less visible vapor). Based on the information gathered by this audit they need to evaluate what can be salvaged from the existing infrastructure and how high in the cloud stack they should venture. Most companies are likely to stick to IaaS. However, major development shops may envisage delving into the PaaS and SaaS sphere. Shifting the current architecture requires us to scrap a good chunk of it, which should be taken literally. However, we already see a sprawl of small cloud island appearing within corporations. As this *unplanned cloud* spreads throughout the organization, coherency becomes a challenge. The requirement for a company-wide cloud approach should then become the number one priority of the CIO, especially when it comes to having a coherent and cost effective development and migration of services on this architecture.

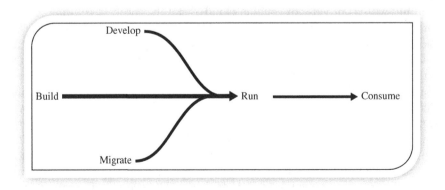

FIGURE 4.3. Five stages of the cloud.

A second challenge is migration of existing or "legacy" applications to "the cloud." The expected average lifetime of ERP product is ~15 years, which means that companies will need to face this aspect sooner than later as they try to evolve toward the new IT paradigm. An applications migration is not a straightforward process. It is risky, and doesn't always guarantee a better service delivery. Firstly, the guarantee that the migration process can be agnostic of the underlying, chosen cloud technology must be provided. If such a process can be automated, a company will still face the same amount of planning, negotiation and testing required for risk mitigation as classical software. It is yet to be proven that companies will be able to balance such expense with the cost cutting, scalability and performance promised by the cloud.

Because migrating to the cloud depends on the concept of decoupling of processes, work needs to be organized using a process (or service) centric model, rather than the standard "silo" one commonly used in IT: server, network, storage, database, and so on. Not all applications will be able to handle such migration without a tedious and costly overall reengineering. However, if companies decide to (re-) develop from scratch, they will face a completely different kind of hurdle: governance, reliability, security/trust, data management, and control/predictability [25] [26]. The ownership of enterprise data conjugated with the integration with others applications integration in and from outside the cloud is one of the key challenges. Future enterprise application development frameworks will need to enable the separation of data management from ownership. From this, it can be extrapolated that SOA, as a style, underlies the architecture and, moreover, the operation of the enterprise cloud.

Challenges for cloud operations can be divided into running the enterprise cloud and running applications on the enterprise cloud. In the first case, companies face difficulties in terms of the changing IT operations of their day today operation. It requires upgrading and updating all the IT department's components. One of these has been notoriously hard to upgrade: the human factor; bringing staff up to speed on the requirements of cloud computing with respect to architecture, implementation, and operation has always been a tedious task.

Once the IT organization has either been upgraded to provide cloud or is able to tap into cloud resource, they face the difficulty of maintaining the services in the cloud. The first one will be to maintain interoperability between in-house infrastructure and service and the CDC (Cloud Data Center).

Furthermore, inasmuch as elasticity is touted as the killer features for enterprise applications, most of the enterprise applications do not really face such wild variations in load to date, such that they need to resort to the cloud for on-demand capacity. More fundamentally, most enterprise apps don't support such features (apart from the few ones built from the ground up for clouds). Before leveraging such features, much more basic functionalities are problematic: monitoring, troubleshooting, and comprehensive capacity planning are actually missing in most offers. Without such features it becomes very hard to gain visibility into the return on investment and the consumption of cloud services.

Today there are two major cloud pricing models: Allocation based and Usage based [27]. The first one is provided by the poster child of cloud computing, namely, Amazon. The principle relies on allocation of resource for a fixed amount of time. The second model does not require any reservation of resource, and the cloud would simply allocate them as a per need basis. When this model combine two typical pricing models: Utility (pay-per-use) and subscription based (fixed per duration charge)—we see the number of variation of offers exploding. Finding the right combination of billing and consumption model for the service is a daunting task. However, the challenge doesn't just stop there. As companies need to evaluate the offers they need to also include the hidden costs such as lost IP, risk, migration, delays and provider overheads. This combination can be compared to trying to choose a new mobile with carrier plan. Not to mention that some providers are proposing to introduce a subscription scheme in order to palliate with their limited resource within their unlimited offer. This is similar to what ISPs would have done with their content rationing strategies. The market dynamics will hence evolve alongside the technology for the enterprise cloud computing paradigm.

4.5 ENTERPRISE CLOUD TECHNOLOGY AND MARKET EVOLUTION

This section discusses the potential factors which will influence this evolution of cloud computing and today's enterprise landscapes to the enterprise computing paradigm, featuring the convergence of business and IT and an open, service oriented marketplace.

4.5.1 Technology Drivers for Enterprise Cloud Computing Evolution

One of the main factors driving this evolution is the concern by all the stakeholders in the cloud ecosystem of vendor lock-in, which includes the barriers of proprietary interfaces, formats, and protocols employed by the cloud vendors. As an increasing number of organizations and enterprises formulate cloud adoption strategies and execution plans, requirements of open, inter-operable standards for cloud management interfaces and protocols, data formats and so on will emerge. This will put pressure on cloud providers to build their offering on open interoperable standards to be considered as a candidate by enterprises. There have been a number initiatives emerging in this space. For example, OGF OCCI [28] for compute clouds, SNIA CDMI [29] for storage and data management, DMTF Virtualization Management (VMAN) [30], and DMTF Cloud Incubator [31], to name a few of these standardization initiatives. Widespread participation in these initiatives is still lacking especially amongst the big cloud vendors like Amazon, Google, and Microsoft, who currently do not actively participate in these efforts. True interoperability across the board in the near future seems unlikely. However, if achieved, it could lead to facilitation of advanced scenarios and thus drive the mainstream adoption of the enterprise cloud computing paradigm. Another reason standards-based cloud offers are critical for the evolution and spread of this paradigm is the fact that standards drive choice and choice drives the market. From another perspective, in the presence of standards-based cloud offers, third party vendors will be able to develop and offer value added management capabilities in the form of independent cloud management tools. Moreover, vendors with existing IT management tools in the market would be able to extend these tools to manage cloud solutions, hence facilitating organizations to preserve their existing investments in IT management solutions and use them for managing their hybrid cloud deployments.

Part of preserving investments is maintaining the assurance that cloud resources and services powering the business operations perform according to the business requirements. Underperforming resources or service disruptions lead to business and financial loss, reduced business credibility, reputation, and marginalized user productivity. In the face of lack of control over the environment in which the resources and services are operating, enterprise would like sufficient assurances and guarantees to eliminate performance issues, and lack of compliance to security or governance standards (e.g. PCI, HPIAA, SOX, etc.) which can potentially lead to service disruptions, business loss, or damaged reputation. Service level agreements (SLA) can prove to be a useful instrument in facilitating enterprises' trust in cloud-based services. Currently, the cloud solutions come with primitive or non existing SLAs. This is surely bound to change; as the cloud market gets crowded with increasing number of cloud offers, providers have to gain some competitive differentiation to capture larger share of the market. This is particularly true for market segments represented by enterprises and large organizations. Enterprise will be particularly interested to choose the offering with sophisticated SLAs providing assurances for the issues mentioned above.

Another important factor in this regard is lack of insights into the performance and health of the resources and service deployed on the cloud, such that this is another area of technology evolution that will be pushed. Currently, cloud providers don't offer sophisticated monitoring and reporting capabilities which can allow customers to comprehend and analyze the operations of these resources and services. However, recently, solutions have started to emerge to address this issue [32–34]. Nonetheless, this is one of the areas where cloud providers need to improve their offerings. It is believed that the situation will then improve because the enterprise cloud adoption phenomenon will make it imperative for the cloud providers to deliver sophisticated monitoring and reporting capabilities for the customers. This requirement would become ever more critical with the introduction of sophisticated SLAs, because customers would like to get insights into the service and resource behaviors for detecting SLA compliance violations. Moreover, cloud providers would need to expose this information through a standardized programmatic interface so customers can feed this information into their planning tools. Another important advancement that would emerge is to enable third-party independent vendors to measure the performance and health of resources and services deployed on cloud. This would prove to be a critical capability empowering third-party organizations to act as independent auditors especially with respect to SLA compliance auditing and for mediating the SLA penalty related issues.

Looking into the cloud services stack (IaaS, PaaS, SaaS) [1], the applications space or SaaS has the most growth potential. As forecasted by the analyst IDC [35], applications will account for 38% of $44.2 billion cloud services market by 2103. Enterprises have already started to adopt some SaaS based solutions; however, these are primarily the edge applications like supplier management, talent management, performance management and so on as compared to the core business processes. These SaaS based applications need to be integrated to the backed applications located on-premise. These integration capabilities would drive the mainstream SaaS adoption by enterprises. Moreover, organizations would opt for SaaS applications from multiple service providers to cater for various operational segments of an enterprise. This adds an extra dimension of complexity because the integration mechanisms need to weave SaaS application from various providers and eventually integrate them to the on-premise core business applications seamlessly. Another emerging trend in the cloud application space is the divergence from the traditional RDBMS based data store backend. Cloud computing has given rise to alternative data storage technologies (Amazon Dynamo, Facebook Cassandra, Google BigTable, etc.) based on key-type storage models as compared to the relational model, which has been the mainstream choice for data storage for enterprise applications. Recently launched NoSQL movement is gaining momentum, and enterprise application developers will start adopting these alternative data storage technologies as a data layer for these enterprise applications.

The platform services segment of the cloud market is still in its early phases. Currently, PaaS is predominantly used for developing and deploying situational applications to exploit the rapid development cycles especially to cope with the scenarios that are constrained by limited timeframe to bring the solutions to the market. However, most of the development platforms and tools addressing this market segment are delivered by small startups and are proprietary technologies. Since the technologies are still evolving, providers are focusing on innovation aspects and gaining competitive edge over other providers. As these technologies evolve into maturity, the PaaS market will consolidate into a smaller number of service providers. Moreover, big traditional software vendors will also join this market which will potentially trigger this consolidation through acquisitions and mergers. These views are along the lines of the research published by Gartner [36]. Key findings published in this report were that through 2011, development platforms and tools targeting cloud deployment will remain highly proprietary and until then, the focus of these service providers would be on innovation over market viability. Gartner predicts that from 2011 to 2015 market competition and maturing developer practises will drive consolidation around a small group of industry-dominant cloud technology providers.

The IaaS segment is typically attractive for small companies or startups that don't have enough capital and human resources to afford internal infrastructures. However, enterprises and large organizations are experimenting with external cloud infrastructure providers as well. According to a Forrester report published last year [37], enterprises were experimenting with IaaS in various contexts for examples R&D-type projects for testing new services and applications and low-priority business applications. The report also quotes a multinational telecommunication company running an internal cloud for wikis and intranet sites and was beginning to test mission critical applications. The report also quotes the same enterprise to have achieved 30% cost reduction by adopting the cloud computing model. However, we will see this trend adopted by an increasing number of enterprises opting for IaaS services. A recent Forrester report [21] published in May 2009 supports this claim as according to the survey, 25% enterprises are either experimenting or thinking about adopting external cloud providers various types of enterprise applications and workloads. As more and more vendors enter the IaaS cloud segment, cloud providers will strive to gain competitive advantage by adopting various optimization strategies or value added services to the customers. Open standards based cloud interfaces will gain attraction for increasing the likelihood of being chosen by enterprises. Cloud providers will provide transparency into their operations and environments through sophisticated monitoring and reporting capabilities for the consumer to track and control their costs based on the consumption and usage information.

A recent report published by Gartner [36] presents an interesting perspective on cloud evolution. The report argues that as cloud services proliferate, services would become complex to be handled directly by the consumers. To cope with these scenarios, meta-services or cloud brokerage services will emerge. These brokerages will use several types of brokers and platforms to enhance service delivery and, ultimately service value. According to Gartner, before these scenarios can be enabled, there is a need for brokerage business to use these brokers and platforms. According to Gartner, the following types of cloud service brokerages (CSB) are foreseen:

- Cloud Service Intermediation. An intermediation broker providers a service that directly enhances a given service delivered one or more service consumers, essentially on top of a given service to enhance a specific capability.
- Aggregation. An aggregation brokerage service combines multiple services into one or more new services.
- Cloud Service Arbitrage. These services will provide flexibility and opportunistic choices for the service aggregator.

The above shows that there is potential for various large, medium, and small organizations to become players in the enterprise cloud marketplace. The dynamics of such a marketplace are still to be explored as the enabling technologies and standards continue to mature.

4.6   BUSINESS DRIVERS TOWARD A MARKETPLACE FOR ENTERPRISE CLOUD COMPUTING

In order to create an overview of offerings and consuming players on the market, it is important to understand the forces on the market and motivations of each player. Porter [39] offers a framework for the industry analysis and business strategy development. Within this framework the actors, products, and business models are clarified and structured.

The Porter model consists of five influencing factors/views (forces) on the market (Figure 4.4). In the traditional economic model, competition among rival companies drives profits to zero, thus forcing companies to strive for a competitive advantage over their rivals. The intensity of rivalry on the market is traditionally influenced by industry-specific characteristics [40]:

- Rivalry: The amount of companies dealing with cloud and virtualization technology is quite high at the moment; this might be a sign for high

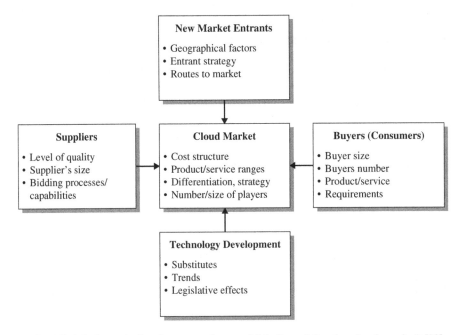

FIGURE 4.4. Porter's five forces market model (adjusted for the cloud market) [38].

rivalry. But also the products and offers are quite various, so many niche products tend to become established.

- Obviously, the cloud-virtualization market is presently booming and will keep growing during the next years. Therefore the fight for customers and struggle for market share will begin once the market becomes saturated and companies start offering comparable products.

- The initial costs for huge data centers are enormous. By building up federations of computing and storing utilities, smaller companies can try to make use of this scale effect as well.

- Low switching costs or high exit barriers influence rivalry. When a customer can freely switch from one product to another, there is a greater struggle to capture customers. From the opposite point of view high exit barriers discourage customers to buy into a new technology. The trends towards standardization of formats and architectures try to face this problem and tackle it. Most current cloud providers are only paying attention to standards related to the interaction with the end user. However, standards for clouds interoperability are still to be developed [41].

Monitoring the cloud market and observing current trends will show when the expected shakeout will take place and which companies will have the most accepted and economic offers by then [42]. After this shakeout, the whole buzz and hype around cloud computing is expected to be over and mature solutions will evolve. It is then that concrete business models will emerge. These business models will consider various fields, including e-business, strategy, supply chain management and information systems [43], [44], but will now need to emphasize the value of ICT-driven innovations for organizations and users [45]. Furthermore, static perspectives on business models will not be viable in such an ICT-centric environment, given that organizations often have to review their business model in order to keep in line with fast changing environments like the cloud market for the ICT sector [46], from development to exploitation [45]. With a few exceptions [47–49], most literature has taken a fairly static perspective on business models.

For dynamic business models for ICT, it is important to incorporate general phases of a product development. Thus, phasing models help to understand how innovation and change affect the evolution of the markets, and its consequences for company strategies and business models [50]. As argued by Kijl [51], the three main phases are R&D, implementation/roll-out, and market phase, which include the subphases of market offerings, maturity, and decline. These three main phases, influencing the business model, are used in a framework, visualized in Figure 4.5.

Figure 4.5 also outlines which external drivers are expected to play a dominant role throughout the phases [52]. Technology is the most important driver for the development of new business models in the ICT sector and will

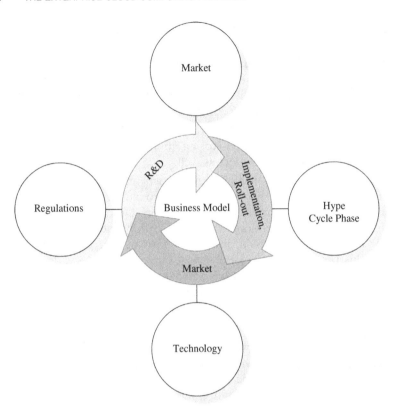

FIGURE 4.5. Dynamic business models (based on [49] extend by influence factors identified by [50]).

undoubtedly continue to be a major influencer of the enterprise cloud computing evolution. However, it can be assumed that market developments and regulation can also trigger opportunities for the development of new products and services in this paradigm. Changes in market opportunities or regulation enable new product and/or service definitions as well as underlying business models. There are already various players in the cloud computing market offering various services [53]. However, they still struggle for market share and it is very likely that they will diversify their offers in order to meet all the market requirements. During these efforts, some of them will reach the mainstream and achieve a critical mass for the market while others will pass away or exist as niche offers after the shakeout. It is increasingly necessary to have a comprehensive model of drivers for business model dynamics [40], [45], [54], including knowledge of actors, products and market. This is also motivated by Porter [40], Kijl [51], and Bouwman and MacInnes [52]. How then would such a business model be manifested?

4.7   THE CLOUD SUPPLY CHAIN

One indicator of what such a business model would look like is in the complexity of deploying, securing, interconnecting and maintaining enterprise landscapes and solutions such as ERP, as discussed in Section 4.3. The concept of a Cloud Supply Chain (C-SC) and hence Cloud Supply Chain Management (C-SCM) appear to be viable future business models for the enterprise cloud computing paradigm. The idea of C-SCM represents the management of a network of interconnected businesses involved in the end-to-end provision of product and service packages required by customers. The established understanding of a supply chain is two or more parties linked by a flow of goods, information, and funds [55], [56] A specific definition for a C-SC is hence: "two or more parties linked by the provision of cloud services, related information and funds." Figure 4.6 represents a concept for the C-SC, showing the flow of products along different organizations such as hardware suppliers, software component suppliers, data center operators, distributors and the end customer.

Figure 4.6 also makes a distinction between innovative and functional products in the C-SC. Fisher classifies products primarily on the basis of their demand patterns into two categories: primarily functional or primarily innovative [57]. Due to their stability, functional products favor competition, which leads to low profit margins and, as a consequence of their properties, to low inventory costs, low product variety, low stockout costs, and low obsolescence [58], [57]. Innovative products are characterized by additional (other) reasons for a customer in addition to basic needs that lead to purchase, unpredictable demand (that is high uncertainties, difficult to forecast and variable demand), and short product life cycles (typically 3 months to 1 year). Cloud services

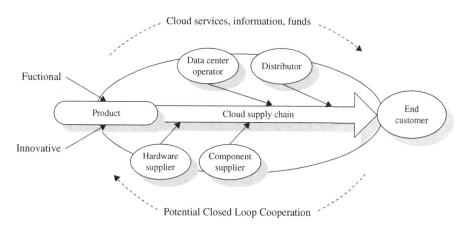

FIGURE 4.6. Cloud supply chain (C-SC).

should fulfill basic needs of customers and favor competition due to their reproducibility. They however also show characteristics of innovative products as the demand is in general unpredictable (on-demand business model) and have due to adjustments to competitors and changing market requirements very short development circles. Table 4.1 presents a comparison of Traditional

TABLE 4.1. Comparison of Traditional and Emerging ICT Supply Chains[a]

	Traditional Supply Chain Concepts		Emerging ICT Concepts
	Efficient SC	Responsive SC	Cloud SC
Primary goal	Supply demand at the lowest level of cost	Respond quickly to demand (changes)	Supply demand at the lowest level of costs and respond quickly to demand
Product design strategy	Maximize performance at the minimum product cost	Create modularity to allow postponement of product differentiation	Create modularity to allow individual setting while maximizing the performance of services
Pricing strategy	Lower margins because price is a prime customer driver	Higher margins, because price is not a prime customer driver	Lower margins, as high competition and comparable products
Manufacturing strategy	Lower costs through high utilization	Maintain capacity flexibility to meet unexpected demand	High utilization while flexible reaction on demand
Inventory strategy	Minimize inventory to lower cost	Maintain buffer inventory to meet unexpected demand	Optimize of buffer for unpredicted demand, and best utilization
Lead time strategy	Reduce but not at the expense of costs	Aggressively reduce even if the costs are significant	Strong service-level agreements (SLA) for ad hoc provision
Supplier strategy	Select based on cost and quality	Select based on speed, flexibility, and quantity	Select on complex optimum of speed, cost, and flexibility
Transportation strategy	Greater reliance on low cost modes	Greater reliance on responsive modes	Implement highly responsive and low cost modes

[a] Based on references 54 and 57.

Supply Chain concepts such as the efficient SC and responsive SC and a new concept for emerging ICT as the cloud computing area with cloud services as traded products.

This mixed characterization is furthermore reflected when it comes to the classification of efficient vs. responsive Supply Chains. Whereas functional products would preferable go into efficient Supply Chains, the main aim of responsive Supply Chains fits the categorization of innovative product. Cachon and Fisher [58] show that within the supply chain the sharing of information (e.g. accounting and billing) is not the only contributor to SC cost, but it is the management and restructuring of services, information, and funds for an optimization of the chain that are expensive [60].

4.8 SUMMARY

In this chapter, the enterprise cloud computing paradigm has been discussed, with respect to opportunities, challenges and strategies for cloud adoption and consumption. With reference to Gartner's hype cycle [61], enterprise cloud computing and related technologies is already in the first phase called "inflated expectation," but it is likely to move quite quickly into the "trough of disillusionment" [62]. At the moment the main adopters of cloud computing are small companies and startups, where the issue of legacy of IT investments is not present. Large enterprises continue to wrestle with the arguments for adopting such a model, given the perceived risks and effort incurred. From an analysis of existing offerings, the current models do not fully meet the criteria of enterprise IT as yet. Progress continues at an accelerated pace, boosted by the rich and vibrant ecosystem being developed by start-up and now major IT vendors. It can hence be foreseen that the enterprise cloud computing paradigm could see a rise within the next 10 years. Evidence is found in the increasing development of enterprise applications tailored for this environment and the reductions in cost for development, testing and operation. However, the cloud model will not predate the classical way of consuming software services to extinction; they will just evolve and adapt. It will have far reaching consequences for years to come within the software, IT services vendors and even IT hardware, as it reshapes the IT landscape.

ACKNOWLEDGMENTS

This chapter combines insights that have been drawn from various EU and Invest-NI funded projects in SAP Research Belfast. These include SLA@SOI (FP7-216556), RESERVOIR (FP7-215605), XtreemOS (FP6-IST-033576), and Virtex (Invest-NI).

REFERENCES

1. NIST, "Working Definition of Cloud Computing," 2009.
2. Cloud Security Alliance, "Guidance for Critical Areas of Focus in Cloud Computing," 2009.
3. Amazon, "Amazon Virtual Private Cloud."
4. OpSource, "OpSource Cloud."
5. Skytap, "Virtual Lab."
6. OpenCirrus, "OpenCirrus Cloud Computing Research Testbed."
7. ENKI, "Outsourced IT Operations."
8. CohesiveFT, "VPN-Cubed."
9. Buyya, R., Yeo, C. S., Venugopal, S., Broberg, J., and Brandic, I., "Cloud computing and emerging IT platforms: Vision, hype, and reality for delivering computing as the 5th utility," *Future Gener. Comput. Syst. 25, 6 (Jun. 2009)*, 2009, pp. 599–616.
10. Ben Pring and Twiggy Lo, "Dataquest Insight: SaaS Adoption Trends in the U.S. and UK," 2009.
11. Hasan, R., Yurcik, W., and Myagmar, S., "The evolution of storage service providers: techniques and challenges to outsourcing storage," *Proceedings of the 2005 ACM Workshop on Storage Security and Survivability (Fairfax, VA, USA, November 11 - 11, 2005). StorageSS '05. ACM*, 2005.
12. McDermott, T, "MES and ERP: Creating Synergy with Industry-Specific Solutions," *APICS—The Performance Advantage, vol. 9, no. 11, November 1999*, 1999, pp. 40–3.
13. Miller, GJ, "Lean and ERP: Can they Co-exist?," *PROACTION Management Consultants—www.proaction.net/HTML_papers/LeanERPCompat.html*.
14. Sandoe, K., Corbitt, G., and Boykin, R., *Enterprise Integration*, New York: 2001.
15. Ferguson, B, "Implementing Supply Chain Management," *Production and Inventory Management Journal, vol. 41, no. 2*, 2000, pp. 64–7.
16. Nash, K.S, "Companies don't learn from previous IT snafus," *ComputerWorld 32–3*, 2000.
17. T.R. Bhatti, "CRITICAL SUCCESS FACTORS FOR THE IMPLEMENTATION OF ENTERPRISE RESOURCE PLANNING (ERP): EMPIRICAL VALIDATION," *The Second International Conference on Innovation in Information Technology (IIT'05)*, p. 2005.
18. Al-Mudimigh A., Zairi M., and Al-Mashiri M., "ERP software implementation: an integrative framework," *European Journal of Information Systems, 10*, 2001, pp. 216–226.
19. Al-Mashari, M., "Enterprise resource planning (ERP) systems: a research agenda," *Industrial Management & Data Systems, Vol. 102, No. 3*, 2002, pp. 165–170.
20. Yasser Jarrar, "ERP Implementation and Critical Success Factors, The Role and Impact of Business Process Management," *Proceedings of The 2000 IEE International Conference on Management of Innovation and Technology, Singapore*, 2000, pp. 167–178.
21. Frank E. Gillet, "Conventional Wisdom is Wrong About Cloud IaaS," 2009.

22. D. Abadi, "Data Management in the Cloud: Limitations and Opportunities," *IEEE Data Engineering Bulletin, 32(1)*, 2009.

23. E. Thomsen, *OLAP Solutions: Building Multi-dimensional Information Systems*, 2002.

24. Oliver Ratzesberger, "Analytics as a Service."

25. Daniel J. and Abadi, H., "Data Management in the Cloud: Limitations and Opportunities," *Bulletin of the IEEE Computer Society Technical Committee on Data Engineering*, 2009.

26. Jay Heiser and Mark Nicolett, "Assessing the Security Risks of Cloud Computing," *Gartner Report*, Jun. 2008.

27. Weiss, A., "Computing in the clouds," *netWorker 11, 4 (Dec. 2007)*, 2007.

28. Open Cloud Computing Interface (OCCI) Working Group, "OCCI."

29. SNIA, "Cloud Data Management Initiative (CDMI)."

30. DMTF, "Virtualization Management Initiative (VMAN)."

31. DMTF, "Open Cloud Standards Incubator."

32. Amazon, "CloudWatch."

33. Hyperic, "CloudStatus."

34. Nimsoft, "Unified Monitoring."

35. IDC, "IT Cloud Services Forecast 2009−2013."

36. Mark Driver, "Cloud Application Infrastructure Technologies Need Seven More Years to Mature," 2008.

37. James Staten, "Is Cloud Ready for Enterprises?," 2008.

38. Daryl C. Plummer and L. Frank Kenney, "Three Types of Cloud Brokerages Will Enhance Cloud Services," 2009.

39. Michael E. Porter, *Competitive Strategy: Techniques for Analyzing Industries and Competitors*, 1980.

40. M.E. Porter, "Competitive Strategy: Techniques for Analyzing Industries and Competitors," *Ed. The Free Press*, 1980.

41. EGEE, "Enabling Grids for E-sciencE An EGEE Comparative study: Grids and Clouds evolution or revolution?," 2008.

42. D. Reeves, *Data center strategies: Vmware: Welcome to the game*, 2008.

43. J. Hedman and T. Kalling, "The business model concept: theoretical underpinnings and empirical illustrations," *European Journal of Information Sciences*, 2003, pp. 49−59.

44. S.M. Shafer, H.J. Smith, and J.C. Linder, "The power of business models. Business Horizons," *European Journal of Information Sciences*, vol. 48, 2005, pp. 199−207.

45. M. de Reuver, H. Bouwman, and I. MacInnes, "What Drives Business Model Dynamics? A Case Survey," *Management of eBusiness, 2007. WCMeB 2007. Eighth World Congress on the*, Jul. 2007, pp. 2−2.

46. A. Afuah and C. Tucci, "Internet Business Models and Strategies," *Boston McGraw-Hill*, 2003.

47. P. Andries, K. Debackere, and B. Van Looy, "Effective business model adaptation strategies for new technology based ventures," *PREBEM Conference on Business Economics*, vol. 9, 2006.

48. I. MacInnes, "Dynamic business model framework for emerging technologies," *International Journal of Services Technology and Management*, vol. 6, 2005, pp. 3–19.

49. V.L. Vaccaro and D.Y. Cohn, "The Evolution of Business Models and Marketing Strategies in the Music Industry," *JMM—The International Journal on Media Management*, vol. 6, 2004, pp. 46–58.

50. A. Afuah and C.L. Tucci, "Internet Business Models and Strategies," *Mcgraw-Hill*, 2001.

51. B. Kijl, "Developing a dynamic business model framework for emerging mobile services," *ITS 16th European Regional Conference*, 2005.

52. H. Bouwman and I. MacInnes, "Dynamic Business Model Framework for Value Webs," *39th Annual Hawaii International Conference on System Sciences*, 2006.

53. M. Crandell, "Defogging cloud computing: A taxonomy—refresh the net," *Gigaom*, Sep. 2008.

54. L.M. Vaquero, L. Rodero-Merino, J. Caceres, and M. Lindner, "A Break in the Clouds: Towards a Cloud Definition," *Strategic Management Journal*, vol. 22, 2009.

55. Tsay, A., Agrawal, N., and Nahmias, S., "Modeling supply chain contracts: a review," *Tayur, S., Ganeshan, R., and Magazine, M., editors, Quantitative Models for Supply Chain Management, Kluwer's International Series in Operations Research & Management Science, chapter 10, pages 299–336. Kluwer Academic Publishers, Boston, MA, USA. F.S.Hillier, series editor*, 1998.

56. Paulitsch, M., "Dynamic Coordination of Supply Chains," 2003.

57. Fisher, M., "What is the right supply chain for your product?," *Harvard Business Review, pages 105–116*, 1997.

58. Lee, H., "Aligning supply chain strategies with product uncertainties," *California Management Review, 44(3):105–119*, 2002.

59. Chopra, S. and Meindl, P., "Supply Chain Management: Strategy, Planning, and Operation," *Prentice-Hall, Inc., Upper Saddle River, New Jersey, USA, 1st edition.*, 2001.

60. Cachon, G. and Fisher, M., "Supply chain inventory management and the value of shared information," *Management Science, 46(8):1032–1048*, 2000.

61. Gartner, "Hype Cycle for Emerging Technologies," 2008.

62. McKinsey&Company, "Clearing the air on cloud computing," Mar. 2009.

PART II

INFRASTRUCTURE AS A SERVICE (IAAS)

CHAPTER 5

VIRTUAL MACHINES PROVISIONING AND MIGRATION SERVICES

MOHAMED EL-REFAEY

5.1 INTRODUCTION AND INSPIRATION

Cloud computing is an emerging research infrastructure that builds on the achievements of different research areas, such as service-oriented architecture (SOA), grid computing, and virtualization technology. It offers infrastructure as a service that is based on pay-as-you-use and on-demand computing models to the end users (exactly the same as a public utility service like electricity, water, gas, etc.). This service is referred to as Infrastructure as a Service (IaaS). To provide this cloud computing service, the provisioning of the cloud infrastructure in data centers is a prerequisite. However, the provisioning for systems and applications on a large number of physical machines is traditionally a time-consuming process with low assurance on deployment's time and cost.

In this chapter, we shall focus on two core services that enable the users to get the best out of the IaaS model in public and private cloud setups. These services are named virtual machine provisioning and migration services. We will also cover their concepts, techniques, and research directions, along with an introductory overview about virtualization technology and its role as a fundamental component/block of the cloud computing architecture stack.

To make the concept clearer, consider this analogy for virtual machine provisioning, to know its value: *Historically*, when there is a need to install a new server for a certain workload to provide a particular service for a client, lots of effort was exerted by the IT administrator, and much time was spent to install and provision a new server, because the administrator has to follow specific checklist and procedures to perform this task on hand. (Check the

---

inventory for a new machine, get one, format, install OS required, and install services; a server is needed along with lots of security batches and appliances.) **Now,** with the emergence of virtualization technology and the cloud computing IaaS model, it is just a matter of minutes to achieve the same task. All you need is to provision a virtual server through a self-service interface with small steps to get what you desire with the required specifications—whether you are provisioning this machine in a public cloud like Amazon Elastic Compute Cloud (EC2) or using a virtualization management software package or a private cloud management solution installed at your data center in order to provision the virtual machine inside the organization and within the private cloud setup. This scenario is an awesome example for illustrating the value of virtualization and the way virtual machines are provisioned.

We can draw the same analogy for migration services. *Previously*, whenever there was a need for performing a server's upgrade or performing maintenance tasks, you would exert a lot of time and effort, because it is an expensive operation to maintain or upgrade a main server that has lots of applications and users. Now, with the advance of the revolutionized virtualization technology and migration services associated with hypervisors' capabilities, these tasks (maintenance, upgrades, patches, etc.) are very easy and need no time to accomplish.

Provisioning a new virtual machine is a matter of minutes, saving lots of time and effort. Migrations of a virtual machine is a matter of milliseconds: saving time, effort, making the service alive for customers, and achieving the SLA/ SLO agreements and quality-of-service (QoS) specifications required.

An overview about the chapter's higlights and sections can be grasped by the mind map shown in Figure 5.1.

5.2   BACKGROUND AND RELATED WORK

In this section, we will have a quick look at previous work, give an overview about virtualization technology, public cloud, private cloud, standardization efforts, high availability through the migration, and provisioning of virtual machines, and shed some lights on distributed management's tools.

5.2.1   Virtualization Technology Overview

Virtualization has revolutionized data center's technology through a set of techniques and tools that facilitate the providing and management of the dynamic data center's infrastructure. It has become an essential and enabling technology of cloud computing environments. Virtualization can be defined as the abstraction of the four computing resources (storage, processing power, memory, and network or I/O). It is conceptually similar to emulation, where a system pretends to be another system, whereas virtualization is a system pretending to be two or more of the same system [1]. As shown in

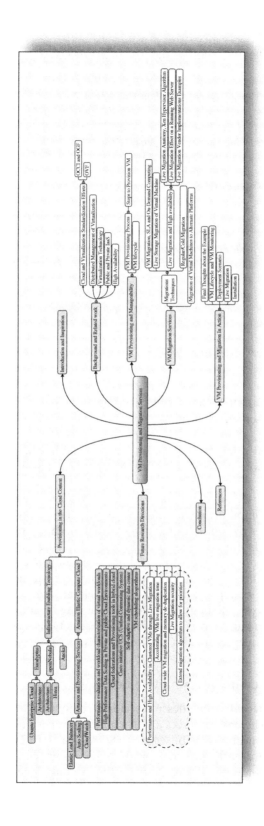

FIGURE 5.1. VM provisioning and migration mind map.

125

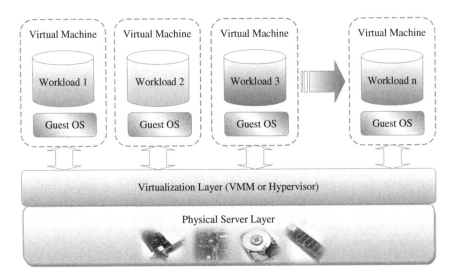

FIGURE 5.2. A layered virtualization technology architecture.

Figure 5.2, the virtualization layer will partition the physical resource of the underlying physical server into multiple virtual machines with different workloads. The fascinating thing about this virtualization layer is that it schedules, allocates the physical resource, and makes each virtual machine think that it totally owns the whole underlying hardware's physical resource (processor, disks, rams, etc.)[2].

Virtual machine's technology makes it very flexible and easy to manage resources in cloud computing environments, because they improve the utilization of such resources by multiplexing many virtual machines on one physical host (server consolidation), as shown in Figure 5.1. These machines can be scaled up and down on demand with a high level of resources' abstraction.

Virtualization enables high, reliable, and agile deployment mechanisms and management of services, providing on-demand cloning and live migration services which improve reliability. Accordingly, having an effective management's suite for managing virtual machines' infrastructure is critical for any cloud computing infrastructure as a service (IaaS) vendor.

5.2.2 Public Cloud and Infrastructure Services

Public cloud or external cloud describes cloud computing in a traditional mainstream sense, whereby resources are dynamically provisioned via publicly accessible Web applications/Web services (SOAP or RESTful interfaces) from an off-site third-party provider, who shares resources and bills on a fine-grained utility computing basis [3], the user pays only for the capacity of the provisioned resources at a particular time.

There are many examples for vendors who publicly provide infrastructure as a service. Amazon Elastic Compute Cloud (EC2)[4] is the best known example, but the market now bristles with lots of competition like GoGrid [5], Joyent Accelerator [6], Rackspace [7], AppNexus [8], FlexiScale [9], and Manjrasoft Aneka [10].

Here, we will briefly cover and describe Amazon EC2 offering. Amazon Elastic Compute Cloud (EC2) is an IaaS service that provides elastic compute capacity in the cloud. These services can be leveraged via Web services (SOAP or REST), a Web-based AWS (Amazon Web Service) management console, or the EC2 command line tools. The Amazon service provides hundreds of pre-made AMIs (Amazon Machine Images) with a variety of operating systems (i.e., Linux, OpenSolaris, or Windows) and pre-loaded software.

It provides you with complete control of your computing resources and lets you run on Amazon's computing and infrastructure environment easily. Amazon EC2 reduces the time required for obtaining and booting a new server's instances to minutes, thereby allowing a quick scalable capacity and resources, up and down, as the computing requirements change. Amazon offers different instances' size according to (a) the resources' needs (small, large, and extra large), (b) the high CPU's needs it provides (medium and extra large high CPU instances), and (c) high-memory instances (extra large, double extra large, and quadruple extra large instance).

5.2.3 Private Cloud and Infrastructure Services

A private cloud aims at providing public cloud functionality, but on private resources, while maintaining control over an organization's data and resources to meet security and governance's requirements in an organization. Private cloud exhibits a highly virtualized cloud data center located inside your organization's firewall. It may also be a private space dedicated for your company within a cloud vendor's data center designed to handle the organization's workloads.

Private clouds exhibit the following characteristics:

- Allow service provisioning and compute capability for an organization's users in a self-service manner.
- Automate and provide well-managed virtualized environments.
- Optimize computing resources, and servers' utilization.
- Support specific workloads.

There are many examples for vendors and frameworks that provide infrastructure as a service in private setups. The best-known examples are Eucalyptus [11] and OpenNebula [12] (which will be covered in more detail later on).

It is also important to highlight a third type of cloud setup named "hybrid cloud," in which a combination of private/internal and external cloud resources exist together by enabling outsourcing of noncritical services and functions in public cloud and keeping the critical ones internal. Hybrid cloud's main function is to release resources from a public cloud and to handle sudden demand usage, which is called "cloud bursting."

5.2.4 Distributed Management of Virtualization

Virtualization's benefits bring their own challenges and complexities presented in the need for a powerful management capabilities. That is why many commercial, open source products and research projects such as OpenNebula [12], IBM Virtualization Manager, Joyent, and VMware DRS are being developed to dynamically provision virtual machines, utilizing the physical infrastrcture. There are also some commercial and scientific infrastructure cloud computing initiatives, such as Globus VWS, Eucalyptus [11] and Amazon, which provide remote interfaces for controling and monitoring virtual resources. One more effort in this context is the RESERVOIR [13] initiative, in which grid interfaces and protocols enable the required interoperability between the clouds or infrastructure's providers. RESERVOIR also, needs to expand substantially on the current state-of-the-art for grid-wide accounting [14], and to increase the flexibility of supporting different billing schemes, and accounting for services with indefinite lifetime, as opposed to finite jobs with support to account for utilization metrics relevant to virtual machines [15].

5.2.5 High Availability

High availability is a system design protocol and an associated implementation that ensures a certain absolute degree of operational continuity during a given measurement period. Availability refers to the ability of a user's community to access the system—whether for submiting new work, updating or altering existing work, or collecting the results of the previous work. If a user cannot access the system, it is said to be unavailable [16]. This means that services should be available all the time along with some planned/unplanned downtime according to a certain SLA (formalize the service availaibiliy objectives, and requirments) which often refers to the monthly availability or downtime of a service; to calculate the service's credits to match the billing cycles. Services that are considered as business critical are often categorized as *high availability* services. Systems running business critical services should be planned and designed from the bottom with the goal of achieving the lowest possible amount of planned and unplanned downtime.

Since a virtual environment is the larger part of any organization, management of these virtual resources within this environemnet becomes a critical mission, and the migration services of these resources became a corner stone in achieving high availability for these services hosted by VMs. So, in the context of virtualized infrastructure, high availability allows virtual machines to automatically be restarted in case of an underlying hardware failure or individual VM failure. If one of your servers fails, the VMs will be restarted on other virtualized servers in the resource pool, restoring the essential services with minimal service interruption.

5.2.6 Cloud and Virtualization Standardization Efforts

Standardization is important to ensure interoperability between virtualization mangement vendors, the virtual machines produced by each one of them, and cloud computing. Here, we will have look at the prevalent standards that make cloud computing and virtualization possible. In the past few years, virtualization standardization efforts led by the Distributed Management Task Force (DMTF) have produced standards for almost all the aspects of virtualization technology. DMTF initiated the VMAN (Virtualization Management Initiative), which delivers broadly supported interoperability and portability standards for managing the virtual computing lifecycle. VMAN's OVF (Open Virtualization Format) in a collaboration between industry key players: Dell, HP, IBM, Microsoft, XenSource, and Vmware. OVF specification provides a common format to package and securely distribute virtual appliances across multiple virtualization platforms. VMAN profiles define a consistent way of managing a heterogeneous virtualized environment [17].

5.2.7 OCCI and OGF

Another standardization effort has been initiated by Open Grid Forum (OGF) through organizing an official new working group to deliver a standard API for cloud IaaS, the Open Cloud Computing Interface Working Group (OCCI-WG). This group is dedicated for delivering an API specification for the remote management of cloud computing's infrastructure and for allowing the development of interoperable tools for common tasks including deployment, autonomic scaling, and monitoring. The scope of the specification will be covering a high-level functionality required for managing the life-cycle virtual machines (or workloads), running on virtualization technologies (or containers), and supporting service elasticity. The new API for interfacing "IaaS" cloud computing facilities will allow [18]:

- **Consumers** to interact with cloud computing infrastructure on an ad hoc basis.
- **Integrators** to offer advanced management services.
- **Aggregators** to offer a single common interface to multiple providers.
- **Providers** to offer a standard interface that is compatible with the available tools.

- **Vendors** of grids/clouds to offer standard interfaces for dynamically scalable service's delivery in their products.

5.3 VIRTUAL MACHINES PROVISIONING AND MANAGEABILITY

In this section, we will have an overview on the typical life cycle of VM and its major possible states of operation, which make the management and automation of VMs in virtual and cloud environments easier than in traditional computing environments.

As shown in Figure 5.3, the cycle starts by a request delivered to the IT department, stating the requirement for creating a new server for a particular service. This request is being processed by the IT administration to start seeing the servers' resource pool, matching these resources with the requirements, and starting the provision of the needed virtual machine. Once it is provisioned and started, it is ready to provide the required service according to an SLA, or a time period after which the virtual is being released; and free resources, in this case, won't be needed.

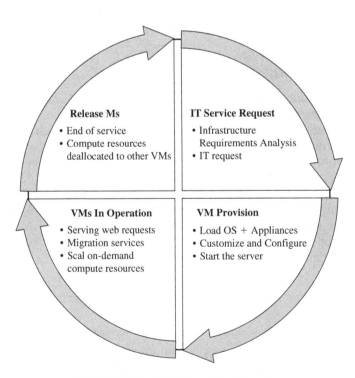

FIGURE 5.3. Virtual machine life cycle.

5.3.1 VM Provisioning Process

Provisioning a virtual machine or server can be explained and illustrated as in Figure 5.4:

Steps to Provision VM. Here, we describe the common and normal steps of provisioning a virtual server:

- Firstly, you need to select a server from a pool of available servers (physical servers with enough capacity) along with the appropriate OS template you need to provision the virtual machine.
- Secondly, you need to load the appropriate software (operating system you selected in the previous step, device drivers, middleware, and the needed applications for the service required).
- Thirdly, you need to customize and configure the machine (e.g., IP address, Gateway) to configure an associated network and storage resources.
- Finally, the virtual server is ready to start with its newly loaded software.

Typically, these are the tasks required or being performed by an IT or a data center's specialist to provision a particular virtual machine.

To summarize, server provisioning is defining server's configuration based on the organization requirements, a hardware, and software component (processor, RAM, storage, networking, operating system, applications, etc.). Normally, virtual machines can be provisioned by manually installing an operating system, by using a preconfigured VM template, by cloning an existing VM, or by importing a physical server or a virtual server from another hosting platform. Physical servers can also be virtualized and provisioned using P2V (physical to virtual) tools and techniques (e.g., virt-p2v).

After creating a virtual machine by virtualizing a physical server, or by building a new virtual server in the virtual environment, a template can be created out of it. Most virtualization management vendors (VMware, XenServer, etc.) provide the data center's administration with the ability to do such tasks in

FIGURE 5.4. Virtual machine provision process.

an easy way. Provisioning from a template is an invaluable feature, because it reduces the time required to create a new virtual machine.

Administrators can create different templates for different purposes. For example, you can create a Windows 2003 Server template for the finance department, or a Red Hat Linux template for the engineering department. This enables the administrator to quickly provision a correctly configured virtual server on demand.

This ease and flexibility bring with them the problem of virtual machine's sprawl, where virtual machines are provisioned so rapidly that documenting and managing the virtual machine's life cycle become a challenge [9].

5.4 VIRTUAL MACHINE MIGRATION SERVICES

Migration service, in the context of virtual machines, is the process of moving a virtual machine from one host server or storage location to another; there are different techniques of VM migration, hot/life migration, cold/regular migration, and live storage migration of a virtual machine [20]. In this process, all key machines' components, such as CPU, storage disks, networking, and memory, are completely virtualized, thereby facilitating the entire state of a virtual machine to be captured by a set of easily moved data files. We will cover some of the migration's techniques that most virtualization tools provide as a feature.

5.4.1 Migrations Techniques

Live Migration and High Availability. *Live migration* (which is also called hot or real-time migration) can be defined as the movement of a virtual machine from one physical host to another while being powered on. When it is properly carried out, this process takes place without any noticeable effect from the end user's point of view (a matter of milliseconds). One of the most significant advantages of live migration is the fact that it facilitates proactive maintenance in case of failure, because the potential problem can be resolved before the disruption of service occurs. Live migration can also be used for load balancing in which work is shared among computers in order to optimize the utilization of available CPU resources.

Live Migration Anatomy, Xen Hypervisor Algorithm. In this section we will explain live migration's mechanism and how memory and virtual machine states are being transferred, through the network, from one host A to another host B [21]; the Xen hypervisor is an example for this mechanism. The logical steps that are executed when migrating an OS are summarized in Figure 5.5. In this research, the migration process has been viewed as a transactional interaction between the two hosts involved:

> **Stage 0: Pre-Migration.** An active virtual machine exists on the physical host A.

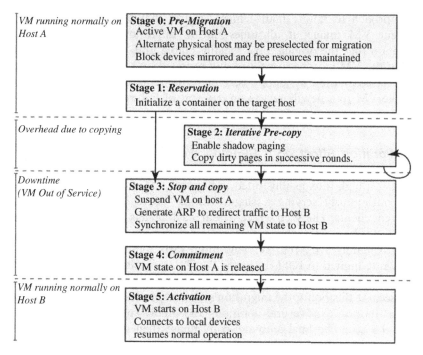

FIGURE 5.5. Live migration timeline [21].

Stage 1: Reservation. A request is issued to migrate an OS from host A to host B (a precondition is that the necessary resources exist on B and on a VM container of that size).

Stage 2: Iterative Pre-Copy. During the first iteration, all pages are transferred from A to B. Subsequent iterations copy only those pages dirtied during the previous transfer phase.

Stage 3: Stop-and-Copy. Running OS instance at A is suspended, and its network traffic is redirected to B. As described in reference 21, CPU state and any remaining inconsistent memory pages are then transferred. At the end of this stage, there is a consistent suspended copy of the VM at both A and B. The copy at A is considered primary and is resumed in case of failure.

Stage 4: Commitment. Host B indicates to A that it has successfully received a consistent OS image. Host A acknowledges this message as a commitment of the migration transaction. Host A may now discard the original VM, and host B becomes the primary host.

Stage 5: Activation. The migrated VM on B is now activated. Post-migration code runs to reattach the device's drivers to the new machine and advertise moved IP addresses.

This approach to failure management ensures that at least one host has a consistent VM image at all times during migration. It depends on the assumption that the original host remains stable until the migration commits and that the VM may be suspended and resumed on that host with no risk of failure. Based on these assumptions, a migration request essentially attempts to move the VM to a new host and on any sort of failure, execution is resumed locally, aborting the migration.

Live Migration Effect on a Running Web Server. Clark et al. [21] did evaluate the above migration on an Apache 1.3 Web server; this served static content at a high rate, as illustrated in Figure 5.6. The throughput is achieved when continuously serving a single 512-kB file to a set of one hundred concurrent clients. The Web server virtual machine has a memory allocation of 800 MB. At the start of the trace, the server achieves a consistent throughput of approximately 870 Mbit/sec. Migration starts 27 sec into the trace, but is initially rate-limited to 100 Mbit/sec (12% CPU), resulting in server's throughput drop to 765 Mbit/sec. This initial low-rate pass transfers 776 MB and lasts for 62 sec. At this point, the migration's algorithm, described in Section 5.4.1, increases its rate over several iterations and finally suspends the VM after a further 9.8 sec. The final stop-and-copy phase then transfers the remaining pages, and the Web server resumes at full rate after a 165-msec outage.

This simple example demonstrates that a highly loaded server can be migrated with both controlled impact on live services and a short downtime. However, the working set of the server, in this case, is rather small. So, this should be expected as a relatively easy case of live migration.

Live Migration Vendor Implementations Examples. There are lots of VM management and provisioning tools that provide the live migration of VM facility, two of which are VMware VMotion and Citrix XenServer "XenMotion."

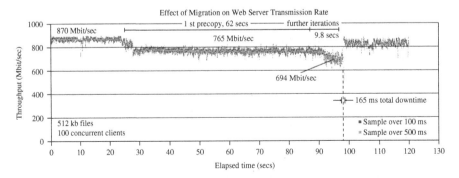

FIGURE 5.6. Results of migrating a running Web server VM [21].

VMware Vmotion. This allows users to (a) automatically optimize and allocate an entire pool of resources for maximum hardware utilization, flexibility, and availability and (b) perform hardware's maintenance without scheduled downtime along with migrating virtual machines away from failing or underperforming servers [22].

Citrix XenServer XenMotion. This is a nice feature of the Citrix XenServer product, inherited from the Xen live migrate utility, which provides the IT administrator with the facility to move a running VM from one XenServer to another in the same pool without interrupting the service (hypothetically for zero-downtime server maintenance, which actually takes minutes), making it a highly available service. This also can be a good feature to balance the workloads on the virtualized environment [23].

Regular/Cold Migration. Cold migration is the migration of a powered-off virtual machine. With cold migration, you have the option of moving the associated disks from one data store to another. The virtual machines are not required to be on a shared storage. It's important to highlight that the two main differences between live migration and cold migration are that live migration needs a shared storage for virtual machines in the server's pool, but cold migration does not; also, in live migration for a virtual machine between two hosts, there would be certain CPU compatibility checks to be applied; while in cold migration this checks do not apply. The cold migration process is simple to implement (as the case for the VMware product), and it can be summarized as follows [24]:

- The configuration files, including the NVRAM file (BIOS settings), log files, as well as the disks of the virtual machine, are moved from the source host to the destination host's associated storage area.
- The virtual machine is registered with the new host.
- After the migration is completed, the old version of the virtual machine is deleted from the source host.

Live Storage Migration of Virtual Machine. This kind of migration constitutes moving the virtual disks or configuration file of a running virtual machine to a new data store without any interruption in the availability of the virtual machine's service. For more details about how this option is working in a VMware product, see reference 20.

5.4.2 VM Migration, SLA and On-Demand Computing

As we discussed, virtual machines' migration plays an important role in data centers by making it easy to adjust resource's priorities to match resource's demand conditions.

This role is completely going in the direction of meeting SLAs; once it has been detected that a particular VM is consuming more than its fair share of resources at the expense of other VMs on the same host, it will be eligible, for this machine, to either be moved to another underutilized host or assign more resources for it, in case that the host machine still has resources; this in turn will highly avoid the violations of the SLA and will also, fulfill the requirements of on-demand computing resources. In order to achieve such goals, there should be an integration between virtualization's management tools (with its migrations and performance's monitoring capabilities), and SLA's management tools to achieve balance in resources by migrating and monitoring the workloads, and accordingly, meeting the SLA.

5.4.3   Migration of Virtual Machines to Alternate Platforms

One of the nicest advantages of having facility in data center's technologies is to have the ability to migrate virtual machines from one platform to another; there are a number of ways for achieving this, such as depending on the source and target virtualization's platforms and on the vendor's tools that manage this facility—for example, the VMware converter that handles migrations between ESX hosts; the VMware server; and the VMware workstation. The VMware converter can also import from other virtualization platforms, such as Microsoft virtual server machines [9].

5.5   VM PROVISIONING AND MIGRATION IN ACTION

Now, it is time to get into business with a real example of how we can manage the life cycle, provision, and migrate a virtual machine by the help of one of the open source frameworks used to manage virtualized infrastructure. Here, we will use ConVirt [25] (open source framework for the management of open source virtualization like Xen [26] and KVM [27], known previously as *XenMan*).

Deployment Scenario. ConVirt deployment consists of at least one ConVirt workstation, where ConVirt is installed and ran, which provides the main console for managing the VM life cycle, managing images, provisioning new VMs, monitoring machine resources, and so on. There are two essential deployment scenarios for ConVirt: A, *basic* configuration in which the Xen or KVM virtualization platform is on the local machine, where ConVirt is already installed; B, an *advanced* configuration in which the Xen or KVM is on one or more remote servers. The scenario in use here is the advanced one. In data centers, it is very common to install centralized management software (ConVirt here) on a dedicated machine for use in managing remote servers in the data center. In our example, we will use this dedicated machine where ConVirt is installed and used to manage a pool of remote servers (two machines). In order to use advanced features of ConVirt (e.g., live migration), you should set up a shared storage for the server pool in use on which the disks of the provisioned virtual machines are stored. Figure 5.7 illustrates the scenario.

Installation. The installation process involves the following:

- Installing ConVirt on at least one computer. See reference 28 for installation details.
- Preparing each managed server to be managed by ConVirt. See reference 28 for managed servers' installation details. We have two managing servers with the following Ips (managed server 1, IP:172.16.2.22; and managed server 2, IP:172.16.2.25) as shown in the deployment diagram (Figure 5.7).
- Starting ConVirt and discovering the managed servers you have prepared.

Notes

- Try to follow the installation steps existing in reference 28 according to the distribution of the operating system in use. In our experiment, we use Ubuntu 8.10 in our setup.
- Make sure that the managed servers include Xen or KVM hypervisors installed.
- Make sure that you can access managed servers from your ConVirt management console through SSH.

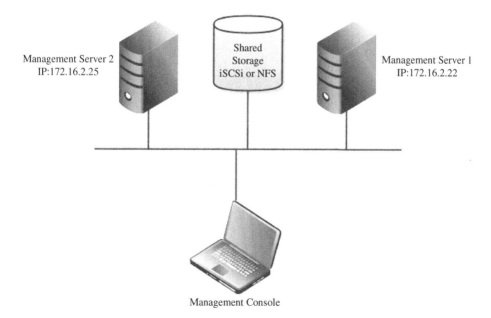

FIGURE 5.7. A deployment scenario network diagram.

Environment, Software, and Hardware. ConVirt 1.1, Linux Ubuntu 8.10, three machines, Dell core 2 due processor, 4G RAM.

Adding Managed Servers and Provisioning VM. Once the installation is done and you are ready to manage your virtual infrastructure, then you can start the ConVirt management console (see Figure 5.8):

Select any of servers' pools existing (QA Lab in our scenario) and on its context menu, select "Add Server."

- You will be faced with a message asking about the virtualization platform you want to manage (Xen or KVM), as shown in Figure 5.9:
- Choose KVM, and then enter the managed server information and credentials (IP, username, and password) as shown in Figure 5.10.
- Once the server is synchronized and authenticated with the management console, it will appear in the left pane/of the ConVirt, as shown in Figure 5.11.
- Select this server, and start provisioning your virtual machine as in Figure 5.12:
- Fill in the virtual machine's information (name, storage, OS template, etc.; Figure 5.13); then you will find it created on the managed server tree powered-off.

Note: While provisioning your virtual machine, make sure that you create disks on the shared storage (NFS or iSCSi). You can do so by selecting

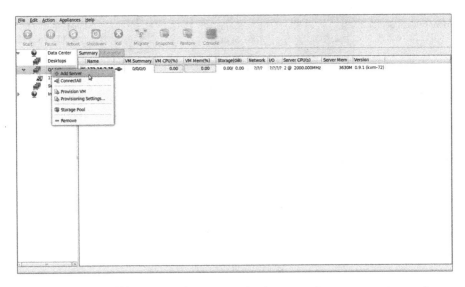

FIGURE 5.8. Adding managed server on the data centre's management console.

FIGURE 5.9. Select virtualization platform.

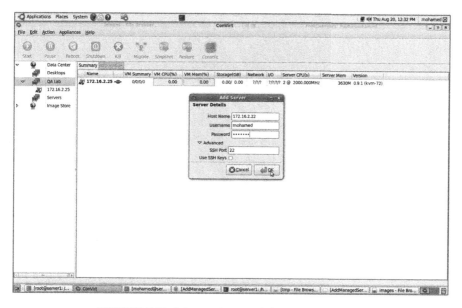

FIGURE 5.10. Managed server info and credentials.

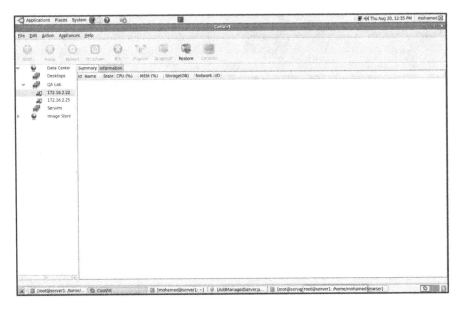

FIGURE 5.11. Managed server has been added.

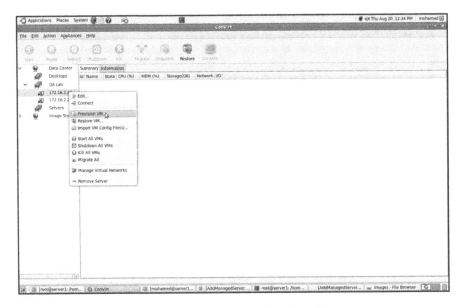

FIGURE 5.12. Provision a virtual machine.

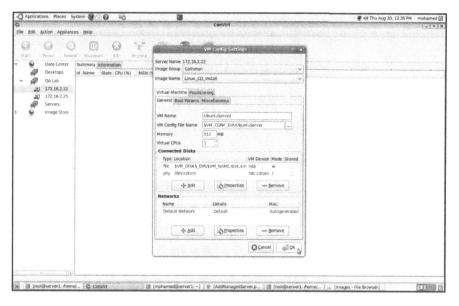

FIGURE 5.13. Configuring virtual machine.

the "provisioning" tab, and changing the VM_DISKS_DIR to point to the location of your shared NFS.

- Start your VM (Figures 5.14 and 5.15), and make sure the installation media of the operating system you need is placed in drive, in order to use it for booting the new VM and proceed in the installation process; then start the installation process as shown in Figure 5.16.
- Once the installation finishes, you can access your provisioned virtual machine from the consol icon on the top of your ConVirt management console.
- Reaching this step, you have created your first managed server and provisioned virtual machine. You can repeat the same procedure to add the second managed server in your pool to be ready for the next step of migrating one virtual machine from one server to the other.

5.5.1 VM Life Cycle and VM Monitoring

You can notice through working with ConVirt that you are able to manage the whole life cycle of the virtual machine; start, stop, reboot, migrate, clone, and so on. Also, you noticed how easy it is to monitor the resources of the managed server and to monitor the virtual machine's guests that help you balance and control the load on these managed servers once needed. In the next section, we are going to discuss how easy it is to migrate a virtual machine from host to host.

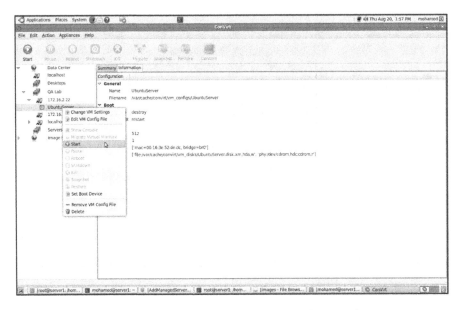

FIGURE 5.14. Provisioned VM ready to be started.

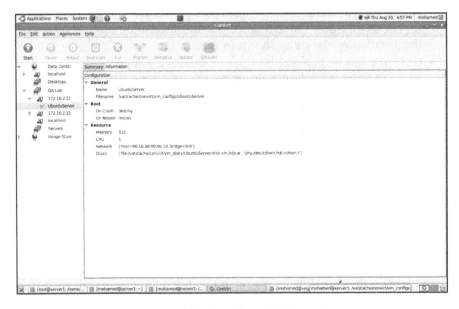

FIGURE 5.15. Provisioned VM started.

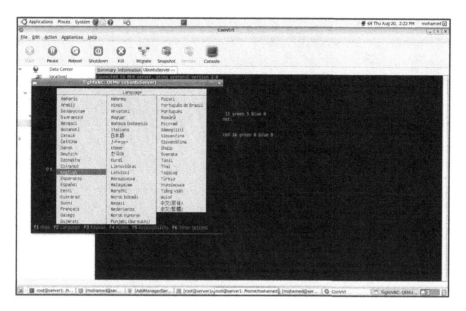

FIGURE 5.16. VM booting from the installation CD to start the installation process.

5.5.2 Live Migration

ConVirt tool allows running virtual machines to be migrated from one server to another [29].This feature makes it possible to organize the virtual machine to physical machine relationship to balance the workload; for example, a VM needing more CPU can be moved to a machine having available CPU cycles, or, in other cases, like taking the host machine for maintenance. For proper VM migration the following points must be considered [29]:

- Shared storage for all Guest OS disks (e.g., NFS, or iSCSI).
- Identical mount points on all servers (hosts).
- The kernel and ramdisk when using para-virtualized virtual machines should, also, be shared. (This is not required, if pygrub is used.)
- Centrally accessible installation media (iso).
- It is preferable to use identical machines with the same version of virtualization platform.
- Migration needs to be done within the same subnet.

Migration Process in ConVirt

- To start the migration of a virtual machine from one host to the other, select it and choose a migrating virtual machine, as shown in Figure 5.17.
- You will have a window containing all the managed servers in your data center (as shown in Figure 5.18). Choose one as a destination and start

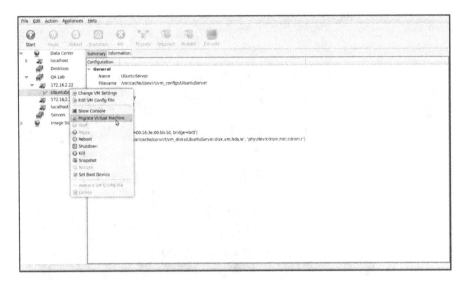

FIGURE 5.17. VM migration.

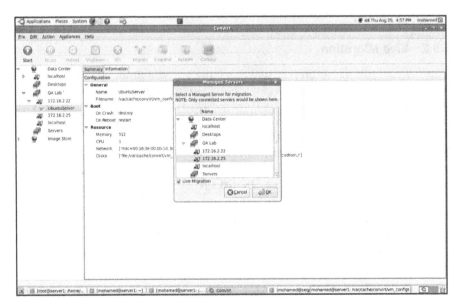

FIGURE 5.18. Select the destination managed server candidate for migration.

migration, or drag the VM and drop it on to another managed server to initiate migration.

- Once the virtual machine has been successfully placed and migrated to the destination host, you can see it still living and working (as shown in Figure 5.19).

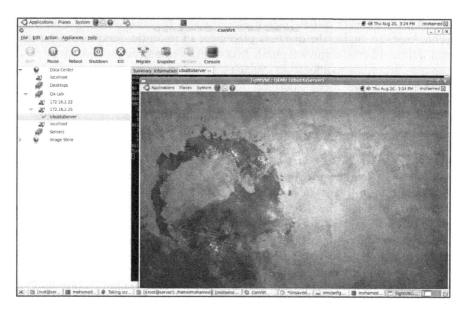

FIGURE 5.19. VM started on the destination server after migration.

5.5.3 Final Thoughts about the Example

This is just a demonstrating example of how to provision and migrate virtual machines; however, there are more tools and vendors that offer virtual infrastructure's management like Citrix XenServer, VMware vSphere, and so on.

5.6 PROVISIONING IN THE CLOUD CONTEXT

In the cloud context, we shall discuss systems that provide the virtual machine provisioning and migration services; Amazon EC2 is a widely known example for vendors that provide public cloud services. Also, Eucalyptus and Open-Nebula are two complementary and enabling technologies for open source cloud tools, which play an invaluable role in infrastructure as a service and in building private, public, and hybrid cloud architecture.

Eucalyptus is a system for implementing on-premise private and hybrid clouds using the hardware and software's infrastructure, which is in place without modification. The current interface to Eucalyptus is compatible with Amazon's EC2, S3, and EBS interfaces, but the infrastructure is designed to support multiple client-side interfaces. Eucalyptus is implemented using commonly available Linux tools and basic Web service's technologies [30]. Eucalyptus adds capabilities, such as end-user customization, self-service provisioning, and legacy application support to data center's virtualization's features, making the IT customer's service easier [11]. On the other hand, OpenNebula is a virtual infrastructure manager that orchestrates storage, network, and virtualization technologies to enable the dynamic placement of multi-tier services on distributed infrastructures, combining both data center's resources and remote cloud's resources according to allocation's policies. OpenNebula provides internal cloud administration and user's interfaces for the full management of the cloud's platform.

5.6.1 Amazon Elastic Compute Cloud

The Amazon EC2 (Elastic Compute Cloud) is a Web service that allows users to provision new machines into Amazon's virtualized infrastructure in a matter of minutes; using a publicly available API (application programming interface), it reduces the time required to obtain and boot a new server. Users get full root access and can install almost any OS or application in their AMIs (Amazon Machine Images). Web services APIs allow users to reboot their instances remotely, scale capacity quickly, and use on-demand service when needed; by adding tens, or even hundreds, of machines. It is very important to mention that there is no up-front hardware setup and there are no installation costs, because Amazon charges only for the capacity you actually use.

EC2 instance is typically a virtual machine with a certain amount of RAM, CPU, and storage capacity.

Setting up an EC2 instance is quite easy. Once you create your AWS (Amazon Web service) account, you can use the on-line AWS console, or simply download the offline command line's tools to start provisioning your instances.

Amazon EC2 provides its customers with three flexible purchasing models to make it easy for the cost optimization:

- *On-Demand* instances, which allow you to pay a fixed rate by the hour with no commitment.
- *Reserved* instances, which allow you to pay a low, one-time fee and in turn receive a significant discount on the hourly usage charge for that instance. It ensures that any reserved instance you launch is guaranteed to succeed (provided that you have booked them in advance). This means that users of these instances should not be affected by any transient limitations in EC2 capacity.
- *Spot* instances, which enable you to bid whatever price you want for instance capacity, providing for even greater savings, if your applications have flexible start and end times.

Amazon and Provisioning Services. Amazon provides an excellent set of tools that help in provisioning service; Amazon Auto Scaling [30] is a set of command line tools that allows scaling Amazon EC2 capacity up or down automatically and according to the conditions the end user defines. This feature ensures that the number of Amazon EC2 instances can scale up seamlessly during demand spikes to maintain performance and can scale down automatically when loads diminish and become less intensive to minimize the costs. Auto Scaling service and CloudWatch [31] (a monitoring service for AWS cloud resources and their utilization) help in exposing functionalities required for provisioning application services on Amazon EC2.

Amazon Elastic Load Balancer [32] is another service that helps in building fault-tolerant applications by automatically provisioning incoming application workload across available Amazon EC2 instances and in multiple *availability zones*.

5.6.2 Infrastructure Enabling Technology

Offering infrastructure as a service requires software and platforms that can manage the Infrastructure that is being shared and dynamically provisioned. For this, there are three noteworthy technologies to be considered: Eucalyptus, OpenNebula, and Aneka.

5.6.3 Eucalyptus

Eucalyptus [11] is an open-source infrastructure for the implementation of cloud computing on computer clusters. It is considered one of the earliest tools developed as a surge computing (in which data center's private cloud could augment its ability to handle workload's spikes by a design that allows it to send overflow work to a public cloud) tool. Its name is an acronym for "elastic utility computing architecture for linking your programs to useful systems." Here are some of the Eucalyptus features [11]:

- Interface compatibility with EC2, and S3 (both Web service and Query/REST interfaces).
- Simple installation and deployment.
- Support for most Linux distributions (source and binary packages).
- Support for running VMs that run atop the Xen hypervisor or KVM. Support for other kinds of VMs, such as VMware, is targeted for future releases.
- Secure internal communication using SOAP with WS security.
- Cloud administrator's tool for system's management and user's accounting.
- The ability to configure multiple clusters each with private internal network addresses into a single cloud.

Eucalyptus aims at fostering the research in models for service's provisioning, scheduling, SLA formulation, and hypervisors' portability.

Eucalyptus Architecture. Eucalyptus architecture, as illustrated in Figure 5.20, constitutes each high-level system's component as a stand-alone Web service with the following high-level components [11].

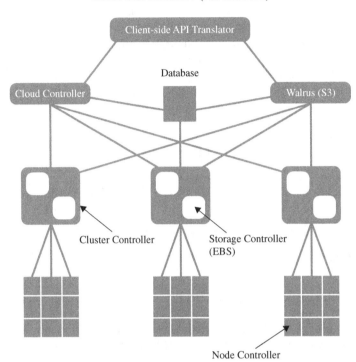

FIGURE 5.20. Eucalyptus high-level architecture.

- **Node controller (NC)** controls the execution, inspection, and termination of VM instances on the host where it runs.
- **Cluster controller (CC)** gathers information about and schedules VM execution on specific node controllers, as well as manages virtual instance network.
- **Storage controller (SC)** is a put/get storage service that implements Amazon's S3 interface and provides a way for storing and accessing VM images and user data.
- **Cloud controller (CLC)** is the entry point into the cloud for users and administrators. It queries node managers for information about resources, makes high-level scheduling decisions, and implements them by making requests to cluster controllers.
- **Walrus (W)** is the controller component that manages access to the storage services within Eucalyptus. Requests are communicated to Walrus using the SOAP or REST-based interface.

Its design is an open and elegant one. It can be very beneficial in testing and debugging purposes before deploying it on a real cloud. For more details about Eucalyptus architecture and design, check reference 11.

Ubuntu Enterprise Cloud and Eucalyptus. Ubuntu Enterprise Cloud (UEC) [33] is a new initiative by Ubuntu to make it easier to provision, deploy, configure, and use cloud infrastructures based on Eucalyptus. UEC brings Amazon EC2-like infrastructure's capabilities inside the firewall.

This is by far the simplest way to install and try Eucalyptus. Just download the Ubuntu server version and install it wherever you want. UEC is also the first open source project that lets you create cloud services in your local environment easily and leverage the power of cloud computing.

5.6.4 VM Dynamic Management Using OpenNebula

OpenNebula [12] is an open and flexible tool that fits into existing data center's environments to build any type of cloud deployment. OpenNebula can be primarily used as a virtualization tool to manage your virtual infrastructure, which is usually referred to as private cloud. OpenNebula supports a hybrid cloud to combine local infrastructure with public cloud-based infrastructure, enabling highly scalable hosting environments. OpenNebula also supports public clouds by providing cloud's interfaces to expose its functionality for virtual machine, storage, and network management. OpenNebula is one of the technologies being enhanced in the Reservoir Project [14], European research initiatives in virtualized infrastructures, and cloud computing.

OpenNebula architecture is shown in Figure 5.21, which illustrates the existence of public and private clouds and also the resources being managed by its virtual manager.

OpenNebula is an open-source alternative to these commercial tools for the dynamic management of VMs on distributed resources. This tool is supporting several research lines in advance reservation of capacity, probabilistic admission control, placement optimization, resource models for the efficient management of groups of virtual machines, elasticity support, and so on. These research lines address the requirements from both types of clouds namely, private and public.

OpenNebula and Haizea. Haizea is an open-source virtual machine-based lease management architecture developed by Sotomayor et al. [34]; it can be used as a scheduling backend for OpenNebula. Haizea uses leases as a fundamental *resource provisioning* abstraction and implements those leases as virtual machines, taking into account the overhead of using virtual machines when scheduling leases. Haizea also provides advanced functionality such as [35]:

- Advance reservation of capacity.
- Best-effort scheduling with backfilling.

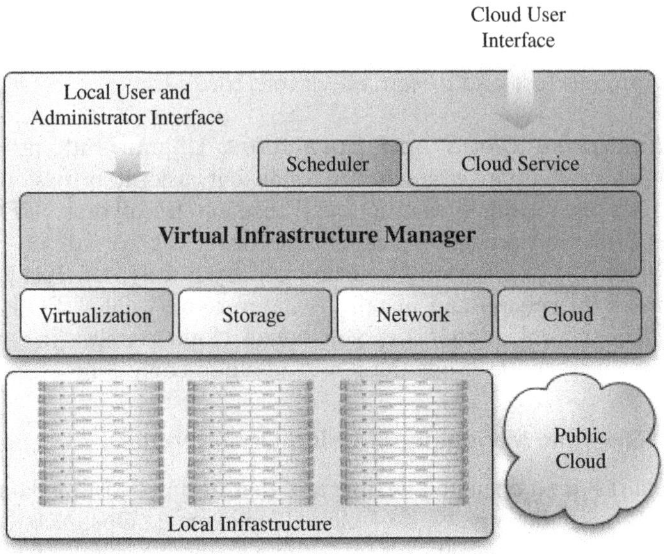

FIGURE 5.21. OpenNebula high-level architecture [14].

- Resource preemption (using VM suspend/resume/migrate).
- Policy engine, allowing developers to write pluggable scheduling policies in Python.

5.6.5 Aneka

Manjrasoft Aneka [10] is a .NET-based platform and framework designed for building and deploying distributed applications on clouds. It provides a set of APIs for transparently exploiting distributed resources and expressing the business logic of applications by using the preferred programming abstractions. Aneka is also a market-oriented cloud platform since it allows users to build and schedule applications, provision resources, and monitor results using pricing, accounting, and QoS/SLA services in private and/or public cloud environments.

It allows end users to build an enterprise/private cloud setup by exploiting the power of computing resources in the enterprise data centers, public clouds such as Amazon EC2 [4], and hybrid clouds by combining enterprise private clouds managed by Aneka with resources from Amazon EC2 or other enterprise clouds built and managed using technologies such as XenServer.

Aneka also provides support for deploying and managing clouds. By using its *Management Studio* and a set of Web interfaces, it is possible to set up either public or private clouds, monitor their status, update their configuration, and perform the basic management operations.

Aneka Architecture. Aneka platform architecture [10], as illustrated in Figure 5.22, consists of a collection of physical and virtualized resources connected through a network. Each of these resources hosts an instance of the Aneka container representing the runtime environment where the distributed applications are executed. The container provides the basic management features of the single node and leverages all the other operations on the services that it is hosting. The services are broken up into fabric, foundation, and execution services. Fabric services directly interact with the node through the platform abstraction layer (PAL) and perform hardware profiling and *dynamic resource provisioning*. Foundation services identify the core system of the Aneka middleware, providing a set of basic features to enable Aneka containers to perform specialized and specific sets of tasks. Execution services directly deal with the scheduling and execution of applications in the cloud.

5.7 FUTURE RESEARCH DIRECTIONS

Virtual machine provision and migration services take their place in research to achieve the best out of its objectives, and here is a list of potential areas' candidates for research:

- Self-adaptive and dynamic data center.

Data centers exist in the premises of any hosting or ISPs that host different Web sites and applications. These sites are being accessed at different timing pattern (morning hours, afternoon, etc.). Thus, workloads against these sites need to be tracked because they vary dynamically over time. The sizing of host machines (the number of virtual machines that host these applications) represents a challenge, and there is a potential research area over here to study the performance impact and overhead due to this dynamic creation of virtual machines hosted in these self-adaptive data centers, in order to manage Web sites properly.

Study of the performance in this dynamic environment will also tackle the the balance that should be exist between a rapid response time of individual applications, the overall performance of the data, and the high availability of the applications and its services.

- Performance evaluation and workload characterization of virtual workloads.

It is very invaluable in any virtualized infrastructure to have a notion about the workload provisioned in each VM, the performance's impacts due to the hypervisors layer, and the overhead due to consolidated workloads for such systems; but yet, this is not a deterministic process. Single-workload benchmark is useful in quantifying the virtualization overhead within a single VM, but not useful in a whole virtualized environment with multiple isolated VMs with varying workloads on each, leading to the inability of capturing the system's

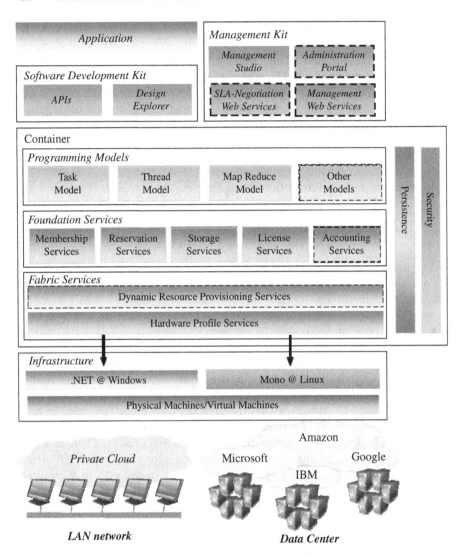

FIGURE 5.22. Manjras oft Aneka layered architecture [10].

behavior. So, there is a big need for a common workload model and methodology for virtualized systems; thus benchmark's results can be compared across different platforms. It will help in the dynamic workload's relocation and migrations' services.

- One of the potential areas that worth study and investigation is the development of fundamental tools and techniques that facilitate the integration and provisioning of distributed and hybrid clouds in federated way, which is critical for enabling of composition and deployment of elastic application services [35, 36].

- High-performance data scaling in private and public cloud environments.

Organizations and enterprises that adopt the cloud computing architectures can face lots of challenges related to (a) the elastic provisioning of compute clouds on their existing data center's infrastructure and (b) the inability of the data layer to scale at the same rate as the compute layer. So, there is a persisting need for implementing systems that are capable of scaling data with the same pace as scaling the infrastructure, or to integrate current infrastructure elastic provisioning systems with existing systems that are designed to scale out the applications and data layers.

- Performance and high availability in clustered VMs through live migration.

Clusters are very common in research centers, enterprises, and accordingly in the cloud. For these clusters to work in a proper way, there are two aspects of great importance, namely, *high availability,* and *high performance* service. This can be achieved through clusters of virtual machines in which high available applications can be achieved through the live migration of the virtual machine to different locations in the cluster or in the cloud. So, the need exists to (a) study the performance, (b) study the performance's improvement opportunities with regard to the migrations of these virtual machines, and (c) decide to which location the machine should be migrated.

- VM scheduling algorithms.
- Accelerating VMs live migration time.
- Cloud-wide VM migration and memory de-duplication.

Normal VM migration is being done within the same physical site location (campus, data center, lab, etc.). However, migrating virtual machines between different locations is an invaluable feature to be added to any virtualization management's tools. For more details on memory status, storage relocation, and so on; check the patent pending technology about this topic [37]. Considering such setup can enable faster and longer-distance VM migrations, cross-site load balancing, power management, and de-duplicating memory throughout multiple sites. It is a rich area for research.

- Live migration security.

Live migration security is a very important area of research, because several security's vulnerabilities exist; check reference 38 for an empirical exploitation of live migration.

- Extend migration algorithm to allow for priorities.
- Cisco initiative UCS (Unified Commuting System) and its role in dynamic just-in-time provisioning of virtual machines and increase of business agility [39].

5.8 CONCLUSION

Virtual machines' provisioning and migration are very critical tasks in today's virtualized systems, data center's technology, and accordingly the cloud computing services.

They have a huge impact on the continuity, and availability of business. In a few minutes, you can provision a complete server with all its appliances to perform a particular functionality, or to offer a service. In a few milliseconds, you can migrate a virtual machine hosted on a physical server within a clustered environment to a completely different server for the purpose of maintenance, workloads' needs, and so on. In this chapter, we covered VM provisioning and migration services techniques, as well as tools and concepts, and also shed some light on potential areas for research.

REFERENCES

1. D. Chisnall, *The Definitive Guide to the Xen Hypervisor*, Upper Saddle River, NJ, Prentice Hall, 2008.
2. M. El-Refaey and M. Rizkaa, Virtual systems workload characterization: An overview, in *Proceedings of the 18th IEEE International Workshops on Enabling Technologies: Infrastructures for Collaborative Enterprises, WETICE 2009*, Groningen, The Netherlands, 29 June–1 July 2009.
3. A. T. Velte, T. J. Velte, and R. Elsenpeter, *Cloud Computing: A Practical Approach*, McGraw-Hill, New York, 2010.
4. Amazon Elastic Compute Cloud (Amazon EC2), http://aws.amazon.com/ec2/, March 15, 2010.
5. Cloud Hosting, Cloud Computing, Hybrid Infrastructure from GoGrid, http://www.gogrid.com/, March 19, 2010.
6. JoyentCloud Computing Companies: Domain, Application & Web Hosting Services, http://www.joyent.com/, March 10, 2010.
7. Rackspace hosting, http://www.rackspace.com/index.php, March 10, 2010.
8. AppNexus—Home, http://www.appnexus.com/, March 9, 2010.
9. FlexiScale cloud computing and hosting: instant Windows and Linux cloud servers on demand, http://www.flexiscale.com/, March 12, 2010.
10. C. Vecchiola, X. Chu, and R. Buyya, Aneka: A Software Platform for .NET-based cloud computing, high speed and large scale scientific computing, in Advances in Parallel Computing, W. Gentzsch, L. Grandinetti, G. Joubert (eds.), ISBN: 978-1-60750-073-5, IOS Press, Amsterdam, Netherlands, 2009, pp. 267–295.

11. D. Nurmi, R. Wolski, C. Grzegorczyk, G. Obertelli, S. Soman, L. Youseff, D. Zagorodnov, The Eucalyptus Open-source Cloud-computing System, in *Proceedings of 9th IEEE International Symposium on Cluster Computing and the Grid*, Shanghai, China, pp. 124–131.

12. B. Sotomayor, R. Santiago Montero, I. Martín Llorente, I. Foster, Capacity Leasing in Cloud Systems using the OpenNebula Engine (short paper). *Workshop on Cloud Computing and its Applications* 2008 (CCA08), October 22–23, 2008, Chicago, Illinois, USA.

13. P. Gardfjäll, E. Elmroth, L. Johnsson, O. Mulmo, and T. Sandholm, Scalable grid-wide capacity allocation with the SweGrid Accounting System (SGAS), *Concurrency and Computation: Practice and Experience*, 20(18): 2089–2122, 2008.

14. I. M. Llorente, Innovation for cloud infrastructure management in OpenNebula/ RESERVOIR, *ETSI Workshop on Grids, Clouds & Service Infrastructures*, Sophia Antipolis, France, December 3, 2009.

15. B. Rochwerger, J. Caceres, R. S. Montero, D. Breitgand, E. Elmroth, A. Galis, E. Levy, I. M. Llorente, and K. Nagin, Y. Wolfsthal, The RESERVOIR Model and architecture for open federated cloud computing, *IBM Systems Journal*, Volume 53, Number 4, 2009.

16. F. Piedad and M. W. Hawkins, *High Availability: Design, Techniques, and Processes*, Prentice Hall PTR, Upper Saddle River, NJ, 2000.

17. DMTF–VMAN, http://www.dmtf.org/standards/mgmt/vman, March 27, 2010.

18. OGF Open Cloud Computing Interface Working Group, http://www.occi-wg.org/doku.php, March 27, 2010.

19. J. Arrasjid, K. Balachandran, D. Conde, G. Lamb, and S. Kaplan, *Deploying the VMware Infrastructure*, The USENIX Association, August 10, 2008.

20. Live Storage Migration of virtual machine, http://www.vmware.com/technology/virtual-storage/live-migration.html, August 19, 2009.

21. C. Clark, K. Fraser, S. Hand, J. G. Hansen, E. Jul, C. Kimpach, I. Pratt, and W. Warfield, Live migration of virtual machines, in *2nd USENIX Symposium on Networked Systems, Design and Implementation (NSDI 05)*, May 2005.

22. VMware VMotion for Live migration of virtual machines, http://www.vmware.com/products/vi/vc/vmotion.html, August 19, 2009.

23. Knowledge Center Home—Citrix Knowledge Center, Article ID: CTX115813 http://support.citrix.com, August 28, 2009.

24. Cold Migration, http://pubs.vmware.com/vsp40_e/admin/wwhelp/wwhimpl/common/html/wwhelp.htm#href=c_cold_migration.html#1_10_21_7_1&single=true, August 20, 2009.

25. ConVirture: Enterprise–class management for open source virtualization, http://www.convirture.com/, August 21, 2009.

26. S. Crosby, D. E. Williams, and J. Garcia, *Virtualization with Xen: Including XenEnterprise, XenServer, and XenExpress*, Syngress Media Inc., ISBN 1-597-49167-5, 2007.

27. I. Habib, Virtualization with KVM, *Linux Journal*, 2008(166):8, February 2008.

28. Installation—ConVirt,   http://www.convirture.com/wiki/index.php?title= Installation, March 27, 2010.

29. VM Migration—ConVirt, http://www.convirture.com/wiki/index.php?title = VM_ Migration, March 25, 2010.

30. Amazon Auto Scaling Service, http://aws.amazon.com/autoscaling/, March 23, 2010.

31. Amazon CloudWatch Service, http://aws.amazon.com/cloudwatch/, March 23, 2010.

32. Amazon Load Balancer Service, http://aws.amazon.com/elasticloadbalancing/. March 21, 2010.

33. S. Wardley, E. Goyer, and N. Barcet, Ubuntu Enterprise Cloud Architecture, http://www.ubuntu.com/cloud/private, March 23, 2010.

34. B. Sotomayor, K. Keahey, and I. Foster. Combining batch execution and leasing using virtual machines ACM, in *Proceedings of the 17th international Symposium on High Performance Distributed Computing*, New York, 2008, pp. 87–96.

35. I. M. LIorente, The OpenNebula Open Source Toolkit to Build Cloud Infrastructures, Seminars LinuxWorld NL, Utrecht, The Netherlands, November 5th, 2009.

36. R. Buyya1, R. Ranjan, and R. N. Calheiros, InterCloud: Utility-Oriented Federation of Cloud Computing Environments for Scaling of Application Services, in *Proceedings of the 10th International Conference on Algorithms and Architectures for Parallel Processing*, ICA3PP 2010, Busan, South Korea, May 21–23, 2010.

37. K. Lawton, Virtualization 3.0: Cloud-wide VM migration and memory de-duplication, *http://www.trendcaller.com/2009/03/virtualization-30-vm-memory-wan. html*, August 25, 2009.

38. J. Oberheide, E. Cooke, and F. Jahanian, Empirical exploitation of live virtual machine migration needs modification, http://www.net-security.org/article.php? id = 1120, August 29, 2009.

39. Cisco Unified Computing System, http://www.cisco.com/go/unifiedcomputing, August 30, 2009.

40. D. Nurmi, R. Wolski, C. Grzegorczyk, G. Obertelli, S. Soman, L. Youseff, and D. Zagorodnov. The Eucalyptus open-source cloud-computing system, in *Proceedings of the 9th IEEE/ACM International Symposium on Cluster Computing and the Grid (CCGrid 2009)*, May 18–May 21, 2010, Shanghai, China.

CHAPTER 6

ON THE MANAGEMENT OF VIRTUAL MACHINES FOR CLOUD INFRASTRUCTURES

IGNACIO M. LLORENTE, RUBÉN S. MONTERO, BORJA SOTOMAYOR, DAVID BREITGAND, ALESSANDRO MARASCHINI, ELIEZER LEVY, and BENNY ROCHWERGER

In 2006, Amazon started offering virtual machines (VMs) to anyone with a credit card for just \$0.10/hour through its Elastic Compute Cloud (EC2) service. Although not the first company to lease VMs, the programmer-friendly EC2 Web services API and their pay-as-you-go pricing popularized the "Infrastructure as a Service" (IaaS) paradigm, which is now closely related to the notion of a "cloud." Following the success of Amazon EC2 [1], several other IaaS cloud providers, or *public clouds*, have emerged—such as Elastic-Hosts [2], GoGrid [3], and FlexiScale [4]—that provide a publicly accessible interface for purchasing and managing computing infrastructure that is instantiated as VMs running on the provider's data center. There is also a growing ecosystem of technologies and tools to build *private clouds*—where in-house resources are virtualized, and internal users can request and manage these resources using interfaces similar or equal to those of public clouds—and *hybrid clouds*—where an organization's private cloud can supplement its capacity using a public cloud.

Thus, within the broader context of cloud computing, this chapter focuses on the subject of IaaS clouds and, more specifically, on the efficient management of virtual machines in this type of cloud. Section 6.1 starts by discussing the characteristics of IaaS clouds and the challenges involved in managing these clouds. The following sections elaborate on some of these challenges, describing the solutions proposed within the virtual machine management activity of

Cloud Computing: Principles and Paradigms, Edited by Rajkumar Buyya, James Broberg and Andrzej Goscinski   Copyright © 2011 John Wiley & Sons, Inc.

RESERVOIR [5] (Resources and Services Virtualization without Barriers), a European Union FP7-funded project. Section 6.2 starts by discussing the problem of managing *virtual infrastructures*; Section 6.3 presents scheduling techniques that can be used to provide advance reservation of capacity within these infrastructures; Section 6.4 focuses on *service-level agreements* (or SLAs) in IaaS clouds and discusses capacity management techniques supporting SLA commitments. Finally, the chapter concludes with a discussion of remaining challenges and future work in IaaS clouds.

6.1   THE ANATOMY OF CLOUD INFRASTRUCTURES

There are many commercial IaaS cloud providers in the market, such as those cited earlier, and all of them share five characteristics: (i) They provide on-demand provisioning of computational resources; (ii) they use virtualization technologies to lease these resources; (iii) they provide public and simple remote interfaces to manage those resources; (iv) they use a pay-as-you-go cost model, typically charging by the hour; and (v) they operate data centers large enough to provide a seemingly unlimited amount of resources to their clients (usually touted as "infinite capacity" or "unlimited elasticity"). Private and hybrid clouds share these same characteristics but, instead of selling capacity over publicly accessible interfaces, focus on providing capacity to an organization's internal users.

Virtualization technologies have been the key enabler of many of these salient characteristics of IaaS clouds by giving providers a more flexible and generic way of managing their resources. Thus, *virtual infrastructure (VI) management*—the management of virtual machines distributed across a pool of physical resources—becomes a key concern when building an IaaS cloud and poses a number of challenges. Like traditional physical resources, virtual machines require a fair amount of configuration, including preparation of the machine's software environment and network configuration. However, in a virtual infrastructure, this configuration must be done on-the-fly, with as little time between the time the VMs are requested and the time they are available to the user. This is further complicated by the need to configure groups of VMs that will provide a specific service (e.g., an application requiring a Web server and a database server). Additionally, a virtual infrastructure manager must be capable of allocating resources efficiently, taking into account an organization's goals (such as minimizing power consumption and other operational costs) and reacting to changes in the physical infrastructure.

Virtual infrastructure management in private clouds has to deal with an additional problem: Unlike large IaaS cloud providers, such as Amazon, private clouds typically do not have enough resources to provide the illusion of "infinite capacity." The immediate provisioning scheme used in public clouds, where resources are provisioned at the moment they are requested, is ineffective in private clouds. Support for additional provisioning schemes, such as best-effort provisioning and advance reservations to guarantee quality of service (QoS) for applications that require resources at specific times (e.g., during known "spikes" in capacity requirements), is required. Thus, efficient resource allocation algorithms and policies and the ability to combine both private and public cloud resources, resulting in a hybrid approach, become even more important.

Several VI management solutions have emerged over time, such as platform ISF [6] and VMware vSphere [7], along with open-source initiatives such as Enomaly Computing Platform [8] and Ovirt [9]. Many of these tools originated out of the need to manage data centers efficiently using virtual machines, before the Cloud Computing paradigm took off. However, managing virtual infrastructures in a private/hybrid cloud is a different, albeit similar, problem than managing a virtualized data center, and existing tools lack several features that are required for building IaaS clouds. Most notably, they exhibit monolithic and closed structures and can only operate, if at all, with some preconfigured placement policies, which are generally simple (round robin, first fit, etc.) and based only on CPU speed and utilization of a fixed and predetermined number of resources, such as memory and network bandwidth. This precludes extending their resource management strategies with custom policies or integration with other cloud systems, or even adding cloud interfaces.

Thus, there are still several gaps in existing VI solutions. Filling these gaps will require addressing a number of research challenges over the next years, across several areas, such as virtual machine management, resource scheduling, SLAs, federation of resources, and security. In this chapter, we focus on three problems addressed by the Virtual Machine Management Activity of RESER-VOIR: distributed management of virtual machines, reservation-based provisioning of virtualized resource, and provisioning to meet SLA commitments.

6.1.1 Distributed Management of Virtual Machines

The first problem is how to manage the virtual infrastructures themselves. Although resource management has been extensively studied, particularly for job management in high-performance computing, managing VMs poses additional problems that do not arise when managing jobs, such as the need to set up custom software environments for VMs, setting up and managing networking for interrelated VMs, and reducing the various overheads involved in using VMs. Thus, VI managers must be able to efficiently orchestrate all these different tasks.

The problem of efficiently selecting or scheduling computational resources is well known. However, the state of the art in VM-based resource scheduling follows a static approach, where resources are initially selected using a greedy allocation strategy, with minimal or no support for other placement policies. To efficiently schedule resources, VI managers must be able to support flexible and complex scheduling policies and must leverage the ability of VMs to suspend, resume, and migrate.

This complex task is one of the core problems that the RESERVOIR project tries to solve. In Section 6.2 we describe the problem of how to manage VMs distributed across a pool of physical resources and describe OpenNebula, the virtual infrastructure manager developed by the RESERVOIR project.

6.1.2 Reservation-Based Provisioning of Virtualized Resources

A particularly interesting problem when provisioning virtual infrastructures is how to deal with situations where the demand for resources is known beforehand—for example, when an experiment depending on some complex piece of equipment is going to run from 2 pm to 4 pm, and computational resources must be available at exactly that time to process the data produced by the equipment. Commercial cloud providers, such as Amazon, have enough resources to provide the illusion of infinite capacity, which means that this situation is simply resolved by requesting the resources exactly when needed; if capacity is "infinite," then there will be resources available at 2 pm.

On the other hand, when dealing with finite capacity, a different approach is needed. However, the intuitively simple solution of reserving the resources beforehand turns out to not be so simple, because it is known to cause resources to be underutilized [10–13], due to the difficulty of scheduling other requests around an inflexible reservation.

As we discuss in Section 6.3, VMs allow us to overcome the utilization problems typically associated with advance reservations and we describe Haizea, a VM-based lease manager supporting advance reservation along with other provisioning models not supported in existing IaaS clouds, such as best-effort provisioning.

6.1.3 Provisioning to Meet SLA Commitments

IaaS clouds can be used to deploy *services* that will be consumed by users other than the one that deployed the services. For example, a company might depend on an IaaS cloud provider to deploy three-tier applications (Web front-end, application server, and database server) for its customers. In this case, there is a distinction between the cloud consumer (i.e., the service owner; in this case, the company that develops and manages the applications) and the end users of the resources provisioned on the cloud (i.e., the service user; in this case, the users that access the applications). Furthermore, service owners will enter into service-level agreements (SLAs) with their end users, covering guarantees such as the timeliness with which these services will respond.

However, cloud providers are typically not directly exposed to the service semantics or the SLAs that service owners may contract with their end users. The capacity requirements are, thus, less predictable and more elastic. The use of reservations may be insufficient, and capacity planning and optimizations are required instead. The cloud provider's task is, therefore, to make sure that resource allocation requests are satisfied with specific probability and timeliness. These requirements are formalized in infrastructure SLAs between the service owner and cloud provider, separate from the high-level SLAs between the service owner and its end users.

In many cases, either the service owner is not resourceful enough to perform an exact service sizing or service workloads are hard to anticipate in advance. Therefore, to protect high-level SLAs, the cloud provider should cater for elasticity on demand. We argue that scaling and de-scaling of an application is best managed by the application itself. The reason is that in many cases, resources allocation decisions are application-specific and are being driven by the application level metrics. These metrics typically do not have a universal meaning and are not observable using black box monitoring of virtual machines comprising the service.

RESERVOIR proposes a flexible framework where service owners may register service-specific elasticity rules and monitoring probes, and these rules are being executed to match environment conditions. We argue that elasticity of the application should be contracted and formalized as part of capacity availability SLA between the cloud provider and service owner. This poses interesting research issues on the IaaS side, which can be grouped around two main topics:

- SLA-oriented capacity planning that guarantees that there is enough capacity to guarantee service elasticity with minimal over-provisioning.
- Continuous resource placement and scheduling optimization that lowers operational costs and takes advantage of available capacity transparently to the service while keeping the service SLAs.

We explore these two topics in further detail in Section 6.4, and we describe how the RESERVOIR project addresses the research issues that arise therein.

6.2 DISTRIBUTED MANAGEMENT OF VIRTUAL INFRASTRUCTURES

Managing VMs in a pool of distributed physical resources is a key concern in IaaS clouds, requiring the use of a *virtual infrastructure manager*. To address some of the shortcomings in existing VI solutions, we have developed the open source OpenNebula[1] virtual infrastructure engine. OpenNebula is capable of managing groups of interconnected VMs—with support for the Xen, KVM, and VMWare platforms—within data centers and private clouds that involve a large amount of virtual and physical servers. OpenNebula can also be used to build hybrid clouds by interfacing with remote cloud sites [14]. This section describes how OpenNebula models and manages VMs in a virtual infrastructure.

[1]http://www.opennebula.org

6.2.1 VM Model and Life Cycle

The primary target of OpenNebula is to manage VMs. Within OpenNebula, a VM is modeled as having the following attributes:

- A capacity in terms of memory and CPU.
- A set of NICs attached to one or more virtual networks.
- A set of disk images. In general it might be necessary to transfer some of these image files to/from the physical machine the VM will be running in.
- A state file (optional) or recovery file that contains the memory image of a running VM plus some hypervisor-specific information.

The life cycle of a VM within OpenNebula follows several stages:

- *Resource Selection*. Once a VM is requested to OpenNebula, a feasible placement plan for the VM must be made. OpenNebula's default scheduler provides an implementation of a rank scheduling policy, allowing site administrators to configure the scheduler to prioritize the resources that are more suitable for the VM, using information from the VMs and the physical hosts. As we will describe in Section 6.3, OpenNebula can also use the Haizea lease manager to support more complex scheduling policies.
- *Resource Preparation*. The disk images of the VM are transferred to the target physical resource. During the boot process, the VM is contextualized, a process where the disk images are specialized to work in a given environment. For example, if the VM is part of a group of VMs offering a service (a compute cluster, a DB-based application, etc.), contextualization could involve setting up the network and the machine hostname, or registering the new VM with a service (e.g., the head node in a compute cluster). Different techniques are available to contextualize a worker node, including use of an automatic installation system (for instance, Puppet or Quattor), a context server (see reference 15), or access to a disk image with the context data for the worker node (OVF recommendation).
- *VM Creation*. The VM is booted by the resource hypervisor.
- *VM Migration*. The VM potentially gets migrated to a more suitable resource (e.g., to optimize the power consumption of the physical resources).
- *VM Termination*. When the VM is going to shut down, OpenNebula can transfer back its disk images to a known location. This way, changes in the VM can be kept for a future use.

6.2.2 VM Management

OpenNebula manages a VMs life cycle by orchestrating three different management areas: *virtualization* by interfacing with a physical resource's hypervisor, such as Xen, KVM, or VMWare, to control (e.g., boot, stop, or shutdown) the VM; *image management* by transferring the VM images from an image repository to the selected resource and by creating on-the-fly temporary images; and *networking* by creating local area networks (LAN) to interconnect the VMs and tracking the MAC addresses leased in each network.

Virtualization. OpenNebula manages VMs by interfacing with the physical resource virtualization technology (e.g., Xen or KVM) using a set of pluggable drivers that decouple the managing process from the underlying technology. Thus, whenever the core needs to manage a VM, it uses high-level commands such as "start VM," "stop VM," and so on, which are translated by the drivers into commands that the virtual machine manager can understand. By decoupling the OpenNebula core from the virtualization technologies through the use of a driver-based architecture, adding support for additional virtual machine managers only requires writing a driver for it.

Image Management. VMs are supported by a set of virtual disks or *images*, which contains the OS and any other additional software needed by the VM. OpenNebula assumes that there is an image repository that can be any storage medium or service, local or remote, that holds the base image of the VMs. There are a number of different possible configurations depending on the user's needs. For example, users may want all their images placed on a separate repository with only HTTP access. Alternatively, images can be shared through NFS between all the hosts. OpenNebula aims to be flexible enough to support as many different image management configurations as possible.

OpenNebula uses the following concepts for its image management model (Figure 6.1):

- *Image Repositories* refer to any storage medium, local or remote, that hold the base images of the VMs. An image repository can be a dedicated file server or a remote URL from an appliance provider, but they need to be accessible from the OpenNebula front-end.
- *Virtual Machine Directory* is a directory on the cluster node where a VM is running. This directory holds all deployment files for the hypervisor to boot the machine, checkpoints, and images being used or saved—all of them specific to that VM. This directory should be shared for most hypervisors to be able to perform live migrations. Any given VM image goes through the following steps along its life cycle:
  - *Preparation* implies all the necessary changes to be made to the machine's image so it is prepared to offer the service to which it is intended. OpenNebula assumes that the images that conform to a particular VM are prepared and placed in the accessible image repository.

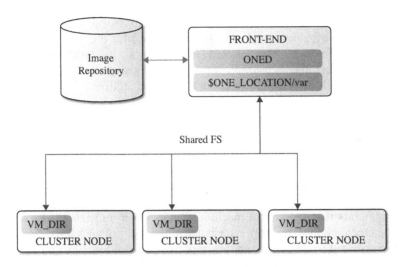

FIGURE 6.1. Image management in OpenNebula.

- Cloning the image means taking the image from the repository and placing it in the VM's directory in the physical node where it is going to be run before the VM is actually booted. If a VM image is to be cloned, the original image is not going to be used, and thus a copy will be used. There is a qualifier (clone) for the images that can mark them as targeting for cloning or not.
- Save/remove. If the save qualifier is disabled, once the VM has been shut down, the images and all the changes thereof are going to be disposed of. However, if the save qualifier is activated, the image will be saved for later use.

Networking. In general, services deployed on a cloud, from a computing cluster to the classical three-tier business application, require several inter-related VMs, with a virtual application network (VAN) being the primary link between them. OpenNebula dynamically creates these VANs and tracks the MAC addresses leased in the network to the service VMs. Note that here we refer to layer 2 LANs; other TCP/IP services such as DNS, NIS, or NFS are the responsibility of the service (i.e., the service VMs have to be configured to provide such services).

The physical hosts that will co-form the fabric of our virtual infrastructures will need to have some constraints in order to effectively deliver virtual networks to our virtual machines. Therefore, from the point of view of networking, we can define our physical cluster as a set of hosts with one or more network interfaces, each of them connected to a different physical network.

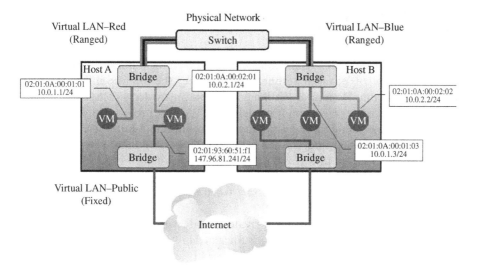

FIGURE 6.2. Networkig model for OpenNebula.

We can see in Figure 6.2 two physical hosts with two network interfaces each; thus there are two different physical networks. There is one physical network that connects the two hosts using a switch, and there is another one that gives the hosts access to the public Internet. This is one possible configuration for the physical cluster, and it is the one we recommend since it can be used to make both private and public VANs for the virtual machines. Moving up to the virtualization layer, we can distinguish three different VANs. One is mapped on top of the public Internet network, and we can see a couple of virtual machines taking advantage of it. Therefore, these two VMs will have access to the Internet. The other two are mapped on top of the private physical network: the Red and Blue VANs. Virtual machines connected to the same private VAN will be able to communicate with each other, otherwise they will be isolated and won't be able to communicate.

6.2.3 Further Reading on OpenNebula

There are a number of scholarly publications that describe the design and architecture of OpenNebula in more detail, including papers showing performance results obtained when using OpenNebula to deploy and manage the back-end nodes of a Sun Grid Engine compute cluster [14] and of a NGINX Web server [16] on both local resources and an external cloud. The OpenNebula virtual infrastructure engine is also available for download at http://www.opennebula.org/, which provides abundant documentation not just on how to install and use OpenNebula, but also on its internal architecture.

6.3   SCHEDULING TECHNIQUES FOR ADVANCE RESERVATION OF CAPACITY

While a VI manager like OpenNebula can handle all the minutiae of managing VMs in a pool of physical resources, scheduling these VMs efficiently is a different and complex matter. Commercial cloud providers, such as Amazon, rely on an immediate provisioning model where VMs are provisioned right away, since their data centers' capacity is assumed to be infinite. Thus, there is no need for other provisioning models, such as best-effort provisioning where requests have to be queued and prioritized or advance provisioning where resources are pre-reserved so they will be guaranteed to be available at a given time period; queuing and reservations are unnecessary when resources are always available to satisfy incoming requests.

However, when managing a private cloud with limited resources, an immediate provisioning model is insufficient. In this section we describe a lease-based resource provisioning model used by the Haizea[2] lease manager, which can be used as a scheduling back-end by OpenNebula to support provisioning models not supported in other VI management solutions. We focus, in particular, on advance reservation of capacity in IaaS clouds as a way to guarantee availability of resources at a time specified by the user.

6.3.1   Existing Approaches to Capacity Reservation

Efficient reservation of resources in resource management systems has been studied considerably, particularly in the context of job scheduling. In fact, most modern job schedulers support advance reservation of resources, but their implementation falls short in several aspects. First of all, they are constrained by the job abstraction; when a user makes an advance reservation in a job-based system, the user does not have direct and unfettered access to the resources, the way a cloud users can access the VMs they requested, but, rather, is only allowed to submit jobs to them. For example, PBS Pro creates a new queue that will be bound to the reserved resources, guaranteeing that jobs submitted to that queue will be executed on them (assuming they have permission to do so). Maui and Moab, on the other hand, simply allow users to specify that a submitted job should use the reserved resources (if the submitting user has permission to do so). There are no mechanisms to directly login to the reserved resources, other than through an interactive job, which does not provide unfettered access to the resources.

Additionally, it is well known that advance reservations lead to utilization problems [10–13], caused by the need to vacate resources before a reservation can begin. Unlike future reservations made by backfilling algorithms, where the start of the reservation is determined on a best-effort basis, advance

[2]http://haizea.cs.uchicago.edu/

reservations introduce roadblocks in the resource schedule. Thus, traditional job schedulers are unable to efficiently schedule workloads combining both best-effort jobs and advance reservations.

However, advance reservations can be supported more efficiently by using a scheduler capable of preempting running jobs at the start of the reservation and resuming them at the end of the reservation. Preemption can also be used to run large parallel jobs (which tend to have long queue times) earlier, and it is specially relevant in the context of urgent computing, where resources have to be provisioned on very short notice and the likelihood of having jobs already assigned to resources is higher. While preemption can be accomplished trivially by canceling a running job, the least disruptive form of preemption is *checkpointing*, where the preempted job's entire state is saved to disk, allowing it to resume its work from the last checkpoint. Additionally, some schedulers also support job migration, allowing checkpointed jobs to restart on other available resources, instead of having to wait until the preempting job or reservation has completed.

However, although many modern schedulers support at least checkpointing-based preemption, this requires the job's executable itself to be checkpointable. An application can be made checkpointable by explicitly adding that function-ality to an application (application-level and library-level checkpointing) or transparently by using OS-level checkpointing, where the operating system (such as Cray, IRIX, and patched versions of Linux using BLCR [17]) checkpoints a process, without rewriting the program or relinking it with checkpointing libraries. However, this requires a checkpointing-capable OS to be available.

Thus, a job scheduler capable of checkpointing-based preemption and migration could be used to checkpoint jobs before the start of an advance reservation, minimizing their impact on the schedule. However, the application- and library-level checkpointing approaches burden the user with having to modify their applications to make them checkpointable, imposing a restriction on the software environment. OS-level checkpointing, on the other hand, is a more appealing option, but still imposes certain software restrictions on resource consumers. Systems like Cray and IRIX still require applications to be compiled for their respective architectures, which would only allow a small fraction of existing applications to be supported within leases, or would require existing applications to be ported to these architectures. This is an excessive restriction on users, given the large number of clusters and applications that depend on the x86 architecture. Although the BLCR project does provide a checkpointing x86 Linux kernel, this kernel still has several limitations, such as not being able to properly checkpoint network traffic and not being able to checkpoint MPI applications unless they are linked with BLCR-aware MPI libraries.

An alternative approach to supporting advance reservations was propo-sed by Nurmi et al. [18], which introduced "virtual advance reservations for queues" (VARQ). This approach overlays advance reservations over traditional job schedulers by first predicting the time a job would spend waiting in a scheduler's queue and then submitting a job (representing the advance reservation) at a time such that, based on the wait time prediction, the probability that it will be running at the start of the reservation is maximized. Since no actual reservations can be done, VARQ jobs can run on traditional job schedulers, which will not distinguish between the regular best-effort jobs and the VARQ jobs. Although this is an interesting approach that can be realistically implemented in practice (since it does not require modifications to existing scheduler), it still depends on the job abstraction.

Hovestadt et al. [19, 20] proposed a planning-based (as opposed to queuing-based) approach to job scheduling, where job requests are immediately planned by making a reservation (now or in the future), instead of waiting in a queue. Thus, advance reservations are implicitly supported by a planning-based system. Additionally, each time a new request is received, the entire schedule is reevaluated to optimize resource usage. For example, a request for an advance reservation can be accepted without using preemption, since the jobs that were originally assigned to those resources can be assigned to different resources (assuming the jobs were not already running).

6.3.2   Reservations with VMs

As we described earlier, virtualization technologies are a key enabler of many features found in IaaS clouds. Virtual machines are also an appealing vehicle for implementing efficient reservation of resources due to their ability to be suspended, potentially migrated, and resumed without modifying any of the applications running inside the VM. However, virtual machines also raise additional challenges related to the overhead of using VMs:

Preparation Overhead. When using VMs to implement reservations, a VM disk image must be either prepared on-the-fly or transferred to the physical node where it is needed. Since a VM disk image can have a size in the order of gigabytes, this preparation overhead can significantly delay the starting time of leases. This delay may, in some cases, be unacceptable for advance reservations that must start at a specific time.

Runtime Overhead. Once a VM is running, scheduling primitives such as checkpointing and resuming can incur in significant overhead since a VM's entire memory space must be saved to disk, and then read from disk. Migration involves transferring this saved memory along with the VM disk image. Similar to deployment overhead, this overhead can result in noticeable delays.

The Haizea project (http://haizea.cs.uchicago.edu/) was created to develop a scheduler that can efficiently support advance reservations efficiently by using the suspend/resume/migrate capability of VMs, but minimizing the overhead of using VMs. The fundamental resource provisioning abstraction in Haizea is the *lease*, with three types of lease currently supported:

- *Advanced reservation leases*, where the resources must be available at a specific time.
- *Best-effort leases*, where resources are provisioned as soon as possible and requests are placed on a queue if necessary.
- *Immediate leases*, where resources are provisioned when requested or not at all.

The Haizea lease manager can be used as a scheduling back-end for the OpenNebula virtual infrastructure engine, allowing it to support these three types of leases. The remainder of this section describes Haizea's leasing model and the algorithms Haizea uses to schedule these leases.

6.3.3 Leasing Model

We define a lease as "a negotiated and renegotiable agreement between a resource provider and a resource consumer, where the former agrees to make a set of resources available to the latter, based on a set of lease terms presented by the resource consumer." The terms must encompass the following: the *hardware resources* required by the resource consumer, such as CPUs, memory, and network bandwidth; a *software environment* required on the leased resources; and an *availability period* during which a user requests that the hardware and software resources be available. Since previous work and other authors already explore lease terms for hardware resources and software environments [21, 22], our focus has been on the availability dimension of a lease and, in particular, on how to efficiently support advance reservations.

Thus, we consider the following availability terms:

- *Start time* may be unspecified (a best-effort lease) or specified (an advance reservation lease). In the latter case, the user may specify either a specific start time or a time period during which the lease start may occur.
- *Maximum duration* refers to the total maximum amount of time that the leased resources will be available.
- Leases can be *preemptable*. A preemptable lease can be safely paused without disrupting the computation that takes place inside the lease.

Haizea's resource model considers that it manages W physical nodes capable of running virtual machines. Each node i has CPUs, megabytes (MB) of memory, and MB of local disk storage. We assume that all disk images required to run virtual machines are available in a *repository* from which they can be transferred to nodes as needed and that all are connected at a bandwidth of B MB/sec by a switched network.

A lease is implemented as a set of N VMs, each allocated resources described by a tuple (p, m, d, b), where p is number of CPUs, m is memory in MB, d is disk space in MB, and b is network bandwidth in MB/sec. A disk image I with a size of $size(I)$ MB must be transferred from the repository to a node before the VM can start. When transferring a disk image to multiple nodes, we use multicasting and model the transfer time as size(I)/B. If a lease is preempted, it is suspended by suspending its VMs, which may then be either resumed on the same node or migrated to another node and resumed there. Suspending a VM results in a memory state image file (of size m that can be saved to either a local filesystem or a global filesystem ($f \in \{local, global\}$). Resumption requires reading that image back into memory and then discarding the file. Suspension of a single VM is done at a rate of s megabytes of VM memory per second, and we define r similarly for VM resumption.

6.3.4   Lease Scheduling

Haizea is designed to process lease requests and determine how those requests can be mapped to virtual machines, leveraging their suspend/resume/migrate capability, in such a way that the leases' requirements are satisfied. The scheduling component of Haizea uses classical backfilling algorithms [23], extended to allow best-effort leases to be preempted if resources have to be freed up for advance reservation requests. Additionally, to address the preparation and runtime overheads mentioned earlier, the scheduler allocates resources explicitly for the overhead activities (such as transferring disk images or suspending VMs) instead of assuming they should be deducted from the lease's allocation. Besides guaranteeing that certain operations complete on time (e.g., an image transfer before the start of a lease), the scheduler also attempts to minimize this overhead whenever possible, most notably by reusing disk image transfers and caching disk images on the physical nodes.

Best-effort leases are scheduled using a queue. When a best-effort lease is requested, the lease request is placed at the end of the queue, which is periodically evaluated using a backfilling algorithm—both aggressive and conservative backfilling strategies [23, 24] are supported—to determine if any leases can be scheduled. The scheduler does this by first checking the earliest possible starting time for the lease on each physical node, which will depend on the required disk images. For example, if some physical nodes have cached the required disk image, it will be possible to start the lease earlier on those nodes. Once these earliest starting times have been determined, the scheduler chooses the nodes that allow the lease to start soonest.

The use of VM suspension/resumption allows the best-effort leases to be scheduled even if there are not enough resources available for their full requested duration. If there is a "blocking" lease in the future, such as an advance reservation lease that would prevent the best-effort lease to run to completion before the blocking lease starts, the best-effort lease can still be scheduled; the VMs in the best-effort lease will simply be suspended before a blocking lease. The remainder of a suspended lease is placed in the queue, according to its submission time, and is scheduled like a regular best-effort lease (except a resumption operation, and potentially a migration operation, will have to be scheduled too).

Advance reservations, on the other hand, do not go through a queue, since they must start at either the requested time or not at all. Thus, scheduling this type of lease is relatively simple, because it mostly involves checking if there are enough resources available during the requested interval. However, the scheduler must also check if any associated overheads can be scheduled in such a way that the lease can still start on time. For preparation overhead, the scheduler determines if the required images can be transferred on time. These transfers are scheduled using an earliest deadline first (EDF) algorithm, where the deadline for the image transfer is the start time of the advance reservation lease. Since the start time of an advance reservation lease may occur long after the lease request, we modify the basic EDF algorithm so that transfers take place as close as possible to the deadline, preventing images from unnecessarily consuming disk space before the lease starts. For runtime overhead, the scheduler will attempt to schedule the lease without having to preempt other leases; if preemption is unavoidable, the necessary suspension operations are scheduled if they can be performed on time.

For both types of leases, Haizea supports *pluggable policies*, allowing system administrators to write their own scheduling policies without having to modify Haizea's source code. Currently, three policies are pluggable in Haizea: determining whether a lease is accepted or not, the selection of physical nodes, and determining whether a lease can preempt another lease.

Our main results so far [25, 26] have shown that, when using workloads that combine best-effort and advance reservation lease requests, a VM-based approach with suspend/resume/migrate can overcome the utilization problems typically associated with the use of advance reservations. Even in the presence of the runtime overhead resulting from using VMs, a VM-based approach results in consistently better total execution time than a scheduler that does not support task preemption, along with only slightly worse performance than a scheduler that does support task preemption. Measuring the wait time and slowdown of best-effort leases shows that, although the average values of these metrics increase when using VMs, this effect is due to short leases not being preferentially selected by Haizea's backfilling algorithm, instead of allowing best-effort leases to run as long as possible before a preempting AR lease (and being suspended right before the start of the AR). In effect, a VM-based approach does not favor leases of a particular length over others, unlike systems that rely more heavily on backfilling. Our results have also shown that, although supporting the deployment of multiple software environments, in the form of multiple VM images, requires the transfer of potentially large disk image files, this deployment overhead can be minimized through the use of image transfer scheduling and caching strategies.

6.3.5   Further Reading on Lease-Based Resource Management

There are several scholarly publications [25–28] available for download at the Haizea Web site (http://haizea.cs.uchicago.edu/) describing Haizea's design and algorithms in greater detail and showing performance results obtained when using Haizea's lease-based model.

6.4   CAPACITY MANAGEMENT TO MEET SLA COMMITMENTS

As was discussed in the previous section, when temporal behavior of services with respect to resource demands is highly predictable (e.g., thanks to well-known business cycle of a service, or predictable job lengths in computational service), capacity can be efficiently scheduled using reservations. In this section we focus on less predictable elastic workloads. For these workloads, exact scheduling of capacity may not be possible. Rather than that, capacity planning and optimizations are required.

IaaS providers perform two complementary management tasks: (1) capacity planning to make sure that SLA obligations are met as contracted with the service providers and (2) continuous optimization of resource utilization given specific workload to make the most efficient use of the existing capacity. It is worthy to emphasize the rationale behind these two management processes.

The first task pertains to the long-term capacity management aimed at cost-efficient provisioning in accordance with contracted SLAs. To protect SLAs with end users, elastic services scale up and down dynamically. This requires an IaaS provider to guarantee elasticity for the service within some contracted capacity ranges. Thus, the IaaS provider should plan capacity of the cloud in such a way that when services change resource demands in response to environment conditions, the resources will be indeed provided with the contracted probability. At the same time, the IaaS cloud provider strives to minimally over-provision capacity, thus minimizing the operational costs. We observe that these goals can be harmonized thanks to statistical multiplexing of elastic capacity demands. The key questions will be (a) in what form to provide capacity guarantees (i.e., infrastructure SLAs) and (b) how to control the risks inherent to over-subscribing. We treat these problems in Sections 6.4.1 and 6.4.2, respectively.

The second task pertains to short- and medium-term optimization of resource allocation under the current workload. This optimization may be guided by different management policies that support high-level business goals of an IaaS provider. We discuss policy-driven continuous resource optimization in Section 6.4.3.

From an architectural viewpoint, we argue in favor of a resource management framework that separates between these two activities and allows combination of solutions to each process, which are best adapted to the needs of a specific IaaS provider.

6.4.1 Infrastructure SLAs

IaaS can be regarded as a giant virtual hardware store, where computational resources such as virtual machines (VM), virtual application networks (VAN) and virtual disks (VD) can be ordered on demand in the matter of minutes or even seconds. Virtualization technology is sufficiently versatile to provide virtual resources on a almost continuous granularity scale. Chandra et al. [29] quantitatively study advantages of fine-grain resource allocation in a shared hosting platform. As this research suggests, fine-grain temporal and spatial resource allocation may lead to substantial improvements in capacity utilization.

These advantages come at a cost of increased management, accounting, and billing overhead. For this reason, in practice, resources are typically provided on a more coarse discrete scale. For example, Amazon EC2 [1] offers *small*, *large*, and *extra large* general-purpose VM instances and high-CPU medium and extra large instances. It is possible that more instance types (e.g., I/O high, memory high, storage high, etc.) will be added in the future should a demand for them arise. Other IaaS providers—for example, GoGrid [3] and FlexiScale [4]—follow similar strategy.

With some caution it may be predicted that this approach, as being considerably more simple management-wise, will remain prevalent in short to medium term in the IaaS cloud offerings.

Thus, to deploy a service on a cloud, service provider orders suitable virtual hardware and installs its application software on it. From the IaaS provider, a given service configuration is a *virtual resource array* of black box resources, which correspond to the number of instances of resource type. For example, a typical three-tier application may contain 10 general-purpose small instances to run Web front-ends, three large instances to run an application server cluster with load balancing and redundancy, and two large instances to run a replicated database.

In an IaaS model it is expected from the service provider that it sizes capacity demands for its service. If resource demands are provided correctly and are indeed satisfied upon request, then desired user experience of the service will be guaranteed. A risk mitigation mechanism to protect user experience in the IaaS model is offered by *infrastructure SLAs* (i.e., the SLAs formalizing capacity availability) signed between service provider and IaaS provider.

The is no universal approach to infrastructure SLAs. As the IaaS field matures and more experience is being gained, some methodologies may become more popular than others. Also some methods may be more suitable for specific workloads than other. There are three main approaches as follows.

- No SLAs. This approach is based on two premises: (a) Cloud always has spare capacity to provide on demand, and (b) services are not QoS-sensitive and can withstand moderate performance degradation. This methodology is best suited for the best effort workloads.

- Probabilistic SLAs. These SLAs allow us to trade capacity availability for cost of consumption. Probabilistic SLAs specify clauses that determine *availability percentile* for contracted resources computed over the SLA evaluation period. The lower the availability percentile, the cheaper the cost of resource consumption. This is justified by the fact that an IaaS provider has less stringent commitments and can over-subscribe capacity to maximize yield without exposing itself to excessive risk. This type of SLA is suitable for small and medium businesses and for many enterprise grade applications.

- Deterministic SLAs. These are, in fact, probabilistic SLAs where resource availability percentile is 100%. These SLAs are most stringent and difficult to guarantee. From the provider's point of view, they do not admit capacity multiplexing. Therefore this is the most costly option for service providers, which may be applied for critical services.

We envision coexistence of all three methodologies above, where each SLA type is most applicable to specific workload type. We will focus on probabilistic SLAs, however, because they represent the more interesting and flexible option and lay the foundation for the rest of discussion on statistical multiplexing of capacity in Section 6.4.2. But before we can proceed, we need to define one more concept, *elasticity rules.*

Elasticity rules are scaling and de-scaling policies that guide transition of the service from one configuration to another to match changes in the environment. The main motivation for defining these policies stems from the pay-as-you-go billing model of IaaS clouds. The service owner is interested in paying only for what is really required to satisfy workload demands minimizing the over-provisioning overhead.

There are three types of elasticity rules:

- Time-driven: These rules change the virtual resources array in response to a timer event. These rules are useful for predictable workloads—for example, for services with well-known business cycles.

- OS Level Metrics-Driven: These rules react on predicates defined in terms of the OS parameters observable in the black box mode (see Amazon Auto-scaling Service). These auto-scaling policies are useful for transparently scaling and de-scaling services. The problem is, however, that in many cases this mechanism is not precise enough.

- Application Metrics-Driven. This is a unique RESERVOIR offering that allows an application to supply application-specific policies that will be transparently executed by IaaS middleware in reacting on the monitoring information supplied by the service-specific monitoring probes running inside VMs.

For a single service, elasticity rules of all three types can be defined, resulting in a complex dynamic behavior of a service during runtime. To protect elasticity rules of a service while increasing the multiplexing gain, RESER-VOIR proposes using probabilistic infrastructure availability SLAs.

Assuming that a business day is divided into a number of *usage windows*, the generic template for probabilistic infrastructure SLAs is as follows.

For each W_i, and each resource type r_j from the virtual resource array, capacity range $C = (r_j^{min}, r_j^{max})$ is available for the service with probability p_i.

Probabilistically guaranteeing capacity ranges allows service providers to define its needs flexibly. For example, for business critical usage window, availability percentile may be higher than for the regular or off-peak hours. Similarly, capacity ranges may vary in size. From the provider's point of view, defining capacity requirements this way allows yield maximization through over-subscribing. This creates a win–win situation for both service provider and IaaS provider.

6.4.2 Policy-Driven Probabilistic Admission Control

Benefits of statistical multiplexing are well known. This is an extensively studied field, especially in computer networking [30–32]. In the context of CPU and bandwidth allocation in shared hosting platforms, the problem was recently studied by Urgaonkar et al. [33]. In this work the resources were treated as contiguous, allowing infinitesimal capacity allocation. We generalize this approach by means of treating each (number of instances of resource *i* in the virtual resources array) as a random variable. The virtual resources array is, therefore, a vector of random variables. Since we assume that each capacity range for each resource type is finite, we may compute both the average resource consumption rate and variance in resource consumption for each service in terms of the capacity units corresponding to each resource type.

Inspired by the approach of Guerin et al. [30], we propose a simple management lever termed *acceptable risk level* (ARL) to control over-subscribing of capacity. We define ARL as the probability of having insufficient capacity to satisfy some capacity allocation requests on demand. The ARL value can be derived from a business policy of the IaaS provider—that is, more aggressive versus more conservative over-subscription.

In general, the optimal ARL value can be obtained by calculating the residual benefit resulting from specific SLA violations. A more conservative, suboptimal ARL value is simply the complement of the most stringent capacity range availability percentile across the SLA portfolio.

An infrastructure SLA commitment for the new application service should be made if and only if the potential effect does not cause the residual benefit to fall below some predefined level, being controlled by the site's business policy. This decision process is referred to as *BSM-aligned admission control.*[3]

---

[3]We will refer to it simply as admission control wherever no ambiguity arises.

Once a service application passes admission control successfully, optimal placement should be found for the virtual resources comprising the service. We treat this issue in Section 6.4.3.

The admission control algorithm calculates *equivalent capacity* required to satisfy the resource demands of the service applications for the given ARL. The equivalent capacity is then matched against the actual available capacity to verify whether it is safe to admit a new service.

In a federated environment (like that provided by RESERVOIR) there is potentially an infinite pool of resources. However, these resources should fit placement constraints that are posed by the service applications and should be reserved using inter-cloud framework agreements. Thus, the BSM-aligned admission control helps the capacity planning process to dimension capacity requests from the partner clouds and fulfill physical capacity requests at the local cloud.

The capacity demands of the deployed application services are being continuously monitored. For each application service, the mean capacity demand (in capacity units) and the standard deviation of the capacity demand are being calculated.

When a new service with unknown history arrives in the system, its mean capacity demand and standard deviation are conservatively estimated from the service elasticity rules and historic data known for other services. Then, an equivalent capacity is approximated using Eq. (6.1). The equivalent capacity is the physical capacity needed to host the new service and all previously deployed services without increasing the probability of congestion (acceptable risk level), ε.

Equivalent capacity is expressed in the form of resource array, where each element represents the number of instances of a resource of a specific type.[4] To verify that physical capacity is sufficient to support the needed equivalent capacity, one may use either the efficient and scalable exact solution (via branch and bound algorithms) to the multiple knapsack problem [48] or the efficient bin-packing approximation algorithm such as First-Fit-Descending, which guarantees approximation ratio within 22% of the optimal algorithm. Using multiple knapsacks is more appropriate when capacity augmentation is not an option. Assuming that value of the resources is proportional to their size, solving the multiple knapsack problem provides a good estimation of value resulting from packing the virtual resources on the given capacity. If capacity can be augmented—for example, more physical capacity can be obtained from a partner cloud provider or procured locally—then solving the bin packing problem is more appropriate since all items (i.e., resources comprising the service) are always packed.

---

[4]When calculating equivalent capacity, we do not know which service will use specific resource instances, but we know that it is sufficient, say, to be able to allocate up to 100 small VM instances and 50 large instances to guarantee all resource requests resulting from the elasticity rules application, so that congestion in resource allocation will not happen with probability larger than ε.

Note that this is different from computing the actual placement of services since at the admission control stage we have "abstract" equivalent capacity. Matching equivalent capacity against physical capacity, as above, guarantees that feasible placement for actual services can be found with probability $1 - \varepsilon$.

If the local and remote physical capacity that can be used by this site in a guaranteed manner is sufficient to support the equivalent capacity calculated, the new service is accepted. Otherwise, a number of possibilities exist, depending on the management policy:

- The service is rejected.
- The total capacity of the site is increased locally and/or remotely (through federation) by the amount needed to satisfy the equivalent capacity constraint and the service is admitted.
- The acceptable risk level is increased, and the service is accepted.

$$B_{eq} = m + \alpha \cdot \sigma \tag{6.1}$$

$$m = \sum_{i}^{n} m_i \tag{6.2}$$

$$\sigma = \sqrt{\sum_{i}^{n} \sigma^2} \tag{6.3}$$

$$\alpha = \sqrt{2} \cdot \operatorname{erfc}^{-1}(2\varepsilon) \approx \sqrt{-2\ln\varepsilon - \ln 2\pi - \ln(-2\ln\varepsilon - \ln 2\pi)} \tag{6.4}$$

Our approach initially overestimates the average capacity demand for the new service. With the passage of time, however, as capacity usage statistics are being collected for the newly admitted application service, the mean and standard deviation for the capacity demands (per resource type) are adjusted for this service. This allows us to reduce the conservativeness when the next service arrives.

Service providers may impose various placement restrictions on VMs comprising the service. For example, it may be required that VMs do not share the same physical host (anti-affinity). As another example, consider heterogeneous physical infrastructure and placement constraints arising from technological incompatibilities.

From the admission control algorithm's vantage point, the problem is that during admission control it may not know which deployment restrictions should be taken into account since which restrictions will be of relevance depends on the dynamic behavior of the services.

Thus, our proposed solution is best suited for services whose elements admit full sharing of the infrastructure. Generalizing this approach to handle various types of deployment restrictions is in the focus of our current research efforts.

In general, to guarantee that a feasible placement for virtual resources will be found with controllable probability in the presence of placement restrictions, resource augmentation is required. The resource augmentation may be quite significant (see references 34 and 35). It is, therefore, prudent on the side of the IaaS provider to segregate workloads that admit full sharing of the infrastructure from those who do not and offer service provider-controlled deployment restrictions as a premium service to recover capacity augmentation costs.

6.4.3 Policy-Driven Placement Optimization

The purpose of statistical admission control is to guarantee that there is enough capacity to find a feasible placement with given probability. Policy-driven placement optimization complements capacity planning and management by improving a given mapping of physical to virtual resources (e.g., VMs).

In the presence of deployment restrictions, efficient capacity planning with guaranteed *minimal* over-provisioning is still an open research problem. Partially the difficulties lie in hardness of solving multiple knapsacks or its more general version, the generalized assignment problem. Both problems are NP-hard in the strong sense (see discussion in Section 6.4.5). In the RESER-VOIR model, where resource augmentation is possible through cloud partner-ship, solutions that may require doubling of existing local capacity in the worst case [34] are applicable. An interesting line of research is to approximate capacity augmentation introduced by specific constraints, such as bin–item and item–item. Based on required augmentation, an IaaS provider may either accept or reject the service.

As shown in reference 36, in the presence of placement constraints of type bin–item, Bi-criteria Multiple Knapsack with Assignment Restrictions (BMKAR) that maximizes the total profit of placed items (subject to a lower bound) and minimizes the total number of containers (i.e., minimizes utilized capacity) does not admit a polynomial algorithm that satisfies the lower bound exactly unless $P = NP$. Two approximation algorithms with performance ratios (running in pseudo-polynomial time) and (running in polynomial time) were presented. These results are best known today for BMKAR, and the bounds are tight.

In our current prototypical placement solution, we formulated the problem as an Integer Linear Programming problem and used branch-and-bound solver (COIN-CBC [37]) to solve the problem exactly. This serves us as a performance baseline for future research. As was shown by Pisinger [38], in the absence of constraints, very large problem instances can be solved exactly in a very efficient manner using a branch-and-bound algorithm. Obviously, as the scale of the problem (in terms of constraints) increases, ILP becomes infeasible. This leads us to focus on developing novel heuristic algorithms extending the state of art, which is discussed in Section 6.4.5.

A number of important aspects should be taken into account in efficient placement optimization.

Penalization for Nonplacement. In BMKAR, as in all classical knapsack problems, no-placement of an item results in 0 profit for that item. In the VM placement with SLA protection problem, nonplacement of an item or a group of items may result in SLA violation and, thus, payment of penalty. The management policy to minimize nonplacements is factored into constraints and an objective function.

Selection Constraints. Selection constraints imply that only when a group of VMs (items) collectively forming a service is placed, this *meta-item* yields profit. Partial placement may even lead to a penalty, since the SLA of a service may be violated. Thus, partial placement should be prevented. In our formulation, this is factored into constraints.

Repeated Solution. Since the placement problem is solved continuously, it is important to minimize the cost of replacement. In particular, we need to minimize the cost of reassignments of VMs to hosts, because this entails VM migrations. We factor the penalty member on migration in our objective function.

Considering ICT-Level Management Policies. There are three policies that we currently consider: *power conservation* (by minimizing the number of physical hosts used for placement), *load balancing* (by spreading load across available physical machines), and *migration minimization* (by introducing a penalty factor for machines migration). We discuss policies below. In general, RESERVOIR provides an open-ended engine that allows to incorporate different policies. Depending on the policy chosen, the optimization problem is cast into a specific form. Currently, we support two placement policies: "load balancing" and "power conservation," with number of migrations minimized in both cases. The first policy is attained through solving GAP with conflicts, and the second one is implemented via bin packing with conflicts.

Inspired by results by Santos et al. [39], who cast infrastructure-level management policies as soft constraints, we factor the load balancing policy into our model using the soft constraints approach.

Whereas the hard constraints take the form of

$$f(\vec{x}) \leq b \tag{6.5}$$

where $\vec{x}$ is the vector of decision variables, with the soft constraints approach, a *constraint violation variable v* is introduced into the hard constraint as shown in Eq. (6.6) and a penalty term $P \cdot v$ is introduced into the objective function to prevent trivial solutions, because soft constraints are always possible to satisfy. If the penalty is a sufficiently large number, the search for an optimal solution will try to minimize it.

$$f(\vec{x}) \leq b + \upsilon \tag{6.6}$$

We exploit the idea that reducing the available capacity at each physical host will force the search for an optimal solution to spread the VEEs over a larger number of knapsacks, thus causing the load to be spread more evenly across the site.

To address power conservation objective as a management policy, we formulate our problem as bin-packing with conflicts.

Since the optimization policy for VEE placement is being continuously solved, it is critical to minimize VEE migrations in order to maintain cost-effectiveness. To model this, we define a migration penalty term MP as shown in Eq. (6.7).

$$MP = \sum_{i=1}^{m} \sum_{j=1}^{n} \text{migr}(j) \cdot \text{abs}(x_{i,j}^{t-1} - x_{i,j}^{t}) \tag{6.7}$$

Since $\text{abs}(\cdot)$, which is a nonlinear, is part of MP, we cannot incorporate MP into the objective function as is. To circumvent this problem, we linearize MP by introducing additional variables, which is a widely used linearization technique.

Management Policies and Management Goals. Policy-based management is an overused term. Therefore, it is, beneficial to define and differentiate our approach to policy-driven admission control and placement optimization in the more precise terms.

Policy-driven management is a management approach based on "if(condition)−then(action)" rules defined to deal with the situations that are likely to arise [40]. These policies serve as a basic building blocks for autonomic computing.

The overall optimality criteria of placement, however, are controlled by the management policies, which are defined at a higher level of abstraction than "if (condition)−then(action)" rules. To avoid ambiguity, we term these policies *management goals*. Management goals, such as "conserve power," "prefer local resources over remote resources," "balance workload," "minimize VM migrations," "minimize SLA noncompliance," and so forth, have complex logical structures. They cannot be trivially expressed by "if(condition)−then(action)" rules even though it is possible to create the elementary rules that will strive to satisfy global management preferences in a reactive or proactive manner.

Regarding the management activity involved in VM placement optimization, a two-phase approach can be used. In the first phase, a feasible placement—that is, a placement that satisfies the hard constraints imposed by the service manifest—can be obtained without concerns for optimality and, thus, with low effort. In the second phase, either a timer-based or a threshold-based *management policy* can invoke a site-wide optimization procedure that aligns capacity allocation with the management goals (e.g., with the goal of using minimal capacity, can be triggered).

Management policies and management goals may be defined at different levels of the management architecture—that is, at the different levels of abstraction. At the topmost level, there are *business* management goals and policies. We briefly discuss them in the next subsection. In the intermediate level there are service-induced goals and policies. Finally, at the infrastructure management level there are ICT management preferences and policies that are our primary focus in this activity. We discuss them in Section 6.4.4.

Business-Level Goals and Policies. Since business goals are defined at such a high level of abstraction, a semantic gap exists between them and the ICT level management goals and policies. Bridging this gap is notoriously difficult. In this work we aim at narrowing this gap and aligning between the high-level business management goals and ICT-level management policies by introducing the notion of acceptable risk level (ARL) of capacity allocation congestion.

Intuitively, we are interested in minimizing the costs of capacity over-provisioning while controlling the risk associated with capacity over-booking.

From minimizing the cost of capacity over-provisioning, we are interested in maximizing yield of the existing capacity. However, at some point, the conflicts (congestions) in capacity allocation may cause excessive SLA penalties that would offset the advantages of yield maximization.

Accounting for benefits from complying with SLAs and for costs of compliance and noncompliance due to congestions, we can compute *residual benefit* for the site. The target value of residual benefit can be controlled by a high-level business policy. To satisfy this business policy, we need to calculate an appropriate congestion probability, ARL. ARL, in turn, would help us calculate equivalent capacity for the site to take advantage of statistical multiplexing in a safe manner.

To allow calculation of residual benefit, capacity allocation behavior under congestion should deterministic. In particular, a policy under congestion may be a Max–Min Fair Share allocation [41] or higher-priority-first (HPF) capacity allocation [39], where services with lower SLA classes are satisfied only after all services with higher SLA classes are satisfied.

For the sake of discussion, let us assume that the HPF capacity allocation policy is used.[5] We use historical data of the capacity demand (in capacity

---

[5]Whether a certain specific policy is being used is of minor importance. It is important, however, that the policy would be deterministic.

units corresponding to different resource types as explained in Section 6.4.2) per service—specifically, the α-percentile of historic capacity demand per application (where α equals the percentile of compliance required in the service SLA). This is used to compute the expected capacity allocation per service under capacity allocation congestion. Thus, we obtain the set of application services, whose SLAs may be violated.[6] Using penalty values defined for each affected SLA, we obtain the residual benefit that would remain after penalties are enforced. Using the management policy that put a lower bound on the expected residual benefit, we compute acceptable risk value, ε, that satisfies this bound.

6.4.4 Infrastructure-Level Management Goals and Policies

In general, infrastructure-level management policies are derived from the business-level management goals. For example, consider our sample business level management goal to "reduce energy expenses by 30% in the next quarter." This broadly defined goal may imply, among other means for achieving it, that we systematically improve consolidation of VMs on physical hosts by putting excessive capacity into a low-power consumption mode. Thus, a site-wide ICT power conservation-level management policy may be formulated as: "minimize number of physical machines while protecting capacity availability SLAs of the application services."

As another example, consider the business-level management goal: "Improve customer satisfaction by achieving more aggressive performance SLOs." One possible policy toward satisfying this business-level goal may be formulated as: "Balance load within the site in order to achieve specific average load per physical host." Another infrastructure-level management policy to improve performance is: "Minimize the number of VM migrations." The rationale for this policy is that performance degradation necessarily occurs during VM migration.

6.4.5 State of the Art

Our approach to capacity management described in Section 6.4.2 is based on the premise that service providers perform sizing of their services. A detailed discussion of the sizing methodologies is out of our scope, and we will only briefly mention results in this area. Capacity planning for Web services was studied by Menascé and Almeida [42]. Doyle et al. [43] considered the problem of how to map requirements of a known media service workload into the corresponding system resource requirements and to accurately size the required system. Based on the past workload history, the capacity planner finds the 95th

---

[6]This is a conservative estimate.

percentile of the service demand (for various resources and on different usage windows) and asks for the corresponding configuration. Urgaonkar et al. [44] studied model-based sizing of three-tier commercial services. Recently, Chen et al. [45] sudied the similar problem and provided novel performance models for multi-tier services.

Doyle et al. [43] presented new models for automating resource provisioning for resources that may interact in complex ways. The premise of the model-based resource provisioning is that internal models capturing service workload and behavior can enable prediction of effects on service performance of the changes to the service workload and resource allotments. For example, the model can answer questions like: "How much memory is needed to reduce this service's storage access rate by 20%?" The paper introduces simple performance models for Web services and proposes a model-based resource allocator that utilizes them and allocates appropriate *resource slices* to achieve needed performance versus capacity utilization. A slice may be mapped to a virtual machine or another resource container providing performance isolation.

In cases when exact model-driven service sizing is not available, learning desirable resource allocation from dynamic service behavior may be possible using black box monitoring of the service network activity as was recently shown by Ben-Yehuda et al. [46] for multi-tier services.

Benefits of capacity multiplexing (under the assumption of known resource demands) in shared hosting platforms were quantitatively studied by Chandra et al. [29].

An approach to capacity over-subscribing that is conceptually similar to ours was recently studied by Urgaonkar et al. [33]. In this work, provisioning CPU and network resources with probabilitistic guarantees on a shared hosting platform were considered. The main difference between our methodology and that of Urgaonkar et al. is that we allocate capacity in integral discrete quanta that encapsulate CPU, memory, network bandwidth, and storage rather than allowing independent infinitesimally small resources allocation along each of this capacity dimensions.

An advance of virtualization technologies and increased awareness about management and power costs of running under-utilized servers have spurred interest in consolidating existing applications on a fewer number of servers in the data center. In most practical settings today a static approach to consolidation, where consolidation is performed as a point-in-time optimization activity, is used [47, 48]. With the static approach, the cost of VM migration are usually not accounted for and relatively time-consuming computations are tolerated. Gupta et al. [48] demonstrated that static consolidation problem can be modeled as a variant of the bin packing problem where items to be packed are the servers being consolidated and bins are the target servers. The sizes of the servers/items being packed are resource utilizations that are obtained from the performance trace data. The authors present a two-stage heuristic algorithm for handling the "bin−item" assignment constraints that inherently restrict any server consolidation problem. The model is able to solve extremely large instances of the problem in a reasonable amount of time.

Autonomic and dynamic optimization of virtual machines placement in a data center received considerable attention (mainly in the research community) recently [49–59].

Bobroff et al. [54] introduce empiric dynamic server migration and consolidation algorithm based on predicting capacity demand of virtual servers using time series analysis.

Mehta and Neogi [49] presented a virtualized servers consolidation planning tool, Recon, that analyzes historical data collected from an existing environment and computes the potential benefits of server consolidation especially in the dynamic setting.

Gmach et al. [50] considered virtualized servers consolidation of multiple servers and their workloads subject to specific quality of service requirements that need to be supported.

Wood et al. [52] presented Sandpiper, a system that automates the task of monitoring and detecting hotspots, determining a new mapping of physical to virtual resources, and initiating the necessary migrations to protect performance.

Singh et al. [53] presented a promising approach to the design of an agile data center with integrated server and storage virtualization technologies.

Verma et al. [51] studied the design, implementation, and evaluation of a power-aware application placement controller in the context of an environment with heterogeneous virtualized server clusters.

Tang et al. [58] presented a performance model-driven approach to application placement that can be extended to VM placement.

Wang et al. [55] defined a nonlinear constrained optimization model for dynamic resource provisioning and presented a novel analytic solution.

Choi et al. [60] proposed machine learning framework that autonomously finds and adjusts utilization thresholds at runtime for different computing requirements.

Kelly [59] studied the problem of allocating discrete resources according to utility functions reported by potential recipients with application to resource allocation in a Utility Data Center (UDC).

Knapsack-related optimization has been relentlessly studied over the last 30 years. The scientific literature on the subject is, therefore, abundant. For excellent treatment of the knapsack problems, we recommend references 61 and 62. The Simple Multiple Knapsack Problem (MKP) is NP-hard in the strong sense. Its generalization, called Generalized Assignment Problem (GAP), is APX-hard [63]. GAP (and therefore MKP) admits two approximations using a greedy algorithm [64]. A Fully Polynomial Time Approximation Scheme (FPTAS) for this problem is unlikely unless $P = NP$ [65]. For some time it was not known whether simple MKP admits the Polynomial Time Approximation Scheme (PTAS). Chekuri and Khanna [63] presented a PTAS for MKP in 2000. Shachnai and Tamir showed that the Class-Constrained Multiple Knapsack also admits PTAS.

Running time of PTASs dramatically increases as ε decreases.[7] Therefore heuristic algorithms optimized for specific private cases and scalable exeat solutions are important.

Pisinger [38] presented a scalable exact branch-and-bound algorithm for solving multiple knapsack problems with hundreds of thousands of items and high ratios of items to bins. This algorithm improves the branch-and-bound algorithm by Martello and Toth [61].

Dawande et al. [34] studied single-criterion and bi-criteria multiple knapsack problems with assignment restrictions. For the bi-criteria problem of minimizing utilized capacity subject to a minimum requirement on assigned weight, they give a (1/3, 2)-approximation algorithm, where the first value refers to profit and the second one refers to capacity augmentation.

Gupta et al. [66] presented a two-stage consolidation heuristic for servers consolidation that handles item–bin and item–item conflicts. No bounds on this heuristic were shown, however.

Epstein and Levin [35] studied the bin packing problem with item–item conflicts. For bipartite graphs they present a 2.5 approximation algorithm for perfect graphs (of conflicts) and a 1.75 approximation algorithm for bipartite graphs.

Additional annotated bibliography and surveys on the knapsack-related problems can be found in references 67 and 68. For survey of the recent results in multi-criteria combinatorial optimization, see reference 69.

An important question for studying scalability of the optimization algorithms is how to produce meaningful benchmarks for the tests. Pisinger [70] studied relative hardness characterization of the knapsack problems. This study may serve as a basis for generating synthetic benchmarks to be used in validating knapsack related solutions.

Business-driven resource provisioning was studied by Marques et al. in [71]. This work proposes a business-oriented approach to designing IT infrastructure in an e-commerce context subject to load surges.

Santos et al. [39] demonstrated that management policies can be effectively and elegantly cast as soft constraints into optimization problem.

From analyzing the state of the art in provisioning and placement optimization, we observe that the mainstream approach is *detection and remediation*. In a nutshell, the SLA compliance of the services is being monitored and when noncompliance or a dangerous trend that may lead to noncompliance is detected, corrective actions (e.g., VEE migrations) are attempted.

6.5 CONCLUSIONS AND FUTURE WORK

Virtualization is one of the cornerstones of Infrastructure-as-a-Service cloud computing and, although virtual machines provide numerous benefits,

[7]Here ε stands for the approximation parameter and should not be confused with the acceptable risk level of Section 6.4.2, which was also denoted ε.

managing them efficiently in a cloud also poses a number of challenges. This chapter has described some of these challenges, along with the ongoing work within the RESERVOIR project to address them. In particular, we have focused on the problems of distributed management of virtual infrastructures, advance reservation of capacity in virtual infrastructures, and meeting SLA commitments.

Managing virtual machines distributed across a pool of physical resources, or virtual infrastructure management, is not a new problem. VM-based data center management tools have been available long before the emergence of cloud computing. However, these tools specialized in long-running VMs and exhibited monolithic architectures that were hard to extend, or were limited by design to use one particular hypervisor. Cloud infrastructures need to support pay-as-you-go and on-demand models where VMs have to be provisioned immediately and fully configured for the user, which requires coordinating storage, network, and virtualization technologies. To this end, we have developed OpenNebula, a virtual infrastructure manager designed with the requirements of cloud infrastructures in mind. OpenNebula is an actively developed open source project, and future work will focus on managing groups of VMs arranged in a service-like structure (e.g., a compute cluster), disk image provision strategies to reduce image cloning times, and improving support for external providers to enable a hybrid cloud model.

We have also developed Haizea, a resource lease manager that can act as a scheduling back-end for OpenNebula, supporting other provisioning models other than the prevalent immediate provisioning models in existing cloud providers. In particular, Haizea adds support for best-effort provisioning and advance reservations, both of which become necessary when managing a finite number of resources. Future work will focus on researching policies for lease admission and lease preemption, particularly those based on economic models, and will also focus on researching adaptive scheduling strategies for advance reservations.

We developed an algorithmic approach to resource over-subscription with probabilistically guaranteed risk of violating SLAs. Our future work in this area will focus on (1) validation of this approach with synthetic and real data through simulating a large-scale IaaS cloud environment, (2) complementing admission control and capacity planning with heuristics for workload throttling, particularly those that take advantage of opportunistic placement in a federated environment, to handle the cases when stochastic properties of the underlying system change abruptly and dramatically, and (3) policies to control cost-effectiveness of resource allocation.

ACKNOWLEDGMENTS

Our work is supported by the European Union through the research grant RESERVOIR Grant Number 215605.

REFERENCES

1. Inc. Amazon. Amazon elastic compute cloud (Amazon ec2). http://aws.amazon.com/ec2/.

2. ElasticHosts Ltd. Elastichosts. http://www.elastichosts.com/.

3. ServePath LLC. Gogrid. http://www.gogrid.com/.

4. xcalibre communications ltd., Flexiscale. http://www.flexiscale.com/.

5. B. Rochwerger, J. Caceres, R. S. Montero, D. Breitgand, E. Elmroth, A. Galis, E. Levy, I. M. Llorente, K. Nagin, and Y. Wolfsthal, The RESERVOIR model and architecture for open federated cloud computing, *IBM Systems Journal*, **53** (4):4:1–4:11, 2009.

6. Platform Computing Corporation. Platform http://www.platform.com/Products/platform-isf.

7. VMware Inc., Vmware DRS, http://www.vmware.com/products/vi/vc/drs.html.

8. Enomaly, Inc. Elastic computing platform. http://www.enomaly.com/.

9. Red Hat. ovirt. http://ovirt.org/.

10. I. Foster, C. Kesselman, C. Lee, R. Lindell, K. Nahrstedt, and A. Roy, A distributed resource management architecture that supports advance reservations and co-allocation, in *Proceedings of the International Workshop on Quality of Service*, 1999.

11. W. Smith, I. Foster, and V. Taylor, Scheduling with advanced reservations, in *Proceedings of the 14th International Symposium on Parallel and Distributed Processing*, IEEE Computer Society, 2000, p. 127.

12. Q. Snell, M. J. Clement, D. B. Jackson, and C. Gregory, The performance impact of advance reservation meta-scheduling, in *Proceedings of the Workshop on Job Scheduling Strategies for Parallel Processing*, Springer-Verlag, London, 2000, pp. 137–153.

13. M. W. Margo, K. Yoshimoto, P. Kovatch, and P. Andrews, Impact of reservations on production job scheduling, in *Proceedings of the 13th Workshop on Job Scheduling Strategies for Parallel Processing*, 116–131, 2007.

14. I. M. Llorente, R. Moreno-Vozmediano, and R. S. Montero, Cloud computing for on-demand grid resource provisioning, in *Advances in Parallel Computing*, IOS Press, volume 18, pp. 177–191, 2009.

15. T. Freeman and K. Keahey, Contextualization: Providing one-click virtual clusters, in *Proceedings of the IEEE Fourth International Conference on eScience*, 301–308, December 2008.

16. R. Moreno, R. S. Montero, and I. M. Llorente, Elastic management of cluster-based services in the cloud, in *Proceedings of the First Workshop on Automated Control for Datacenters and Clouds (ACDC 2009)*, 19–24, June 2009.

17. P. H. Hargrove and J. C. Duell, Berkeley Lab checkpoint/restart (blcr) for linux clusters, *Journal of Physics: Conference Series*, **46**:494–499, 2006.

18. D. C. Nurmi, R. Wolski, and J. Brevik, Varq: Virtual advance reservations for queues, in *Proceedings of the 17th International Symposium on High Performance Distributed Computing*, ACM, New York, 2008, pp. 75–86.

19. M. Hovestadt, O. Kao, A. Keller, and A. Streit, Scheduling in hpc resource management systems: Queuing vs. planning, *Lecture Notes in Computer Science 2862*, Springer, Berlin, 2003, pp. 1–20.

20. F. Heine, M. Hovestadt, O. Kao, and A. Streit, On the impact of reservations from the grid on planning-based resource management, in *Proceedings of the 5th International Conference on Computational Science (ICCS 2005), Volume 3516 of Lecture Notes in Computer Science (LNCS,)* Springer, Berlin, 2005, pp. 155–162.

21. T. Freeman, K. Keahey, I. T. Foster, A. Rana, B. Sotomayor, and F. Wuerthwein, Division of labor: Tools for growing and scaling grids, in *Proceedings of the International Conference on Service Oriented Computing*, 40–51, 2006.

22. K. Keahey and T. Freeman, Contextualization: Providing one-click virtual clusters, in *Proceedings of the IEEE Fourth International Conference on eScience*, 2008.

23. Ahuva W. Mu'alem and Dror G. Feitelson, Utilization, predictability, workloads, and user runtime estimates in scheduling the IBM SP2 with backfilling, *IEEE Transactions on Parallel and Distributed Systems*, 12(6):529–543, 2001.

24. D. A. Lifka, The ANL/IBM SP scheduling system, in *Proceedings of the Workshop on Job Scheduling Strategies for Parallel Processing*, Springer-Verlag, London, 1995, pp. 295–303.

25. B. Sotomayor, K. Keahey, and I. Foster, Combining batch execution and leasing using virtual machines, in *Proceedings of the 17th International Symposium on High Performance Distributed Computing*, ACM, New York, 2008, pp. 87–96.

26. B. Sotomayor, R. S. Montero, I. M. Llorente, and Ian Foster, Resource leasing and the art of suspending virtual machines, in *Proceedings of the 11th IEEE International Conference on High Performance Computing and Communications (HPCC-09)*, 59–68, June 2009.

27. B. Sotomayor, A resource management model for VM-based virtual workspaces. *Master's thesis*, University of Chicago, February 2007.

28. B. Sotomayor, K. Keahey, I. Foster, and T. Freeman, Enabling cost-effective resource leases with virtual machines, in *Hot Topics session in ACM/IEEE International Symposium on High Performance Distributed Computing 2007 (HPDC 2007)*, 2007.

29. A. Chandra, P. Goyal, and P. Shenoy, Quantifying the benefits of resource multiplexing in on-demand data centers, in *Proceedings of the First ACM Workshop on Algorithms and Architectures for Self-Managing Systems (Self-Manage 2003)*, January 2003.

30. R. Guerin, H. Ahmadi, and M. Nagshineh, Equivalent Capacity and its application to bandwidth allocation in high speed networks, *IEEE Journal on Selected Areas in Communication*, 9(7):968–981, 1991.

31. Zhi-Li Zhang, J. Kurose, J. D. Salehi, and D. Towsley, Smoothing, statistical multiplexing, and call admission control for stored video, *IEEE Selected Areas in Communications*, 15(6):1148–1166, 1997.

32. E. W. Knightly and N. B. Shroff, Admission control for statistical qos: Theory and practice. *IEEE Network*, 13(2):20–29, 1999.

33. B. Urgaonkar, B. Urgaonkar, P. Shenoy, P. Shenoy, and T. Roscoe, Resource overbooking and application profiling in shared hosting platforms, in *Proceedings of the 5th Symposium on Operating Systems Design and Implementation (OSDI'02)*, 2002, pp. 239–254.

34. M. Dawande, J. Kalagnanam, P. Keskinocak, R. Ravi, and F. S. Salman, Approximation algorithms for the Multiple Knapsack Problem with assignment

restrictions, *Journal of Combinatorial Optimization*, **4**:171–186, 2000. http://www. research.ibm.com/pdos/doc/papers/mkar.ps.

35. L. Epstein and A. Levin, On bin packing with conflicts, *SIAM Journal on Optimization*, **19**(3):1270–1298, 2008.

36. M. Dawande and J. Kalagnanam, The Multiple Knapsack Problem with Color Constraints, *Technical Report*, IBM T. J. Watson Research, 1998.

37. J. Forrest and R. Lougee-Heimer, Cbc user guide. http://www.coinor.org/Cbc/index.html, 2005.

38. D. Pisinger, An exact algorithm for large multiple knapsack problems, *European Journal of Operational Research*, **114**:528–541, 1999.

39. C. A. Santos, A. Sahai, X. Zhu, D. Beyer, V. Machiraju, and S. Singhal, Policy-based resource assignment in utility computing Environments, in *Proceedings of The 15th IFIP/IEEE Distributed Systems: Operations and Management*, Davis, CA, November 2004.

40. D. Verma, Simplifying network administration using policy-based management, *IEEE Network*, **16**(2):20–26, Jul 2002.

41. S. Keshav, *An Engineering Approach to Computing Networking*. Addison-Wesley Professional Series, Addison-Wesley, Reading, MA, 1997.

42. Daniel A. Menascé and Virgilio A. F. Almeida, *Capacity Planning for Web Performance: metrics, models, and methods*. Prentice-Hall, 1998.

43. R. P. Doyle, J. S. Chase, O. M. Asad, W. Jin, and A. M. Vahdat., Model-based resource provisioning in a Web service utility, in *Proceedings of the USENIX Symposium on Internet Technologies and Systems (USITS)*, p. 5, 2003.

44. B. Urgaonkar, G. Pacifici, P. Shenoy, M. Spreitzer, and A. Tantawi, An analytical model for multi-tier internet services and its applications, in *Proceedings of the 2005 ACM SIGMETRICS International Conference on Measurement and Modeling of Computer Systems*, ACM, New York, 2005, pp. 291–302.

45. Y. Chen, S. Iyer, D. Milojicic, and A. Sahai, A systematic and practical approach to generating policies from service level objectives, in *Proceedings of the 11th IFIP/IEEE International Symposium on Integrated Network Management*, 89–96, 2009.

46. M. Ben-Yehuda, D. Breitgand, M. Factor, H. Kolodner, and V. Kravtsov, NAP: A building block for remediating performance bottlenecks via black box network analysis, in *Proceedings of the 6th International Conference on Autonomic Computing and Communications (ICAC'09)*, Barcelona, Spain, 179–188, June 2009.

47. T. Yuyitung and A. Hillier, Virtualization analysis for VMware, *Technical Report*, CiRBA, 2007.

48. R. Gupta, S. K. Bose, S. Sundarrajan, M. Chebiyam, and A. Chakrabarti, A two stage heuristic algorithm for solving the server consolidation problem with item–item and bin–item incompatibility constraints, in *Proceedings of the IEEE International Conference on Services Computing (SCC'08)*, Vol. 2, Honolulu, HI, July 2008, pp. 39–46.

49. S. Mehta and A. Neogi, Recon: A tool to recommend dynamic server consolidation in multi-cluster data centers, *Proceedings of the IEEE Network Operations and Management Symposium (NOMS 2008)*, Salvador, Bahia, Brasil, April 2008, pp. 363–370.

50. D. Gmach, J. Rolia, L. Cherkasova, G. Belrose, T. Turicchi, and A. Kemper, An integrated approach to resource pool management: Policies, efficiency and quality metrics, in *Proceedings of the 38th Annual IEEE/IFIP International Conference on Dependable Systems and Networks (DSN'2008)*, 2008.

51. A. Verma, P. Ahuja, and A. Neogi, pmapper: Power and migration cost aware application placement in virtualized systems, in *Proceedings of the 9th ACM/IFIP/ USENIX International Conference on Middleware*, 2008, Springer-Verlag, New York, pp. 243–264.

52. T. Wood, P. Shenoy, A. Venkataramani, and M. Yousif. Black-box and gray-box strategies for virtual machine migration, in *Proceedings of the USENIX Symposium on Networked System Design and Implementation (NSDI'07)*, Cambridge, MA, April 2007.

53. A. Singh, M. Korupolu, and D. Mohapatra, Server-storage virtualization: Integration and load balancing in data centers, in *Proceedings of the 7th International Symposium on Software Composition (SC 2008)*, Budapest, Hungary, Article No. 53, March 2008.

54. N. Bobroff, A. Kochut, and K. Beaty, Dynamic placement of virtual machines for managing SLA violations, in *Proceedings of the 10th IFIP/IEEE International Symposium on Integrated Network Management, IM '07*, pp. 119–128, 2007. Best Paper award, IM'07.

55. X. Wang, Z. Du, Y. Chen, S. Li, D. Lan, G. Wang, and Y. Chen, An autonomic provisioning framework for outsourcing data center based on virtual appliances, *Cluster Computing*, **11**(3):229–245, 2008.

56. C. Hyser, B. McKee, R. Gardner, and J. Watson. Autonomic Virtual Machine Placement in the Data Center, Technical Report, HP Laboratories, February 2008.

57. L. Grit, D. Irwin, A. Yumerefendi, and J. Chase, Virtual machine hosting for networked clusters: Building the foundations for "autonomic" orchestration, in *Proceedings of the 2nd International Workshop on Virtualization Technology in Distributed Computing*, Washington, DC, IEEE Computer Society, 2006, p. 7.

58. C. Tang, M. Steinder, M. Spreitzer, and G. Pacifici, A scalable application placement controller for enterprise data centers, in *Proceedings of the 16th International World Wide Web Conference (WWW07)*, Bannf, Canada, 331–340, May 2007.

59. T. Kelly, Utility-directed allocation, in *Proceedings of the First Workshop on Algorithms and Architectures for Self-Managing Systems*, 2003.

60. H. W. Choi, H. Kwak, A. Sohn, and K. Chung. Autonomous learning for efficient resource utilization of dynamic VM migration, in *Proceedings of the 22nd Annual International Conference on Supercomputing*, New York, ACM, 2008, pp. 185–194.

61. S. Martello and P. Toth, *Knapsack Problems, Algorithms and Computer Implementations*, John Wiley & Sons, New York, 1990.

62. H. Kellerer, U. Pferschy, and D. Pisinger, *Knapsack Problems*, Springer, Berlin, 2004.

63. C. Chekuri and S. Khanna, A PTAS for the multiple knapsack problem, in *Proceedings of the Eleventh Annual ACM-SIAM Symposium on Discrete Algorithms*, 2000, pp. 213–222.

64. D. B. Shmoys and E. Tardos, An approximation algorithm for the generalized assignment problem, *Mathematical Programming*, **62**:461–474, 1993.

65. M. R. Garey and David S. Johnson, *Computers and Intractability: A Guide to the Theory of NP-Completeness*, W. H. Freeman, New York, 1979.

66. R. Gupta, S. K. Bose, S. Sundarrajan, M. Chebiyam, and A. Chakrabarti, A two stage heuristic algorithm for solving the server consolidation problem with item–item and bin–item incompatibility constraints, in *Proceedings of the 2008 IEEE International Conference on Services Computing*, Washington, DC, IEEE Computer Society, 2008, pp. 39–46.

67. E. Yu-Hsien Lin, A Bibliographical Survey On Some Well-Known Non-Standard Knapsack Problems, 1998.

68. A. Frèville, The multidimensional 0–1 knapsack problem: An overview. *European Journal of Operational Research*, **155**(1):1–21, 2004.

69. M. Ehrgott and X. Gandibleux, A survey and annotated bibliography of multi-objective combinatorial optimization, *OR Spectrum*, **22**(4):425–460, 2000.

70. D. Pisinger, Where are the hard knapsack problems? *Computers & Operations Research*, **32**(9):2271–2284, 2005.

71. J. Marques, F. Sauve, and A. Moura, Business-oriented capacity planning of IT infrastructure to handle load surges, in *Proceedings of The 10th IEEE/ IFIP Network Operations and Management Symposium (NOMS06)*, Vancouver, Canada, April 2006.

72. X. Zhu, D. Young, B. J. Watson, Z. Wang, J. Rolia, S. Singhal, B. McKee, C. Hyser, D. Gmach, R. Gardner, T. Christian, and L. Cherkasova, 1000 Islands: Integrated capacity and workload management for the next generation data center, in *Proceedings of The 5th IEEE International Autonomic Computing Conference (ICAC'08)*, Chicago. IL, June 2008, pp. 172–181.

CHAPTER 7

ENHANCING CLOUD COMPUTING ENVIRONMENTS USING A CLUSTER AS A SERVICE

MICHAEL BROCK and ANDRZEJ GOSCINSKI

7.1 INTRODUCTION

The emergence of cloud computing has caused a significant change in how IT infrastructures are provided to research and business organizations. Instead of paying for expensive hardware and incur excessive maintenance costs, it is now possible to rent the IT infrastructure of other organizations for a minimal fee.

While the existence of cloud computing is new, the elements used to create clouds have been around for some time. Cloud computing systems have been made possible through the use of large-scale clusters, service-oriented archi-tecture (SOA), Web services, and virtualization.

While the idea of offering resources via Web services is commonplace in cloud computing, little attention has been paid to the clients themselves—specifically, human operators. Despite that clouds host a variety of resources which in turn are accessible to a variety of clients, support for human users is minimal.

Proposed in this chapter is the Cluster as a Service (CaaS), a Web service for exposing via WSDL and for discovering and using clusters to run jobs.[1] Because the WSDL document is the most commonly exploited object of a Web service, the inclusion of state and other information in the WSDL document makes the

[1]Jobs contain programs, data and management scripts. A process is a program that is in execution. When clients use a cluster, they submit jobs and when the jobs which are run by clusters creating one or more processes.

Cloud Computing: Principles and Paradigms, Edited by Rajkumar Buyya, James Broberg and Andrzej Goscinski Copyright © 2011 John Wiley & Sons, Inc.

internal activity of the Web services publishable. This chapter offers a cloud higher layer abstraction and support for users. From the virtualization point of view the CaaS is an interface for clusters that makes their discovery, selection, and use easier.

The rest of this chapter is structured as follows. Section 7.2 discusses three well-known clouds. Section 7.3 gives a brief explanation of the dynamic attribute and Web service-based Resources Via Web Services (RVWS) framework [1, 2], which forms a basis of the CaaS. Section 7.4 presents the logical design of our CaaS solution. Section 7.5 presents a proof of concept where a cluster is published, found, and used. Section 7.6 provides a conclusion.

7.2 RELATED WORK

In this section, four major clouds are examined to learn what is offered to clients in terms of higher layer abstraction and support for users—in particular, service and resource publication, discovery, selection, and use. While the focus of this chapter is to simplify the exposure of clusters as Web services, it is important to learn what problems exist when attempting to expose any form of resource via a Web service.

Depending on what services and resources are offered, clouds belong to one of three basic cloud categories: Infrastructure as a Service (IaaS), Platform as a Service (PaaS), and Software as a Service (SaaS). IaaS clouds make basic computational resources (e.g., storage, servers) available as services over the Internet. PaaS clouds offer easy development and deployment for environments scalable applications. SaaS clouds allow complete end user applications to be deployed, managed, and delivered as a service usually through a browser over the Internet. SaaS clouds only support provider's applications on their infrastructure.

The well-known four clouds—EC2 [3], Azure [4], AppEngine [5], and Salesforce [16]—represent these three basic cloud categories well.

7.2.1 Amazon Elastic Compute Cloud (EC2)

An IaaS cloud, EC2 offers "elastic" access to hardware resources that EC2 clients use to create virtual servers. Inside the virtual servers, clients either host the applications they wish to run or host services of their own to access over the Internet. As demand for the services inside the virtual machine rises, it is possible to create a duplicate (instance) of the virtual machine and distribute the load across the instances.

The first problem with EC2 is its low level of abstraction. Tutorials [6–8] show that when using EC2, clients have to create a virtual machine, install software into it, upload the virtual machine to EC2, and then use a command line tool to start it. Even though EC2 has a set of pre-built virtual machines that

EC2 clients can use [9], it still falls on the clients to ensure that their own software is installed and then configured correctly.

It was only recently that Amazon announced new scalability features, specifically Auto-Scaling [10] and Elastic Load Balancing [10]. Before the announcement of these services, it fell to EC2 clients to either modify their services running on EC2 or install additional management software into their EC2 virtual servers. While the offering of Auto-Scaling and Elastic Load Balancing reduces the modification needed for services hosted on EC2, both services are difficult to use and require client involvement [11, 12]. In both cases, it is required of the EC2 client to have a reserve of virtual servers and then configure Auto-Scaling and Elastic Load Balancing to make use of the virtual servers based on demand.

Finally, EC2 does not provide any means for publishing services by other providers, nor does it provide the discovery and selection of services within EC2. An analysis of EC2 documentation [13] shows that network multicasting (a vital element to discovery) is not allowed, thus making discovery and selection of services within EC2 difficult. After services are hosted inside the virtual machines on EC2, clients are required to manually publish their services to a discovery service external to EC2.

7.2.2 Google App Engine

Google App Engine [5] is a PaaS cloud that provides a complete Web service environment: All required hardware, operating systems, and software are provided to clients. Thus, clients only have to focus on the installation or creation of their own services, while App Engine runs the services on Google's servers.

However, App Engine is very restricted in what language can be used to build services. At the time of writing, App Engine only supports the Java and Python programming languages. If one is not familiar with any of the supported programming languages, the App Engine client has to learn the language before building his or her own services. Furthermore, existing applications cannot simply be placed on App Engine: Only services written completely in Java and Python are supported.

Finally, App Engine does not contain any support to publish services created by other service providers, nor does it provide discovery and selection services. After creating and hosting their services, clients have to publish their services to discovery services external to App Engine. At the time of writing, an examination of the App Engine code pages [24] also found no matches when the keyword "discovery" was used as a search string.

7.2.3 Microsoft Windows Azure

Another PaaS cloud, Microsoft's Azure [4] allows clients to build services using developer libraries which make use of communication, computational, and storage services in Azure and then simply upload the completed services.

To ease service-based development, Azure also provides a discovery service within the cloud itself. Called the .NET Service Bus [14], services hosted in Azure are published once and are locatable even if they are frequently moved. When a service is created/started, it publishes itself to the Bus using a URI [15] and then awaits requests from clients.

While it is interesting that the service can move and still be accessible as long as the client uses the URI, how the client gets the URI is not addressed. Furthermore, it appears that no other information such as state or quality of service (QoS) can be published to the Bus, only the URI.

7.2.4 Salesforce

Salesforce [16] is a SaaS cloud that offers customer relations management (CRM) software as a service. Instead of maintaining hardware and software licenses, clients use the software hosted on Salesforce servers for a minimal fee. Clients of Salesforce use the software as though it is their own one and do not have to worry about software maintenance costs. This includes the provision of hardware, the installation, and all required software and the routine updates.

However, Salesforce is only applicable for clients who need existing software. Salesforce only offers CRM software and does not allow the hosting of custom services. So while it is the cloud with the greatest ease of use, Salesforce has the least flexibility.

7.2.5 Cloud Summary

While there is much promise with the four major clouds presented in this chapter, all have a problem when it comes to publishing a discovering required services and resources. Put simply, discovery is close to nonexistent and some clouds require significant involvement from their clients.

Of all the clouds examined, only Azure offers a discovery service. However, the discovery service in Azure only addresses static attributes. The .NET Service Bus only allows for the publication of unique identifiers.

Furthermore, current cloud providers assume that human users of clouds are experienced programmers. There is no consideration for clients that are specialists in other fields such as business analysis and engineering. Hence, when interface tools are provided, they are primitive and only usable by computing experts. Ease of use needs to be available to both experienced and novice computing users.

What is needed is an approach to provide higher layer abstraction and support for users through the provision of simple publication, discovery, selection, and use of resources. In this chapter, the resource focused on is a cluster. Clients should be able to easily place required files and executables on the cluster and get the results back without knowing any cluster specifics. We propose to exploit Web services to provide a higher level of abstraction and offer these services.

7.3 RVWS DESIGN

While Web services have simplified resource access and management, it is not possible to know if the resource(s) behind the Web service is (are) ready for requests. Clients need to exchange numerous messages with required Web services to learn the current activity of resources and thus face significant overhead loss if most of the Web services prove ineffective. Furthermore, even in ideal circumstances where all resources behind Web services are the best choice, clients still have to locate the services themselves. Finally, the Web services have to be stateful so that they are able to best reflect the current state of their resources.

This was the motivation for creating the RVWS framework. The novelty of RVWS is that it combines dynamic attributes, stateful Web services (aware of their past activity), stateful and dynamic WSDL documents [1], and brokering [17] into a single, effective, service-based framework. Regardless of clients accessing services directly or discovering them via a broker, clients of RVWS-based distributed systems spend less time learning of services.

7.3.1 Dynamic Attribute Exposure

There are two categories of dynamic attributes addressed in the RVWS framework: state and characteristic. State attributes cover the current activity of the service and its resources, thus indicating readiness. For example, a Web service that exposes a cluster (itself a complex resource) would most likely have a dynamic state attribute that indicates how many nodes in the cluster are busy and how many are idle.

Characteristic attributes cover the operational features of the service, the resources behind it, the quality of service (QoS), price and provider information. Again with the cluster Web service example, a possible characteristic is an array of support software within the cluster. This is important information as cluster clients need to know what software libraries exist on the cluster.

Figure 7.1 shows the steps on how to make Web services stateful and how the dynamic attributes of resources are presented to clients via the WSDL document.

To keep the stateful Web service current, a Connector [2] is used to detect changes in resources and then inform the Web service. The Connector has three logical modules: Detection, Decision, and Notification. The Detection module routinely queries the resource for attribute information (1−2). Any changes in the attributes are passed to the Decision module (3) that decides if the attribute change is large enough to warrant a notification. This prevents excessive communication with the Web service. Updated attributes are passed on to the Notification module (4), which informs the stateful Web service (5) that updates its internal state. When clients requests the stateful WSDL document (6), the Web service returns the WSDL document with the values of all attributes (7) at the request time.

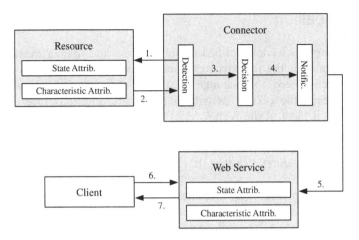

FIGURE 7.1. Exposing resource attributes.

7.3.2 Stateful WSDL Document Creation

When exposing the dynamic attributes of resources, the RVWS framework allows Web services to expose the dynamic attributes through the WSDL documents of Web services. The Web Service Description Language (WSDL) [18] governs a schema that describes a Web service and a document written in the schema. In this chapter, the term WSDL refers to the *stateless* WSDL document. Stateful WSDL document refers to the WSDL document created by RVWS Web services.

All information of service resources is kept in a new WSDL section called Resources. Figure 7.2 shows the structure of the Resources section with the rest of the WSDL document. For each resource behind the Web service, a ResourceInfo section exists.

Each ResourceInfo section has a resource-id attribute and two child sections: state and characteristic. All resources behind the Web service have unique identifiers. When the Connector learns of the resource for the first time, it publishes the resource to the Web service.

Both the state and characteristics elements contain several description elements, each with a name attribute and (if the provider wishes) one or more attributes of the service. Attributes in RVWS use the {name: op value} notations. An example attribute is {cost: <= $5}.

The state of a resource could be very complex and cannot be described in just one attribute. For example, variations in each node in the cluster all contribute significantly to the state of the cluster. Thus the state in RVWS is described via a collection of attributes, all making up the whole state.

The characteristics section describes near-static attributes of resources such as their limitations and data parameters. For example, the type of CPU on a node in a cluster is described in this section.

```
<definitions xmlns:wsdl="http://schemas.xmlsoap.org/wsdl/">
    <resources>
        <resource-info identifier="resourceID">
            <state>
                <description name="" attribute₁="value₁" …
                             attributeₙ="valueₙ">

                    …Other description Elements…
                </description>

                …Other description Elements…
            </state>

            <characteristics>
                <description name="" />

                …Other description Elements…
            </characteristics>
        </resource-info>

        …Other resource-info elements
    </resources>

    <types>...</types>

     message name="MethodSoapIn">...</message>
    <message name="MethodSoapOut">...</message>

    <portType name="CounterServiceSoap">...</portType>

    <binding name="CounterServiceSoap"
             type="tns:CounterServiceSoap">...</wsdl:binding>

    <wsdl:service name="CounterService">...</wsdl:service>
</wsdl:definitions>
```

FIGURE 7.2. New WSDL section.

7.3.3   Publication in RVWS

While the stateful WSDL document eliminates the overhead incurred from manually learning the attributes of the service and its resource(s), the issues behind discovering services are still unresolved.

To help ease the publication and discovery of required services with stateful WSDL documents, a Dynamic Broker was proposed (Figure 7.3) [17]. The goal of the Dynamic Broker is to provide an effective publication and discovery service based on service, resource, and provider dynamic attributes.

When publishing to the Broker (1), the provider sends attributes of the Web service to the Dynamic Broker. The dynamic attributes indicate the functionality, cost, QoS, and any other attributes the provider wishes to have published about the service. Furthermore, the provider is able to publish information about itself, such as the provider's contact details and reputation.

After publication (1), the Broker gets the stateful WSDL document from the Web service (2). After getting the stateful WSDL document, the Dynamic Broker extracts all resource dynamic attributes from the stateful WSDL documents and stores the resource attributes in the resources store.

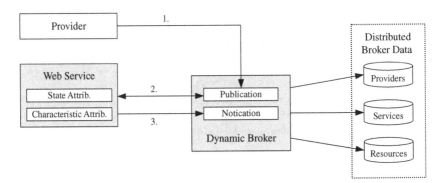

FIGURE 7.3. Publication.

The Dynamic Broker then stores the (stateless) WSDL document and service attributes from (1) in the service store. Finally, all attributes about the provider are placed in the providers store.

As the Web service changes, it is able to send a notification to the Broker (3) which then updates the relevant attribute in the relevant store. Had all information about each service been kept in a single stateful WSDL document, the dynamic broker would have spent a lot of time load, thereby editing and saving huge XML documents to the database.

7.3.4 Automatic Discovery and Selection

The automatic service discovery that takes into consideration dynamic attributes in their WSDL documents allows service (e.g., a cluster) discovery.

When discovering services, the client submits to the Dynamic Broker three groups of requirements (1 in Figure 7.4): service, resource, and provider. The Dynamic Broker compares each requirement group on the related data store (2). Then, after getting matches, the Broker applies filtering (3). As the client using the Broker could vary from human operators to other software units, the resulting matches have to be filtered to suit the client. Finally, the filtered results are returned to the client (4).

The automatic service selection that takes into consideration dynamic attributes in their WSDL documents allows for both a single service (e.g., a cluster) selection and an orchestration of services to satisfy workflow requirements (Figure 7.5).

The SLA (service-level agreement) reached by the client and cloud service provider specifies attributes of services that form the client's request or workflow. This is followed by the process of services' selection using Brokers. Thus, selection is carried out automatically and transparently. In a system comprising many clouds, the set of attributes is partitioned over many distributed service databases, for autonomy, scalability, and performance.

The automatic selection of services is performed to optimize a function reflecting client requirements. Time-critical and high-throughput tasks benefit by executing a computing intensive application on multiple clusters exposed as services of one or many clouds.

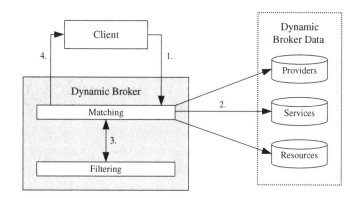

FIGURE 7.4. Matching parameters to attributes.

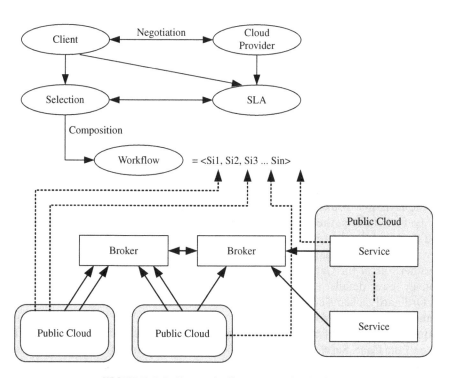

FIGURE 7.5. Dynamic discovery and selection.

The dynamic attribute information only relates to clients that are aware of them. Human clients know what the attributes are, owning to the section being clearly named. Software-client-designed pre-RVWS ignore the additional information as they follow the WSDL schema that we have not changed.

7.4   CLUSTER AS A SERVICE: THE LOGICAL DESIGN

Simplification of the use of clusters could only be achieved through higher layer abstraction that is proposed here to be implemented using the service-based Cluster as a Service (CaaS) Technology. The purpose of the CaaS Technology is to ease the publication, discovery, selection, and use of existing computational clusters.

7.4.1   CaaS Overview

The exposure of a cluster via a Web service is intricate and comprises several services running on top of a physical cluster. Figure 7.6 shows the complete CaaS technology.

A typical cluster is comprised of three elements: nodes, data storage, and middleware. The middleware virtualizes the cluster into a single system image; thus resources such as the CPU can be used without knowing the organization of the cluster. Of interest to this chapter are the components that manage the allocation of jobs to nodes (scheduler) and that monitor the activity of the cluster (monitor). As time progresses, the amount of free memory, disk space, and CPU usage of each cluster node changes. Information about how quickly the scheduler can take a job and start it on the cluster also is vital in choosing a cluster.

To make information about the cluster publishable, a Publisher Web service and Connector were created using the RVWS framework. The purpose of the publisher Web service was to expose the dynamic attributes of the cluster via the stateful WSDL document. Furthermore, the Publisher service is published to the Dynamic Broker so clients can easily discover the cluster.

To find clusters, the CaaS Service makes use of the Dynamic Broker. While the Broker is detailed in returning dynamic attributes of matching services, the results from the Dynamic Broker are too detailed for the CaaS Service. Thus another role of the CaaS Service is to "summarize" the result data so that they convey fewer details.

Ordinarily, clients could find required clusters but they still had to manually transfer their files, invoke the scheduler, and get the results back. All three tasks require knowledge of the cluster and are conducted using complex tools. The role of the CaaS Service is to (i) provide easy and intuitive file transfer tools so clients can upload jobs and download results and (ii) offer an easy to use interface for clients to monitor their jobs. The CaaS Service does this by

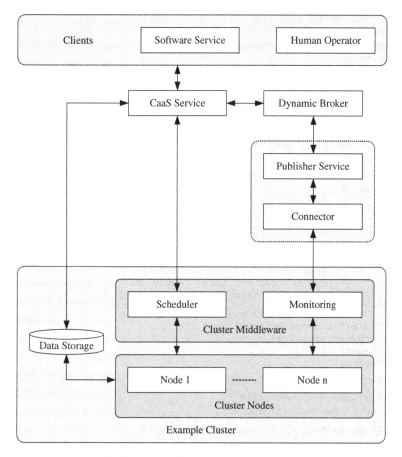

FIGURE 7.6. Complete CaaS system.

allowing clients to upload files as they would any Web page while carrying out the required data transfer to the cluster transparently.

Because clients to the cluster cannot know how the data storage is managed, the CaaS Service offers a simple transfer interface to clients while addressing the transfer specifics. Finally, the CaaS Service communicates with the cluster's scheduler, thus freeing the client from needing to know how the scheduler is invoked when submitting and monitoring jobs.

7.4.2 Cluster Stateful WSDL Document

As stated in Section 7.4.1, the purpose of the Publisher Web service is to expose the dynamic attributes of a cluster via a stateful WSDL document. Figure 7.7 shows the resources section to be added to the WSDL of the Publisher Web service.

Inside the state and characteristic elements, an XML element for each cluster node was created. The advantage of the XML structuring of our cluster

```
<definitions xmlns:wsdl="http://schemas.xmlsoap.org/wsdl/">
  <resources>
    <resource-info resource-identifier="resourceId">
      <state element-identifier="elementId">

        <cluster-state element-identifier="cluster-state-root">

          <cluster-node-name free-disk="" free-memory="" native-os-name=""
            native-os-version="" processes-count=""
            processes-running="" cpu-usage-percent=""
            element-identifier="stateElementId"
            memory-free-percent="" />

          ...Other Cluster Node State Elements...
        </cluster-state>
      </state>

      <characteristics element-identifier="characteristicElementId">

        <cluster-characteristics node-count=""
          element-identifier="cluster-characteristics-root">

          <cluster-node-name core-count="" core-speed="" core-speed-unit=""
            hardware-architecture="" total-disk="" total-memory=""
            total-disk-unit="" total-memory-unit=""
            element-identifier="characteristicElementId" />

          ...Other Cluster Node Characteristic Elements...
        </cluster-characteristics>
      </characteristics>
    </resource-info>
  </resources>

  <types>...
  <message name="MethodSoapIn">...
  <message name="MethodSoapOut">...

  <portType name="CounterServiceSoap">...

  <binding name="CounterServiceSoap" ...>...

  <wsdl:service name="CounterService">...
</wsdl:definitions>
```

FIGURE 7.7. Cluster WSDL.

attributes means that comparing client requirements to resource attributes only requires using XPath queries.

For the CaaS Service to properly support the role of cluster discovery, detailed information about clusters and their nodes needs to be published to the WSDL of the cluster and subsequently to the Broker (Table 7.1).

7.4.3 CaaS Service Design

The CaaS service can be described as having four main tasks: cluster discovery and selection, result organization, job management, and file management. Based on these tasks, the CaaS Service has been designed using

TABLE 7.1. Cluster Attributes

Type	Attribute Name	Attribute Description	Source
Characteristics	core-count	Number of cores on a cluster node	Cluster node
	core-speed	Speed of each core	
	core-speed-unit	Unit for the core speed (e.g., gigahertz)	
	hardware-architecture	Hardware architecture of each cluster node (e.g., 32-bit Intel)	
	total-disk	Total amount of physical storage space	
	total-disk-unit	Storage amount unit (e.g., gigabytes)	
	total-memory	Total amount of physical memory	
	total-memory-unit	Memory amount measurement (e.g., gigabytes)	
	software-name	Name of an installed piece of software.	
	software-version	Version of a installed piece of software	
	software-architecture	Architecture of a installed piece of software	
	node-count	Total number of nodes in the cluster. Node count differs from core-count as each node in a cluster can have many cores.	Generated
State	free-disk	Amount of free disk space	Cluster node
	free-memory	Amount of free memory	
	os-name	Name of the installed operating system	
	os-version	Version of the running operating system	
	processes-count	Number of processes	
	processes-running	Number of processes running	
	cpu-usage-percent	Overall percent of CPU used. As this metric is for the node itself, this value becomes averaged over cluster core	Generated
	memory-free-percent	Amount of free memory on the cluster node	

intercommunicating modules. Each module in the CaaS Service encapsulates one of the tasks and is able to communicate with other modules to extend its functionality.

Figure 7.8 presents the modules with the CaaS Service and illustrates the dependencies between them. To improve the description, elements from Figure 7.6 have been included to show what other entities are used by the CaaS service.

The modules inside the CaaS Web service are only accessed through an interface. The use of the interface means the Web service can be updated over time without requiring clients to be updated nor modified.

Invoking an operation on the CaaS Service Interface (discovery, etc.) invokes operations on various modules. Thus, to best describe the role each module plays, the following sections outline the various tasks that the CaaS Service carries out.

Cluster Discovery. Before a client uses a cluster, a cluster must be discovered and selected first. Figure 7.9 shows the workflow on finding a required cluster. To start, clients submit cluster requirements in the form of attribute values to the CaaS Service Interface (1). The requirements range from the number of nodes in the cluster to the installed software (both operating systems and software APIs). The CaaS Service Interface invokes the Cluster Finder module (2) that communicates with the Dynamic Broker (3) and returns service matches (if any).

To address the detailed results from the Broker, the Cluster Finder module invokes the Results Organizer module (4) that takes the Broker results and returns an organized version that is returned to the client (5–6). The organized

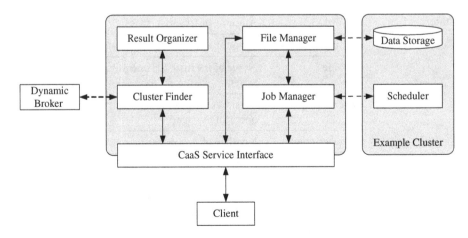

FIGURE 7.8. CaaS Service design.

results instruct the client what clusters satisfy the specified requirements. After reviewing the results, the client chooses a cluster.

Job Submission. After selecting a required cluster, all executables and data files have to be transferred to the cluster and the job submitted to the scheduler for execution. As clusters vary significantly in the software middleware used to create them, it can be difficult to place jobs on the cluster. To do so requires knowing how jobs are stored and how they are queued for execution on the cluster. Figure 7.10 shows how the CaaS Service simplifies the use of a cluster to the point where the client does not have to know about the underlying middleware.

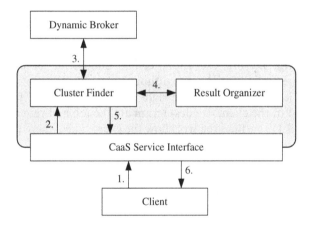

FIGURE 7.9. Cluster discovery.

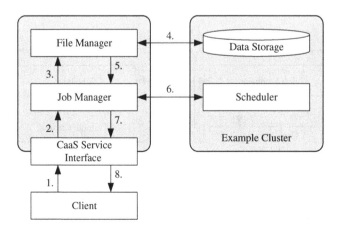

FIGURE 7.10. Job submission.

All required data, parameters, such as estimated runtime, are uploaded to the CaaS Service (1). Once the file upload is complete, the Job Manager is invoked (2). It resolves the transfer of all files to the cluster by invoking the File Manager (3) that makes a connection to the cluster storage and commences the transfer of all files (4).

Upon completion of the transfer (4), the outcome is reported back to the Job Manager (5). On failure, a report is sent and the client can decide on the appropriate action to take. If the file transfer was successful, the Job Manager invokes the scheduler on the cluster (6).

The same parameters the client gave to the CaaS Service Interface are submitted to the scheduler; the only difference being that the Job Manager also informs the scheduler where the job is kept so it can be started. If the outcome of the scheduler (6) is successful, the client is then informed (7–8). The outcome includes the response from the scheduler, the job identifier the scheduler gave to the job, and any other information the scheduler provides.

Job Monitoring. During execution, clients should be able to view the execution progress of their jobs. Even though the cluster is not the owned by the client, the job is. Thus, it is the right of the client to see how the job is progressing and (if the client decides) terminate the job and remove it from the cluster. Figure 7.11. outlines the workflow the client takes when querying about job execution.

First, the client contacts the CaaS service interface (1) that invokes the Job Manager module (2). No matter what the operation is (check, pause, or terminate), the Job Manager only has to communicate with the scheduler (3) and reports back a successful outcome to the client (4–5).

Result Collection. The final role of the CaaS Service is addressing jobs that have terminated or completed their execution successfully. In both

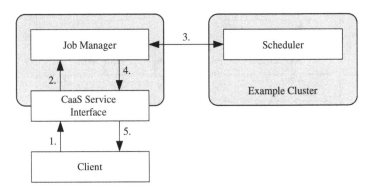

FIGURE 7.11. Job monitoring.

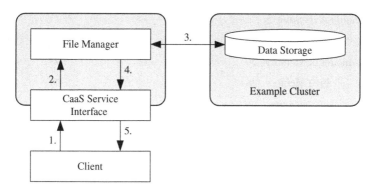

FIGURE 7.12. Job result collection.

cases, error or data files need to be transferred to the client. Figure 7.12 presents the workflow and CaaS Service modules used to retrieve error or result files from the cluster.

Clients start the error or result file transfer by contacting the CaaS Service Interface (1) that then invokes the File Manager (2) to retrieve the files from the cluster's data storage (3). If there is a transfer error, the File Manager attempts to resolve the issue first before informing the client. If the transfer of files (3) is successful, the files are returned to the CaaS Service Interface (4) and then the client (5). When returning the files, URL link or a FTP address is provided so the client can retrieve the files.

7.4.4 User Interface: CaaS Web Pages

The CaaS Service has to support *at least* two forms of client: software clients and human operator clients. Software clients could be other software applications or services and thus are able to communicate with the CaaS Service Interface directly.

For human operators to use the CaaS Service, a series of Web pages has been designed. Each page in the series covers a step in the process of discovering, selecting, and using a cluster. Figure 7.13 shows the Cluster Specification Web page where clients can start the discovery of a required cluster.

In Section A the client is able to specify attributes about the required cluster. Section B allows specifying any required software the cluster job needs. Afterwards, the attributes are then given to the CaaS service that performs a search for possible clusters and the results are displayed in a Select Cluster Web page (Figure 7.14).

Next, the client goes to the job specification page, Figure 7.15. Section A allows specifying the job. Section B allows the client to specify and upload all data files and job executables. If the job is complex, Section B also allows specifying a job script. Job scripts are script files that describe and manage

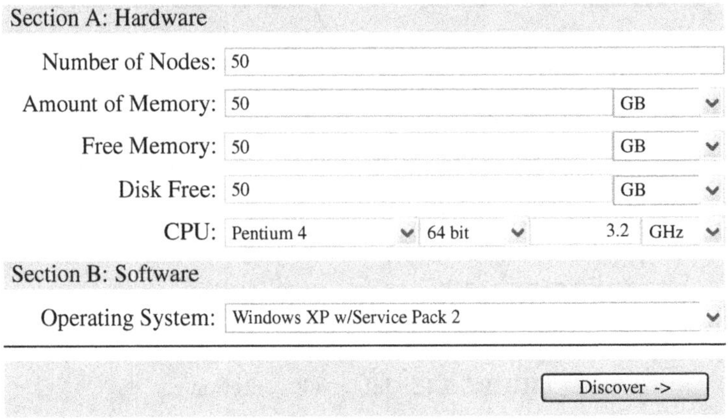

Section A: Hardware

Number of Nodes:	50
Amount of Memory:	50 — GB ⌄
Free Memory:	50 — GB ⌄
Disk Free:	50 — GB ⌄
CPU:	Pentium 4 ⌄ — 64 bit ⌄ — 3.2 GHz ⌄

Section B: Software

Operating System:	Windows XP w/Service Pack 2 ⌄

Discover ->

FIGURE 7.13. Web page for cluster specification.

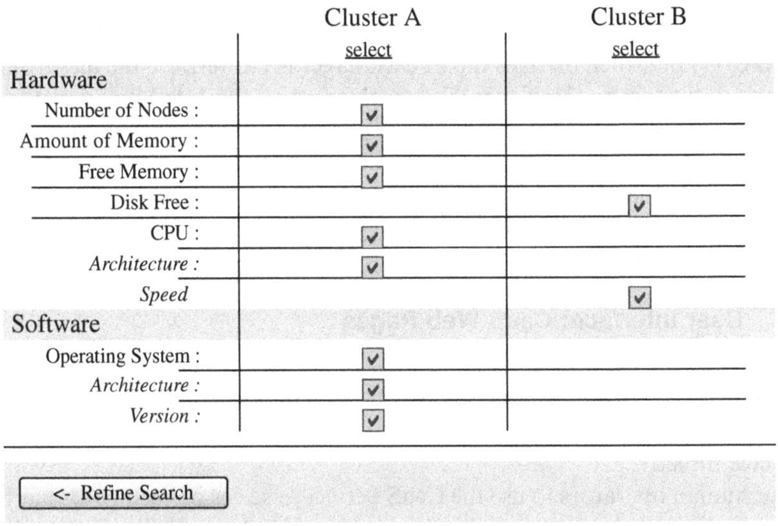

	Cluster A select	Cluster B select
Hardware		
Number of Nodes :	☑	
Amount of Memory :	☑	
Free Memory :	☑	
Disk Free :		☑
CPU :	☑	
Architecture :	☑	
Speed		☑
Software		
Operating System :	☑	
Architecture :	☑	
Version :	☑	

<- Refine Search

FIGURE 7.14. Web page for showing matching clusters.

various stages of a large cluster job. Section C allows specifying an estimated time the job would take to complete.

Afterword, the CaaS Service attempts to submit the job; the outcome is shown in the Job Monitoring page, Figure 7.16. Section A tells the client whether the job is submitted successfully. Section B offers commands to allow the client to take an appropriate action.

When the job is complete, the client is able to collect the results from the Collect Results page (Figure 7.17). Section A shows the outcome of the job.

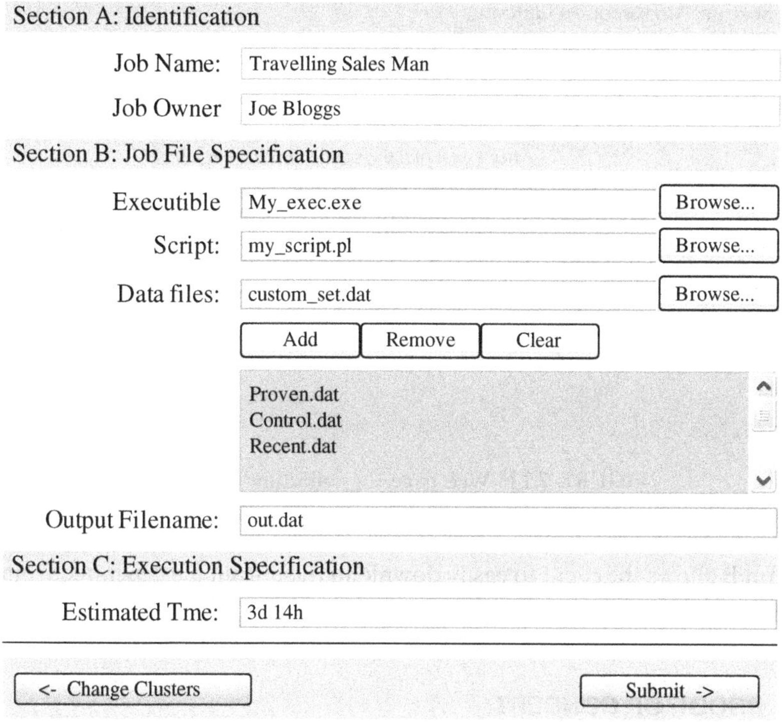

Section A: Identification

Job Name: Travelling Sales Man

Job Owner Joe Bloggs

Section B: Job File Specification

Executible My_exec.exe Browse...

Script: my_script.pl Browse...

Data files: custom_set.dat Browse...

Add Remove Clear

Proven.dat
Control.dat
Recent.dat

Output Filename: out.dat

Section C: Execution Specification

Estimated Tme: 3d 14h

<- Change Clusters Submit ->

FIGURE 7.15. Web page for job specification.

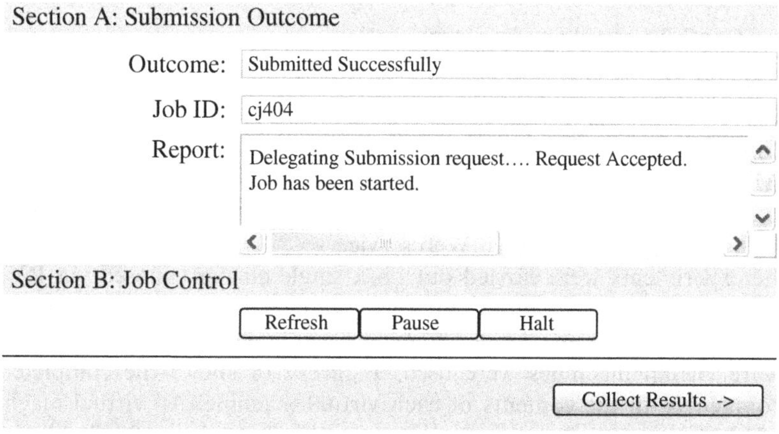

Section A: Submission Outcome

Outcome: Submitted Successfully

Job ID: cj404

Report: Delegating Submission request.... Request Accepted.
Job has been started.

Section B: Job Control

Refresh Pause Halt

Collect Results ->

FIGURE 7.16. Web page for monitoring job execution.

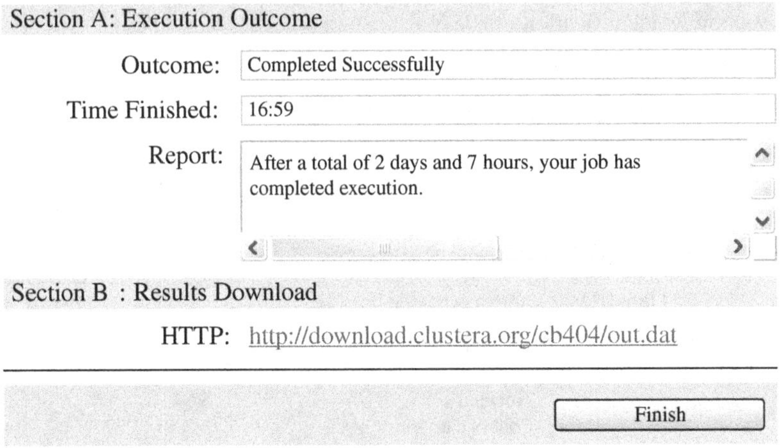

Section A: Execution Outcome

Outcome: | Completed Successfully |

Time Finished: | 16:59 |

Report: | After a total of 2 days and 7 hours, your job has completed execution. |

Section B : Results Download

HTTP: http://download.clustera.org/cb404/out.dat

[Finish]

FIGURE 7.17. Web page for collecting result files.

Section B allows the client to easily download the output file generated from the completed/aborted job via HTTP or using an FTP client.

7.5 PROOF OF CONCEPT

To demonstrate the RVWS framework and CaaS Technology, a proof of concept was performed where an existing cluster was published, discovered, selected, and used. It was expected that the existing cluster could be easily used all through a Web browser and without any knowledge of the underlying middleware.

7.5.1 CaaS Technology Implementation

The CaaS Service was implemented using Windows Communication Foundations (WCF) of .NET 3.5 that uses Web services. An open source library for building SSH clients in .NET (sharpSSH) [19] was used to build the Job and File Managers. Because schedulers are mostly command driven, the commands and outputs were wrapped into a Web service. Each module outlined in Section 7.4.3 is implemented as its own Web service.

The experiments were carried out on a single cluster exposed via RVWS; communication was carried out only through the CaaS Service. To manage all the services and databases needed to expose and use clusters via Web services, VMware virtual machines were used. Figure 7.18 shows the complete test environment with the contents of each virtual machine. All virtual machines have 512 MB of virtual memory and run the Windows Server 2003. All virtual machines run .NET 2.0; the CaaS virtual machine runs .NET 3.5.

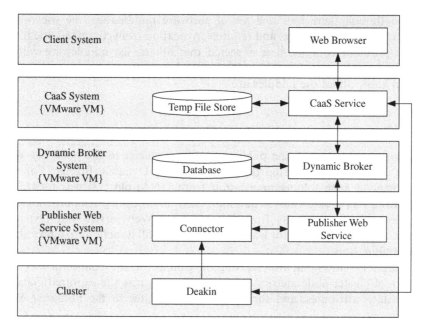

FIGURE 7.18. Complete CaaS environment.

The first virtual machine is the Publisher Web service system. It contains the Connector, Publisher Web service [17], and all required software libraries. The Dynamic Broker virtual machine contains the Broker and its database. The final virtual machine is the CaaS virtual machine; it has the CaaS Service and a temporary data store. To improve reliability, all file transfers between the cluster and the client are cached. The client system is an Asus Notebook with 2 gigabytes of memory and an Intel Centrino Duo processor, and it runs the Windows XP operating system.

7.5.2 Cluster Behind the CaaS

The cluster used in the proof of concept consists of 20 nodes plus two head nodes (one running Linux and the other running Windows). Each node in the cluster has two Intel Cloverton Quad Core CPUs running at 1.6 GHz, 8 gigabytes of memory, and 250 gigabytes of data storage, and all nodes are connected via gigabit Ethernet and Infiniband. The head nodes are the same except they have 1.2 terabytes of data storage.

In terms of middleware, the cluster was constructed using Sun GridEngine [20], OpenMPI [21], and Ganglia [22]. GridEngine provided a high level of abstraction where jobs were placed in a queue and then allocated to cluster nodes based on policies. OpenMPI provided a common distribute application API that hid the underlying communication system. Finally, Ganglia provided easy access to current cluster node usage metrics.

Even though there is a rich set of software middleware, the use of the middleware itself is complex and requires invocation from command line tools. In this proof of concept, it is expected that all the list middleware will be abstracted so clients only see the cluster as a large supercomputer and do not have to know about the middleware.

7.5.3 Experiments and Results

The first experiment was the publication of the cluster to the publisher Web service and easily discovering the cluster via the Dynamic Broker. For this experiment, a gene folding application from UNAFold [23] was used. The application was used because it had high CPU and memory demands. To keep consistency between results from the publisher Web service and Dynamic Broker, the cluster Connector was instructed to log all its actions to a text file to later examination.

Figure 7.19 shows that after starting the Connector, the Connector was able to learn of cluster node metrics from Ganglia, organize the captured Ganglia metrics into attributes, and forwarded the attributes to the Publisher Web service.

Figure 7.20 shows that the data from the Connector was also being presented in the stateful WSDL document. As the Connector was detecting slight changes in the cluster (created from the management services), the stateful WSDL of the cluster Web service was requested and the same information was found in the stateful WSDL document.

```
22/01/2009 1:51:52 PM-Connector[Update]:
    Passing 23 attribute updates to the web service...
* Updating west-03.eit.deakin.edu.au-state in
    free-memory to 7805776
* Updating west-03.eit.deakin.edu.au-state in
    ready-queue-last-five-minutes to 0.00
```

   Other attribute updates from various cluster nodes...
...

FIGURE 7.19. Connector output.

```
<rvwi:state rvwi:element-identifier= "resource-state">
  <cluster-state>
    <west-03.eit.deakin.edu.au free-memory="7805776" />
```

   ...Other Cluster Node Entries...
```
  </cluster-state>
```

   ...Rest of Stateful WSDL...

FIGURE 7.20. Updated WSDL element.

In the consistency stage, a computational and memory intense job was started on a randomly selected node and the stateful WSDL of the Publisher Web service requested to see if the correct cluster node was updated. The WSDL document indicated that node 20 was running the job (Figure 7.21). This was confirmed when the output file of the Connector was examined. As the cluster changed, both the Connector and the Publisher Web service were kept current.

After publication, the Dynamic Broker was used to discover the newly published Web service. A functional attribute of {main: = monitor} was specified for the discovery. Figure 7.22 shows the Dynamic Broker discovery results with the location of the Publisher Web service and its matching dynamic attribute.

At this point, all the cluster nodes were being shown because no requirements on the state nor the characteristics of the cluster were specified. The purpose of the selection stage of this experiment is intended to ensure that when given client attribute values, the Dynamic Broker only returned matching attribute.

For this stage, only loaded cluster nodes were required; thus a state attribute value of {cpu_usage_percent: > 10} was specified. Figure 7.23 shows the Dynamic Broker results only indicating node 20 as a loaded cluster node.

```
<west-20.eit.deakin.edu.au
    cpu-system-usage="1.5"
    cpu-usage-percent="16.8"
    free-memory="12104"
    memory-free-percent="0.001489594" />
```

FIGURE 7.21. Loaded cluster node element.

```
<ArrayOfServiceMatch>
  <ServiceMatch>
    <Url >http://einstein/rvws/rvwi_cluster /
    ClusterMonitorService.asmx</Url>

    <Wsdl>...Service Stateful WSDL...</Wsdl>

    <Metadata>
      <service-meta>
        <Functionalty main="monitor" />

        ...Other Provider Attributes...
      </service-meta>
    </Metadata>
  </ServiceMatch>
</ArrayOfServiceMatch>
```

FIGURE 7.22. Service match results from dynamic broker.

```
<west-20.eit.deakin.edu.au
     cpu-usage-percent="64.3" />
```

FIGURE 7.23. The only state element returned.

```
<west-03.eit.deakin.edu.au cpu-usage-percent="12.5" />
<west-20.eit.deakin.edu.au cpu-usage-percent="63" />
```

FIGURE 7.24. Cluster nodes returned from the broker.

The final test was to load yet another randomly selected cluster node. This time, the cluster node was to be discovered using only the Dynamic Broker and without looking at the Connector or the Publisher Web service. Once a job was placed on a randomly selected cluster node, the Dynamic Broker was queried with the same attribute values that generated Figure 7.23.

Figure 7.24 shows the Dynamic Broker results indicating node 3 as a loaded cluster node. Figure 7.25 shows an excerpt from the Connector text file that confirmed that node 3 had recently changed state.

Figure 7.26 shows the filled-in Web form from the browser. Figure 7.27 shows the outcome of our cluster discovery. This outcome is formatted like that shown in Figure 7.14. As the cluster was now being successfully published, it was possible to test the rest of the CaaS solution.

Figure 7.26 shows the filled in Web form from the browser. Figure 7.27 shows the outcome of our cluster discovery, formatted like that shown in Figure 7.14. Because only the Deakin cluster was present, that cluster was chosen to run our job. For our example job, we specified the script, data files, and a desired return file.

Figure 7.28 shows the complete form. For this proof of concept, the cluster job was simple: Run UNIX grep over a text file and return another text file with lines that match our required pattern. While small, all the functionality of the CaaS service is used: The script and data file had to be uploaded and then submitted, to the scheduler, and the result file had to be returned.

Once our job was specified, clicking the "Submit" button was expected to upload the files to the CaaS virtual machine and then transfer the files to the cluster. Once the page in Figure 7.29 was presented to us, we examined both the CaaS virtual machine and cluster data store. In both cases, we found our script and data file.

After seeing the output of the Job Monitoring page, we contacted the cluster and queried the scheduler to see if information on the page was correct. The job listed on the page was given the ID of 3888, and we found the same job listed as running with the scheduler.

One final test was seeing if the Job Monitoring Web page was able to check the state of our job and (if finished) allows us to collect our result file. We got confirmation that our job had completed, and we were able to proceed to the Results Collection page.

```
22/01/2009 2:00:58 PM-Connector[Update]:
    Passing 36 attribute updates to the web service...
* Updating west-03.eit.deakin.edu.au-state in
  cpu-usage-percent to 12.5
```

FIGURE 7.25. Text file entry from the connector.

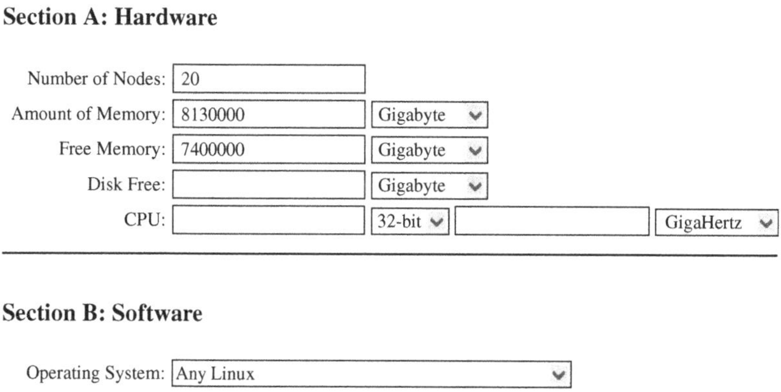

Section A: Hardware

Number of Nodes:	20	
Amount of Memory:	8130000	Gigabyte ⌄
Free Memory:	7400000	Gigabyte ⌄
Disk Free:		Gigabyte ⌄
CPU:		32-bit ⌄ GigaHertz ⌄

Section B: Software

Operating System: [Any Linux ⌄]

FIGURE 7.26. Cluster specification.

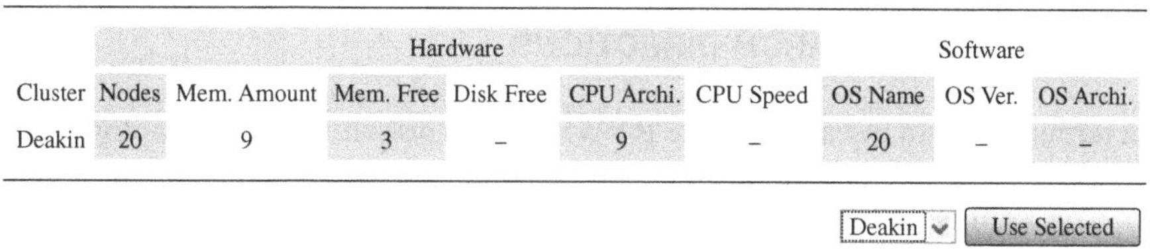

		Hardware					Software		
Cluster	Nodes	Mem. Amount	Mem. Free	Disk Free	CPU Archi.	CPU Speed	OS Name	OS Ver.	OS Archi.
Deakin	20	9	3	–	9	–	20	–	–

[Deakin ⌄] [Use Selected]

FIGURE 7.27. Cluster selection.

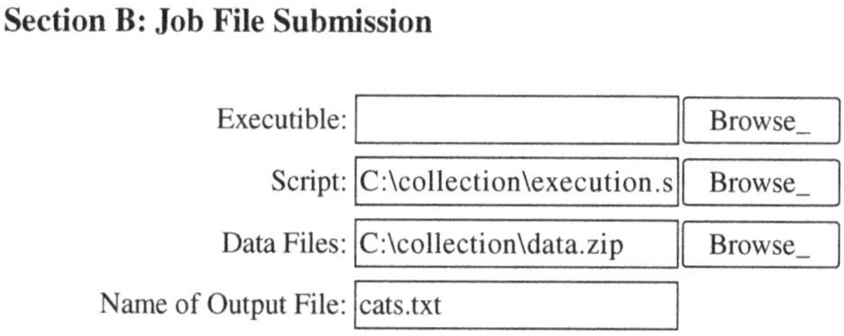

Section B: Job File Submission

Executible:		Browse_
Script:	C:\collection\execution.s	Browse_
Data Files:	C:\collection\data.zip	Browse_
Name of Output File:	cats.txt	

FIGURE 7.28. Job specification.

Section A: Submission Outcome

Outcome: Your job 38888 ("execution.sh") has been submitted

Job ID: 38888

Report:
```
26/05/2009 10:39:03 AM: You job is still running.
26/05/2009 10:39:55 AM: You job appears to have finished.
26/05/2009 10:39:55 AM: Please collect your result files.
```

FIGURE 7.29. Job monitoring.

Section B: Result File Download

HTTP: cats.txt

FTP:

FIGURE 7.30. Result collection.

The collection of result file(s) starts when the "Collect Results" button (shown in Figure 7.16) is clicked. It was expected that by this time the result file would have been copied to the CaaS virtual machine. Once the collection Web page was displayed (Figure 7.30), we checked the virtual machine and found our results file.

7.6   FUTURE RESEARCH DIRECTIONS

In terms of future research for the RVWS framework and CaaS technology, the fields of load management, security, and SLA negotiation are open. Load management is a priority because loaded clusters should be able to offload their jobs to other known clusters. In future work, we plan to expose another cluster using the same CaaS technology and evaluate its performance with two clusters.

At the time of writing, the Dynamic Broker within the RVWS framework considers all published services and resources to be public: There is no support for paid access or private services. In the future, the RVWS framework has to be enhanced so that service providers have greater control over how services are published and who accesses them.

SLA negotiation is also a field of interest. Currently, if the Dynamic Broker cannot find matching services and resources, the Dynamic Broker returns no results. To better support a service-based environment, the Dynamic Broker needs to be enhanced to allow it to delegate service attributes with service providers. For example, the Dynamic Broker needs to be enhanced to try and "barter" down the price of a possible service if it matches all other requirements.

7.7 CONCLUSION

While cloud computing has emerged as a new economical approach for sourcing organization IT infrastructures, cloud computing is still in its infancy and suffers from poor ease of use and a lack of service discovery. To improve the use of clouds, we proposed the RVWS framework to improve publication, discovery, selection, and use of cloud services and resources.

We have achieved the goal of this project by the development of a technology for building Cluster as a Service (CaaS) using the RVWS framework. Through the combination of dynamic attributes, Web service's WSDL and brokering, we successfully created a Web service that quickly and easily published, discovered, and selected a cluster and allowed us to specify a job and we execute it, and we finally got the result file back.

The easy publication, discovery, selection, and use of the cluster are significant outcomes because clusters are one of the most complex resources in computing. Because we were able to simplify the use of a cluster, it is possible to use the same approach to simplify any other form of resource from databases to complete hardware systems. Furthermore, our proposed solution provides a new higher level of abstraction for clouds that supports cloud users. No matter the background of the user, all users are able to access clouds in the same easy-to-use manner.

REFERENCES

1. M. Brock and A. Goscinski, State aware WSDL, in *Sixth Australasian Symposium on Grid Computing and e-Research (AusGrid 2008)*. Wollongong, Australia, 82, January 2008, pp. 35–44.

2. M. Brock and A. Goscinski, Publishing dynamic state changes of resources through state aware WSDL, in *International Conference on Web Services (ICWS)* 2008. Beijing, September 23–26, 2008, pp. 449–456.

3. Amazon, Amazon Elastic Compute Cloud. http://aws.amazon.com/ec2/, 1 August 2009.

4. Microsoft, Azure, http://www.microsoft.com/azure/default.mspx, 5 May 2009.

5. Google, App Engine. http://code.google.com/appengine/, 17 February 2009.

6. P. Chaganti, Cloud computing with Amazon Web services, Part 1: Introduction. Updated 15 March 2009, http://www.ibm.com/developerworks/library/ar-cloudaws1/.

7. P. Chaganti, Cloud computing with Amazon Web services, Part 2: Storage in the cloud with Amazon simple storage service (S3). Updated 15 March 2009, http://www.ibm.com/developerworks/library/ar-cloudaws2/.

8. P. Chaganti, Cloud computing with Amazon Web services, Part 3: Servers on demand with EC2. Updated 15 March 2009, http://www.ibm.com/developer-works/library/ar-cloudaws3/.

9. Amazon, Amazon Machine Images. http://developer.amazonwebservices.com/connect/kbcategory.jspa?categoryID = 171, 28 July 2009.

10. Amazon, Auto Scaling. http://aws.amazon.com/autoscaling/, 28 July 2009.

11. Amazon, Auto Scaling Developer Guide. Updated 15 May 2009, http://docs.amazonwebservices.com/AutoScaling/latest/DeveloperGuide/, 28 July 2009.

12. Amazon, Elastic Load Balancing Developer Guide. Updated 15 May 2009, http://docs.amazonwebservices.com/ElasticLoadBalancing/latest/DeveloperGuide/, 28 July 2009.

13. Amazon, Amazon EC2 Technical FAQ. http://developer.amazonwebservices.com/connect/entry.jspa?externalID=1145, 15 May 2009.

14. A. Skonnard, A Developer's Guide to the Microsoft .NET Service Bus. December 2008.

15. M. Mealling and R. Denenberg, Uniform resource identifiers (URIs), URLs, and uniform resource names (URNs): Clarifications and recommendations, http://tools.ietf.org/html/rfc3305, 28 June 2009.

16. Salesforce.com, CRM—salesforce.com, http://www.salesforce.com/.

17. M. Brock and A. Goscinski, Supporting service oriented computing with distributed brokering and dynamic WSDL, Computing Series, 8 December, 2008, Technical Report, C08/05, Deakin University. 2008.

18. World Wide Web Consortium, Web Services Description Language (WSDL) Version 2.0. Updated 23 May 2007, http://www.w3.org/TR/wsdl20-primer/, 21 June 2007.

19. T. Gal, sharpSSH—A secure shell (SSH) library for .NET. Updated 30 October 2005, http://www.codeproject.com/KB/IP/sharpssh.aspx, 1 March 2009.

20. Sun Microsystems, GridEngine, http://gridengine.sunsource.net/, 9 March 2009.

21. Indiana University, Open MPI: Open source high performance computing. Updated 14 July 2009, http://www.open-mpi.org/, 31 August 2009.

22. Ganglia, Ganglia. Updated 9 September 2008, http://ganglia.info/, 3 November 2008.

23. M. Zuker and N. R. Markham, UNAFold. Updated 18 January 2005, http://dinamelt.bioinfo.rpi.edu/unafold/, 1 April 2009.

24. Google, Developer's Guide—Google App Engine. http://code.google.com/appengine/docs/, 28 June 2009.

CHAPTER 8

SECURE DISTRIBUTED DATA STORAGE IN CLOUD COMPUTING

YU CHEN, WEI-SHINN KU, JUN FENG, PU LIU, and ZHOU SU

8.1 INTRODUCTION

Cloud computing has gained great attention from both industry and academia since 2007. With the goal of providing users more flexible services in a transparent manner, all services are allocated in a "cloud" that actually is a collection of devices and resources connected through the Internet. One of the core services provided by cloud computing is data storage. This poses new challenges in creating secure and reliable data storage and access facilities over remote service providers in the cloud. The security of data storage is one of the necessary tasks to be addressed before the blueprint for cloud computing is accepted.

In the past decades, data storage has been recognized as one of the main concerns of information technology. The benefits of network-based applications have led to the transition from server-attached storage to distributed storage. Based on the fact that data security is the foundation of information security, a great quantity of efforts has been made in the area of distributed storage security [1–3]. However, this research in cloud computing security is still in its infancy [4].

One consideration is that the unique issues associated with cloud computing security have not been recognized. Some researchers think that cloud computing security will not be much different from existing security practices and that the security aspects can be well-managed using existing techniques such as digital signatures, encryption, firewalls, and/or the isolation of virtual environments, and so on [4]. For example, SSL (Secure Sockets Layer) is a protocol that provides reliable secure communications on the Internet for things such as Web browsing, e-mail, instant messaging, and other data transfers.

Cloud Computing: Principles and Paradigms, Edited by Rajkumar Buyya, James Broberg and Andrzej Goscinski   Copyright © 2011 John Wiley & Sons, Inc.

Another consideration is that the specific security requirements for cloud computing have not been well-defined within the community. Cloud security is an important area of research. Many consultants and security agencies have issued warnings on the security threats in the cloud computing model [5]. Besides, potential users still wonder whether the cloud is secure. There are at least two concerns when using the cloud. One concern is that the users do not want to reveal their data to the cloud service provider. For example, the data could be sensitive information like medical records. Another concern is that the users are unsure about the integrity of the data they receive from the cloud. Therefore, within the cloud, more than conventional security mechanisms will be required for data security.

This chapter presents the recent research progress and some results of secure distributed data storage in cloud computing. The rest of this chapter is organized as follows. Section 8.2 indicates the results of the migration from traditional distributed data storage to the cloud-computing-based data storage platform. Aside from discussing the advantages of the new technology, we also illustrate a new vulnerability through analyzing three current commercial cloud service platforms. Section 8.3 presents technologies for data security in cloud computing from four different perspectives:

8.3.1 Database Outsourcing and Query Integrity Assurance

8.3.2 Data Integrity in Untrustworthy Storage

8.3.3 Web-Application-Based Security

8.3.4 Multimedia Data Security Storage

Section 8.4 discusses some open questions and existing challenges in this area and outlines the potential directions for further research. Section 8.5 wraps up this chapter with a brief summary.

8.2 CLOUD STORAGE: FROM LANs TO WANs

Cloud computing has been viewed as the future of the IT industry. It will be a revolutionary change in computing services. Users will be allowed to purchase CPU cycles, memory utilities, and information storage services conveniently just like how we pay our monthly water and electricity bills. However, this image will not become realistic until some challenges have been addressed. In this section, we will briefly introduce the major difference brought by distributed data storage in cloud computing environment. Then, vulnerabilities in today's cloud computing platforms are analyzed and illustrated.

8.2.1 Moving From LANs to WANs

Most designs of distributed storage take the form of either storage area networks (SANs) or network-attached storage (NAS) on the LAN level, such as the networks of an enterprise, a campus, or an organization. SANs are constructed on top of block-addressed storage units connected through dedicated high-speed networks. In contrast, NAS is implemented by attaching specialized file servers to a TCP/IP network and providing a file-based interface to client machine [6]. For SANs and NAS, the distributed storage nodes are managed by the same authority. The system administrator has control over each node, and essentially the security level of data is under control. The reliability of such systems is often achieved by redundancy, and the storage security is highly dependent on the security of the system against the attacks and intrusion from outsiders. The confidentiality and integrity of data are mostly achieved using robust cryptographic schemes.

However, such a security system would not be robust enough to secure the data in distributed storage applications at the level of wide area networks, specifically in the cloud computing environment. The recent progress of network technology enables global-scale collaboration over heterogeneous networks under different authorities. For instance, in a peer-to-peer (P2P) file sharing environment, or the distributed storage in a cloud computing environment, the specific data storage strategy is transparent to the user [3]. Furthermore, there is no approach to guarantee that the data host nodes are under robust security protection. In addition, the activity of the medium owner is not controllable to the data owner. Theoretically speaking, an attacker can do whatever she wants to the data stored in a storage node once the node is compromised. Therefore, the confidentiality and the integrity of the data would be violated when an adversary controls a node or the node administrator becomes malicious.

8.2.2 Existing Commercial Cloud Services

As shown in Figure 8.1, data storage services on the platform of cloud computing are fundamentally provided by applications/software based on the Internet. Although the definition of cloud computing is not clear yet, several pioneer commercial implementations have been constructed and opened to the public, such as Amazon's Computer Cloud AWS (Amazon Web service) [7], the Microsoft Azure Service Platform [8], and the Google App Engine (GAE) [9].

In normal network-based applications, user authentication, data confidentiality, and data integrity can be solved through IPSec proxy using encryption and digital signature. The key exchanging issues can be solved by SSL proxy. These methods have been applied to today's cloud computing to secure the data on the cloud and also secure the communication of data to and from the cloud. The service providers claim that their services are secure. This section describes three secure methods used in three commercial cloud services and discusses their vulnerabilities.

Amazon's Web Service. Amazon provides Infrastructure as a Service (IaaS) with different terms, such as Elastic Compute Cloud (EC2), SimpleDB, Simple

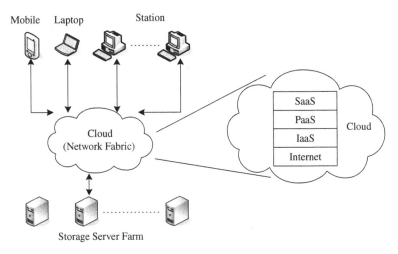

FIGURE 8.1. Illustration of cloud computing principle.

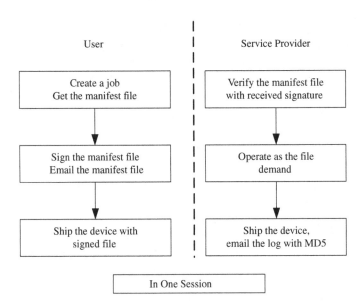

FIGURE 8.2. AWS data processing procedure.

Storage Service (S3), and so on. They are supposed to ensure the confidentiality, integrity, and availability of the customers' applications and data. Figure 8.2 presents one of the data processing methods adopted in Amazon's AWS [7], which is used to transfer large amounts of data between the AWS cloud and portable storage devices.

When the user wants to upload the data, he/she stores some parameters such as AccessKeyID, DeviceID, Destination, and so on, into an import metadata file called the *manifest file* and then signs the manifest file and e-mails the signed manifest file to Amazon. Another metadata file named the *signature file* is used by AWS to describe the cipher algorithm that is adopted to encrypt the job ID and the bytes in the manifest file. The signature file can uniquely identify and authenticate the user request. The signature file is attached with the storage device, which is shipped to Amazon for efficiency. On receiving the storage device and the signature file, the service provider will validate the signature in the device with the manifest file sent through the email. Then, Amazon will e-mail management information back to the user including the number of bytes saved, the MD5 of the bytes, the status of the load, and the location on the Amazon S3 of the AWS Import−Export Log. This log contains details about the data files that have been uploaded, including the key names, number of bytes, and MD5 checksum values.

The downloading process is similar to the uploading process. The user creates a manifest and signature file, e-mails the manifest file, and ships the storage device attached with signature file. When Amazon receives these two files, it will validate the two files, copy the data into the storage device, ship it back, and e-mail to the user with the status including the MD5 checksum of the data. Amazon claims that the maximum security is obtained via SSL endpoints.

Microsoft Windows Azure. The Windows Azure Platform (Azure) is an Internet-scale cloud services platform hosted in Microsoft data centers, which provides an operating system and a set of developer services that can be used individually or together [8]. The platform also provides scalable storage service. There are three basic data items: blobs (up to 50 GB), tables, and queues (<8k). In the Azure Storage, based on the blob, table, and queue structures, Microsoft promises to achieve confidentiality of the users' data. The procedure shown in Figure 8.3 provides security for data accessing to ensure that the data will not be lost.

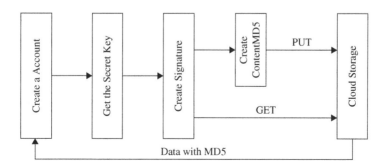

FIGURE 8.3. Security data access procedure.

PUT http://jerry.blob.core.windows.net/movie/mov.avi

?comp=block &blockid=BlockId1 &timeout=30

HTTP/1.1 Content-Length: 2174344

Content-MD5: FJXZLUNMuI/KZ5KDcJPcOA==

Authorization:SharedKeyjerry:F5a+dUDvef+PfMb4T8Rc2jHcwfK58KecSZY+l2naIao=

x-ms-date: Sun, 13 Sept 2009 22:30:25 GMT

x-ms-version: 2009-04-14

GET http://jerry.blob.core.windows.net/movies/mov.avi

HTTP/1.1

Authorization:SharedKeyjerry:ZF3lJMtkOMi4y/nedSk5Vn74IU6/fRMwiPsL+uYSDjY=

x-ms-date: Sun, 13 Sept 2009 22:40:34 GMT

x-ms-version: 2009-04-14

FIGURE 8.4. Example of a REST request.

To use Windows Azure Storage service, a user needs to create a storage account, which can be obtained from the Windows Azure portal web interface. After creating an account, the user will receive a 256-bit secret key. Each time when the user wants to send the data to or fetch the data from the cloud, the user has to use his secret key to create a HMAC SHA256 signature for each individual request for identification. Then the user uses his signature to authenticate request at server. The signature is passed with each request to authenticate the user requests by verifying the HMAC signature.

The example in Figure 8.4 is a REST request for a PUT/GET block operation [10]. Content-MD5 checksums can be provided to guard against network transfer errors and data integrity. The Content-MD5 checksum in the PUT is the MD5 checksum of the data block in the request. The MD5 checksum is checked on the server. If it does not match, an error is returned. The content length specifies the size of the data block contents. There is also an authorization header inside the HTTP request header as shown above in Figure 8.4.

At the same time, if the Content-MD5 request header was set when the blob has been uploaded, it will be returned in the response header. Therefore, the user can check for message content integrity. Additionally, the secure HTTP connection is used for true data integrity [7].

Google App Engine (GAE). The Google App Engine (GAE) [9] provides a powerful distributed data storage service that features a query engine and transactions. An independent third-party auditor, who claims that GAE can be secure under the SAS70 auditing industry standard, issued Google Apps an unqualified SAS70 Type II certification. However, from its on-line storage

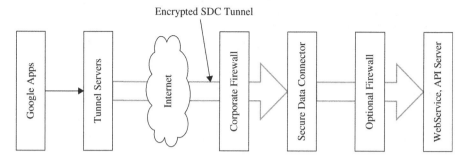

FIGURE 8.5. Illustration of Google SDC working flow.

technical document of lower API [9], there are only some functions such as GET and PUT. There is no content addressing the issues of securing storage services. The security of data storage is assumed guaranteed using techniques such as by SSL link, based on our knowledge of security method adopted by other services.

Figure 8.5 is one of the secure services, called Google Secure Data Connector (SDC), based on GAE [9]. The SDC constructs an encrypted connection between the data source and Google Apps. As long as the data source is in the Google Apps domain to the Google tunnel protocol servers, when the user wants to get the data, he/she will first send an authorized data requests to Google Apps, which forwards the request to the tunnel server. The tunnel servers validate the request identity. If the identity is valid, the tunnel protocol allows the SDC to set up a connection, authenticate, and encrypt the data that flows across the Internet. At the same time, the SDC uses resource rules to validate whether a user is authorized to access a specified resource. When the request is valid, the SDC performs a network request. The server validates the signed request, checks the credentials, and returns the data if the user is authorized.

The SDC and tunnel server are like the proxy to encrypt connectivity between Google Apps and the internal network. Moreover, for more security, the SDC uses signed requests to add authentication information to requests that are made through the SDC. In the signed request, the user has to submit identification information including the owner_id, viewer_id, instance_id, app_id, public_key, consumer_key, nonce, token, and signature within the request [9] to ensure the integrity, security, and privacy of the request.

8.2.3 Vulnerabilities in Current Cloud Services

Previous subsections describe three different commercial cloud computing secure data storage schemes. Storage services that accept a large amount of data (>1 TB) normally adopt strategies that help make the shipment more convenient, just as the Amazon AWS does. In contrast, services that only accept a smaller data amount (≤ 50 GB) allow the data to be uploaded or downloaded via the Internet, just as the Azure Storage Service does. To provide data integrity, the Azure Storage Service stores the uploaded data MD5 checksum in the database and returns it to the user when the user wants to retrieve the data. Amazon AWS computes the data MD5 checksum and e-mails it to the user for integrity checking. The SDC is based on GAE's attempt to strengthen Internet authentication using a signed request. If these services are grouped together, the following scheme can be derived.

As shown in Figure 8.6, when user_1 stores data in the cloud, she can ship or send the data to the service provider with MD5_1. If the data are transferred through the Internet, a signed request could be used to ensure the privacy, security, and integrity of the data. When the service provider receives the data and the MD5 checksum, it stores the data with the corresponding checksum (MD5_1). When the service provider gets a verified request to retrieve the data from another user or the original user, it will send/ship the data with a MD5 checksum to the user. On the Azure platform, the original checksum MD5_1will be sent, in contrast, a re-computed checksum MD5_2 is sent on Amazon's AWS.

The procedure is secure for each individual session. The integrity of the data during the transmission can be guaranteed by the SSL protocol applied. However, from the perspective of cloud storage services, data integrity depends on the security of operations while in storage in addition to the security of the uploading and downloading sessions. The uploading session can only ensure that the data received by the cloud storage is the data that the user uploaded; the downloading session can guarantee the data that the user retrieved is the data cloud storage recorded. Unfortunately, this procedure applied on cloud storage services cannot guarantee data integrity.

To illustrate this, let's consider the following two scenarios. First, assume that Alice, a company CFO, stores the company financial data at a cloud storage service provided by Eve. And then Bob, the company administration chairman, downloads the data from the cloud. There are three important concerns in this simple procedure:

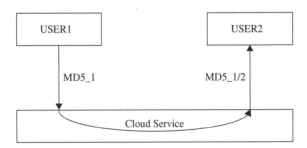

FIGURE 8.6. Illustration of potential integrity problem.

1. Confidentiality. Eve is considered as an untrustworthy third party, Alice and Bob do not want reveal the data to Eve.
2. Integrity. As the administrator of the storage service, Eve has the capability to play with the data in hand. How can Bob be confident that the data he fetched from Eve are the same as what was sent by Alice? Are there any measures to guarantee that the data have not been tampered by Eve?
3. Repudiation. If Bob finds that the data have been tampered with, is there any evidence for him to demonstrate that it is Eve who should be responsible for the fault? Similarly, Eve also needs certain evidence to prove her innocence.

Recently, a potential customer asked a question on a cloud mailing-group regarding data integrity and service reliability. The reply from the developer was "*We won't lose your data—we have a robust backup and recovery strategy — but we're not responsible for you losing your own data…*" [11]. Obviously, it is not persuasive to the potential customer to be confident with the service.

The repudiation issue opens a door for potentially blackmailers when the user is malicious. Let's assume that Alice wants to blackmail Eve. Eve is a cloud storage service provider who claims that data integrity is one of their key features. For that purpose, Alice stored some data in the cloud, and later she downloaded the data. Then, she reported that her data were incorrect and that it is the fault of the storage provider. Alice claims compensation for her so-called loss. How can the service provider demonstrate her innocence?

Confidentiality can be achieved by adopting robust encryption schemes. However, the integrity and repudiation issues are not handled well on the current cloud service platform. One-way SSL session only guarantees one-way integrity. One critical link is missing between the uploading and downloading sessions: There is no mechanism for the user or service provider to check whether the record has been modified in the cloud storage. This vulnerability leads to the following questions:

- **Upload-to-Download Integrity.** Since the integrity in uploading and downloading phase are handled separately, how can the user or provider know the data retrieved from the cloud is the same data that the user uploaded previously?
- **Repudiation Between Users and Service Providers.** When data errors happen without transmission errors in the uploading and downloading sessions, how can the user and service provider prove their innocence?

8.2.4 Bridge the Missing Link

This section presents several simple ideas to bridge the missing link based on digital signatures and authentication coding schemes. According to whether there is a third authority certified (TAC) by the user and provider and whether the user and provider are using the secret key sharing technique (SKS), there are four solutions to bridge the missing link of data integrity between the uploading and downloading procedures. Actually, other digital signature technologies can be adopted to fix this vulnerability with different approaches.

Neither TAC nor SKS.

Uploading Session

1. *User*: Sends data to service provider with MD5 checksum and MD5 Signature by User (MSU).
2. *Service Provider*: Verifies the data with MD5 checksum, if it is valid, the service provider sends back the MD5 and MD5 Signature by Provider (MSP) to user.
3. MSU is stored at the user side, and MSP is stored at the service provider side.

Once the uploading operation finished, both sides agreed on the integrity of the uploaded data, and each side owns the MD5 checksum and MD5 signature generated by the opposite site.

Downloading Session

1. *User*: Sends request to service provider with authentication code.
2. *Service Provider*: Verifies the request identity, if it is valid, the service provider sends back the data with MD5 checksum and MD5 Signature by Provider (MSP) to user.
3. User verifies the data using the MD5 checksum.

When disputation happens, the user or the service provider can check the MD5 checksum and the signature of MD5 checksum generated by the opposite side to prove its innocence. However, there are some special cases that exist. When the service provider is trustworthy, only MSU is needed; when the user is trustworthy, only MSP is needed; if each of them trusts the other side, neither MSU nor MSP is needed. Actually, that is the current method adopted in cloud computing platforms. Essentially, this approach implies that when the identity is authenticated that trust is established.

With SKS but without TAC.

Uploading Session

1. *User*: Sends data to service provider with MD checksum 5.
2. *Service Provider*: Verifies the data with MD5 checksum, if it is valid, the service provider sends back the MD5 checksum.
3. The service provider and the user share the MD5 checksum with SKS.

Then, both sides agree on the integrity of the uploaded data, and they share the agreed MD5 checksum, which is used when disputation happens.

Downloading Session

1. *User*: Sends request to the service provider with authentication code.
2. *Service Provider*: Verifies the request identity, if it is valid, the service provider sends back the data with MD5 checksum.
3. User verifies the data through the MD5 checksum.

When disputation happens, the user or the service provider can take the shared MD5 together, recover it, and prove his/her innocence.

With TAC but without SKS.

Uploading Session

1. *User*: Sends data to the service provider along with MD5 checksum and MD5 Signature by User (MSU).
2. *Service Provider*: Verifies the data with MD5 checksum, if it is valid, the service provider sends back the MD5 checksum and MD5 Signature by Provider (MSP) to the user.
3. MSU and MSP are sent to TAC.

On finishing the uploading phase, both sides agree on the integrity of the uploaded data, and TAC owns their agreed MD5 signature.

Downloading Session

1. *User*: Sends request to the service provider with authentication code.
2. *Service Provider*: Verifies the request with identity, if it is valid, the service provider sends back the data with MD5 checksum.
3. User verifies the data through the MD5 checksum.

When disputation happens, the user or the service provider can prove his innocence by presenting the MSU and MSP stored at the TAC.

Similarly, there are some special cases. When the service provider is trustworthy, only the MSU is needed; when the user is trustworthy, only the MSP is needed; if each of them trusts the other, the TAC is not needed. Again, the last case is the method adopted in the current cloud computing platforms. When the identity is authenticated, trust is established.

With Both TAC and SKS.

Uploading Session

1. *User*: Sends data to the service provider with MD5 checksum.
2. *Service Provider*: verifies the data with MD5 checksum.

3. Both the user and the service provider send MD5 checksum to TAC.

4. TAC verifies the two MD5 checksum values. If they match, the TAC distributes MD5 to the user and the service provider by SKS.

Both sides agree on the integrity of the uploaded data and share the same MD5 checksum by SKS, and the TAC own their agreed MD5 signatures.

Downloading Session

1. *User*: Sends request to the service provider with authentication code.

2. *Service Provider*: Verifies the request identity, if it is valid, the service provider sends back the data with MD5 checksum.

3. User verifies the data through the MD5 checksum.

When disputation happens, the user or the service provider can prove their innocence by checking the shared MD5 checksum together. If the disputation cannot be resolved, they can seek further help from the TAC for the MD5 checksum.

Here are the special cases. When the service provider is trustworthy, only the user needs the MD5 checksum; when the user is trustworthy, only the service provider needs MD5 checksum; if both of them can be trusted, the TAC is not needed. This is the method used in the current cloud computing platform.

8.3 TECHNOLOGIES FOR DATA SECURITY IN CLOUD COMPUTING

This section presents several technologies for data security and privacy in cloud computing. Focusing on the unique issues of the cloud data storage platform, this section does not repeat the normal approaches that provide confidentiality, integrity, and availability in distributed data storage applications. Instead, we select to illustrate the unique requirements for cloud computing data security from a few different perspectives:

- *Database Outsourcing and Query Integrity Assurance.* Researchers have pointed out that storing data into and fetching data from devices and machines behind a cloud are essentially a novel form of database outsourcing. Section 8.3.1 introduces the technologies of Database Outsourcing and Query Integrity Assurance on the clouding computing platform.

- *Data Integrity in Untrustworthy Storage.* One of the main challenges that prevent end users from adopting cloud storage services is the fear of losing data or data corruption. It is critical to relieve the users' fear by providing technologies that enable users to check the integrity of their data. Section 8.3.2 presents two approaches that allow users to detect whether the data has been touched by unauthorized people.

- *Web-Application-Based Security.* Once the dataset is stored remotely, a Web browser is one of the most convenient approaches that end users can use to access their data on remote services. In the era of cloud computing, Web security plays a more important role than ever. Section 8.3.3 discusses the most important concerns in Web security and analyzes a couple of widely used attacks.
- *Multimedia Data Security.* With the development of high-speed network technologies and large bandwidth connections, more and more multimedia data are being stored and shared in cyber space. The security requirements for video, audio, pictures, or images are different from other applications. Section 8.3.4 introduces the requirements for multimedia data security in the cloud.

8.3.1 Database Outsourcing and Query Integrity Assurance

In recent years, database outsourcing has become an important component of cloud computing. Due to the rapid advancements in network technology, the cost of transmitting a terabyte of data over long distances has decreased significantly in the past decade. In addition, the total cost of data management is five to ten times higher than the initial acquisition costs. As a result, there is a growing interest in outsourcing database management tasks to third parties that can provide these tasks for a much lower cost due to the economy of scale. This new outsourcing model has the benefits of reducing the costs for running Database Management Systems (DBMS) independently and enabling enterprises to concentrate on their main businesses [12]. Figure 8.7 demonstrates the general architecture of a database outsourcing environment with clients. The database owner outsources its data management tasks, and clients send queries to the untrusted service provider. Let T denote the data to be outsourced. The data T are is preprocessed, encrypted, and stored at the service provider. For evaluating queries, a user rewrites a set of queries Q against T to queries against the encrypted database.

The outsourcing of databases to a third-party service provider was first introduced by Hacigümüs et al. [13]. Generally, there are two security concerns

FIGURE 8.7. The system architecture of database outsourcing.

in database outsourcing. These are data privacy and query integrity. The related research is outlined below.

Data Privacy Protection. Hacigümüs et al. [37] proposed a method to execute SQL queries over encrypted databases. Their strategy is to process as much of a query as possible by the service providers, without having to decrypt the data. Decryption and the remainder of the query processing are performed at the client side. Agrawal et al. [14] proposed an order-preserving encryption scheme for numeric values that allows any comparison operation to be directly applied on encrypted data. Their technique is able to handle updates, and new values can be added without requiring changes in the encryption of other values. Generally, existing methods enable direct execution of encrypted queries on encrypted datasets and allow users to ask identity queries over data of different encryptions. The ultimate goal of this research direction is to make queries in encrypted databases as efficient as possible while preventing adversaries from learning any useful knowledge about the data. However, researches in this field did not consider the problem of query integrity.

Query Integrity Assurance. In addition to data privacy, an important security concern in the database outsourcing paradigm is query integrity. Query integrity examines the trustworthiness of the hosting environment. When a client receives a query result from the service provider, it wants to be assured that the result is both correct and complete, where correct means that the result must originate in the owner's data and not has been tampered with, and complete means that the result includes all records satisfying the query. Devanbu et al. [15] authenticate data records using the Merkle hash tree [16], which is based on the idea of using a signature on the root of the Merkle hash tree to generate a proof of correctness. Mykletun et al. [17] studied and compared several signature methods that can be utilized in data authentication, and they identified the problem of completeness but did not provide a solution. Pang et al. [18] utilized an aggregated signature to sign each record with the information from neighboring records by assuming that all the records are sorted with a certain order. The method ensures the completeness of a selection query by checking the aggregated signature. But it has difficulties in handling multipoint selection query of which the result tuples occupy a noncontinuous region of the ordered sequence.

The work in Li et al. [19] utilizes Merkle hash tree-based methods to audit the completeness of query results, but since the Merkle hash tree also applies the signature of the root Merkle tree node, a similar difficulty exists. Besides, the network and CPU overhead on the client side can be prohibitively high for some types of queries. In some extreme cases, the overhead could be as high as processing these queries locally, which can undermine the benefits of database outsourcing. Sion [20] proposed a mechanism called the challenge token and uses it as a probabilistic proof that the server has executed the query over the entire database. It can handle arbitrary types of queries including joins and does not assume that the underlying data is ordered. However, the approach is not applied to the adversary model where an adversary can first compute the complete query result and then delete the tuples specifically corresponding to the challenge tokens [21]. Besides, all the aforementioned methods must modify the DBMS kernel in order to provide proof of integrity.

Recently, Wang et al. [22] proposed a solution named dual encryption to ensure query integrity without requiring the database engine to perform any special function beyond query processing. Dual encryption enables cross-examination of the outsourced data, which consist of (a) the original data stored under a certain encryption scheme and (b) another small percentage of the original data stored under a different encryption scheme. Users generate queries against the additional piece of data and analyze their results to obtain integrity assurance.

For auditing spatial queries, Yang et al [23] proposed the MR-tree, which is an authenticated data structure suitable for verifying queries executed on outsourced spatial databases. The authors also designed a caching technique to reduce the information sent to the client for verification purposes. Four spatial transformation mechanisms are presented in Yiu et al. [24] for protecting the privacy of outsourced private spatial data. The data owner selects transformation keys that are shared with trusted clients, and it is infeasible to reconstruct the exact original data points from the transformed points without the key. However, both aforementioned researches did not consider data privacy protection and query integrity auditing jointly in their design. The state-of-the-art technique that can ensure both privacy and integrity for outsourced spatial data is proposed in Ku et al. [12]. In particular, the solution first employs a one-way spatial transformation method based on Hilbert curves, which encrypts the spatial data before outsourcing and hence ensures its privacy. Next, by probabilistically replicating a portion of the data and encrypting it with a different encryption key, the authors devise a mechanism for the client to audit the trustworthiness of the query results.

8.3.2 Data Integrity in Untrustworthy Storage

While the transparent cloud provides flexible utility of network-based resources, the fear of loss of control on their data is one of the major concerns that prevent end users from migrating to cloud storage services. Actually it is a potential risk that the storage infrastructure providers become self-interested, untrustworthy, or even malicious. There are different motivations whereby a storage service provider could become untrustworthy—for instance, to cover the consequence of a mistake in operation, or deny the vulnerability in the system after the data have been stolen by an adversary. This section introduces two technologies to enable data owners to verify the data integrity while the files are stored in the remote untrustworthy storage services.

Actually, before the term "cloud computing" appears as an IT term, there are several remote data storage checking protocols that have been suggested [25], [26]. Later research has summarized that in practice a remote data possession checking protocol has to satisfy the following five requirements [27]. Note that the *verifier* could be either the data owner or a trusted third party, and the *prover* could be the storage service provider or storage medium owner or system administrator.

- *Requirement #1*. It should not be a pre-requirement that the verifier has to possess a complete copy of the data to be checked. And in practice, it does not make sense for a verifier to keep a duplicated copy of the content to be verified. As long as it serves the purpose well, storing a more concise contents digest of the data at the verifier should be enough.
- *Requirement #2*. The protocol has to be very robust considering the untrustworthy prover. A malicious prover is motivated to hide the violation of data integrity. The protocol should be robust enough that such a prover ought to fail in convincing the verifier.
- *Requirement #3*. The amount of information exchanged during the verification operation should not lead to high communication overhead.
- *Requirement #4*. The protocol should be computationally efficient.
- *Requirement #5*. It ought to be possible to run the verification an unlimited number of times.

A PDP-Based Integrity Checking Protocol. Ateniese et al. [28] proposed a protocol based on the provable data procession (PDP) technology, which allows users to obtain a probabilistic proof from the storage service providers. Such a proof will be used as evidence that their data have been stored there. One of the advantages of this protocol is that the proof could be generated by the storage service provider by accessing only a small portion of the whole dataset. At the same time, the amount of the metadata that end users are required to store is also small—that is, $O(1)$. Additionally, such a small amount data exchanging procedure lowers the overhead in the communication channels too.

Figure 8.8 presents the flowcharts of the protocol for provable data possession [28]. The data owner, the *client* in the figure, executes the protocol to verify that a dataset is stored in an outsourced storage machine as a collection of n blocks. Before uploading the data into the remote storage, the data owner pre-processes the dataset and a piece of metadata is generated. The metadata are stored at the data owner's side, and the dataset will be transmitted to the storage server. The cloud storage service stores the dataset and sends the data to the user in responding to queries from the data owner in the future.

As part of pre-processing procedure, the data owner (client) may conduct operations on the data such as expanding the data or generating additional metadata to be stored at the cloud server side. The data owner could execute the PDP protocol before the local copy is deleted to ensure that the uploaded copy has been stored at the server machines successfully. Actually, the data owner may encrypt a dataset before transferring them to the storage machines. During the time that data are stored in the cloud, the data owner can generate a

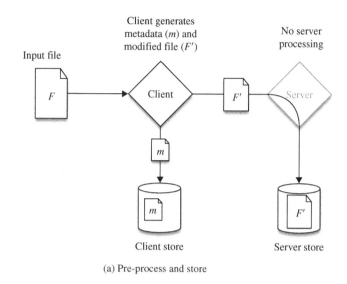

FIGURE 8.8. Protocol for provable data possession [28].

"challenge" and send it to the service provider to ensure that the storage server has stored the dataset. The data owner requests that the storage server generate a metadata based on the stored data and then send it back. Using the previously stored local metadata, the owner verifies the response.

On the behalf of the cloud service provider's side, the server may receive multiple challenges from different users at the same time. For the sake of availability, it is highly desired to minimize not only the computational overhead of each individual calculation, but also the number of data blocks to be accessed. In addition, considering the pressure on the communication networks, minimal bandwidth consumption also implies that there are a limited amount of metadata included in the response generated by the server. In the protocol shown in Figure 8.8, the PDP scheme only randomly accesses one subdata block when the sample the stored dataset [28]. Hence, the PDP scheme probabilistically guarantees the data integrity. It is mandatory to access the whole dataset if a deterministic guarantee is required by the user.

An Enhanced Data Possession Checking Protocol. Sebe et al. [27] pointed out that the above PDP-based protocol does not satisfy Requirement #2 with 100% probability. An enhanced protocol has been proposed based on the idea of the Diffie–Hellman scheme. It is claimed that this protocol satisfies all five requirements and is computationally more efficient than the PDP-based protocol [27]. The verification time has been shortened at the setup stage by taking advantage of the trade-offs between the computation times required by the prover and the storage required at the verifier. The setup stage sets the following parameters:

p and q : two primary factors chosen by the verifier;

$N = pq$: a public RSA modulus created by the verifier;

$\Phi(N) = (p-1)(q-1)$: the private key of the verifier, which is the secret only known by the verifier;

l: an integer that is chosen depending on the trade-offs between the computation time required at the prover and the storage required at the verifier;

t: a security parameter;

PRNG: a pseudorandom number generator, which generates t-bit integer values.

The protocol is presented as follows:
At first, the verifier generates the digest of data m:

1. Break the data m into n pieces, each is l-bit. Let $m_1, m_2, \ldots, m_n$ $(n = \lceil |m|/l \rceil)$ be the integer values corresponding to fragments of m.
2. For each fragment m_i, compute and store $M_i = m_i \bmod \Phi(N)$.

The challenge–response verification protocol is as follows:

1. The verifier
   1.1 generates a random seed S and a random element $\alpha \in Z_N \setminus \{1, N-1\}$ and
   1.2 sends the challenge (α, S) to the prover.

2. Upon receiving the challenge, the prover:
   2.1 generates n pseudorandom values $c_i \in [1,2^t]$, for $i = 1$ to n, using *PRNG* seeded by S,
   2.2 calculates $r = \sum_{i=1}^{n} c_i m_i$ and $R = \alpha^r \bmod N$, and
   2.3 sends R to the verifier.
3. The verifier:
   3.1 regenerates the n pseudorandom values $c_i \in [1,2^t]$, for $i = 1$ to n, using *PRNG* seeded by S,
   3.2 calculates $r' = \sum_{i=1}^{n} c_i m_i \bmod \Phi(N)$ and $R' = \alpha^{r'} \bmod N$, and
   3.3 checks whether $R = R'$.

Due to the space constraints, this section only introduces the basic principles and the working flows of the protocols for data integrity checking in untrustworthy storages. The proof of the correctness, security analysis, and the performance analysis of the protocols are left for the interested readers to explore deeper in the cited research papers [25, 26–28].

8.3.3 Web-Application-Based Security

In cloud computing environments, resources are provided as a service over the Internet in a dynamic, virtualized, and scalable way [29, 30]. Through cloud computing services, users access business applications on-line from a Web browser, while the software and data are stored on the servers. Therefore, in the era of cloud computing, Web security plays a more important role than ever. The Web site server is the first gate that guards the vast cloud resources. Since the cloud may operate continuously to process millions of dollars' worth of daily on-line transactions, the impact of any Web security vulnerability will be amplified at the level of the whole cloud.

Web attack techniques are often referred as the class of attack. When any Web security vulnerability is identified, attacker will employ those techniques to take advantage of the security vulnerability. The types of attack can be categorized in Authentication, Authorization, Client-Side Attacks, Command Execution, Information Disclosure, and Logical Attacks [31]. Due to the limited space, this section introduces each of them briefly. Interested readers are encouraged to explore for more detailed information from the materials cited.

Authentication. Authentication is the process of verifying a claim that a subject made to act on behalf of a given principal. Authentication attacks target a Web site's method of validating the identity of a user, service, or application, including Brute Force, Insufficient Authentication, and Weak Password Recovery Validation. Brute Force attack employs an automated process to guess a person's username and password by trial and error. In the Insufficient Authentication case, some sensitive content or functionality are protected by "hiding" the specific location in obscure string but still remains accessible directly through a specific URL. The attacker could discover those URLs through a Brute Force probing of files and directories. Many Web sites provide password recovery service. This service will automatically recover the user name or password to the user if she or he can answer some questions defined as part of the user registration process. If the recovery questions are either easily guessed or can be skipped, this Web site is considered to be Weak Password Recovery Validation.

Authorization. Authorization is used to verify if an authenticated subject can perform a certain operation. Authentication must precede authorization. For example, only certain users are allowed to access specific content or functionality.

Authorization attacks use various techniques to gain access to protected areas beyond their privileges. One typical authorization attack is caused by Insufficient Authorization. When a user is authenticated to a Web site, it does not necessarily mean that she should have access to certain content that has been granted arbitrarily. Insufficient authorization occurs when a Web site does not protect sensitive content or functionality with proper access control restrictions. Other authorization attacks are involved with session. Those attacks include Credential/Session Prediction, Insufficient Session Expiration, and Session Fixation.

In many Web sites, after a user successfully authenticates with the Web site for the first time, the Web site creates a session and generate a unique "session ID" to identify this session. This session ID is attached to subsequent requests to the Web site as "Proof" of the authenticated session.

Credential/Session Prediction attack deduces or guesses the unique value of a session to hijack or impersonate a user.

Insufficient Session Expiration occurs when an attacker is allowed to reuse old session credentials or session IDs for authorization. For example, in a shared computer, after a user accesses a Web site and then leaves, with Insufficient Session Expiration, an attacker can use the browser's back button to access Web pages previously accessed by the victim.

Session Fixation forces a user's session ID to an arbitrary value via Cross-Site Scripting or peppering the Web site with previously made HTTP requests. Once the victim logs in, the attacker uses the predefined session ID value to impersonate the victim's identity.

Client-Side Attacks. The Client-Side Attacks lure victims to click a link in a malicious Web page and then leverage the trust relationship expectations of the victim for the real Web site. In Content Spoofing, the malicious Web page can trick a user into typing user name and password and will then use this information to impersonate the user.

Cross-Site Scripting (XSS) launches attacker-supplied executable code in the victim's browser. The code is usually written in browser-supported scripting languages such as JavaScript, VBScript, ActiveX, Java, or Flash. Since the code will run within the security context of the hosting Web site, the code has the ability to read, modify, and transmit any sensitive data, such as cookies, accessible by the browser.

Cross-Site Request Forgery (CSRF) is a serve security attack to a vulnerable site that does not take the checking of CSRF for the HTTP/HTTPS request. Assuming that the attacker knows the URLs of the vulnerable site which are not protected by CSRF checking and the victim's browser stores credentials such as cookies of the vulnerable site, after luring the victim to click a link in a malicious Web page, the attacker can forge the victim's identity and access the vulnerable Web site on victim's behalf.

Command Execution. The Command Execution attacks exploit server-side vulnerabilities to execute remote commands on the Web site. Usually, users supply inputs to the Web-site to request services. If a Web application does not properly sanitize user-supplied input before using it within application code, an attacker could alter command execution on the server. For example, if the length of input is not checked before use, buffer overflow could happen and result in denial of service. Or if the Web application uses user input to construct statements such as SQL, XPath, C/C++ Format String, OS system command, LDAP, or dynamic HTML, an attacker may inject arbitrary executable code into the server if the user input is not properly filtered.

Information Disclosure. The Information Disclosure attacks acquire sensitive information about a web site revealed by developer comments, error messages, or well-know file name conventions. For example, a Web server may return a list of files within a requested directory if the default file is not present. This will supply an attacker with necessary information to launch further attacks against the system. Other types of Information Disclosure includes using special paths such as "." and ".." for Path Traversal, or uncovering hidden URLs via Predictable Resource Location.

Logical Attacks. Logical Attacks involve the exploitation of a Web application's logic flow. Usually, a user's action is completed in a multi-step process. The procedural workflow of the process is called application logic. A common Logical Attack is Denial of Service (DoS). DoS attacks will attempt to consume all available resources in the Web server such as CPU, memory, disk space, and so on, by abusing the functionality provided by the Web site. When any one of any system resource reaches some utilization threshold, the Web site will no long be responsive to normal users. DoS attacks are often caused by Insufficient Anti-automation where an attacker is permitted to automate a process repeatedly. An automated script could be executed thousands of times a minute, causing potential loss of performance or service.

8.3.4   Multimedia Data Security Storage

With the rapid developments of multimedia technologies, more and more multimedia contents are being stored and delivered over many kinds of devices, databases, and networks. Multimedia Data Security plays an important role in the data storage to protect multimedia data. Recently, how storage multimedia contents are delivered by both different providers and users has attracted much attentions and many applications. This section briefly goes through the most critical topics in this area.

Protection from Unauthorized Replication. Contents replication is required to generate and keep multiple copies of certain multimedia contents. For example, content distribution networks (CDNs) have been used to manage content distribution to large numbers of users, by keeping the replicas of the same contents on a group of geographically distributed surrogates [32, 33]. Although the replication can improve the system performance, the unauthorized replication causes some problems such as contents copyright, waste of replication cost, and extra control overheads.

Protection from Unauthorized Replacement. As the storage capacity is limited, a replacement process must be carried out when the capacity exceeds its limit. It means the situation that a currently stored content [34] must be removed from the storage space in order to make space for the new coming content. However, how to decide which content should be removed is very important. If an unauthorized replacement happens, the content which the user doesn't want to delete will be removed resulting in an accident of the data loss. Furthermore, if the important content such as system data is removed by unauthorized replacement, the result will be more serious.

Protection from Unauthorized Pre-fetching. The Pre-fetching is widely deployed in Multimedia Storage Network Systems between server databases and end users' storage disks [35]. That is to say, If a content can be predicted to be requested by the user in future requests, this content will be fetched from the server database to the end user before this user requests it, in order to decrease user response time. Although the Pre-fetching shows its efficiency, the unauthorized pre-fetching should be avoided to make the system to fetch the necessary content.

8.4   OPEN QUESTIONS AND CHALLENGES

Almost all the current commercial cloud service providers claim that their platforms are secure and robust. On one hand, they adopt robust cipher algorithms for confidentiality of stored data; on the other hand, they depend on network communication security protocols such as SSL, IPSec, or others to protect data in transmission in the network. For the service availability and high performance, they choose virtualization technologies and apply strong authentication and authorization schemes in their cloud domains. However, as a new infrastructure/platform leading to new application/service models of the future's IT industry, the requirement for a security cloud computing is different from the traditional security problems. As pointed out by Dr. K. M. Khan [4]:

> Encryption, digital signatures, network security, firewalls, and the isolation of virtual environments all are important for cloud computing security, but these alone won't make cloud computing reliable for consumers.

8.4.1   Concerns at Different Levels

The cloud computing environment consists of three levels of abstractions [4]:

1. *The cloud infrastructure providers*, which is at the back end, own and manage the network infrastructure and resources including hardware devices and system software.
2. *The cloud service providers*, which offer services such as on-demand computing, utility computing, data processing, software services, and platforms for developing application software.
3. *The cloud consumers*, which is at the front end of the cloud computing environment and consists of two major categories of users: (a) *application developers*, who take advantage of the hardware infrastructure and the software platforms to construct application software for ultimate end users; and (b) *end users*, who carry out their daily works using the on-demand computing, software services, and utility services.

Regarding data/information security, the users at different levels have variant expectations and concerns due to the roles they play in the data's life cycle.

From the perspective of cloud consumers, normally who are the data owners, the concerns are essentially raised from the loss of control when the data are in a cloud. As the dataset is stored in unknown third-party infrastructure, the owner loses not only the advantages of endpoint restrictions and management, but also the fine-grained credential quality control. The uncertainty about the privacy and the doubt about the vulnerability are also resulted from the disappearing physical and logical network boundaries [36].

The main security concerns of the end users include confidentiality, loss of control of data, and the undisclosed security profiles of the cloud service and infrastructure providers. The users' data are transmitted between the local machine and cloud service provider for variant operations, and they are also persistently stored in the cloud infrastructure provider's facilities. During this procedure, data might not be adequately protected while they are being moved within the systems or across multiple sites owned by these providers. The data owner also cannot check the security assurances before using the service from the cloud, because the actual security capabilities associated with the providers are transparent to the user/owner.

The problem becomes more complicated when the service and infrastructure providers are not the same, and this implies additional communication links in the chain. Involving a third party in the services also introduces an additional vector of attack. Actually, in practice there are more challenging scenarios. For instance, consider that multiple end users have different sets of security requirements while using the same service offered by an individual cloud service provider. To handle such kind of complexity, one single set of security provisions does not fit all in cloud computing. The scenarios also imply that the back-end infrastructure and/or service providers must be capable of supporting multiple levels requirements of security similar to those guaranteed by front-end service provider.

From the perspective of the cloud service providers, the main concern with regard to protecting users' data is the transfer of data from devices and servers within the control of the users to its own devices and subsequently to those of the cloud infrastructure, where the data is stored. The data are stored in cloud service provider's devices on multiple machines across the entire virtual layer. The data are also hosted on devices that belong to infrastructure provider. The cloud service provider needs to ensure users that the security of their data is being adequately addressed between the partners, that their virtual environments are isolated with sufficient protection, and that the cleanup of outdated images is being suitably managed at its site and cloud infrastructure provider's storage machines.

Undoubtedly, the cloud infrastructure providers' security concerns are not less than those of end users or cloud service providers. The infrastructure provider knows that a single point of failure in its infrastructure security mechanisms would allow hackers to take out thousands of data bytes owned by the clients, and most likely data owned by other enterprises. The cloud infrastructure providers need to ask the following questions:

- How are the data stored in its physical devices protected?
- How does the cloud infrastructure manage the backup of data, and the destruction of outdated data, at its site?
- How can the cloud infrastructure control access to its physical devices and the images stored on those devices?

8.4.2 Technical and Nontechnical Challenges

The above analysis has shown that besides technical challenges, the cloud computing platform (infrastructure and service) providers are also required to meet a couple of nontechnical issues—for example, the lack of legal requirements on data security to service providers [36]. More specifically, the following technical challenges need to be addressed in order to make cloud computing acceptable for common consumers:

- Open security profiling of services that is available to end users and verifiable automatically. Service providers need to disclose in detail the levels of specific security properties rather than providing blanket assurances of "secure" services.
- The cloud service/infrastructure providers are required to enable end users to remotely control their virtual working platforms in the cloud and monitor others' access to their data. This includes the capability of fine-grained accessing controls on their own data, no matter where the data files are stored and processed. In addition, it is ideal to possess the capability of restricting any unauthorized third parties from manipulating users' data, including the cloud service provider, as well as cloud infrastructure providers.
- Security compliance with existing standards could be useful to enhance cloud security. There must be consistency between the security requirements and/or policies of service consumers and the security assurances of cloud providers [4].
- It is mandatory for the providers to ensure that software is as secure as they claim. These assurances may include certification of the security of the systems in question. A certificate—issued after rigorous testing according to agreed criteria (e.g., ISO/IEC 15408)—can ensure the degree of reliability of software in different configurations and environments as claimed by the cloud providers.

Regarding the above technical issues, actually they have been and will be addressed by constant development of new technologies. However, some special efforts are needed to meet the nontechnical challenges. For instance, one of the most difficult issue to be solved in cloud computing is the users' fear of losing control over their data. Because end users feel that they do not clearly know where and how their data are handled, or when the users realize that their data are processed, transmitted, and stored by devices under the control of some strangers, it is reasonable for them to be concerned about things happening in the cloud. In traditional work environments, in order to keep a dataset secure, the operator just keeps it away from the threat. In cloud computing, however, it seems that datasets are moved closer to their threats; that is, they are transmitted to, stored in, and manipulated by remote devices controlled by third parties, not by the owner of the data set. It is recognized that this is partly a psychological issue; but until end users have enough information and insight that make them believe cloud computing security and its dynamics, the fear is unlikely to go away.

End-user license agreements (EULAs) and vendor privacy policies are not enough to solve this psychological issue. Service-level agreements (SLAs) need to specify the preferred security assurances of consumers in detail. Proper business models and risk assessments related to cloud computing security need to be defined. In this new security-sensitive design paradigm, the ability to change one's mind is crucial, because consumers are more security-aware than ever before. They not only make the service-consuming decision on cost and service, they also want to see real, credible security measures from cloud providers.

8.5 SUMMARY

In this chapter we have presented the state-of-the-art research progress and results of secure distributed data storage in cloud computing. Cloud computing has acquired considerable attention from both industry and academia in recent years. Among all the major building blocks of cloud computing, data storage plays a very important role. Currently, there are several challenges in implementing distributed storage in cloud computing environments. These challenges will need to be addressed before users can enjoy the full advantages of cloud computing. In addition, security is always a significant issue in any computing system. Consequently, we surveyed a number of topics related to the challenging issues of securing distributed data storage, including database outsourcing and query integrity assurance, data integrity in untrustworthy storage, Web-application-based security, and multimedia data security. It is anticipated that the technologies developed in the aforementioned research will contribute to paving the way for securing distributed data storage environments within cloud computing.

REFERENCES

1. J. A. Garay, R. Gennaro, C. Jutla, and T. Rabin, Secure distributed storage and retrieval, in *Proceedings of the 11th International workshop on Distributed Algorithms*, Saarbrucken, pp. 275–289 Germany, September 1997.

2. V. Kher and Y. Kim, Securing distributed storage: Challenges, techniques, and systems, in *Proceedings of the 2005 ACM Workshop on Storage Security and Survivability*, Fairfax, VA, November 11, 2005.

3. R. Ranjan, A. Harwood, and R. Buyya, Peer-to-peer-based resource discovery in global grids: A tutorial, *IEEE Communications Surveys & Tutorials*, **10**(2), 2008, pp. 6–33.

4. K. M. Khan, Security dynamics of cloud computing, *Cutter IT Journal*, June/July 2009, pp. 38–43.

5. J. Heiser and M. Nicolett, Assessing the Security Risks of Cloud Computing, Gartner Inc., June 2, 2008.

6. G. A. Gibson and R. V. Meter, Network attached storage architecture, *Communications of the ACM*, **43**(11): 37–45, 2000.

7. Amazon Import/Export Developer Guid", Version 1.2, http://aws.amazon.com/documentation/, August 2009.

8. Microsoft Azure Services Platform, http://www.microsoft.com/azure/default.mspx, 2009.

9. Google, What is Google App Engine?, http://code.google.com/appengine/docs/whatisgoogleappengine.html, September 2009.

10. Microsoft Azura MSDN API, http://msdn.microsoft.com/en-us/library/dd179394.aspx, 2009.

11. Google mail, http://groups.google.com/group/google-appengine/browse-thread/thread/782aea7f85ecbf98/8a9a505e8aaee07a?show_docid = 8a9a505e8aaee07a#

12. W.-S. Ku, L. Hu, C. Shahabi, and H. Wang, Query integrity assurance of location-based services accessing outsourced spatial databases, in *Proceedings of the International Symposium on Spatial and Temporal Databases* (SSTD), 2009, pp. 80–97.

13. H. Hacigümüs, S. Mehrotra, and B. R. Iyer, Providing database as a service, in *Proceedings of the IEEE International Conference on Data Engineering* (ICDE), 2002, p. 29.

14. R. Agrawal, J. Kiernan, R. Srikant, and Y. Xu, Order-preserving encryption for numeric data, in *Proceedings of the ACM International Conference on Management of Data* (SIGMOD), 2004, pp. 563–574.

15. P. T. Devanbu, M. Gertz, C. U. Martel, and S. G. Stubblebine, Authentic third-party data publication, in *Proceedings of the IFIP Working Conference on Data and Applications Security* (DBSec), 2000, pp. 101–112.

16. R. C. Merkle, A certified digital signature, in *Proceedings of the Annual International Cryptology Conference* (CRYPTO), 1989, pp. 218–238.

17. E. Mykletun, M. Narasimha, and G. Tsudik, Authentication and integrity in outsourced databases, in *Proceedings of the Network and Distributed System Security Symposium* (NDSS), 2004.

18. H.-H. Pang, A. Jain, K. Ramamritham, and K.-L. Tan, Verifying completeness of relational query results in data publishing, in *Proceedings of the ACM International Conference on Management of Data* (SIGMOD), 2005, pp. 407–418.

19. F. Li, M. Hadjieleftheriou, G. Kollios, and L. Reyzin, Dynamic authenticated index structures for outsourced databases, in *Proceedings of the ACM International Conference on Management of Data* (SIGMOD), 2006, pp. 121–132.

20. R. Sion, Query execution assurance for outsourced databases, in *Proceedings of the International Conference on Very Large Data Bases* (VLDB), 2005, pp. 601–612.

21. M. Xie, H. Wang, J. Yin, and X. Meng, Integrity auditing of outsourced data, in *Proceedings of the International Conference on Very Large Data Bases* (VLDB), 2007, pp. 782–793.

22. H. Wang, J. Yin, C.-S. Perng, and P. S. Yu, Dual encryption for query integrity assurance, in *Proceedings of the ACM Conference on Information and Knowledge Management* (CIKM), 2008, pp. 863–872.

23. Y, Yang, S, Papadopoulos, D, Papadias, and G. Kollios, Spatial outsourcing for location-based services, in *IEEE International Conference on Data Engineering* (ICDE), 2008, pp. 1082–1091.

24. M.-L. Yiu, G. Ghinita, C. S. Jensen, and P. Kalnis, Outsourcing search services on private spatial data, in *Proceedings of the IEEE International Conference on Data Engineering* (ICDE), 2009, pp. 1140–1143.

25. Y. Deswarte, J.-J. Quisquater, and A. Saidane, Remote integrity checking, in *Integrity and Internal Control in Information Systems VI*, Kluwer Academic Publishers, Boston, 2003, pp. 1–11.

26. D. L. Gazzaoni-Filho and P. S. Licciardi-Messeder-Barreto, Demonstrating data possession and uncheatable data transfer, *Cryptology ePrint Archive*, Report 2006/150, http://eprint.iacr.org/, 2006.

27. F. Sebe, J. Domingo-Ferrer, A. Martinez-Balleste, Y. Deswarte, and J.-J. Quisquater, Efficient remote data possession checking in critical information infrastructure, *IEEE Transactions on Knowledge and Data Engineering*, **20**(8): 1034–1038, 2008.

28. G. Ateniese, R. Burns, R. Curtmola, J. Herring, L. Kissner, Z. Peterson, and D. Song, Provable data possession at untrusted stores, in *Proceedings 14th ACM Conference on Computer and Communication Security* (CCS'07), 2007, pp. 598–609.

29. M. D. Dikaiakos, D. Katsaros, G. Pallis, A. Vakali, P. Mehra: Guest editors introduction: Cloud computing, *IEEE Internet Computing*, **12**(5), 2009, pp. 10–13.

30. S. Murugesan, Cloud computing: IT's day in the sun?, in *Cutter Consortium*, 2009, http://www.cutter.com/content/itjournal/fulltext/2009/06/index.html.

31. Web Application Security Consortium, www.webappsec.org, 2009.

32. M. A. Niazi and A. R. Baig, Phased approach to simulation of security algorithms for ambient intelligent (ami) environments, the *Winter Simulation Conference*, Washington D.C., December 9–12, 2007.

33. Z. Su, J. Katto, and Y. Yasuda, Optimal replication algorithm for scalable streaming media in contents delivery networks, *IEICE Transactions on Information and Systems*, **E87**(12):2723–2732, 2004.

34. A. Rowstron and P. Druschel, Storage management and caching in PAST, a large-scale, persistent peer-to-peer storage utility, in *Proceedings of the Eighth Workshop on Hot Topics in Operating Systems*, Banff, Canada, 2001, pp. 75–80.

35. Z. Su, T. Washizawa, J. Katto, and Y. Yasuda, Integrated pre-fetching and replacing algorithm for graceful image caching, *IEICE Transactions on Communications*, **E89-B**(9):2753–2763, 2003.

36. A. Stamos, A. Becherer, and N. Wilcox, Cloud computing models and vulnerabilities: Raining on the trendy new parade, in *Blackhat USA 2009*, Las Vegas, Nevada.

37. H. Hacigümüs, B. R. Iyer, C. Li, and S. Mehrotra, Executing SQL over encrypted data in the database-service-provider model, in *Proceedings of the ACM International Conference on Management of Data* (SIGMOD), 2002, pp. 216–227.

PART III

PLATFORM AND SOFTWARE AS A SERVICE (PᴀᴀS/IᴀᴀS)

CHAPTER 9

ANEKA—INTEGRATION OF PRIVATE AND PUBLIC CLOUDS

CHRISTIAN VECCHIOLA, XINGCHEN CHU, MICHAEL MATTESS, and RAJKUMAR BUYYA

9.1 INTRODUCTION

A growing interest in moving software applications, services, and even infrastructure resources from in-house premises to external providers has been witnessed recently. A survey conducted by F5 Networks between June and July 2009[1] showed that such a trend has now reached a critical mass; and an increasing number of IT managers have already adopted, or are considering adopting, this approach to implement IT operations. This model of making IT resources available, known as Cloud Computing [1], opens new opportunities to small, medium-sized, and large companies. It is not necessary anymore to bear considerable costs for maintaining the IT infrastructures or to plan for peak demand. Instead, infrastructure and applications can scale elastically according to the business needs at a reasonable price. The possibility of instantly reacting to the demand of customers without long-term planning is one of the most appealing features of cloud computing, and it has been a key factor in making this trend popular among technology and business practitioners.

As a result of this growing interest, the major players in the IT industry such as Google, Amazon, Microsoft, Sun, and Yahoo have started offering cloud-computing-based solutions that cover the entire IT computing stack, from hardware to applications and services. These offerings have become quickly

[1]The survey, available at http://www.f5.com/pdf/reports/cloud-computing-survey-results-2009.pdf, interviewed 250 IT companies with at least 2500 employees worldwide and targeted the following personnel: managers, directors, vice presidents, and senior vice presidents.

Cloud Computing: Principles and Paradigms, Edited by Rajkumar Buyya, James Broberg and Andrzej Goscinski   Copyright © 2011 John Wiley & Sons, Inc.

popular and led to the establishment of the concept of "Public Cloud," which represents a publicly accessible distributed system hosting the execution of applications and providing services billed on a pay-per-use basis. After an initial enthusiasm for this new trend, it soon became evident that a solution built on outsourcing the entire IT infrastructure to third parties would not be applicable in many cases, especially when there are critical operations to be performed and security concerns to consider. Moreover, with the public cloud distributed anywhere on the planet, legal issues arise and they simply make it difficult to rely on a virtual public infrastructure for any IT operation. As an example, data location and confidentiality are two of the major issues that scare stakeholders to move into the cloud—data that might be secure in one country may not be secure in another. In many cases though, users of cloud services don't know where their information is held and different jurisdictions can apply. It could be stored in some data center in either Europe, (a) where the European Union favors very strict protection of privacy, or (b) America, where laws such as the U.S. Patriot Act[2] invest government and other agencies with virtually limitless powers to access information including that belonging to companies. In addition, enterprises already have their own IT infra-structures. In spite of this, the distinctive feature of cloud computing still remains appealing, and the possibility of replicating in-house (on their own IT infrastructure) the resource and service provisioning model proposed by cloud computing led to the development of the "Private Cloud" concept.

Private clouds are virtual distributed systems that rely on a private infra-structure and provide internal users with dynamic provisioning of comput-ing resources. Differently from public clouds, instead of a pay-as-you-go model, there could be other schemes in place, which take into account the usage of the cloud and proportionally bill the different departments or sections of the enterprise. Private clouds have the advantage of keeping in-house the core business operations by relying on the existing IT infrastructure and reducing the burden of maintaining it once the cloud has been set up. In this scenario, security concerns are less critical, since sensitive information does not flow out of the private infrastructure. Moreover, existing IT resources can be better utilized since the Private cloud becomes accessible to all the division of the enterprise. Another interesting opportunity that comes with private clouds is the possibility of testing applications and systems at a comparatively lower price rather than public clouds before deploying them on the public virtual infrastructure. In April 2009, a Forrester Report [2] on the benefits of delivering in-house cloud computing solutions for enterprises

---

[2]The U.S. Patriot Act is a statute enacted by the United States Government that increases the ability of law enforcement agencies to search telephone, e-mail communications, medical, financial, and other records; it eases restrictions on foreign intelligence gathering within the United States. The full text of the act is available at the Web site of the Library of the Congress at the following address: http://thomas.loc.gov/cgi-bin/query/z?c107:H.R.3162.ENR (accessed December 5, 2009).

highlighted some of the key advantages of using a private cloud computing infrastructure:

- *Customer Information Protection.* Despite assurances by the public cloud leaders about security, few provide satisfactory disclosure or have long enough histories with their cloud offerings to provide warranties about the specific level of security put in place in their system. Security in-house is easier to maintain and to rely on.
- *Infrastructure Ensuring Service Level Agreements (SLAs).* Quality of service implies that specific operations such as appropriate clustering and failover, data replication, system monitoring and maintenance, disaster recovery, and other uptime services can be commensurate to the application needs. While public clouds vendors provide some of these features, not all of them are available as needed.
- *Compliance with Standard Procedures and Operations.* If organizations are subject to third-party compliance standards, specific procedures have to be put in place when deploying and executing applications. This could be not possible in the case of virtual public infrastructure.

In spite of these advantages, private clouds cannot easily scale out in the case of peak demand, and the integration with public clouds could be a solution to the increased load. Hence, hybrid clouds, which are the result of a private cloud growing and provisioning resources from a public cloud, are likely to be best option for the future in many cases. Hybrid clouds allow exploiting existing IT infrastructures, maintaining sensitive information within the premises, and naturally growing and shrinking by provisioning external resources and releasing them when needed. Security concerns are then only limited to the public portion of the cloud, which can be used to perform operations with less stringent constraints but that are still part the system workload.

Platform as a Service (PaaS) solutions offer the right tools to implement and deploy hybrid clouds. They provide enterprises with a platform for creating, deploying, and managing distributed applications on top of existing infrastructures. They are in charge of monitoring and managing the infrastructure and acquiring new nodes, and they rely on virtualization technologies in order to scale applications on demand. There are different implementations of the PaaS model; in this chapter we will introduce Manjrasoft Aneka, and we will discuss how to build and deploy hybrid clouds based on this technology. Aneka [3] is a programming and management platform for building and deploying cloud computing applications. The core value of Aneka is its service-oriented architecture that creates an extensible system able to address different application scenarios and deployments such as public, private, and heterogeneous clouds. On top of these, applications that can be expressed by means of different programming models can transparently execute under the desired service-level agreement.

The remainder of this chapter is organized as follows: In the next section we will briefly review the technologies and tools for Cloud Computing by presenting both the commercial solution and the research projects currently available, we will then introduce Aneka in Section 9.3 and provide an overview of the architecture of the system. In Section 9.4 we will detail the resource provisioning service that represents the core feature for building hybrid clouds. Its architecture and implementation will be described in Section 9.5, together with a discussion about the desired features that a software platform support hybrid clouds should offer. Some thoughts and future directions for practitioners will follow, before the conclusions.

9.2 TECHNOLOGIES AND TOOLS FOR CLOUD COMPUTING

Cloud computing covers the entire computing stack from hardware infrastructure to end-user software applications. Hence, there are heterogeneous offerings addressing different niches of the market. In this section we will concentrate mostly on the Infrastructure as a Service (IaaS) and Platform as a Service (PaaS) implementations of the cloud computing model by first presenting a subset of the most representative commercial solutions and then discussing the few research projects and platforms, which attracted considerable attention.

Amazon is probably the major player for what concerns the Infrastructure-as-a-Service solutions in the case of public clouds. Amazon Web Services [4] deliver a set of services that, when composed together, form a reliable, scalable, and economically accessible cloud. Within the wide range of services offered, it is worth noting that Amazon Elastic Compute Cloud (EC2) [5] and Simple Storage Service (S3) [6] allow users to quickly obtain virtual compute resources and storage space, respectively. GoGrid [7] provides customer with a similar offer: it allows users to deploy their own distributed system on top of their virtual infrastructure. By using the GoGrid Web interface users can create their custom virtual images, deploy database and application servers, and mount new storage volumes for their applications. Both GoGrid and Amazon EC2 charge their customers on a pay-as-you-go basis, and resources are priced per hours of usage. 3Tera AppLogic [8] lays at the foundation of many public clouds, it provides a grid operating system that includes workload distribution, metering, and management of applications. These are described in a platform-independent manner, and AppLogic takes care of deploying and scaling them on demand. Together with AppLogic, which can also be used to manage and deploy private clouds, 3Tera also provides cloud hosting solutions and, because of its grid operating system, makes the transition from the private to the public virtual infrastructure simple and completely transparent. Solutions that are completely based on a PaaS approach for public clouds are Microsoft Azure and Google AppEngine. Azure [9] allows developing scalable applications for the cloud. It is a cloud services operating system that serves as the development, runtime, and control environment for the Azure Services Platform. By using the Microsoft Azure SDK, developers can create services that leverage the .NET framework. These services are then uploaded to the Microsoft Azure portal and executed on top of Windows Azure. Additional services such as workflow management and execution, web services orchestration, and SQL data storage are provided to empower the hosted applications. Azure customers are billed on a pay-per-use basis and by taking into account the different services: compute, storage, bandwidth, and storage transactions. Google AppEngine [10] is a development platform and a runtime environment focusing primarily on web applications that will be run on top of Google's server infrastructure. It provides a set of APIs and an application model that allow developers to take advantage of additional services provided by Google such as *Mail, Datastore, Memcache*, and others. Developers can create applications in Java, Python, and JRuby. These applications will be run within a sandbox, and AppEngine will take care of automatically scaling when needed. Google provides a free limited service and utilizes daily and per minute quotas to meter and price applications requiring professional service.

Different options are available for deploying and managing private clouds. At the lowest level, virtual machine technologies such as Xen [11], KVM [12], and VMware [13] can help building the foundations of a virtual infrastructure. On top of this, virtual machine managers such as VMWare vCloud [14] and Eucalyptus [15] allow the management of a virtual infrastructure and turning a cluster or a desktop grid into a private cloud. Eucalyptus provides a full compatibility with the Amazon Web Services interfaces and supports different virtual machine technologies such as Xen, VMWare, and KVM. By using Eucalyptus, users can test and deploy their cloud applications on the private premises and naturally move to the public virtual infrastructure provided by Amazon EC2 and S3 in a complete transparent manner. VMWare vCloud is the solution proposed by VMWare for deploying virtual infrastructure as either public or private clouds. It is built on top of the VMWare virtual machine technology and provides an easy way to migrate from the private premises to the public infrastructure that leverages VMWare for infrastructure virtualization. For what concerns the Platform-as-a-Service solutions, we can notice DataSynapse, Elastra, Zimory Pools, and the already mentioned App-Logic. DataSynapse [16] is a global provider of application virtualization software. By relying on the VMWare, virtualization technology provides a flexible environment that converts a data center into a private cloud. Elastra [17] cloud server is a platform for easily configuring and deploying distributed application infrastructures on clouds: by using a simple control panel, administrators can visually describe the distributed application in terms of components and connections and then deploying them on one or more cloud providers such Amazon EC2 or VMware ESX. Cloud server can provision resources from either private or public clouds, thus deploying application on hybrid infrastructures. Zimory [18], a spinoff company from Deutsche Telekom, provides a software infrastructure layer that automates the use of resource pools based on Xen, KVM, and VMware virtualization technologies. It allows creating an internal cloud composed by sparse private and public resources that both host the Zimory's software agent and provides facilities for quickly migrating applications from one data center to another and utilizing at best the existing infrastructure.

The wide range of commercial offerings for deploying and managing private and public clouds mostly rely on a few key virtualization technologies, on top of which additional services and features are provided. In this sense, an interesting research project combining public and private clouds and adding advanced services such as resource reservation is represented by the coordinated use of OpenNebula [19] and Haizea [20]. OpenNebula is a virtual infrastructure manager that can be used to deploy and manage virtual machines on local resources or on external public clouds, automating the setup of the virtual machines regardless of the underlying virtualization layer (Xen, KVM, or VMWare are currently supported) or external cloud such as Amazon EC2. A key feature of OpenNebula's architecture is its highly modular design, which facilitates integration with any virtualization platform and third-party component in the cloud ecosystem, such as cloud toolkits, virtual image managers, service managers, and VM schedulers such as Haizea. Haizea is a resource lease manager providing leasing capabilities not found in other cloud systems, such as advance reservations and resource preemption. Integrated together, Open-Nebula and Haizea constitute a virtual management infrastructure providing flexible and advanced capabilities for resource management in hybrid clouds. A similar set of capabilities is provided by OpenPEX [21], which allows users to provision resources ahead of time through advance reservations. It also incorporates a bilateral negotiation protocol that allows users and providers to come to an agreement by exchanging offers and counter offers. OpenPEX natively supports Xen as a virtual machine manager (VMM), but additional plug-ins can be integrated into the system to support other VMMs. Nimbus [22], formerly known as Globus Workspaces, is another framework that provides a wide range of extensibility points. It is essentially a framework that allows turning a cluster into an Infrastructure-as-a-Service cloud. What makes it interesting from the perspective of hybrid clouds is an extremely modular architecture that allows the customization of many tasks: resource scheduling, network leases, accounting, propagation (intra VM file transfer), and fine control VM management.

All of the previous research platforms are mostly IaaS implementation of the cloud computing model: They provide a virtual infrastructure management layer that is enriched with advanced features for resource provisioning and scheduling. Aneka, which is both a commercial solution and a research platform, positions itself as a Platform-as-a-Service implementation. Aneka provides not only a software infrastructure for scaling applications, but also a wide range of APIs that help developers to design and implement applications that can transparently run on a distributed infrastructure whether this be the local cluster or the cloud. Aneka, as OpenNebula and Nimbus, is characterized by a modular architecture that allows a high level of customization and integration with existing technologies, especially for what concerns resource provisioning. Like Zimory, the core feature of Aneka is represented by a configurable software agent that can be transparently deployed on both physical and virtual resources and constitutes the runtime environment for the cloud. This feature, together with the resource provisioning infrastructure, is at the heart of Aneka-based hybrid clouds. In the next sections we will introduce the key feature of Aneka and describe in detail the architecture of the resource provisioning service that is responsible of integrating cloud resources into the existing infrastructure.

9.3 ANEKA CLOUD PLATFORM

Aneka [3] is a software platform and a framework for developing distributed applications on the cloud. It harnesses the computing resources of a heterogeneous network of workstations and servers or data centers on demand. Aneka provides developers with a rich set of APIs for transparently exploiting these resources by expressing the application logic with a variety of programming abstractions. System administrators can leverage a collection of tools to monitor and control the deployed infrastructure. This can be a public cloud available to anyone through the Internet, a private cloud constituted by a set of nodes with restricted access within an enterprise, or a hybrid cloud where external resources are integrated on demand, thus allowing applications to scale.

Figure 9.1 provides a layered view of the framework. Aneka is essentially an implementation of the PaaS model, and it provides a runtime environment for executing applications by leveraging the underlying infrastructure of the cloud. Developers can express distributed applications by using the API contained in the Software Development Kit (SDK) or by porting existing legacy applications to the cloud. Such applications are executed on the Aneka cloud, represented by a collection of nodes connected through the network hosting the Aneka container. The container is the building block of the middleware and represents the runtime environment for executing applications; it contains the core functionalities of the system and is built up from an extensible collection of services that allow administrators to customize the Aneka cloud. There are three classes of services that characterize the container:

- *Execution Services.* They are responsible for scheduling and executing applications. Each of the programming models supported by Aneka defines specialized implementations of these services for managing the execution of a unit of work defined in the model.
- *Foundation Services.* These are the core management services of the Aneka container. They are in charge of metering applications, allocating

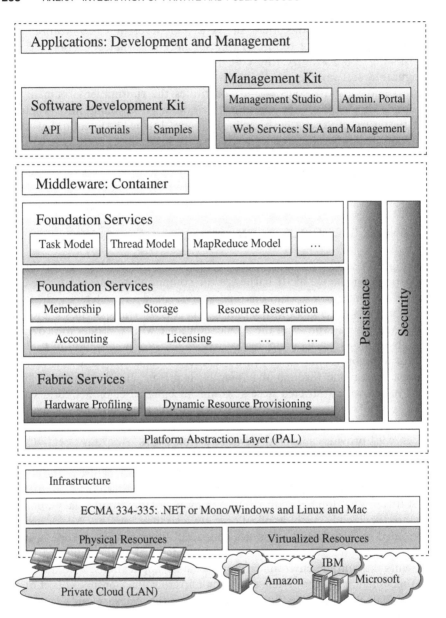

FIGURE 9.1. Aneka framework architecture.

resources for execution, managing the collection of available nodes, and keeping the services registry updated.
- *Fabric Services:* They constitute the lowest level of the services stack of Aneka and provide access to the resources managed by the cloud. An

important service in this layer is the *Resource Provisioning Service,* which enables horizontal scaling[3] in the cloud. Resource provisioning makes Aneka elastic and allows it to grow or to shrink dynamically to meet the QoS requirements of applications.

The container relies on a platform abstraction layer that interfaces it with the underlying host, whether this is a physical or a virtualized resource. This makes the container portable over different runtime environments that feature an implementation of the ECMA 334 [23] and ECMA 335 [24] specifications (such as the .NET framework or Mono).

Aneka also provides a tool for managing the cloud, allowing administrators to easily start, stop, and deploy instances of the Aneka container on new resources and then reconfigure them dynamically to alter the behavior of the cloud.

9.4 ANEKA RESOURCE PROVISIONING SERVICE

The most significant benefit of cloud computing is the elasticity of resources, services, and applications, which is the ability to automatically scale out based on demand and users' quality of service requests. Aneka as a PaaS not only features multiple programming models allowing developers to easily build their distributed applications, but also provides resource provisioning facilities in a seamless and dynamic fashion. Applications managed by the Aneka container can be dynamically mapped to heterogeneous resources, which can grow or shrink according to the application's needs. This elasticity is achieved by means of the resource provisioning framework, which is composed primarily of services built into the Aneka fabric layer.

Figure 9.2 provides an overview of Aneka resource provisioning over private and public clouds. This is a typical scenario that a medium or large enterprise may encounter; it combines privately owned resources with public rented resources to dynamically increase the resource capacity to a larger scale.

Private resources identify computing and storage elements kept in the premises that share similar internal security and administrative policies. Aneka identifies two types of private resources: *static* and *dynamic* resources. Static resources are constituted by existing physical workstations and servers that may be idle for a certain period of time. Their membership to the Aneka cloud is manually configured by administrators and does not change over time. Dynamic resources are mostly represented by virtual instances that join and leave the Aneka cloud and are controlled by resource pool managers that provision and release them when needed.

---

[3]Horizontal scaling is the process of adding more computing nodes to a system. It is counterposed to vertical scaling, which is the process of increasing the computing capability of a single computer resource.

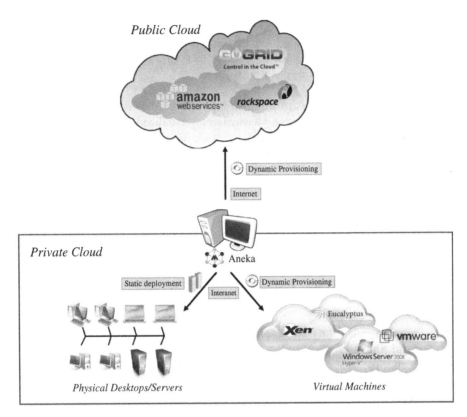

FIGURE 9.2. Aneka resource provisioning over private and public clouds.

Public resources reside outside the boundaries of the enterprise and are provisioned by establishing a service-level agreement with the external provider. Even in this case we can identify two classes: *on-demand* and *reserved* resources. On-demand resources are dynamically provisioned by resource pools for a fixed amount of time (for example, an hour) with no long-term commitments and on a pay-as-you-go basis. Reserved resources are provisioned in advance by paying a low, one-time fee and mostly suited for long-term usage. These resources are actually the same as static resources, and no automation is needed in the resource provisioning service to manage them.

Despite the specific classification previously introduced, resources are managed uniformly once they have joined the Aneka cloud and all the standard operations that are performed on statically configured nodes can be transparently applied to dynamic virtual instances. Moreover, specific operations pertaining to dynamic resources, such as join and leave, are seen as connection and disconnection of nodes and transparently handled. This is mostly due to the indirection layer provided by the Aneka container that abstracts the specific nature of the hosting machine.

9.4.1 Resource Provisioning Scenario

Figure 9.3 illustrates a possible scenario in which the resource provisioning service becomes important. A private enterprise maintains a private cloud, which consists of (a) five physical dedicated desktops from its engineering department and (b) a small data center managed by Xen Hypervisor providing virtual machines with the maximum capacity of 12 VMs. In most of the cases, this setting is able to address the computing needs of the enterprise. In the case of peak computing demand, additional resources can be provisioned by leveraging the virtual public infrastructure. For example, a mission critical application could require at least 30 resources to complete within an hour, and the customer is willing to spend a maximum of 5 dollars to achieve this goal. In this case, the Aneka Resource Provisioning service becomes a fundamental infrastructure component to address this scenario.

In this case, once the client has submitted the application, the Aneka scheduling engine detects that the current capacity in terms of resources (5 dedicated nodes) is not enough to satisfy the user's QoS requirement and to complete the application on time. An additional 25 resources must be provisioned. It is the responsibility of the Aneka Resource Provisioning service to acquire these resources from both the private data center managed by Xen Hypervisor and the Amazon public cloud. The provisioning service is configured by default with a cost-effective strategy, which privileges the use of local resources instead of the dynamically provisioned and chargeable ones. The computing needs of the application require the full utilization of the local data center that provides the Aneka cloud with 12 virtual machines. Such capacity is still not enough to complete the mission critical application in time; and the

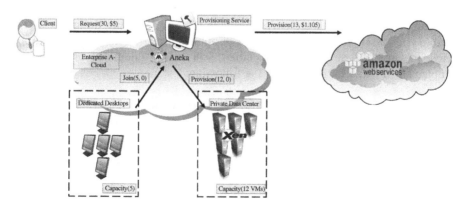

FIGURE 9.3. Use case of resource provisioning under Aneka.

remaining 13 resources are rented from Amazon for a minimum of one hour, which incurs a few dollars' cost.[4]

This is not the only scenario that Aneka can support, and different provisioning patterns can be implemented. Another simple strategy for provisioning resources could be minimizing the execution time to let the application finish as early as possible; this requires Aneka to request more powerful resources from the Amazon public cloud. For example, in the previous case instead of provisioning 13 small instances from Amazon, a major number of resources, or more powerful resources, can be rented by spending the entire budget available for the application. The resource provisioning infrastructure can also serve broader purposes such as keeping the length of the system queue, or the average waiting time of a job in the queue, under a specified value. In these cases, specific policies can be implemented to ensure that the throughput of the system is kept at a reasonable level.

9.5 HYBRID CLOUD IMPLEMENTATION

Currently, there is no widely accepted standard for provisioning virtual infrastructure from Infrastructure as a Service (IaaS) providers, but each provider exposes its own interfaces and protocols. Hence, it is not possible to seamlessly integrate different providers into one single infrastructure. The resource provisioning service implemented in Aneka addresses these issues and abstracts away the differences of providers' implementation. In this section we will briefly review what the desired features of a hybrid cloud implementation are and then we will give a closer a look at the solution implemented in Aneka together with a practical application of the infrastructure developed.

9.5.1 Design and Implementation Guidelines

The particular nature of hybrid clouds demands additional and specific functionalities that software engineers have to consider while designing software systems supporting the execution of applications in hybrid and dynamic environments. These features, together with some guidelines on how to implement them, are presented in the following:

- *Support for Heterogeneity.* Hybrid clouds are produced by heterogeneous resources such as clusters, public or private virtual infrastructures, and workstations. In particular, for what concerns a virtual machine manager, it must be possible to integrate additional cloud service providers (mostly

---

[4]At the time of writing (October 2010), the cost for a small Linux-based instance in Amazon EC2 is 0.085 cent/hour and the total cost bore by the customer will be in this case 1.105 UD. We expect this price to decrease even more in the next years.

IaaS providers) without major changes to the entire system design and codebase. Hence, the specific code related to a particular cloud resource provider should be kept isolated behind interfaces and within pluggable components.

- *Support for Dynamic and Open Systems.* Hybrid clouds change their composition and topology over time. They form as a result of dynamic conditions such as peak demands or specific Service Level Agreements attached to the applications currently in execution. An open and extensible architecture that allows easily plugging new components and rapidly integrating new features is of a great value in this case. Specific enterprise architectural patterns can be considered while designing such software systems. In particular, *inversion of control* and, more precisely, *dependency injection*[5] in component-based systems is really helpful.

- *Support for Basic VM Operation Management.* Hybrid clouds integrate virtual infrastructures with existing physical systems. Virtual infrastructures are produced by virtual instances. Hence, software frameworks that support hypervisor-based execution should implement a minimum set of operations. They include requesting a virtual instance, controlling its status, terminating its execution, and keeping track of all the instances that have been requested.

- *Support for Flexible Scheduling Policies.* The heterogeneity of resources that constitute a hybrid infrastructure naturally demands for flexible scheduling policies. Public and private resources can be differently utilized, and the workload should be dynamically partitioned into different streams according to their security and quality of service (QoS) requirements. There is then the need of being able to transparently change scheduling policies over time with a minimum impact on the existing infrastructure and almost now downtimes. Configurable scheduling policies are then an important feature.

- *Support for Workload Monitoring.* Workload monitoring becomes even more important in the case of hybrid clouds where a subset of resources is leased and resources can be dismissed if they are no longer necessary. Workload monitoring is an important feature for any distributed middleware, in the case of hybrid clouds, it is necessary to integrate this feature with scheduling policies that either directly or indirectly govern the management of virtual instances and their leases.

---

[5]Dependency injection is a technique that allows configuring and connecting components within a software container (such as a Web or an application server) without hard coding their relation but for example by providing an abstract specification—for example, a configuration file that specifies which component to instantiate and to connect them together. A detailed description of this programming pattern can be found at the following link: http://martinfowler.com/articles/injection. html (accessed December 2009).

Those presented are, according to the authors, the most relevant features for successfully supporting the deployment and the management of hybrid clouds. In this list we did not extensively mention security that is transversal to all features listed. A basic recommendation for implementing a security infra-structure for any runtime environment is to use a *Defense in Depth*[6] security model whenever it is possible. This principle is even more important in heterogeneous systems such as hybrid clouds, where both applications and resources can represent treats to each other.

9.5.2 Aneka Hybrid Cloud Architecture

The Resource Provisioning Framework represents the foundation on top of which Aneka-based hybrid clouds arc implemented. In this section we will introduce the components that compose this framework and briefly describe their interactions.

The basic idea behind the Resource Provisioning Framework is depicted in Figure 9.4. The resource provisioning infrastructure is represented by a collection of resource pools that provide access to resource providers, whether they are external or internal, and managed uniformly through a specific component called a resource pool manager. A detailed description of the components follows:

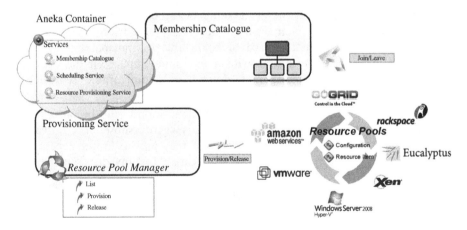

FIGURE 9.4. System architecture of the Aneka Resource Provisioning Framework.

---

[6]Defense in depth is an information assurance (IA) strategy in which multiple layers of defense are placed throughout an information technology (IT) system. More information is available at the following link: http://www.nsa.gov/ia/_files/support/defenseindepth.pdf (accessed December 2009).

- *Resource Provisioning Service*. This is an Aneka-specific service that implements the service interface and wraps the resource pool manager, thus allowing its integration within the Aneka container.
- *Resource Pool Manager*. This manages all the registered resource pools and decides how to allocate resources from those pools. The resource pool manager provides a uniform interface for requesting additional resources from any private or public provider and hides the complexity of managing multiple pools to the Resource Provisioning Service.
- *Resource Pool*. This is a container of virtual resources that mostly come from the same resource provider. A resource pool is in charge of managing the virtual resources it contains and eventually releasing them when they are no longer in use. Since each vendor exposes its own specific interfaces, the resource pool (a) encapsulates the specific implementation of the communication protocol required to interact with it and (b) provides the pool manager with a unified interface for acquiring, terminating, and monitoring virtual resources.

The request for additional resources is generally triggered by a scheduler that detects that the current capacity is not sufficient to satisfy the expected quality of services ensured for specific applications. In this case a provisioning request is made to the Resource Provisioning Service. According to specific policies, the pool manager determines the pool instance(s) that will be used to provision resources and will forward the request to the selected pools. Each resource pool will translate the forwarded request by using the specific protocols required by the external provider and provision the resources. Once the requests are successfully processed, the requested number of virtual resources will join the Aneka cloud by registering themselves with the Membership Catalogue Service, which keeps track of all the nodes currently connected to the cloud. Once joined the cloud the provisioned resources are managed like any other node.

A release request is triggered by the scheduling service when provisioned resources are no longer in use. Such a request is then forwarded to the interested resources pool (with a process similar to the one described in the previous paragraph) that will take care of terminating the resources when more appropriate. A general guideline for pool implementation is to keep provisioned resources active in a local pool until their lease time expires. By doing this, if a new request arrives within this interval, it can be served without leasing additional resources from the public infrastructure. Once a virtual instance is terminated, the Membership Catalogue Service will detect a disconnection of the corresponding node and update its registry accordingly.

It can be noticed that the interaction flow previously described is completely independent from the specific resource provider that will be integrated into the system. In order to satisfy such a requirement, modularity and well-designed interfaces between components are very important. The current design, implemented in Aneka, maintains the specific implementation details within the *ResourcePool* implementation, and resource pools can be dynamically configured and added by using the dependency injection techniques, which are already implemented for configuring the services hosted in the container. The current implementation of Aneka allows customizing the Resource Provisioning Infrastructure by specifying the following elements:

- *Resource Provisioning Service.* The default implementation provides a lightweight component that generally forwards the requests to the resource Pool Manager. A possible extension of the system can be the implementation of a distributed resource provisioning service that can operate at this level or at the Resource Pool Manager level.
- *Resource Pool Manager.* The default implementation provides the basic management features required for resource and provisioning request forwarding.
- *Resource Pools.* The Resource Pool Manager exposes a collection of resource pools that can be used. It is possible to add any implementation that is compliant to the interface contract exposed by the Aneka provisioning API, thus adding a heterogeneous open-ended set of external providers to the cloud.
- *Provisioning Policy.* Scheduling services can be customized with resource provisioning aware algorithms that can perform scheduling of applications by taking into account the required QoS.

The architecture of the Resource Provisioning Framework shares some features with other IaaS implementations featuring configurable software containers, such as OpenNebula [19] and Nimbus [22]. OpenNebula uses the concept of *cloud drivers* in order to abstract the external resource providers and provides a pluggable scheduling engine that supports the integration with advanced schedulers such Haizea [20] and others. Nimbus provides a plethora of extension points into its programming API, and among these there are hooks for scheduling and resource management and the remote management (RM) API. The first ones control when and where a virtual machine will run, while the RM API act as unified interface to Infrastructure as a Service (IaaS) implementations such as Amazon EC2 and OpenNebula. By providing a specific implementation of RM API, it is possible to integrate other cloud providers.

In the next paragraph, we will detail the implementation of the Amazon EC2 resource pool to provide a practical example of a resource pool implementation.

9.5.3 Use Case—The Amazon EC2 Resource Pool

Amazon EC2 is one of the most popular cloud resource providers. At the time of writing it is listed among the top 10 companies providing cloud computing services.[7] It provides a Web service interface for accessing, managing, and controlling virtual machine instances. The Web-service-based interface simplifies the integration of Amazon EC2 with any application. This is the case of Aneka, for which a simple Web service client has been developed to allow the interaction with EC2. In order to interact with Amazon EC2, several parameters are required:

- *User Identity*. This represents the account information used to authenticate with Amazon EC2. The identity is constituted by a pair of encrypted keys that are the access key and the secret key. These keys can be obtained from the Amazon Web services portal once the user has signed in, and they are required to perform any operation that involves Web service access.
- *Resource Identity*. The resource identity is the identifier of a public or a private Amazon Machine Image (AMI) that is used as template from which to create virtual machine instances.
- *Resource Capacity*. This specifies the different type of instance that will be deployed by Amazon EC2. Instance types vary according to the number of cores, the amount of memory, and other settings that affect the performance of the virtual machine instance. Several types of images are available, those commonly used are: *small*, *medium*, and *large*. The capacity of each type of resource has been predefined by Amazon and is charged differently.

This information is maintained in the *EC2ResourcePoolConfiguration* class and need to be provided by the administrator in order to configure the pool. Hence, the implementation of *EC2ResourcePool* is forwarding the request of the pool manager to EC2 by using the Web service client and the configuration information previously described. It then stores the metadata of each active virtual instance for further use.

In order to utilize at best the virtual machine instances provisioned from EC2, the pool implements a cost-effective optimization strategy. According to the current business model of Amazon, a virtual machine instance is charged by using one-hour time blocks. This means that if a virtual machine instance is used for 30 minutes, the customer is still charged for one hour of usage. In order to provide a good service to applications with a smaller granularity in terms of execution times, the *EC2ResourcePool* class implements a local cache that keeps track of the released instances whose time block is not expired yet. These instances will be reused instead of activating new instances from Amazon.

With the cost-effective optimization strategy, the pool is able to minimize the cost of provisioning resources from Amazon cloud and, at the same time, achieve high utilization of each provisioned resource.

---

[7]Source: http://www.networkworld.com/supp/2009/ndc3/051809-cloud-companies-to-watch.html (accessed December 2009). A more recent review ranked Amazon still in the top ten (Source: http://searchcloudcomputing.techtarget.com/generic/0,295582,sid201_gci1381115,00.html#slideshow)

9.5.4 Implementation Steps for Aneka Resource Provisioning Service

The resource provisioning service is a customized service which will be used to enable cloud bursting by Aneka at runtime. Figure 9.5 demonstrates one of the application scenarios that utilize resource provisioning to dynamically provision virtual machines from Amazon EC2 cloud.

The general steps of resource provisioning on demand in Aneka are the following:

- The application submits its tasks to the scheduling service, which, in turns, adds the tasks into the scheduling queue.
- The scheduling algorithm finds an appropriate match between a task and a resource. If the algorithm could not find enough resources for serving all the tasks, it requests extra resources from the scheduling service.
- The scheduling service will send a ResourceProvisionMessage to provision service and will ask provision service to get X number of resources as determined by the scheduling algorithm.

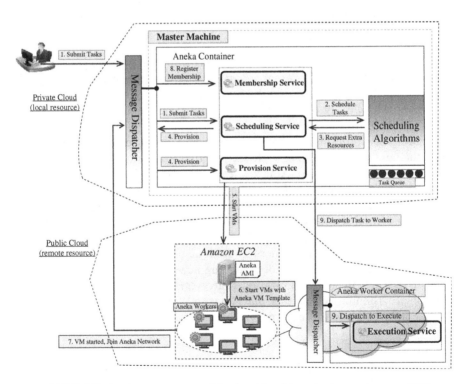

FIGURE 9.5. Aneka resource provisioning (cloud bursting) over Amazon EC2.

- Upon receiving the provision message, the provision service will delegate the provision request to a component called resource pool manager, which is responsible for managing various resource pools. A resource pool is a logical view of a cloud resource provider, where the virtual machines can be provisioned at runtime. Aneka resource provisioning supports multiple resource pools such as Amazon EC2 pool and Citrix Xen server pool.

- The resource pool manager knows how to communicate with each pool and will provision the requested resources on demand. Based on the requests from the provision service, the pool manager starts X virtual machines by utilizing the predefined virtual machine template already configured to run Aneka containers.

- A worker instance of Aneka will be configured and running once a virtual resource is started. All the work instances will then connect to the Aneka master machine and will register themselves with Aneka membership service.

- The scheduling algorithm will be notified by the membership service once those work instances join the network, and it will start allocating pending tasks to them immediately.

- Once the application is completed, all the provisioned resources will be released by the provision service to reduce the cost of renting the virtual machine.

9.6 VISIONARY THOUGHTS FOR PRACTITIONERS

The research on the integration of public and private clouds is still at its early stage. Even though the adoption of cloud computing technologies is still growing, delivering IT services via the cloud will be the norm in future. The key areas of interest that need to be explored include security standardization; pricing models; and management and scheduling policies for heterogeneous environments. At the time of writing, only limited research has been carried out in these fields.

As briefly addressed in the introduction, security is one of the major concerns in hybrid clouds. While private clouds significantly reduce the security risks concerned by retaining sensitive information within corporate boundaries, in the case of hybrid clouds the workload that is delegated to the public portion of the infrastructure is subject to the same security risks that are prevalent in public clouds. In this sense, workload partitioning and classification can help in reducing the security risks for sensitive data. Keeping sensitive operations within the boundaries of the private part of the infrastructure and ensuring that the information flow in the cloud is kept under control is a naïve and probably often limited solution. The major issues that need to be addressed are the following: security of virtual execution environments (either hypervisors or managed runtime environments for PaaS implementations), data retention, possibility of massive outages, provider trust, and also jurisdiction issues that can break the confidentiality of data. These issues become even more crucial in the case of hybrid clouds because of the dynamic nature of the way in which public resources are integrated into the system. Currently, the security measures and tools adopted for traditional distributed systems are used. Cloud computing brings not only challenges for security, but also advantages. Cloud service providers can make sensible investments on the security infrastructure and provide more secured environments than those provided by small enterprises. Moreover, a cloud's virtual dynamic infrastructure makes it possible to achieve better fault tolerance and reliability, greater resiliency to failure, rapid reconstruction of services, and a low-cost approach to disaster recovery.

The lack of standardization is another important area that has to be covered. Currently, each vendor publishes their own interfaces, and there is no common agreement on a standard for exposing such services. This condition limits the adoption of inter-cloud services on a global scale. As discussed in this chapter, in order to integrate IaaS solutions from different vendors it is necessary to implement ad hoc connectors. The lack of standardization covers not only the programming and management interface, but also the use of abstract representations for virtual images and active instances. An effort in this direction is the Open Virtualization Format (OVF) [25], an open standard for packaging and distributing virtual appliances or more generally software to be run in virtual machines. However, even if endorsed by the major representative companies in the field (Microsoft, IBM, Dell, HP, VMWare, and XenSource) and released as a preliminary standard by the Distributed Management Task Force, the OVF specification only captures the static representation of a virtual instance; it is mostly used as a canonical way of distributing virtual machine images. Many vendors and implementations simply use OVF as an import format and convert it into their specific runtime format when running the image. Additional effort has to be spent on defining a common method to represent live instances of applications and in providing a standard approach to customizing these instances during startup. Research in this area will be necessary to completely eliminate vendor lock-in.[8] In addition, when building a hybrid cloud based on legacy hardware and virtual public infrastructure, additional compatibility issues arise due to the heterogeneity of the runtime environments: almost all the hypervisors support the x86 machine model, which could constitute a technology barrier in the seamless transition from private environments to public ones. Finally, as discussed by Keahey et al. [26], there is a need for providing (a) a standardized way for describing and comparing the quality of service (QoS) offerings of different cloud services providers and (b) a standardized approach to benchmark those services. These

---

[8]In cloud computing, vendor lock-in relates to the condition in which a large installed base of a customer is maintained within the virtual infrastructure of one vendor who does not disclose the internals of their system, thus preventing the possibility of the customer moving their installed base to another provider without considerable costs.

are all areas that have to be explored in order to take advantage of hetero-geneous clouds, which, due to their dynamic nature, require automatic methods for optimizing and monitoring the publicly provisioned services. An important step in providing a standardization path and to foster the adoption of cloud computing is the Open Cloud Manifesto,[9] which provides a starting point for the promotion of open clouds characterized by interoperability between providers and true scalability for applications.

Since the integration of external resources comes with a price, it is interesting to study how to optimize the usage of such resources. Currently, resources are priced in time blocks, and often their granularity does not meet the needs of enterprises. Virtual resource pooling, as provided by Aneka, is an initial step in closing this gap, but new strategies for optimizing the usage of external provisioned resources can be devised. For example, intelligent policies that can predict when to release a resource by relying on the statistics of the workload can be investigated. Other policies could identify the optimal number of resources to provision according to the application needs, the budget allocated for the execution of the application, and the workload. Research in this direction will become even more consistent when different pricing models will be introduced by cloud providers. In this future scenario, the introduction of a market place for brokering cloud resources and services will definitely give more opportunities to fully realize the vision of cloud computing. Each vendor will be able to advertise their services and customers will have more options to choose from, eventually by relying on meta-brokering services. Once realized, these opportunities will make the accessibility of cloud computing technology more natural and at a fairer price, thus simplifying the integration of existing computing infrastructure owned within the premises.

We believe that one of the major areas of interest in the next few years for what concerns the implementation and the deployment of hybrid clouds will be the scheduling of applications and the provisioning of resources for these applications. In particular, due to the heterogeneous nature of hybrid clouds, additional coordination between the private and the public service management becomes fundamental. Hence, cloud schedulers will necessarily be integrated with different aspects such as federate policy management tools, seamless hybrid integration, federated security, information asset management, coordi-nated provisioning control, and unified monitoring.

9.7 SUMMARY AND CONCLUSIONS

In this chapter we have presented the characteristics of hybrid clouds and discussed their implementation and deployment by using Aneka. Hybrid clouds emerge when an existing private infrastructure grows into a virtual public

[9]The Open Cloud Manifesto is available at: http://www.opencloudmanifesto.org (Accessed, December, 2009).

infrastructure in order to handle its workload. We envision that this specific scenario will be the most common in the future because hybrid clouds can overcome specific disadvantages of both public and private clouds. They can scale on demand and leverage the horse power of third-party data centers and maintain the elaboration of sensitive information within the premises of the enterprise. Different solutions are available for implementing hybrid clouds; the most relevant to the discussed scenario are IaaS and PaaS implementaions. Among these we presented the solution proposed by Aneka, which is an implementation of the PaaS model for cloud computing. The Aneka container—the basic building block of Aneka clouds—can be easily deployed on different hardware: a desktop PC, a workstation, a server, a cluster, and even a virtual machine. This flexibility allows the quick setup of heterogeneous execution environments on top of which distributed applications can run transparently. Such a feature constitutes a key element for integrating computing resources from external providers into the private infrastructure.

In order to support this scenario, we first highlighted which are the desired features of a reference model for hybrid cloud and then presented how these characteristics are reflected into Aneka. Three major components compose the provisioning framework: Resource Provisioning Service, Resource Pool Manager, and Resource Pools. A fundamental role is played by resource pools, which represent collections of computing nodes belonging to the same domain. The abstraction provided by resource pools makes it possible to integrate and leverage either public or private clouds uniformly. As a proof of concept of the presented solution, we discussed a use case scenario that involves the creation of a hybrid cloud composed by a set of workstations that has been augmented by initially provisioning resources from a cluster managed by a Xen Hypervisor and then by leveraging a public virtual infrastructure such as Amazon EC2.

As a conclusion to the chapter, we introduced and discussed the future directions of the research in hybrid clouds, we highlighted the major challenges that have to be faced in order to promote a wider adoption of hybrid clouds, and provided some insights into the initial efforts taken toward this direction.

In the future we aim to extend the resource provisioning framework by providing more advanced scheduling techniques for heterogeneous environments. Additionally, we would like to extend the number of resource provider actually supported. Currently, we are developing support for VMWare, Eucalyptus, and InterGrid [27].

ACKNOWLEDGMENTS

We would like to thank Dileban Karunamoorthy and Mukaddim Pathan for their useful insights on structuring the content of the chapter and their suggestions for improving the presentation of the content.

REFERENCES

1. M. Armbrust, A. Fox, R. Griffith, A.D. Joseph, R. Katz, A. Konwinski, G. Lee, D. Patterson, A. Rabkin, I. Stoika, and M. Zaharia, Above the clouds: A Berkeley view of cloud computing, Technical Report, UC Berkeley Reliable Adaptive Distributed Systems Laboratory, February 2009.

2. J. Staten, S. Yates, J. Ryme, F. Gillett, and L. E. Nelson, Deliver Cloud Benefits Inside Your Walls: Economic and Self-Service Gains Are Within Reach, *Forrester Research Inc.*, April 2009.

3. C. Vecchiola, X. Chu, and R. Buyya, *Aneka: A software platform for .NET cloud computing*, in *High Performance & Large Scale Computing*, W. Gentzsch, L. Grandinetti, and G. Joubert (eds.), IOS Press, Amsterdam, 2009.

4. Amazon Web Services, http://aws.amazon.com (accessed October 21, 2010).

5. Amazon Elastic Compute Cloud, http://aws.amazon.com/ec2/ (accessed October 21, 2010).

6. Amazon Simple Storage Service, http://aws.amazon.com/s3/ (accessed October 21, 2010).

7. GoGrid, http://www.gogrid.com (accessed October 21, 2010).

8. 3tera AppLogic, http://www.3tera.com/AppLogic/ (accessed October 21, 2010).

9. Microsoft Azure, http://www.microsoft.com/windowsazure/ (accessed October 21, 2010).

10. Google AppEngine, http://code.google.com/appengine/ (accessed October 21, 2010).

11. Xen Hypervisor, http://xen.org/ (accessed October 21, 2010).

12. Kernel-based Virtual Machine, http://www.linux-kvm.org/page/Main_Page (accessed October 21, 2010).

13. VMWare Business Infrastructure Virtualization, http://www.vmware.com/ (accessed October 21, 2010).

14. VMWare vCloud, http://www.vmware.com/solutions/cloud-computing/ (accessed October 21, 2010).

15. D. Nurmi, R. Wolski, C. Grzegorczyk, G. Obertelli, S. Soman, L. Youseff, and D. Zagorodnov, The Eucalyptus open-source cloud computing system, in *Proceedings of 9th IEEE/ACM International Symposium on Cluster Computing and the Grid (CCGrid 2009)*, Shanghai, China, May 2009.

16. Datasynapse, http://www.datasynapse.com (accessed October 21, 2010).

17. Elastra—Manage IT complexity, http://www.elastra.com (accessed October 21, 2010).

18. Zimory, http://www.zimory.com (accessed October 21, 2010).

19. I. Llorente, R. Moreno-Vozmediano, and R. Montero, Cloud computing for on-demand grid resource provisioning, in *Advances in Parallel Computing*, IOS Press, Amsterdam, 2009, p. 18.

20. B. Sotomayor, K. Keahey, and I. Foster, Combining batch execution and leasing using virtual machines, in *HPDC '08: Proceedings of the 17th International Symposium on High Performance Distributed Computing*, ACM, 2008, pp. 87–96.

21. S. Venugopal, J. Broberg, and R. Buyya, OpenPEX: An open provisioning and execution systems for virtual machines, in *Proceedings of the 17th International Conference on Advanced Computing and Communications (ADCOM 2009)*, Bengaluru, India, December 14–18, 2009.

22. K. Keahey, I. Foster, T. Freeman, and X. Zhang, Virtual workspaces: Achieving quality of service and quality of life on the grid, *Scientific Programming*, **13**(4): 265–276, 2005.

23. J. Jagger, N. Perry, and P. Sestoft, *C# Annotated Standard*, Morgan Kaufmann, San Francisco, 2007.

24. J.S. Miller, S. Ragsdale, *The Common Language Infrastructure Annotated Standard*, Addison-Wesley, Reading, MA, 2004.

25. Open Virtualization Format Specification, Distributed Management Task Force, http://www.dmtf.org/sites/default/files/standards/documents/DSP0243_1.1.0.pdf (accessed October 21, 2010)

26. K. Keahey, M. Tsugawa, A. Matsunaga, and J. A. B. Fortés, Sky computing, *IEEE Internet Computing*, **13**(5):43–51, 2009.

27. A. Di Costanzo, M. Dias de Assunção, and R. Buyya, Harnessing cloud technologies for a virtualized distributed computing infrastructure, *IEEE Internet Computing*, **13**(5):14–22, 2009.

CHAPTER 10

CometCloud: AN AUTONOMIC CLOUD ENGINE

HYUNJOO KIM and MANISH PARASHAR

10.1 INTRODUCTION

Clouds typically have highly dynamic demands for resources with highly heterogeneous and dynamic workloads. For example, the workloads associated with the application can be quite dynamic, in terms of both the number of tasks processed and the computation requirements of each task. Furthermore, different applications may have very different and dynamic quality of service (QoS) requirements; for example, one application may require high throughput while another may be constrained by a budget, and a third may have to balance both throughput and budget. The performance of a cloud service can also vary based on these varying loads as well as failures, network conditions, and so on, resulting in different "QoS" to the application.

Combining public cloud platforms and integrating them with existing grids and data centers can support on-demand scale-up, scale-down, and scale-out. Users may want to use resources in their private cloud (or data center or grid) first before scaling out onto a public cloud, and they may have a preference for a particular cloud or may want to combine multiple clouds. However, such integration and interoperability is currently nontrivial. Furthermore, integrating these public cloud platforms with exiting computational grids provides opportunities for on-demand scale-up and scale-down, that is cloudbursts.

In this chapter, we present the CometCloud autonomic cloud engine. The overarching goal of CometCloud is to realize a virtual computational cloud with resizable computing capability, which integrates local computational environments and public cloud services on-demand, and provide abstractions and mechanisms to support a range of programming paradigms and

Cloud Computing: Principles and Paradigms, Edited by Rajkumar Buyya, James Broberg and Andrzej Goscinski Copyright © 2011 John Wiley & Sons, Inc.

applications requirements. Specifically, CometCloud enables policy-based autonomic *cloudbridging* and *cloudbursting*. Autonomic cloudbridging enables on-the-fly integration of local computational environments (data centers, grids) and public cloud services (such as Amazon EC2 [10] and Eucalyptus [20]), and autonomic cloudbursting enables dynamic application scale-out to address dynamic workloads, spikes in demands, and other extreme requirements.

CometCloud is based on a decentralized coordination substrate, and it supports highly heterogeneous and dynamic cloud/grid infrastructures, integration of public/private clouds, and cloudbursts. The coordination substrate is also used to support a decentralized and scalable task space that coordinates the scheduling of task, submitted by a dynamic set of users, onto sets of dynamically provisioned workers on available private and/or public cloud resources based on their QoS constraints such as cost or performance. These QoS constraints along with policies, performance history, and the state of resources are used to determine the appropriate size and mix of the public and private clouds that should be allocated to a specific application request.

This chapter also demonstrates the ability of CometCloud to support the dynamic requirements of real applications (and multiple application groups) with varied computational requirements and QoS constraints. Specifically, this chapter describes two applications enabled by CometCloud, a computationally intensive value at risk (VaR) application and a high-throughput medical image registration. VaR is a market standard risk measure used by senior managers and regulators to quantify the risk level of a firm's holdings. A VaR calculation should be completed within the limited time, and the computational requirements for the calculation can change significantly. Image registration is the process to determine the linear/nonlinear mapping between two images of the same object or similar objects. In image registration, a set of image registration methods are used by different (geographically distributed) research groups to process their locally stored data. The set of images will be typically acquired at different time, or from different perspectives, and will be in different coordinate systems. It is therefore critical to align those images into the same coordinate system before applying any image analysis.

The rest of this chapter is organized as follows. We present the CometCloud architecture in Section 10.2. Section 10.3 elaborates policy-driven autonomic cloudbursts,—specifically, autonomic cloudbursts for real-world applications, autonomic cloudbridging over a virtual cloud, and runtime behavior of CometCloud. Section 10.4 states the overview of VaR and image registration applications. We evaluate the autonomic behavior of CometCloud in Section 10.5 and conclude this paper in Section 10.6.

10.2   COMETCLOUD **ARCHITECTURE**

CometCloud is an autonomic computing engine for cloud and grid environments. It is based on the Comet [1] decentralized coordination substrate, and it supports highly heterogeneous and dynamic cloud/grid infrastructures, integration of public/private clouds, and autonomic cloudbursts. CometCloud is based on a peer-to-peer substrate that can span enterprise data centers, grids, and clouds. Resources can be assimilated on-demand and on-the-fly into its peer-to-peer overlay to provide services to applications. Conceptually, CometCloud is composed of a programming layer, a service layer, and an infrastructure layer; these layers are described in more detail in the following section. CometCloud (and Comet) adapts the Squid [2] information discovery scheme to deterministically map the information space onto the dynamic set of peer nodes. The resulting structure is a locality preserving semantic distributed hash table (DHT) on top of a self-organizing structured overlay. It maintains content locality and guarantees that content-based queries, using flexible content descriptors in the form of keywords, partial keywords, and wildcards, are delivered with bounded costs. Comet builds a tuple-based coordination space abstraction using Squid, which can be associatively accessed by all system peers without requiring the location information of tuples and host identifiers. CometCloud also provides transient spaces that enable applications to explicitly exploit context locality.

10.2.1 CometCloud Layered Abstractions

A schematic overview of the CometCloud architecture is presented in Figure 10.1. The infrastructure layer uses the Chord self-organizing overlay [3], and the Squid [2] information discovery and content-based routing substrate built on top of Chord. The routing engine [4] supports flexible content-based

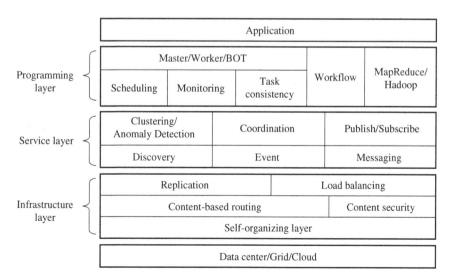

FIGURE 10.1. The CometCloud architecture for autonomic cloudbursts.

routing and complex querying using partial keywords, wildcards, or ranges. It also guarantees that all peer nodes with data elements that match a query/message will be located. Nodes providing resources in the overlay have different roles and, accordingly, different access privileges based on their credentials and capabilities. This layer also provides replication and load balancing services, and it handles dynamic joins and leaves of nodes as well as node failures. Every node keeps the replica of its successor node's state, and it reflects changes to this replica whenever its successor notifies it of changes. It also notifies its predecessor of any changes to its state. If a node fails, the predecessor node merges the replica into its state and then makes a replica of its new successor. If a new node joins, the joining node's predecessor updates its replica to reflect the joining node's state, and the successor gives its state information to the joining node. To maintain load balancing, load should be redistributed among the nodes whenever a node joins and leaves.

The service layer provides a range of services to supports autonomics at the programming and application level. This layer supports the Linda-like [5] tuple space coordination model, and it provides a virtual shared-space abstraction as well as associative access primitives. The basic coordination primitives are listed below:

- *out* (ts, t): a nonblocking operation that inserts tuple t into space ts.
- *in* (ts, t'): a blocking operation that removes a tuple t matching template t' from the space ts and returns it.
- *rd* (ts, t'): a blocking operation that returns a tuple t matching template t' from the space ts. The tuple is not removed from the space.

The *out* is for inserting a tuple into the space, and *in* and *rd* are for reading a tuple from the space are implemented. *in* removes the tuple after read, and *rd* only reads the tuple. We support range query, hence "*" can be used for searching all tuples. The above uniform operators do not distinguish between local and remote spaces, and consequently the Comet is naturally suitable for context-transparent applications. However, this abstraction does not maintain geographic locality between peer nodes and may have a detrimental effect on the efficiency of the applications imposing context-awareness, for example mobile applications. These applications require that context locality be maintained in addition to content locality; that is, they impose requirements for context-awareness. To address this issue, CometCloud supports dynamically constructed transient spaces that have a specific scope definition (e.g., within the same geographical region or the same physical subnet). The global space is accessible to all peer nodes and acts as the default coordination platform. Membership and authentication mechanisms are adopted to restrict access to the transient spaces. The structure of the transient space is exactly the same as the global space. An application can switch between spaces at runtime and can simultaneously use multiple spaces. This layer also provides asynchronous (publish/subscribe) messaging and evening services. Finally, on-line clustering services support autonomic management and enable self-monitoring and control. Events describing the status or behavior of system components are clustered, and the clustering is used to detect anomalous behaviors.

The programming layer provides the basic framework for application development and management. It supports a range of paradigms including the master/worker/BOT. Masters generate tasks and workers consume them. Masters and workers can communicate via virtual shared space or using a direct connection. Scheduling and monitoring of tasks are supported by the application framework. The task consistency service handles lost tasks. Even though replication is provided by the infrastructure layer, a task may be lost due to network congestion. In this case, since there is no failure, infrastructure level replication may not be able to handle it. This can be handled by the master, for example, by waiting for the result of each task for a predefined time interval and, if it does not receive the result back, regenerating the lost task. If the master receives duplicate results for a task, it selects the first one and ignores other subsequent results. Other supported paradigms include workflow-based applications as well as Mapreduce [6] and Hadoop [7].

10.2.2 Comet Space

In Comet, a tuple is a simple XML string, where the first element is the tuple's tag and is followed by an ordered list of elements containing the tuple's fields. Each field has a name followed by its value. The tag, field names, and values must be actual data for a tuple and can contain wildcards ("*") for a template tuple. This lightweight format is flexible enough to represent the information for a wide range of applications and can support rich matching relationships [8]. Further more, the cross-platform nature of XML makes this format suitable for information exchange in distributed heterogeneous environments.

A tuple in Comet can be retrieved if it exactly or approximately matches a template tuple. Exact matching requires the tag and field names of the template tuple to be specified without any wildcard, as in Linda. However, this strict matching pattern must be relaxed in highly dynamic environments, since applications (e.g., service discovery) may not know exact tuple structures. Comet supports tuple retrievals with incomplete structure information using approximate matching, which only requires the tag of the template tuple be specified using a keyword or a partial keyword. Examples are shown in Figure 10.2. In this figure, tuple (a) tagged "contact" has fields "name, phone, email, dep" with values "Smith, 7324451000, smith@gmail.com, ece" and can be retrieved using tuple template (b) or (c).

Comet adapts Squid information discovery scheme and employs the Hilbert space-filling curve (SFC) [9] to map tuples from a semantic information space to a linear node index. The semantic information space, consisting of based-10 numbers and English words, is defined by application users. For example, a computational storage resource may belong to the 3D storage space with

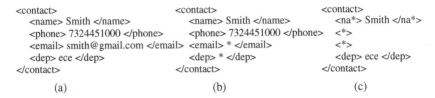

FIGURE 10.2. Example of tuples in CometCloud.

coordinates "space," "bandwidth," and "cost." Each tuple is associated with k keywords selected from its tag and field names, which are the keys of a tuple. For example, the keys of tuple (a) in Figure 10.2 can be "name, phone" in a 2D student information space. Tuples are local in the information space if their keys are lexicographically close, or if they have common keywords. The selection of keys can be specified by the applications.

A Hilbert SFC is a locality preserving continuous mapping from a k-dimensional (kD) space to a 1D space. It is locality preserving in that points that are close on the curve are mapped from close points in the kD space. The Hilbert curve readily extends to any number of dimensions. Its locality-preserving property enables the tuple space to maintain content locality in the index space. In Comet, the peer nodes form a one-dimensional overlay, which is indexed by a Hilbert SFC. Applying the Hilbert mapping, the tuples are mapped from the multi-dimensional information space to the linear peer index space. As a result, Comet uses the Hilbert SFC constructs the distribute hash table (DHT) for tuple distribution and lookup. If the keys of a tuple only include complete keywords, the tuple is mapped as a point in the information space and located on at most one node. If its keys consist of partial keywords, wildcards, or ranges, the tuple identifies a region in the information space. This region is mapped to a collection of segments on the SFC and corresponds to a set of points in the index space. Each node stores the keys that map to the segment of the curve between itself and the predecessor node. For example, as shown in Figure 10.3, five nodes (with id shown in solid circle) are indexed using SFC from 0 to 63, the tuple defined as the point (2, 1) is mapped to index 7 on the SFC and corresponds to node 13, and the tuple defined as the region $(2-3, 1-5)$ is mapped to two segments on the SFC and corresponds to nodes 13 and 32.

10.3 AUTONOMIC BEHAVIOR OF COMETCLOUD

10.3.1 Autonomic Cloudbursting

The goal of autonomic cloudbursts is to seamlessly and securely integrate private enterprise clouds and data centers with public utility clouds on-demand, to provide the abstraction of resizable computing capacity. It enables the

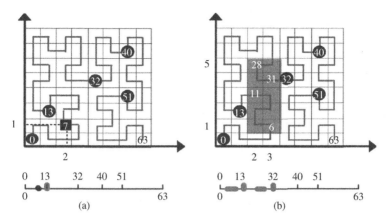

FIGURE 10.3. Examples of mapping tuples from 2D information space to 1D index space [1].

dynamic deployment of application components (which typically run on internal organizational compute resources) onto a public cloud to address dynamic workloads, spikes in demands, and other extreme requirements. Furthermore, given the increasing application and infrastructure scales, as well as their cooling, operation, and management costs, typical over-provisioning strategies are no longer feasible. Autonomic cloudbursts can leverage utility clouds to provide on-demand scale-out and scale-in capabilities based on a range of metrics.

The overall approach for supporting autonomic cloudbursts in CometCloud is presented in Figure 10.4. CometCloud considers three types of clouds based on perceived security/trust and assigns capabilities accordingly. The first is a highly trusted, robust, and secure cloud, usually composed of trusted/secure nodes within an enterprise, which is typically used to host masters and other key (management, scheduling, monitoring) roles. These nodes are also used to store states. In most applications, the privacy and integrity of critical data must be maintained; as a result, tasks involving critical data should be limited to cloud nodes that have required credentials. The second type of cloud is one composed of nodes with such credentials—that is, the cloud of secure workers. A privileged Comet space may span these two clouds and may contain critical data, tasks, and other aspects of the application-logic/workflow. The final type of cloud consists of casual workers. These workers are not part of the space but can access the space through the proxy and a request handler to obtain (possibly encrypted) work units as long as they present required credentials. Nodes can be added or deleted from any of these clouds by purpose. If the space needs to be scale-up to store dynamically growing workload as well as requires more computing capability, then autonomic cloudbursts target secure worker to scale up. But only if more computing capability is required, then unsecured workers are added.

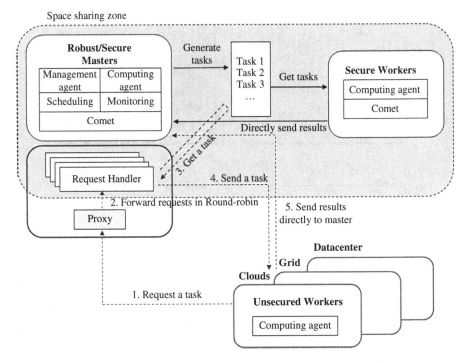

FIGURE 10.4. Autonomic cloudbursts using CometCloud.

Key motivations for autonomic cloudbursts include:

- *Load Dynamics.* Application workloads can vary significantly. This includes the number of application tasks as well the computational requirements of a task. The computational environment must dynamically grow (or shrink) in response to these dynamics while still maintaining strict deadlines.

- *Accuracy of the Analytics.* The required accuracy of risk analytics depends on a number of highly dynamic market parameters and has a direct impact on the computational demand—for example the number of scenarios in the Monte Carlo VaR formulation. The computational environment must be able to dynamically adapt to satisfy the accuracy requirements while still maintaining strict deadlines.

- *Collaboration of Different Groups.* Different groups can run the same application with different dataset policies . Here, policy means user's SLA bounded by their condition such as time frame, budgets, and economic models. As collaboration groups join or leave the work, the computational environment must grow or shrink to satisfy their SLA.

- *Economics.* Application tasks can have very heterogeneous and dynamic priorities and must be assigned resources and scheduled accordingly.

Budgets and economic models can be used to dynamically provision computational resources based on the priority and criticality of the application task. For example, application tasks can be assigned budgets and can be assigned resources based on this budget. The computational environment must be able to handle heterogeneous and dynamic provisioning and scheduling requirements.

- *Failures.* Due to the strict deadlines involved, failures can be disastrous. The computation must be able to manage failures without impacting application quality of service, including deadlines and accuracies.

10.3.2 Autonomic Cloudbridging

Autonomic cloudbridging is meant to connect CometCloud and a virtual cloud which consists of public cloud, data center, and grid by the dynamic needs of the application. The clouds in the virtual cloud are heterogeneous and have different types of resources and cost policies, besides, the performance of each cloud can change over time by the number of current users. Hence, types of used clouds, the number of nodes in each cloud, and resource types of nodes should be decided according to the changing environment of the clouds and application's resource requirements.

Figure 10.5 shows an overview of the operation of the CometCloud-based autonomic cloudbridging. The scheduling agent manages autonomic

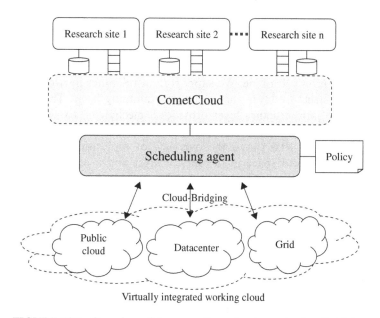

FIGURE 10.5. Overview of the operation of autonomic cloudbridging.

cloudbursts over the virtual cloud, and there can be one or more scheduling agents. A scheduling agent is located at a robust/secure master site. If multiple collaborating research groups work together and each group requires generating tasks with its own data and managing the virtual cloud by its own policy, then it can have a separate scheduling agent in its master site. The requests for tasks generated by the different sites are logged in the CometCloud virtual shared space that spans master nodes at each of the sites. These tasks are then consumed by workers, which may run on local computational nodes at the site, a shared data center, and a grid or on a public cloud infrastructure. A scheduling agent manages QoS constraints and autonomic cloudbursts of its site according to the defined policy. The workers can access the space using appropriate credentials, access authorized tasks, and return results back to the appropriate master indicated in the task itself.

A scheduling agent manages autonomic cloudbridging and guarantees QoS within user policies. Autonomic cloudburst is represented by changing resource provisioning not to violate defined policy. We define three types of policies.

- *Deadline-Based.* When an application needs to be completed as soon as possible, assuming an adequate budget, the maximum required workers are allocated for the job.
- *Budget-Based.* When a budget is enforced on the application, the number of workers allocated must ensure that the budget is not violated.
- *Workload-Based.* When the application workload changes, the number of workers explicitly defined by the application is allocated or released.

10.3.3 Other Autonomic Behaviors

Fault-Tolerance. Supporting fault-tolerance during runtime is critical to keep the application's deadline. We support fault-tolerance in two ways which are in the infrastructure layer and in the programming layer. The replication substrate in the infrastructure layer provides a mechanism to keep the same state as that of its successor's state, specifically coordination space and overlay information. Figure 10.6 shows the overview of replication in the overlay. Every node has a local space in the service layer and a replica space in the infrastructure layer. When a tuple is inserted or extracted from the local space, the node notifies this update to its predecessor and the predecessor updates the replica space. Hence every node keeps the same replica of its successor's local space. When a node fails, another node in the overlay detects the failure and notifies it to the predecessor of the failed node. Then the predecessor of the failed node merges the replica space into the local space, and this makes all the tuples from the failed node recovered. Also the predecessor node makes a new replica for the local space of its new successor. We also support fault-tolerance in the programming layer. Even though replica of each node is maintained, some tasks can be lost during runtime because of network

CometCloud

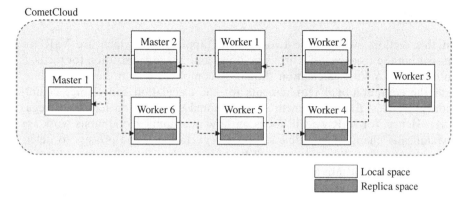

| | Local space |
| | Replica space |

FIGURE 10.6. Replication overview in the CometCloud overlay.

congestion or task generation during failure. To address this issue, the master checks the space periodically and regenerates lost tasks.

Load Balancing. In a cloud environment, executing application requests on underlying grid resources consists of two key steps. The first, which we call VM *Provisioning*, consists of creating VM instances to host each application request, matching the specific characteristics and requirements of the request. The second step is mapping and scheduling these requests onto distributed physical resources (*Resource Provisioning*). Most virtualized data centers currently provide a set of general-purpose VM classes with generic resource configurations, which quickly become insufficient to support the highly varied and interleaved workloads. Furthermore, clients can easily under- or overestimate their needs because of a lack of understanding of application requirements due to application complexity and/or uncertainty, and this often results in over-provisioning due to a tendency to be conservative.

The decentralized clustering approach specifically addresses the distributed nature of enterprise grids and clouds. The approach builds on a decentralized messaging and data analysis infrastructure that provides monitoring and density-based clustering capabilities. By clustering workload requests across data center job queues, the characterization of different resource classes can be accomplished to provide autonomic VM provisioning. This approach has several advantages, including the capability of analyzing jobs across a dynamic set of distributed queues, the nondependency on a priori knowledge of the number of clustering classes, and the amenity for online application and timely adaptation to changing workloads and resources. Furthermore, the robust nature of the approach allows it to handle changes (joins/leaves) in the job queue servers as well as their failures while maximizing the quality and efficiency of the clustering.

10.4 OVERVIEW OF COMETCLOUD-BASED APPLICATIONS

In this section, we describe two types of applications which are VaR for measuring the risk level of a firm's holdings and image registration for medical informatics. A VaR calculation should be completed within the limited time, and the computational requirements for the calculation can change significantly. Besides, the requirement for additional computation happens irregularly. Hence, for VaR we will focus on how autonomic cloudbursts work for dynamically changing workloads. Image registration is the process to determine the linear/nonlinear mapping T between two images of the same object or similar objects that are acquired at different time, or from different perspectives. Besides, because a set of image registration methods are used by different (geographically distributed) research groups to process their locally stored data, jobs can be injected from multiple sites. Another distinguished difference between two applications is that data size of image registration is much larger than that of VaR. For a 3D image, the image size is usually a few tens of megabytes. Hence, image data should be separated from its task tuple, and instead it locates on a separate storage server and its location is indicated in the task tuple. For image registration, because it usually needs to be completed as soon as possible within budget limit, we will focus on how CometCloud works using budget-based policy.

10.4.1 Value at Risk (VaR)

Monte Carlo VaR is a very powerful measure used to judge the risk of portfolios of financial instruments. The complexity of the VaR calculation stems from simulating portfolio returns. To accomplish this, Monte Carlo methods are used to "guess" what the future state of the world may look like. Guessing a large number of times allows the technique to encompass the complex distributions and the correlations of different factors that drive portfolio returns into a discreet set of *scenarios*. Each of these Monte Carlo scenarios contains a state of the world comprehensive enough to value all instruments in the portfolio, thereby allowing us to calculate a return for the portfolio under that scenario.

The process of generating Monte Carlo scenarios begins by selecting primitive instruments or *invariants*. To simplify simulation modeling, invariants are chosen such that they exhibit returns that can be modeled using a stationary normal probability distribution [11]. In practice these invariants are returns on stock prices, interest rates, foreign exchange rates, and so on. The universe of invariants must be selected such that portfolio returns are driven only by changes to the invariants.

To properly capture the nonlinear pricing of portfolios containing options, we use Monte Carlo techniques to simulate many realizations of the invariants. Each realization is referred to as a scenario. Under each of these scenarios, each option is priced using the invariants and the portfolio is valued. As outlined above, the portfolio returns for scenarios are ordered from worst loss to best gain, and a VaR number is calculated.

10.4.2 Image Registration

Nonlinear image registration [12] is the computationally expensive process to determine the mapping T between two images of the same object or similar objects acquired at different time, in different position or with different acquisition parameters or modalities. Both intensity/area based and landmark based methods have been reported to be effective in handling various registration tasks. Hybrid methods which integrate both techniques have demonstrated advantages in the literature [13–15].

Alternative landmark point detection and matching method are developed as a part of hybrid image registration algorithm for both 2D and 3D images [16]. The algorithm starts with automatic detection of a set of landmarks in both fixed and moving images, followed by a coarse to fine estimation of the nonlinear mapping using the landmarks. Intensity template matching is further used to obtain the point correspondence between landmarks in the fixed and moving images. Because there is a large portion of outliers in the initial landmark correspondence, a robust estimator, RANSAC [17], is applied to reject outliers. The final refined inliers are used to robustly estimate a Thin Spline Transform (TPS) [18] to complete the final nonlinear registration.

10.5 IMPLEMENTATION AND EVALUATION

In this section, we evaluate basic CometCloud operations first, and then compare application runtime varying the number of nodes after describing how the applications were implemented using CometCloud. Then we evaluate VaR using workload-based policy and Image registration using budget-based policy. Also we evaluate CometCloud with/without a scheduling agent. For deadline-based policy that doesn't have a budget limit, because it allocates as many workers as possible, we applied it just to compare results with and without scheduling agent for budget-based policy.

10.5.1 Evaluation of CometCloud

Basic CometCloud Operations. In this experiment we evaluated the costs of basic tuple insertion and exact retrieval operations on the Rutgers cloud. Each machine was a peer node in the CometCloud overlay and the machines formed a single CometCloud peer group. The size of the tuple in the experiment was fixed at 200 bytes. Aing-pong-like process was used in the experiment, in which an application process inserted a tuple into the space using the *out* operator, read the same tuple using the *rd* operator, and deleted it using the *in* operator. In the experiment, the *out* and exact matching *in/rd* operators used a three-dimensional information space. For an *out* operation, the measured time corresponded to the time interval between when the tuple was posted into the space and when the response from the destination was received. For an *in* or *rd* operation, the measured time was the time interval between when the template was posted into the space and when the matching tuple was returned to the application, assuming that a matching tuple existed in the space. This time included the time for routing the template, matching tuples in the repository, and returning the matching tuple. The average performances were measured for different system sizes.

Figure 10.7a plots the average measured performance and shows that the system scales well with increasing number of peer nodes. When the number of peer nodes increases 32 times (i.e., from 2 to 64), the average round-trip time increases only about 1.5 times, due to the logarithmic complexity of the routing algorithm of the Chord overlay. *rd* and *in* operations exhibit similar

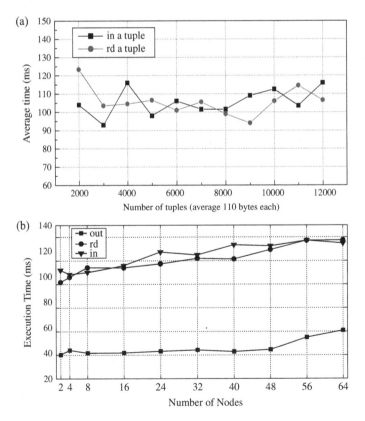

FIGURE 10.7. Evaluation of CometCloud primitives on the Rutgers cloud. (a) Average time for out, in, and rd operators for increasing system sizes. (b) Average time for in and rd operations with increasing number of tuples. System size fixed at 4 nodes.

TABLE 10.1. The Overlay Join Overhead on Amazon EC2

Number of Nodes	Time (msec)
10	353
20	633
40	1405
80	3051
100	3604

performance, as shown in Figure 10.7a. To further study the *in/rd* operator, the average time for *in/rd* was measured using an increasing number of tuples. Figure 10.7b shows that the performance of *in/rd* is largely independent of the number of tuples in the system: The average time is approximately 105 ms as the number of tuples is increased from 2000 to 12,000.

Overlay Join Overhead. To share the Comet space, a node should join the CometCloud overlay and each node should manage a finger table to keep track of changing neighbors. When a node joins the overlay, it first connects to a predefined bootstrap node and sends its information such as IP address to the bootstrap. Then the bootstrap node makes a finger table for the node and sends it back to the node. Hence, the more nodes join the overlay at the same time, the larger join overhead happens. Table 10.1 shows the join overhead varying the number of joining nodes at the same time. We evaluated it on Amazon EC2, and the figure shows that the join overhead is less than 4 seconds even when 100 nodes join the overlay at the same time.

10.5.2 Application Runtime

All tasks generated by the master are inserted into the Comet space and each should be described by XML tags that are described differently for the purpose of an application. Data to be computed can be included in a task or outside of the task such as in a file server. To show each case, let VaR tasks include data inside the tuple and image registration tasks include data outside of the tuple because image data are relatively larger than VaR data. A typical *out* task for VaR is described as shown below.

```
< VarAppTask >
  < TaskId > taskid < /TaskId >
  < DataBlock > data_blocks < /DataBlock >
  < MasterNetName > master_name < /MasterNetName >
< /VarAppTask >
```

In image registration, each worker processes a whole image, hence the number of images to be processed is the number of tasks. Besides, because the image size is too large to be conveyed on a task, when the master generates tasks, it just includes the data location for the task as a tag. After a worker takes a task from the Comet space, it connects to the data location and gets data. A typical *out* task for image registration is described as shown below.

```
< ImageRegAppTask >
  < TaskId > taskid < /TaskId >
  < ImageLocation > image_location < /ImageLocation >
  < MasterNetName > master_name < /MasterNetName >
< /ImageRegAppTask >
```

Figure 10.8 shows the total application runtime of CometCloud-based (a) VaR and (b) image registration on Amazon EC2 for different number of scenarios. In this experiment, we ran a master on the Rutgers cloud and up to 80 workers on EC2 instances. Each worker ran on a different instance. We assumed that all workers were unsecured and did not share the Comet space. As shown in Figure 10.8a, and as expected, the application runtime of VaR decreases as the number of EC2 workers increases up to some points. However, when the number of workers is larger than some values, the application runtime increases (see 40 and 80 workers). This is because of the communication overhead that workers ask tasks to the proxy. Note that the proxy is the access point for unsecured workers even though a request handler sends a task to the worker after the proxy forwards the request to the request handler. If the computed data size is large and it needs more time to be completed, then workers will have less access the proxy and the communication overhead of the proxy will decrease. Figure 10.8b shows the performance improvement of image registration when the number of workers increases. The same as in VaR, when the number of workers increases, the application runtime decreases. In this application, one image takes around 1 minute to be completed, hence the communication overhead does not appear in the graph.

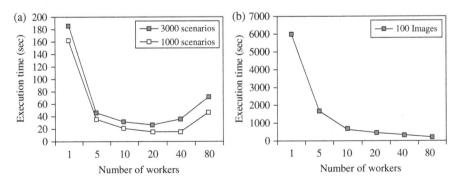

FIGURE 10.8. Evaluation of CometCloud-based applications on Amazon EC2. (a) VaR. (b) Image registration.

10.5.3 Autonomic Cloudbursts Behaviors

VaR Using Workload-Based Policy. In this experiment, autonomic cloud-burst is represented by the number of changing workers. When the application workload increases (or decreases), a predefined number of workers are added (or released), based on the application workload. Specifically, we defined *workload-specific* and *workload-bounded* policies. In workload-specific, a user can specify the workload that nodes are allocated or released. In workload-bounded, whenever the workload increases by more than a specified threshold, a predefined number of workers is added. Similarly, if the workload decreases by more than the specified threshold, the predefined number of workers is released.

Figure 10.9 demonstrates autonomic cloudbursts in CometCloud based on two of the above polices—that is, workload-specific and workload-bounded. The figure plots the changes in the number of worker as the workload changes. For the workload-specific policy, the initial workload is set to 1000 simulations and the initial number of workers is set to 8. The workload is then increased or decreased by 200 simulations at a time, and the number of worked added or released set to 3. For workload-bounded policy, the number of workers is initially 8 and the workload is 1000 simulations. In this experiment, the workload is increased by 200 and decreased by 400 simulations, and 3 workers are added or released at a time. The plots in Figure 10.9 clearly demonstrate the cloudburst behavior. Note that the policy used as well as the thresholds can be changed on-the-fly.

Image Registration Using Budget-Based Policy. The virtual cloud environment used for the experiments consisted of two research sites located at Rutgers University and the University of Medicine and Dentistry of New Jersey: one public cloud (i.e., Amazon Web Service (AWS) EC2 [10]) and one private data center at Rutgers (i.e., TW). The two research sites hosted their own image servers and job queues, and workers running on EC2 or TW access these image servers to get the image described in the task assigned to them (see Figure 10.5). Each image

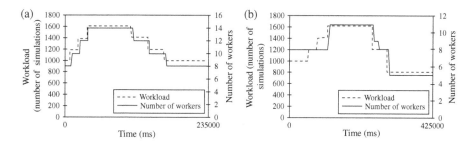

FIGURE 10.9. Policy-based autonomic cloudburst using CometCloud. (a) Workload-specific policy. (b) Workload-bounded policy.

server has 250 images resulting in a total of 500 tasks. Each image is two-dimensional, and its size is between 17 kB and 65 kB. The costs associated with running tasks on EC2 and TW nodes were computed based on costing models presented in references 10 and 9, respectively. On EC2, we used standard small instances with a computing cost of $0.10/hour, data transfer costs of $0.10/GB for inward transfers, and $0.17/GB for outward transfers. Because the computing cost is charged by hourly base, users should pay for the full hour even though they use just a few minutes. However, in this experiment, we calculated the cost by seconds because the total runtime is less than an hour.

Costs for the TW data center included hardware investment, software, electricity, and so on, and were estimated based on the discussion in [9], which says that a data center costs $120K/life cycle per rack and has a life cycle of 10 years. Hence, we set the cost for TW to $1.37/hour per rack. In the experiments we set the maximum number of available nodes to 25 for TW and 100 for EC2. Note that TW nodes outperform EC2 nodes, but are more expensive. We used budget-based policy for scheduling where the scheduling agent tries to complete tasks as soon as possible without violating the budget. We set the maximum available budget in the experiments to $3 to complete all tasks. The motivation for this choice is as follows. If the available budget was sufficiently high, then all the available nodes on TW will be allocated, and tasks would be assigned until the all the tasks were completed. If the budget is too small, the scheduling agent would not be able to complete all the tasks within the budget. Hence, we set the budget to an arbitrary value in between. Finally, the monitoring component of the scheduling agent evaluated the performance every 1 minute.

Evaluation of CometCloud-Based Image Registration Application Enabled Scheduling Agent. The results from the experiments are plotted in Figure 10.10. Note that since the scheduling interval is 1 min, the x axis corresponds to both time (in minutes) and the scheduling iteration number. Initially, the CometCloud scheduling agent does not know the cost of completing a task. Hence, it initially allocated 10 nodes each from TW and EC2. Figure 10.10a shows the scheduled number of workers on TW and EC2 and Figure 10.10b shows costs per task for TW and EC2. In the beginning, since the budget is sufficient, the scheduling agent tries to allocate TW nodes even though they cost more than EC2 node. In the second scheduling iteration, there are 460 tasks still remaining, and the agent attempts to allocate 180 TW nodes and 280 EC2 nodes to finish all tasks as soon as possible within the available budget. If TW and EC2 could provide the requested nodes, all the tasks would be completed by next iteration. However, since the maximum available number of TW nodes is only 25, it allocates these 25 TW nodes and estimates that a completion time of 7.2 iterations. The agent then decides on the number of EC2 workers to be used based on the estimated rounds.

In case of the EC2, it takes around 1 minute to launch (from the start of virtual machine to ready state for consuming tasks); as a result, by the 4th

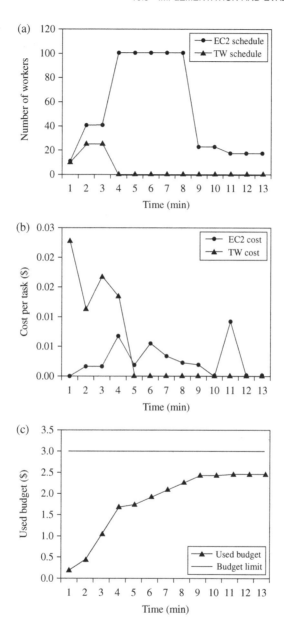

FIGURE 10.10. Experimental evaluation of medical image registration using Comet-Cloud. Results were obtained using the scheduling agent. (a) Scheduled number of nodes. (b) Calculated cost per task. (c) Cumulative budget usage over time.

iteration the cost per task for EC2 increases. At this point, the scheduling agent decides to decrease the number of TW nodes, which are expensive, and instead it decides to increase the number of EC2 nodes using the available budget. By the 9th iteration, 22 tasks are still remaining. The scheduling agent now decides to release 78 EC2 nodes because they will not have jobs to execute. The reason why the remaining jobs have not completed at the 10th iteration (i.e., 10 minutes) even though 22 nodes are still working is that the performance of EC2 decreased for some reason in our experiments. Figure 10.10c shows the used budget over time. It shows that all the tasks were completed within the budget and took around 13 minutes.

Comparison of Execution Time and Used Budget with/without Scheduling Agent. Figure 10.11 shows a comparison of execution time and used budget with/without the CometCloud scheduling agent. In the case where only EC2 nodes are used, when the number of EC2 nodes is decreased from 100 to 50 and 25, the execution time increases and the used budget decreases as shown in Figures 10.11a and 10.11b. Comparing the same number of EC2 and TW nodes (25 EC2 and 25 TW), the execution time for 25 TW nodes is approximately half that for 25 EC2 nodes; however, the cost for 25 TW nodes is significantly more than that for 25 EC2 nodes. When the CometCloud autonomic scheduling agent is used, the execution time is close to that obtained using 25 TW nodes, but the cost is much smaller and the tasks are completed within the budget. An interesting observation from the plots is that if you don't have any limits on the number of EC2 nodes used, then a better solution is to allocate as many EC2 nodes as you can. However, if you only have a limited number of nodes to use and want to be guaranteed that your job is completed in limited budget, then the autonomic scheduling approach achieves an acceptable trade-off. Note that launching EC2 nodes at runtime impacts application performance because it

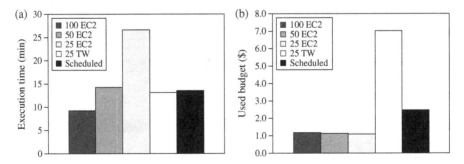

FIGURE 10.11. Experimental evaluation of medical image registration using Comet-Cloud - Comparison of performance and costs with/without autonomic scheduling. (a) Execution time varying the number of nodes of EC2 and TW. (b) Used budget over time varying the number of nodes for EC2 and TW.

takes about a minute: A node launched at time t minutes only starts working at time $t + 1$ minutes. Since different cloud service will have different performance and cost profiles, the scheduling agent will have to use historical data and more complex models to compute schedules, as we extend CometCloud to include other service providers.

10.6 CONCLUSION AND FUTURE RESEARCH DIRECTIONS

In this chapter, we investigated autonomic cloudbursting and autonomic cloudbridging to support real-world applications such as VaR and a medical image registration application using the CometCloud framework. CometCloud enables a virtual computational cloud that integrates local computational environments (data centers) and public cloud services on-the-fly and provides a scheduling agent to manage cloudbridging. CometCloud supports on-line risk analytics that should be time-critically completed and has dynamically changing workload and medical informatics which has large data and receives requests from different distributed researcher groups with varied computational requirements and QoS constraints. The policy-driven scheduling agent uses the QoS constraints along with performance history and the state of the resources to determine the appropriate size and mix of the public and private cloud resources that should be allocated to a specific request. These applications were deployed on private clouds at Rutgers University, the Cancer Institute of New Jersey, and a public cloud at Amazon EC2. The results demonstrated the effectiveness of autonomic cloudbursts as well as policy-based autonomic scheduling and showed the feasibility to run similar types of applications using CometCloud.

We are supporting high-level application models such as Hadoop/MapReduce and workflow abstraction. Also, we are deploying more applications such as Ensemble Kalman Filter, partial differential equation (PDE), pharmaceutical informatics, Mandelbrot, and replica exchange on Amazon EC2. To prove the feasibility of autonomic cloudbursting and autonomic cloudbridging for more heterogeneous clouds, we plan to extend the virtual cloud such as TeraGrid and Eucalyptus.

ACKNOWLEDGMENTS

The authors would like to thank Zhen Li, Shivangi Chaudhari, and Lin Yang for their contributions to this work. The research presented in this chapter was supported in part by National Science Foundation via grants numbers IIP 0758566, CCF-0833039, DMS-0835436, CNS 0426354, IIS 0430826, and CNS 0723594, by Department of Energy via the grant number DE-FG02-06ER54857, by The Extreme Scale Systems Center at ORNL and the Department of Defense, and by an IBM Faculty Award and was conducted as part of the NSF Center for Autonomic Computing at Rutgers University. Experiments on the EC2 were supported by a grant from Amazon Web Services.

REFERENCES

1. Z. Li and M. Parashar, A computational infrastructure for grid-based asynchronous parallel applications, in *Proceedings of the 16th International Symposium on High Performance Distributed Computing*. ACM, New York, 2007, pp. 229–230.

2. C. Schmidt and M. Parashar, Squid: Enabling search in dht-based systems, *Journal of Parallel and Distributed Computing*, **68**(7):962–975, 2008.

3. I. Stoica, R. Morris, D. Karger, M. F. Kaashoek, and H. Balakrishnan, Chord: A scalable peer-to-peer lookup service for internet applications, in *Proceedings of the 2001 Conference on Applications, Technologies, Architectures, and Protocols for Computer Communications*, 2001, pp. 149–160.

4. C. Schmidt and M. Parashar, Enabling flexible queries with guarantees in p2p systems, *IEEE Internet Computing*, **8**(3):19–26, 2004.

5. N. Carriero and D. Gelernter, Linda in context, *Communications of the ACM*, **32**(4):444–458, 1989.

6. J. Dean and S. Ghemawat, Mapreduce: Simplified data processing on large clusters, *Communications of the ACM*, **51**(1):107–113, 2008.

7. Hadoop, http://hadoop.apache.org/core/.

8. R. Tolksdorf and D. Glaubitz, Coordinating web-based systems with documents in xmlspaces, in *Proceedings of the Sixth IFCIS International Conference on Cooperative Information Systems*, Springer-Verlag, New York, 2001, pp. 356–370.

9. B. Moon, H. V. Jagadish, C. Faloutsos, and J. H. Saltz, Analysis of the clustering properties of the hilbert space-filling curve, *IEEE Transactions on Knowledge and Data Engineering*, **13**(1):124–141, 2001.

10. Amazon elastic compute cloud. http://aws.amazon.com/ec2/.

11. A. Meucci, *Risk and Asset Allocation*, Springer-Verlag, New York, 2005.

12. T. Vercauteren, X. Pennec, A. Perchant, and N. Ayache, Symmetric logdomain diffeomorphic registration: A demons-based approach, in *Proceedings of the International Conference on Medical Image Computing and Computer Assisted Intervention*, Vol. 5241, 2008, pp. 754–761.

13. C. DeLorenzo, X. Papademetris, K. Wu, K. P. Vives, D. Spencer, and J. S. Duncan, Nonrigid 3D brain registration using intensity/feature information, in *Proceedings of the International Conference on Medical Image Computing and Computer Assisted Intervention*, Vol. 4190, 2004, pp. 1611–3349.

14. B. Fischer and J. Modersitzki, Combination of automatic and landmark based registration: The best of both worlds, *SPIE Medical Imaging*, 2003, pp. 1037–1047.

15. A. Azar, C. Xu, X. Pennec, and N. Ayache, An interactive hybrid nonrigid registration framework for 3D medical images, in *Proceedings of the International Symposium on Biomedical Imaging*, 2006, pp. 824–827.

16. L. Yang, L. Gong, H. Zhang, J. L. Nosher, and D. J. Foran, A method for parallel platform based acceleration of landmark based image registration, in *Proceedings of the European Conference on Parallel Computing*, Netherlands, 2009.

17. M. A. Fischler and R. C. Bolles, Random sample consensus: A paradigm for model fitting with applications to image analysis and automated cartography, *Communications of the ACM*, **24**:381–395, 1981.

18. H. Chui and A. Rangarajan, A new point matching algorithm for nonrigid registration, *Computer Vision and Image Understanding*, **89**(2):114–141, 2003.

19. Apc, http://apcmedia.com/salestools/CMRP-5T9PQG R3 EN.pdf

20. D. Nurmi, R. Wolski, C. Grzegorczyk, G. Obertelli, S. Soman, L. Youseff, and D. Zagorodnov, The Eucalyptus open-source cloudcomputing system, in *Proceedings of the 9th IEEE/ACM International Symposium on Cluster Computing and the Grid (CCGrid 2009)*, 2009, pp. 124-131.

CHAPTER 11

T-SYSTEMS' CLOUD-BASED SOLUTIONS FOR BUSINESS APPLICATIONS

MICHAEL PAULY

11.1 INTRODUCTION

Thanks to the widespread acceptance of the Internet, cloud computing has become firmly established in the private sphere. And now enterprises appear poised to adopt this technology on a large scale. This is a further example of the consumerization of IT—with technology in the consumer world driving developments in the business world.

T-Systems is one of Europe's largest ICT service providers. It offers a wide range of IT, telecommunications, and integrated ICT services, and it boasts extensive experience in managing complex outsourcing projects. The company offers hosting and other services from its 75 data centers with over 50,000 servers and over 125.000 MIPS—in Europe, Asia, the Americas and Africa. In addition, it is a major provider of desktop and network services. T-Systems approaches cloud computing from the viewpoint of an organization with an established portfolio of dynamic, scalable services delivered via networks. The service provider creates end-to-end offerings that integrate all elements, in collaboration with established hardware and software vendors.

Cloud computing is an opportunity for T-Systems to leverage its established concept for services delivered from data centers. Cloud computing entails the industrialization of IT production, enabling customers to use services and resources on demand. Business, however, cannot adopt wholesale the principles of cloud computing from the consumer world. Instead, T-Systems aligns cloud computing with the specific requirements of large enterprises. This can mean

Cloud Computing: Principles and Paradigms, Edited by Rajkumar Buyya, James Broberg and Andrzej Goscinski Copyright © 2011 John Wiley & Sons, Inc.

rejecting cloud principles where these conflict with statutory requirements or security imperatives [1].

11.2   WHAT ENTERPRISES DEMAND OF CLOUD COMPUTING

Whether operated in-house or by an external provider, ICT is driven by two key factors (Figure 11.1): cost pressure and market pressure. Both of these call for increases in productivity.

11.2.1   Changing Markets

Today's markets are increasingly dynamic. Products and skills rapidly become obsolete, eroding competitiveness. So incumbents need to find and implement new ideas at an ever faster pace. Also, new businesses are entering the market more rapidly, and they are extending their portfolios by forging alliances with other players.

The Internet offers the opportunity to implement new business models and integrate new stakeholders into processes—at speeds that were previously unimaginable. One excellent example is the automotive industry, which has brought together OEMs, suppliers, dealers, and customers on shared Internet

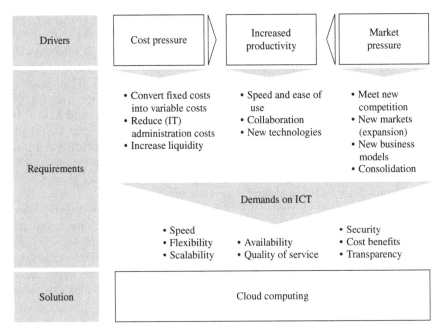

FIGURE 11.1. The route to cloud computing—industrialization of IT.

platforms. In line with Web 2.0 principles, customers can influence vehicle development. This and other examples demonstrate the revolutionary potential of cloud computing.

Markets and market participants are changing at an unprecedented pace. New competitors are constantly entering the ring, and established enterprises are undergoing transformation. Value grids are increasing the number of joint ventures. This often leads to acquisitions, mergers, and divestments and gives rise to new enterprises and business models.

At the same time, markets have become more flexible. This not only enables enterprises to move into new lines of business with greater ease and speed, it also changes prevailing market conditions. Customers respond faster to changes in the supply of goods and services, market shares shift, some supply-and-demand relationships vanish completely, and individual markets shrink or disappear. These phenomena have, for instance, radically transformed the retail industry in recent years.

Against this background, companies not only need to scale up, but also to scale down—for example, if demand falls, or if they take a strategic decision to abandon a line of business or territory.

There is a need to respond to all these factors. Pressure is rising not only on management, but also on ICT—because business processes supported by ICT have to be rapidly modified to meet new imperatives. While the focus was on saving money, ICT outsourcing was the obvious answer. But traditional outsourcing cannot deliver the speed and agility markets now demand.

Today's legacy ICT infrastructures have evolved over many years and lack flexibility. Moreover, few organizations can afford the capital investment required to keep their technology up to date. At the same time, ICT resources need to be quickly scaled up and down in line with changing requirements.

Intriguingly, ICT triggered this trend toward faster, more flexible businesses. Now, this has come full circle—with more dynamic businesses calling for more dynamic ICT.

11.2.2 Increased Productivity

Today, enterprise ICT and business processes are closely interwoven—so that the line between processes and technology is becoming blurred. As a result, ICT is now a critical success factor: It significantly influences competitiveness and value creation. The impact of fluctuations in the quality of ICT services (for example, availability) is felt immediately. The nonavailability of ERP (enterprise resource planning) and e-mail systems brings processes grinding to a halt and makes collaboration impossible. And the resulting time-to-market delays mean serious competitive disadvantage.

The demands are also increasing when it comes to teamwork and collaboration. Solutions not only have to deliver speed plus ease of use, they also have to support simultaneous work on the same documents, conduct team meetings with participants on different continents, and provide the necessary infrastructure (anywhere access, avoidance of data redundancy, etc.). That is no easy task in today's environment.

11.2.3 Rising Cost Pressure

Globalization opens up new markets. But it also means exposure to greater competition. Prices for goods and services are falling at the same time that the costs for power, staff, and raw materials are rising. The financial crisis has aggravated the situation, with market growth slowing or stagnating. To master these challenges, companies have to improve their cost structures.

This generally means cutting costs. Staff downsizing and the divestment of loss-making units are often the preferred options. However, replacing fixed costs with variable costs can also contribute significantly—without resorting to sensitive measures such as layoffs. This improves liquidity. Money otherwise tied up in capital investment can be put to good use elsewhere. In extreme cases, this can even avert insolvency; most commonly, the resulting liquidity is used to increase equity, mitigating financial risk.

A radical increase in the flexibility of the ICT landscapes can deliver significant long-term benefits. It fundamentally transforms cost structures, since ICT-related expenses are a significant cost factor. ICT spending (for example, administration and energy costs) offers considerable potential for savings.

However, those savings must not be allowed to impact the quality of ICT services. The goal must be standardized, automated (i.e., industrialized), and streamlined ICT production. The high quality of the resulting ICT services increases efficiency and effectiveness and enhances reliability, thereby cutting costs and improving competitiveness.

In other words, today's businesses expect a great deal from their ICT. It not only has to open up market opportunities, it also has to be secure and reliable. This means that ICT and associated services have to deliver speed, flexibility, scalability, security, cost-effectiveness, and transparency. And cloud computing promises to meet all these expectations.

11.3 DYNAMIC ICT SERVICES

Expectations differ considerably, depending on company size and industry. For example, a pharmaceuticals multinational, a traditional midsize retailer, and a startup will all have very different ICT requirements, particularly when it comes to certification.

However, they all face the same challenges: the need to penetrate new markets, to launch new services, to supply sales models, or to make joint offerings with partners. This is where dynamic ICT delivers tangible benefits.

At first sight, it may seem paradoxical to claim that standardization can create flexibility. But industrialized production within the scope of outsourcing is not restrictive. In fact, quite the opposite: Industrialization provides the basis for ICT services that are dynamic, fast, in line with real-world requirements, and secure and reliable. ICT services of this kind are the foundation of a cloud that provides services on demand. Only by industrializing ICT is it possible to create the conditions for the flexible delivery of individual ICT services, and for combining them in advantageous ways.

Standardized production also enables ICT providers to achieve greater economies of scale. However, this calls for highly effective ICT management—on the part of both the service provider and the customer. Proven concepts and methodologies from the manufacturing industry can be applied to ICT. The following are particularly worth mentioning:

- Standardization
- Automation
- Modularization
- Integrated creation of ICT services

11.3.1 Steps Toward Industrialized ICT

Standardization and automation greatly reduce production costs and increase the efficiency and flexibility of ICT. However, they come at a price: There is less scope for customization. This is something that everyone with a personal e-mail account from one of the big providers has encountered. Services of this kind fulfill their purpose, but offer only very stripped-down functionality and are usually free of charge. More sophisticated e-mail solutions are available only via fee-based "premium" offerings. In other words, lower costs and simpler processes go hand in hand. And this is why companies have to streamline their processes. When it comes to standardization, ICT service providers focus on the technology while businesses focus on services and processes.

The growing popularity of standard software reflects this. In the ERP space, this trend has been evident for years, with homegrown solutions being replaced by standard packages. A similar shift can be observed in CRM, with a growing number of slimmed-down offerings available as software as a service (SaaS) from the cloud.

At the same time, standards-based modularization enables new forms of customization. However, greater customization of the solutions delivered to businesses reduces efficiency for providers, thereby pushing up prices. In the world of ICT, there is a clear conflict between customization and cost.

Standardization has the appeal (particularly for service providers) of cutting ICT production costs. This means that ICT providers have to take these arguments in favor of standardization seriously and adapt their production accordingly. For enterprise customers, security and compliance are also key considerations, alongside transparent service delivery, data storage, and transfer. These parameters must be clearly defined in contracts and service-level agreements (SLAs).

11.3.2   Customization through Modularization

Modular production enables ICT to be tailored to customers' specific requirements—in conjunction with standardization. Modularization allows providers to pool resources as the basis for delivering the relevant services [2].

Modularization is essentially a set of standardized individual modules that can be combined. The resulting combinations give rise to sophisticated applications tailored to the needs of the specific company. Standardized interfaces (e.g., APIs) between individual modules play a pivotal role. And one of the great strengths of modules is their reusability.

The more easily and flexibly such modules can be combined, the greater the potential benefits. Providers have to keep the number of modules as low as possible while meeting as many of their customers' requirements as possible, and this is far from easy.

One example of modularization in a different context is combining Web services from various sources (mashups). In the cloud era, providers of modules of this kind claim that they enable users with no programming skills to support processes with ICT. However, experience shows that where such skills are lacking, a specialist integrator is generally called in as an implementation partner.

The benefit of modular services is that they can be flexibly combined, allowing standard offerings to be tailored to specific requirements. At the same time, they prevent customized solutions from straying too far from the standard, which would significantly drive up the costs of later modifications.

11.3.3   Integrated Creation of ICT Services

Each of the elements outlined above can have significant advantages. But only an integrated approach to creating ICT services—combining standardization, automation and modularization—can deliver the entire range of benefits. This gives the provider standardized, automated production processes and enables the desired services to be delivered to the customer quickly and flexibly.

In the context of outsourcing, this form of industrialization yields its full potential when providers and users have a close, two-way relationship with corresponding connectivity. This enables businesses to play an active part in production (ICT supply chain), tailoring ICT services to their changing needs. However, the technology that supports this relationship must be based on standards. Cloud computing promises to make switching to a different provider quick and easy, but that is only possible if users are careful to avoid provider lock-in.

11.4 IMPORTANCE OF QUALITY AND SECURITY IN CLOUDS

11.4.1 Quality (End-to-End SLAs)

If consumers' Internet or ICT services are unavailable, or data access is slow, the consequences are rarely serious. But in business, the nonavailability of a service can have a grave knock-on effect on entire mission-critical processes—bringing production to a standstill, or preventing orders from being processed.

In such instances, quality is of the essence. The user is aware of the performance of systems as a whole, including network connectivity. In complex software applications, comprising multiple services and technical components, each individual element poses a potential risk to the smooth running of processes. Cloud-service providers therefore have to offer end-to-end availability, backed by clearly defined SLAs.

The specific quality requirements are determined by weighing up risk against cost. The importance of a particular process and the corresponding IT solution are assessed. The findings are then compared with the service levels on offer. As a rule, higher service levels come at a higher price. Where a process is not critical, businesses are often willing to accept relatively low availability to minimize costs. But if a process is critical, they will opt for a higher service level, with a corresponding price tag. So the quality question is not about combining the highest service levels, but about selecting the right levels for each service.

11.4.2 Compliance and Security

Compliance and security are increasingly important for cloud-computing providers. Security has been the subject of extensive media coverage and debate. And surveys consistently pinpoint it as the greatest obstacle to cloud computing. In a 2008 cio.com study, IT decision-makers cited security and loss of control over data as the key drawbacks of cloud computing.

However, for businesses looking to deploy a form of cloud computing, legal issues (e.g., privacy and liability) are considerably more important. And this is why cloud providers have to find ways of enabling customers to meet statutory requirements.

Consumer Cloud Versus Enterprise Cloud. The Internet has given rise to new forms of behavior, even when concluding contracts on-line. When presented with general terms and conditions, many consumers simply check the relevant box and click "OK," often not realizing that they are entering into a legally binding agreement. Standard contracts are now commonly used for consumer services offered from the cloud. However, this does not meet the demands of businesses.

Cloud computing raises no new legal issues, but it makes existing ones more complex. This increased complexity is due to two factors. On the one hand, cloud computing means that data no longer have to reside in a single location.

On the other hand, business scenarios involving multiple partners are now conceivable. It is therefore often impossible to say exactly where data are stored and what national legislation applies. And where data are handled by multiple providers from different countries (sometimes on the basis of poorly structured contracts), the issue of liability becomes correspondingly complex.

Cloud Computing from an Enterprise Perspective. With this in mind, businesses should insist on comprehensive, watertight contracts that include provisions for the recovery and return of their data, even in the event of provider bankruptcy. Moreover, they should establish the country where servers and storage systems are located. Cloud principles notwithstanding, services still have to be performed and data stored at specific physical locations. Where data are located determines whose law applies and also determines which government agencies can access it. In addition to these "hard" factors, enterprises have to consider that data-privacy cultures differ from country to country.

Having the legal basis for liability claims is one thing; successfully prosecuting them is quite another. This is why it is important to know the contractually agreed legal venue. Moreover, it is useful to have a single end-to-end service level agreement defining availability across all services.

Even stricter statutory requirements apply where data are of a personal nature (e.g., employee details in an HR system). Financial data are also subject to stringent restrictions. In many parts of Europe, personal data enjoys special protection. But even encryption cannot guarantee total security. Solutions that process and store data in encrypted form go a long way toward meeting statutory data-protection requirements. However, they are prohibited in some countries. As a result, there are limits to secure data encryption in the cloud.

Companies listed on the U.S. stock exchange are subject to the Sarbanes–Oxley Act (SOX), requiring complete data transparency and audit trails. This poses particular challenges for cloud providers. To comply with SOX 404, CEOs, CFOs, and external auditors have to report annually on the adequacy of internal control systems for financial reporting. ICT service providers are responsible for demonstrating the transparency of financial transactions. However, providing this evidence is especially difficult, if not impossible, in a cloud environment. This is a challenge that cloud providers must master—if necessary, by departing from cloud principles.

Service providers also have to ensure that data are not lost and do not fall into the wrong hands. The EU has data-security regulations that apply for all European companies. For example, personal details may only be disclosed to third parties with the consent of the individual involved. Moreover, public-sector organizations generally insist on having sensitive data processed in their home country. This is a particularly thorny issue when it comes to patents, since attitudes to intellectual property differ greatly around the world.

Moreover, some industries and markets have their own statutory requirements. It is therefore essential that customers discuss their specific needs with the provider. And the provider should be familiar with industry-specific practices and acquire appropriate certification.

Providers also have to safeguard data against loss, and businesses that use cloud services should seek a detailed breakdown of disaster-recovery and business-continuity plans.

Other legal issues may arise directly from the technology behind cloud computing. On the one hand, conventional software licensing (based on CPUs) can run counter to cloud-computing business models. On the other hand, licenses are sometimes subject to geographical restrictions, making it difficult to deploy them across borders.

What Enterprises Need. Cloud computing and applicable ICT legislation are based on diametrically opposed principles. The former is founded on liberalism and unfettered development—in this case, of technical opportunities. The latter imposes tight constraints on the handling of data and services, as well as on the relationship between customers and providers. And it seems unlikely that these two perspectives will be reconciled in the near future.

Cloud providers have to meet the requirements of the law and of customers alike. As a rule, this leads them to abandon some principles of "pure" cloud computing—and to adopt only those elements that can be aligned with applicable legislation and without risk. However, deployment scenarios involving services from a public cloud are not inconceivable. So providers have to critically adapt cloud principles.

Furthermore, providers working for major corporations have to be dependable in the long term, particularly where they deliver made-to-measure solutions for particular business processes. This is true whether the process is critical or not. If a provider goes out of business, companies can expect to be without the service for a long time. So before selecting a cloud provider, customers should take a long hard look at candidates' services, ability to deliver on promises, and, above all, how well SLAs meet their needs [4].

11.5 DYNAMIC DATA CENTER—PRODUCING BUSINESS-READY, DYNAMIC ICT SERVICES

11.5.1 Flexibility Across All Modules

Agility at the infrastructure level alone is not enough to provide fast, flexible ICT services. Other dynamic levels and layers are also required (Figure 11.2) [3]. Ultimately, what matters to the user is the flexibility of the system or service as a whole. So service quality is determined by the slowest component.

Adaptable processing and storage resources at the computing level must be supported by agile LAN and WAN infrastructures. Flexibility is also important when it comes to application delivery, scalability, and extensibility via functional modules. Management processes must allow for manual intervention,

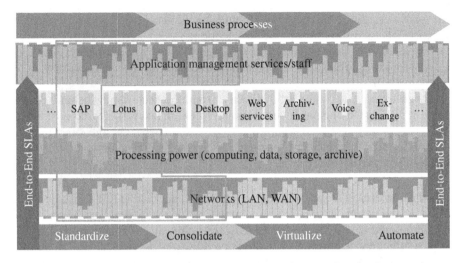

FIGURE 11.2. Flexibility at all levels is a basic requirement for cloud computing.

where necessary, and automatically link the various layers. These factors enable the creation of end-to-end SLAs across all components.

Every dynamic ICT service is based on a resource pool from which computing, data, and storage services can be delivered as required. Dynamic network and application services are also available. Moreover, the (business) applications are optimized for deployment with pooled resources.

When customers opt for a dynamic service, they require an SLA that covers not only individual components, but also the service as a whole, including any WAN elements.

Toward Dynamic, Flexible ICT Services. The first step is to standardize the customer's existing environment. IT systems running different software releases have to be migrated, often to a single operating system. Hardware also has to be standardized—for example, by bringing systems onto a specific processor generation (such as x86). Eliminating disparate operating systems and hardware platforms at this stage makes it considerably easier to automate further down the line.

The second step is technical consolidation. This not only reduces the number of physical servers, but also slims down data storage. Identical backup and restore mechanisms are introduced at this stage; and small, uneconomical data centers are closed.

The third step involves separating the logical from the physical. Virtualization means that services no longer depend on specific hardware. This has particular benefits in terms of maintenance. Moreover, virtualization enables server resources to be subdivided and allocated to different tasks.

Process automation is more than just another component—it is key to meeting the rising demand for IT services. What's more, it slashes costs, improves efficiency (for example, by preventing errors), and accelerates standard procedures. Providers' ability to offer cloud-computing services will largely depend on whether they can implement mechanisms for automatic management, allocation, and invoicing of resources.

In the business world, automation must also support seamless integration of financial, accounting, and ordering systems.

11.5.2 T-Systems' Core Cloud Modules: Computing, Storage

Computing. The computing pool is based on server farms located in different data centers. Logical server systems are created automatically at these farms. The server systems comply with predefined standards. They are equipped with the network interface cards required for communications and integration with storage systems. No internal hard drives or direct-attached storage systems are deployed.

The configuration management database (CMDB) plays a key role in computing resource pools (Figure 11.3). This selects and configures the required physical server (1). Once a server has been selected from the pool, virtualization technology is selected in line with the relevant application and the demands it has to meet (2). At the same time, the configuration requirements are sent to the network configuration management system (3) and to the storage configuration management system (4). Once all the necessary elements are in place, the storage systems are mounted on the servers, after which the operating-system images are booted (5).

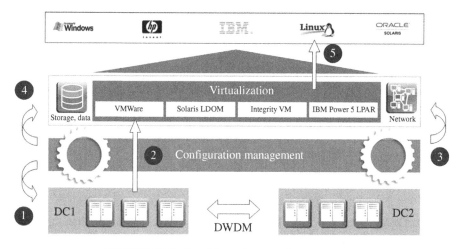

FIGURE 11.3. Provision of computing resources.

Cloud computing enables a customer's application to be switched from server to server within a defined group at virtually any interval (from minutes to hours or days). This means that the configuration database must be updated automatically to accurately reflect the current state of systems and configurations at all times.

The CMDB also supports other tasks that are not required in conventional ICT environments. These include enhanced monitoring and reporting, quality management, and corresponding resource planning. Moreover, an ongoing inventory of systems and their configurations is essential for rapid troubleshooting.

Operating systems are provided in the form of images stored on a central storage system. These are in read-only mode to ensure rapid startup. To limit the number of operating systems and releases—and minimize related administrative effort—only one version of each operating system is maintained. This is employed to configure and boot the servers. This high degree of standardization significantly reduces administration overhead.

Applications Are Also Virtualized. Speed is of the essence for cloud-computing providers. Decoupling operating systems from applications plays a key role here, because it reduces both initial and subsequent application-provisioning time (following a failure, for example). Making applications available is simply a matter of mounting them. This approach has other advantages: Applications can quickly be moved from one server to another, and updates can be managed independently of operating systems.

However, the full benefits can only be realized if there is a high degree of automation and standardization in the IT infrastructure and the applications themselves.

Storage. The necessary storage is provided and configured in much the same way as the computing resources. IP-based storage systems are deployed. To reduce hardware-configuration effort, the computing systems use neither SAN nor direct-attached storage.

Using fiber-channel (FC) cards in the servers and deploying an FC network increases overall system complexity substantially. The IP storage systems are linked via Gbit Ethernet. Storage is automatically allocated to the server systems that require it.

Storage resources are located in different fire zones as well as in different data centers, preventing data loss in the event of a disaster. The storage system handles replication of data between data centers and fire zones, so computing resources are not needed for this purpose (Figure 11.4).

Backup-Integrated Storage. In addition to storage resources, backups are necessary to safeguard against data loss. For this reason, and in the interests of automation, the Dynamic Data Center model directly couples backup to

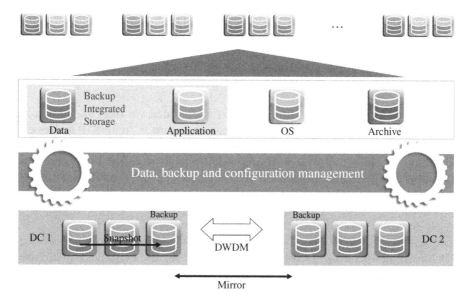

FIGURE 11.4. Storage resources: backup-integrated, read-only, and archive storage.

storage; in other words, backup-integrated storage (BIS) is provided, along with full management functionality.

To accelerate backup and reduce the volume of data transferred, data are backed up on hard disks within the storage system by means of snapshotting. This simplifies the structure of the computing systems (as no backup LAN is necessary) and minimizes the potential for temporal bottlenecks.

Storage systems normally provide for a 35-day storage period. Usually, the last three days are accessible on-line, with the rest being accessible from a remote site.

Archive and Other Storage. Archive systems are also available for long-term data storage. Like BIS, these are hard-disk-based and linked via IP to the respective systems. Data for archiving is replicated within the archive system and in a separate fire zone, as well as at a remote data center. Replication is handled by the archive system itself.

Archive storage can be managed in two ways. Archiving can be initiated either from the applications themselves, which then handle administration of all data, or via a document management system.

Some systems require a hard-disk cache. This is not worth backing up via BIS, since data in a cache change rapidly, and the original data are stored and backed up elsewhere in the system.

Communications. The computing and storage modules are integrated via an automatically configured LAN or corresponding virtual networks (VPNs). The servers deployed in the computing module are equipped with multiple network cards as standard. Depending on requirements, these are grouped to form the necessary networks.

Networks are segregated from each other by means of VPN technology. Backup-integrated storage eliminates the need for a separate backup network.

Customer Network. Access for customers is provided via Internet/VPN connections. Services are assigned to companies by means of unique IP addresses.

As standard, access to Dynamic Data Centers is protected via redundant, clustered firewalls. Various versions are available to cater to a range of different customer and application requirements. Virtual firewalls are configured automatically. Due to the high level of standardization, access is entirely IP-based.

Storage and Administration Network. A separate storage network is provided for accessing operating-system images, applications, and customer and archive data. Configuration is handled automatically. An additional network, segregated from the others, is available for managing IT components. Used purely for systems configuration and other administration tasks, this network has no access to the customer's data or content.

11.5.3 Dynamic Services—A Brief Overview

The Dynamic Data Center concept underlies all T-Systems Dynamic Services. All the resources required by a given service are automatically provided by the data center. This lays the foundations for a portfolio of solutions aimed at business customers.

Dynamic Applications for Enterprises. Enterprises require applications that support specific processes. This applies both to traditional outsourcing and to business relationships in the cloud. T-Systems has tailored its portfolio to fulfill these requirements.

- *Communications and Collaboration.* These are key components for any company. Work on projects often entails frequent changes in user numbers. As a result, enterprises need flexible means of handling communications and collaboration. T-Systems offers the two leading e-mail systems, Microsoft Exchange and IBM Lotus Domino via Dynamic Services, ensuring their rapid integration into existing environments.
- *ERP and CRM.* Dynamic systems are available to support core ERP and CRM processes. T-Systems offers SAP and Navision solutions in this space.
- *Development and Testing.* Software developers often need access—at short notice and for limited periods of time—to server systems running a variety of operating system versions and releases. Dynamic Services offer the

flexibility needed to meet these demands. Configured systems that are not currently required can be locked and mothballed. So when computing resources are no longer needed, no further costs are incurred. That is the advantage of Dynamic Services for developers.

- *Middleware.* When it comes to middleware, Dynamic Services can lay the foundation for further (more complex) services. In addition, businesses can deploy them directly and integrate them into their own infrastructure. The common term for offerings of this type is platform-as-a-service (PaaS). T-Systems' middleware portfolio includes dynamic databases, Web servers, portals, and archiving components.

- *Front-Ends and Devices.* Not only business applications, but also users' PC systems, can be provided via the cloud. These systems, including office applications, can be made available to users via Dynamic Desktop Services.

Introducing New Services in a Dynamic Data Center. Cloud computing is developing at a rapid pace. This means that providers have to continuously review and extend their offerings. Here, too, a standardized approach is key to ensuring that the services delivered meet business customers' requirements.

First, automatic mechanisms have to be developed for standardizing the installation of typical combinations of operating system, database, and application software. These mechanisms must also support automated procedures for starting and stopping applications. The software components and their automatic management functions are subject to release and patch management procedures agreed with the vendors.

Deploying the combination of version and patches authorized by the vendor enables a provider to assume end-to-end responsibility for a service. Automatic monitoring and monthly reports are put in place for each service. An operating manual is developed and its recommendations tested in a pilot installation before the production environment goes live. The operating manual includes automatic data backup procedures.

Next, a variety of quality options are developed. These can include redundant resources across multiple fire zones. A concept for segregating applications from each other is also created. This must include provisions for selectively enabling communications with other applications via defined interfaces, implemented in line with customer wishes. Only after EU legislation (particularly regarding liability) has been reviewed is the application rolled out to data centers worldwide.

11.5.4   Dynamic Data Centers Across the Globe

T-Systems delivers Dynamic Services from multiple data centers around the world (Figure 11.5). These are mostly designed as twin-core facilities; in other words, each location has two identical data centers several kilometers apart.

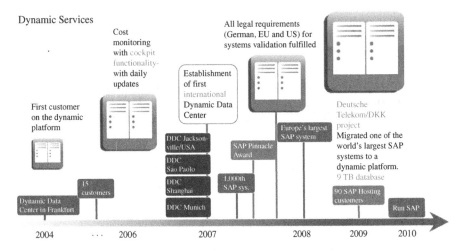

FIGURE 11.5. The development of Dynamic Services.

All Dynamic Data Centers are based on the original concept used for the first data center of this kind in Frankfurt. There are currently facilities in the United States, Brazil, Germany, Singapore, and Malaysia.

11.6 CASE STUDIES

The industrialization of outsourcing not only impacts costs, it also affects customers' business processes and sourcing strategies. In terms of sourcing, the effects depend on the company's current ICT and on the size of the enterprise. This is particularly obvious in the case of startups or businesses with an existing ICT infrastructure.

Dynamic ICT Services for Startups. Startups often have no ICT infrastructure and lack the knowledge required to establish and operate one. However, to put their business concepts into practice, companies of this kind need rapid access to reliable, fully functional ICT services. And because it is difficult to predict how a startup will grow, its ICT has to offer maximum scalability and flexibility, thereby enabling the company to meet market requirements. Moreover, few venture capitalists are prepared to invest in inflexible hardware and software that has to be depreciated over a number of years.

By deploying dynamic ICT services, a startup can find its feet in those early, uncertain stages—without maintaining in-house ICT. And if demand falls, the company does not have to foot the bill for unneeded resources. Instead, it can quickly and easily scale down—and invest more capital in core tasks.

Dynamic ICT Services at Companies with Existing ICT Infrastructures. In comparison to startups, most large companies already have established ICT departments, with the skills needed to deliver the desired services. These in-house units often focus on ICT security rather than flexibility. After all, a company's knowledge and expertise resides to a large extent in its data. These data must be secure and available at all times—because it is often a business-critical asset, the loss of which could jeopardize the company's future.

In addition to cost savings, companies that use Dynamic Services benefit from greater transparency—it is clear at all times which resources are available and which are currently being used.

The opportunity to source ICT as a service opens up a wide range of new options. For example, an international player with a complex legacy environ-ment can introduce Dynamic Services for SAP Solutions for a specific business segment by adding resources to its German company and then rolling these out to its other national subsidiaries. This kind of dynamic ICT provisioning also enables fast, flexible penetration of new markets, without the need for advance planning and long-term operation of additional ICT resources. And seasonal fluctuations in business can be dealt with even more easily.

Figure 11.6 shows the flexible and dynamic provisioning of resources. Provisioning starts during the implementation phase, with a development and test environment over a one-month period. This is followed by go-live of the production environment. Additional development and training resources can be accessed rapidly, if and when required.

11.6.1 Example: Dynamic Infrastructure Services

A mid-sized furniture manufacturer with over 800 employees leverages dynamic infrastructure services. Within the scope of make-to-order manufacturing, the company produces couches and armchairs in line with customers' specific needs. On average, it makes some 1500 couches and armchairs daily. During the

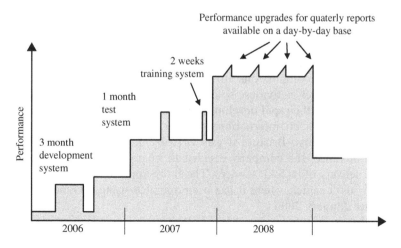

FIGURE 11.6. Flexible ICT provisioning for dynamic markets.

summer months, this figure is almost halved—and use of the company's in-house IT falls accordingly. In June 2005, the IT department outsourced data backup and provisioning of mainframe resources to T-Systems. The service provider now provides these as services, on a pay-per-use basis. As a result, the furniture manufacturer no longer has to maintain in-house IT resources sized for peak loads. Instead, its IT infrastructure is provided as a service [infrastructure as a service (IaaS)].

If the data volume or number of users suddenly rises or falls, the company can scale its resources up or down—and costs increase or decrease accordingly. At the same time, it benefits from a solution that is always at the leading edge of technology, without having to invest in that technology itself. Through regular reporting, the customer also gains new transparency into the services it uses. Around-the-clock monitoring provides maximum protection against system failure and downtime. And the service provider backs up data from production planning, on-line sales, transactions, e-mails, and the ERP system at one of its data centers.

11.6.2   Example: Dynamic Services for SAP

Infrastructure services like these enable the delivery of more complex services. In this context, T-Systems specializes in business-critical applications supported by SAP. So far about 100 European-based companies use Dynamic Services from T-Systems. Among them are Shell, Philips, Linde, and MAN.

In this case a global group with a workforce of almost 500,000 in 60 countries operates in various business segments. However, its core business is direct sales: The enterprise sells its products via sales partners, who process 110,000 orders each week using the central SAP system. If these orders are not processed, payment will not be received; as a result, system failure could significantly impact the company. Furthermore, around one million calls (in Germany alone) are handled each year in the CRM module, as are tasks ranging from a simple change of address to changes in financing arrangements. The group's IT strategy is therefore focused on ensuring efficient, effective IT support for its international direct sales.

Due to weekly commissions for sales employees and the unpredictable nature of call-center activities, system-sizing estimates can vary by up to 500%. In addition, the rapid development of the company's SAP R/3 solution, in conjunction with an international rollout, has significantly increased IT resource requirements. Because it was virtually impossible to quantify these factors in advance, the company decided to migrate to a dynamic platform for future delivery of its SAP services. The entire application was transferred to T-Systems' data center, where it has been operated using a Dynamic Services model since January 2006.

With the move, the group has implemented a standardization strategy that enables flexible adaptation of business processes and makes for more straightforward and transparent group-wide reporting. With a conventional infrastructure sized for peak loads, SAP R/3 operating costs would have been twice as high as with the current dynamic solution. Furthermore, the company now has the opportunity to scale its resources up or down by 50% within a single day.

11.6.3 DKK: Europe's Largest SAP Installation Is Run in a Private Cloud

Many simple applications and small-scale, non-core systems already run in the cloud. And now, some enterprises are having larger-scale, mission-critical apps delivered in this way, or via their own secure clouds. For example, Deutsche Telekom currently utilizes ICT services from a private cloud for some of its business-critical processes.

This move was motivated by the desire to establish a highly scalable, on-demand system for processing invoicing and payments and for managing customer accounts and receivables. Deutsche Telekom's revenue management system, DKK, handles more than 1.5 million payments a day from approximately 30 million customers, making it one of the largest SAP installations in the world (Figure 11.5).

T-Systems migrated the legacy server environment, comprising two monolithic systems with a capacity of some 50,000 SAPS, to a highly standardized, rapidly scalable solution based on Dynamic Services for SAP. Performance improved by more than 20%, while costs sank by 30%.

The customer can freely scale ICT resources up or down. Furthermore, a disaster recovery solution was established at a second, remote data center for failure protection. The system currently handles nine terabytes of data.

The significant cost reductions are the result of vendor-independent standardization of hardware with clustered deployment of commodity components, backup-integrated storage, and extensively standardized processes and procedures.

Quantifiable improvements, in technical terms, include a 45% drop in server response times and a 40% reduction in batch-job processing times. Even client response times have shrunk by close to 10%. This means that the new platform significantly exceeds the targeted 20% improvement in overall system performance. The dynamic cloud solution has proved more cost-effective, and delivers better performance, than an environment operated on traditional lines.

The transition to the new platform did not involve modifications to the custom-developed SAP ABAP programs. Returning to a conventional environment would be even more straightforward, since no changes to the operating system would be required, and the application's business logic would not be affected.

11.6.4 Migrating Globally Distributed SAP Systems to a Dynamic Platform

Even experienced ICT providers with a successful track record in transformation projects have to perform risk analysis, including fallback scenarios. To reduce the risk of migrations (in both directions), cloud providers that serve large enterprises require skills in both conventional operations and cloud computing.

In one transformation engagement, when the contract was signed, the customer was operating 232 SAP systems worldwide, with a total capacity of 1.2 million SAPS. Initially, T-Systems assumed responsibility for the systems within the scope of a conventional outsourcing agreement, without changing the mode of operation. The original environment was then gradually replaced by a commercial cloud solution (managed private cloud). This approach has since become established practice for the T-Systems. Within the agreed timeframe of 18 months, 80% of the systems were migrated. This major project involved not only SAP software, but also non-SAP systems, which were brought onto the new platform via dedicated interfaces.

Projects on this scale have a lasting influence on a service provider's datacenter infrastructure, and they drive IT industrialization. In this particular engagement, the most compelling arguments for the customer were (a) the security and reliability of the provider's data centers and (b) the smooth interaction between the SAP interfaces. Transparency throughout the entire systems landscape, lower costs, and greater responsiveness to changing requirements were the key customer benefits.

11.7 SUMMARY: CLOUD COMPUTING OFFERS MUCH MORE THAN TRADITIONAL OUTSOURCING

Cloud computing is an established concept from the private world that is gaining ground in the business world. This trend can help large corporations master some of their current challenges—for example, cost and market pressures that call for increased productivity. While conventional outsourcing can help enterprises cut costs, it cannot deliver the flexibility they need. And greater flexibility brings even greater savings. Cloud computing poses a challenge to traditional outsourcing models. If the paradigm shift becomes a reality, IT users will have even more choice when it comes to selecting a provider—and cloud computing will become a further alternative to existing sourcing options.

Cloud computing makes for a more straightforward and flexible relationship between providers and their customers. Contracts can be concluded more rapidly, and resources are available on demand. What's more, users benefit from end-to-end services delivered dynamically in line with their specific business requirements. And companies only pay for the services they actually use, significantly lowering IT investment. In a nutshell, cloud computing means that IT services are available as and when they are needed—helping pare back costs.

When it comes to selecting a sourcing model, cost and flexibility are only two of the many factors that have to be taken into account. Further important aspects are data privacy, security, compliance with applicable legislation, and quality of service. The public cloud cannot offer a solution to these issues, which is why private clouds are well worth considering.

Providers of cloud computing for large corporations need to be able to intelligently combine their offerings with customer-specific IT systems and services. In some cases, they can also leverage resources and services from the public cloud.

But first, companies must consider which services and resources can be outsourced to the cloud, and they must also define how important each one is for the organization. Services that are not mission critical do not require robust service levels and can be delivered via the public cloud. But business-critical IT processes call for clearly defined SLAs, which, in turn, pushes up costs. Private clouds are an effective way of meeting these requirements.

In both cloud-computing models, services are delivered on a standardized basis. This reflects a general trend toward the industrialization of IT. Provision of services via a private cloud requires higher standards of quality than via the public cloud. By means of industrialization, cloud-computing providers enable more efficient use of their IT infrastructures, thereby increasing productivity. This not only cuts production costs, it also reduces the environmental footprint of businesses' IT.

Case studies show that the general principles of cloud computing have already been successfully adapted and employed for business-critical applications hosted in a private cloud. However, enterprises must carefully weigh up the pros and cons of each model and decide which resources can be provided via the public cloud and which require a private cloud.

ACKNOWLEDGMENTS

I would like to thank various colleagues, especially Dr. Martin Reti for his comments and extensive discussions on this chapter.

REFERENCES

1. M. Reti and M. Pauly, Cloud Computing—Alternative Sourcing Strategy for Business ICT, White Paper, T-Systems, Frankfurt/Main, March 2009.
2. T. Chou, *Seven Software Business Models*, Active Book Press, 2008.
3. M. Pauly, Dynamic Services—Flexible ICT Resources Implemented Based on Need, White Paper, T-Systems, Frankfurt/Main, March, 2008.
4. J. Staten, *Is Cloud Computing Ready for the Enterprise? Not Yet, But This Disruptive Innovation Is Maturing Fast*, Forrester Research, March 7, 2008.

CHAPTER 12

WORKFLOW ENGINE FOR CLOUDS

SURAJ PANDEY, DILEBAN KARUNAMOORTHY,
and RAJKUMAR BUYYA

12.1 INTRODUCTION

A workflow models a process as consisting of a series of steps that simplifies the complexity of execution and management of applications. Scientific workflows in domains such as high-energy physics and life sciences utilize distributed resources in order to access, manage, and process a large amount of data from a higher level. Processing and managing such large amounts of data require the use of a distributed collection of computation and storage facilities. These resources are often limited in supply and are shared among many competing users. The recent progress in virtualization technologies and the rapid growth of cloud computing services have opened a new paradigm in distributed computing for utilizing existing (and often cheaper) resource pools for on-demand and scalable scientific computing. Scientific Workflow Management Systems (WfMS) need to adapt to this new paradigm in order to leverage the benefits of cloud services.

Cloud services vary in the levels of abstraction and hence the type of service they present to application users. Infrastructure virtualization enables providers such as Amazon[1] to offer virtual hardware for use in compute- and data-intensive workflow applications. Platform-as-a-Service (PaaS) clouds expose a higher-level development and runtime environment for building and deploying workflow applications on cloud infrastructures. Such services may also expose domain-specific concepts for rapid-application development. Further up in the cloud stack are Software-as-a-Service providers who offer end users with

[1] http://aws.amazon.com

Cloud Computing: Principles and Paradigms, Edited by Rajkumar Buyya, James Broberg and Andrzej Goscinski   Copyright © 2011 John Wiley & Sons, Inc.

standardized software solutions that could be integrated into existing workflows.

This chapter presents workflow engines and its integration with the cloud computing paradigm. We start by reviewing existing solutions for workflow applications and their limitations with respect to scalability and on-demand access. We then discuss some of the key benefits that cloud services offer workflow applications, compared to traditional grid environments. Next, we give a brief introduction to workflow management systems in order to highlight components that will become an essential part of the discussions in this chapter. We discuss strategies for utilizing cloud resources in workflow applications next, along with architectural changes, useful tools, and services. We then present a case study on the use of cloud services for a scientific workflow application and finally end the chapter with a discussion on visionary thoughts and the key challenges to realize them. In order to aid our discussions, we refer to the workflow management system and cloud middleware developed at CLOUDS Lab, University of Melbourne. These tools, referred to as Cloudbus toolkit [1], henceforth, are mature platforms arising from years of research and development.

12.2 BACKGROUND

Over the recent past, a considerable body of work has been done on the use of workflow systems for scientific applications. Yu and Buyya [2] provide a comprehensive taxonomy of workflow management systems based on workflow design, workflow scheduling, fault management, and data movement. They characterize and classify different approaches for building and executing workflows on Grids. They also study existing grid workflow systems highlighting key features and differences.

Some of the popular workflow systems for scientific applications include DAGMan (Directed Acyclic Graph MANager) [3, 4], Pegasus [5], Kepler [6], and Taverna workbench [7]. DAGMan is a workflow engine under the Pegasus workflow management system. Pegasus uses DAGMan to run the executable workflow. Kepler provides support for Web-service-based workflows. It uses an actor-oriented design approach for composing and executing scientific application workflows. The computational components are called actors, and they are linked together to form a workflow. The Taverna workbench enables the automation of experimental methods through the integration of various services, including WSDL-based single operation Web services, into workflows. For a detailed description of these systems, we refer you to Yu and Buyya [2].

Scientific workflows are commonly executed on shared infrastructure such as Tera-Grid,[2] Open Science Grid,[3] and dedicated clusters [8]. Existing workflow systems tend to utilize these global Grid resources that are made available

---

[2] http://www.teragrid.org
[3] http://www.opensciencegrid.org

through prior agreements and typically at no cost. The notion of leveraging virtualized resources was new, and the idea of using resources as a utility [9, 10] was limited to academic papers and was not implemented in practice. With the advent of cloud computing paradigm, economy-based utility computing is gaining widespread adoption in the industry.

Deelman et al. [11] presented a simulation-based study on the costs involved when executing scientific application workflows using cloud services. They studied the cost performance trade-offs of different execution and resource provisioning plans, and they also studied the storage and communication fees of Amazon S3 in the context of an astronomy application known as Montage [5, 10]. They conclude that cloud computing is a cost-effective solution for data-intensive applications.

The Cloudbus toolkit [1] is our initiative toward providing viable solutions for using cloud infrastructures. We propose a wider vision that incorporates an inter-cloud architecture and a market-oriented utility computing model. The Cloudbus workflow engine [12], presented in the sections to follow, is a step toward scaling workflow applications on clouds using market-oriented computing.

12.3 WORKFLOW MANAGEMENT SYSTEMS AND CLOUDS

The primary benefit of moving to clouds is application scalability. Unlike grids, scalability of cloud resources allows real-time provisioning of resources to meet application requirements at runtime or prior to execution. The elastic nature of clouds facilitates changing of resource quantities and characteristics to vary at runtime, thus dynamically scaling up when there is a greater need for additional resources and scaling down when the demand is low. This enables workflow management systems to readily meet quality-of-service (QoS) requirements of applications, as opposed to the traditional approach that required advance reservation of resources in global multi-user grid environments. With most cloud computing services coming from large commercial organizations, service-level agreements (SLAs) have been an important concern to both the service providers and consumers. Due to competitions within emerging service providers, greater care is being taken in designing SLAs that seek to offer (a) better QoS guarantees to customers and (b) clear terms for compensation in the event of violation. This allows workflow management systems to provide better end-to-end guarantees when meeting the service requirements of users by mapping them to service providers based on characteristics of SLAs. Economically motivated, commercial cloud providers strive to provide better services guarantees compared to grid service providers. Cloud providers also take advantage of economies of scale, providing compute, storage, and bandwidth resources at substantially lower costs. Thus utilizing public cloud services could be economical and a cheaper alternative (or add-on) to the more expensive dedicated resources. One of the benefits of using virtualized resources for workflow execution, as opposed to having direct access to the physical machine, is the reduced need for securing the physical resource from malicious code using techniques such as sandboxing. However, the long-term effect of using virtualized resources in clouds that effectively share a "slice" of the physical machine, as opposed to using dedicated resources for high-performance applications, is an interesting research question.

12.3.1 Architectural Overview

Figure 12.1 presents a high-level architectural view of a Workflow Management System (WfMS) utilizing cloud resources to drive the execution of a scientific

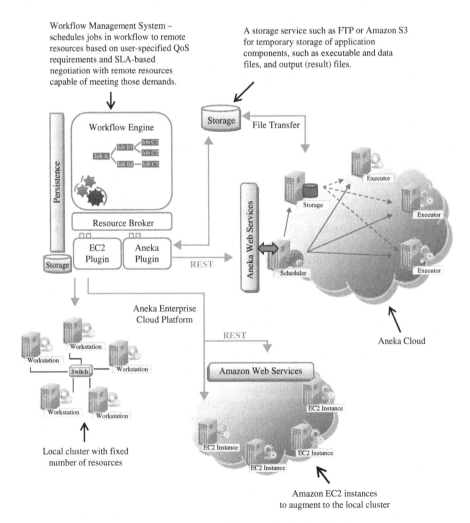

FIGURE 12.1. Workflow engine in the cloud.

workflow application. The workflow system comprises the workflow engine, a resource broker [13], and plug-ins for communicating with various technological platforms, such as Aneka [14] and Amazon EC2. A detailed architecture describing the components of a WfMS is given in Section 12.4.

User applications could only use cloud services or use cloud together with existing grid/cluster-based solutions. Figure 12.1 depicts two scenarios, one where the Aneka platform is used in its entirety to complete the workflow, and the other where Amazon EC2 is used to supplement a local cluster when there are insufficient resources to meet the QoS requirements of the application. Aneka [13], described in further detail in Section 12.5, is a PaaS cloud and can be run on a corporate network or a dedicated cluster or can be hosted entirely on an IaaS cloud. Given limited resources in local networks, Aneka is capable of transparently provisioning additional resources by acquiring new resources in third-party cloud services such as Amazon EC2 to meet application demands. This relieves the WfMS from the responsibility of managing and allocating resources directly, to simply negotiating the required resources with Aneka.

Aneka also provides a set of Web services for service negotiation, job submission, and job monitoring. The WfMS would orchestrate the workflow execution by scheduling jobs in the right sequence to the Aneka Web Services.

The typical flow of events when executing an application workflow on Aneka would begin with the WfMS staging in all required data for each job onto a remote storage resource, such as Amazon S3 or an FTP server. In this case, the data would take the form of a set of files, including the application binaries. These data can be uploaded by the user prior to execution, and they can be stored in storage facilities offered by cloud services for future use. The WfMS then forwards workflow tasks to Aneka's scheduler via the Web service interface. These tasks are subsequently examined for required files, and the storage service is instructed to stage them in from the remote storage server, so that they are accessible by the internal network of execution nodes. The execution begins by scheduling tasks to available execution nodes (also known as worker nodes). The workers download any required files for each task they execute from the storage server, execute the application, and upload all output files as a result of the execution back to the storage server. These files are then staged out to the remote storage server so that they are accessible by other tasks in the workflow managed by the WfMS. This process continues until the workflow application is complete.

The second scenario describes a situation in which the WfMS has greater control over the compute resources and provisioning policies for executing workflow applications. Based on user-specified QoS requirements, the WfMS schedules workflow tasks to resources that are located at the local cluster and in the cloud. Typical parameters that drive the scheduling decisions in such a scenario include deadline (time) and budget (cost) [15, 16]. For instance, a policy for scheduling an application workflow at minimum execution cost would utilize local resources and then augment them with cheaper cloud resources, if needed, rather than using high-end but more expensive cloud resources. On the contrary, a policy that scheduled workflows to achieve minimum execution time would always use high-end cluster and cloud resources, irrespective of costs. The resource provisioning policy determines the extent of additional resources to be provisioned on the public clouds. In this second scenario, the WfMS interacts directly with the resources provisioned. When using Aneka, however, all interaction takes place via the Web service interface.

The following sections focuses on the integration of workflow management systems and clouds and describes in detail practical issues involved in using clouds for scientific workflow applications.

12.4   ARCHITECTURE OF WORKFLOW MANAGEMENT SYSTEMS

Scientific applications are typically modeled as workflows, consisting of tasks, data elements, control sequences and data dependencies. *Workflow management systems* are responsible for managing and executing these workflows. According to Raicu et al. [17], scientific workflow management systems are engaged and applied to the following aspects of scientific computations: (1) describing complex scientific procedures (using GUI tools, workflow specific languages), (2) automating data derivation processes (data transfer components), (3) high-performance computing (HPC) to improve throughput and performance (distributed resources and their coordination), and (4) provenance management and query (persistence components). The Cloudbus Workflow Management System [12] consists of components that are responsible for handling tasks, data and resources taking into account users' QoS requirements. Its architecture is depicted in Figure 12.2. The architecture consists of three major parts: (a) the user interface, (b) the core, and (c) plug-ins. The user interface allows end users to work with workflow composition, workflow execution planning, submission, and monitoring. These features are delivered through a Web portal or through a stand-alone application that is installed at the user's end. Workflow composition is done using an XML-based Workflow Language (xWFL). Users define task properties and link them based on their data dependencies. Multiple tasks can be constructed using copy-paste functions present in most GUIs.

The components within the core are responsible for managing the execution of workflows. They facilitate in the translation of high-level workflow descriptions (defined at the user interface using XML) to task and data objects. These objects are then used by the execution subsystem. The scheduling component applies user-selected scheduling policies and plans to the workflows at various stages in their execution. The tasks and data dispatchers interact with the resource interface plug-ins to continuously submit and monitor tasks in the workflow. These components form the core part of the workflow engine.

The plug-ins support workflow executions on different environments and platforms. Our system has plug-ins for querying task and data characteristics

Workflow Management System

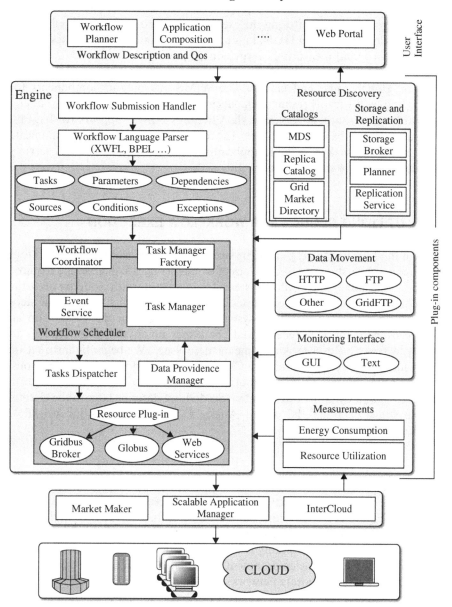

FIGURE 12.2. Architecture of Workflow Management System.

(e.g., querying metadata services, reading from trace files), transferring data to and from resources (e.g., transfer protocol implementations, and storage and replication services), monitoring the execution status of tasks and applications (e.g., real-time monitoring GUIs, logs of execution, and the scheduled retrieval of task status), and measuring energy consumption.

The resources are at the bottom layer of the architecture and include clusters, global grids, and clouds. The WfMS has plug-in components for interacting with various resource management systems present at the front end of distributed resources. Currently, the Cloudbus WfMS supports Aneka, Pbs, Globus, and fork-based middleware. The resource managers may communicate with the market maker, scalable application manager, and InterCloud services for global resource management [18].

12.5 UTILIZING CLOUDS FOR WORKFLOW EXECUTION

Taking the leap to utilizing cloud services for scientific workflow applications requires an understanding of the types of clouds services available, the required component changes in workflow systems for interacting with cloud services, the set of tools available to support development and deployment efforts, the steps involved in deploying workflow systems and services on the cloud, and an appreciation of the key benefits and challenges involved. In the sections to follow, we take a closer look at some of these issues. We begin by introducing the reader to the Aneka Enterprise Cloud service. We do this for two reasons. First, Aneka serves as a useful tool for utilizing clouds, including platform abstraction and dynamic provisioning. Second, we describe later in the chapter a case study detailing the use of Aneka to execute a scientific workflow application on clouds.

12.5.1 Aneka

Aneka is a distributed middleware for deploying platform-as-a-service (PaaS) offerings (Figure 12.3). Developed at CLOUDS Lab, University of Melbourne, Aneka is the result of years of research on cluster, grid, and cloud computing for high-performance computing (HPC) applications. Aneka, which is both a development and runtime environment, is available for public use (for a cost),[4] can be installed on corporate networks, or dedicated clusters, or can be hosted on infrastructure clouds like Amazon EC2. In comparison, similar PaaS services such as Google AppEngine [19] and Windows Azure [20] are in-house platforms hosted on infrastructures owned by the respective companies. Aneka was developed on Microsoft's.NET Framework 2.0 and is compatible with other implementations of the ECMA 335 standard [21], such as Mono. Aneka

---

[4] http://www.manjrasoft.com

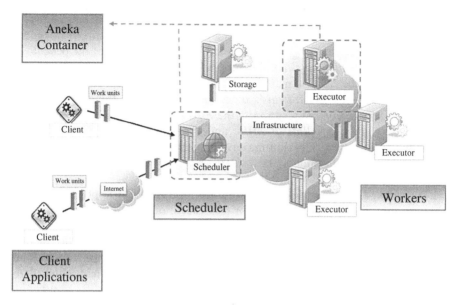

FIGURE 12.3. A deployment of Aneka Enterprise Cloud.

can run on popular platforms such as Microsoft Windows, Linux, and Mac OS X, harnessing the collective computing power of a heterogeneous network.

The runtime environment consists of a collection of Aneka containers running on physical or virtualized nodes. Each of these containers can be configured to play a specific role such as scheduling or execution. The Aneka distribution also provides a set of tools for administrating the cloud, reconfiguring nodes, managing users, and monitoring the execution of applications. The Aneka service stack provides services for infrastructure management, application execution management, accounting, licensing, and security. For more information we refer you to Vecchiola et al. [14].

Aneka's *Dynamic Resource Provisioning* service enables horizontal scaling depending on the overall load in the cloud. The platform is thus elastic in nature and can provision additional resources on-demand from external physical or virtualized resource pools, in order to meet the QoS requirements of applications. In a typical scenario, Aneka would acquire new virtualized resources from external clouds such as Amazon EC2, in order to meet the minimum waiting time of applications submitted to Aneka. Such a scenario would arise when the current load in the cloud is high, and there is a lack of available resources to timely process all jobs.

The development environment provides a rich set of APIs for developing applications that can utilize free resources of the underlying infrastructure. These APIs expose different programming abstractions, such as the *task model, thread model,* and *MapReduce* [22]. The *task programming model* is of particular importance to the current discussion. It models "independent bag of tasks" (BoT) applications that are composed of a collection of *work units* independent of each other, and it may be executed in any given order. One of the benefits of the *task programming model* is its simplicity, making it easy to run legacy applications on the cloud. An application using the *task model* composes one or more task instances and forwards them as work units to the scheduler. The scheduling service currently supports the *First-In-First-Out*, *First-In-First-Out with Backfilling, Clock-Rate Priority,* and *Preemption-Based Priority Queue* scheduling algorithms. The runtime environment also provides two specialized services to support this model: the *task scheduling service* and the *task execution service*.

The storage service provides a temporary repository for application files— that is, input files that are required for task execution, and output files that are he result of execution. Prior to dispatching work units, any files required are staged-in to the storage service from the remote location. This remote location can be either the client machine, a remote FTP server, or a cloud storage service such as Amazon S3. The work units are then dispatched to executors, which download the files before execution. Any output files produced as a result of the execution are uploaded back to the storage service. From here they are staged-out to the remote storage location.

12.5.2 Aneka Web Services

Aneka exposes three SOAP Web services for service negotiation, reservation, and task submission, as depicted in Figure 12.4. The negotiation and reservation services work in concert, and they provide interfaces for negotiating

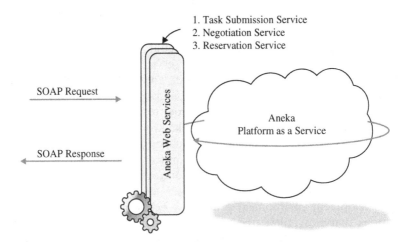

FIGURE 12.4. Aneka Web services interface.

resource use and reserving them in Aneka for predetermined timeslots. As such, these services are only useful when Aneka has limited resources to work with and no opportunities for provisioning additional resources. The *task Web service* provides a SOAP interface for executing jobs on Aneka. Based on the *task programming model*, this service allows remote clients to submit jobs, monitor their status, and abort jobs.

12.5.3 General Approach

Traditional WfMSs were designed with a centralized architecture and were thus tied to a single machine. Moving workflow engines to clouds requires (a) architectural changes and (b) integration of cloud management tools.

Architectural Changes. Most components of a WfMS can be separated from the core engine so that they can be executed on different cloud services. Each separated component could communicate with a centralized or replicated workflow engine using events. The manager is responsible for coordinating the distribution of load to its subcomponents, such as the Web server, persistence, monitoring units, and so forth.

In our WfMS, we have separated the components that form the architecture into the following: user interface, core, and plug-ins. The user interface can now be coupled with a Web server running on a "large" instance of cloud that can handle increasing number of users. The Web request from users accessing the WfMS via a portal is thus offloaded to a different set of resources.

Similarly, the core and plug-in components can be hosted on different types of instances separately. Depending on the size of the workload from users, these components could be migrated or replicated to other resources, or reinforced with additional resources to satisfy the increased load. Thus, employing distributed modules of the WfMS on the basis of application requirements helps scale the architecture.

Integration of Cloud Management Tools. As the WfMS is broken down into components to be hosted across multiple cloud resources, we need a mechanism to (a) access, transfer, and store data and (b) enable and monitor executions that can utilize this approach of scalable distribution of components.

The cloud service provider may provide APIs and tools for discovering the VM instances that are associated to a user's account. Because various types of instances can be dynamically created, their characteristics such as CPU capacity and amount of available memory are a part of the cloud service provider's specifications. Similarly, for data storage and access, a cloud may provide data sharing, data movement, and access rights management capabilities to user's applications. Cloud measurement tools may be in place to account for the amount of data and computing power used, so that users are charged on the pay-per-use basis. A WfMS now needs to access these tools to discover and characterize the resources available in the cloud. It also needs to interpret the access rights (e.g., access control lists provided by Amazon), use the data movement APIs, and share mechanisms between VMs to fully utilize the benefits of moving to clouds. In other words, traditional catalog services such as the Globus Monitoring and Discovery Service (MDS) [23], Replica Location Services, Storage Resource Brokers, Network Weather Service [24], and so on could be easily replaced by more user-friendly and scalable tools and APIs associated with a cloud service provider. We describe some of these tools in the following section.

12.5.4 Tools for Utilizing Clouds in WfMS

The range of tools and services offered by cloud providers play an important role in integrating WfMSs with clouds (Figure 12.5). Such services can facilitate in the deployment, scaling, execution, and monitoring of workflow systems. This section discusses some of the tools and services offered by various service providers that can complement and support WfMSs.

A WfMS manages dynamic provisioning of compute and storage resources in the cloud with the help of tools and APIs provided by service providers. The provisioning is required to dynamically scale up/down according to application requirements. For instance, data-intensive workflow applications may require

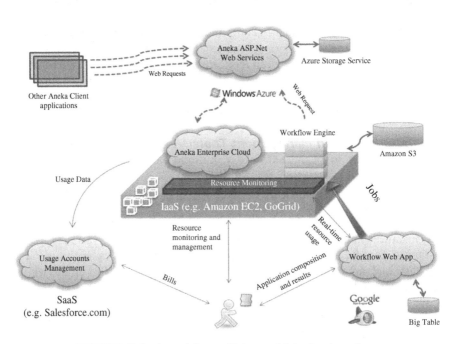

FIGURE 12.5. A workflow utilizing multiple cloud services.

large amount of disk space for storage. A WfMS could provision dynamic volumes of large capacity that could be shared across all instances of VMs (similar to snapshots and volumes provided by Amazon). Similarly, for compute-intensive tasks in an workflow, a WfMS could provision specific instances that would help accelerate the execution of these compute-intensive tasks.

A WfMS implements scheduling policies to assign tasks to resources based on applications' objectives. This task-resource mapping is dependent on several factors: compute resource capacity, application requirements, user's QoS, and so forth. Based on these objectives, a WfMS could also direct a VM provisioning system to consolidate data center loads by migrating VMs so that it could make scheduling decisions based on locality of data and compute resources.

A persistence mechanism is often important in workflow management systems and for managing metadata such as available resources, job queues, job status, and user data including large input and output files. Technologies such as Amazon S3, Google's BigTable, and the Windows Azure Storage Services can support most storage requirements for workflow systems, while also being scalable, reliable, and secure. If large quantities of user data are being dealt with, such as a large number of brain images used in functional magnetic resonance imaging (fMRI) studies [12], transferring them online can be both expensive and time-consuming. In such cases, traditional post can prove to be cheaper and faster. Amazon's AWS Import/Export[5] is one such service that aims to speed up data movement by transferring large amounts of data in portable storage devices. The data are shipped to/from Amazon and offloaded into/from S3 buckets using Amazon's high-speed internal network. The cost savings can be significant when transferring data on the order of terabytes.

Most cloud providers also offer services and APIs for tracking resource usage and the costs incurred. This can complement workflow systems that support budget-based scheduling by utilizing real-time data on the resources used, the duration, and the expenditure. This information can be used both for making scheduling decisions on subsequent jobs and for billing the user at the completion of the workflow application.[6]

Cloud services such as Google App Engine and Windows Azure provide platforms for building scalable interactive Web applications. This makes it relatively easy to port the graphical components of a workflow management system to such platforms while benefiting from their inherent scalability and reduced administration. For instance, such components deployed on Google App Engine can utilize the same scalable systems that drive Google applications, including technologies such as BigTable [25] and GFS [26].

---

[5] http://aws.amazon.com/importexport/

[6] http://aws.amazon.com/devpay/

12.6 CASE STUDY: EVOLUTIONARY MULTIOBJECTIVE OPTIMIZATIONS

This section presents a scientific application workflow based on an iterative technique for optimizing multiple search objectives, known as evolutionary multiobjective optimization (EMO) [27]. EMO is a technique based on genetic algorithms. Genetic algorithms are search algorithms used for finding optimal solutions in a large space where deterministic or functional approaches are not viable. Genetic algorithms use heuristics to find an optimal solution that is acceptable within a reasonable amount of time. In the presence of many variables and complex heuristic functions, the time consumed in finding even an acceptable solution can be too large. However, when multiple instances are run in parallel in a distributed setting using different variables, the required time for computation can be drastically reduced.

12.6.1 Objectives

The following are the objectives for modeling and executing an EMO workflow on clouds:

- Design an execution model for EMO, expressed in the form of a workflow, such that multiple distributed resources can be utilized.
- Parallelize the execution of EMO tasks for reducing the total completion time.
- Dynamically provision compute resources needed for timely completion of the application when the number of tasks increase.
- Repeatedly carry out similar experiments as and when required.
- Manage application execution, handle faults, and store the final results for analysis.

12.6.2 Workflow Solution

In order to parallelize the execution of EMO, we construct a workflow model for systematically executing the tasks. A typical workflow structure is depicted in Figure 12.6.

In our case study, the EMO application consists of five different topologies, upon which the iteration is done. These topologies are defined in five different binary files. Each file becomes the input files for the top level tasks (A0emo1, A0emo, ...). We create a separate branch for each topology file. In Figure 12.6, there are two branches, which get merged on level 6. The tasks at the root level operate on the topologies to create new population, which is then merged by the task named "emomerge." In Figure 12.6, we see two "emomerge" tasks in the 2nd level, one task in the 6th level that merges two branches and then splits the population to two branches again, two tasks on the 8th and 10th

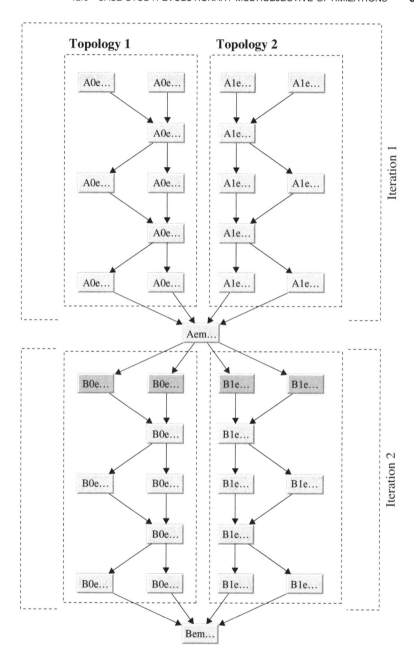

FIGURE 12.6. EMO workflow structure (boxes represent task, arrows represent data-dependencies between tasks).

levels, and the final task on the 12th level. In the example figure, each topology is iterated two times in a branch before getting merged. The merged population is then split. This split is done two times in the figure. The tasks labeled B0e and B1e (depicted as darker shade in Figure 12.6) is the start of second iteration.

12.6.3 Deployment and Results

EMO Application. We use ZDT2 [27] as a test function for the objective function. The workflow for this problem is depicted in Figure 12.6.

In our experiments, we carry out 10 iterations within a branch for 5 different topologies. We merge and split the results of each of these branches 10 times. For this scenario, the workflow constituted of a total of 6010 tasks. We varied the tasks by changing the number of merges from 5 to 10. In doing so, the structure and the characteristics of the tasks in the workflow would remain unchanged. This is necessary for comparing the execution time when the number of task increases from 1600 to 6000 when we alter the number of merges from 5 to 10.

Compute Resource. We used 40 Amazon EC2 compute resources for executing the EMO application. Twenty resources were instantiated at US-east-1a, and 20 were instantiated at US-east-1d. Among these resources, one was used for the workflow engine, one was used for Aneka's master node and the rest were worker nodes. The characteristics of these resources are listed in Table 12.1.

The workflow engine, along with a database for persistence, the IBM TSpace [28] based coordination server, and the Tomcat Web container, was instantiated on a medium instance VM.

Output of EMO Application. After running the EMO workflow, we expect to see optimized values for the two objectives given by the ZDT2 test function. Figure 12.7 depicts the graph that plots the *front* obtained after iterating the EMO workflow depicted in Figure 12.6. The front at Level 2 is not the optimal. After first iteration, the front is optimized. Iteration 2 does not significantly change the front, hence the overlapping of the data for Iteration 1 and 2.

Experimental Results When Using Clouds. Because the EMO workflow is an iterative approach, increasing the number of iterations would increase the quality of optimization in the results. Analogously, the greater the number of tasks completing in the workflow, the greater the number of iterations, hence the better the optimization.

Because the iterations can be carried out for an arbitrarily large number of times, it is usually a best practice to limit the time for the overall calculation. Thus, in our experiment we set the deadline to be 95 minutes. We then analyze the number of tasks completing within the first 95 minutes in two classes of experiments.

TABLE 12.1. Characteristics of Amazon Compute Resources (EC2) Used in Our Experiment

Characteristics	Aneka Master/Worker	Workflow Engine
Platform	Windows 2000 Server	Linux
CPU (type)	1 EC2 Compute Units[a] (small)	5 EC2 Compute Units[b] (medium)
Memory	1.7 GB	1.7 GB
Instance storage	160 GB	350GB
Instance location	US-east-1a (19) US-east-1b(20)	US-east-1a
Number of instances	39	1
Price per hour	$US 0.12	$US 0.17

[a]Small instance (default) 1.7 GB of memory, 1 EC2 compute unit (1 virtual core with 1 EC2 compute unit), 160 GB of instance storage, 32-bit platform.
[b]High-CPU medium instance 1.7 GB of memory, 5 EC2 compute units (2 virtual cores with 2.5 EC2 compute units each), 350 GB of instance storage, 32-bit platform.
Source: Amazon.

Experiment 1: Seven Additional EC2 Instances Were Added. In this experiment, we started executing the tasks in the EMO workflow initially using 20 EC2 compute resources (one node for workflow engine, one node for Aneka master, 18 Aneka worker nodes). We instantiate seven more small instances to increase the total number of resources to 25. They were available for use after 25 minutes of execution. At the end of 95 minutes, a total of 1612 tasks were completed.

Experiment 2: Twenty Additional EC2 Instances Were Added. In this experiment, we started executing the tasks in the EMO workflow using 20

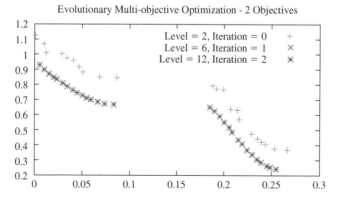

FIGURE 12.7. A graph that plots the pareto-front obtained after executing EMO for ZTD2 test problem.

EC2 compute resources, similar to Experiment 1. We instantiated 20 more EC2 instances after noticing the linear increase in task completion rate. These instances however were available for use after 40 minutes of execution. At the end of 95 minutes, a total of 3221 tasks were completed.

Analysis of the Results. In both experiments, the initial task completion rate increased linearly until we started more instances, as depicted in Figure 12.8. As the number of resources was increased, the rate of task completing increased drastically. This is due to the submission of queued tasks in Aneka to the newly available resources, which would have remained queued if resources were not added.

In the figure, the completion rate curve rises up to a point until all the queued tasks are submitted. The curve then rises gradually because the EMO application is a workflow. Tasks in the workflow get submitted gradually as their parents finish executions. Hence, the completion rate has similar slope

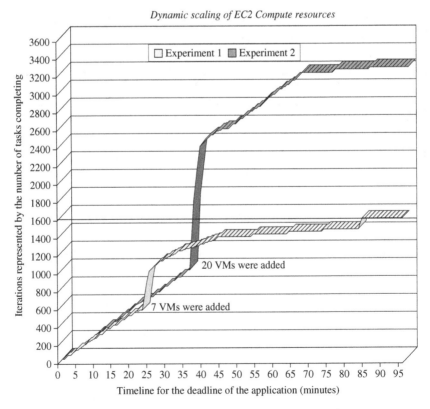

FIGURE 12.8. Number of tasks completing in time as the number of compute resources provisioned were increased at runtime.

as the initial rate, even after increasing the number of resources (30 to 45 minutes for Experiment 1; 45 to 70 minutes for Experiment 2). When more tasks began completing as a result of adding new resources, the workflow engine was able to submit additional tasks for execution. As a result, tasks started competing for resources and hence were being queued by Aneka. Because of this queuing at Aneka's scheduler, the curve flattens after 45 minutes for Experiment 1 and after 70 minutes for Experiment 2.

The most important benefit of increasing the resources dynamically at runtime is the increase in the total number of tasks completing, and hence the quality of final result. This is evident from the two graphs depicted in Figure 12.8. If a total of 25 resources were used, Experiment 1 would complete 1612 tasks by the end of the 95-minute deadline, whereas Experiment 2 would complete executing nearly 3300 tasks within the same deadline if 20 additional resources were added. The quality of results would be twice as good for Experiment 2 as for Experiment 1. However, if a user wants to have the same quality of output as in Experiment 1 but in much shorter time, he should increase the number of resources used well before the deadline. A line just above 1600 in Figure 12.8 depicts the cutoff point where the user could terminate all the VM instances and obtain the same quality of results as Experiment 1 would have obtained by running for 95 minutes. It took ~45 minutes less time for Experiment 2 to execute the same number of tasks as Experiment 1. This drastic reduction in time was seen even when both experiments initially started with the same number of resources. In terms of cost of provisioning additional resources, Experiment 2 is cheaper because there are fewer overheads in time spent queuing and managing task submissions, since the tasks would be submitted as soon as they arrive at Aneka's master node. If Amazon were to charge EC2 usage cost per minute rather than per hour, Experiment 2 would save 45 minutes of execution time at the cost of 20 more resources.

We also analyzed the utilization of instantiated compute resources by Aneka, as depicted in Figure 12.9. At the time of recording the graph, there were 21 worker nodes in the Aneka cloud, with a combined power of 42 GHz.

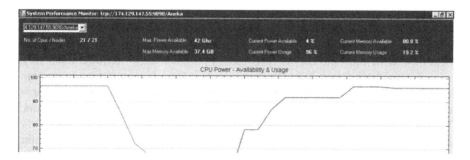

FIGURE 12.9. Distributed compute resource utilized by Aneka network.

The graph shows a steep rise in the system utilization (labeled as *usage* in the figure) as tasks were submitted for execution. The compute power available (labeled as *available*) decreased to 4% with 80.8% memory available. This decrease in utilization was due to the use of all the available resources for execution of tasks submitted to Aneka by the workflow engine executing EMO workflow.

12.7 VISIONARY THOUGHTS FOR PRACTITIONERS

The cloud computing paradigm is emerging and is being adopted at a rapid rate. Gartner ranks it at the top of the hype cycle for the year 2010 [29]. As the technology is being adopted by practitioners industry-wide, there are numerous challenges to overcome. Moreover, these challenges could be addressed via a realistic vision of the cloud computing models of the near future. This section discusses some of them.

Software and service giants such as Google, Amazon, and Microsoft own large data centers for providing a variety of cloud services to customers. These independent and disparate initiatives would eventually lead to an interconnection model where users can choose a combination of services from different providers in their applications. Our vision provides an entity responsible for brokerage of resources across different cloud providers, termed the market maker [16]. These inter-cloud environments would then facilitate executions of workflow applications at distributed data centers. Large scientific experiments would then be able to use inter-cloud resources, brokered through the market maker.

The essence of using cloud services is to be able to dynamically scale the applications running on top of it. Automating resource provisioning and VM instance management in clouds based on multiobjectives (cost, time, and other QoS parameters) can help achieve this goal. The automation process should be transparent to the end users who would just be interested in running workflow applications under their time and budget constraints. Users would specify either flexible or tight deadline for the cost they pay for using cloud services. It becomes the responsibility of the workflow engine running in the cloud to dynamically scale the application to satisfy multiple users' request.

In order to facilitate fair but competitive use of cloud resources for workflow applications, a service negotiation module must be in place. This entity would negotiate with multiple service providers to match users' requirements to a service provider's capabilities. Once a match is found, required resources can then be allocated to the user application. A cloud market directory service is needed to maintain a catalog of services from various cloud service providers. Data and their communication play a vital role in any data-intensive workflow application. When running such applications on clouds, storage and transfer costs need to be taken into account in addition to the execution cost. The right choice of compute location and storage service provider would result in minimizing the total cost billed to a user. A cloud market maker could handle these task and communication issues at the time of negotiation between various cloud service providers.

12.8 FUTURE RESEARCH DIRECTIONS

In Section 12.7, we described some visions and inherent difficulties faced by practitioners when using various cloud services. Drawing upon these visions, we list below some future research directions in the form of broad research directions:

- How to facilitate inter-cloud operations in terms of coherent data exchange, task migration, and load balancing for workflow application.
- When and where to provision cloud resources so that workflow applications can meet their deadline constraints and also remain within their budget.
- How to balance the use of cloud and local resources so that workflow applications can meet their objectives.
- How to match workflow application requirements to any service provider's capabilities when there are numerous vendors with similar capabilities in a cloud.

12.9 SUMMARY AND CONCLUSIONS

To summarize, we have presented a comprehensive description of using workflow engine in cloud computing environments. We discussed the limitations of existing workflow management systems and proposed changes that need to be incorporated when moving to clouds. We also described cloud tools that could help applications use cloud services.

To demonstrate a practical scenario of deploying a workflow engine in clouds, we described in detail our workflow management system and a.NET-based cloud computing platform, Aneka. We presented a case study of an evolutionary multiobjective optimization algorithm. By modeling this application in the form of a workflow, we obtained an order-of-magnitude improvement in the application runtime when compute resources were provisioned at runtime. Thousands of tasks were completed in a short period of time as additional resources were provisioned, eventually decreasing the total runtime of the application.

Based on our experience in using cloud services, we conclude that large applications can certainly benefit by using cloud resources. The key benefits are in terms of decreased runtime, on-demand resource provisioning, and ease of resource management. However, these services come at a price whereby users have to pay cloud service providers on the basis of the resource usage.

Although clouds offer many benefits, they can't and will not replace grids. Clouds will augment grids. Users will use cloud services together with their in-house solutions (cluster/enterprise grids) to enhance the performance of their applications as and when needed.

ACKNOWLEDGMENTS

This work is partially supported through Australian Research Council (ARC) Discovery Project grant. We would like to thank Christian Vecchiola from University of Melbourne for his help in defining the EMO application. We also thank Adam Barker for reviewing and providing feedback on this chapter.

REFERENCES

1. R. Buyya, S. Pandey, and C. Vecchiola, Cloudbus toolkit for market-oriented cloud computing, in *Proceedings of the 1st International Conference on Cloud Computing (CloudCom 2009, Springer, Germany)*, Beijing, China, December 1–4, 2009.

2. J. Yu and R. Buyya, A taxonomy of workflow management systems for grid computing, *Journal of Grid Computing*, **3**(3–4):171–200, 2005.

3. DAGMan Application. http://www.cs.wisc.edu/condor/dagman/ (November 2009).

4. T. Tannenbaum, D. Wright, K. Miller, and M. Livny. Condor—A distributed job scheduler, in *Beowulf Cluster Computing with Linux*, MIT Press, Cambridge, MA, 2002.

5. E. Deelman, J. Blythe, Y. Gil, C. Kesselman, G. Mehta, and K. Vahi. Mapping abstract complex workflows onto grid environments, *Journal of Grid Computing*, **1**: 25–39, 2003.

6. B. Ludäscher, I. Altintas, C. Berkley, D. Higgins, E. Jaeger, M. Jones, E. A. Lee, J. Tao, and Y. Zhao, Scientific workflow management and the Kepler system, *Concurrency and Computation: Practice and Experience*, **18**(10):1039–1065, 2006.

7. T. Oinn, M. Addis, J. Ferris, D. Marvin, M. Senger, M. Greenwood, T. Carver, K. Glover, M. R. Pocock, A. Wipat, and P. Li, Taverna: A tool for the composition and enactment of bioinformatics workflows, in *Bioinformatics*, **20**(17): 3045–3054, 2004.

8. I. Foster and C. Kesselman (eds.), *The Grid: Blueprint for a Future Computing Infrastructure*, Morgan Kaufmann Publishers, San Francisco, 1999.

9. R. Buyya, *Economic-Based Distributed Resource Management and Scheduling for Grid Computing*, PhD Thesis, Monash University, Melbourne, Australia, April 2002.

10. R. Buyya, D. Abramson, and J. Giddy, An economy driven resource management architecture for global computational power grids, in *Proceedings of the 7th International Conference on Parallel and Distributed Processing Techniques and Applications*, Las Vegas, June 26–29, 2000.

11. E. Deelman, G. Singh, M. Livny, B. Berriman, and J. Good, The cost of doing science on the cloud: the montage example, in *Proceedings of the 2008 ACM/IEEE Conference on Supercomputing*, NJ, 2008, pp. 1–12.

12. S. Pandey, W. Voorsluys, M. Rahman, R. Buyya, J. Dobson, and K. Chiu, A grid workflow environment for brain imaging analysis on distributed systems, *Concurrency and Computation: Practice and Experience*, **21**(16):2118–2139, 2009.

13. S. Venugopal, K. Nadiminti, H. Gibbins, and R. Buyya, Designing a resource broker for heterogeneous grids, *Software: Practice and Experience*, **38**(8): 793–825, 2008.

14. C. Vecchiola, X. Chu, and R. Buyya, Aneka: A software platform for .NET-based cloud computing, in *High Performance and Large Scale Computing*, IOS Press, Amsterdam, Netherlands, 2009.

15. J. Yu and R. Buyya, Scheduling scientific workflow applications with deadline and budget constraints using genetic algorithms, *Scientific Programming Journal*, **14** (3–4): 217–230, 2006.

16. Suraj Pandey, Linlin Wu, Siddeswara Guru, and Rajkumar Buyya, A Particle Swarm Optimization (PSO)-based Heuristic for Scheduling Workflow Applications in Cloud Computing Environments, Proceedings of the 24th IEEE International Conference on Advanced Information Networking and Applications (AINA 2010), Perth, Australia, April 20–23, pp. 400–407, 2010. – Best Paper Award.

17. I. Raicu, Y. Zhao, I. Foster, and A. Szalay, Accelerating large-scale data exploration through data diffusion, in *Proceedings of the 2008 International Workshop on Data-Aware Distributed Computing*, ACM, 2008, pp. 9–18.

18. C. Vecchiola, S. Pandey, and R. Buyya, High-performance cloud computing: A view of scientific applications, in *Proceedings of the 10th International Symposium on Pervasive Systems, Algorithms and Networks* Kaohsiung, Taiwan, December 14–16, 2009.

19. Google AppEngine, http://code.google.com/appengine/ (November 2009).

20. Windows Azure Platform, http://www.microsoft.com/windowsazure/window sazure/ (November 2009).

21. Standard ECMA-335, http://www.ecma-international.org/publications/standards/ Ecma-335.htm (November 2009).

22. C. Jin and R. Buyya, MapReduce programming model for .NET-based cloud computing, in *Proceedings of the 15th International European Parallel Computing Conference*, Delft, The Netherlands, August 25–28, 2009.

23. K. Czajkowski, S. Fitzgerald, I. Foster, and C. Kesselman, Grid information services for distributed resource sharing, in *10th IEEE International Symposium on High Performance Distributed Computing*, Los Alamitos, CA, 7–9 August 2001.

24. R. Wolski, N. T. Spring, and J. Hayes. The network weather service: A distributed resource performance forecasting service for metacomputing, *Future Generation Computer Systems*, **15**(5–6):757–768, 1999.

25. F. Chang, J. Dean, S. Ghemawat, W. C. Hsieh, D. A. Wallach, M. Burrows, T. Chandra, A. Fikes, and R. E. Gruber, Bigtable: A distributed storage system for structured data, in *Proceedings of the 7th USENIX Symposium on Operating Systems Design and Implementation*, Berkeley, CA, USENIX Association, 2006, p. 15.

26. S. Ghemawat, H. Gobioff, and S. T. Leung, The google file system, *SIGOPS Operating System Review*, **37**(5), 2003, 29–43.

27. C. Vecchiola, M. Kirley, and R. Buyya, Multi-objective problem solving with offspring on enterprise clouds, in *Proceedings of the 10th International Conference on High-Performance Computing in Asia-Pacific Region* (HPC Asia 2009), Kaohsiung, Taiwan, March 2–5, 2009.

28. IBM TSpaces, http://www.almaden.ibm.com/cs/tspaces/ (November 2009).

29. Gartner's Hype Cycle for 2009. http://www.gartner.com/technology/research/hype-cycles/index.jsp (Accessed October, 2010).

CHAPTER 13

UNDERSTANDING SCIENTIFIC APPLICATIONS FOR CLOUD ENVIRONMENTS

SHANTENU JHA, DANIEL S. KATZ, ANDRE LUCKOW, ANDRE MERZKY, and KATERINA STAMOU

13.1 INTRODUCTION

Distributed systems and their specific incarnations have evolved significantly over the years. Most often, these evolutionary steps have been a consequence of external technology trends, such as the significant increase in network/bandwidth capabilities that have occurred. It can be argued that the single most important driver for cloud computing environments is the advance in virtualization technology that has taken place. But what implications does this advance, leading to today's cloud environments, have for scientific applications? The aim of this chapter is to explore how clouds can support scientific applications.

Before we can address this important issue, it is imperative to (a) provide a working model and definition of clouds and (b) understand how they differ from other computational platforms such as grids and clusters. At a high level, cloud computing is defined by Mell and Grance [1] as a model for enabling convenient, on-demand network access to a shared pool of configurable computing resources (e.g., networks, servers, storage, applications, and services) that can be rapidly provisioned and released with minimal management effort or service provider interaction.

We view clouds not as a monolithic isolated platform but as part of a large distributed ecosystem. But are clouds a natural evolution of distributed systems, or are they a fundamental new paradigm? Prima facie, cloud concepts are derived from other systems, such as the implicit model of clusters as static

Cloud Computing: Principles and Paradigms, Edited by Rajkumar Buyya, James Broberg and Andrzej Goscinski   Copyright © 2011 John Wiley & Sons, Inc.

bounded sets of resources, which leads to batch-queue extensions to virtualization. Another example is provided by ideas prevalent in grids to address dynamic application requirements and resource capabilities, such as pilot jobs, that are being redesigned and modified for clouds. In either case, clouds are an outgrowth of the systems and ideas that have come before them, and we want to consciously consider our underlying assumptions, to make sure we are not blindly carrying over assumptions about previous types of parallel and distributed computing.

We believe that there is novelty in the resource management and capacity planning capabilities for clouds. Thanks to their ability to provide an illusion of unlimited and/or *immediately available* resources, as currently provisioned, clouds in conjunction with traditional HPC and HTC grids provide a balanced infrastructure supporting scale-out and scale-up, as well as capability (HPC) and quick turn-around (HTC) computing for a range of application (model) sizes and requirements. The novelty in resource management and capacity planning capabilities is likely to influence changes in the usage mode, as well deployment and execution management/planning. The ability to exploit these attributes could lead to applications with new and interesting usage modes and dynamic execution on clouds and therefore new application capabilities. Additionally, clouds are suitable infrastructure for dynamic applications—that is, those with execution time resource requirements that cannot be determined exactly in advance, either due to changes in runtime requirements or due to interesting changes in application structure (e.g., different solver with different resource requirement).

Clouds will have a broad impact on legacy scientific applications, because we anticipate that many existing legacy applications will adapt to and take advantage of new capabilities. However, it is unclear if clouds as currently presented are likely to change (many of) the fundamental reformulation of the development of scientific applications. In this chapter, we will thus focus on scientific applications that can benefit from a dynamic execution model that we believe can be facilitated by clouds. Not surprisingly, and in common with many distributed applications, coarse-grained or task-level parallelism is going to be the basis of many programming models aimed at data-intensive science executing in cloud environments. However, even for common programming approaches such as MapReduce (based on task-level parallelism), the ability to incorporate dynamic resource placement and management as well as dynamic datasets is an important requirement with concomitant performance advantages. For example, the Map and Reduce phases involve different computations, thus different loads and resources; dynamical formulations of applications are better suited to supporting such load-balancing. Clouds are thus emerging as an important class of distributed computational resource, for both data-intensive and compute-intensive applications.

There are novel usage modes that can be supported when grids and clouds are used concurrently. For example, the usage of clouds as the computational equivalent of a heat bath establishes determinism—that is, well-bounded time-to-completion with concomitant advantages that will accrue as a consequence.

But to support such advanced usage modes, there is a requirement for programming systems, models, and abstractions that enable application developers to express decompositions and which support dynamic execution. Many early cloud applications employ ad hoc solutions, which results in a lack of generality and the inability of programs to be extensible and independent of infrastructure details. The IDEAS design objectives—Interoperability, Distributed scale-out, Extensibility, Adaptivity, and Simplicity—summarize the design goals for distributed applications. In this chapter we demonstrate several examples of how these objectives can be accomplished using several cloud applications that use SAGA.

13.1.1 Fundamental Issues

In this chapter, we want to consider a set of fundamental questions about scientific applications on clouds, such as: What kind of scientific applications are suitable for clouds? Are there assumptions that were made in developing applications for grids that should consciously be thrown out, when developing applications for clouds? In other words, from an application's perspective, how is a cloud different from a traditional grid? What kind of scientific applications can utilize both clouds and grids, and under what conditions? The issue of how applications and environments are developed is a chicken-and-egg situation. One might ask which applications are suitable for a given environment. Similarly, one might ask which environment can support a given application. Applications are developed to run in specific environments, while environments are developed to run specific applications. This coupling is a Zen-like paradox.

Clouds as a Type of Distributed Infrastructure. Before we can analyze if there is a fundamentally different class of applications that can be supported on cloud systems, it is imperative to ask, What is the difference between clouds and other distributed infrastructure?

To structure the differences between grid and cloud applications, if any, let us use the three phases of an applications life cycle: (i) development, (ii) deployment, and (iii) execution [2]. In development, if we think of the three vectors (execution unit, communication, and coordination) aiding our analysis, then neither resource management or scheduling influence the above three vector values. In deployment, clouds can be clearly differentiated from clusters and grids. Specifically, the runtime environment [as defined by the virtual machine (VM)] is controlled by the user/application and can be set up as such; this is in contrast to traditional computational environments. By providing simplicity and ease of management, it is hoped that the changes at the execution level may feed back to the application development level.

Some uncertainty lies in the fact that there are some things we understand, while there are some things that are dependent on evolving technologies and are thus unclear. For example, at the execution level, clouds differ from clusters/

grids in at least a couple of different ways. In cloud environments, user-level jobs are not typically exposed to a scheduling system; a user-level job consists of requesting the instantiation of a VM. Virtual machines are either assigned to the user or not (this is an important attribute that provides the illusion of infinite resources). The assignment of a job to a VM must be done by the user (or a middleware layer). In contrast, user-level jobs on grids and clusters are exposed to a scheduling system and are assigned to execute at a later stage. Also a description of a grid/cluster job typically contains an explicit workload description. In contrast, for clouds, a user-level job typically contains the container (a description of the resource requested) but does not necessarily contain the workload itself. In other words, the physical resources are not provisioned to the workload but are provisioned to the container. This model is quite similar to resource reservations where one can obtain a "container" of resources to which jobs can be later be bound. Interestingly, at this level of formulation, pilot jobs can be considered to provide a model of resource provisioning similar to the one that clouds natively provide.

An additional issue is compositional and deployment flexibility. A number of applications are difficult to build, due to runtime dependencies or complicated nonportable build systems. There is often a need to control the runtime environment at a fine-grained level, which is often difficult with grids; this often provides a rationale for using cloud environments. Clouds offer an opportunity to build virtual machines once, then to load them on various systems, working around issues related to portability on the physical systems, because the VM images can be static, while real systems (both hardware and software) are often changing.

A third issue is scheduling flexibility. Clouds offer the ability to create usage modes for applications to support the situation where, when the set of resources needed to run an application changes (perhaps rapidly), the resources can actually be changed (new resources can be added, or existing resources can be removed from the pool used by the job).

Scientific Cloud Applications as Distributed Applications. We have previously [2] introduced the concept of *Distributed Application Vectors* to structure the analysis and understanding of the main characteristics with a view to understanding the primary design requirements and constraints. Specifically, we determined that understanding the execution units, communication requirements, coordination mechanisms, and execution environment of a distributed application was a necessary (minimally complete) set of requirements. We will argue that both the vectors and the abstractions (patterns) for cloud-based applications are essentially the same as those for grid-based applications, further lending credibility to the claim that cloud-based applications are of the broader distributed applications class.

Most applications have been modified to utilize clouds. Usually, the modifications have not been at the application level, but more at the point at which the application uses the infrastructure. It appears that there is not a major distinction between a classic grid application or a scientific cloud application; they are both incarnations of distributed applications—with the same development concerns and requirements, but with different deployment and execution contexts. In other words: Cloud applications are essentially a type of distributed applications, but with different infrastructure usage than grid applications. Due to a better control on the software environment, there is the ability to do some things better on clouds; thus, some types of applications are better suited/adapted to clouds. Programming models, such as MapReduce, that support data-intensive applications are not exclusively cloud-based, but due to the programming systems and tools as well as other elements of the ecosystem, they are likely to find increased utilization. Thus, at this level, there are no fundamental new development paradigms for cloud-based applications *a priori*.

We also formally characterized [2] patterns that can be used to capture aspects of distributed coordination, communication, and execution. Specifically, we identified three important elements ("vectors") influencing the overall development of distributed applications, coordination, communication, and execution and showed how these and data access patterns can be associated with a primary distributed application concern (reproduced and extended in Table 13.1).

We will discuss how using cloud capabilities will enable applications to exploit new scenarios, for example, the dynamic adjustment of application parameters (such as the accuracy) or the dynamic addition of new resources to an application. In order to motivate and structure these applications and their usage modes, we will provide a brief overview of a classification of scientific cloud applications in the next section. We will then discuss SAGA, which is an API for distributed applications as a viable programming system for clouds. We establish this with three distinct applications that have been developed for clouds using SAGA, further bolstering the connection between cloud applications and distributed applications. We end this chapter with a discussion of issues of relevance to scientific applications on clouds—including design objectives, interoperability with grids, and application performance considerations.

TABLE 13.1. A Classification of Some Commonly Occurring Patterns in Distributed Computing.[a]

Coordination	Communication	Deployment	Data Access
Client-server	Pub-sub	Replication	Co-access
P2P	Stream	At-home	One-to-one
Master-worker (TF, BoT)	Point-to-point	Brokering	One-to-many
Consensus	Broadcast	Co-allocation	Scatter-gather
Data processing pipeline			All-to-all

[a]The patterns are placed into a category that represents the predominant context in which they appear and address; this is not to imply that each pattern addresses only one issue exclusively. *Source*: Adapted from Jha et al. [2].

13.2 A CLASSIFICATION OF SCIENTIFIC APPLICATIONS AND SERVICES IN THE CLOUD

Common models of clouds [1,3,4] introduce composite hierarchies of different layers, each implementing a different service model (see Figure 13.1). The services of each layer can be composed from the services of the layer underneath, and each layer may include one or more services that share the same or equivalent levels of abstraction. The proposed layers consist of the following: the Software as a Service (SaaS) layer, the platform as a service (PaaS) layer, and the Infrastructure as a Service (IaaS) layer. The IaaS layer can be further divided into the computational resources, storage, and communications sublayers, the software kernel layer, and the hardware/firmware layer that consists of the actual physical system components. As shown in Figure 13.1, clouds can also be classified according to their deployment model into public and private clouds. A public cloud is generally available on pay-per-use basis. Several infrastructures have emerged that enable the creation of so-called private clouds—that is, clouds that are only accessible from within an organization.

Based on the proposed service layers, we will derive a classification from the application's perspective, with our aim to provide suggestions and raise further discussions on how scientific applications could possibly foster in the cloud

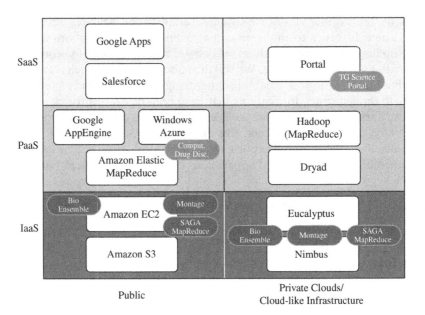

FIGURE 13.1. Cloud taxonomy and application examples: Clouds provide services at different levels (IaaS, PaaS, SaaS). The amount of control available to users and developers decreases with the level of abstraction. According to their deployment model, clouds can be categorized into public and private clouds.

environment. Although our taxonomy is targeted toward specific cloud environments, we strongly believe that a scientific application should and must remain interoperable regardless of the execution backend or the initial development infrastructure.

The identification of how cloud application services fit into the layers may allow software developers to better comprehend the nature of parameters introduced in each layer. Such an assumption could lead into easier and more efficient implementation of cloud-operable scientific applications. Research work from the traditional cluster/grid era systems has already determined important features like scalability, extensibility, and high availability that should play an integral role in a distributed application's core functionality.

Before we discuss scientific cloud applications in Section 13.3, here we will explain the details of the layers in the cloud model.

13.2.1 Software as a Service (SaaS) Layer

The software as a service layer is the highest layer in the proposed model. SaaS provides ready-to-run services that are deployed and configured for the user. In general, the user has no control over the underlying cloud infrastructure with the exception of limited configuration settings. Regarding scientific applications, such a layer may represent an access point for the end user to reach a service, like a portal or a visualization tool. Scientific portals have been used by many grid services.

A strong characteristic of SaaS services is that there is no client side software requirement. All data manipulated in such systems are held in remote infrastructures where all the processing takes place. One of the most prominent advantages of applications that are presented in this layer is universal accessibility regardless of the client system's software availability. This scheme provides flexibility to the end user and transparency of any complex mechanism involved. Some widely used examples of services that belong to this category are Google Apps and Salesforce. A prominent example from the science community is the TeraGrid Science Gateways [5].

These gateways provide among other things several domain specific web portals, which can be used to access computational and data services.

13.2.2 Platform as a Service (PaaS) Layer

The Platform as a Service (PaaS) layer provides the capability to deploy custom applications on the cloud providers infrastructure. These applications are developed using the programming languages and APIs defined by the cloud provider. Similar to SaaS, the user has only limited control over the underlying cloud infrastructures: He can deploy and configure applications created using the vendor's programming environment. The process of implementing and deploying a cloud application becomes more accessible while allowing the programmer to focus on important issues like the formulation of the scientific algorithm. A developer does not have to worry about complex programming details, scalability, load balancing, or other system issues that may hinder the overall process of building an application. All such criteria are already specified by the given API that abstracts underlying architectural parameters.

A well-known PaaS example is the Google App Engine [6] that equips developers with a Python and Java API and runtime environment for the implementation of web applications. Windows Azure [7] is Microsoft's PaaS platform and offers different types of runtime environments and storage services for applications. While, in particular, Google App Engine is primarily geared toward Web applications (such as science portals), Windows Azure is also well-suited for compute- and data-intensive applications. Watson et al. [8] use Windows Azure—in particular the data storage and VM execution environment—to conduct data mining for computational drug discovery.

Another PaaS abstraction that is used for parallel processing of large amounts of data is MapReduce (MR) [9]. The framework solely requires the user to define two functions: the *map* and the *reduce* function. Both functions operate on key/value pairs: The map function transforms an input key/value pair representing a data row to an output key/value pair; the reduce function is used to merge all outputs of the map functions. Generally, the MapReduce framework handles all complexities and orchestrates the distribution of the the data as well as of the map and reduce tasks. Hadoop [10] is a well-known example of an open-source MapReduce framework. Amazon's Elastic MapReduce [11] provides a hosted MapReduce service.

Another example of an environment for data-intensive computing is Microsoft Dryad [12]. The framework allows the programmer to efficiently use resources for running data parallel applications. In Dryad a computation has the form of a directed graph (DAG), where the program instances that compose the computation are represented as graph vertices and the one-way communication channels between the instances are represented as graph edges. The Dryad infrastructure includes computational frameworks like Google's MapReduce. A port of Dryad to Windows Azure is planned, but at the time of writing is not available.

PaaS clouds provider higher-level abstractions for cloud applications, which usually simplifies the application development process and removes the need to manage the underlying software and hardware infrastructure. PaaS offers automatic scalability, load balancing, and failure tolerance. However, the benefits are also associated with some drawbacks: Generally, PaaS services usually provide highly proprietary environments with only limited standard support. App Engine, for example, supports parts of the Java Enterprise API, but uses a custom BigTable-based [13] data store.

13.2.3 Infrastructure-as-a-Service Layer

The infrastructure-as-a-service (Iaas) layer provides low-level, virtualized resources, such as storage, networks, and other fundamental computing resources via self-services to the user. In general, the user can deploy and run arbitrary software, which usually includes operating systems as well as applications. However, the user has no knowledge of the exact location and specifics of the underlying physical resources. Cloud providers usually offer instant elasticity; that is, new resources can be rapidly and elastically provisioned to scale-up or scale-out applications dynamically.

Computational cloud resources are represented through virtual machine instances (VMs), where the user is usually granted full administrative access and has the ability to build and deploy any kind of service infrastructure. Such VMs usually come with an OS already installed. The developer may choose a VM to rent that has the OS she wants. Amazon EC2 [14] is the prime example of such a service and currently offers a variety of VM images, where one may choose to work on a Windows platform or on some Linux-based platforms. The developer can further configure and add extra libraries to the selected OS to accommodate an application. Rackspace [15] and GoGrid [16] provide similar services. Eucalyptus [17] and Nimbus [18] offer EC2 compatible infrastructures, which can be deployed in-house in a private cloud. Several scientific clouds utilize these frameworks—for example, Science Cloud [19] and Future Grid [20].

VMs are provided to the user under SLAs, where the cloud provider guarantees a certain level of system's performance to their clients. They usually involve fees on behalf of the user utilizing the leased computational resources, while open source/research cloud infrastructures don't include any financial requirement. When a team of scientists rents some virtual resources to run their experiments, they usually also lease data storage to store their data/results remotely and access them within the time limits of their agreement with the service provider. Examples of public cloud storage service are Amazon S3 [21] and Rackspace Cloud Files [22]. Walrus [23] is a S3 interface compatible service, which can be deployed on private cloud infrastructures. Another common cloud-like infrastructure is distributed file systems, such as the Google File System (GFS) [24] and the Hadoop File System (HDFS) [25]. Both systems are optimized for storing and retrieving large amounts of data.

13.2.4 Discussion of Cloud Models

Several scientific applications from different domains (e.g., life sciences, high-energy physics, astrophysics, computational chemistry) have been ported to cloud environments (see references 26–28 for examples). The majority of these applications rely on IaaS cloud services and solely utilize static execution modes: A scientist leases some virtual resources in order to deploy their testing services. One may select different number of instances to run their tests on. An instance of a VM is perceived as a node or a processing unit. There can be a multiple number of instances under the same VM, depending on the SLA one has agreed on. Once the service is deployed, a scientist can begin testing on the virtual nodes; this is similar to how one would use a traditional set of local clusters.

Furthermore, most of this research has solely attempted to manually customize legacy scientific applications in order to accommodate them into a cloud infrastructure. Benchmark tests on both EC2 virtual instances and conventional computational clusters indicated no significant difference in the results with respect to total running time (wall clock) and number of processors used. So far, there hasn't been much discussions on implementing scientific applications targeted to a cloud infrastructure. Such first-principle applications require programatic access to cloud capabilities as dynamic provisioning in an infrastructure-independent way to support dynamic execution modes.

In summary, clouds provide services at different levels (IaaS, PaaS, SaaS). In general, the amount of control available to users and developers decreases with the level of abstraction. Only IaaS provides sufficient programmatic control to express decompositions and dynamic execution modes, which seems central to many scientific applications.

13.3 SAGA-BASED SCIENTIFIC APPLICATIONS THAT UTILIZE CLOUDS

In this chapter we take the scope of "cloud applications" to be those distributed applications that are able to explicitly benefit from the cloud's inherent elasticity—where elasticity is a kind of dynamic execution mode—and from the usage modes provided by clouds. This excludes those applications that are trivially mapped to a small static set of small resources, which can of course be provided by clouds but do not really capture the predominant advantages and features of clouds.

Earlier work of the chapter authors [28] has shown that the Simple API for Grid Applications (SAGA) [29] provides a means to implement first-principle distributed applications. Both the SAGA standard [30] and the various SAGA implementations [31,32] ultimately strive to provide higher-level programming abstractions to developers, while at the same time shielding them from the heterogeneity and dynamics of the underlying infrastructure. The low-level decomposition of distributed applications can thus be expressed via the relatively high-level SAGA API.

SAGA has been used to develop scientific applications that can utilize an ever-increasing set of infrastructure, ranging from vanilla clouds such as EC2, to "open source" clouds based upon Eucalyptus, to regular HPC and HTC grids, as well to a proposed set of emerging "special-purpose" clouds. SAGA has also been used in conjunction with multiple VM management systems such as OpenNebula (work in progress) and Condor (established). In those cases where the application decomposition properties can be well-mapped to the respective underlying cloud and its usage usage modes (as discussed before), the resulting applications are fit to utilize cloud environments. In other words, if clouds can be defined as elastic distributed systems that support specific usage modes, then it seems viable to expect explicit application level support for those usage modes, in order to allow applications to express that usage mode in the first place.

If we now consider the variety of scientific applications (see reference 2), it seems clear that (i) no single usage mode will be able to accommodate them all and (ii) no single programming abstraction will be able to cover their full scope. Instead, we see a continuum of requirements and solutions that try to map the application structure to the specific distributed runtime environment. This is exactly where SAGA tries to contribute: It provides a *framework* for implementing higher-level programming abstractions (where it does not provide those abstractions itself), each expressing or demanding a certain usage mode. The SAGA layer allows to abstract the specific way in which that usage mode is provided—either implicitly by adding additional structure to the distributed environment, or explicitly by exploiting support for that usage mode, for example, the elasticity in a specific cloud.

This section will discuss several SAGA-based scientific cloud applications, but we assert that the discussion holds just as well for applications that express their decomposition in other ways programatically. We do not claim that SAGA is the ultimate approach to develop cloud applications, but given our experience so far, it at least seems to be a viable approach that allows applications to directly benefit from the features that clouds, as specific distributed environments, provide: (a) support for specific usage modes and (b) elasticity of resources. Below we will present a number of examples that illustrate and verify that approach.

13.3.1 MapReduce

As discussed in Section 13.2, MapReduce (MR) is a prominent example for a PaaS: The MR framework allows users to (a) define their own specific map and reduce algorithms and (b) utilize the respective PaaS infrastructure with its MR supporting usage modes (elasticity, communication, etc.). With the emergence of the currently observed broad spectrum of cloud infrastructures, it became, however, necessary to implement the MR framework for each of them. Furthermore, MR has traditionally not been heavily used by the scientific computation community, so that efficient implementations on the "legacy" grid and cluster platforms have been largely missing, which raises the barrier for adoption of MR for scientific applications.

The SAGA MapReduce [33] provides a MR development and runtime environment that is implemented using the SAGA. The main advantage of a SAGA-based approach is that it is infrastructure-independent while still providing a maximum of control over the deployment, distribution, and runtime decomposition. In particular, the ability to control the distribution and placement of the computation units (workers) is critical in order to implement the ability to move computational work to the data. This is required to keep data network transfer low and, in the case of commercial clouds, the monetary cost of computing the solution low.

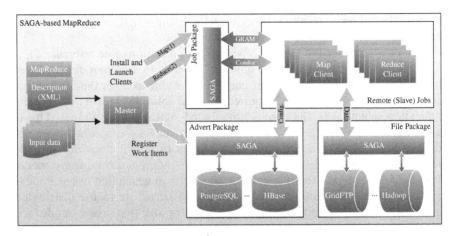

FIGURE 13.2. SAGA MapReduce framework. A master-worker paradigm is used to implement the MapReduce pattern. The diagram shows several different infrastructure options that can be utilized by the application.

Figure 13.2 show the architecture of the SAGA MR framework. Several SAGA adaptors have been developed to utilize SAGA MapReduce seamlessly on different grid and cloud infrastructures [28]. For this purpose, adaptors for the SAGA job and file package are provided. The SAGA job API is used to orchestrate mapping and reduction tasks, while the file API is utilized to access data. In addition to the local adaptors for testing, we use the Globus adaptors for grids and the AWS adaptors for cloud environments. Furthermore, we provide various adaptors for cloud-like infrastructure, such as different open-source distributed file systems (e.g., HDFS [25] and CloudStore [34]), and key/value stores (e.g., HBase [35]).

Tables 13.2 and 13.3 show some selected performance data for SAGA MapReduce; further details can be found in references 28 and 33. These tests established interoperability across a range of distinct infrastructure concurrently. Ongoing work is currently adding dynamic resource placement and job management to the framework, and it is also experimenting with automated data/compute colocation. The SAGA-based MapReduce implementation has shown to be easily applicable to sequence search applications, which in turn can make excellent use of the MapReduce algorithm and of a variety of middleware backends.

13.3.2 SAGA Montage

Montage [36, 37], an astronomical image mosaicking application that is also one of the most commonly studied workflow applications, has also been studied [38] with SAGA. Montage is designed to take multiple astronomical

TABLE 13.2. Performance Data for Different Configurations of Worker Placements[a]

Number of workers		Data	T_S	T_{Spawn}	$T_S -$
TeraGrid	AWS	Size (MB)	(sec)	(sec)	T_{Spawn} (sec)
4	—	10	8.8	6.8	2.0
—	1	10	4.3	2.8	1.5
—	2	10	7.8	5.3	2.5
—	3	10	8.7	7.7	1.0
—	4	10	13.0	10.3	2.7
—	4 (1)	10	11.3	8.6	2.7
—	4 (2)	10	11.6	9.5	2.1
—	2	100	7.9	5.3	2.6
—	4	100	12.4	9.2	3.2
—	10	100	29.0	25.1	3.9
—	4 (1)	100	16.2	8.7	7.5
—	4 (2)	100	12.3	8.5	3.8
—	6 (3)	100	18.7	13.5	5.2
—	8 (1)	100	31.1	18.3	12.8
—	8 (2)	100	27.9	19.8	8.1
—	8 (4)	100	27.4	19.9	7.5

[a]The master places the workers either on clouds or on the TeraGrid (TG). The configurations, separated by horizontal lines, are classified as either all workers on the TG or having all workers on EC2. For the latter, unless otherwise explicitly indicated by a number in parentheses, every worker is assigned to a unique VM. In the final set of rows, the number in parentheses indicates the number of VMs used. It is interesting to note the significant spawning times, and its dependence on the number of VM, which typically increase with the number of VMs. T_{Spawn} does not include instantiation of the VM.

TABLE 13.3. Performance Data for Different Configurations of Worker Placements on TG, Eucalyptus–Cloud, and EC2.[a]

Number of Workers			Size	T_S	T_{Spawn}	$T_S -$
TG	AWS	Eucalyptus	(MB)	(sec)	(sec)	T_{Spawn} (sec)
—	1	1	10	5.3	3.8	1.5
—	2	2	10	10.7	8.8	1.9
—	1	1	100	6.7	3.8	2.9
—	2	2	100	10.3	7.3	3.0
1	—	1	10	4.7	3.3	1.4
1	—	1	100	6.4	3.4	3.0
2	2	—	10	7.4	5.9	1.5
3	3	—	10	11.6	10.3	1.6
4	4	—	10	13.7	11.6	2.1
5	5	—	10	33.2	29.4	3.8
10	10	—	10	33.2	28.8	2.4

[a]The first set of data establishes cloud–cloud interoperability. The second set (rows 5–11) shows interoperability between grids and clouds (EC2). The experimental conditions and measurements are similar to those in Table 13.2.

images (from telescopes or other instruments) and stitch them together into a mosaic that appears to be from a single instrument.

Montage initially focused on being scientifically accurate and useful to astronomers, without being concerned about computational efficiency, and it is being used by many production science instruments and astronomy projects [39]. Montage was envisioned to be customizable, so that different astronomers could choose to use all, much, or some of the functionality, and so that they could add their own code if so desired. For this reason, Montage is a set of modules or tools, each an executable program, that can run on a single computer, a parallel system, or a distributed system. The first version of Montage used a script to run a series of these modules on a single processor, with some modules being executed multiple times on different data. A Montage run is a set of tasks, each having input and output data, and many of the tasks are the same executable run on different data, referred to as a stage.

Later Montage releases delivered two new execution modes, suitable for grid and also cloud environments [40], in addition to sequentially execution. First, each stage can be wrapped by an MPI executable that calls the tasks in that stage in a round-robin manner across the available processors. Second, the Montage workflow can be described as a directed acyclic graph (DAG), and this DAG can be executed on a grid. In the released version of Montage, this is done by mDAG, a Montage module that produces an abstract DAG (or A-DAG, where abstract means that no specific resources are assigned to execute the DAG), Pegasus [41, 42], which communicates with grid information systems and maps the abstract DAG to a concrete resource assignment, creating a concrete DAG (or C-DAG), and DAGMan [43], which executes C-DAG nodes on their internally specified resources.

The generality of Montage as a workflow application has led it to become an exemplar for those in the computer science workflow community, such as those working on: Pegasus, ASKALON [44], quality-of-service (QoS)-enabled GridFTP [45], SWIFT [46], SCALEA-G [47], VGrADS [48], and so on.

A lot of interesting work has been done around the accommodation of workflow and generally data-intensive applications into the cloud. Such applications have a large amount and number of data dependencies, which are usually represented using a DAG to define the sequence of those dependencies. Different approaches have been used to test how well a traditional application like Montage could fit in and utilize virtual resources without compromising any of its functionality or performance [49], including a SAGA-based workflow system, called "digedag," has been developed. This allows one to run Montage applications on a heterogeneous set of backends, with acceptable performance penalties [38]. Individual nodes of Montage workflows are usually sequential (i.e., nonparallel) computations, with moderate data input and output rates. Those nodes thus map very well to resources that are usually available in today's IaaS clouds, such as AWS/EC2 or Eucalyptus. SAGA-based Montage workflows can thus seamlessly scale out, and simultaneously span grid, cloud, and cluster environments. It must be noted that workflows with other

TABLE 13.4. Execution Measurements

#	Resources	Middleware	Walltime (sec)	Standard Deviation (sec)	Difference from Local (sec)
1	L	F	68.7	9.4	—
2	L	S	131.3	8.7	62.6
3	L	C	155.0	16.6	86.3
4	L	F, S	89.8	5.7	21.1
5	L	F, C	117.7	17.7	49.0
6	L	F, C	133.5	32.5	64.8
7	L	F, S, C	144.8	18.3	76.1
8	Q	S	491.6	50.6	422.9
9	E	A	354.2	23.3	285.5
10	E, Q	S, A	363.6	60.9	294.0
11	L, Q, E	F, S, A	409.6	60.9	340.9
12	L	D	168.8	5.3	100.1
13	P	D	309.7	41.5	241.0

Resources: L, local; P, Purdue; Q, Queen Bee; E, AWS/EC2
Middleware: F, FORK/SAGA; S, SSH/SAGA; A, AWS/SAGA; C, Condor/SAGA; D, Condor/DAGMan.

compute/data characteristics could not be mapped onto cloud resources prevalent today: The usage modes supported by AWS/EC2 and the like do not, at the moment, cover massive parallel applications, low-latency pipeline, and so on.

Table 13.4 gives the results (mean + standard deviation) for several SAGA Montage experiments. The AWS/EC2 times (#9, #10, #11) are cleared of the EC2 startup times—those are discussed in detail in reference 28. If multiple resources are specified, the individual DAG nodes are mapped to the respective resources in round-robin fashion. Note that the table also gives the times for the traditional DAGMan execution to a local and a remote Condor pool (#12, #13).

13.3.3 Ensemble of Biomolecular Simulations

Several classes of applications are well-suited for distributed environments. Probably the best-known and most powerful examples are those that involve an ensemble of decoupled tasks, such as simple parameter sweep applications [50]. In the following we investigate an ensemble of (parallel HPC) MD simulations. Ensemble-based approaches represent an important and promising attempt to overcome the general limitations of insufficient timescales, as well as specific limitations of inadequate conformational sampling arising from kinetic trappings. The fact that one single long-running simulation can be substituted for an ensemble of simulations makes these ideal candidates for distributed environments. This provides an important general motivation for researching ways to support scale-out and thus enhance sampling and to thereby increase "effective" timescales studied.

The physical system we investigate is the HCV internal ribosome entry site and is recognized specifically by the small ribosomal subunit and eukaryotic initiation factor 3 (eIF3) before viral translation initiation. This makes it a good candidate for new drugs targeting HCV. The initial conformation of the RNA is taken from the NMR structure (PDB ID: 1PK7). By using multiple replicas, the aim is to enhance the sampling of the conformational flexibility of the molecule as well as the equilibrium energetics.

To efficiently execute the ensemble of batch jobs without the necessity to queue each individual job, the application utilizes the SAGA BigJob framework [51]. BigJob is a Pilot Job framework that provides the user a uniform abstraction to grids and clouds independent of any particular cloud or grid provider that can be instantiated dynamically. Pilot Jobs are an execution abstraction that have been used by many communities to increase the predictability and time-to-solution of such applications. Pilot Jobs have been used to (i) improve the utilization of resources, (ii) reduce the net wait time of a collection of tasks, (iii) facilitate bulk or high-throughput simulations where multiple jobs need to be submitted which would otherwise saturate the queuing system, and (iv) implement application-specific scheduling decisions and policy decisions.

As shown in Figure 13.3, BigJob currently provides an abstraction to grids, Condor pools, and clouds. Using the same API, applications can

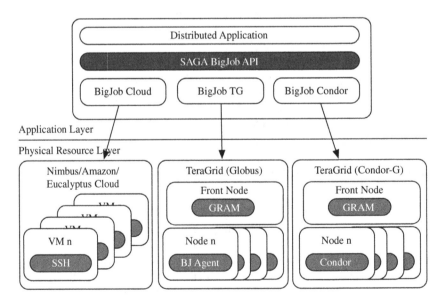

FIGURE 13.3. An overview of the SAGA-based Pilot Job: The SAGA Pilot-Job API is currently implemented by three different back-ends: one for grids, one for Condor, and one for clouds.

dynamically allocate resources via the big-job interface and bind sub-jobs to these resources.

In the following, we use an ensemble of MD simulations to investigate different BigJob usage modes and analyze the time-to-completion, T_C, in different scenarios.

Scenario A: T_C for Workload for Different Resource Configurations. In this scenario and as proof of scale-out capabilities, we use SAGA BigJob to run replicas across different types of infrastructures. At the beginning of the experiment a particular set of Pilot Jobs is started in each environment. Once a Pilot Job becomes active, the application assigns replicas to this job. We measure T_C for different resource configurations using a workload of eight replicas each running on eight cores. The following setups have been used:

Scenario A1: Resource I and III—Clouds and GT2-based grids.

Scenario A2: Resource II and III—Clouds and Condor grids.

Scenario A3: Resource I, II, and III—Clouds, GT2, and Condor grids.

For this experiment, the LONI clusters Poseidon and Oliver are used as grid and Condor resources, and Nimbus is used as a cloud resource.

Figure 13.4 shows the results. For the first three bars, only one infrastructure was used to complete the eight-replica workload. Running the whole scenario in the Science Cloud resulted in a quite poor but predictable performance; the standard deviation for this scenario is very low. The LONI resources are about three times faster than the Science Cloud, which corresponds to our earlier findings. The performance of the Condor and grid BigJob is similar, which can be expected since the underlying physical LONI resources are the same. Solely, a slightly higher startup overhead can be observed in the Condor runtimes.

In the next set of three experiments, multiple resources were used. For Scenario A1 (the fourth bar from left), two replicas were executed on the Science Cloud. The offloading of two replicas to an additional cloud resource resulted in a light improvement of T_C compared to using just LONI resources. Thus, the usage of cloud resources must be carefully considered since T_C is determined by the slowest resource, that is, Nimbus. As described earlier, the startup time for Nimbus images is, particularly for such short runs, significant. Also, NAMD performs significantly worse in the Nimbus cloud than on Poseidon or Oliver. Since the startup time on Nimbus averages to 357 sec and each eight-core replica runs for about 363 sec, at least 720 sec must be allowed for running a single replica on Nimbus. Thus, it can be concluded that if resources in the grids or Condor pool are instantly available, it is not reasonable to start additional cloud resources. However, it must be noted that there are virtual machines types with a better performance available—for example, in the Amazon cloud. These VMs are usually associated with higher costs (up to \$2.40 per CPU hour) than the Science Cloud VMs. For a further

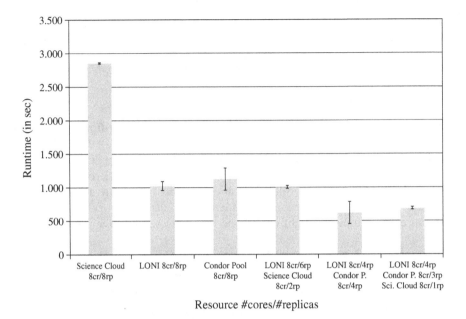

FIGURE 13.4. Collective usage of grid, Condor, and cloud resources for workload of eight replicas. The experiments showed that if the grid and Condor resource Poseidon has only a light load, no benefits for using additional cloud resources exist. However, the introduction of an additional Condor or grid resource significantly decreases T_C.

discussion of cost trade-offs for scientific computations in clouds, see Deelman et al. [52].

Scenario B: T_C for Workload for Different Resource Configurations.

Given that clouds provide the illusion of infinite capacity, or at least queue wait-times are nonexistent, it is likely that when using multiple resource types and with loaded grids/clusters (e.g., TeraGrid is currently over-subscribed and typical queue wait-times often exceed 24 hours), most sub-jobs will end up on the cloud infrastructure. Thus, in Scenario B, the resource assignment algorithm we use is as follows: We submit tasks to non-cloud resources first and periodically monitor the progress of the tasks. If insufficient jobs have finished when time equal to T_X has elapsed (determined per criteria outlined below), then we move the workload to utilize clouds. The underlying basis is that clouds have an explicit cost associated with them; and if jobs can be completed on the TeraGrid/Condor-pool while preserving the performance constraints, we opt for such a solution. However, if queue loads prevent the performance requirements from being met, we move the jobs to a cloud resource, which we have shown has less fluctuation in T_C of the workload.

For this experiment we integrated a progress manager that implements the described algorithm into the replica application. The user has the possibility to

TABLE 13.5. Usage of Cloud Pilot Jobs to Ensure Deadline

Result	Number of Occurrences	Average T_C (minutes)
No VM started	6	7.8
1 VM started	1	36.4
2 VMs started	1	47.3
3 VMs started	2	44.2

specify a maximum runtime and a check interval. At the beginning of each check interval, the progress manager compares the number of jobs done with the total number of jobs and estimates the total number of jobs that can be completed within the requested timeframe. If the total number of jobs is higher than this estimate, the progress monitor instantiates another BigJob object request additional cloud resources for a single replica. In this scenario, each time an intermediate target is not met, four additional Nimbus VMs sufficient for running another eight core replica are instantiated. Table 13.5 summarizes the results.

In the investigated scenario, we configured a maximum runtime of 45 min and a progress check interval of 4 min. We repeated the same experiment 10 times at different times of the day. In 6 out of 10 cases the scenario was completed in about 8 minutes. However, the fluctuation in particular in the waiting time on typical grid resources can be very high. Thus, in four cases, it was necessary to start additional VMs to meet the application deadline. In two cases, three Pilot Jobs each with eight cores had to be started, and in one case a single Pilot Job was sufficient. In a single case the deadline was missed solely because not enough cloud resources were available; that is, we were only able to start two instead of three Pilot Jobs.

13.4 DISCUSSION

It is still unclear what the predominant usage mode of cloud infrastructures will be. As shown, there are a large number of applications that are able to utilize clouds, including both data-intensive applications (i.e., those that require data-compute affinity) and compute-intensive applications. While clouds can support different compute-intensive usage modes (e.g., distributed, tightly coupled and loosely coupled applications), tightly coupled applications are less well suited for clouds because current cloud infrastructures lack high-end, low-latency interconnects. Another interesting type of application includes programs that are able to utilize clouds in addition to traditional grids in a hybrid mode. Using dynamic and adaptive execution modes, the time-to-solution for many applications can be reduced and exceptional runtime situations (e.g., failures or scheduling delays) can be handled.

Developing and running applications on dynamic computational infrastructures such as clouds presents new and significant challenges. This includes the need for programming systems such as SAGA, which is able to express the different usage modes, associated runtime trade-offs, and adaptations. Other issues include: decomposing applications, components and workflows; determining and provisioning the appropriate mix of grid/cloud resources, and dynamically scheduling them across the hybrid execution environment while satisfying/balancing multiple possibly changing objectives for performance, resilience, budgets, and so on.

13.4.1 IDEAS Revisited

In computational science applications that utilize distributed infrastructure (such as computational grids and clouds), dealing with heterogeneity and scale of the underlying infrastructure remains a challenge. As shown in Table 13.6, SAGA and SAGA-based abstractions help to advance the IDEAS design objectives: Interoperability, Distributed scale-out, Extensibilty, Adaptivity and Simplicity:

- **Interoperability.** In all three examples, application-level interoperability is provided by the SAGA programming system. SAGA decouples applications from the underlying physical resources and provides infrastructure-independent control over the application deployment, decomposition, and runtime execution.
- **Distributed Scale-Out.** SAGA-based applications and frameworks, such as SAGA BigJob and Digedag, support the distributed scale-out of applications to multiple and possibly heterogeneous infrastructures—for example, different types of clouds and grids.
- **Extensibility.** The example clouds applications are extensible in several directions; new functionality and usage modes can simply be incorporated using SAGA. Additional distributed cloud and grid infrastructures can be included by configuration using a different middleware adaptor.

TABLE 13.6. **Design objectives addressed by the different applications: Interoperability, infrastructure independence; Distributed Scale-Out, ability to use multiple distributed resources concurrently; Extensibility, extensibility and general purpose uptake; Adaptivity, ability to respond to changes; and Simplicity, greater simplicity without sacrificing functionality and performance.**

Application	Interoperability	Distr. Scale-Out	Extensibility	Adaptivity	Simplicity
SAGA MapReduce	Y	Y	Y		Y
SAGA Montage	Y	Y	Y		Y
Biomolecular Ensemble	Y	Y	Y	Y	Y

- **Adaptivity.** Distributed applications that utilize SAGA are able to explicitly benefit from the cloud properties such as elasticity and to pursue dynamic execution modes. Examples of such usage mode include the usage of additional resources to meet a deadline or to meet an increased resource demand due to a certain runtime condition.
- **Simplicity.** SAGA provides a simple, high-level programming abstraction to express core distributed functionality. Simplicity arises from the fact that the API is very focused and reduced to the most essential functionalities.

13.4.2 Interoperability of Scientific Applications across Clouds and HPC/Grids

It is still unclear what kind of programming models and programming systems will emerge for clouds. It has been shown that traditional distributed applications can be easily ported to IaaS environments. The nature of applications as well as the provided system-level interfaces will play an important role for interoperability. While several technical infrastructure features, as well as economical policies, influence the design of programming models for the cloud era, it is important for effective scientific application development that any such system should not be constrained to a specific infrastructure—that is, it should support infrastructure interoperability at the application-level.

The SAGA programming system provides a standard interface and can support powerful programming models. SAGA allows application developers to implement common and basic distributed functionality, such as application decomposition, distributed job submission, and distributed file movement/management, independently of the underlying infrastructure. The SAGA cloud adaptors provide the foundation for accessing cloud storage and compute resource via the SAGA API. The ability to design and develop applications in an infrastructure-independent way leads to new kinds of application, such as dynamic applications. Such applications have dynamic runtime requirements and are able to adapt to changing runtime environments and resource availabilities. SAGA provides developers with new capability while introducing a new set of challenges and trade-offs. Application developers are, for example, able to utilize new execution modes in conjunction with "traditional" distributed applications but must, however, consider new trade-offs, for example, when selecting a resource.

The MapReduce programming model has exemplified a novel way to construct distributed applications for the cloud. It has been perceived as a programming pattern to lead the implementation of some future scientific applications. There has been a lot of testing on simple applications performing map and reduce computations on VMs as well as on traditional local clusters in order to first verify the scalability of performance that the proposed model successfully offers and then, most importantly, guarantee interoperability between VMs and local clusters for a given application. As shown, SAGA MapReduce is able to run across different cloud and cloud-like back-end infrastructures.

As highlighted earlier, SAGA provides the basis for dynamic applications. Such applications greatly benefit from the ability of clouds to dynamically provision resources. The biomolecular ensemble application, for example, easily scales out to cloud and grid infrastructures and is able to utilize additional cloud resources to ensure the progress toward a deadline. Furthermore, SAGA enables applications and higher-level frameworks such as BigJob to deploy dynamic schedulers that determine the appropriate mix of cloud/grid resources and are able to adaptively respond to special runtime situations, such as faults.

Similarly, the development of workflow applications such as SAGA Montage can be both simple and efficient using the right tools. While SAGA Montage can easily be run across grid and clouds, the current version follows a traditional static execution model. In the future, the decision of where to run Montage components should be made at runtime, taking into account the current system and network utilization. Furthermore, capabilities, such as the ability to dynamically reschedule tasks, should be considered.

13.4.3 Application Performance Considerations

Undoubtedly, the most important characteristic for the establishment of a scientific application is its overall performance. There are proposals on including HPC tools and scientific libraries in EC2 AMIs and have them ready to run on request. This might lead to re-implementing some HPC tools and deploying public images on Amazon or other vendors specifically for scientific purposes (e.g., the SGI Cyclone Cloud [53]). Still, in order to include ready-to-use MPI clusters on EC2, there are several challenges to be met: The machine images must be manually prepared, which involves setting up the operating system, the application's software environment and the security credentials. However, this step is only initially required and comparable with moving an application to a new grid resource. Furthermore, the virtual machines must be started and managed by the application. As shown, several middleware frameworks, such as BigJob, are already able to utilize and manage cloud resources taking the burden off the application. Depending on the cloud infrastructure used, the spawning of VMs usually involves some overhead for resource allocation and for staging the VM to the target machine. At the end of the run, the results must be obtained and stored persistently, and the cluster must be terminated.

Another concern that scientists have to deal with in a cloud environment are different computational overheads as well as high and sometimes unpredictable communication latencies and limited bandwidths. For applications that are HPC applications, where the coupling of communication and computation is relatively tight and where there is relatively frequent communication including global communication, clouds can be used, but with added performance overhead, at least on today's clouds. These overheads have various sources, some of which can be reduced. How much of this overhead must exist and will exist in the future is unclear.

There are two types of overhead: (i) added computational overhead of a VM and (ii) communication overhead when communicating between VMs. The first type of overhead results from the use of VMs and the fact that the underlying hardware is shared. While clouds nowadays deploy highly efficient virtualization solutions that impose very low overheads on applications (see reference 51), unanticipated load increases on the cloud providers infrastructure can affect the runtime of scientific applications. The communication overhead mainly results from the fact that most clouds do not use networking hardware that is as low-overhead as that of dedicated HPC systems. There are at least two routes to parallelism in VMs. The first is a single VM across multiple cores; the second is parallelism across VMs. The latter type is especially affected from these communication overheads; that is, tightly coupled workloads (e.g., MPI jobs) are likely to see a degraded performance if they run across multiple VMs.

Also, the common perception of clouds does not include the ability to co-locate different parts of a single application on a single physical cluster. Again, some of this network-related overhead can be reduced. At the time of writing this chapter, it is unclear to the authors if there is community consensus on what the performance of HPC applications on clouds is expected to be compared to bare-metal, whether the future model is that of a single VM over multiple-cores, or if there will be an aggregation of multiple VMs to form a single application, and thus importantly it is unclear what the current limitations on performance are. Additionally, there is also work in progress to develop pass-through communication and I/O, where the VM would not add overhead, though this is not yet mature.

13.5 CONCLUSIONS

As established earlier, both cloud and grid applications are incarnations of distributed applications. Applications require only small modifications to run on clouds, even if most of them only utilize "legacy" modes; that is, they usually run on a set of static resources [54]. Additionally, cloud applications are generally able to take advantage of existing abstractions and interfaces.

With the emergence of clouds and a general increase in the importance of data-intensive applications, programming models for data-intensive applications have gained significant attention; a prominent example is MapReduce. It is important to remember that these are not grid- or cloud-specific programming models; they can be used in either or both contexts. Most applications can in principle use either a grid or a cloud; whether they use a grid or a cloud is dependent upon the level of control and decomposition that needs to be asserted and/or retained. Additional factors that determine this decision include the offering of the programming model, as well as a mapping to the capabilities of infrastructure that addresses the desired affinities, such as compute–communication and compute–data affinities [54].

The usability and effectiveness of a programming model is dependent upon the desired degree of control in the application development, deployment, and execution. To efficiently support coordinated execution across heterogeneous grid and cloud infrastructures, programming tools and systems are required. It is important to ensure that such programming systems and tools provide open interfaces and support the IDEAS design objectives. Furthermore, these tools must address the cloud's inherent elasticity and support applications with dynamic resource requirements and execution modes. Programming systems such as SAGA provide developers with ability to express application decompositions and coordinations via a simple, high-level API. Having established that cloud applications are conceptually akin to grid applications, we have shown, via several scientific applications, how SAGA has proven to be a programming system to develop applications that can utilize grids and clouds effectively.

REFERENCES

1. P. Mell and T. Grance, *The NIST definition of cloud computing*.

2. S. Jha et al., Programming Abstractions for Large-scale Distributed Applications, submitted to *ACM Computing Surveys*; draft at http://www.cct.lsu.edu/~sjha/publications/dpa_surveypaper.pdf.

3. L. Youseff, M. Butrico, and D. Da Silva, Toward a unified ontology of cloud computing, in *Proceedings of the Grid Computing Environments Workshop*, GCE '08, November 2008, 1–10.

4. M. Armbrust et al., Above the clouds: A Berkeley View of Cloud Computing, *Technical Report UCB/EECS-2009–28*, EECS Department, University of California, Berkeley, February 2009.

5. N. Wilkins-Diehr, D. Gannon, G. Klimeck, S. Oster, and S. Pamidighantam, TeraGrid science gateways and their impact on science. *Computer*, **41**(11):32–41, 2008.

6. Google App Engine, http://code.google.com/appengine/.

7. Windows Azure, http://www.microsoft.com/windowsazure/.

8. P. Watson, D. Leahy, H. Hiden, S. Woodman, and J. Berry, *An Azure Science Cloud for Drug Discovery*, Microsoft External Research Symposium, 2009.

9. J. Dean and S. Ghemawat, MapReduce: Simplified data processing on large clusters, in *Proceedings of the 6th Conference on Symposium on Operating Systems Design & Implementation*, Berkeley, CA, USENIX Association, 2004, pp. 137–150.

10. Hadoop: Open Source Implementation of MapReduce, http://hadoop.apache.org/.

11. Amazon Elastic MapReduce, http://aws.amazon.com/elasticmapreduce/.

12. M. Isard, M. Budiu, Y. Yu, A. Birrell, and D. Fetterly, Dryad: Distributed data-parallel programs from sequential building blocks, *SIGOPS Operating System Review*, **41**(3):59−72, 2007.

13. F. Chang et al., Bigtable: A distributed storage system for structured data, in *Proceedings of the 7th USENIX Symposium on Operating Systems Design and Implementation*, pages 15−15, Berkeley, CA, USA, 2006. USENIX Association,

14. Amazon EC2 Web Service, http://ec2.amazonaws.com.

15. Rackspace Cloud, http://www.rackspacecloud.com/.

16. GoGrid Cloud Hosting, http://www.gogrid.com/.

17. Eucalyptus, http://open.eucalyptus.com/.

18. K. Keahey, I. Foster, T. Freeman, and X. Zhang, Virtual workspaces: Achieving quality of service and quality of life in the grid, *Scientific Programming*, **13** (4):265−275, 2005.

19. Science Cloud. http://scienceclouds.org/.

20. Future Grid. http://www.futuregrid.org/.

21. Amazon S3 Web Service. http://s3.amazonaws.com.

22. Rackspace Cloud Files. http://www.rackspacecloud.com/cloud_hosting_ pro-ducts/files/.

23. Eucalyptus Walrus. http://open.eucalyptus.com/wiki/EucalyptusStorage_ v1.4.

24. S. Ghemawat, H. Gobioff, and S. Leung, The Google File System, *SIGOPS Operating System Reviews*, **37**(5):29−43, 2003.

25. HDFS. http://hadoop.apache.org/common/docs/current/hdfs_design. html.

26. C. Evangelinos and C. Hill, Cloud computing for parallel scientific HPC applications: Feasibility of running coupled atmosphere-ocean climate models on Amazon's EC2, *Cloud Computing and Its Applications* (CCA-08), 2008.

27. M.-E. Bégin, Grids and Clouds—Evolution or Revolution, https://edms.cern. ch/file/925013/3/EGEE-Grid-Cloud.pdf, 2008.

28. A. Merzky, K. Stamou, and S. Jha, Application level interoperability between clouds and grids, in *Proceedings of the Grid and Pervasive Computing Conference*, May 2009, pp. 143−150.

29. T. Goodale et al., SAGA: A simple API for grid applications, high-level application programming on the grid, *Computational Methods in Science and Technology*, **12**(1):7−20, 2006.

30. T. Goodale, S. Jha, H. Kaiser, T. Kielmann, P. Kleijer, A. Merzky, J. Shalf, and C. Smith, A Simple API for Grid Applications (SAGA), *OGF Document Series 90*, http://www.ogf.org/documents/GFD.90.pdf.

31. H. Kaiser, A. Merzky, S. Hirmer, and G. Allen, The SAGA C++ Reference Implementation, in *Object-Oriented Programming, Systems, Languages and Applications (OOPSLA'06)—Library-Centric Software Design (LCSD'06)*, Portland, OR, USA, October 22−26 2006.

32. JSaga. http://grid.in2p3.fr/jsaga/index.html.

33. C. Miceli, M. Miceli, S. Jha, H. Kaiser, and A. Merzky, Programming abstractions for data intensive computing on clouds and grids, in *Proceedings of the 9th IEEE/ACM International Symposium on Cluster Computing and the Grid*, May 2009, pp. 478−483.

34. CloudStore, http://kosmosfs.sourceforge.net.

35. HBase, http://hadoop.apache.org/hbase/.

36. The Montage project, http://montage.ipac.caltech.edu/.

37. G. B. Berriman, J. C. Good, D. Curkendall, J. Jacob, D. S. Katz, T. A. Prince, and R. Williams. Montage: An on-demand image mosaic service for the NVO, Astronomical Data Analysis Software and Systems (ADASS) XII, 2002.

38. A Merzky, K Stamou, S Jha, and D Katz, A fresh perspective on developing and executing DAG-based distributed applications: A case-study of SAGA-based Montage, in *Proceedings of the IEEE Conference on eScience 2009*, Oxford.

39. G. B. Berriman, J. C. Good, A. C. Laity, J. C. Jacob, D. S. Katz, E. Deelman, G. Singh, M.-H. Su, R. Williams, and T. Prince, Science applications of Montage: An astronomical image mosaic engine, presented at IAU XXXVI General Assembly, 2006.

40. E. Deelman et al., The cost of doing science on the cloud: The Montage example, *Proceedings of SC08*, Austin, Texas, 2008.

41. E. Deelman, J. Blythe, Y. Gil, C. Kesselman, G. Mehta, and K. Vahi, Mapping abstract complex workflows onto grid environments, *Journal of Grid Computing*, 1(1):25–39, 2003.

42. E. Deelman, J. Blythe, Y. Gil, C. Kesselman, G. Mehta, S. Patil, M.-H. Su, K. Vahi, and M. Livny, Pegasus: Mapping scientific workflows onto the grid, in *Proceedings of the Across Grids Conference*, 2004.

43. Condor DAGMAn, http://www.cs.wisc.edu/condor/dagman/.

44. M. Wieczorek, R. Prodan, and T. Fahringer, Scheduling of scientific workflows in the askalon grid environment, *ACM SIGMOD Record*, 34(3):52–62, 2005.

45. M. Humphrey and S. Park, Data throttling for data-intensive workflows, in *Proceedings of the IEEE International Parallel and Distributed Processing Symposium*, 1–11, 2008.

46. Y. Zhao et al., Swift: Fast, reliable, loosely coupled parallel computation, *IEEE Congress on Services*, pages 199–206, 2007.

47. H. Truong, T. Fahringer, and S. Dustda, Dynamic instrumentation, performance monitoring and analysis of grid scientific workflows, *Journal of Grid Computing*, 2005(3):1–18, 2005.

48. VGRaDS: Montage, a project providing a portable, compute-intensive service delivering custom mosaics on demand.

49. G. Juve, E. Deelman, K. Vahi, G. Mehta, B. Berriman, B. Berman, and P. Maechling, Scientific workflow applications on Amazon EC2, in *Proceedings of the Workshop on Cloud-based Services and Applications in conjunction with 5th IEEE International Conference on e-Science (e-Science 2009)*, 2009.

50. H. Casanova, G. Obertelli, F. Berman, and R. Wolski, The apples parameter sweep template: User-level middleware for the grid, *Scientific Programming*, 8 (3):111–126, 2000.

51. A. Luckow, L. Lacinski, and S. Jha. Saga bigjob: An extensible and interoperable pilot-job abstraction for distributed applications and systems, in *Proceedings of the 10th IEEE/ACM International Symposium on Cluster, Cloud and Grid Computing*, 2010.

52. E. Deelman, G. Singh, M. Livny, B. Berriman, and J. Good, The cost of doing science on the cloud: the montage example, in *Proceedings of the 2008 ACM/IEEE Conference on Supercomputing*, IEEE Press, New York, 2008, pp. 1–12.

53. SGI Cyclone–HPC Cloud, http://www.sgi.com/products/hpc_cloud/cyclone/index.html.

54. S. Jha, A. Merzky, and G. Fox, Using clouds to provide grids with higher levels of abstraction and explicit support for usage modes, *Concurrency and Computation: Practice & Experience*, **21**(8):1087–1108, 2009.

CHAPTER 14

THE MapReduce PROGRAMMING MODEL AND IMPLEMENTATIONS

HAI JIN, SHADI IBRAHIM, LI QI, HAIJUN CAO, SONG WU
and XUANHUA SHI

14.1 INTRODUCTION

Recently the computing world has been undergoing a significant transformation from the traditional noncentralized distributed system architecture, typified by distributed data and computation on different geographic areas, to a centralized cloud computing architecture, where the computations and data are operated somewhere in the "cloud"—that is, data centers owned and maintained by third party.

The interest in cloud computing has been motivated by many factors [1] such as the low cost of system hardware, the increase in computing power and storage capacity (e.g., the modern data center consists of hundred of thousand of cores and petascale storage), and the massive growth in data size generated by digital media (images/audio/video), Web authoring, scientific instruments, physical simulations, and so on. To this end, still the main challenge in the cloud is how to effectively store, query, analyze, and utilize these immense datasets. The traditional data-intensive system (data to computing paradigm) is not efficient for cloud computing due to the bottleneck of the Internet when transferring large amounts of data to a distant CPU [2]. New paradigms should be adopted, where computing and data resources are co-located, thus minimizing the communication cost and benefiting from the large improvements in IO speeds using local disks, as shown in Figure 14.1. Alex Szalay and Jim Gray stated in a commentary on 2020 computing [3]:

> In the future, working with large data sets will typically mean sending computations to data rather than copying the data to your work station.

Cloud Computing: Principles and Paradigms, Edited by Rajkumar Buyya, James Broberg and Andrzej Goscinski   Copyright © 2011 John Wiley & Sons, Inc.

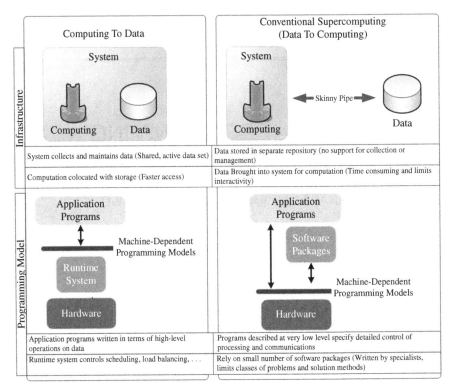

FIGURE 14.1. Traditional Data-to-Computing Paradigm versus Computing-to-Data Paradigm [10].

Google has successfully implemented and practiced the new data-intensive paradigm in their Google MapReduce System (e.g., Google uses its MapReduce framework to process 20 petabytes of data per day [4]). The MapReduce system runs on top of the Google File System (GFS) [5], within which data are loaded, partitioned into chunks, and each chunk is replicated. Data processing is co-located with data storage: When a file needs to be processed, the job scheduler consults a storage metadata service to get the host node for each chunk and then schedules a "map" process on that node, so that data locality is exploited efficiently.

At the time of writing, due to its remarkable features including simplicity, fault tolerance, and scalability, MapReduce is by far the most powerful realization of data-intensive cloud computing programming. It is often advocated as an easier-to-use, efficient and reliable replacement for the traditional data-intensive programming model for cloud computing. More significantly, MapReduce has been proposed to form the basis of the data-center software stack [6].

MapReduce has been widely applied in various fields including data- and compute-intensive applications, machine learning, graphic programming, multi-core programming, and so on. Moreover, many implementations have been developed in different languages for different purposes.

Its popular open-source implementation, Hadoop [7], was developed primarily by Yahoo!, where it processes hundreds of terabytes of data on at least 10,000 cores [8], and is now used by other companies, including Facebook, Amazon, Last.fm, and the *New York Times* [9]. Research groups from the enterprise and academia are starting to study the MapReduce model for better fit for the cloud, and they explore the possibilities of adapting it for more applications.

14.2 MapReduce PROGRAMMING MODEL

MapReduce is a software framework for solving many large-scale computing problems. The MapReduce abstraction is inspired by the Map and Reduce functions, which are commonly used in functional languages such as Lisp [4]. The MapReduce system allows users to easily express their computation as *map* and *reduce* functions (more details can be found in Dean and Ghemawat [4]):

- The map function, written by the user, processes a key/value pair to generate a set of intermediate key/value pairs:

  ```
  map (key1, value1) → list (key2, value2)
  ```

- The reduce function, also written by the user, merges all intermediate values associated with the same intermediate key:

  ```
  reduce (key2, list (value2)) → list (value2)
  ```

14.2.1 The Wordcount Example

As a simple illustration of the Map and Reduce functions, Figure 14.2 shows the pseudo-code and the algorithm and illustrates the process steps using the widely used "Wordcount" example. The Wordcount application counts the number of occurrences of each word in a large collection of documents.

The steps of the process are briefly described as follows: The input is read (typically from a distributed file system) and broken up into key/value pairs (e.g., the Map function emits a word and its associated count of occurrence, which is just "1"). The pairs are partitioned into groups for processing, and they are sorted according to their key as they arrive for reduction. Finally, the key/value pairs are reduced, once for each unique key in the sorted list, to

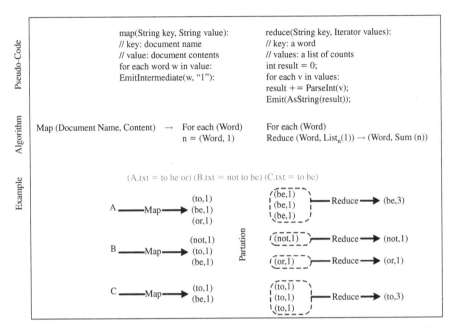

FIGURE 14.2. The Wordcount example.

produce a combined result (e.g., the Reduce function sums all the counts emitted for a particular word).

14.2.2 Main Features

In this section we list the main features of MapReduce for data-intensive application:

- Data-Aware. When the MapReduce-Master node is scheduling the Map tasks for a newly submitted job, it takes in consideration the data location information retrieved from the GFS-Master node.
- Simplicity. As the MapReduce runtime is responsible for parallelization and concurrency control, this allows programmers to easily design parallel and distributed applications.
- Manageability. In traditional data-intensive applications, where data are stored separately from the computation unit, we need two levels of management: (i) to manage the input data and then move these data and prepare them to be executed; (ii) to manage the output data. In contrast, in the Google MapReduce model, data and computation are allocated, taking advantage of the GFS, and thus it is easier to manage the input and output data.

- Scalability. Increasing the number of nodes (data nodes) in the system will increase the performance of the jobs with potentially only minor losses.
- fault Tolerance and Reliability. The data in the GFS are distributed on clusters with thousands of nodes. Thus any nodes with hardware failures can be handled by simply removing them and installing a new node in their place. Moreover, MapReduce, taking advantage of the replication in GFS, can achieve high reliability by (1) rerunning all the tasks (completed or in progress) when a host node is going off-line, (2) rerunning failed tasks on another node, and (3) launching backup tasks when these tasks are slowing down and causing a bottleneck to the entire job.

14.2.3 Execution Overview

As shown in Figure 14.3, when the user program calls the MapReduce function, the following sequence of actions occurs. More details can be found in Dean and Ghemawat [4]:

The MapReduce library in the user program first splits the input files into M pieces of typically 16 to 64 megabytes (MB) per piece. It then starts many copies

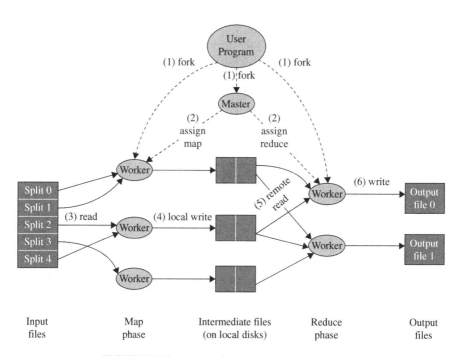

FIGURE 14.3. MapReduce execution overview [4].

of the program on a cluster. One is the "master" and the rest are "workers." The master is responsible for scheduling (assigns the map and reduce tasks to the worker) and monitoring (monitors the task progress and the worker health).

When map tasks arise, the master assigns the task to an idle worker, taking into account the data locality. A worker reads the content of the corresponding input split and emits a key/value pairs to the user-defined Map function. The intermediate key/value pairs produced by the Map function are first buffered in memory and then periodically written to a local disk, partitioned into R sets by the partitioning function.

The master passes the location of these stored pairs to the reduce worker, which reads the buffered data from the map worker using remote procedure calls (RPC). It then sorts the intermediate keys so that all occurrences of the same key are grouped together. For each key, the worker passes the corresponding intermediate value for its entire occurrence to the Reduce function. Finally, the output is available in R output files (one per reduce task).

14.2.4 Spotlight on Google MapReduce Implementation

Google's MapReduce implementation targets large clusters of Linux PCs connected through Ethernet switches [11]. Tasks are forked using remote procedure calls. Buffering and communication occurs by reading and writing files on the GFS. The runtime library is written in C++ with interfaces in Python and Java [12]. MapReduce jobs are spread across its massive computing clusters. For example, the average MapReduce job in September 2007 ran across approximately 400 machines, and the system delivered approximately 11,000 machine years in a single month as shown in Table 14.1 [4].

TABLE 14.1. MapReduce Statistics for Different Months [4]

	Aug. '04	Mar. '06	Sep. '07
Number of jobs (1000s)	29	171	2,217
Avg. completion time (sec)	634	874	395
Machine years used	217	2,002	11,081
Map input data (TB)	3,288	52,254	403,152
Map output data (TB)	758	6,743	34,774
Reduce output data (TB)	193	2,970	14,018
Avg. machines per job	157	268	394
Unique implementations			
Map	395	1,958	4,083
Reduce	269	1,208	2,418

14.3 MAJOR MAPREDUCE IMPLEMENTATIONS FOR THE CLOUD

In the following sections, we will introduce some of the major MapReduce implementations around the world as shown in Table 14.2, and we will provide a comparison of these different implementations, considering their functionality, platform, the associated storage system, programming environment, and so on, as shown in Table 14.3.

14.3.1 Hadoop

Hadoop [7] is a top-level Apache project, being built and used by a community of contributors from all over the world [13]. It was advocated by industry's premier Web players—Google, Yahoo!, Microsoft, and Facebook—as the engine to power the cloud [14]. The Hadoop project is stated as a collection of various subprojects for reliable, scalable distributed computing [7]. It is defined as follows [7]:

TABLE 14.2. MapReduce Cloud Implementations

Owner	Imp Name and Website	Start Time	Last Release	Distribution Model
Google	Google MapReduce http://labs.google .com/papers/ mapreduce.html	2004	—	Internal use by Google
Apache	Hadoop http://hadoop .apache.org/	2004	Hadoop0.20.0 April 22, 2009	Open source
GridGain	GridGain http://www .gridgain.com/	2005	GridGain 2.1.1 February 26, 2009	Open source
Nokia	Disco http://discoproject .org/	2008	Disco 0.2.3 September 9, 2009	Open source
Geni.com	SkyNet http://skynet .rubyforge.org	2007	Skynet0.9.3 May 31, 2008	Open source
Manjrasoft	MapReduce.net (Optional service of Aneka) http://www .manjrasoft.com/ products.html	2008	Aneka 1.0 March 27, 2009	Commercial

TABLE 14.3. Comparison of MapReduce Implementations

	Google MapReduce	Hadoop	Disco	MapReduce.NET	Skynet	GridGain
Focus	Data-intensive	Data-intensive	Data-intensive	Data- and compute-intensive	Data-intensive	Compute-intensive and data-intensive
Architecture Platform	Master–Slave Linux	Master–Slave Cross-platform	Master–slave Linux, Mac OS X	Master–Slave .Net Windows	P2P OS-independent	Master–slave Windows, Linux, Mac OS X
Storage System	GFS	HDFS, CloudStore, S3	GlusterFS	WinDFS, CIFS, and NTFS	Message queuing: Tuplespace and MySQL	Data grid
Implementation Technology	C++	JAVA	Erlang	C#	Ruby	Java
Programming Environment	Java and Python	JAVA, shell utilities using Hadoop streaming, C++ Using Hadoop pipes	Python	C#	Ruby	Java
Deployment	Deployed on Google clusters	Private and public cloud (EC2)	Private and public cloud (EC2)	Using Aneka, can be deployed on private and public Cloud	Web application (Rails)	Private and public cloud
Some Users and Applications	Google	Baidu [46], NetSeer [47], A9.com [48], Facebook [49] …	Nokia Research center [21]	Vel Tech University [50]	Geni.com [17]	MedVoxel [51], Pointloyalty [52], Traficon [53], …

The Apache Hadoop project develops open-source software for reliable, scalable, distributed computing. Hadoop includes these subprojects:

- Hadoop Common: The common utilities that support the other Hadoop subprojects.
- Avro: A data serialization system that provides dynamic integration with scripting languages.
- Chukwa: A data collection system for managing large distributed systems.
- HBase: A scalable, distributed database that supports structured data storage for large tables.
- HDFS: A distributed file system that provides high throughput access to application data.
- Hive: A data warehouse infrastructure that provides data summarization and ad hoc querying.
- MapReduce: A software framework for distributed processing of large data sets on compute clusters.
- Pig: A high-level data-flow language and execution framework for parallel computation.
- ZooKeeper: A high-performance coordination service for distributed applications.

HadoopMapReduce Overview. The Hadoop common [7], formerly Hadoop core, includes file System, RPC, and serialization libraries and provides the basic services for building a cloud computing environment with commodity hardware. The two fundamental subprojects are the MapReduce framework and the Hadoop Distributed File System (HDFS).

The Hadoop Distributed File System is a distributed file system designed to run on clusters of commodity machines. It is highly fault-tolerant and is appropriate for data-intensive applications as it provides high speed access the application data.

The Hadoop MapReduce framework is highly reliant on its shared file system (i.e., it comes with plug-ins for HDFS, CloudStore [15], and Amazon Simple Storage Service S3 [16]).

The Map/Reduce framework has master/slave architecture. The master, called JobTracker, is responsible for (a) querying the NameNode for the block locations, (b) scheduling the tasks on the slave which is hosting the task's blocks, and (c) monitoring the successes and failures of the tasks. The slaves, called TaskTracker, execute the tasks as directed by the master.

Hadoop Communities. Yahoo! has been the largest contributor to the Hadoop project [13]. Yahoo! uses Hadoop extensively in its Web search and advertising businesses [13]. For example, in 2009, Yahoo! launched, according to them, the world's largest Hadoop production application, called

Yahoo! Search Webmap. The Yahoo! Search Webmap runs on a more than 10,000 core Linux cluster and produces data that are now used in every Yahoo! Web search query [8].

Besides Yahoo!, many other vendors have introduced and developed their own solutions for the enterprise cloud; these include IBM Blue Cloud [17], Cloudera [18], Opensolaris Hadoop Live CD [19] by Sun Microsystems, and Amazon Elastic MapReduce [20], as shown in Table 14.4. Besides the

TABLE 14.4. Some Major Enterprise Solutions Based on Hadoop

Or Name	Solution and Website	Brief Description
Yahoo!	Yahoo! Distribution of Hadoop, http://developer.yahoo.com/hadoop/distribution/	The Yahoo! distribution is based entirely on code found in the Apache Hadoop project. It includes code patches that Yahoo! has added to improve the stability and performance of their clusters. In all cases, these patches have already been contributed back to Apache.
Cloudera	Cloudera Hadoop Distribution, http://www.cloudera.com/	Cloudera provides enterprise-level support to users of Apache Hadoop. The Cloudera Hadoop Distribution is an easy-to-install package of Hadoop software. It includes everything you need to configure and deploy Hadoop using standard Linux system administration tools. In addition, Cloudera provides a training program aimed at producers and users of large volumes of data.
Amazon	Amazon Elastic MapReduce, http://aws.amazon.com/elasticmapreduce/	*"Web service that enables businesses, researchers, data analysts, and developers to easily and cost-effectively process vast amounts of data. It utilizes a hosted Hadoop framework running on the web-scale infrastructure of Amazon Elastic Compute Cloud (Amazon EC2) [17] and Amazon Simple Storage Service (Amazon S3)."*
Sun Microsystems	Hadoop Live CD, http://opensolaris.org/os/project/livehadoop/	This project's initial CD development tool aims to provide users who are new to Hadoop with a fully functional Hadoop cluster that is easy to start up and use.
IBM	Blue Cloud, http://www-03.ibm.com/press/us/en/pressrelease/22613.wss	Targets clients who want to explore the extreme scale of cloud computing infrastructures quickly and easily. *"Blue Cloud will include Xen and PowerVM virtualized Linux operating system images and Hadoop parallel workload scheduling. It is supported by IBM Tivoli software that manages servers to ensure optimal performance based on demand."*

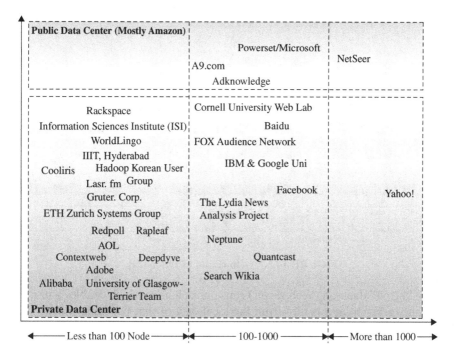

FIGURE 14.4. Organizations using Hadoop to run distributed applications, along with their cluster scale.

aforementioned vendors, many other organizations are using Hadoop solutions to run large distributed computations as shown in Figure 14.4 [9].

14.3.2 Disco

Disco is an open-source MapReduce implementation developed by Nokia [21]. The Disco core is written in Erlang, while users of Disco typically write jobs in Python. Disco was started at Nokia Research Center as a lightweight framework for rapid scripting of distributed data processing tasks. Furthermore, Disco has been successfully used, for instance, in parsing and reformatting data, data clustering, probabilistic modeling, data mining, full-text indexing, and log analysis with hundreds of gigabytes of real-world data.

Disco is based on the master-slave architecture as shown is Figure 14.5. When the Disco master receives jobs from clients, it adds them to the job queue, and runs them in the cluster when CPUs become available. On each node there is a Worker supervisor that is responsible for spawning and monitoring all the running Python worker processes within that node. The Python worker runs the assigned tasks and then sends the addresses of the resulting files to the master through their supervisor.

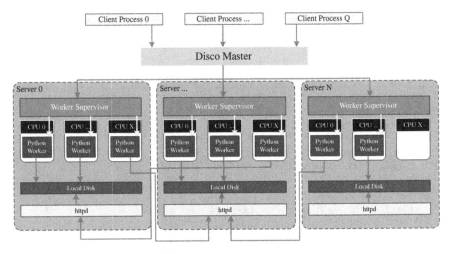

FIGURE 14.5. Architecture of Disco [21].

An "httpd" daemon (Web server) runs on each node which enables a remote Python worker to access files from the local disk of that particular node.

14.3.3 Mapreduce.NET

Mapreduce.NET [22] is a realization of MapReduce for the.NET platform. It aims to provide support for a wider variety of data-intensive and compute-intensive applications (e.g., MRPGA is an extension of MapReduce for GA applications based on MapReduce.NET [23]).

MapReduce.NET is designed for the Windows platform, with emphasis on reusing as many existing Windows components as possible. As shown in Figure 14.6, the MapReduce.Net runtime library is assisted by several components services from Aneka [24, 25] and runs on WinDFS.

Aneka is a.NET-based platform for enterprise and public cloud computing. It supports the development and deployment of.NET-based cloud applications in public cloud environments, such as Amazon EC2.

Besides Aneka, MapReduce.NET is using WinDFS, a distributed storage service over the.NET platform. WinDFS manages the stored data by providing an object-based interface with a flat name space. Moreover, MapReduce.NET can also work with the Common Internet File System (CIFS) or NTFS.

14.3.4 Skynet

Skynet [17, 26] is a Ruby implementation of MapReduce, created by Geni. Skynet is "an adaptive, self-upgrading, fault-tolerant, and fully distributed system with no single point of failure" [17]. At the heart of Skynet is plug-in based message queue architecture, with the message queuing allowing workers to

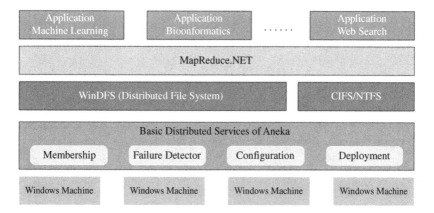

FIGURE 14.6. Architecture of Mapreduce.NET [22].

watch out for each other. If a worker fails, another worker will notice and pick up that task. Currently, there are two message queue implementations available: one built on Rinda [27] that uses Tuplespace [28] and one built on MySQL.

Skynet works by putting "tasks" on a message queue that are picked up by skynet workers. Skynet workers execute the tasks after loading the code at startup; Skynet tells the worker where all the needed code is. The workers put their results back on the message queue.

14.3.5 GridGain

GridGain [29] is an open cloud platform, developed in Java, for Java. GridGain enables users to develop and run applications on private or public clouds. The MapReduce paradigm is at core of what GridGain does. It defines the process of splitting an initial task into multiple subtasks, executing these subtasks in parallel and aggregating (reducing) results back to one final result. New features have been added in the GridGain MapReduce implementation such as: distributed task session, checkpoints for long running tasks, early and late load balancing, and affinity co-location with data grids.

14.4 MAPREDUCE IMPACTS AND RESEARCH DIRECTIONS

Since J. Dean and S. Ghemawat proposed the MapReduce model [4], it has received much attention from both industry and academia. Many projects are exploring ways to support MapReduce on various types of distributed architecture and for a wider range of applications as shown in Figure 14.7.

For instance, QT Concurrent [30] is a C++ library for multi-threaded application; it provides a MapReduce implementation for multi-core computers. Stanford's Phoenix [31] is a MapReduce implementation that targets

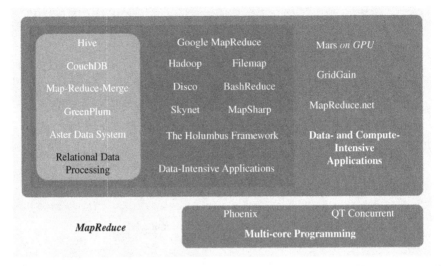

FIGURE 14.7. MapReduce different implementations.

shared memory architecture, while Kruijf and Sankaralingam implemented MapReduce for the Cell B.E. architecture [32]. Mars [33] is a MapReduce framework on graphic processors (GPUs). The Mars framework aims to provide a generic framework for developers to implement data- and computation-intensive tasks correctly, efficiently, and easily on the GPU.

Hadoop [7], Disco [21], Skynet [26], and GridGain [29] are open-source implementations of MapReduce for large-scale data processing. Map-Reduce-Merge [34] is an extension on MapReduce. It adds to MapReduce a merge phase to easily process data relationships among heterogeneous datasets. Microsoft Dryad [35] is a distributed execution engine for coarse-grain data parallel applications. In Dryad, computation tasks are expressed as directed acyclic graph (DAG).

Other efforts [36, 37] focus on enabling MapReduce to support a wider range of applications. S. Chen and S. W. Schlosser from Intel are working on making MapReduce suitable for performing earthquake simulation, image processing and general machine learning computations [36]. MRPSO [38] utilizes Hadoop to parallelize a compute-intensive application, called Particle Swarm Optimization. Research groups from Cornell, Carnegie Mellon, University of Maryland, and PARC are also starting to use Hadoop for both Web data and non-data-mining applications, like seismic simulation and natural language processing [39].

At present, many research institutions are working to optimize the performance of MapReduce for the cloud. We can classify these works in two directions:

The first one is driven by the simplicity of the MapReduce scheduler. In Zaharia et al. [40] the authors introduced a new scheduling algorithm called the

Longest Approximate Time to End (LATE) to improve the performance of Hadoop in a heterogeneous environment by running "speculative" tasks—that is, looking for tasks that are running slowly and might possibly fail—and replicating them on another node just in case they don't perform. In LATE, the slow tasks are prioritized based on how much they hurt job response time, and the number of speculative tasks is capped to prevent thrashing.

The second one is driven by the increasing maturity of virtualization technology—for example, the successful adoption and use of virtual machines (VMs) in various distributed systems such as grid [41] and HPC applications [42, 43]. To this end, some efforts have been proposed to efficiently run MapReduce on VM-based cluster, as in Cloudlet [44] and Tashi [45].

14.5 CONCLUSION

To summarize, we have presented the MapReduce programming model as an important programming model for next-generation distributed systems, namely cloud computing. We have introduced the MapReduce metaphor and identified some of major MapReduce features. We have introduced some of the major MapReduce implementations for cloud computing, especially data- and compute-intensive cloud computing owned by different organizations.

We have presented the different impacts of the MapReduce model in the computer science discipline, along with different efforts around the world. It can be observed that while there has been a lot of effort in the development of different implementations of MapReduce, there is still more to be achieved in terms of MapReduce optimizations and implementing this simple model in different areas.

14.5.1 Acknowledgments

This work is supported by National 973 Key Basic Research Program under Grant 2007CB310900, NSFC under Grants 61073024 and 60973037, Program for New Century Excellent Talents in University under Grant NCET-07-0334, Information Technology Foundation of MOE and Intel under Grant MOE-INTEL-09-03, National High-Tech R&D Plan of China under Grant 2006AA01A115, Important National Science & Technology Specific Projects under Grant 2009ZX03004-002, China Next Generation Internet Project under Grant CNGI2008-109, and Key Project in the National Science & Technology Pillar Program of China under Grant 2008BAH29B00.

REFERENCES

1. I. Foster, Yong Zhao, I. Raicu and S. Lu, Cloud computing and grid computing 360-degree compared, in *Proceedings of the Grid Computing Environments Workshop (GCE '08)*, 2008, pp. 1–10.

2. A. Szalay, A. Bunn, J. Gray, I. Foster, I. Raicu. The Importance of Data Locality in Distributed Computing Applications, in *Proceedings of NSF Workflow*, 2006.

3. A. S. Szalay, P. Z. Kunszt, A. Thakar, J. Gray, D. Slutz, and R. J. Brunner, Designing and mining multi-terabyte astronomy archives: The Sloan Digital Sky Survey, in *Proceedings of the SIGMOD International Conference on Management of Data*, 2000, pp. 451–462.

4. J. Dean and S. Ghemawat, MapReduce: Simplified data processing on large clusters, *Communications of the ACM*, **51**(1):107–113, 2008.

5. S. Ghemawat, H. Gobioff, and S. T. Leung, The Google File System, in *Proceedings of the 19th ACM Symposium on Operating Systems Principles*, Lake George, NY, October, 2003, pp. 29–43.

6. D. A. Patterson, Technical perspective: The data center is the computer, *Communications of the ACM*, **51**(1):105, 2008, pp. 105–105.

7. Hadoop: http://lucene.apache.org/

8. Yahoo!, Yahoo! Developer Network, http://developer.yahoo.com/blogs/hadoop/2008/02/yahoo-worlds-largest-production-hadoop.html (accessed September 2009).

9. Hadoop, Applications powered by Hadoop: http://wiki.apache.org/hadoop/PoweredB

10. Presentation by Randal E. Bryant, Presented in conjunction with the 2007 Federated Computing Research Conference, http://www.cs.cmu.edu/~bryant/presentations/DISC-FCRC07.ppt.

11. L. Barroso, J. Dean, and U. Holzle, Web search for a planet: The Google cluster architecture, *IEEE Micro*, **23**(2), 2003, pp. 22–28.

12. MapReduce in Wikipedia, http://en.wikipedia.org/wiki/MapReduce (accessed September 2009).

13. Hadoop in Wikipedia, http://en.wikipedia.org/wiki/Hadoop (accessed September 2009).

14. CNET news, http://news.cnet.com/8301-13505_3-10196871-16.html (accessed September 2009).

15. CloudStore (Formerly Kosmos File System), http://kosmosfs.sourceforge.net/

16. Amazon Simple Storage Service, http://aws.amazon.com/s3/

17. Ruby MapReduce Implementation, http://en.oreilly.com/rails2008/public/schedule/detail/2022 (accessed September 2009).

18. Cloudera Homepage, http://www.cloudera.com/

19. OpensolarisHadoop Live CD, http://opensolaris.org/os/project/livehadoop/

20. Amazon Elastic MapReduce, http://aws.amazon.com/elasticmapreduce/

21. Disco Project Homepage, http://discoproject.org/

22. C. Jin and R. Buyya, MapReduce programming model for.NET-based cloud computing, in *Proceedings of the 15th International European Parallel Computing Conference (EuroPar 2009)*, Delft, The Netherlands, August 25–28, 2009, pp. 417–428.

23. C. Jin, C. Vecchiola, and R. Buyya, MRPGA: An Extension of MapReduce for Parallelizing Genetic Algorithms, in *Proceedings of 4th IEEE International Conference on e-Science*, Indiana, USA, 2008, pp. 214–221.

24. X. Chu, K. Nadiminti, J. Chao, S. Venugopal, and R. Buyya, Aneka: Next-Generation Enterprise Grid Platform for e-Science and e-Business Applications, *Proceedings of the 3rd IEEE International Conference and Grid Computing*, Bangalore, India, December 10–13, 2007, pp. 151–159.

25. Manjrasoft Products, http://www.manjrasoft.com/products.html (accessed September 2009).

26. Skynet, http://skynet.rubyforge.org/

27. Rinda Doc page, http://www.ruby-doc.org/stdlib/libdoc/rinda/rdoc/index.html

28. Tuplespace in Wikipedia, http://en.wikipedia.org/wiki/Tuple_space (accessed September 2009).

29. GridGain, http://www.gridgain.com/

30. QT concurrent Page, http://labs.trolltech.com/page/Projects/Threads/QtConcurrent

31. C. Ranger, R. Raghuraman, A. Penmetsa, G. Bradski, C. Kozyrakis, Evaluating MapReduce for Multi-core and Multiprocessor Systems, in *Proceedings of the 13th International Symposium on High-Performance Computer Architecture (HPCA)*, Phoenix, AZ, February 2007, pp. 13–24.

32. M. Kruijf and K. Sankaralingam, MapReduce for the Cell B. E. Architecture, TR1625, Technical Report, Department of Computer Sciences, the University of Wisconsin—Madison, 2007.

33. B. S. He, W. B. Fang, Q. Luo, N. K. Govindaraju, and T. Y. Wang, Mars: A MapReduce framework on graphics processors, in *Proceedings of the 17th International Conference on Parallel Architectures and Compilation Techniques*, Toronto, Ontario, Canada, 2008, pp. 260–269.

34. H. C. Yang, A. Dasdan, R. L. Hsiao, and D. S. P. Jr, Map-reduce-merge: Simplified relational data processing on large clusters, in *Proceedings of SIGMOD*, 2007, pp. 1029–1040.

35. M. Isard, M. Budiu, Y. Yu, A. Birrell, and D. Fetterly, Dryad: Distributed data-parallel programs from sequential building blocks, in *Proceedings of the European Conference on Computer Systems (EuroSys)*, Lisbon, Portugal, March, 2007, pp. 59–72.

36. S. Chen, and S. W. Schlosser, Map-Reduce Meets Wider Varieties of Applications, IRP-TR-08-05, Technical Report, Intel Research Pittsburgh, May 2008.

37. R. E. Bryant, Data-Intensive Supercomputing: The Case for DISC, CMU-CS-07-128, Technical Report, Department of Computer Science, Carnegie Mellon University, May 2007.

38. A. W. McNabb, C. K. Monson, and K. D. Seppi, Parallel PSO Using MapReduce, in *Proceedings of the Congress on Evolutionary Computation*, Singapore, 2007, pp. 7–14.

39. Presentations by Steve Schlosser and Jimmy Lin at the 2008 Hadoop Summit, http://developer.yahoo.com/hadoop/summit/ (accessed September 2009).

40. M. Zaharia, A. Konwinski, A. D. Joseph, R. Katz, and I. Stoica, Improving mapreduce performance in heterogeneous environments in, *Proceedings of the 8th USENIX Symposium on Operating Systems Design and Implementation*, 2008, pp. 29–42.

41. R. Figueiredo, P. Dinda, and J. Fortes, A Case for Grid Computing on Virtual Machines, in *Proceedings of the 23rd International Conference on Distributed Computing Systems*, 2003, pp. 550–559.

42. M. F. Mergen, V. Uhlig, O. Krieger, and J. Xenidis, Virtualization for high-performance computing. SIGOPS operating systems review, **40**(2):8–11, 2006.

43. W. Huang, J. Liu, B. Abali, and D. K. Panda, A case for high performance computing with virtual machines, in *Proceedings of the 20th ACM International Conference on Supercomputing (ICS'06)*, Cairns, Australia, June 2006, pp. 125–134.

44. S. Ibrahim, H. Jin, B. Cheng, H. J. Cao, W. Song and L. Qi, Cloudlet: Towards MapReduce implementation on Virtual machines, in *Proceedings of the 18th ACM International Symposium on High Performance Distributed Computing (HPDC-18)*, Germany, 2009, pp. 65–66.

45. Tashi Homepage, http://www.pittsburgh.intel-research.net/projects/tashi/, 2009.

46. Baidu search engine, www.baidu.com

47. NetSeerHomePage, http://www.netseer.com/

48. A9.com Homepage, www.a9.com

49. Facebook Homepage, www.facebook.com/

50. Manjrasoft customers, http://www.manjrasoft.com/customers.html (accessed September 2009).

51. Medvoxel homepage, http://www.medvoxel.com/

52. Pointoyalty Homepage, http://www.pointloyalty.ru/

53. Traficon Homepage, http://www.traficon.com/

54. Amazon Elastic MapReduce, http://aws.amazon.com/ec2/

55. IBM Blue Cloud Announcement, http://www-03.ibm.com/press/us/en/pressrelease/22613.wss, (accessed September 2009).

PART IV

MONITORING AND MANAGEMENT

CHAPTER 15

AN ARCHITECTURE FOR FEDERATED CLOUD COMPUTING

BENNY ROCHWERGER, CONSTANTINO VÁZQUEZ, DAVID BREITGAND, DAVID HADAS, MASSIMO VILLARI, PHILIPPE MASSONET, ELIEZER LEVY, ALEX GALIS, IGNACIO M. LLORENTE, RUBÉN S. MONTERO, YARON WOLFSTHAL, KENNETH NAGIN, LARS LARSSON, and FERMÍN GALÁN

15.1 INTRODUCTION

Utility computing, a concept envisioned back in the 1960s, is finally becoming a reality. Just as we can power a variety of devices, ranging from a simple light bulb to complex machinery, by plugging them into the wall, today we can satisfy, by connecting to the Internet, many of our computing needs, ranging from full pledge productivity applications to raw compute power in the form of virtual machines. Cloud computing [1], in all its different forms, is rapidly gaining momentum as an alternative to traditional IT, and the reasons for this are clear: In principle, it allows individuals and companies to fulfill all their IT needs with minimal investment and controlled expenses (both capital and operational).

Cloud computing enables companies and individuals to lease resources on-demand from a virtually unlimited pool. The "pay as you go" billing model applies charges for the actually used resources per unit time. This way, a business can optimize its IT investment and improve availability and scalability.

While cloud computing holds a lot of promise for enterprise computing, there are a number of inherent deficiencies in current offerings such as:

Cloud Computing: Principles and Paradigms, Edited by Rajkumar Buyya, James Broberg and Andrzej Goscinski   Copyright © 2011 John Wiley & Sons, Inc.

- **Inherently Limited Scalability of Single-Provider Clouds.** Although most infrastructure cloud providers today claim infinite scalability, in reality it is reasonable to assume that even the largest players may start facing scalability problems as cloud computing usage rate increases. In the long term, scalability problems may be expected to worsen as cloud providers serve an increasing number of on-line services, each accessed by massive amounts of global users at all times.

- **Lack of Interoperability Among Cloud Providers.** Contemporary cloud technologies have not been designed with interoperability in mind. This results in an inability to scale through business partnerships across clouds providers. In addition, it prevents small and medium cloud infrastructure providers from entering the cloud provisioning market. Overall, this stifles competition and locks consumers to a single vendor.

- **No Built-In Business Service Management Support.** Business Service Management (BSM) is a management strategy that allows businesses to align their IT management with their high-level business goals. The key aspect of BSM is service-level agreement (SLA) management. Current cloud computing solutions are not designed to support the BSM practices that are well established in the daily management of the enterprise IT departments. As a result, enterprises looking at transforming their IT operations to cloud-based technologies face a non-incremental and potentially disruptive step.

To address these issues, we present in this chapter a model for business-driven federation of cloud computing providers, where each provider can buy and sell, on-demand, capacity from other providers (see Figure 15.1).

In this chapter we analyze the requirements for an enterprise-grade cloud computing offering and identify the main functional components that should be part of such offering. In addition, we develop from the requirement the basic principles that we believe are the cornerstone of future cloud computing offerings. The remainder of this chapter is organized as follows: In Section 15.2 we will present use cases and requirements, and in Section 15.3 we expand on the principles of cloud computing derived from these requirements. In Section 15.4 we will present a model for federated cloud computing infra-structure and provide definitions of the concepts used and in Section 15.5 we describe the seurity considerations for such system. We conclude with a summary in Section 15.6.

15.2 A TYPICAL USE CASE

As a representative of an enterprise-grade application, we have chosen to analyze SAP™ systems and to derive from them general requirements that such application might have from a cloud computing provider.

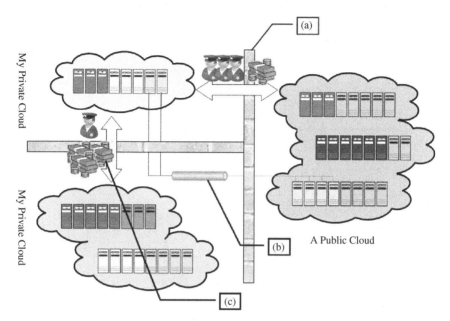

FIGURE 15.1. Model for federated cloud computing: (a) Different cloud providers collaborate by sharing their resources while keeping thick walls in between them; that is, each is an independent autonomous entity. (b) Applications running in this cloud of clouds should be unaware of location; that is, virtual local networks are needed for the inter-application components to communicate. (c) Cloud providers differentiate from each in terms of cost and trust level; for example, while a public cloud maybe cheap, companies will be reluctant to put in there sensitive services.

15.2.1 SAP Systems

SAP systems are used for a variety of business applications that differ by version and functionality [such as customer relationship management (CRM) and enterprise resource planning (ERP)]. For a given application type, the SAP system components consist of generic parts customized by configuration and parts custom-coded for a specific installation. Certain SAP applications are composed of several loosely coupled systems. Such systems have independent databases and communicate asynchronously by message with each other.

An SAP system is a typical three-tier system (see Figure 15.2) as follows:

- Requests are handled by the SAP Web dispatcher.
- In the middle tier, there are two types of components: multiple stateful dialog instances (DIs) and a single central instance (CI) that performs central services such as application-level locking, messaging, and registration of DIs. The number of DIs can be changed while the system is running to adapt to load.
- A single database management system (DBMS) serves the SAP system.

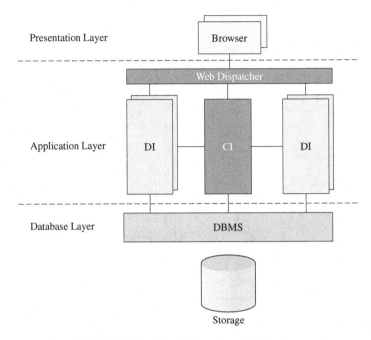

Presentation Layer

Application Layer

Database Layer

FIGURE 15.2. Abstraction of an SAP system.

The components can be arranged in a variety of configurations, from a minimal configuration where all components run on a single machine, to larger ones where there are several DIs, each running on a separate machine, and a separate machine with the CI and the DBMS (see Figure 15.3)

15.2.2 The Virtualized Data Center Use Case

Consider a data center that consolidates the operation of different types of SAP applications and all their respective environments (e.g., test, production) using virtualization technology. The applications are offered as a service to external customers, or, alternatively, the data center is operated by the IT department of an enterprise for internal users (i.e., enterprise employees).

A special variation that deserves mentioning is when the data center serves an on-demand, Software as a Service (SaaS) setup, where customers are external and where each customer (tenant) gets the same base version of the application. However, each tenant configures and customizes the application to suit his specific needs. It is reasonable to assume that a tenant in this case is a small or medium business (SMB) tenant.

We briefly mention here a few aspects that are typical of virtualized data centers:

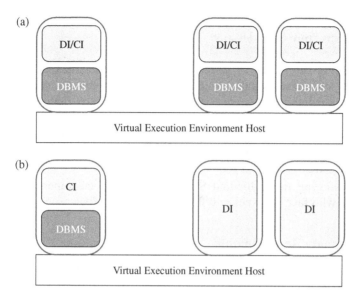

FIGURE 15.3. Sample SAP system deployments. (a) All components run in the same virtual execution environment (represented as rounded rectangles); (b) the large components (CI and DBMS) run each on a dedicated virtual execution environment. The virtual execution environment host refers to the set of components managing the virtual environments.

- The infrastructure provider must manage the life cycle of the application for hundreds or thousands of tenants while keeping a very low total cost of ownership (TCO). This includes setting up new tenants, backing up the databases, managing the customizations and configurations of tenants, and getting patches and newer versions of the software from SAP (the service provider).
- Setting up a new tenant in the SaaS for SMBs case is completely automated by a Web-based wizard. The new tenant runs through a series of configuration questions and uploads master data items (e.g., product catalog and customer lists). Following these steps, the tenant is up and running, typically using a trial version. The provisioning of the resources (storage, database, and application server) is part of this automated setup.
- The customers are billed a fixed monthly subscription fee or a variable fee based on their usage of the application.
- There are several well-known approaches to multi-tenancy of the same database schema [2]. Regardless of the approach taken, multi-tenancy calls for flexible virtualization schemes where, for example, the DBMS component and the storage system are shared between multiple tenants. The main reason for this sharing is to keep the TCO per tenant at a minimum.

In summary, the key challenges in all these use cases from the point of view of the infrastructure provider are:

- Managing thousands of different service components that comprise a variety of service applications executed by thousands of virtual execution environments, on top of a complex infrastructure that also includes network and storage systems.
- Consolidating many applications on the same infrastructure, thereby increasing HW utilization and optimizing power consumption, while keeping the operational cost at minimum.
- Guaranteeing the individual SLAs of the many customers of the data center who face different and fluctuating workloads.

15.2.3 Primary Requirements

From the use case discussed in the previous section, we derived the following main requirements from a cloud computing infrastructure:

- **Automated and Fast Deployment.** The cloud should support automated provisioning of complex service applications based on a formal contract specifying theinfrastructure SLAs. The same contract should be reused to provision multiple instances of the same application for different tenants with different customizations.
- **Dynamic Elasticity.** The cloud should dynamically adjust resource allocation parameters (memory, CPU, network bandwidth, storage) of individual virtual execution environments seamlessly. Moreover, the number of virtual execution environments must be dynamically and seamlessly adjusted to adapt to the changing load.
- **Automated Continuous Optimization.** The cloud should continuously optimize alignment of infrastructure resources management with the high-level business goals.

15.3 THE BASIC PRINCIPLES OF CLOUD COMPUTING

In this section we unravel a set of principles that enable Internet scale cloud computing services. We seek to highlight the fundamental requirement from the providers of cloud computing to allow virtual applications to freely migrate, grow, and shrink.

15.3.1 Federation

All cloud computing providers, regardless of how big they are, have a finite capacity. To grow beyond this capacity, cloud computing providers should be able to form federations of providers such that they can collaborate and share their resources. The need for federation-capable cloud computing offerings is also derived from the industry trend of adopting the cloud computing paradigm internally within companies to create *private clouds* and then being able to extend these clouds with resources leased on-demand from *public clouds*.

Any federation of cloud computing providers should allow virtual application to be deployed across federated sites. Furthermore, virtual applications need to be completely location free and allowed to migrate in part or as a whole between sites. At the same time, the security privacy and independence of the federation members must be maintained to allow competing providers to federate.

15.3.2 Independence

Just as in other utilities, where we get service without knowing the internals of the utility provider and with standard equipment not specific to any provider (e.g., telephones), for cloud computing services to really fulfill the computing as a utility vision, we need to offer cloud computing users full independence. Users should be able to use the services of the cloud without relying on any provider-specific tool, and cloud computing providers should be able to manage their infrastructure without exposing internal details to their customers or partners.

As a consequence of the independence principle, all cloud services need to be encapsulated and generalized such that users will be able to acquire equivalent virtual resources at different providers.

15.3.3 Isolation

Cloud computing services are, by definition, hosted by a provider that will simultaneously host applications from many different users. For these users to move their computing into the cloud, they need warranties from the cloud computing provider that their stuff is completely isolated from others. Users must be ensured that their resources cannot be accessed by others sharing the same cloud and that adequate performance isolation is in place to ensure that no other user may possess the power to directly effect the service granted to their application.

15.3.4 Elasticity

One of the main advantages of cloud computing is the capability to provide, or release, resources on-demand. These "elasticity" capabilities should be enacted automatically by cloud computing providers to meet demand variations, just as electrical companies are able (under normal operational circumstances) to automatically deal with variances in electricity consumption levels. Clearly the behavior and limits of automatic growth and shrinking should be driven by contracts and rules agreed on between cloud computing providers and consumers.

The ability of users to grow their applications when facing an increase of real-life demand need to be complemented by the ability to scale. Cloud computing services as offered by a federation of infrastructure providers is expected to offer any user application of any size the ability to quickly scale up its application by unrestricted magnitude and approach Internet scale. At the same time, user applications should be allowed to scale down facing decreasing demand. Such scalability although depended on the internals of the user application is prime driver for cloud computing because it help users to better match expenses with gain.

15.3.5   Business Orientation

Before enterprises move their mission critical applications to the cloud, cloud computing providers will need to develop the mechanisms to ensure quality of service (QoS) and proper support for service-level agreements (SLAs). More than ever before, cloud computing offers challenges with regard to the articulation of a meaningful language that will help encompass business requirements and that has translatable and customizable service parameters for infrastructure providers.

15.3.6   Trust

Probably the most critical issue to address before cloud computing can become the preferred computing paradigm is that of establishing trust. Mechanisms to build and maintain trust between cloud computing consumers and cloud computing providers, as well as between cloud computing providers among themselves, are essential for the success of any cloud computing offering.

15.4   A MODEL FOR FEDERATED CLOUD COMPUTING

In our model for federated cloud computing we identify two major types of actors: *Service Providers (SPs)* are the entities that need computational resources to offer some service. However, SPs do not own these resources; instead, they lease them from *Infrastructure Providers (IPs)*, which provide them with a seemingly infinite pool of computational, network, and storage resources.

A *Service Application* is a set of software components that work collectively to achieve a common goal. Each component of such service applications executes in a dedicated VEE. SPs deploy service applications in the the cloud by providing to a IP, known as the *primary site*, with a *Service Manifest*—that is, a document that defines the structure of the application as well as the contract and SLA between the SP and the IP.

To create the illusion of an infinite pool of resources, IPs shared their unused capacity with each other to create a *federation cloud*. A *Framework Agreement*

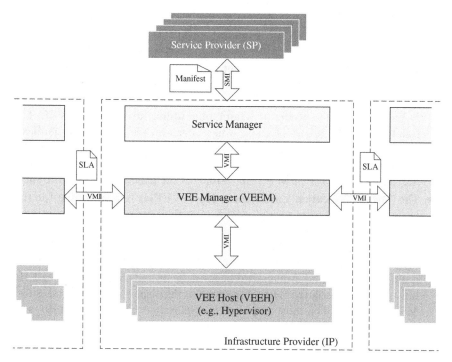

FIGURE 15.4. The RESERVOIR architecture: major components and interfaces.

is document that defines the contract between two IPs—that is, it states the terms and conditions under which one IP can use resources from another IP.

Within each IP, optimal resource utilization is achieved by partitioning physical resources, through a virtualization layer, into *Virtual Execution Environments (VEEs)*—fully isolated runtime environments that abstract away the physical characteristics of the resource and enable sharing. We refer to the virtualized computational resources, alongside the virtualization layer and all the management enablement components, as the *Virtual Execution Enviroment Host (VEEH)*.

With these concepts in mind, we can proceed to define a reference architecture for federated cloud computing. The design and implementation of such architecure are the main goals of the RESERVOIR European research project. The RESERVOIR architecture [3], shown in Figure 15.4, identifies the major functional components needed within an IP to fully support the cloud computing paradigm. The rationale behind this particular layering is to keep a clear separation of concerns and responsibilities and to hide low-level infrastructure details and decisions from high-level management and service providers.

- **The Service Manager** is the only component within an IP that interacts with SPs. It receives Service Manifests, negotiates pricing, and handles billing. Its two most complex tasks are (1) deploying and provisioning VEEs based on the Service Manifest and (2) monitoring and enforcing SLA compliance by throttling a service application's capacity.

- **The Virtual Execution Environment Manager (VEEM)** is responsible for the optimal placement of VEEs into VEE Hosts subject to constraints determined by the Service Manager. The continuous optimization process is driven by a site-specific programmable utility function. The VEEM is free to place and move VEEs anywhere, even on the remote sites (subject to overall cross-site agreements), as long as the placement satisfies the constraints. Thus, in addition to serving local requests (from the local Service Manager), VEEM is responsible for the federation of remote sites.

- **The Virtual Execution Environment Host (VEEH)** is responsible for the basic control and monitoring of VEEs and their resources (e.g., creating a VEE, allocating additional resources to a VEE, monitoring a VEE, migrating a VEE, creating a virtual network and storage pool, etc.). Given that VEEs belonging to the same application may be placed on multiple VEEHs and even extend beyond the boundaries of a site, VEEHs must support isolated virtual networks that span VEEHs and sites. Moreover, VEEHs must support transparent VEE migration to any compatible VEEH within the federated cloud, regardless of site location or network and storage configurations.

The layered design stresses the use of standard, open, and generic protocols and interfaces to support vertical and horizontal interoperability between layers. Different implementations of each layer will be able to interact with each other. The Service Management Interface (SMI) with its service manifest exposes a standardized interface into the RESERVOIR cloud for service providers. The service provider may then choose among RESERVOIR cloud providers, knowing that they share a common language to express their business requirements. The VEE Management Interface (VMI) simplifies the introduction of different and independent IT optimization strategies without disrupting other layers or peer VEEMs. Furthermore, VMI's support of VEEM-to-VEEM communication simplifies cloud federation by limiting the horizontal interoperability to one layer of the stack. The VEE Host Interface (VHI) will support plugging-in of new virtualization platforms (e.g., hypervisors), without requiring VEEM recompilation or restart. RESERVOIR's loosely coupled stack reference architecture should promote a variety of innovative approaches to support cloud computing.

15.4.1 Features of Federation Types

Federations of clouds may be constructed in various ways, with disparate feature sets offered by the underlying implementation architecture. This section is devoted to present these differentiating features. Using these features as a base, a number of federation scenarios are defined, comprised of subsets of this feature set.

The first feature to consider is the framework agreement support: Framework agreements, as defined in the previous section, may either be supported by the architecture or not. If framework agreements are not supported, this implies that federation may only be carried out in a more ad hoc opportunistic manner. Another feature is the *opportunistic placement support*. If framework agreements are not supported by the architecture, or if there is not enough spare capacity even including the framework agreements, a site may choose to perform opportunistic placement. It is a process where remote sites are queried on-demand as the need for additional resources arises, and the local site requests a certain SLA-governed capacity for a given cost from the remote sites.

One interesting feature to take into account is the *advance resource reservation support*. This feature may be used both when there is an existing framework agreement and when opportunistic placement has been performed. Both types of advance reservations are only valid for a certain time, since they impact the utilization of resources at a site. Because of this impact, they should be billed as actual usage during the active time interval.

The ability to migrate machines across sites defines the *federated migration support*. There are two types of migration: cold and hot (or live). In cold migration, the VEE is suspended and experiences a certain amount of downtime while it is being transferred. Most modern operating systems have support for being suspended, which includes saving all RAM contents to disk and later restoring the runtime state to its prior state. Hot or live migration does not allow for system downtime, and it works by transferring the runtime state while the VEE is still running.

Focusing on networks, there can be *cross-site virtual network support*: VEEs belonging to a service are potentially connected to virtual networks, should this be requested by the SP. Ideally, these virtual networks will span across sites. However, this requires substantial effort and advanced features of the underlying architecture. In the same line, the federation can offer *public IP addresses retention post cross-site migration*. With fully virtualized networks, this may be a directly supported feature; but even if virtualized networks are not available, it may still be possible to maintain public IP addresses by manipulating routing information.

Information disclosure within the federation has also to be taken into account. The sites in the federation may provide information to different degrees (for instance, the information exchange between sites may be larger within the same administrative domain than outside it). Information regarding deployed VEEs will be primarily via the monitoring system, whereas some information may also potentially be exposed via the VMI as response to a VEE deployment request.

The last identified feature useful to define scenario is the *VMI operation support*: Depending on the requirements of the federation scenario, only a subset of the VMI operations may be made available. Which operations are required may be related to the amount of information that is exposed by the remote sites; access to more information may also increase the possibility and need to manipulate the deployed VEEs.

15.4.2 Federation Scenarios

In this section, a number of federation scenarios are presented, ranging from a baseline case to a full-featured federation. These scenarios have various requirements on the underlying architecture, and we use the features presented in previous section as the basis for differentiating among them.

The *baseline federation* scenario provides only the very basic required for supporting opportunistic placement of VEEs at a remote site. Migration is not supported, nor does it resize the VEEs once placed at the remote site. Advanced features such as virtual networks across site boundaries are also not supported. The baseline federation should be possible to build on top of most public cloud offerings, which is important for interoperability. The *basic federation* scenario includes a number of features that the baseline federation does not, such as framework agreements, cold migration, and retention of public IP addresses. Notably missing is (a) support for hot migration and (b) cross-site virtual network functionality. This scenario offers a useful cloud computing federation with support for site collaboration in terms of framework agreements without particularly high technological requirements on the underlying architecture in terms of networking support. The *advanced federation* scenario offers advanced functionality such as cross-site virtual network support. The feature most notably missing is hot migration, and the monitoring system also does not disclose VEE substate metadata information. The *full-featured* federation scenario offers the most complete set of features, including hot migration of VEEs.

15.4.3 Layers Enhancement for Federation

Taking into account the different types of federation, a summary of the features needed in the different layers of the RESERVOIR architecture to achieve federation is presented.

Service Manager. The *baseline federation* is the most basic federation scenario, but even here the SM must be allowed to specify placement restrictions when a service is deployed. Deployment restrictions are associated to an specific VEE (although the restriction expression could involve other VEEs, as can be seen in the affinity restrictions above) and passed down to the VEEM along with any other specific VEE metadata when the VEE is issued for creation through VMI. They specify a set of constraints that must be held when the VEE is created, so they can be seen as some kind of "contour conditions" that determine the domain that can be used by the placement algorithm run at VEEM layer. Two kinds of deployment restrictions are envisioned: First, there are *affinity restrictions*, related to the relations between VEEs; and second, there can be *site restrictions*, related to sites.

In the *basic federation* scenario, federation uses framework agreement (FA) between organizations to set the terms and conditions for federation. Framework agreements are negotiated and defined by individuals, but they are encoded at the end in the service manager (SM)—in particular, within the business information data base (BIDB). The pricing information included in the FA is used by the SM to calculate the cost of resources running in remote systems (based on the aggregated usage information that it received from the local VEEM) and correlate this information with the charges issued by those remote sites. The SM should be able to include as part of the VEE metadata a "price hint vector" consisting on a sequence of numbers, each one representing an estimation of the relative cost of deploying the VEE on each federated site. The SM calculate this vector based on the FA established with the other sites.

Given that the *advanced federation* scenario supports migration, the placement restrictions have to be checked not only at service deployment time but also for migration. In addition, the SM could update the deployment restrictions during the service lifespan, thereby changing the "contour conditions" used by the placement algorithm. When the VEE is migrated across sites, its deployment restrictions are included along with any other metadata associated with the VEE. On the other hand, no additional functionality is needed from the service manager to implement the *full-featured federation*.

Virtual Execution Environment Manager. Very little is needed in the *baseline federation* scenario of the VEEM. The only requirement will be the ability to deploy a VEE in the remote site, so it will need a plug-in that can communicate with the remote cloud by invoking the public API. This will satisfy the opportunistic placement requirement. For the different features offered by the *basic federation* scenario, the VEEM will need framework agreement, since it is necessary that the VEEM implement a way to tell whether it can take care of the VEE or not, attending to the SLAs defined in the framework agreement. The best module in the VEEM for the SLA evaluation to take place is the admission control of the policy engine. Also, cold migration is needed; therefore the VEEM needs the ability to signal the hypervisor to save the VEE state (this is part of the VEEM life-cycle module) and also the ability to transfer the state files to the remote site. Additionally, the VEEM need to be able to signal the hypervisor to restore the VEE state and resume its execution (also part of the VEEM life-cycle module). Regarding advance resource reservation support, the policy engine must be capable of reserving capacity in the physical infrastructure given a timeframe for certain VEEs.

In the *advanced federation* scenario, the ability to create cross-site virtual networks for the VEEs has to be achieved using the functionality offered by the virtual application network (VAN) as part of the virtual host interface API. Therefore, the VEEM needs to correctly interface with the VAN and be able to express the virtual network characteristics in a VEEM-to-VEEM connection.

In the full-featured federation scenario the live migration feature offered by this scenario will need to be supported also in the VHI API. The VEEM will just need to invoke the functionality of live migration to the hypervisor part of the VHI API to achieve live migration across administrative domains.

Virtual Execution Environment Host. The ability to monitor a federation is needed. The RESERVOIR monitoring service supports the asynchronous monitoring of a cloud data centers' VEEHs, their VEEs, and the applications running inside the VEEs. To support federation, the originating data center must be able to monitor VEEs and their applications running at a remote site. When an event occurs related to a VEE running on a remote site, it is published and a remote proxy forwards the request to the subscribing local proxy, which in turn publishes the event to the waiting local subscribers. The monitoring framework is agnostic to type and source of data being monitored and supports the dynamic creation of new topics.

No further functionality is required for the *basic federation* in the VEEH apart from the features described for the baseline scenario. On the other hand, for the *advanced federation* one, several features are needed. First, it must have the ability to implement federated network service with virtual application network (VANs), a novel overlay network that enables virtual network services across subnets and across administrative boundaries [8,9]. VANs enables the establishment of large-scale virtual networks, free of any location dependency, that in turn allows completely "migratable" virtual networks. (1) The offered virtual network service is fully isolated, (2) it enables sharing of hosts, network devices, and physical connections, and (3) hides network related physical characteristics such as link throughputs, location of hosts, and so forth. Also, the ability to do federated migration with non-shared storage service is required. RESERVOIR enhances the standard VM migration capability typically available in every modern hypervisor with support for environments in which the source and the destination hosts do not share storage; typically the disk(s) of the migrated VM resided in the shared storage.

Regarding the *full-featured federation* scenario, hot migration is the functionality that affects the most what is demanded from VEEH in this scenario. RESERVOIR's separation principle requires that each RESERVOIR site be an autonomous entity. Site configuration, topology, and so on, are not shared between sites. So one site is not aware of the host addresses on another site. However, currently VM migration between hosts require that the source and destination hypervisors know each other's addresses and transfer a VM directly from the source host to the destination host. In order to overcome this apparent contradiction, RESERVOIR introduces a novel federated migration channel to transfer a VEE from one host to another host without directly addressing the destination host. Instead of transferring the VEE directly to the destination host, it passes through proxies at the source site and destination site, solving the unknown hypervisor location problem.

15.5 SECURITY CONSIDERATIONS

As previously reported, virtualized service-oriented infrastructures provide computing as a commodity for today's competitive businesses. Besides cost-effectiveness, they also ensure optimized use of system and network resources, reduced carbon footprints, and simplify management of their underlying resources. Businesses around the world are therefore giving enormous attention to virtualized SOI technology nowadays [4]. The capability of using virtual resources across the Internet is making up throughout a new kind of computation infrastructures. These platforms presented an unspecified environment where it is possible to run any type of VEEs. However, the salient features of these virtualization infrastructures give rise to a number of security concerns. These security threats are now emerging as the biggest obstacle in the widespread deployment of virtual infrastructures for cloud computing. Security concerns are multiplying with an increasing number of reported cloud computing incidents and other on-line services incidents such as the Kaminsky DNS vulnerability [5]. According to a survey results published in the Guardian newspaper, cloud computing security was the foremost concern for the year 2009 [6]. The higher stakes and broader scope of the security requirements of virtualization infrastructures require comprehensive security solutions because they are critical to ensure the anticipated adoption of virtualization solutions by their users and providers. The conception of a comprehensive security model requires a realistic threat model. Without such a threat model, security designers risk wasting time and effort implementing safeguards that do not address any realistic threat.

Or, just as dangerously, they run the risk of concentrating their security measures on one threat while leaving the underlying architecture dangerously exposed to others. Threats of large-scale cross-border virtualization infrastructures are broadly classified into two major categories, namely, *external threats* and *internal threats*, so as to complement the Dolev–Yao threat model [4].

15.5.1 External Threats

The Internet represents the same origin of threats for the communication across the RESERVOIR sites (VMI interfaces) and outside the RESERVOIR sites both for the SMI interface and service interface (SI—interface for service user on Internet). Some threats, related to communication, can be classified as: *men-in-the-middle, TCP hijacking (spoofing), service manifest attacks (malicious manifest/SLA format injection), migration and security policies and identity theft/impersonation (SP or RESERVOIR site pretends to be someone else)*, and so on. The main goals of these threats are to gain *unauthorized access* to systems and to impersonate another entity on the network. These techniques allow the attackers to eavesdrop as well as to change, delete, or divert data. All the interfaces could be instead exposed to the following attacks: *denial of service (DoS or distributed DoS), flooding, buffer overflow, p2p-attacks,* and so on.

These kind of threats are aimed toward provoking a *system crash*, leading to the inability to perform ordinary functions. All the interfaces (SMI, VMI and SI) are affected by the same issues, but we have to underline that the solutions in some cases are different. Considering the VMI interfaces, the RESERVOIR system administrator has the full capability to manage security policies and to apply them on both the sides (endpoints of site A and site B). It is possible for each RESERVOIR site to select its own security framework; however, in the case of communication between SM and SP (SMI), the RESERVOIR cloud has to use a common security framework shared with many different partners (SPs). All threats related to SI are managed through a simple monitoring, because no action can be performed.

15.5.2 Internal Threats

Each RESERVOIR site has a logical representation with three different layers, but these layers can be compounded by one or more hardware components. Figure 15.5 gives an overview of these entities and relative mapping with a simplified view of the hardware. It is possible to split the site in two different virtual zones: *control and execution zone*; in the *control zone* the components are: Service Manager (SM), VEEM (in bridge configuration between control

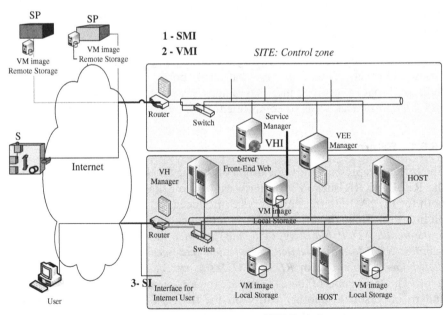

FIGURE 15.5. RESERVOIR site: internal representation.

and execution zone), network components (router, switch, cable, etc.), SMI/ VMI interfaces, and VHI internal interface.

In the *execution zone* instead there are: VEEH, VEEM (in-bridge configuration between control and execution zone), VHI internal interface, network components (router, switch, cable, etc.), network storage (NAS, databases, etc.), and SI (user access interfaces).

The *control zone* can be considered a trusted area. Some threats can appear through the SMI and VEEM interfaces, since they fall into the same cases of external threats. The firewall located next to the router increases the trustworthiness. In this zone the weak ring of the system is represented by the VEEM. It is the bridge between two areas, and it allows the exchange of data among the zones. Figure 15.5 shows a firewall close to the VEEM, added to prevent any attacks from the execution area. The zone with a high level of risk is represented by the *execution zone*. This area shares all the hardware components. The hypervisor (VEEH) uses the network, storage, CPU, and ram (host) to load and execute all the VEEs. To better explain the role of each component, it can be useful to evaluate chronologically all the phases necessary to execute a virtual execution environment (VEEH); once all the requirements from the VEEM are received, it downloads the VM image from the SP, stores the image into the NAS, performs the setup configuration, and executes the VM. The internal threats related to these phases can be classified as follows: (1) threats linked to authentication/communication of SPs and other RESERVOIR site; (2) threats related to misbehavior of service resource allocation—to alter the agreement (manifest) during the translation between service manager and VEEM malicious component on SM; (3) data export control legislation—on an international cloud or between two clouds; (4) threats linked to fake command for placement of VEEs and compromising the data integrity of the distributed file system (NFS, SAMBA, CIFS); (5) storage data compromising (fake VEE image); (6) threats linked to compromise data privacy; (7) threats linked to the underlying hypervisor and OS (VEE could break hypervisor/ underlying OS security and access other VEE); and (8) data partitioning between VEE.

To avoid any fraudulent access, the VEEH has to verify *authentication/ communication* of SPs and other RESERVOIR sites. Thus, the same behavior is analyzed for all the communications in external threats.

Relatively to the latter group of threats (3,4,5−6,7,8), the RESERVOIR site has to guarantee different types of isolation—that is, *runtime isolation, network isolation,* and *storage isolation.*

Runtime isolation resolves all the security problems with the underlying OS. The hypervisor security mechanisms need to be used to provide the isolation.

Network isolation is addressed via the dynamic configuration of network policies and via virtual circuits that involve routers and switches.

To avoid fake VEE image loading and do not compromise data privacy, *storage isolation* has to be performed and secure protocols has to be used. Protocols like NFS, SAMBA, and CIFS are not secure.

Virtual execution environment, downloaded from any generic SP, can expose the infrastructure toward back door threats, spoofing threats and malicious code execution (virus, worm, and Trojan horse). The RESERVOIR site administrator needs to know at any time the state of threats, with a strong monitoring of the *execution zone*, through the runtime intrusion detection.

15.6 SUMMARY AND CONCLUSIONS

Cloud computing as a new computing paradigm has the potential of dramatically changing the way we use computers. Just as in the early days of the power grid, nobody could have imagined fully automated robotic production plants, or the high-definition TVs in our houses, today we can't really predict what will happen once the computing utility dream becomes a reality. As this new paradigm becomes prevalent, there are many exciting opportunities: Cloud computing providers will probably achieve levels of efficiency and utilization that seem imaginary just a few years ago, while consumers of cloud computing services will be able to free resources and focuses on their business. However, along the way there are many challenges that the industry needs to deal with. First of all, just in the case of the power grid, interoperability between cloud providers and standardization are a fundamental need. Second, cloud providers will need to build mechanisms to ensure the service levels; without proper warranties on the levels of reliability, serviceability, and availability, companies are going to be reluctant to move any of the more critical operations to the cloud. Last, but not least, the need to build trust is essential and probably the hardest because it is not a technical issue only.

In this chapter we presented the RESERVOIR model for cloud computing that deals with these issues and extended on federation and security. RESERVOIR's work on business orientation management is left for future publications.

15.6.1 Acknowledgments

We would like to thank the following people Irit Loy and Shimon Agassi from IBM, Juan Caceres and Luis Vaquero from Telefónica I&D, Stuart Clayman from UCL, and Erik Elmroth and Johan Tordsson from Umeå; without their help, this work would not have been possible.

The research leading to these results is partially supported by the European Community's Seventh Framework Programme (FP7/2001-2013) under grant agreement 215605.

REFERENCES

1. M. Armbrust et al., *Above the Clouds: A Berkeley View of Cloud Computing*, Technical Report, University of California, Berkeley, 2009.

2. S. Aulbach, T. Gurst, D. Jacobs, A. Kemper, and J. Rittinger, Multi-tenant databases for software as a service, in *Proceedings of the ACM SIGMOD International Conference on Management of Data*, June 2008, pp. 1195–1206.

3. B. Rochwerger et al., The reservoir model and architecture for open federated cloud computing, *IBM Journal of Research and Development*, **53**(4), 2009.

4. D. Dolev, and A. C. Yao, On the Security of Public Key Protocols, in *Proceedings of the IEEE 22nd Annual Symposium on Foundations of Computer Science*, 1982, pp. 350–357.

5. M. Olney, P. Mullen, K. Miklavcic, and D. Kaminsky, 2008 DNS Vulnerability, Sourcefire Vulnerability Research Team Report, July 2008.

6. K. Bevan, What will frighten us next year?, the guardian newspaper, December 2008. http://www.guardian.co.uk/technology/2008/dec/11/security-cloud-computing

7. N. Kolakowski, IBM User Group Survey Says Virtualization, Cloud Computing on the Rise, http://www.eweek.com/c/a/IT-Infrastructure/IBM-User-Group-Survey-Says-Virtualization-Cloud-Computing-on-the-Rise, January 2009.

8. D. Hadas, S. Guenender, and B. Rochwerger, 2009, Virtual Network Services For Federated Cloud Computing, IBM Research Report H-0269, http://domino.watson.ibm.com/library/cyberdig.nsf/papers/3ADF4AD46CBB0E6B852576770056B848

9. A. Landau, D. Hadas and M. Ben-Yehuda, 2010, Plugging the hypervisor abstraction leaks caused by virtual networking, SYSTOR '10: Proceedings of the 3rd Annual Haifa Experimental Systems Conference, pp. 1–9, http://doi.acm.org/10.1145/1815695.1815716

CHAPTER 16

SLA MANAGEMENT IN CLOUD COMPUTING: A SERVICE PROVIDER'S PERSPECTIVE

SUMIT BOSE, ANJANEYULU PASALA, DHEEPAK RAMANUJAM A, SRIDHAR MURTHY and GANESAN MALAIYANDISAMY

16.1 INSPIRATION

In the early days of web-application deployment, performance of the application at peak load was a single important criterion for provisioning server resources [1]. Provisioning in those days involved deciding hardware configuration, determining the number of physical machines, and acquiring them upfront so that the overall business objectives could be achieved. The web applications were hosted on these dedicated individual servers within enterprises' own server rooms. These web applications were used to provide different kinds of e-services to various clients. Typically, the service-level objectives (SLOs) for these applications were response time and throughput of the application end-user requests. The capacity buildup was to cater to the estimated peak load experienced by the application. The activity of determining the number of servers and their capacity that could satisfactorily serve the application end-user requests at peak loads is called *capacity planning* [1].

An example scenario where two web applications, application A and application B, are hosted on a separate set of dedicated servers within the enterprise-owned server rooms is shown in Figure 16.1. The planned capacity for each of the applications to run successfully is three servers. As the number of web applications grew, the server rooms in the organization became large and such server rooms were known as data centers. These data centers were owned and managed by the enterprises themselves.

Cloud Computing: Principles and Paradigms,   Edited by Rajkumar Buyya, James Broberg and Andrzej Goscinski   Copyright © 2011 John Wiley & Sons, Inc.

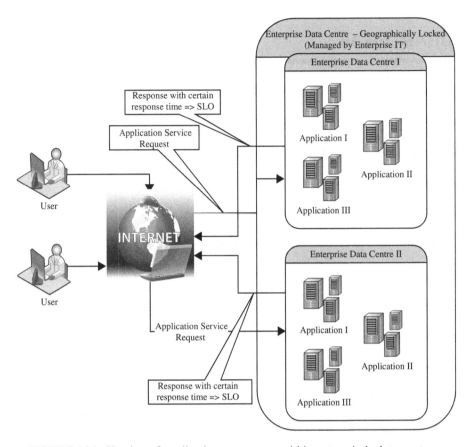

FIGURE 16.1. Hosting of applications on servers within enterprise's data centers.

Furthermore, over the course of time, the number of web applications and their complexity have grown. Therefore, the complexity of managing the data centers also increased. Accordingly, enterprises realized that it was economical to outsource the application hosting activity to third-party infrastructure providers because:

- The enterprises need not invest in procuring expensive hardware upfront without knowing the viability of the business.
- The hardware and application maintenance were non-core activities of their business.
- As the number of web applications grew, the level of sophistication required to manage the data centers increased manyfold—hence the cost of maintaining them.

Enterprises developed the web applications and deployed on the infrastructure of the third-party service providers. These providers get the required hardware and make it available for application hosting. It necessitated the enterprises to enter into a legal agreement with the infrastructure service providers to guarantee a minimum quality of service (QoS). Typically, the QoS parameters are related to the availability of the system CPU, data storage, and network for efficient execution of the application at peak loads. This legal agreement is known as the service-level agreement (SLA). For example, one SLA may state that the application's server machine will be available for 99.9% of the key business hours of the application's end users, also called core time, and 85% of the non-core time. Another SLA may state that the service provider would respond to a reported issue in less than 10 minutes during the core time, but would respond in one hour during non-core time. These SLAs are known as the infrastructure SLAs, and the infrastructure service providers are known as Application Service Providers (ASPs). This scenario is depicted in Figure 16.2, where the enterprise applications are hosted on the dedicated servers belonging to an ASP. Consequently, a set of tools for monitoring and measurement of availability of the infrastructure were required and developed. However, availability of the infrastructure doesn't automatically guarantee the availability of the application for its end users. These tools helped in tracking the SLA adherence. The responsibility for making the application available to its end users is with the enterprises. Therefore, the enterprises' IT team performs capacity planning, and the infrastructure provider procures the same.

The dedicated hosting practice resulted in massive redundancies within the ASP's data centers due to the underutilization of many of their servers. This is because the applications were not fully utilizing their servers' capacity at non-peak loads. To reduce the redundancies and increase the server utilization in data centers, ASPs started co-hosting applications with complementary work-load patterns. Co-hosting of applications means deploying more than one application on a single server. This led to further cost advantage for both the ASPs and enterprises. Figure 16.3 shows the enterprise and the third-party perspective before and after the applications are co-located. Figure 16.3a and Figure 16.3c shows the underutilized capacity of a server during dedicated hosting. However, Figure 16.3b shows the scenario when the same system is multiplexed between two applications, application A and application B; and the capacity of the server visible to the enterprise owning application A is only the amount consumed by it. However, Figure 16.3d depicts the ASP's perspective of the server capacity utilization when two applications, application A and application B, having complementary workload patterns are co-located.

However, newer challenges such as application performance isolation and security guarantees have emerged and needed to be addressed. Performance isolation implies that one application should not steal the resources being utilized by other co-located applications. For example, assume that application A is required to use more quantity of a resource than originally allocated to it for duration of time t. For that duration the amount of the same resource available to application B is decreased. This could adversely affect the performance of application B. Similarly, one application should not access and destroy the data

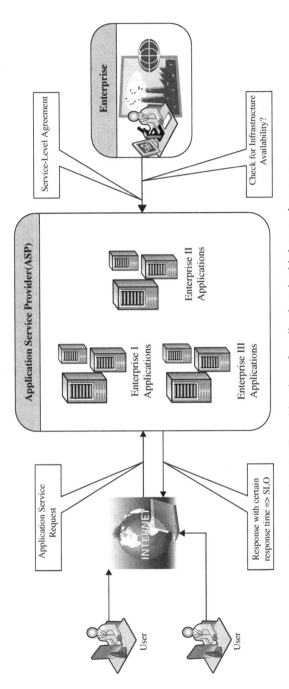

FIGURE 16.2. Dedicated hosting of applications in third party data centers.

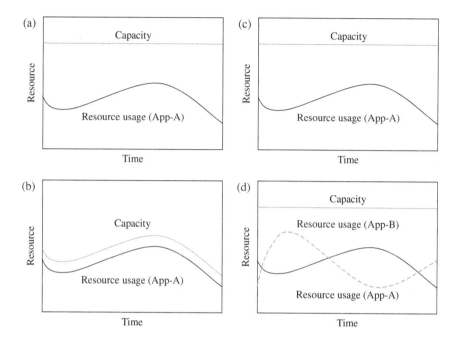

FIGURE 16.3. Service consumer and service provider perspective before and after the MSP's hosting platforms are virtualized and cloud-enabled. (a) Service consumer perspective earlier. (b) Service consumer perspective now. (c) Service provider perspective earlier. (d) Service provider perspective now.

and other information of co-located applications. Hence, appropriate measures are needed to guarantee security and performance isolation. These challenges prevented ASPs from fully realizing the benefits of co-hosting.

Virtualization technologies have been proposed to overcome the above challenges. The ASPs could exploit the containerization features of virtualization technologies to provide performance isolation and guarantee data security to different co-hosted applications [2, 3]. The applications, instead of being hosted on the physical machines, can be encapsulated using virtual machines. These virtual machines are then mapped to the physical machines. System resource allocation to these virtual machines can be made in two modes: (1) conserving and (2) nonconserving. In the conserving mode, a virtual machine demanding more system resources (CPU and memory) than the specified quota cannot be allocated the spare resources that are remain un-utilized by the other co-hosted virtual machines. In the nonconserving mode the spare resources that are not utilized by the co-hosted virtual machines can be used by the virtual machine needing the extra amount of resource. If the resource requirements of a virtual machine cannot be fulfilled from the current physical host, then the virtual machine can be migrated to another physical machine capable of fulfilling the additional resource requirements. This new development enabled the ASPs to allocate system resources to different competing applications on demand. Because, the system resources are allocated to the applications based on their needs at different times, the notion of capacity planning is redundant. This is because the enterprises and the ASPs need not provision their resources for the peak load.

Adoption of virtualization technologies required ASPs to get more detailed insight into the application runtime characteristics with high accuracy. Based on these characteristics, ASPs can allocate system resources more efficiently to these applications on-demand, so that application-level metrics can be monitored and met effectively. These metrics are request rates and response times. Therefore, different SLAs than the infrastructure SLAs are required. These SLAs are called application SLAs. These service providers are known as Managed Service Providers (MSP) because the service providers were responsible for managing the application availability too. This scenario is shown in Figure 16.4, where both application A and application B share the same set of virtualized servers.

To fulfill the SLOs mentioned in the application SLA and also make their IT infrastructure elastic, an in-depth understanding of the application's behavior is required for the MSPs. Elasticity implies progressively scaling up the IT infrastructure to take the increasing load of an application. The customer is billed based on their application usage of infrastructure resources for a given period only. The infrastructure can be augmented by procuring resources dynamically from multiple sources, including other MSPs, if resources are scarce at their data centers. This kind of new hosting infrastructure is called cloud platform. The cloud platforms introduce another set of challenges to fulfill the SLOs agreed between the cloud owners and the application owners. Due to nonavailability of high-level design documents, the cloud owners have to treat the customer application that might include many third-party components and packaged applications, as a black box. To address these challenges in meeting SLAs, service providers are required to follow a meticulous process for understanding and characterizing the applications runtime behavior better.

16.2   TRADITIONAL APPROACHES TO SLO MANAGEMENT

Traditionally, load balancing techniques and admission control mechanisms have been used to provide guaranteed quality of service (QoS) for hosted web applications. These mechanisms can be viewed as the first attempt towards managing the SLOs. In the following subsections we discuss the existing approaches for load balancing and admission control for ensuring QoS.

16.2.1   Load Balancing

The objective of a load balancing is to distribute the incoming requests onto a set of physical machines, each hosting a replica of an application, so that the

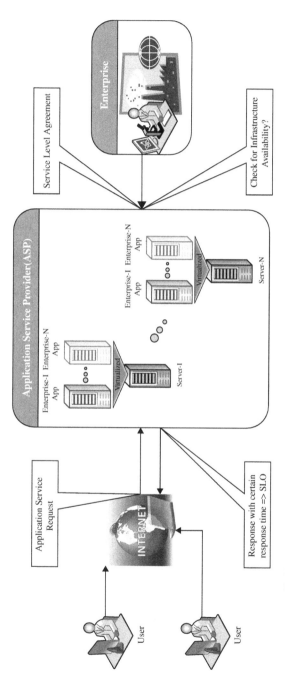

FIGURE 16.4. Shared hosting of applications on virtualized servers within ASP's data centers.

419

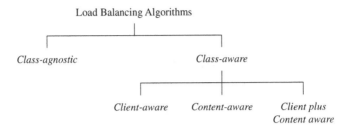

FIGURE 16.5. General taxonomy of load-balancing algorithms.

load on the machines is equally distributed [4]. The load balancing algorithm executes on a physical machine that interfaces with the clients. This physical machine, also called the front-end node, receives the incoming requests and distributes these requests to different physical machines for further execution. This set of physical machines is responsible for serving the incoming requests and are known as the back-end nodes. Typically, the algorithm executing on the front-end node is agnostic to the nature of the request. This means that the front-end node is neither aware of the type of client from which the request originates nor aware of the category (e.g., browsing, selling, payment, etc.) to which the request belongs to. This category of load balancing algorithms is known as class-agnostic. There is a second category of load balancing algorithms that is known as class-aware. With class-aware load balancing and requests distribution, the front-end node must additionally inspect the type of client making the request and/or the type of service requested before deciding which back-end node should service the request. Inspecting a request to find out the class or category of a request is difficult because the client must first establish a connection with a node (front-end node) that is not responsible for servicing the request. Figure 16.5 shows the general taxonomy of different load-balancing algorithms.

16.2.2 Admission Control

Admission control algorithms play an important role in deciding the set of requests that should be admitted into the application server when the server experiences "very" heavy loads [5, 6]. During overload situations, since the response time for all the requests would invariably degrade if all the arriving requests are admitted into the server, it would be preferable to be selective in identifying a subset of requests that should be admitted into the system so that the overall pay-off is high. The objective of admission control mechanisms, therefore, is to police the incoming requests and identify a subset of incoming requests that can be admitted into the system when the system faces overload situations. Figure 16.6 shows the general taxonomy of the admission control mechanisms. The algorithms proposed in the literature are broadly categorized

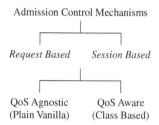

FIGURE 16.6. General taxonomy for admission control mechanisms.

into two types: (1) request-based algorithms and (2) session-based algorithms. Request-based admission control algorithms reject new requests if the servers are running to their capacity. The disadvantage with this approach is that a client's session may consist of multiple requests that are not necessarily unrelated. Consequently, some requests are rejected even if there are others that are honored. Contrary to request-based algorithms, session-based admission control mechanisms try to ensure that longer sessions are completed and any new sessions are rejected. Accordingly, once a session is admitted into the server, all future requests belonging to that session are admitted as well, even though new sessions are rejected by the system. Furthermore, the decision to reject a request can depend on the type of user making the request or the nature of the request being made. For example, a new request or a new session initiated by a high-priority user may be admitted while the requests from low-priority users are rejected. Similarly, requests that are likely to consume more system resources can be rejected during overload situations. Such admission control mechanisms are called QoS-aware control mechanisms.

16.3 TYPES OF SLA

Service-level agreement provides a framework within which both seller and buyer of a service can pursue a profitable service business relationship. It outlines the broad understanding between the service provider and the service consumer for conducting business and forms the basis for maintaining a mutually beneficial relationship. From a legal perspective, the necessary terms and conditions that bind the service provider to provide services continually to the service consumer are formally defined in SLA.

SLA can be modeled using web service-level agreement (WSLA) language specification [7]. Although WSLA is intended for web-service-based applications, it is equally applicable for hosting of applications. Service-level parameter, metric, function, measurement directive, service-level objective, and penalty are some of the important components of WSLA and are described in Table 16.1.

TABLE 16.1. Key Components of a Service-Level Agreement

Service-Level Parameter	Describes an observable property of a service whose value is measurable.
Metrics	These are definitions of values of service properties that are measured from a service-providing system or computed from other metrics and constants. Metrics are the key instrument to describe exactly what SLA parameters mean by specifying how to measure or compute the parameter values.
Function	A function specifies how to compute a metric's value from the values of other metrics and constants. Functions are central to describing exactly how SLA parameters are computed from resource metrics.
Measurement directives	These specify how to measure a metric.

There are two types of SLAs from the perspective of application hosting. These are described in detail here.

Infrastructure SLA. The infrastructure provider manages and offers guarantees on availability of the infrastructure, namely, server machine, power, network connectivity, and so on. Enterprises manage themselves, their applications that are deployed on these server machines. The machines are leased to the customers and are isolated from machines of other customers. In such dedicated hosting environments, a practical example of service-level guarantees offered by infrastructure providers is shown in Table 16.2.

Application SLA. In the application co-location hosting model, the server capacity is available to the applications based solely on their resource demands. Hence, the service providers are flexible in allocating and de-allocating computing resources among the co-located applications. Therefore, the service

TABLE 16.2. Key Contractual Elements of an Infrastructural SLA

Hardware availability	• 99% uptime in a calendar month
Power availability	• 99.99% of the time in a calendar month
Data center network availability	• 99.99% of the time in a calendar month
Backbone network availability	• 99.999% of the time in a calendar month
Service credit for unavailability	• Refund of service credit prorated on downtime period
Outage notification guarantee	• Notification of customer within 1 hr of complete downtime
Internet latency guarantee	• When latency is measured at 5-min intervals to an upstream provider, the average doesn't exceed 60 msec
Packet loss guarantee	• Shall not exceed 1% in a calendar month

TABLE 16.3. Key contractual components of an application SLA

Service-level parameter metric	• Web site response time (e.g., max of 3.5 sec per user request)
	• Latency of web server (WS) (e.g., max of 0.2 sec per request) • Latency of DB (e.g., max of 0.5 sec per query)
Function	• Average latency of WS = (latency of web server 1 + latency of web server 2) /2 • Web site response time = Average latency of web server + latency of database
Measurement directive	• DB latency available via http://mgmtserver/em/latency
	• WS latency available via http://mgmtserver/ws/instanceno/latency
Service-level objective	• Service assurance
	• web site latency < 1 sec when concurrent connection < 1000
Penalty	• 1000 USD for every minute while the SLO was breached

providers are also responsible for ensuring to meet their customer's application SLOs. For example, an enterprise can have the following application SLA with a service provider for one of its application, as shown in Table 16.3.

It is also possible for a customer and the service provider to mutually agree upon a set of SLAs with different performance and cost structure rather than a single SLA. The customer has the flexibility to choose any of the agreed SLAs from the available offerings. At runtime, the customer can switch between the different SLAs.

However, from the SLA perspective there are multiple challenges for provisioning the infrastructure on demand. These challenges are as follows:

a. The application is a black box to the MSP and the MSP has virtually no knowledge about the application runtime characteristics. Therefore, the MSP needs to determine the right amount of computing resources required for different components of an application at various workloads.

b. The MSP needs to understand the performance bottlenecks and the scalability of the application.

c. The MSP analyzes the application before it goes on-live. However, subsequent operations/enhancements by the customer's to their applications or auto updates beside others can impact the performance of the applications, thereby making the application SLA at risk.

d. The risk of capacity planning is with the service provider instead of the customer. If every customer decides to select the highest grade of SLA simultaneously, there may not be a sufficient number of servers for provisioning and meeting the SLA obligations of all the customers.

16.4   LIFE CYCLE OF SLA

Each SLA goes through a sequence of steps starting from identification of terms and conditions, activation and monitoring of the stated terms and conditions, and eventual termination of contract once the hosting relationship ceases to exist. Such a sequence of steps is called SLA life cycle and consists of the following five phases:

1. Contract definition
2. Publishing and discovery
3. Negotiation
4. Operationalization
5. De-commissioning

Here, we explain in detail each of these phases of SLA life cycle.

Contract Definition. Generally, service providers define a set of service offerings and corresponding SLAs using standard templates. These service offerings form a catalog. Individual SLAs for enterprises can be derived by customizing these base SLA templates.

Publication and Discovery. Service provider advertises these base service offerings through standard publication media, and the customers should be able to locate the service provider by searching the catalog. The customers can search different competitive offerings and shortlist a few that fulfill their requirements for further negotiation.

Negotiation. Once the customer has discovered a service provider who can meet their application hosting need, the SLA terms and conditions needs to be mutually agreed upon before signing the agreement for hosting the application. For a standard packaged application which is offered as service, this phase could be automated. For customized applications that are hosted on cloud platforms, this phase is manual. The service provider needs to analyze the application's behavior with respect to scalability and performance before agreeing on the specification of SLA. At the end of this phase, the SLA is mutually agreed by both customer and provider and is eventually signed off. SLA negotiation can utilize the WS-negotiation specification [8].

Operationalization. SLA operation consists of SLA monitoring, SLA accounting, and SLA enforcement. SLA monitoring involves measuring parameter values and calculating the metrics defined as a part of SLA and determining the deviations. On identifying the deviations, the concerned parties are notified. SLA accounting involves capturing and archiving the SLA adherence for compliance. As part of accounting, the application's actual performance and the performance guaranteed as a part of SLA is reported. Apart from the frequency and the duration of the SLA breach, it should also provide the penalties paid for each SLA violation. SLA enforcement involves taking appropriate action when the runtime monitoring detects a SLA violation. Such actions could be notifying the concerned parties, charging the penalties besides other things. The different policies can be expressed using a subset of the Common Information Model (CIM) [9]. The CIM model is an open standard that allows expressing managed elements of data center via relationships and common objects.

De-commissioning. SLA decommissioning involves termination of all activities performed under a particular SLA when the hosting relationship between the service provider and the service consumer has ended. SLA specifies the terms and conditions of contract termination and specifies situations under which the relationship between a service provider and a service consumer can be considered to be legally ended.

16.5 SLA MANAGEMENT IN CLOUD

SLA management of applications hosted on cloud platforms involves five phases.

1. Feasibility
2. On-boarding
3. Pre-production
4. Production
5. Termination

Different activities performed under each of these phases are shown in Figure 16.7. These activities are explained in detail in the following subsections.

16.5.1 Feasibility Analysis

MSP conducts the feasibility study of hosting an application on their cloud platforms. This study involves three kinds of feasibility: (1) technical feasibility, (2) infrastructure feasibility, and (3) financial feasibility. The technical feasibility of an application implies determining the following:

1. Ability of an application to scale out.
2. Compatibility of the application with the cloud platform being used within the MSP's data center.
3. The need and availability of a specific hardware and software required for hosting and running of the application.
4. Preliminary information about the application performance and whether they can be met by the MSP.

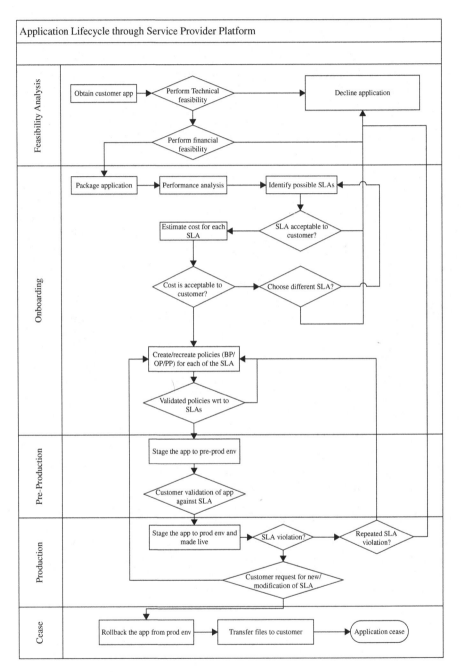

FIGURE 16.7. Flowchart of the SLA management in cloud.

Performing the infrastructure feasibility involves determining the availability of infrastructural resources in sufficient quantity so that the projected demands of the application can be met. The financial feasibility study involves determining the approximate cost to be incurred by the MSP and the price the MSP charges the customer so that the hosting activity is profitable to both of them. A feasibility report consists of the results of the above three feasibility studies. The report forms the basis for further communication with the customer. Once the provider and customer agree upon the findings of the report, the outsourcing of the application hosting activity proceeds to the next phase, called "on-boarding" of application. Only the basic feasibility of hosting an application has been carried in this phase. However, the detailed runtime characteristics of the application are studied as part of the on-boarding activity.

16.5.2 On-Boarding of Application

Once the customer and the MSP agree in principle to host the application based on the findings of the feasibility study, the application is moved from the customer servers to the hosting platform. Moving an application to the MSP's hosting platform is called on-boarding [10]. As part of the on-boarding activity, the MSP understands the application runtime characteristics using runtime profilers. This helps the MSP to identify the possible SLAs that can be offered to the customer for that application. This also helps in creation of the necessary policies (also called rule sets) required to guarantee the SLOs mentioned in the application SLA. The application is accessible to its end users only after the on-boarding activity is completed.

On-boarding activity consists of the following steps:

a. Packing of the application for deploying on physical or virtual environments. Application packaging is the process of creating deployable components on the hosting platform (could be physical or virtual). Open Virtualization Format (OVF) standard is used for packaging the application for cloud platform [11].

b. The packaged application is executed directly on the physical servers to capture and analyze the application performance characteristics. It allows the functional validation of customer's application. Besides, it provides a baseline performance value for the application in nonvirtual environment. This can be used as one of the data points for customer's performance expectation and for application SLA. Additionally, it helps to identify the nature of application—that is, whether it is CPU-intensive or I/O-intensive or network-intensive and the potential performance bottlenecks.

c. The application is executed on a virtualized platform and the application performance characteristics are noted again. Important performance characteristics like the application's ability to scale (out and up) and performance bounds (minimum and maximum performance) are noted.

d. Based on the measured performance characteristics, different possible SLAs are identified. The resources required and the costs involved for each SLA are also computed.

e. Once the customer agrees to the set of SLOs and the cost, the MSP starts creating different policies required by the data center for automated management of the application. This implies that the management system should automatically infer the amount of system resources that should be allocated/de-allocated to/from appropriate components of the application when the load on the system increases/decreases. These policies are of three types: (1) business, (2) operational, and (3) provisioning. Business policies help prioritize access to the resources in case of contentions. Business policies are in the form of weights for different customers or group of customers. Operational policies are the actions to be taken when different thresholds/conditions are reached. Also, the actions when thresholds/ conditions/triggers on service-level parameters are breached or about to be breached are defined. The corrective action could be different types of provisioning such as scale-up, scale-down, scale-out, scale-in, and so on, of a particular tier of an application. Additionally, notification and logging action (notify the enterprise application's administrator, etc.) are also defined. Operational policies (OP) are represented in the following format:

$$OP \ = \ \text{collection of } \langle \text{Condition, Action} \rangle$$

Here the action could be workflow defining the sequence of actions to be undertaken. For example, one OP is

$$OP \ = \ \langle \text{average latency of web server } > 0.8 \text{ sec, scale-out the web-server tier} \rangle$$

It means, if average latency of the web server is more than 0.8 sec then automatically scale out the web-server tier. On reaching this threshold, MSP should increase the number of instances of the web server.

Provisioning policies help in defining a sequence of actions corresponding to external inputs or user requests. Scale-out, scale-in, start, stop, suspend, resume are some of the examples of provisioning actions. A provisioning policy (PP) is represented as

$$PP \ = \ \text{collection of } \langle \text{Request, Action} \rangle$$

For example, a provisioning policy to start a web site consists of the following sequence: start database server, start web-server instance 1, followed by start the web-server instance 2, and so on. On defining these policies, the packaged applications are deployed on the cloud platform and the application is tested to validate whether the policies are able to meet the SLA requirements. This step is iterative and is repeated until all the infrastructure conditions necessary to satisfy the application SLA are identified.

Once the different infrastructure policies needed to guarantee the SLOs mentioned in the SLA are completely captured, the on-boarding activity is said to be completed.

16.5.3   Preproduction

Once the determination of policies is completed as discussed in previous phase, the application is hosted in a simulated production environment. It facilitates the customer to verify and validate the MSP's findings on application's runtime characteristics and agree on the defined SLA. Once both parties agree on the cost and the terms and conditions of the SLA, the customer sign-off is obtained. On successful completion of this phase the MSP allows the application to go on-live.

16.5.4   Production

In this phase, the application is made accessible to its end users under the agreed SLA. However, there could be situations when the managed application tends to behave differently in a production environment compared to the preproduction environment. This in turn may cause sustained breach of the terms and conditions mentioned in the SLA. Additionally, customer may request the MSP for inclusion of new terms and conditions in the SLA. If the application SLA is breached frequently or if the customer requests for a new non-agreed SLA, the on-boarding process is performed again. In the case of the former, on-boarding activity is repeated to analyze the application and its policies with respect to SLA fulfillment. In case of the latter, a new set of policies are formulated to meet the fresh terms and conditions of the SLA.

16.5.5   Termination

When the customer wishes to withdraw the hosted application and does not wish to continue to avail the services of the MSP for managing the hosting of its application, the termination activity is initiated. On initiation of termination, all data related to the application are transferred to the customer and only the essential information is retained for legal compliance. This ends the hosting relationship between the two parties for that application, and the customer sign-off is obtained.

16.6   AUTOMATED POLICY-BASED MANAGEMENT

This section explains in detail the operationalization of the "Operational" and "Provisioning" policies defined as part of the on-boarding activity. The policies specify the sequence of actions to be performed under different circumstances.

Operational policies specify the functional relationship between the system-level infrastructural attributes and the business level SLA goals. Knowledge of such a relationship helps in identifying the quantum of system resources to be allocated to the various components of the application for different system attributes at various workloads, workload compositions, and operating conditions, so that the SLA goals are met. Figure 16.8 explains the importance of such a relationship. For example, consider a three-tier web application consisting of web server, application server, and database server. Each of the servers is encapsulated using a virtual machine and is hosted on virtualized servers. Furthermore, assume that the web tier and the database tier of the application have been provisioned with sufficient resources at a particular work-load. The effect of varying the system resources (such as CPU) on the SLO, which in this case is the average response time for customer requests, is shown in Figure 16.8.

To understand the system resource requirements for each of the tiers of an application at different workloads necessitates the deployment of the application on a test system. The test system is used to collect the low-level system metrics such as usage of memory and CPU at different workloads, as well as to observe the corresponding high-level service level objectives such as average response time. The metrics thus collected are used to derive the functional relationship between the SLOs and low-level system attributes. These functional relations are called policies. For example, a classification technique is used to derive policies [12, 13].

The triggering of operational and provisional policies results in a set of actions to be executed by the service provider platform. It is possible that some of these actions contend for the same resources. In such a case, execution of certain actions needs to be prioritized over the execution of others. The rules that govern this prioritization of request execution in case of resource contention are specified

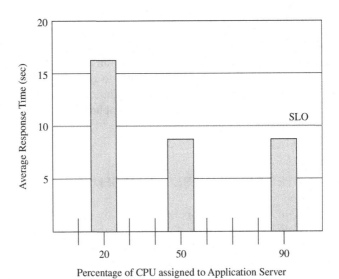

FIGURE 16.8. Performance of a multi-tier application for varied CPU allocation.

as a part of business policy. Some of the parameters often used to prioritize action and perform resource contention resolution are:

- The SLA class (Platinum, Gold, Silver, etc.) to which the application belongs to.
- The amount of penalty associated with SLA breach.
- Whether the application is at the threshold of breaching the SLA.
- Whether the application has already breached the SLA.
- The number of applications belonging to the same customer that has breached SLA.
- The number of applications belonging to the same customer about to breach SLA.
- The type of action to be performed to rectify the situation.

Priority ranking algorithms use these parameters to derive scores. These scores are used to rank each of the actions that contend for the same resources. Actions having high scores get higher priority and hence, receive access to the contended resources.

Furthermore, automatic operationalization of these policies consists of a set of components as shown in Figure 16.9. The basic functionality of these components is described below:

1. Prioritization Engine. Requests from different customers' web applications contending for the same resource are identified, and accordingly their execution is prioritized. Business policies defined by the MSP helps in identifying the requests whose execution should be prioritized in case of resource contentions so that the MSP can realize higher benefits.

2. Provisioning Engine. Every user request of an application will be enacted by the system. The set of steps necessary to enact the user requests are defined in the provisioning policy, and they are used to fulfill the application request like starting an application, stopping an application, and so on. These set of steps can be visualized as a workflow. Hence, the execution of provisioning policy requires a workflow engine [14].

3. Rules Engine. The operation policy defines a sequence of actions to be enacted under different conditions/trigger points. The rules engine evaluates the data captured by the monitoring system [15], evaluates against the predefined operation rules, and triggers the associated action if required. Rules engine and the operational policy is the key to guaranteeing SLA under a self healing system.

4. Monitoring System. Monitoring system collects the defined metrics in SLA. These metrics are used for monitoring resource failures, evaluating operational policies, and auditing and billing purpose.

5. Auditing. The adherence to the predefined SLA needs to be monitored and recorded. It is essential to monitor the compliance of SLA because

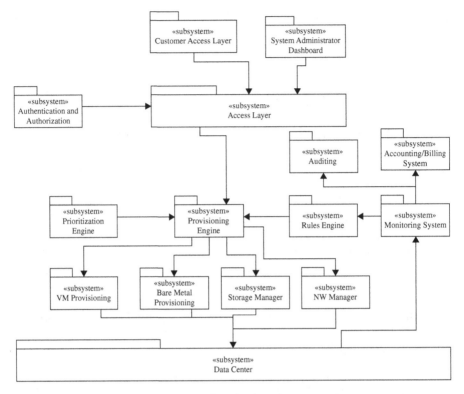

FIGURE 16.9. Component diagram of policy-based automated management system.

any noncompliance leads to strict penalties. The audit report forms the basis for strategizing and long-term planning for the MSP.

6. Accounting/Billing System. Based on the payment model, chargebacks could be made based on the resource utilized by the process during the operation. The fixed cost and recurring costs are computed and billed accordingly.

The interactions among these components are shown in Figure 16.9 and described below.

The policies and packaged application are deployed on the platform after completing the on-boarding activity. The customer is provided with options to start the application in any of the agreed SLAs. The application request is sent via the access layer to the system. Using the provisioning policy, the provisioning engine determines how and in what sequence the different components/tiers of an application should be started and configured. If the start operation requires a resource that is also contended by a different application request, then provisioning engine interacts with the prioritization engine to determine the request that should have access to the contended resource in case of conflict. This conflict resolution is guided by the business policy defined in the prioritization engine. Once an application begins execution, it is continuously monitored by the monitoring system. Monitoring involves collecting statistics about the key metrics and evaluating them against the rules defined in the operational policy for validating the SLA adherence. SLA violation triggers rules that initiate appropriate corrective action automatically. For example, whenever the performance of the application degrades and chances of violating the agreed SLO limits are high, the rules that help scale out the bottleneck tier of the application is triggered. This ensures that the performance does not degenerate to a level of violating the SLA. Periodically, the amount of resource utilized by the application is calculated. On calculating the resource utilization, the cost is computed correspondingly and the bill is generated. The bill along with the report on the performance of the application is sent to the customer.

Alternatively, the monitoring system can interact with the rules engine through an optimization engine, as shown in Figure 16.10. The role of the optimization system is to decide the migration strategy that helps optimize certain objective functions for virtual machine migration. The objective could be to minimize the number of virtual machines migrated or minimize the number of physical machines affected by the migration process. The following example highlights the importance of the optimization engine within a policy based management system [16].

Assume an initial assignment of seven virtual machines (VM) to the three physical machines (PM) at time t_1 as shown in Figure 16.11. Also, each of the three PMs has memory and CPU capacity of 100. At time t_1, the CPU usage by VM_1, VM_2, and VM_3 on PM_A are 40, 40, and 20, respectively, and the memory

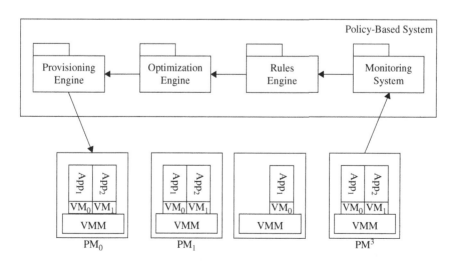

FIGURE 16.10. Importance of optimization in the policy-based management system.

consumption is 20, 10, and 40 respectively. Similarly, at time t_1 the CPU and memory requirements of VM_4, VM_5, and VM_6 on PMB are 20, 10, 40 and 20, 40, 20, respectively. VM_7 only consumes 20% of CPU and 20% of memory on PM_C. Thus, PM_B and PM_C are underloaded but PM_A is overloaded. Assume VM_1 is the cause of the overload situation in PM_A.

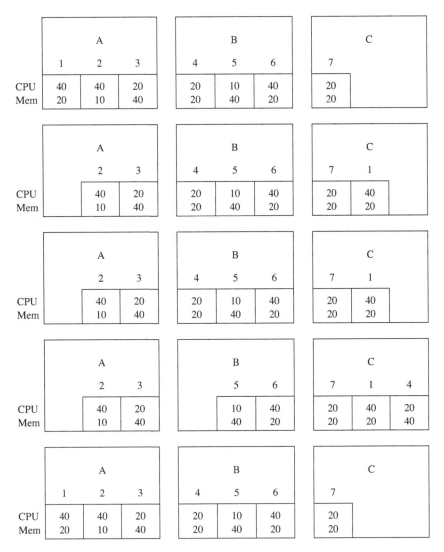

FIGURE 16.11. (a) Initial configuration of the VMs and the PMs at time t_1. (b) Configuration resulting from event-based migration of VM_1 at time t_1. (c) Resource requirement situation at time $t_2 > t_1$. (d) Configuration resulting from "event-based" migration of VM_4 at time $t_2 > t_1$. (e) Alternate configuration resulting from optimization-based migration at time $t_2 > t_1$.

In the above scenario, event-based migration will result in migration of VM_1 out of PM_A to PM_C. Furthermore, consider that at time t_2 ($t_2 > t_1$), PM_B is overloaded as the memory requirement of VM_4 increases to 40. Consequently, an event-based scheme results in migration of VM_4 to PM_C. At time t_3 ($t_3 > t_2$), a new VM, VM_8, with CPU and memory requirements of 70 each, needs to be allocated to one of the PMs; then a new PM, PM_D, needs to be switched on for hosting it. In such a scenario, VM_8 cannot be hosted on any of the three existing PMs: PM_A, PM_B, and PM_C. However, assume that the duration of the time window $t_2 - t_1$ is such that the QoS and SLA violations due to the continued hosting of VM_1 on PM_A are well within the permissible limits. In such a case, the migration of both VMs—VM_1 to PM_B and VM_4 to PM_A—at time t_2 ensures lesser number of PM are switched on. This results in a global resource assignment that may be better than local resource management.

In such environment, consider a case wherein a virtual machine is over-loaded. The optimization module needs to not only determine the virtual machine that needs to be migrated out of its current physical machine but also determine the new physical machine where the migrating virtual machine should be hosted. The Sandpiper technique [17] has been proposed for monitoring and detecting hotspots, determining new assignments of virtual resources to physical resources, and initiating the necessary migrations.

16.7 CONCLUSION

The chapter presented a detailed overview of SLA and its importance from the service provider's perspective. It described a brief history of how the SLA that evolved from a state of infrastructure availability was the prime consideration today where complex application SLO could be included as part of it. The chapter provided the necessary mechanisms that make it possible for a service provider to evaluate the infrastructure needs to meet the provisions mentioned in the SLA. A complete view of the process involved and also an overview of the architectural stack for achieving the same are presented.

REFERENCES

1. D. Mensce and V. Almeida, *Capacity Planning for web Performance: Metrics, Models and Methods*, Prentice-Hall, Englewood Cliffs, NJ, 1998.

2. P. Barham, B. Dragovic, K. Fraser, S. Hand, T. Harris, A. Ho, R. Neugebauer, I. Pratt, and A. Warfield, Xen and the art of virtualization, in *Proceedings of the 19th ACM Symposium on Operating Systems Principles*, New York, October 19–22, 2003, pp. 164–177.

3. G. Popek and R. Goldberg, Formal requirements for virtualizable third generation architectures, *Communications of ACM*, **17**(7):412–421, 1974.

4. E. de Souza E. Silva, and M. Gerla, Load balancing in distributed systems with multiple classes and site constraints, in *Proceedings of the 10th International*

Symposium on Computer Performance Modeling, Measurement and Evaluation, Paris, France, December 19–21 1984, pp. 17–33.

5. J. Carlstrom and R. Rom, Application-aware admission control and scheduling in web servers, in *Proceedings of the 21st IEEE Infocom,* New York, June 23–27, 2002, pp. 824–831.

6. X. Chen, P. Mohapatra, and H. Chen, An admission control scheme for predictable server response time for web accesses, in *Proceedings of the 10th International Conference on World Wide web,* Hong Kong, China, May 1–5, 2001, pp. 545–554.

7. Web Service Level Agreement (WSLA) Language Specification Version 1.0, *www.research.ibm.com/wsla/WSLASpecV1–20030128.pdf,* accessed on April 16, 2010.

8. Web Services Agreement Specification (WS Agreement), *http://ogsa.gridforum.org/ Public_Comment_Docs/Documents/Oct-2006/WS-AgreementSpecificationDraftFinal_sp_tn_jpver_v2.pdf,* accessed on April 16, 2010.

9. Common Information Model (CIM) Standards, DMTF standard version 2.25.0, March 2010, *http://www.dmtf.org/standards/cim/cim_schema_v2250/,* accessed on April 16, 2010.

10. S. Bose, N. Tiwari, A. Pasala, and S. Padmanabhuni, SLA Aware "on-boarding" of applications on the cloud, *SETLabs Briefings,* 7(7):27–32, 2009.

11. Open Virtualization Format Specification, DMTF standard version 1.0.0, Doc. no. DSP0243, February 2009, *http://www.dmtf.org/standards/published_documents/ DSP0243_1.0.0.pdf,* accessed on April 16, 2010.

12. Y. Udupi, A. Sahai, and S. Singhal, A classification-based approach to policy refinement, in *Proceedings of the 10th IFIP/IEEE International Symposium on Integrated Network Management,* Munich, Germany, May 21–25, 2007, pp. 785–788.

13. Y. Chen, S. Iyer, X. Liu, D. Milojicic, and A. Sahai, SLA decomposition: Translating service level objectives to system level thresholds, in *Proceedings of the 4th International Conference on Autonomic Computing (ICAC),* Florida, June 11–15, 2007, pp. 3–3.

14. K. Gor, D. Ra, S. Ali, L. Alves, N. Arurkar, I. Gupta, A. Chakrabarti, A. Sharma, and S. Sengupta, Scalable enterprise level workflow and infrastructure management in a grid computing environment, in *Proceedings of the 5th IEEE International Symposium on Cluster Computing and the Grid (CCGrid),* Cardiff, UK, May 9–12, 2005, pp. 661–667.

15. B. Van Halle, *Business Rules Applied: Building Better Systems Using Business Rules Approach,* John Wiley & Sons, Hoboken, NJ, 2002.

16. S. Bose and S. Sudarrajan, Optimizing migration of virtual machines across datacenters, in *Proceeding of the 38th International Conference on Parallel Processing (ICPP) Workshops,* Vienna, Austria, September 22–25 2009, pp. 306–313.

17. T. Wood, P. Shenoy, and A. Venkataramani, Black-box and Gray-box strategies for virtual machine migration, in *Proceedings of the 4th USENIX Symposium on Networked Systems Design and Implementation (NSDI),* Cambridge, MA, April 11–13, 2007, pp. 229–242.

CHAPTER 17

PERFORMANCE PREDICTION FOR HPC ON CLOUDS

ROCCO AVERSA, BENIAMINO DI MARTINO, MASSIMILIANO RAK, SALVATORE VENTICINQUE, and UMBERTO VILLANO

17.1 INTRODUCTION

High-performance computing (HPC) is one of the contexts in which the adoption of the cloud computing paradigm is debated. Traditionally, HPC users are accustomed to managing directly very complex parallel systems and performing a very fine-tuning of their applications on the target hardware. The matter is to ascertain if it may be convenient to deploy such applications on a cloud, where users "voluntarily" lose almost all control on the execution environment, leaving the management of datacenters to the cloud owner.

In order to understand fully the implications of this issue, it is probably necessary to take a step back and to clarify how the cloud paradigm can be applied to HPC. As outlined in other chapters of this book, cloud computing may be exploited at three different levels: IaaS (Infrastructure as a Service), PaaS (Platform as a Service), and AaaS (Application as a Service). In one way or another, all of them can be useful for HPC. However, nowadays the most common solution is the adoption of the IaaS paradigm. IaaS lets users run applications on fast pay-per-use machines they don't want to buy, to manage, or to maintain. Furthermore, the total computational power can be easily increased (by additional charge). For the sporadic HPC user, this solution is undoubtedly attractive: no investment in rapidly-obsolescing machines, no power and cooling nightmares, and no system software updates.

An IaaS cloud environment hinges on a virtualization engine. Basically, this engine provides by means of a hypervisor the illusion of multiple independent replicas of every physical machine in the cloud. Each replica has its own address

Cloud Computing: Principles and Paradigms, Edited by Rajkumar Buyya, James Broberg and Andrzej Goscinski   Copyright © 2011 John Wiley & Sons, Inc.

space, devices, and network connections and is capable of running any software (O.S. included) that could be run on a stand-alone machine. Currently, a number of different virtual machine (VM) environments are readily available and can be used to provide server virtualization (VMWare [1], Xen [2],VirtualBox [3]). The virtual engines differ in the approach used to run the host operating systems [unmodified (fully virtualized approach) or aware of the presence of the hypervisor (paravirtualized approach)] on the exploitation of hardware CPU virtualization technologies (like Intel VT and AMD-V) and on the type of licensing (opensource or closed-source). On the top of such virtualization engines, which physically manage the hardware, cloud environments offer a service-oriented interface for managing the virtual machines (create, destroy, suspend, migrate from a physical system to another, change the amount of available memory or the number of virtual CPUs assigned), as well as a large set of ancillary services for managing the secure access to resources and for auditing (and billing).

At the state of the art, there exist many solutions for building up a cloud environment. VMWare cloud OS is integrated in the VMWare virtualization solutions. Opennebula [4, 26], Enomaly [5], and Eucalyptus [6] are open-source software layers that provide a service-oriented interface on the top of existing virtual engines (mainly, VMWare and Xen). Virtual workspaces [7, 16, 27], and related projects (Nimbus, Kupa, WISPY) build up the service-oriented interface for the virtual engines by exploiting a grid infrastructure (see Section 17.2 for further details).

As mentioned above, the most common solution to exploit cloud power in the context of HPC is to get a pay-per-use infrastructure. But, unlike other cloud users, most HPC users usually exploit parallel hardware, and so they would like to get parallel hardware to execute their explicitly-parallel applications. They want to receive from the cloud a (possibly high) number of powerful machines with fast interconnect that could resemble a high-performance computing cluster. Stated another way, they exploit the cloud as a provider of cluster-on-demand (CoD) systems. They ask for, and obtain from the cloud, clusters that they can configure according to their software requirements. This is possible since these are in fact virtual clusters, whose management (even in terms of the number of nodes and their configurations) is completely delegated to the cloud user.

The key of the issue discussed in this chapter (the profitability of cloud for HPC) is all in the difference between a real cluster system and the virtual cluster received from the cloud. On the one hand, a virtual cluster may be economically convenient, is fully configurable, and requires no long-term investment. On the other hand, it is not as fast as a physical cluster. Furthermore, understanding the limits of the cloud interconnect is essentially impossible. After all, a cloud is a cloud, and you cannot put your hands on its components. This is great for the end user, but is frustrating for the advanced HPC user who wishes to identify the real hardware its application is running on.

Another source of confusion for most users is the relationship between clouds and grids. Cloud environments, from the HPC point of view, are a centralized resource of computational power. On the other hand, the grid paradigm proposes a distributed approach to computational resources, "gluing" together distributed datacenters to build up a computational grid, accessible in a simple and standardized way. After all, their objective is the same: offering computational power to final users. But this is obtained following two different approaches: centralized for clouds and distributed for grids. It is easy to find on the net many open (and often useless) discussions comparing the two paradigms. In this chapter we will not deal further with the problem, limiting ourselves to discuss the profitability of the two paradigms in the HPC context and to point out the possibility to integrate both of them in a unified view.

The above-discussed issues focus on the technological state of the art of cloud and HPC, describing the architectural solutions offered. The problem initially raised (whether clouds may be convenient for HPC or not) can now be translated into the question, Is the performance loss due to the adoption of the cloud approach acceptable in the HPC context? In short, the performance losses linked to virtualization, relatively slow networks, and cloud overheads are the main reason for the very slow diffusion of virtualization and cloud techniques into HPC environments. However, there are very good motivations for the adoption of VMs in this context. As everyone involved in HPC knows, during recent years there has been a continuous proliferation of different operating system versions. Many applications have strict requirements for their execution environments. Often the applications' environment requirements are mutually incompatible, and it is not reasonable to modify or to re-install system software on-the-fly to make applications work. Moreover, partitioning the computing hardware into closed environments with different characteristics is not decidedly an efficient solution.

In light of the above, it is reasonable to think that, notwithstanding the inevitable performance loss, cloud techniques will progressively spread into HPC environments. As an example, Rocks, the widely used Linux distribution for HPC clusters, provides support for virtual clusters starting from release 5.1 [8]. Virtual clusters are independent and separately configurable clusters sharing the same HPC hardware. However, the availability of virtualization software out-of-the-box might be not sufficient to decide to switch to virtualized environments for the typical HPC users, namely, scientists running high-performance codes. Before making the choice, they would be aware of the performance losses involved. But, unfortunately, these have not yet been extensively evaluated and analyzed.

As pointed out above, the performance problem is hard due to the intrinsically "intangible" and flexible nature of cloud systems. This makes difficult (and maybe useless) to compare the performance of a given application that executes in two different virtual environments received from a cloud. So, given the extreme simplicity to ask from a cloud for additional computing resources (with additional costs), it is almost impossible to make a choice that maximizes the performance/cost ratio.

In the remainder of this chapter, we will try to discuss this matter, pointing out the importance of performance evaluation and prediction. First, we will deal with the grid–cloud relationship, outlining the state of the art for their integration. Then we will focus on virtual clusters and on research contributions about performance evaluation of clouds.

The presentation is organized as follows: The next section (17.2) introduces the fundamentals of cloud computing paradigm applied to HPC, aiming at defining the concepts and terminology concerning virtual clusters. Section 17.3 instead focuses on the relationship between grid and cloud, highlighting their similarities and differences, the opportunity of their integration, and the approaches proposed to this end. Section 17.4 focuses on performance-related problems, which affect the adoption of cloud computing for HPC, pointing out the need for methods, techniques, and tools for performance prediction of clouds. The final section (17.5) presents our conclusions.

17.2 BACKGROUND

As outlined in the introduction, the main question related to the adoption of the cloud paradigm in HPC is related to the evaluation (and, possibly, to the reduction) of possible performance losses compared to physical HPC hardware. In clouds, performance penalties may appear at two different levels:

- Virtual Engine (VE). These are related to the performance loss introduced by the virtualization mechanism. They are strictly related to the VE technology adopted.
- Cloud Environment (CE). These are the losses introduced at a higher level by the cloud environment, and they are mainly due to overheads and to the sharing of computing and communication resources.

The actual hardware used in the cloud, along with the losses at the VE and CE levels, will determine the actual performance of applications running in the cloud. As will be discussed later, for HPC users the final perceived performance will be not so much affected by VE and CE levels as by the class of the physical hardware (computing and interconnect) making up the cloud. Even if the computing nodes adopted in cloud are not too different from those making up (economical) HPC clusters, it is a fact that these usually adopt suitable network switches, like Myrinet or Infiniband, which provide high bandwidth and low latency. These networks typically are not available, at the state of the art, in commercial cloud environments. In practice, their relatively slow interconnects can easily dwarf the effect of VE and CE overheads. However, we will not consider here this hardware factor, because it is not under the cloud user's control. Additional considerations on the cloud hardware and its impact on the performance of HPC applications will be presented in Section 17.3.

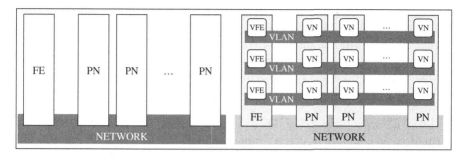

FIGURE 17.1. Physical and virtual cluster.

The configuration and performance analysis of virtual clusters poses problems that are considerably more complex than those involved in the use of physical clusters. The objective of this section is to present the main problems and to introduce a clear and sound terminology, which is still lacking in the literature.

A traditional cluster—that is, a physical cluster—can be schematized as in Figure 17.1. It is essentially made up of a front-end (typically used only for administration purposes, often the only node with a public IP address) and a number of (physical) processing nodes. These are, turn, provided with a single CPU or with multiple CPUs sharing a common memory and I/O resources. The multiple CPUs may be multiple cores on a single processor chip, a traditional single-core CPUs working in SMP mode, a "fictitious" CPU obtained by hyperthreading, or a mixture of all the above.

A physical cluster can execute multiple jobs in parallel, by assigning to every job a subset of the total number of CPUs. Usually the choice is to use non-overlapping subsets of CPUs, in order to avoid processor sharing among multiple jobs. But, even doing so, the interconnection network (and the front-end) are inevitably shared.

This may, or may not, introduce significant overheads, depending on the type of computations and their communication requirements and, above all, on the characteristics of the interconnect. Anyway, very often this overhead is tolerable.

A parallel application running in a physical cluster is composed of processes. To exploit all the available computing resources, the application should use at least a number of processes equal to the number of available CPUs (or, in the case of concurrent jobs, equal to the number of CPU exclusively reserved for the job). Redundant application decompositions (i.e., applications made up of a number of processes higher than the number of CPUs) are possible and, in some cases, they may even be more efficient.

The main problem with physical clusters is that all jobs running on the cluster, whether concurrent or non-concurrent, have to share the same operating system (OS), the system and application libraries, and the operating environment (system applications and tools). The frequently recurring requirements for mutually exclusive or incompatible libraries and support software make physical cluster management a nightmare for system administrators.

Basically, a virtual cluster is made up of a virtual front-end and a number of virtual nodes (see Figure 17.1). Virtual front-ends are obtained by virtualization of a physical front-end machine, and virtual nodes are obtained by virtualization of physical processing nodes.

Even if, strictly speaking, in a virtual cluster the front-end could be virtualized as compute nodes, a simpler and less resource-demanding solution is to use a physical front-end. Both with physical or virtual front-ends, virtual cluster may have an execution environment of its own (OS, libraries, tools, etc.) that is loaded and initialized when the cluster is created. The advantages of cluster virtualization are clear: Every application can set up a proper execution environment, which does not interfere with all other applications and virtual clusters running on the hardware. Moreover, the network traffic of every virtual cluster is encapsulated in a separate VLAN. However, most likely all VLANs will share the physical network resources.

As shown in Figure 17.1, every virtual processing node can host one or several virtual machines (VMs), each running a private OS instance. These may belong to the same or to different virtual clusters. At least in theory, the number of VMs is limited only by resource consumption (typically, physical memory). In turn, each VM is provided with several virtual CPUs (VCPUs). A virtual machine manager running in every node makes it possible to share the physical CPUs among the VCPUs defined on the node (which may belong to a single virtual cluster or to several virtual clusters). Typically, it is possible to define VCPU affinity and to force every VCPU to run on a subset of the physical CPUs available.

It is worth noting that, given a physical node provided with n CPUs, there are two possibilities to exploit all the computing resources available:

- Using n VMs (each running its OS instance) with one, or even several, VCPUs;
- Using a single VM with at least n VCPUs.

On the other hand, the use in a node of v VCPUs, with $v > n$, whether in a single or in multiple VMs, leads to a fictitious multiplication of computing resources. In nodes where CPU resources are multiplied, the virtual clusters not only share memory, communication hardware, and the virtual machine manager, but also share CPU cycles, with a more direct effect on overall computing performance.

17.3   GRID AND CLOUD

"Grid vs Cloud" is the title of an incredible number of recent Web blogs and articles in on-line forums and magazines, where many HPC users express their

own opinion on the relationship between the two paradigms [11, 28, 29, 40]. Cloud is simply presented, by its supporters, as an evolution of the grid. Some consider grids and clouds as alternative options to do the same thing in a different way. However, there are very few clouds on which one can build, test, or run compute-intensive applications. In fact it still necessary to deal with some open issues. One is when, in term of performance, a cloud is better than a grid to run a specific application. Another problem to be addressed concerns the effort to port a grid application to a cloud. In the following it will be discussed how these and other arguments suggest that we investigate the integration of grids and clouds to improve the exploitation of computing resources in HPC.

17.3.1 Grid and Cloud as Alternatives

Both grid and cloud are technologies that have been conceived to provide users with handy computing resources according to their specific requirements.

Grid was designed with a bottom-up approach [9, 30, 31, 39]. Its goal is to share a hardware or a software among different organizations by means of common protocols and policies. The idea is to deploy interoperable services in order to allow the access to physical resources (CPU, memory, mass storage, etc.) and to available software utilities. Users get access to a real machine. Grid resources are administrated by their owners. Authorized users can invoke grid services on remote machines without paying and without service level guarantees. A grid middleware provides a set of API (actually services) to program a heterogeneous, geographically distributed system.

On the other hand, cloud technology was designed using a top-down approach. It aims at providing its users with a specific high-level functionality: a storage, a computing platform, a specialized service. They get virtual resources from the cloud. The underlying hardware/software infrastructure is not exposed. The only information the user needs to know is the quality of service (QoS) of the services he is paying for. Bandwidth, computing power, and storage represent parameters that are used for specifying the QoS and for billing. Cloud users ask for a high-level functionality (service, platform, infrastructure), pay for it, and become owners of a virtual machine. From a technological point of view, virtualization is exploited to build an insulated environment, which is configured to meet users' requirements and is exploited for easy reconfiguration and backup. A single enterprise is the owner of the cloud platform (software and underlying hardware), whereas customers become owners of the virtual resources they pay for.

Cloud supporters claim that the cloud is easy to be used [9], is scalable [10], and always gives users exactly what they want. On the other hand, grid is difficult to be used, does not give performance guarantees, is used by narrow communities of scientists to solve specific problems, and does not actually support interoperability [9].

Grid fans answer [11] that grid users do not need a credit card, that around the world there are many examples of successful projects, and that a great number of computing nodes connected across the net execute large-scale scientific applications, addressing problems that could not be solved otherwise. Grid users can use a reduced set of functionalities and can develop simple applications, or they can get, theoretically, an infinite amount of resources.

As always, truth is in the middle. Some users prefer to pay since they need a specific service with strict requirements and require a guaranteed QoS. Cloud can provide this. Many users of the scientific community look for some sort of supercomputing architecture to solve intensive computations that process a huge amount of data, and they do not care about getting a guaranteed performance level. The grid can provide it. But, even on this last point, there are divergent opinions.

17.3.2   Grid and Cloud Integration

To understand why grids and clouds should be integrated, we have to start by considering what the users want and what these two technologies can provide. Then we can try to understand how cloud and grid can complement each other and why their integration is the goal of intensive research activities [12]. We know that a supercomputer runs faster than a virtualized resource. For example, a LU benchmark on EC2 (the cloud platform provided by Amazon) runs slower, and some overhead is added to start VMs [13]. On the other hand, the probability to execute an application in fixed time on a grid resource depends on many parameters and cannot be guaranteed. As experimented in Foster [13], if 400 msec is the time that an EC2 requires to execute an LU benchmark, then the probability of obtaining a grid resource in less that 400 msec is very low (34%), even if the same benchmark can take less than 100 msec to complete.

If you want to get your results as soon as possible, you are adopting the cloud end-user perspective. If you want to look for the optimum resources that solve the problem, overcoming the boundaries of a single enterprise, you are using the grid perspective that aims at optimizing resources sharing and system utilization.

The integration of cloud and grid, or at least their integrated utilization, has been proposed [14] since there is a trade-off between application turnaround and system utilization, and sometimes it is useful to choose the right compromise between them.

Some issues to be investigated have been pointed out:

- Integration of virtualization into existing e-infrastructures
- Deployment of grid services on top of virtual infrastructures
- Integration of cloud-base services in e-infrastructures
- Promotion of open-source components to build clouds
- Grid technology for cloud federation

In light of the above, the integration of the two environments is a debated issue [9]. At the state of the art, two main approaches have been proposed:

- *Grid on Cloud.* A cloud IaaS (Infrastructure as a Service) approach is adopted to build up and to manage a flexible grid system [15]. Doing so, the grid middleware runs on a virtual machine. Hence the main drawback of this approach is performance. Virtualization inevitably entails performance losses as compared to the direct use of physical resources.
- *Cloud on Grid*: The stable grid infrastructure is exploited to build up a cloud environment. This solution is usually preferred [7, 16] because the cloud approach mitigates the inherent complexity of the grid. In this case, a set of grid services is offered to manage (create, migrate, etc.) virtual machines. The use of *Globus workspaces* [16], along with a set of grid services for the Globus Toolkit 4, is the prominent solution, as in the Nimbus project [17].

The integration could simplify the task of the HPC user to select, to configure, and to manage resources according to the application requirements. It adds flexibility to exploit available resources, but both of the above-presented approaches have serious problems for overall system management, due to the complexity of the resulting architectures. Performance prediction, application tuning, and benchmarking are some of the relevant activities that become critical and that cannot be performed in the absence of performance evaluation of clouds.

17.4 HPC IN THE CLOUD: PERFORMANCE-RELATED ISSUES

This section will discuss the issues linked to the adoption of the cloud paradigm in the HPC context. In particular, we will focus on three different issues:

1. The difference between typical HPC paradigms and those of current cloud environments, especially in terms of performance evaluation.
2. A comparison of the two approaches in order to point out their advantages and drawbacks, as far as performance is concerned.
3. New performance evaluation techniques and tools to support HPC in cloud systems.

As outlined in the previous sections, the adoption of the cloud paradigm for HPC is a flexible way to deploy (virtual) clusters dedicated to execute HPC applications. The switch from a physical to a virtual cluster is completely transparent for the majority of HPC users, who have just terminal access to the cluster and limit themselves to "launch" their tasks.

The first and well-known difference between HPC and cloud environments is the different economic approach: (a) buy-and-maintain for HPC and

(b) pay-per-use in cloud systems. In the latter, every time that a task is started, the user will be charged for the used resources. But it is very hard to know in advance which will be the resource usage and hence the cost. On the other hand, even if the global expense for a physical cluster is higher, once the system has been acquired, all the costs are fixed and predictable (in fact, they are so until the system is not faulty). It would be great to predict, albeit approximately, the resource usage of a target application in a cloud, in order to estimate the cost of its execution.

These two issues above are strictly related, and a performance problem becomes an economic problem. Let us assume that a given application is well-optimized for a physical cluster. If it behaves on a virtual cluster as on the physical one, it will use the cloud resources in an efficient way, and its execution will be relatively cheap. This is not so trivial as it may seem, as the pay-per-use paradigm commonly used in commercial clouds (see Table 17.1) charges the user for virtual cluster up-time, not for CPU usage. Almost surprisingly, this means that processor idle time has a cost for cloud users.

For clarity's sake, it is worth presenting a simple but interesting example regarding performance and cost. Let us consider two different virtual clusters with two and four nodes, respectively. Let us assume that the application is well-optimized and that, at least for a small number of processors, it gets linear speed-up. The target application will be executed in two hours in the first cluster and in one hour in the second one. Let the execution cost be X dollars per hour per machine instance (virtual node). This is similar to the charging scheme of EC2. The total cost is given by

$$\langle \text{cost per hour per instance} \rangle * \langle \text{numberofinstances} \rangle * \langle \text{hours} \rangle$$

In the first case (two-node cluster) the cost will be $X*2*2$, whereas in the second one it will be $X*1*4$. It turns out that the two configurations have the same cost for the final user, even if the first execution is slower than the second. Now if we consider an application that is not well-optimized and has a speed-up less than the ideal one, the running time on the large virtual cluster will be longer than two hours; as a consequence, the cost of the run of the second virtual cluster

TABLE 17.1. Example of Cost Criteria

Cloud Provider	Index	Description
Amazon	$/hour	Cost (in $) per hour of activity of the virtual machines.
Amazon	$/GB	Cost (in $) per Gigabyte transferred outside the cloud zone (transfers inside the same zone have no price)
GoGrid	$*RAM/hour	Cost (in $) by RAM memory allocated per hour

will be higher than that on the small one. In conclusion: In clouds, performance counts two times. Low performance means not only long waiting times, but also high costs. The use of alternative cost factors (e.g., the RAM memory allocated, as for GoGrid in Table 17.1) leads to completely different considerations and requires different application optimizations to reduce the final cost of execution.

In light of the above, it is clear that the typical HPC user would like to know how long his application will run on the target cluster and which configuration has the highest performance/cost ratio. The advanced user, on the other hand, would also know if there is a way to optimize its application so as to reduce the cost of its run without sacrificing performance. The high-end user, who cares more for performance than for the cost to be sustained, would like instead to know how to choose the best configuration to maximize the performance of his application. In other words, in the cloud world the hardware configuration is not fixed, and it is not the starting point for optimization decisions. Configurations can be easily changed in order to fit the user needs. All the three classes of users should resort to performance analysis and prediction tools. But, unfortunately, prediction tools for virtual environments are not available, and the literature presents only partial results on the performance analysis of such systems.

An additional consequence of the different way that HPC users exploit a virtual cluster is that the cloud concept makes very different the system dimensioning—that is, the choice of the system configuration fit for the user purposes (cost, maximum response time, etc.). An HPC machine is chosen and acquired, aiming to be at the top of available technology (under inevitable money constraints) and to be able to sustain the highest system usage that may eventually be required. This can be measured in terms of GFLOPS, in terms of number of runnable jobs, or by other indexes depending on the HPC applications that will be actually executed. In other words, the dimensioning is made by considering the *peak system usage*. It takes place at system acquisition time, by examining the machine specifications or by assembling it using hardware components of known performance. In this phase, simple and global performance indexes are used (e.g., bandwidth and latency for the interconnect, peak FLOPS for the computing nodes, etc.).

In clouds, instead, the system must be dimensioned by finding out an optimal trade-off between application performance and used resources. As mentioned above, the optimality is a concept that is fairly different, depending on the class of users. Someone would like to obtain high performance at any cost, whereas others would privilege economic factors. In any case, as the choice of the system is not done once and for all, the dimensioning of the virtual clusters takes place every time the HPC applications have to be executed on new datasets. In clouds, the system dimensioning is a task under the control of the user, not of the system administrator. This completely changes the scenario and makes the dimensioning a complex activity, eager for performance data and indexes that can be measured fairly easily in the HPC world on physical

TABLE 17.2. Differences Between "Classical" HPC and HPC in Cloud Environments

Problem	HPC	HPC in Clouds
Cost	Buy-and-maintain paradigm	Pay-per-use paradigm
Performance optimization	Tuning of the application to the hardware	Joint tuning of application and system
System dimensioning	At system acquisition time, using global performance indexes under system administrator control	At every application execution, using application oriented performance indexes, under user control

systems, but that are not generally available for complex and rapidly changing systems as virtual clusters.

Table 17.2 summarizes the differences between HPC classical environments and HPC in clouds. To summarize the above discussion, in systems (the clouds) where the availability of performance data is crucial to know how fast your applications will run and how much you will pay, there is great uncertainty about what to measure and how to measure, and there are great difficulties when attempting to interpret the meaning of measured data.

17.4.1 HPC Systems and HPC on Clouds: A Performance Comparison

The second step of our analysis is a performance comparison between classical HPC systems and the new cloud paradigm. This will make it possible to point out the advantages and disadvantages of the two approaches and will enable us to understand if and when clouds can be useful for HPC.

The performance characterization of HPC systems is usually carried out by executing benchmarks. However, the only ones that make measurements of virtual clusters at different levels and provide available results in the literature [18–22, 33, 34, 36] are the following:

- The **LINPACK** benchmark, a so-called kernel benchmark, which aims at measuring the peak performance (in FLOPSs) of the target environment.
- The **NAS Parallel Benchmarks (NPB)**, a set of eight programs designed to help to evaluate the performance of parallel supercomputers, derived from computational fluid dynamics (CFD) applications and consisting of five kernels and three pseudo-applications. As performance index, together with FLOPS, it measures response time, network bandwidth usage, and latency.
- **mpptest,** a microbenchmark that measures the performance of some of the basic MPI message passing routines in a variety of different conditions. It measures (average) response time, network bandwidth usage and latency.

When these benchmarks are executed on physical machines (whether clusters or other types of parallel hardware), they give a coarse-level indication of the system potentialities. In the HPC world, these benchmarks are of common use and widely diffused, but their utility is limited. Users usually have an in-depth knowledge of the target hardware used for executing their applications, and a comparison between two different (physical) clusters makes sense only for Top500 classification or when they are acquired. HPC users usually outline the potentiality and the main features of their system through (a) a brief description of the hardware and (b) a few performance indexes obtained using some of the above-presented benchmarks. In any case, these descriptions are considered useless for application performance optimization, because they only aim at providing a rough classification of the hardware.

Recently, the benchmarking technique has been adopted in a similar way, tackling also the problem of the utility of the cloud paradigm for scientific applications. In particular, the papers focusing on the development of applications executed in virtual clusters propose the use of a few benchmarks to outline the hardware potentialities [22, 23]. These results are of little interest for our comparison. On the other hand, papers that present comparisons between virtual and physical clusters [18, 20–22, 36, 37] use benchmarks to find out the limits of cloud environments, as discussed below. In the following, we will focus on these results.

We can start our analysis from benchmark-based comparison of virtual clusters and physical HPC systems. In the literature there are results on all three types of benchmarks mentioned above, even if the only cloud provider considered is Amazon EC2 (there are also results on private clusters, but in those cases the analysis focuses on virtual engine level and neglects the effects of the cloud environment, and so it is outside the scope of this chapter).

Napper and Bientinesi [20] and Ostermann et al. [21] adopted the LINPACK benchmark, measuring the GFLOPS provided by virtual clusters composed of Amazon EC2 virtual machines. Both studies point out that the values obtained in the VCs are an order of magnitude lower than equivalent solutions on physical clusters. The best result found in the literature is about 176 GFLOPS, to be compared to 37.64 TFLOPS of the last (worst) machine in Top500 list. Even if it is reasonable that VCs peak performances are far from the supercomputer ones, it is worth noting that the GFLOPS tends to decrease (being fixed the memory load) when the number of nodes increases. In other words, virtual clusters are not so efficient as physical clusters, at least for this benchmark. As shown later, the main cause of this behavior is the inadequate internal interconnect.

An analysis by real-world codes, using the NPB (NAS parallel benchmark) benchmark suite, was proposed in Walker [18], Ostermann et al. [21]. NPBs are a collection of MPI-based HPC applications. The suite is organized so as to stress different aspects of an HPC systems—for example, computation, communication, or I/O.

Walker [18] compared a virtual EC2 cluster to a physical cluster composed of TeraGrid machines with similar hardware configuration (i.e., the hardware under the virtual cluster was the same adopted by the physical cluster). This comparison pointed out that the overheads introduced by the virtualization layer and the cloud environment level were fairly high. It should be noted that Walker adopted for his analysis two virtual clusters made up of a very limited number of nodes (two and four). But, even for such small systems, the applications did not scale well with the number of nodes.

The last kind of benchmark widely adopted in the literature is the MPI kernel benchmark, which measures response time, bandwidth, and latency for MPI communication primitives. These tests, proposed by almost all the authors who tried to run scientific applications on cloud-based virtual clusters, are coherent with the results presented above. In all the cases in the literature, bandwidth and, above all, latency have unacceptable values for HPC applications.

In the literature, at the best of the authors' knowledge, there are currently no other examples of virtual cluster benchmarking, even if the ongoing diffusion of the paradigm will lead probably to a fast growth of this kind of results in the next years. As mentioned above, the benchmarking technique is able to put in evidence the main drawback linked to the adoption of cloud systems for HPC: the unsatisfactory performance of the network connection between virtual clusters. In any case, the performance offered by virtual clusters is not comparable to the one offered by physical clusters.

Even if the results briefly reported above are of great interest and can be of help to get insight on the problem, they do not take into account the differences between HPC machines and HPC in the cloud, which we have summarized at the start of this section. Stated another way, the mentioned analyses simply measure global performance indexes. But the scenario can drastically change if different performance indexes are measured.

Just to start, the *application response time* is perhaps the performance index of great importance in a cloud context. In fact, it is a measurement of interest for the final user and, above all, has a direct impact on the cost of the application execution. An interesting consideration linked to response time was proposed by Ian Foster in his blog [11]. The overall application response time (RT) is given by the formula $RT = \langle job\ submission\ time \rangle + \langle execution\ time \rangle$.

In common HPC environments (HPC system with batch queue, grids, etc.) the job submission time may be fairly long (even minutes or hours, due to necessity to get all the required computing resources together). On the other hand, in a cloud used to run HPC workload (a virtual cluster dedicated to the HPC user), queues (and waiting time) simply disappear. The result is that, even if the virtual cluster may offer a much lower computational power, the final response time may be comparable to that of (physical) HPC systems.

In order to take into account this important difference between physical and virtual environments, Foster suggests to evaluate the response time in terms of *probability of completion*, which is a stochastic function of time, and represents the probability that the job will be completed before that time. Note that the stochastic behavior mainly depends on the job submission time, whereas execution time is usually a deterministic value. So in a VC the probability of completion is a threshold function (it is zero before the value corresponding to execution time of actual task, and one after). In a typical HPC environment, which involves batch and queuing systems, the job submission time is stochastic and fairly long, thus leading to a global completion time higher than the one measured on the VC.

This phenomenon opens the way to a large adoption of the cloud approach, at least for middle- or small-dimension HPC applications, where the computation power loss due to the use of the cloud is more tolerable. In Jha et al. [9] and in the on-line discussion [13] it is well shown that the cloud approach could be very interesting for substituting the ecosystem of HPC clusters that are usually adopted for solving middle-dimension problems. This is a context in which the grid paradigm was never largely adopted because of the high startup overhead.

17.4.2 Supporting HPC in the Cloud

The above-presented analysis shows how the cloud approach has good chances to be widely adopted for HPC [32, 35, 38], even if there are limits one should be aware of, before trying to switch to virtualized systems. Moreover, the differences between "physical computing" and "virtual computing," along with their impact on performance evaluation, clearly show that common performance indexes, techniques, and tools for performance analysis and prediction should be suitably adapted to comply with the new computing paradigm.

To support HPC applications, a fundamental requirement from a cloud provider is that an adequate service-level agreement (SLA) is granted. For HPC applications, the SLA should be different from the ones currently offered for the most common uses of cloud systems, oriented at transactional Web applications. The SLA should offer guarantees useful for the HPC user to predict his application performance behavior and hence to give formal (or semi-formal) statements about the parameters involved. At the state of the art, cloud providers offer their SLAs in the form of a contract (hence in natural language, with no formal specification). Two interesting examples are Amazon EC2 (http://aws.amazon.com/ec2-sla/) and GoGrid (http://www.gogrid.com/legal/sla.php).

The first one (Amazon) stresses fault tolerance parameters (such as service uptime), offering guarantees about system availability. There are instead no guarantees about network behavior (for both internal and external network), except that it will "work" 95% of the time. Moreover, Amazon guarantees that the virtual machine instances will run using a dedicated memory (i.e., there will be no other VM allocated to on the physical machine using the same memory). This statement is particularly relevant for HPC users, because it is of great help for the performance predictability of applications.

On the other hand, GoGrid, in addition to the availability parameters, offers a clear set of guarantees on network parameters, as shown in Table 17.3. This kind of information is of great interest, even if the guaranteed network latency (order of milliseconds) is clearly unacceptable for HPC applications. GoGrid

TABLE 17.3. Service-Level Agreement of GoGrid Network

Parameter	Description	GoGrid SLA
Jitter	Variation in latency	< 0.5msec
Latency	Amount of time it takes for a packet to travel from one point to another	< 5 msec
Maximum jitter	Highest permissible jitter within a given period when there is no network outage	10 msec within any 15-min period
Network outage	Unscheduled period during which IP services are not useable due to capacity-constraints or hardware failures	None
Packet loss	Latency in excess of 10 seconds	< 0.1%

does not offer guarantees about the sharing of physical computing resources with other virtual machines.

In conclusion, even if the adoption of SLA could be (part of) a solution for HPC performance tuning, giving a clear reference for the offered virtual cluster performances, current solutions offer too generic SLA contracts or too poor values for the controlled parameters.

As regards performance measurement techniques and tools, along with their adaption for virtualized environments, it should be noted that very few performance-oriented services are offered by cloud providers or by third parties. Usually these services simply consist of more or less detailed performance monitoring tools, such as CloudWatch offered by Amazon, or CloudStatus, offered by Hyperic (and integrated in Amazon). These tools essentially measure the performance of the cloud internal or external network and should help the cloud user to tune his applications. In exactly the same way as SLAs, they can be useful only for the transactional applications that are the primary objective of cloud systems, since, at the state of the art, they do not offer any features to predict the behavior of long-running applications, such as HPC codes.

An interesting approach, although still experimental, is the one offered by solutions as C-meter [21] and PerfCloud [24], which offer frameworks that dynamically benchmark the target VMs or VCs offered by the cloud. The idea is to provide a benchmark-on-demand service to take into account the extreme variability of the cloud load and to evaluate frequently its actual state. The first framework [25] supports the GrenchMark benchmark (which generates synthetic workloads) and is oriented to Web applications. The second one, instead, supports many different benchmarks typical of the HPC environment (the above-mentioned NPB and MPP tests, the SkaMPI benchmark, etc.). More detailed, the PerfCloud project aims at providing performance evaluation and prediction services in grid-based clouds. Besides providing services for on-demand benchmarking of virtual clusters, the PerfCloud framework uses the benchmarking results to tune a simulator used for predict the performance of HPC applications.

17.5 SUMMARY AND CONCLUSIONS

The conclusions of this overview on performance-related issues of cloud for HPC are not particularly encouraging. From the analysis of existing work, a number of considerations arise. Here we will try to summarize those that in our opinion are the most relevant ones.

First of all, current cloud interconnects are simply not suitable for HPC uses. The performance of a gigabit or 10-gigabit Ethernet is very good for running workloads made up of monolithic tasks, but it is inadequate for the majority of HPC parallel tasks. Upgrading existing clouds so as to provide high-performance interconnects is not just an economic matter. Up until now, drivers for these interconnects are not supported by state-of-the-art virtual engines. And, as we have repeated many times in this chapter, virtual engines are an integral part of clouds.

Secondly, the SLAs that have proven to be extremely useful in different contexts have finally appeared in the commercial cloud field. This is a good starting point. But the problem is that their current formulation is (once again) completely inadequate to express a quality of service that could be of interest for HPC users. These need SLA defined in a more formal way, along with guarantees of particular parameters (essentially, low communication latency, even if associated to higher jitter values).

But maybe the most important of the issues discussed here is that the criteria for computing the cost of an application run do not encourage HPC users to resort to clouds. Commercial cloud providers try to give machines in exclusive use for computationally intensive tasks, and hence the cost to pay for this is proportional to the total duration of the run. This is natural, after all. But this choice penalizes the user that submits unoptimized applications, who pays even for the application idle time. And this, from his point of view, is unfair. Because an application well-optimized for a physical HPC system could likely be a non-optimized application in the virtual world of clouds (e.g., due to the low-performance interconnect), this is particularly disappointing. Furthermore, the mentioned problem makes it particularly difficult to estimate the cost of the run of an application (at least, of its first run).

We would like to conclude by pointing out that the HPC community has a lot of work to do in order to make cloud more useful for their needs. The use of virtualization and of leased computing resources is unstoppable and is an unavoidable technologic trend, at least due to the power savings that it implies. High-end HPC users would difficultly resort to clouds. Or, at least, they would not resort to present-day clouds. But the majority of "simple" HPC tasks could immediately profit from the scale economy that the cloud concept implies. It is up to the scientific community to "level the ground" to make cloud use simple and profitable for most HPC users. This requires the availability of more insight on the performance of virtual environments, the development of virtual-enabled drivers for high-speed interconnects, and a pervasive use of performance evaluation techniques. A successive step is the study and development of performance prediction tools, which have proved to be very useful in the "physical machines" world, even if they have never been in widespread use in the HPC community (maybe because up until now most users do not pay for their program inefficiencies). Performance prediction of virtual and cloud-based systems is indeed possible, and some of the authors of this chapter are already working on it [24], but a lot of research and development work is still necessary to have tools that could be used by the typical user without hassle.

REFERENCES

1. J. Sugerman, G. Venkitachalam, and B. H. Lim, Virtualizing I/O devices on VMware workstation's hosted virtual machine monitor, *USENIX Annual Technical Conference*, 2001.

2. Xen Hypervisor, http://xen.org/

3. VirtuaBox, http://www.virtualbox.org

4. B. Sotomayor, R. S. Montero, I. M. Llorente, and I. Foster , Capacity leasing in cloud systems using the OpenNebula engine, in *Workshop on Cloud Computing and its Applications 2008* (CCA08), October 2008, Online Publication.

5. Enormaly Inc, http://www.enomaly.com

6. D. Nurmi, R. Wolski, C. Grzegorczyk, G. Obertelli, S. Soman, L. Youseff, and D. Zagorodnov, The Eucalyptus open-source cloud-computing system, in *Proceedings of the 9th IEEE/ACM International Symposium on Cluster Computing and the Grid (CCGrid 2009)*, May 2009, pp. 124–131.

7. K. Keahey, I. T. Foster, T. Freeman, and X. Zhang, Virtual workspaces: Achieving quality of service and quality of life in the grid, *Scientific Programming*, 4(13):265–275, 2005.

8. P. M. Papadopoulos, M. J. Katz, and G. Bruno, NPACI Rocks: Tools and techniques for easily deploying manageable linux clusters, *Concurrency and Computation: Practice and Experience*, 7-8(15):707–725, 2003.

9. S. Jha, A. Merzky, and G. Fox, Using clouds to provide grids with higher levels of abstraction and explicit support for usage modes, *Concurrency and Computation: Practice Experiences*, 21(8):1087–1108, 2009.

10. J. Myerson, Cloud Computing Versus Grid Computing, *IBM*, 2009, http://www.ibm.com/developerworks/web/library/wa-cloudGrid/

11. I. Foster, A critique of "Using Clouds to Provide Grids...", http://ianfoster.typepad.com/blog/2008/09/a-critique-of-u.html, September 2008.

12. T. Rings, G. Caryer , J. Gallop, J. Grabowski, T. Kovacikova, S. Schulz, and I. Stokes-Rees, Grid and cloud computing: Opportunities for integration with the next generation network, *Journal of Grid Computing*, 2009.

13. I. Foster, What's Faster—A Supercomputer or EC2?, http://ianfoster.typepad.com/blog/2009/08/whats-fastera-supercomputer-or-ec2.html, accessed September 2009.

14. GridTalk-Grid Briefings, Grids and clouds: The new computing, http://www.olivier-art.com/gridTalk/Documents/GridBriefing_Grids_and_clouds.pdf, January 2009.

15. L. Cherkasova, D. Gupta, E. Ryabinkin, R. Kurakin, V. Dobretsov, and A. Vahdat, Optimizing grid site manager performance with virtual machines, in *Proceedings of the 3rd USENIX Workshop on Real Large Distributed Systems (WORLDS '06)*, Seattle, November 5, 2006.

16. I. T. Foster, T. Freeman, K. Keahey, D. Scheftner, B. Sotomayor, and X. Zhang, Virtual clusters for grid communities, in *Proceedings of Cluster Computing and Grid*, IEEE Computer Society, 2006, pp. 513–520.

17. L. Youseff, R. Wolski, B. Gorda, and C. Krintz, Paravirtualization for HPC Systems, in *Proceedings of ISPA Workshops*, Lecture Notes in Computer Science, Vol. 4331, Springer, 2006, pp. 474–486.

18. E. Walker, Benchmarking Amazon ec2, *USENIX Login*, **33**(5):18–23, 2008.

19. W. Voorsluys, J. Broberg, S. Venugopal, and R. Buyya, Cost of virtual machine live migration in clouds: A performance evaluation, in *Proceedings of the First International Conference on Cloud Computing*, CloudCom 2009, Beijing, China, December 1–4, 2009.

20. J. Napper and P. Bientinesi, Can cloud computing reach the top500?, in *Proceedings of the Combined Workshops on Unconventional High Performance Computing Workshop Plus Memory Access Workshop*, May 2009.

21. S. Ostermann, A. Iosup, N. Yigitbasi, R. Prodan, T. Fahringer, and D. Epema, An Early Performance Analysis of Cloud Computing Services for Scientific Computing, TU Delft/PDS Technical Report PDS-2008–12, December 2008.

22. C. Evangelinos and C. N. Hill, Cloud computing for parallel scientific hpc applications: Feasibility of running coupled atmosphere–ocean climate models on amazon's ec2, Cloud Computing and Its Applications, October 2008.

23. E. Deelman, G. Singh, M. Livny, B. Berriman, and J. Good, The cost of doing science on the cloud: The Montage example, in *Proceedings of the 2008 ACM/IEEE Conference on Supercomputing*, November 2008, pp. 1–12.

24. E. P. Mancini, M. Rak, and U. Villano: PerfCloud: Grid Services for performance-oriented development of cloud computing applications, in *Proceedings of WETICE 2009*, 2009, pp. 201–206.

25. N. Yigitbasi, A. Iosup, D. Epema, and S. Ostermann, C-Meter: A Framework for Performance Analysis of Computing Clouds, in *Proceedings of the 9th IEEE/ACM International Symposium on Cluster Computing and the Grid*, **53**(4), 2009, pp. 472–477.

26. B. Rochwerger, J. Caceres, R. S. Montero, D. Breitgand, E. Elmroth, A. Galis, E. Levy, I. M. Llorente, K. Nagin, and Y. Wolfsthal, The RESERVOIR model and architecture for open federated cloud computing, *IBM Systems Journal*, **53**(4):535–545, 2009.

27. K. Keahey, and T. Freeman, Contextualization: Providing one-click virtual clusters, in *eScience 2008*, Indianapolis, IN, December 2008.

28. Israeli Association of Grid Technology, Comparing Grid and Cloud Computing, http://www.Grid.org.il/_Uploads/dbsAttachedFiles/Comparing-Cloud-Grid.pdf, June 20, 2008.

29. R. Buyya, D. Abramson, and J. Giddy, A case for economy grid architecture for service-oriented grid computing, in *Proceedings of the IPDPS, 10th IEEE International Heterogeneous Computing Workshop*, San Francisco, April 23, 2001, p. 20083.1, IEEE Computer Society.

30. R. Buyya, D. Abramson, and J. Giddy, Nimrod-G: An architecture for a resource management and scheduling system in a global computational grid, in *Proceedings of the 4th International Conference on High Performance Computing in Asia-Pacific Region*, Beijing, China, May 2000.

31. R. Buyya, D. Abramson, J. Giddy, and H. Stockinger, Economic models for resource management and scheduling in grid computing, *Concurrency and Computation: Practice and Experience*, **14**(13–15):1507–1542, 2002.

32. G. M. Christina Hoffa and J. G. Berriman, On the Use of Cloud Computing for Scientific Workflows, http://pegasus.isi.edu/publications/2008/Hoffa-CloudComputing.pdf

33. T. Sterling and D. Stark, A high-performance computing forecast: Partly cloudy, *Computing in Science and Engineering*, **11**(4):42–49, 2009.

34. B. Carpenter, IPv6 and the Future of the Internet, *The Internet Society Member Briefing*, July 23, 2001. http://www.isoc.org/briefings/001/

35. J. Brandt, A. Gentile, J. Mayo, P. Pebay, D. Roe, D. Thompson, and M. Wong, Resource monitoring and management with OVIS to enable HPC in cloud computing environments, in *Proceedings of the 2009 IEEE International Symposium on Parallel & Distributed Processing* (IPDPS), IPDPS, May, 2009, pp. 1–8.

36. W. Sobel, S. Subramanyam, A. Sucharitakul, J. Nguyen, H. Wong, A. Klepchukov, S. Patil, A. Fox, and D. Patterson, Cloudstone: Multi-platform, multi-language benchmark and measurement tools for web 2.0, in *Proceedings of Cloud Computing and Its Applications*, 2008.

37. J. Ekanayake and G. Fox, High performance parallel computing with clouds and cloud technologies, in *Proceedings of the First International Conference on Cloud Computing*, CloudCom 2009, Beijing, China, December 1–4, 2009.

38. Y. Tanaka, H. Nakada, S. Sekiguchi, T. Suzumura, and S. Matsuoka, Ninf-G: A reference implementation of RPC-based programming middleware for grid computing, *Journal of Grid Computing*, **1**(1):41–51, 2003.

39. M. Armbrust, A. Fox, R. Griffith, A. D. Joseph, R. H. Katz, A. Konwinski, G. Lee, D. A. Patterson, A. Rabkin, I. Stoica, and M. Zaharia, Above the Clouds: A Berkeley View of Cloud Computing, Technical Report, TR. UCB/EECS-2009–28, EECS Department, University of California, Berkeley, February 2009.

40. M. D. de Assuncao, A. di Costanzo, and R. Buyya, Evaluating the cost-benefit of using cloud computing to extend the capacity of clusters, in *Proceedings of the 18th ACM international Symposium on High Performance Distributed Computing (HPDC '09)*, June 2009, pp. 141–150.

PART V

APPLICATIONS

CHAPTER 18

BEST PRACTICES IN ARCHITECTING CLOUD APPLICATIONS IN THE AWS CLOUD

JINESH VARIA

18.1 INTRODUCTION

For several years, software architects have discovered and implemented several concepts and best practices to build highly scalable applications. In today's "era of tera," these concepts are even more applicable because of ever-growing datasets, unpredictable traffic patterns, and the demand for faster response times. This chapter will reinforce and reiterate some of these traditional concepts and discuss how they may evolve in the context of cloud computing. It will also discuss some unprecedented concepts, such as elasticity, that have emerged due to the dynamic nature of the cloud.

This chapter is targeted toward *cloud architects* who are gearing up to move an enterprise-class application from a fixed physical environment to a virtualized cloud environment. The focus of this chapter is to highlight concepts, principles, and best practices in creating new *cloud applications* or migrating existing applications to the cloud.

18.2 BACKGROUND

As a cloud architect, it is important to understand the benefits of cloud computing. In this section, you will learn some of the business and technical benefits of cloud computing and different Amazon Web services (AWS) available today.

Cloud Computing: Principles and Paradigms,   Edited by Rajkumar Buyya, James Broberg and Andrzej Goscinski   Copyright © 2011 John Wiley & Sons, Inc.

18.2.1 Business Benefits of Cloud Computing

There are some clear business benefits to building applications in the cloud. A few of these are listed here:

Almost Zero Upfront Infrastructure Investment. If you have to build a large-scale system, it may cost a fortune to invest in real estate, physical security, hardware (racks, servers, routers, backup power supplies), hardware management (power management, cooling), and operations personnel. Because of the high upfront costs, the project would typically require several rounds of management approvals before the project could even get started. Now, with utility-style cloud computing, there is no fixed cost or startup cost.

Just-in-Time Infrastructure. In the past, if your application became popular and your systems or your infrastructure did not scale, you became a victim of your own success. Conversely, if you invested heavily and did not get popular, you became a victim of your failure. By deploying applications in-the-cloud with just-in-time self-provisioning, you do not have to worry about pre-procuring capacity for large-scale systems. This increases agility, lowers risk, and lowers operational cost because you scale only as you grow and only pay for what you use.

More Efficient Resource Utilization. System administrators usually worry about procuring hardware (when they run out of capacity) and higher infrastructure utilization (when they have excess and idle capacity). With the cloud, they can manage resources more effectively and efficiently by having the applications request and relinquish resources on-demand.

Usage-Based Costing. With utility-style pricing, you are billed only for the infrastructure that has been used. You are not paying for allocated infrastructure but instead for unused infrastructure. This adds a new dimension to cost savings. You can see immediate cost savings (sometimes as early as your next month's bill) when you deploy an optimization patch to update your cloud application. For example, if a caching layer can reduce your data requests by 70%, the savings begin to accrue immediately and you see the reward right in the next bill. Moreover, if you are building platforms on the top of the cloud, you can pass on the same flexible, variable usage-based cost structure to your own customers.

Reduced Time to Market. Parallelization is one of the great ways to speed up processing. If one compute-intensive or data-intensive job that can be run in parallel takes 500 hours to process on one machine, with cloud architectures [1], it would be possible to spawn and launch 500 instances and process the same job in 1 hour. Having available an elastic infrastructure provides the application with the ability to exploit parallelization in a cost-effective manner reducing time to market.

18.2.2 Technical Benefits of Cloud Computing

Some of the technical benefits of cloud computing includes:

Automation—"Scriptable Infrastructure": You can create repeatable build and deployment systems by leveraging programmable (API-driven) infrastructure.

Auto-scaling: You can scale your applications up and down to match your unexpected demand without any human intervention. Auto-scaling encourages automation and drives more efficiency.

Proactive Scaling: Scale your application up and down to meet your anticipated demand with proper planning understanding of your traffic patterns so that you keep your costs low while scaling.

More Efficient Development Life Cycle: Production systems may be easily cloned for use as development and test environments. Staging environments may be easily promoted to production.

Improved Testability: Never run out of hardware for testing. Inject and automate testing at every stage during the development process. You can spawn up an "instant test lab" with preconfigured environments only for the duration of testing phase.

Disaster Recovery and Business Continuity: The cloud provides a lower cost option for maintaining a fleet of DR servers and data storage. With the cloud, you can take advantage of geo-distribution and replicate the environment in other location within minutes.

"Overflow" the Traffic to the Cloud: With a few clicks and effective load balancing tactics, you can create a complete overflow-proof application by routing excess traffic to the cloud.

18.2.3 Understanding the Amazon Web Services Cloud

The Amazon Web Services (AWS) cloud provides a highly reliable and scalable infrastructure for deploying Web-scale solutions, with minimal support and administration costs, and more flexibility than you've come to expect from your own infrastructure, either on-premise or at a datacenter facility. AWS offers variety of infrastructure services today. The diagram below will introduce you to the AWS terminology and help you understand how your application can interact with different Amazon Web Services (Figure 18.1) and how different services interact with each other. Amazon Elastic Compute Cloud (Amazon EC2)[2] is a Web service that provides resizable compute capacity in the cloud. You can bundle the operating system, application software, and associated configuration settings into an Amazon machine image (AMI). You can then use these AMIs to provision multiple virtualized instances as well as decommission them using simple Web service calls to scale capacity up and down quickly, as your capacity requirement changes. You can purchase either (a) on-demand

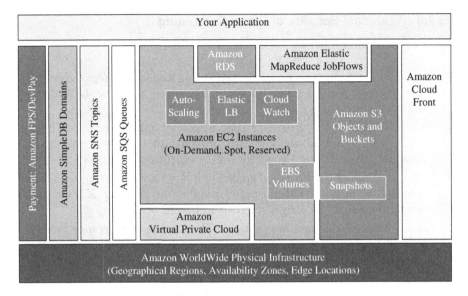

FIGURE 18.1. Amazon Web Services.

instances, in which you pay for the instances by the hour, or (b) reserved instances, in which you pay a low, one-time payment and receive a lower usage rate to run the instance than with an on-demand instance or spot instances where you can bid for unused capacity and further reduce your cost. Instances can be launched in one or more geographical regions. Each region has multiple availability zones. Availability zones are distinct locations that are engineered to be insulated from failures in other availability zones and provide inexpensive, low-latency network connectivity to other availability zones in the same region.

Elastic IP addresses allow you to allocate a static IP address and programmatically assign it to an instance. You can enable monitoring on an Amazon EC2 instance using Amazon CloudWatch [3] in order to gain visibility into resource utilization, operational performance, and overall demand patterns (including metrics such as CPU utilization, disk reads and writes, and network traffic). You can create an *auto-scaling group* using the auto-scaling feature [4] to automatically scale your capacity on certain conditions based on metric that Amazon CloudWatch collects. You can also distribute incoming traffic by creating an *elastic load balancer* using the Elastic Load Balancing service [5]. Amazon Elastic Block Storage (EBS)[6] *volumes* provide network-attached persistent storage to Amazon EC2 instances. Point-in-time consistent *snapshots* of EBS volumes can be created and stored on Amazon Simple Storage Service (Amazon S3)[7].

Amazon S3 is highly durable and distributed data store. With a simple Web services interface, you can store and retrieve large amounts of data as *objects* in *buckets* (containers) at any time, from anywhere on the Web using standard

HTTP verbs. Copies of objects can be distributed and cached at 14 *edge locations* around the world by creating a *distribution* using Amazon Cloud-Front service [8], a Web service for content delivery (static or streaming content). Amazon SimpleDB[9] is a Web service that provides the core functionality of a database—real-time lookup and simple querying of structured data—without the operational complexity. You can organize the dataset into *domains* and can run queries across all of the data stored in a particular domain. Domains are collections of *items* that are described by *attribute–value pairs*. Amazon Relational Database Service (Amazon RDS)[10] provides an easy way to set up, operate, and scale a relational database in the cloud. You can launch a *DB instance* and get access to a full-featured MySQL database and not worry about common database administration tasks like backups, patch management, and so on.

Amazon Simple Queue Service (Amazon SQS)[11] is a reliable, highly scalable, hosted distributed queue for storing *messages* as they travel between computers and application components.

Amazon Elastic MapReduce [12] provides a hosted Hadoop framework running on the web-scale infrastructure of Amazon Elastic Compute Cloud (Amazon EC2) and Amazon Simple Storage Service (Amazon S3) and allows you to create customized *JobFlows*. JobFlow is a sequence of MapReduce *steps*.

Amazon Simple Notifications Service (Amazon SNS) provides a simple way to notify applications or people from the cloud by creating *Topics* and using a publish-subscribe protocol.[12]

Amazon Virtual Private Cloud (Amazon VPC)[13] allows you to extend your corporate network into a private cloud contained within AWS. Amazon VPC uses an IPSec tunnel mode that enables you to create a secure connection between a gateway in your data center and a gateway in AWS.

AWS also offers various payment and billing services [14] that leverages Amazon's payment infrastructure.

All AWS infrastructure services offer utility-style pricing that require no long-term commitments or contracts. For example, you pay by the hour for Amazon EC2 instance usage and pay by the gigabyte for storage and data transfer in the case of Amazon S3. More information about each of these services and their pay-as-you-go pricing is available on the AWS Web site.

18.3 CLOUD CONCEPTS

The cloud reinforces some old concepts of building highly scalable Internet architectures [15] and introduces some new concepts that entirely change the way applications are built and deployed. Hence, when you progress from concept to implementation, you might get the feeling that "Everything's changed, yet nothing's different." The cloud changes several processes, patterns, practices, and philosophies and reinforces some traditional service-oriented architectural principles that you have learned because they are even more important than before. In this section, you will see some of those new cloud concepts and reiterated SOA concepts.

Traditional applications were built with some pre-conceived mindsets that made economic and architectural-sense at the time they were developed. The cloud brings some new philosophies that you need to understand, and these are discussed below.

18.3.1 Building Scalable Architectures

It is critical to build a scalable architecture in order to take advantage of a scalable infrastructure.

The cloud is designed to provide conceptually infinite scalability. However, you cannot leverage all that scalability in infrastructure if your architecture is not scalable. Both have to work together. You will have to identify the monolithic components and bottlenecks in your architecture, identify the areas where you cannot leverage the on-demand provisioning capabilities in your architecture, and work to *refactor* your application in order to leverage the scalable infrastructure and take advantage of the cloud.

Characteristics of a truly scalable application:

- Increasing resources results in a proportional increase in performance.
- A scalable service is capable of handling heterogeneity.
- A scalable service is operationally efficient.
- A scalable service is resilient.
- A scalable service should become more cost effective when it grows (cost per unit reduces as the number of units increases).

These are things that should become an inherent part of your application; and if you design your architecture with the above characteristics in mind, then both your architecture and infrastructure will work together to give you the scalability you are looking for.

18.3.2 Understanding Elasticity

Figure 18.2 illustrates the different approaches a cloud architect can take to scale their applications to meet the demand.

Scale-Up Approach. Not worrying about the scalable application architecture and investing heavily in larger and more powerful computers (vertical scaling) to accommodate the demand. This approach usually works to a point, but either it could cost a fortune (see "Huge capital expenditure" in Figure 18.2) or the demand could outgrow capacity before the new "big iron" is deployed (see "You just lost your customers" in diagram).

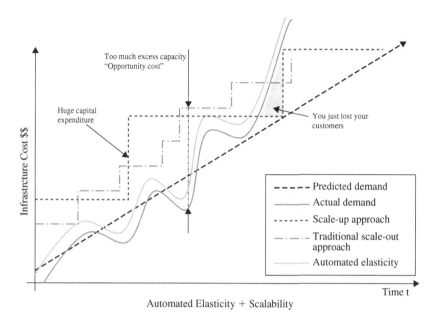

FIGURE 18.2. Automated elasticity.

The Traditional Scale-Out Approach. Creating an architecture that scales horizontally and investing in infrastructure in small chunks. Most of the businesses and large-scale Web applications follow this pattern by distributing their application components, federating their datasets, and employing a service-oriented design. This approach is often more effective than a scale-up approach. However, this still requires predicting the demand at regular intervals and then deploying infrastructure in chunks to meet the demand. This often leads to excess capacity ("burning cash") and constant manual monitoring ("burning human cycles"). Moreover, it usually does not work if the application is a victim of a viral fire (often referred to as the Slashdot Effect [16]).

Note: Both approaches have initial startup costs, and both approaches are reactive in nature.

Traditional infrastructure generally necessitates predicting the amount of computing resources your application will use over a period of several years. If you underestimate, your applications will not have the horsepower to handle unexpected traffic, potentially resulting in customer dissatisfaction. If you overestimate, you're wasting money with superfluous resources.

The on-demand and elastic nature of *the cloud approach* (automated elasticity), however, enables the infrastructure to be closely aligned (as it expands and contracts) with the actual demand, thereby increasing overall utilization and reducing cost.

Elasticity is one of the fundamental properties of the cloud. Elasticity is the power to scale computing resources up and down easily and with minimal friction. It is important to understand that elasticity will ultimately drive most of the benefits of the cloud. As a cloud architect, you need to internalize this concept and work it into your application architecture in order to take maximum benefit of the cloud.

Traditionally, applications have been built for fixed, rigid, and pre-provisioned infrastructure. Companies never had the need to provision and install servers on a daily basis. As a result, most software architectures do not address the rapid deployment or reduction of hardware. Since the provisioning time and upfront investment for acquiring new resources was too high, software architects never invested time and resources in optimizing for hardware utilization. It was acceptable if the hardware on which the application is running was underutilized. The notion of "elasticity" within an architecture was overlooked because the idea of having new resources in minutes was not possible.

With the cloud, this mindset needs to change. Cloud computing streamlines the process of acquiring the necessary resources; there is no longer any need to place orders ahead of time and to hold unused hardware captive. Instead, cloud architects can request what they need mere minutes before they need it or automate the procurement process, taking advantage of the vast scale and rapid response time of the cloud. The same is applicable to releasing the unneeded or underutilized resources when you don't need them. If you cannot embrace the change and implement elasticity in your application architecture, you might not be able to take the full advantage of the cloud. As a cloud architect, you should think creatively and think about ways you can implement elasticity in your application. For example, infrastructure that used to run daily nightly builds and performs regression and unit tests every night at 2:00 AM for two hours (often termed as the "QA/Build box") was sitting idle for rest of the day. Now, with elastic infrastructure, one can run nightly builds on boxes that are "alive" and being paid for only for 2 hours in the night. Likewise, an internal trouble ticketing Web application that always used to run on peak capacity (5 servers 24 × 7 × 365) to meet the demand during the day can now be provisioned to run on-demand (five servers from 9 AM to 5 PM and two servers for 5 PM to 9 AM) based on the traffic pattern.

Designing intelligent elastic cloud architectures, so that infrastructure runs only when you need it, is an art in itself. Elasticity should be one of the architectural design requirements or a system property. The questions that you need to ask are as follows: What components or layers in my application architecture can become elastic? What will it take to make that component *elastic*? What will be the impact of implementing elasticity to my overall system architecture?

In the next section, you will see specific techniques to implement elasticity in your applications. To effectively leverage the cloud benefits, it is important to architect with this mindset.

18.3.3 Not Fearing Constraints

When you decide to move your applications to the cloud and try to map your system specifications to those available in the cloud, you will notice that cloud might not have the exact specification of the resource that you have on-premise. For example, "Cloud does not provide X amount of RAM in a server" or "My database needs to have more IOPS than what I can get in a single instance."

You should understand that cloud provides *abstract resources* that become powerful when you combine them with the on-demand provisioning model. You should not be afraid and constrained when using cloud resources because it is important to understand that even if you might not get an exact replica of your hardware in the cloud environment, you have the ability to get more of those resources in the cloud to compensate that need.

For example, if the cloud does not provide you with exact or greater amount of RAM in a server, try using a distributed cache like memcached [17] or partitioning your data across multiple servers. If your databases need more IOPS and it does not directly map to that of the cloud, there are several recommendations that you can choose from depending on your type of data and use case. If it is a read-heavy application, you can distribute the read load across a fleet of synchronized slaves. Alternatively, you can use a *sharding* [18] algorithm that routes the data where it needs to be or you can use various database clustering solutions.

In retrospect, when you combine the on-demand provisioning capabilities with the flexibility, you will realize that apparent constraints can actually be broken in ways that will actually improve the scalability and overall performance of the system.

18.3.4 Virtual Administration

The advent of cloud has changed the role of System Administrator to a "Virtual System Administrator." This simply means that daily tasks performed by these administrators have now become even more interesting as the administrators learn more about applications and decide what's best for the business as a whole. The System Administrator no longer has a need to provision servers and install software and wire up network devices since all of that grunt work is replaced by few clicks and command line calls. The cloud encourages automation because the infrastructure is programmable. System administrators need to move up the technology stack and learn how to manage abstract cloud resources using scripts.

Likewise, the role of Database Administrator is changed into a "Virtual Database Administrator" (DBA) in which he/she manages resources through a Web-based console, executes scripts that add new capacity programmatically if the database hardware runs out of capacity, and automates the day-to-day processes. The virtual DBA has to now learn new deployment methods (virtual machine images), embrace new models (query parallelization, geo-redundancy, and asynchronous replication [19]), rethink the architectural approach for data (sharding [20], horizontal partitioning [15], federating [21]), and leverage different storage options available in the cloud for different types of datasets.

In the traditional enterprise company, application developers may not work closely with the network administrators and network administrators may not have a clue about the application. As a result, several possible optimizations in the network layer and application architecture layer are overlooked. With the cloud, the two roles have merged into one to some extent. When architecting future applications, companies need to encourage more cross-pollination of knowledge between the two roles and understand that they are merging.

18.4   CLOUD BEST PRACTICES

In this section, you will learn about best practices that will help you build an application in the cloud.

18.4.1   Design for Failure and Nothing Will Fail

Rule of Thumb: Be a pessimist when designing architectures in the cloud; assume things will fail. In other words, always design, implement, and deploy for automated recovery from failure.

In particular, assume that your hardware *will* fail. Assume that outages *will* occur. Assume that some disaster *will* strike your application. Assume that you *will* be slammed with more than the expected number of requests per second some day. Assume that with time your application software will fail too. By being a pessimist, you end up thinking about recovery strategies during design time, which helps in designing an overall system better.

If you realize that things fail over time and incorporate that thinking into your architecture, as well as build mechanisms to handle that failure before disaster strikes to deal with a scalable infrastructure, you will end up creating a fault-tolerant architecture that is optimized for the cloud.

Questions that you need to ask: What happens if a node in your system fails? How do you recognize that failure? How do I replace that node? What kind of scenarios do I have to plan for? What are my single points of failure? If a load balancer is sitting in front of an array of application servers, what if that load balancer fails? If there are master and slaves in your architecture, what if the master node fails? How does the failover occur and how is a new slave instantiated and brought into sync with the master?

Just like designing for hardware failure, you have to also design for software failure. Questions that you need to ask: What happens to my application if the dependent services changes its interface? What if downstream service times out or returns an exception? What if the cache keys grow beyond memory limit of an instance?

Build mechanisms to handle that failure. For example, the following strategies can help in event of failure:

1. Have a coherent backup and restore strategy for your data and automate it.
2. Build process threads that resume on reboot.
3. Allow the state of the system to re-sync by reloading messages from queues.
4. Keep preconfigured and preoptimized virtual images to support strategies 2 and 3 on launch/boot.
5. Avoid in-memory sessions or stateful user context; move that to data stores.

Good cloud architectures should be impervious to reboots and re-launches. In GrepTheWeb (discussed in the next section), by using a combination of Amazon SQS and Amazon SimpleDB, the overall controller architecture is very resilient to the types of failures listed in this section. For instance, if the instance on which controller thread was running dies, it can be brought up and resume the previous state as if nothing had happened. This was accomplished by creating a preconfigured Amazon machine image, which, when launched, dequeues all the messages from the Amazon SQS queue and reads their states from an Amazon SimpleDB domain on reboot.

Designing with an assumption that underlying hardware will fail will prepare you for the future when it actually fails.

This design principle will help you design operations-friendly applications, as also highlighted in Hamilton's paper [19]. If you can extend this principle to proactively measure and balance load dynamically, you might be able to deal with variance in network and disk performance that exists due to the multi-tenant nature of the cloud.

AWS-Specific Tactics for Implementing This Best Practice

1. Failover gracefully using Elastic IPs: Elastic IP is a static IP that is dynamically remappable. You can quickly remap and failover to another set of servers so that your traffic is routed to the new servers. It works great when you want to upgrade from old to new versions or in case of hardware failures.
2. Utilize multiple availability zones: Availability zones are conceptually like logical datacenters. By deploying your architecture to multiple availability zones, you can ensure high availability.
3. Maintain an Amazon Machine Image so that you can restore and clone environments very easily in a different availability zone; maintain multiple database slaves across availability zones and set up hot replication.

4. Utilize Amazon CloudWatch (or various real-time open source monitoring tools) to get more visibility and take appropriate actions in case of hardware failure or performance degradation. Set up an Auto scaling group to maintain a fixed fleet size so that it replaces unhealthy Amazon EC2 instances by new ones.

5. Utilize Amazon EBS and set up cron jobs so that incremental snapshots are automatically uploaded to Amazon S3 and data are persisted independent of your instances.

6. Utilize Amazon RDS and set the retention period for backups, so that it can perform automated backups.

18.4.2 Decouple your Components

The cloud reinforces the SOA design principle that *the more loosely coupled the components of the system, the bigger and better it scales.*

The key is to build components that do not have tight dependencies on each other, so that if one component were to die (fail), sleep (not respond), or remain busy (slow to respond) for some reason, the other components in the system are built so as to continue to work as if no failure is happening. In essence, loose coupling isolates the various layers and components of your application so that each component interacts asynchronously with the others and treats them as a "black box." For example, in the case of Web application architecture, you can isolate the app server from the Web server and from the database. The app server does not know about your Web server and vice versa; this gives decoupling between these layers, and there are no dependencies code-wise nor functional perspectives. In the case of batch-processing architecture, you can create *asynchronous* components that are independent of each other.

Questions you need to ask: Which business component or feature could be isolated from current monolithic application and can run stand-alone separately? And then how can I add more instances of that component without breaking my current system and at the same time serve more users? How much effort will it take to encapsulate the component so that it can interact with other components asynchronously?

Decoupling your components, building *asynchronous* systems, and scaling horizontally become very important in the context of the cloud. It will not only allow you to scale out by adding more instances of same component but will also allow you to design innovative hybrid models in which a few components continue to run in on-premise while other components can take advantage of the cloudscale and use the cloud for additional compute-power and bandwidth. That way with minimal effort, you can "overflow" excess traffic to the cloud by implementing smart load balancing tactics.

One can build a loosely coupled system using *messaging queues*. If a queue/buffer is used to connect any two components together (as shown in Figure 18.3 under Loose Coupling), it can support concurrency, high availability, and load

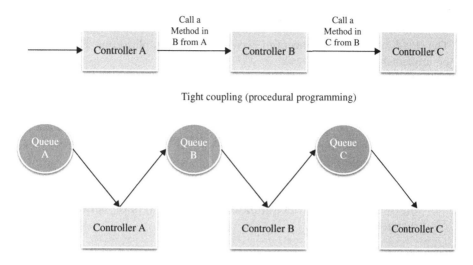

Tight coupling (procedural programming)

Loose coupling (independent phases using queues)

FIGURE 18.3. Decoupling components using Queues.

spikes. As a result, the overall system continues to perform even if parts of components are momentarily unavailable. If one component dies or becomes temporarily unavailable, the system will buffer the messages and get them processed when the component comes back up.

You will see heavy use of queues in GrepTheWeb architecture epitomized in the next section. In GrepTheWeb, if lots of requests suddenly reach the server (an Internet-induced overload situation) or the processing of regular expressions takes a longer time than the median (slow response rate of a component), the Amazon SQS queues buffer the requests in a durable fashion so that those delays do not affect other components.

AWS Specific Tactics for Implementing This Best Practice

1. Use Amazon SQS to isolate components [22].
2. Use Amazon SQS as buffers between components [22].
3. Design every component such that it expose a service interface and is responsible for its own scalability in all appropriate dimensions and interacts with other components asynchronously.
4. Bundle the logical construct of a component into an Amazon Machine Image so that it can be deployed more often.
5. Make your applications as stateless as possible. Store session state outside of component (in Amazon SimpleDB, if appropriate).

18.4.3 Implement Elasticity

The cloud brings a new concept of elasticity in your applications. Elasticity can be implemented in three ways:

1. *Proactive Cyclic Scaling.* Periodic scaling that occurs at fixed interval (daily, weekly, monthly, quarterly).
2. *Proactive Event-Based Scaling.* Scaling just when you are expecting a big surge of traffic requests due to a scheduled business event (new product launch, marketing campaigns).
3. *Auto-scaling Based on Demand.* By using a monitoring service, your system can send triggers to take appropriate actions so that it scales up or down based on metrics (utilization of the servers or network i/o, for instance).

To implement elasticity, one has to first automate the deployment process and streamline the configuration and build process. This will ensure that the system can scale without any human intervention.

This will result in immediate cost benefits as the overall utilization is increased by ensuring your resources are closely aligned with demand rather than potentially running servers that are underutilized.

Automate your Infrastructure. One of the most important benefits of using a cloud environment is the ability to use the cloud's APIs to automate your deployment process. It is recommended that you take the time to create an automated deployment process early on during the migration process and not wait until the end. Creating an automated and repeatable deployment process will help reduce errors and facilitate an efficient and scalable update process.

To automate the deployment process:

- Create a library of "recipes"—that is, small frequently used scripts (for installation and configuration).
- Manage the configuration and deployment process using agents bundled inside an AMI.
- Bootstrap your instances.

Bootstrap Your Instances. Let your instances ask you a question at boot: "*Who am I and what is my role?*" Every instance should have a role ("DB server," "app server," "slave server" in the case of a Web application) to play in the environment. This role may be passed in as an argument during launch that instructs the AMI when instantiated the steps to take after it has booted. On boot, instances should grab the necessary resources (code, scripts, configuration) based on the role and "attach" itself to a cluster to serve its function.

Benefits of bootstrapping your instances:

1. It re-creates the (Dev, staging, Production) environment with few clicks and minimal effort.
2. It affords more control over your abstract cloud-based resources.
3. It reduces human-induced deployment errors.
4. It creates a self-healing and self-discoverable environment which is more resilient to hardware failure.

AWS-Specific Tactics to Automate Your Infrastructure

1. Define auto-scaling groups for different clusters using the Amazon auto-scaling feature in Amazon EC2.
2. Monitor your system metrics (CPU, memory, disk I/O, network I/O) using Amazon CloudWatch and take appropriate actions (launching new AMIs dynamically using the auto-scaling service) or send notifications.
3. Store and retrieve machine configuration information dynamically: Utilize Amazon SimpleDB to fetch config data during the boot-time of an instance (e.g., database connection strings). SimpleDB may also be used to store information about an instance such as its IP address, machine name, and role.
4. Design a build process such that it dumps the latest builds to a bucket in Amazon S3; download the latest version of an application from during system startup.
5. Invest in building resource management tools (automated scripts, preconfigured images) or use smart open source configuration management tools like Chef [23], Puppet [24], CFEngine [25], or Genome [26].
6. Bundle Just Enough Operating System (JeOS [27]) and your software dependencies into an Amazon Machine Image so that it is easier to manage and maintain. Pass configuration files or parameters at launch time and retrieve user data [28] and instance metadata after launch.
7. Reduce bundling and launch time by booting from Amazon EBS volumes [29] and attaching multiple Amazon EBS volumes to an instance. Create snapshots of common volumes and share snapshots [30] among accounts wherever appropriate.
8. Application components should not assume health or location of hardware it is running on. For example, dynamically attach the IP address of a new node to the cluster. Automatically failover to the new cloned instance in case of a failure.

18.4.4 Think Parallel

The cloud makes parallelization effortless. Whether it is requesting data from the cloud, storing data to the cloud, or processing data (or executing jobs) in the cloud, as a cloud architect you need to internalize the concept of parallelization when designing architectures in the cloud. It is advisable to not only implement parallelization wherever possible but also automate it because the cloud allows you to create a repeatable process every easily.

When it comes to accessing (retrieving and storing) data, the cloud is designed to handle massively parallel operations. In order to achieve maximum performance and throughput, you should leverage *request parallelization*. Multi-threading your requests by using multiple concurrent threads will store or fetch the data faster than requesting it sequentially. Hence, wherever possible, the processes of a cloud application should be made thread-safe through a share-nothing philosophy and leverage multi-threading.

When it comes to processing or executing requests in the cloud, it becomes even more important to leverage parallelization. A general best practice, in the case of a Web application, is to distribute the incoming requests across multiple Web servers using load balancer. In the case of a batch processing application, your master node can spawn up multiple slave worker nodes that process a task in parallel (as in distributed processing frameworks like Hadoop [31]).

The beauty of the cloud shines when you combine elasticity and parallelization. Your cloud application can bring up a cluster of compute instances that are provisioned within minutes with just a few API calls, perform a job by executing tasks in parallel, store the results, and terminate all the instances. The GrepTheWeb application discussed in the next section is one such example.

AWS Specific Tactics for Parallelization

1. Multi-thread your Amazon S3 requests as detailed in a best practices paper [32] [62].
2. Multi-thread your Amazon SimpleDB GET and BATCHPUT requests [33–35].
3. Create a JobFlow using the Amazon Elastic MapReduce Service for each of your daily batch processes (indexing, log analysis, etc.) which will compute the job in parallel and save time.
4. Use the Elastic Load Balancing service and spread your load across multiple Web app servers *dynamically.*

18.4.5 Keep Dynamic Data Closer to the Compute and Static Data Closer to the End User

In general it's a good practice to keep your data as close as possible to your compute or processing elements to reduce latency. In the cloud, this best practice is even more relevant and important because you often have to deal with Internet latencies. Moreover, in the cloud, you are paying for bandwidth in and out of the cloud by the gigabyte of data transfer, and the cost can add up very quickly.

If a large quantity of data that need to be processed resides outside of the cloud, it might be cheaper and faster to "ship" and transfer the data to the cloud first and then perform the computation. For example, in the case of a data warehousing application, it is advisable to move the dataset to the cloud and then perform parallel queries against the dataset. In the case of Web applications that store and retrieve data from relational databases, it is advisable to move the database as well as the app server into the cloud all at once.

If the data are generated in the cloud, then the applications that consume the data should also be deployed in the cloud so that they can take advantage of in-cloud free data transfer and lower latencies. For example, in the case of an e-commerce Web application that generates logs and clickstream data, it is advisable to run the log analyzer and reporting engines in the cloud.

Conversely, if the data are static and not going to change often (e.g., images, video, audio, PDFs, JS, CSS files), it is advisable to take advantage of a content delivery service so that the static data are cached at an edge location closer to the end user (requester), thereby lowering the access latency. Due to the caching, a content delivery service provides faster access to popular objects.

AWS-Specific Tactics for Implementing This Best Practice

1. Ship your data drives to Amazon using the Import/Export service [36]. It may be cheaper and faster to move large amounts of data using the sneakernet [37] than to upload using the Internet.
2. Utilize the same availability zone to launch a cluster of machines.
3. Create a distribution of your Amazon S3 bucket and let Amazon CloudFront caches content in that bucket across all the 14 edge locations around the world.

18.4.6 Security Best Practices

In a multi-tenant environment, cloud architects often express concerns about security. *Security should be implemented in every layer of the cloud application architecture.*

Physical security is typically handled by your service provider (Security Whitepaper [38]), which is an additional benefit of using the cloud. Network and application-level security is your responsibility, and you should implement the best practices as applicable to your business. In this section, you will learn about some specific tools, features, and guidelines on how to secure your cloud application in the AWS environment. It is recommended to take advantage of these tools and features mentioned to implement basic security and then implement additional security best practices using standard methods as appropriate or as they see fit.

Protect Your Data in Transit. If you need to exchange sensitive or confidential information between a browser and a Web server, configure SSL on your server instance. You'll need a certificate from an external certification authority like VeriSign [39] or Entrust [40]. The public key included in the certificate authenticates your server to the browser and serves as the basis for creating the shared session key used to encrypt the data in both directions.

Create a virtual private cloud by making a few command line calls (using Amazon VPC). This will enable you to use your own logically isolated resources within the AWS cloud, and then connect those resources directly to your own data center using industry-standard encrypted IPSec VPN connections.

You can also set up [41] an OpenVPN server on an Amazon EC2 instance and install the OpenVPN client on all user PCs.

Protect your Data at Rest. If you are concerned about storing sensitive and confidential data in the cloud, you should encrypt the data (individual files) before uploading it to the cloud. For example, encrypt the data using any open source [42] or commercial [43] PGP-based tools before storing it as Amazon S3 objects and decrypt it after download. This is often a good practice when building HIPPA-compliant applications [44] that need to store protected health information (PHI).

On Amazon EC2, file encryption depends on the operating system. Amazon EC2 instances running Windows can use the built-in Encrypting File System (EFS) feature [45] available in Windows. This feature will handle the encryption and decryption of files and folders automatically and make the process transparent to the users [46]. However, despite its name, EFS doesn't encrypt the entire file system; instead, it encrypts individual files. If you need a full encrypted volume, consider using the open-source TrueCrypt [47] product; this will integrate very well with NTFS-formatted EBS volumes. Amazon EC2 instances running Linux can mount EBS volumes using encrypted file systems using a variety of approaches (EncFS [48], Loop-AES [49], dm-crypt [50], TrueCrypt [51]). Likewise, Amazon EC2 instances running OpenSolaris can take advantage of ZFS [52] encryption support [53]. Regardless of which approach you choose, encrypting files and volumes in Amazon EC2 helps protect files and log data so that only the users and processes on the server can see the data in clear text, but anything or anyone outside the server sees only encrypted data.

No matter which operating system or technology you choose, encrypting data at rest presents a challenge: managing the keys used to encrypt the data. If you lose the keys, you will lose your data forever; and if your keys become compromised, the data may be at risk. Therefore, be sure to study the key management capabilities of any products you choose and establish a procedure that minimizes the risk of losing keys.

Besides protecting your data from eavesdropping, also consider how to protect it from disaster. Take periodic snapshots of Amazon EBS volumes to ensure that it is highly durable and available. Snapshots are incremental in nature and stored on Amazon S3 (separate geo-location) and can be restored back with a few clicks or command line calls.

Manage Multiple Users and their permissions with IAM. AWS Identity and Access Management (IAM) enables you to create multiple Users and manage the permissions for each of these Users within your AWS Account. A User is an identity (within your AWS Account) with unique security credentials that can be used to access AWS Services. IAM eliminates the need to share passwords or access keys, and makes it easy to enable or disable a User's access as appropriate.

IAM enables you to implement security best practices, such as least privilege, by granting unique credentials to every User within your AWS account and only grant permission to access the AWS Services and resources required for the Users to perform their job. IAM is secure by default; new Users have no access to AWS until permissions are explicitly granted.

IAM is natively integrated into most AWS Services. No service APIs have changed to support IAM, and applications and tools built on top of the AWS service APIs will continue to work when using IAM. Applications only need to begin using the access keys generated for a new User.

You should minimize the use of your AWS Account credentials as much as possible when interacting with your AWS Services and take advantage of IAM User credentials to access AWS Services and resources.

Protect your AWS Credentials. AWS supplies two types of security credentials: AWS access keys and X.509 certificates. Your AWS access key has two parts: your *access key ID* and your *secret access key*. When using the REST or Query API, you have to use your secret access key to calculate a signature to include in your request for authentication. To prevent in-flight tampering, all requests should be sent over HTTPS.

If your Amazon Machine Image (AMI) is running processes that need to communicate with other AWS Web services (for polling the Amazon SQS queue or for reading objects from Amazon S3, for example), one common design mistake is embedding the AWS credentials in the AMI. Instead of embedding the credentials, they should be passed in as arguments during launch and encrypted before being sent over the wire [54].

If your secret access key becomes compromised, you should obtain a new one by rotating [55] to a new access key ID. As a good practice, it is recommended that you incorporate a key rotation mechanism into your application architecture so that you can use it on a regular basis or occasionally (when an disgruntled employee leaves the company) to ensure that compromised keys can't last forever.

Alternately, you can use X.509 certificates for authentication to certain AWS services. The certificate file contains your public key in a base64-encoded DER certificate body. A separate file contains the corresponding base64-encoded PKCS#8 private key. AWS supports multi-factor authentication [56] as an additional protector for working with your account information on aws. Amazon.com and AWS Management Console [57].

Secure Your Application. Every Amazon EC2 instance is protected by one or more *security groups* [58]—that is, named sets of rules that specify which ingress (i.e., incoming) network traffic should be delivered to your instance. You can specify TCP and UDP ports, ICMP types and codes, and source addresses. Security groups give you basic firewall-like protection for running instances. For example, instances that belong to a Web application can have the security group settings shown in Figure 18.4.

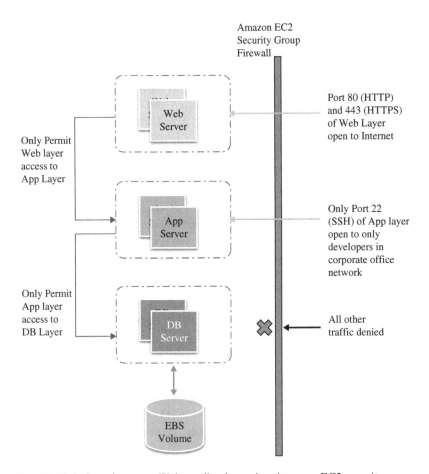

FIGURE 18.4. Securing your Web application using Amazon EC2 security groups.

Another way to restrict incoming traffic is to configure software-based firewalls on your instances. Windows instances can use the built-in firewall [59]. Linux instances can use *netfilter* [60] and *iptables*.

Over time, errors in software are discovered and require patches to fix. You should ensure the following basic guidelines to maximize security of your application:

- Regularly download patches from the vendor's Web site and update your AMIs.

- Redeploy instances from the new AMIs and test your applications to ensure that the patches don't break anything. Ensure that the latest AMI is deployed across *all* instances.

- Invest in test scripts so that you can run security checks periodically and automate the process.

- Ensure that the third-party software is configured to the most secure settings.

- Never run your processes as *root* or *Administrator* login unless absolutely necessary.

All the standard security practices in the pre-cloud era, such as adopting good coding practices and isolating sensitive data, are still applicable and should be implemented.

In retrospect, the cloud abstracts the complexity of the physical security from you and gives you the control through tools and features so that you can secure your application.

18.5 GREPTHEWEB CASE STUDY

The Alexa Web Search[1] Web service allows developers to build customized search engines against the massive data that Alexa generates (using a Web crawl) every night. One of the features of their Web service allows users to query the Alexa search index and get Million Search Results (MSR) back as output. Developers can run queries that return up to 10 million results.

The resulting set, which represents a small subset of all the documents on the Web, can then be processed further using a regular expression language. This allows developers to filter their search results using criteria that are *not* indexed by Alexa, thereby giving the developer power to do more sophisticated searches. Developers can run regular expressions against the actual documents, even when there are millions of them, to search for patterns and retrieve the subset of documents that matched that regular expression. This application is

---

[1]The service has been deprecated for business reasons; however, the architecture and design principles are still relevant.

currently in production at Amazon.com and is code-named *GrepTheWeb* because it can "grep" (a popular Unix command-line utility to search patterns) the actual Web documents. GrepTheWeb allows developers to either (a) perform specialized searches such as selecting documents that have a particular HTML tag or META tag, (b) find documents with particular punctuations ("Hey!", he said. "Why Wait?"), or (c) search for mathematical equations ("$f(x) = \sum x + W$"), source code, e-mail addresses, or other patterns such as "(dis)integration of life."

The functionality is impressive, but even more impressive was GrepThe-Web's architecture and implementation. In the next section, you will zoom in to see different levels of the architecture of GrepTheWeb.

18.5.1 Architecture

Figure 18.5 shows a high-level depiction of the architecture. The output of the Million Search Results Service, which is a sorted list of links gzipped (compressed using the Unix gzip utility) into a single file, is given to GrepTheWeb as input. It takes a regular expression as a second input. It then returns a filtered subset of document links sorted and gzipped into a single file. Since the overall process is asynchronous, developers can get the status of their jobs by calling GetStatus() to see whether the execution is completed.

Matching a regular expression against millions of documents is not trivial. Different factors could combine to cause the processing to take a lot of time:

- Regular expressions could be complex.
- Dataset could be large, even hundreds of terabytes.
- There could be unknown request patterns; for example, any number of people can access the application at any given point in time.

Hence, the design goals of GrepTheWeb included the ability to scale in all dimensions (more powerful pattern-matching languages, more concurrent users

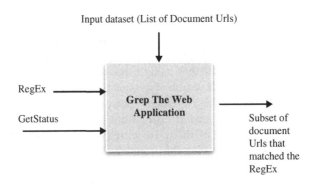

FIGURE 18.5. GrepTheWeb Architecture—Zoom Level 1.

of common datasets, larger datasets, better result quality) while keeping the costs of processing as low as possible.

The approach was to build an application that scales not only with demand, but also without a heavy upfront investment and without the cost of maintaining idle machines. To get a response in a reasonable amount of time, it was important to distribute the job into multiple tasks and to perform a distributed Grep operation that runs those tasks on multiple nodes in parallel.

Zooming in further, GrepTheWeb architecture is as shown in Figure 18.6. It uses the following AWS components:

- **Amazon S3.** For retrieving input datasets and for storing the output dataset.
- **Amazon SQS.** For durably buffering requests acting as a "glue" between controllers.
- **Amazon SimpleDB.** For storing intermediate status, for storing log, and for user data about tasks.
- **Amazon EC2.** For running a large distributed processing Hadoop cluster on-demand.
- **Hadoop.** For distributed processing, automatic parallelization, and job scheduling.

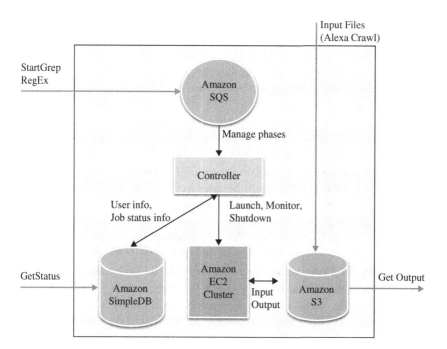

FIGURE 18.6. GrepTheWeb Architecture—Zoom Level 2.

FIGURE 18.7. Phases of GrepTheWeb architecture.

18.5.2 Workflow

GrepTheWeb is modular. It does its processing in four phases as shown in Figure 18.7. The launch phase is responsible for validating and initiating the processing of a GrepTheWeb request, instantiating Amazon EC2 instances, launching the Hadoop cluster on them, and starting all the job processes. The monitor phase is responsible for monitoring the EC2 cluster; it also maps, reduces, and checks for success and failure. The shutdown phase is responsible for billing and shutting down all Hadoop processes and Amazon EC2 instances, while the cleanup phase deletes Amazon SimpleDB transient data.

Detailed Workflow for Figure 18.8

1. On application start, queues are created if not already created and all the controller threads are started. Each controller thread starts polling their respective queues for any messages.
2. When a StartGrep user request is received, a launch message is enqueued in the launch queue.
3. *Launch Phase*: The launch controller thread picks up the launch message, executes the launch task, updates the status and timestamps in the Amazon SimpleDB domain, enqueues a new message in the monitor queue, and deletes the message from the launch queue after processing.
   a. The launch task starts Amazon EC2 instances using a JRE pre-installed AMI, deploys required Hadoop libraries, and starts a Hadoop Job (run Map/Reduce tasks).
   b. Hadoop runs map tasks on Amazon EC2 slave nodes in parallel. Each map task takes files (multithreaded in background) from Amazon S3, runs a regular expression (Queue Message Attribute) against the file from Amazon S3, and writes the match results along with a description of up to five matches locally, and then the combine/reduce task combines and sorts the results and consolidates the output.
   c. The final results are stored on Amazon S3 in the output bucket.
4. *Monitor Phase:* The monitor controller thread picks up this message, validates the status/error in Amazon SimpleDB, executes the monitor task, updates the status in the Amazon SimpleDB domain, enqueues a new message in the shutdown queue and billing queue, and deletes the message from monitor queue after processing.

a. The monitor task checks for the Hadoop status (JobTracker success/failure) in regular intervals, and it updates the SimpleDB items with status/error and Amazon S3 output file.

5. *Shutdown Phase*: The shutdown controller thread picks up this message from the shutdown queue, executes the shutdown task, updates the status and timestamps in Amazon SimpleDB domain, and deletes the message from the shutdown queue after processing. Likewise, the billing controller thread picks up the message from the billing queue and executes the billing task of sending usage information to the billing service.

   a. The shutdown task kills the Hadoop processes, terminates the EC2 instances after getting EC2 topology information from Amazon SimpleDB, and disposes of the infrastructure.

   b. The billing task gets EC2 topology information, SimpleDB Box Usage, and Amazon S3 file and query input and calculates the billing and passes it to the billing service.

6. *Cleanup Phase*: Archives the SimpleDB data with user info.

7. Users can execute GetStatus on the service endpoint to get the status of the overall system (all controllers and Hadoop) and download the filtered results from Amazon S3 after completion.

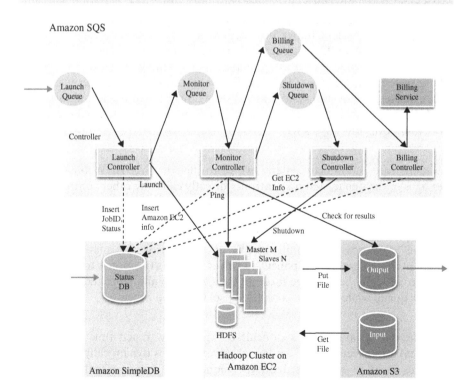

FIGURE 18.8. GrepTheWeb Architecture—Zoom Level 3.

18.5.3   Implementing Best Practices

In the next four subsections, you will see how GrepTheWeb implements the best practices using different Amazon Web Services.

Elastic Storage Provided by Amazon S3. In GrepTheWeb, Amazon S3 acts as an input as well as an output data store. The input to GrepTheWeb is the Web itself (compressed form of Alexa's Web Crawl), stored on Amazon S3 as objects and updated frequently. Because the Web Crawl dataset can be huge (usually in terabytes) and always growing, there was a need for a distributed, elastic, persistent storage. Amazon S3 proved to be a perfect fit.

Loose Coupling Using Amazon SQS. Amazon SQS was used as message-passing mechanism between components. It acts as "glue" that wired different functional components together. This not only helped in making the different components loosely coupled, but also helped in building an overall more failure resilient system.

Buffer. If one component is receiving and processing requests faster than other components (an unbalanced producer consumer situation), buffering will help make the overall system more resilient to bursts of traffic (or load). Amazon SQS acts as a transient buffer between two components (controllers) of the GrepTheWeb system. If a message is sent directly to a component, the receiver will need to consume it at a rate dictated by the sender. For example, if the billing system was slow or if the launch time of the Hadoop cluster was more than expected, the overall system would slow down, because it would just have to wait. With message queues, sender and receiver are decoupled and the queue service smooths out any "spiky" message traffic.

Isolation. Interaction between any two controllers in GrepTheWeb is through messages in the queue, and no controller directly calls any other controller. All communication and interaction happens by storing messages in the queue (en-queue) and retrieving messages from the queue (de-queue). This makes the entire system loosely coupled and makes the interfaces simple and clean. Amazon SQS provided a uniform way of transferring information between the different application components. Each controller's function is to retrieve the message, process the message (execute the function), and store the message in another queue while they are completely isolated from others.

Asynchrony. Because it was difficult to know how much time each phase would take to execute (e.g., the launch phase decides dynamically how many instances need to start based on the request and hence execution time is unknown), Amazon SQS helped by making the system behave in an asynchronous fashion. Now, if the launch phase takes more time to process or the monitor phase fails, the other components of the system are not affected and the overall system is more stable and highly available.

Storing Statuses in Amazon SimpleDB. One use for a database in cloud applications is to track statuses. Since the components of the system run asynchronously, there is a need to obtain the status of the system at any given point in time. Moreover, since all components are autonomous and discrete, there is a need for a query-able data store that captures the state of the system.

Because Amazon SimpleDB is schema-less, there is no need to define the structure of a record beforehand. Every controller can define its own structure and append data to a "job" item. For example: For a given job, "run email address regex over 10 million documents," the launch controller will add/update the "launch_status" attribute along with the "launch_starttime," while the monitor controller will add/update the "monitor_status" and "hadoop_status" attributes with enumeration values (running, completed, error, none). A GetStatus() call will query Amazon SimpleDB and return the state of each controller and also the overall status of the system.

Component services can query Amazon SimpleDB anytime because controllers independently store their states—one more nice way to create asynchronous highly available services. Although a simplistic approach was used in implementing the use of Amazon SimpleDB in GrepTheWeb, a more sophisticated approach, where there was complete, almost real-time monitoring, would also be possible—For example, storing the Hadoop JobTracker status to show how many maps have been performed at a given moment.

Amazon SimpleDB is also used to store active Request IDs for historical and auditing/billing purposes.

In summary, Amazon SimpleDB is used as a status database to store the different states of the components and a historical/log database for querying high-performance data.

Intelligent Elasticity Implemented Using Amazon EC2. In GrepTheWeb, the controller code runs on Amazon EC2 instances. The launch controller spawns master and slave instances using a preconfigured Amazon machine image (AMI). Since the dynamic provisioning and decommissioning happens using simple Web service calls, GrepTheWeb knows how many master and slave instances need to be launched.

The launch controller makes an educated guess, based on reservation logic, of how many slaves are needed to perform a particular job. The reservation logic is based on the complexity of the query (number of predicates, etc.) and the size of the input dataset (number of documents to be searched). This was also kept configurable so that overall processing time can be reduced by simply specifying the number of instances to launch. After launching the instances and starting the Hadoop cluster on those instances, Hadoop will appoint a master

Example
Regular Expression "A(.*)zon"
Format of the line in the Input dataset [URL] [Title] [charset] [size] [S3 Object Key of .gz file] [offset] http://www.amazon.com/gp/browse.html?node=3435361   Amazon Web   us-ascii   3509   /2008/01/08/51/1/51_1_20080108072442_crawl100.arc.gz   70150864
Mapper Implementation Key = line number and value = line in the input dataset Create a signed URL (using Amazon AWS credentials) using the contents of key-value Read (fetch) Amazon S3 Object (file) into a buffer Run regular expression on that buffer If there is match, collect the output in new set of key-value pairs (key = line, value = up to 5 matches)
Reducer Implementation Pass-through (Built-in Identity Function) and write the results back to S3.

FIGURE 18.9. Map reduce operation (in GrepTheWeb).

and slaves, handles the negotiating, handshaking, and security token distribution (SSH keys, certificates), and runs the grep job.

18.5.4 GrepTheWeb Hadoop implementation

Hadoop is an open source distributed processing framework that allows computation of large datasets by splitting the dataset into manageable chunks, spreading it across a fleet of machines and managing the overall process by launching jobs, processing the job no matter where the data are physically located and, at the end, aggregating the job output into a final result.

Hadoop is a good fit for the GrepTheWeb application. Because each grep task can be run in parallel independently of other grep tasks, using the parallel approach embodied in Hadoop is a perfect fit.

For GrepTheWeb, the actual documents (the web) are crawled ahead of time and stored on Amazon S3. Each user starts a grep job by calling the StartGrep function at the service endpoint. When triggered, masters and slave nodes (Hadoop cluster) are started on Amazon EC2 instances. Hadoop splits the input (document with pointers to Amazon S3 objects) into multiple manageable chunks of 100 lines each and assign the chunk to a slave node to run the map task [61]. The map task reads these lines and is responsible for fetching the files from Amazon S3, running the regular expression on them and writing the results locally. If there is no match, there is no output. The map tasks then passes the results to the reduce phase, which is an identity function (pass through) to aggregate all the outputs. The "final" output is written back to Amazon S3.

18.6 FUTURE RESEARCH DIRECTIONS

The day is not too far when applications will cease to be aware of physical hardware. Much like plugging in a microwave in order to power it doesn't require any knowledge of electricity, one should be able to *plug in* an application to the cloud in order to receive the power it needs to run, just like a utility. As an architect, you will manage abstract compute, storage, and network resources instead of physical servers. Applications will continue to function even if the underlying physical hardware fails or is removed or replaced. Applications will adapt themselves to fluctuating demand patterns by deploying resources *instantaneously* and automatically, thereby achieving highest utilization levels at all times. Scalability, security, high availability, fault-tolerance, testability, and elasticity will be configurable properties of the application architecture and will be an automated and intrinsic part of the platform on which they are built.

However, we are not there yet. Today, you can build applications in the cloud with some of these qualities by implementing the best practices highlighted in the chapter. Best practices in cloud computing architectures will continue to evolve, and as researchers we should focus not only on enhancing the cloud but also on building tools, technologies, and processes that will make it easier for developers and architects to plug in applications to the cloud easily.

18.7 CONCLUSION

This chapter has provided prescriptive guidance to cloud architects for designing efficient cloud applications.

By focusing on concepts and best practices—like designing for failure, decoupling the application components, understanding and implementing elasticity, combining it with parallelization, and integrating security in every aspect of the application architecture—cloud architects can understand the design considerations necessary for building highly scalable cloud applications.

The GrepTheWeb architecture epitomizes how highly scalable architectures are built in the cloud today. The AWS cloud offers highly reliable pay-as-you-go infrastructure services. The AWS-specific tactics highlighted in the chapter will help design cloud applications using these services. As a researcher, it is advised that you play with these commercial services, learn from the work of others, build on the top, and enhance and further invent cloud computing.

ACKNOWLEDGMENTS

The author is profoundly grateful to Jeff Barr, Steve Riley, Paul Horvath, Prashant Sridharan, and Scot Marvin for providing comments on early drafts of this chapter. Special thanks to Matt Tavis for providing valuable insight. Without his contributions, the chapter would not have been possible.

REFERENCES

1. J. Varia, Cloud Architectures, http://jineshvaria.s3.amazonaws.com/public/cloudarchitectures-varia.pdf, 2007-07-01.

2. Amazon EC2 Detail Page, http://aws.amazon.com/ec2.

3. Amazon CloudWatch Detail Page, http://aws.amazon.com/cloudwatch/

4. Auto-scaling feature, http://aws.amazon.com/auto-scaling

5. Elastic Load Balancing feature, http://aws.amazon.com/elasticloadbalancing

6. Elastic Block Store, http://aws.amazon.com/ebs

7. Amazon S3, http://aws.amazon.com/s3

8. Amazon CloudFront, http://aws.amazon.com/cloudfront

9. Amazon SimpleDB, http://aws.amazon.com/simpledb

10. Amazon RDS, http://aws.amazon.com/rds

11. Amazon SQS, http://aws.amazon.com/sqs

12. Amazon ElasticMapReduce, http://aws.amazon.com/elasticmapreduce and Amazon Simple Notification Services (Amazon SNS)

13. Amazon Virtual Private Cloud, http://aws.amazon.com/vpc

14. Amazon Flexible Payments Service, http://aws.amazon.com/fps and Amazon DevPay, http://aws.amazon.com/devpay

15. T. Schlossnagle, *Scalable Internet Architectures*, Sams Publishing, 2006-07-31.

16. Wikipedia Article, http://en.wikipedia.org/wiki/Slashdot_effect

17. Memcached Web site, http://www.danga.com/memcached/

18. D. Pritchett, Shard Lessons, http://www.addsimplicity.com/adding_simplicity_an_engi/2008/08/shard-lessons.html, 2008-08-24.

19. J. Hamilton, On designing and deploying Internet-scale services, 2007, in *21st Large Installation System Administration conference (LISA '07)*, http://mvdirona.com/jrh/talksAndPapers/JamesRH_Lisa.pdf

20. D. Obasanjo, Building Scalable Databases: Pros and Cons of Various Database Sharding Schemes, http://www.25hoursaday.com/weblog/2009/01/16/BuildingScalableDatabasesProsAndConsOfVariousDatabaseShardingSchemes.aspx, 2009-01-16.

21. M. Lurie, The Federation: Database Interoperability, http://www.ibm.com/developerworks/data/library/techarticle/0304lurie/0304lurie.html, 2003-04-23.

22. Amazon SQS Team, Building Scalable, Reliable Amazon EC2 Applications with Amazon SQS, http://sqs-public-images.s3.amazonaws.com/Building_Scalabale_EC2_applications_with_SQS2.pdf, 2008.

23. Chef, http://wiki.opscode.com/display/chef/Home

24. Puppet, http://reductivelabs.com/trac/puppet/

25. CFEngine, http://www.cfengine.org/

26. Genome, http://genome.et.redhat.com/

27. Wikipedia Article, http://en.wikipedia.org/wiki/Just_enough_operating_system

28. Instance metadata and userdata, http://docs.amazonwebservices.com/AWSEC2/latest/DeveloperGuide/index.html?AESDG-chapter-instancedata.html

29. Boot From Amazon EBS feature, http://developer.amazonwebservices.com/connect/entry.jspa?externalID = 3121

30. How to Share a Snapshot section, http://aws.amazon.com/ebs/

31. Hadoop website, http://hadoop.apache.org/

32. Amazon S3 Team, Amazon S3 Error Best Practices, http://docs.amazonwebservices.com/AmazonS3/latest/index.html?ErrorBestPractices.html, 2006-03-01.

33. Amazon SimpleDB Team, Query 201: Tips and Tricks for Amazon SimpleDB Query, http://developer.amazonwebservices.com/connect/entry.jspa?externalID = 1232&categoryID = 176, 2008-02-07.

34. Amazon SimpleDB Team, Building for Performance and Reliability with Amazon SimpleDB, http://developer.amazonwebservices.com/connect/entry.jspa?externalID = 1394&categoryID = 176, 2008-04-11.

35. Amazon SimpleDB Team, Query 101: Building Amazon SimpleDB Queries, http://developer.amazonwebservices.com/connect/entry.jspa?externalID = 1231& categoryID = 176, 2008-02-07.

36. Amazon Import Export Services, http://aws.amazon.com/importexport

37. Wikipedia Article, http://en.wikipedia.org/wiki/Sneakernet

38. Amazon Security Team, Overview of Security Processes, http://awsmedia.s3 .amazonaws.com/pdf/AWS_Security_Whitepaper.pdf, 2009-06-01.

39. Verisign SSL, http://www.verisign.com/ssl/

40. EnTrust SSL, http://www.entrust.net/ssl-products.htm

41. E. Hammond, Escaping Restrictive/Untrusted Networks with OpenVPN on EC2, http://alestic.com/2009/05/openvpn-ec2, 2009-05-02.

42. GNUPG, http://www.gnupg.org

43. PGP, http://www.pgp.com/

44. Amazon Web Services Team, Creating HIPPA-Compliant Medical Data Applications with AWS, http://awsmedia.s3.amazonaws.com/AWS_HIPAA_ Whitepaper_Final.pdf, 2009-04-01.

45. R. Bragg, The Encrypting File System, http://technet.microsoft.com/en-us/library/ cc700811.aspx, 2009.

46. Microsoft Support Team, Best Practices For Encrypting File System (Windows), http://support.microsoft.com/kb/223316, 2009.

47. TrueCrypt, http://www.truecrypt.org/

48. EnCFS, http://www.arg0.net/encfs

49. AES, http://loop-aes.sourceforge.net/loop-AES.README

50. DM-Crypt, http://www.saout.de/misc/dm-crypt/

51. TrueCrypt, http://www.truecrypt.org/

52. ZFS filesystem, http://www.opensolaris.org/os/community/zfs/

53. Solaris Security Team, ZFS Encryption Project (OpenSolaris), http://www.open-solaris.org/os/project/zfs-crypto/, 2009-05-01.

54. S. Swidler, How to keep your AWS credentials on an EC2 instance securely, http:// clouddevelopertips.blogspot.com/2009/08/how-to-keep-your-aws-credentials-on-ec2.html, 2009-08-31.

55. AWS announcement, http://aws.amazon.com/about-aws/whats-new/2009/08/31/ seamlessly-rotate-your-access-credentials/

56. Multi-factor Authentication, http://aws.amazon.com/mfa/

57. AWS Management Console, http://aws.amazon.com/console/

58. Amazon EC2 User Guide, Security Group description, http://docs.amazonwebser-vices.com/AWSEC2/2009-07-15/UserGuide/index.html?using-network-security.html

59. Microsoft Windows Firewall, http://technet.microsoft.com/en-us/library/cc779199 (WS.10).aspx, March 2003

60. Netfilter Website, http://www.netfilter.org/

61. Hadoop Map/Reduce Tutorial, The Apache Software foundation, http://hadoop .apache.org/common/docs/ro.19.2./mapred_tutorial.html, 2008

62. Amazon S3 Team, Best Practices for using Amazon S3, http://developer.amazon-webservices.com/connect/entry.jspa?externalID = 1904, 2008-11-26.

CHAPTER 19

MASSIVELY MULTIPLAYER ONLINE GAME HOSTING ON CLOUD RESOURCES

VLAD NAE, RADU PRODAN, and ALEXANDRU IOSUP

19.1 INTRODUCTION

Massively Multiplayer On-Line Games (MMOGs) have emerged in the past decade as a new type of large-scale distributed application characterized by a huge real-time virtual world entertaining millions of players spread across the globe. Today's MMOGs operate as client–server architectures, in which the game server simulates a world via computing and database operations, receives and processes commands from the clients, and interoperates with a billing and accounting system [1, 2]. Based on the actions submitted by the players, the game servers compute the global state of the game world represented by the position and interactions of the entities, and they send appropriate real-time responses to the players containing the new relevant state information. Depending on the game, typical response times to ensure fluent play must be between 100 msec in on-line *First Person Shooter (FPS)* action games and 1−2 sec for *Role-Playing Games (RPG)*. A good game experience is critical in keeping the players engaged, and it has an immediate consequence on the income of the MMOG operators. Failing to deliver timely simulation updates leads to a degraded game experience and triggers player departure.

To support thousands of concurrent players and many more other game entities, MMOG operators install and operate a large static infrastructure consisting of hundreds to thousands of computers onto which they distribute the load of a game in order to provide the required quality of service. For example, the operating infrastructure of the Massively Multiplayer On-Line

Cloud Computing: Principles and Paradigms,   Edited by Rajkumar Buyya, James Broberg and Andrzej Goscinski   Copyright © 2011 John Wiley & Sons, Inc.

Role-Playing Game (MMORPG) World of Warcraft,[1] has over 10,000 computers. In an earlier study [3] we demonstrated that the resource demand of MMOGs is highly dynamic and thus a large portion of the statically allocated resources is unnecessary, which leads to a very inefficient resource utilization. In addition, this enterprise limitation has negative economic impacts by preventing any but the largest hosting centers from joining the market; this dramatically increases prices, because those centers must be capable of handling peaks in demand, even if the resources are not needed for much of the time.

In this chapter we propose a new MMOG ecosystem consisting of a game operator responsible for the management of a distributed game session and multiple data centers providing virtualized resources required for running the session. This new model extends our previous work based on the assumption that the software that implements the game servers is pre-deployed and installed on the data center machines based on off-line agreements (signed beforehand) between the game operators and the hosting data centers. This approach has an obvious limitation if the game operator underestimates the success of its MMOG (such a scenario did happen in reality, causing huge economic losses) and the load of a game session exceeds the capacities of the data centers with which the operator has signed off-line leasing agreements.

We plan to address this limitation by applying *cloud computing* principles, which emerged in the recent years as a hot topic that promises a cheap alternative to supercomputers and expensive specialized data centers. Through the concept of *virtualization*, compute clouds provide generic functionality for on-demand hosting and provisioning of computing resources capable of running nearly any kind of application, including MMOGs. Aggregating in theory an unbounded number of resources from a large number of different providers, compute clouds have the potential to eliminate the scalability barriers in MMOG hosting through a novel concept of *"scaling by credit card,"* where the only limits are imposed by the financial reasons, as opposed to the physical data center limitations of today.

In the next section we introduce some more background information on MMOG and resource virtualization. Section 19.3 surveys the most relevant related work. In Section 19.4 we describe the MMOG application hosting, operation, and virtualization models used by our enhanced MMOG ecosystem. In Section 19.5 we study the impact of using virtualized resources for running single and multiple MMOG sessions using different MMOG hosting and operation policies, and Section 19.7 describes the conclusions we have reached.

19.2 BACKGROUND

In this section we introduce a few background concepts on MMOG and virtualization required for a better positioning and understanding of our approach.

---

[1]Blizzard Entertainment, Inc., *World Of Warcraft*, http://www.worldofwarcraft.com/.

19.2.1   MMOG

On-line entertainment including gaming is a huge growth sector worldwide. MMOGs grew from 10,000 subscribers in 1997 to 6.7 million in 2003, and the rate is accelerating to an estimated 60 million people by 2011. The release of World of Warcraft in 2005 saw a single game break the barrier of 4 million subscribers worldwide. The market size shows equally impressive numbers, estimated by the Entertainment Software Association (ESA) to 7 billion USD with an avid growth over 300% in the last 10 years. In comparison, the Motion Picture Association of America (MPAA) reports a size of 8.99 billion USD and the Recording Industry Association of America (RIAA) reports a size of 12.3 billion USD, which stagnated (and even decreased by 2%) in the last 10 years. It is therefore expected that the game industry will soon grow larger than both movie and music market sizes.

The relative success of each game is characterized by the number of registered players. Figure 19.1 displays the number of MMORPG players over time for the U.S. and European markets based on the survey of Wood-cock[2] for dates until June 2006 and then based on our own research afterwards.

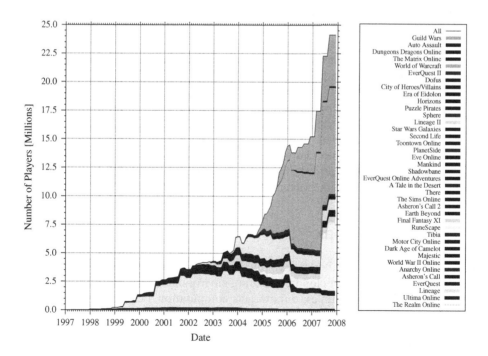

FIGURE 19.1. Number of MMORPG players over time.

[2]B. S. Woodcock, *An Analysis of MMOG Subscription Growth*, 2008, http://www.mmogchart.com/.

The chart shows that there are currently six games with more than 500,000 players each. The total number of MMORPG players is well-approximated by the exponential trend $\alpha \cdot e^{\beta \cdot x}$, where $\alpha = 7 \times 10^{-9}$ and $\beta = 0.028$ give a Pearson's coefficient of determination $R^2 = 0.974$. Assuming the same rate of growth, we can estimate over 60 million players by 2011 in the U.S. and EU markets alone. The large number of MMOG players for each title, as well as for the MMOG ecosystem as a whole, is one main motivation for our work.

19.2.2   Virtualization

Similar to many types of scientific computing software, MMOG are implemented in the C language with lots of low-level library dependencies that makes the deployment and installation process a hard problem that requires manual intervention. In this context, virtualization is a key technology for hiding from the users the low-level physical characteristics of a computing platform by showing another abstract, higher-level emulated platform instead represented by a so-called *virtual machine* (VM). The two most common virtualization environments today are [4] VMWare and Xen [5], and there exist other solutions used by smaller communities such as Oceano, VMPlants, Kadeploy, Shirako, VW, XGE, VD caches, KVM, Virtual Box, vsersers, OpenVZ, and Qemu. Although the new virtualization layer adds a certain degree of overheads (that we will model in Section 19.4.4), the time for creating one VM image embedding the required software is relatively constant and can be automatically deployed on all supported platforms. This process ensures deployment and provisioning scalability that represents a significant benefit.

The largest part of the scientific community, including Amazon, has chosen Xen as their virtualization platform as it is open source and, therefore, can be freely used and adapted to various needs, if required. The advantages of virtualization are rather important when using heterogeneous computing resources. A VM image only needs to be created once and then used on all machines having the same virtualization software installed.

19.3   RELATED WORK

There have been a number of research activities in assessing the performance of virtualized resources in cloud computing environments and in general [6–13]. In contrast to these studies, ours targets computational cloud resources for a new application class (MMOG).

Close to our work is the seminal study of Amazon S3 [8], which includes an evaluation of file transfer between Amazon EC2 and S3. Several other small-scale performance studies of Amazon EC2 have been recently conducted such as the study of Amazon EC2 performance using the NPB benchmark suite [9] and the early comparative study of Eucalyptus and EC2 performance [13]. Our work complements these studies by proposing a detailed analytical model for VM instantiation overheads by analyzing the services offered multiple cloud providers.

In Deelman et al. [7], the authors perform a performance and cost study of executing a scientific astronomy workflow on simulated Amazon EC2 and S3 resources. They proved that by provisioning the right amount of storage and compute resources, cost can be significantly reduced with no significant impact on application performance. Our work focused on another application class and provides a more fine-grained VM instantiation overhead breakdown by considering multiple cloud providers (not restricted to Amazon EC2).

The Globus project studied different scheduling strategies that allow the integration of VM management into batch execution systems like PBS [14]. The virtualization features such as suspend, migrate, and resume allow new scheduling strategies which can be used in future grid or cloud environments [13].

Aneka [15] is a.NET-based service-oriented platform for desktop grid computing that provides (a) a configurable service container hosting, (b) pluggable services for discovering, scheduling, and balancing various types of workloads, and (c) a flexible and extensible API supporting various programming models including threading, batch processing, MPI, and dataflow. The work in [16] targets interconnecting clouds for dynamically creating an atmospheric computing environment and describes a meta-negotiation infrastructure to establish global cloud exchanges and markets. Recent work [17] describes an approach of extending a local cluster by cloud resources using two schedulers: one for the cluster and one for the cloud, using different strategies. The possible benefit of not violating deadlines and higher throughput of the cluster is analyzed.

The EGEE project released an interesting report comparing the Amazon EC2 and S3 services with the EGEE grid infrastructure [18]. Three interesting aspects about cost and functionality are compared, with the conclusion that for long-lasting large-scale experiments, such as those conducted for the LHC, cloud services would be too expensive compared to the computing center resources owned by the project members.

19.4 MODEL

We model a platform for a MMOG ecosystem consisting of a global network of conventional data centers complemented by a set of virtualized cloud computing providers that host in cooperation one MMOG session. An MMOG session is managed by one game operator that is responsible for the real-time experience of the connected players and which negotiates with existing data center and cloud providers the necessary resources in order to achieve this goal. Our multi-data center model extends on related work limited to Web services and single data centers [19–23].

19.4.1 Application

MMOGs are large-scale simulations of persistent *game worlds* comprising various objects or *entities* such as avatars (in-game representation of the players), bots or nonplayer characters (mobile entities that have the ability to act independently), movable objects (passive entities such as boxes or guns which can be manipulated but do not initiate interactions), and immutable entities or decor.

The mostly employed architectural model for MMOGs is client/server [1], with game operators maintaining the servers that simulate a distributed game world. The clients dynamically connect to a joint *game session* and interact with each other by sending play actions such as movements, shootings, operations on game objects, or chat. The vast majority of game servers follow a similar computational model implementing an infinite loop, where in each loop iteration (also called tick) there are certain steps to be performed such as processing events coming from the connected clients and other servers, processing the states of the active entities, and broadcasting state update to the connected clients at a required rate. To accommodate the thousands of concurrent players into one single MMOG session, the current practice is to parallelize it and distribute the load across multiple resources using several parallelization techniques.

Spatial scaling of a game session is achieved through a conventional parallelization technique called *zoning*, based on similar data locality concepts as in scientific parallel processing (see Figure 19.2). Zoning is currently

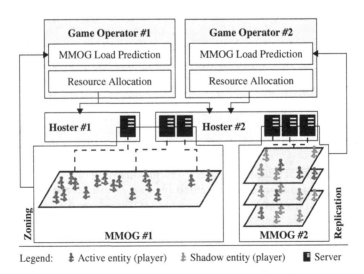

FIGURE 19.2. The MMOG ecosystem architecture.

being applied on MMORPGs (World of Warcraft)[3] by partitioning of the game world into zones to be handled independently by separate machines. In production MMORPGs, zones are typically predefined static geographical areas, where the transition among zones can only happen through certain portals such as special doors or teleportation.

The second technique, called *replication* (see Figure 19.2), targets parallelization of game sessions with a large density of players located and interacting within each other's proximity. Such situations are typical for fast-paced FPS games in which players gather in certain hotspot action areas that congest game servers that are no longer capable of delivering state updates at the required rate. To address this problem, replication defines a novel method of distributing load by replicating the same game zone on several machines and distributing the entities. Each server computes the state for a subset of entities called active entities, while the remaining ones, called shadow entities (which are active in the other participating servers), are synchronized across servers.

The third parallelization technique, called *instancing,* is a simplification of replication which distributes the session load by starting multiple instances of widely populated zones. The instances are completely independent of each other, meaning that two entities from different instances will not see each other, even if located at the same coordinates.

19.4.2 Hosting

The novel enhanced hosting model introduced in this article consists of conventional data centers that operate pre-installed game servers [3] and additional general purpose providers of virtualized cloud resources (see Figure 19.2). In the remainder of the chapter, we will refer to both types of resource providers as *hosters.*

We consider the hosting platform as consisting of hosters (data centers and cloud providers) scattered around the world, where each hoster pools together resources that may serve several games simultaneously (see Figure 19.2). The hosters operate two major services. A *load prediction* service, presented in detail in Nae et al. [24], is in charge of projecting the future distribution of entities in the game world that is demonstrated to have the highest impact on the server load. We devised accurate analytical models for translating the entity distribution prediction and possible interactions into estimating the game server load. Based on the projected load, a *resource allocation* service [3] provisions additional local servers to the game session (through the zoning, replication, or instancing) that accommodate the player load while guaranteeing the real-time quality of service. For example, by timely foreseeing critical hot spots (i.e., excessively populated area of interest generating a large number of interactions), one can dynamically provision additional servers on some new resources

---

[3]*MMORPG.COM, Your Headquarters for Massive Multiplayer Online Role-Playing Games.* http://www.mmorpg.com/

and take timely load balancing actions that transparently redistribute the game load before the servers become overloaded.

Our hosting model considers the *size* and *duration* of the minimal resource allocation which may be not only for a resource as a whole (e.g., a server in Web data centers [9] or a processor in a grid system), but also for a fraction of that resource (e.g., a virtual machine running on a physical node [25], or a channel of an optical network). The minimal duration for which a resource may be allocated may be between a few seconds (servicing one user request by a Web service) and several months (a typical value for Web server hosting). We define the *resource bulk* as the minimum number of resources that can be allocated for one request, expressed as the multiple of a minimal resource size. Similarly, we define the *time bulk* as the minimum duration for which a resource allocation can be performed expressed as multiple of a minimal time period. A hoster may choose to allocate resources for MMOGs only in bulks under a certain space−time *hosting policy*.

19.4.3 Operation

A game operator can handle simultaneously multiple MMOG sessions of different genres, designs with different interactivity types and counts, and different latency tolerance. Based on the exhibited game load, the operator submits resource requests to the hosters by specifying the type, number, and duration for which the resources are desired (either statically or dynamically computed), and the hosters respond with offers based on their local time−space renting policy. We currently consider four resource types that are relevant for MMOG hosting: *CPU*, *memory*, *input* from the external network (*Ext[in]*), and output to the external network (*Ext[out]*) of a data center.

Depending on the hoster's service model (either best-effort or advance reservation-based), resource requests are queued or immediately fitted in the schedule, respectively. Using one or several important metrics (e.g., virtualization overheads, geographical proximity, data locality, resource proportionality), the game operator applies a *resource selection policy* using one or several of the following ordering mechanisms:

- *Classifying* groups several resources into classes based on metric value ranges.
- *Sorting* orders the resources based on the metric values.
- *Filtering* eliminates the resources with inadequate metric values.
- *Prioritizing* gives higher allocation priority to resources with important metric values.

Once the available resources are selected, they are *allocated* to the game operators. From the game operator's point of view, we say that the resources have been *provisioned*. From here on, we use the terms resource allocation and resource provisioning interchangeably. The allocated resources are reserved for executing the MMOG servers for the entire duration of the game operator's request.

19.4.4 Virtualization Model

VM instantiation is the process by which a VM is started on a selected resource. A *heavy VM* behaves as a full operating system and middleware stack, as opposed to a *light VM* that only installs a minimal control and communication layer on top of the existing operating system and middleware stack. For example, a VMware or Xen deployment is a heavy VM, while a Condor glide-in deployment is a light VM. In this section we present a model for the instantiation of a heavy VM on a cloud resource.

This section presents a model for VM instantiation that considers four performance aspects expressed by the corresponding *virtualization overheads*: VM image preparation t_c, VM transfer t_x, VM start t_s, and VM removal t_r. Performance-wise, the total time needed to instantiate a VM can be expressed as

$$T = t_c + t_x + t_s + t_r$$

Conventional data centers do not exhibit this overhead, but are restricted to pre-deployed software that lack the flexibility of dynamic provisioning and on-the-fly deployment of MMOG servers. We detail these observed overheads in the remainder of this section.

We distinguish two models for VM instantiation:

- *VMI-Plain*, where a VM suspension/resume is not allowed
- *VMI-SR*, where a VM suspend/resume is allowed

The main differences between these two models are that t_c and t_s are, respectively, higher and lower for VMI-SR than for VMI-Plain and that VMI-SR enables VM migration across (identical) resources. The suspension/resume mechanism is worthwhile when the user submits jobs that require the same VM and the size of the required VM is small. For both models, the images are stored uncompressed.

For the VMI-Plain *image preparation*, VM images are pre-created, but they can be extensively configured. For VMI-SR, VM image creation follows the same process as for VMI-Plain the first time a VM is created; afterwards, the VM is only suspended/resumed. We model the VM image preparation as follows:

$$t_c = \begin{cases} 0, & \text{VM pre-created or cached,} \\ t_{\text{suspend}}, & \text{VM to be suspended,} \\ t_{\text{image}}, & \text{on-the-fly image creation and/or configuration} \end{cases}$$

where $t_{\text{suspend}} = f(\text{size}(\text{VM}_{\text{mem}}))$ and VM_{mem} is the memory size of the instantiated VM (RAM and disk).

For the *VM transfer*, our model considers (a) the minimal time necessary to transfer one uncompressed VM image and the configuration scripts and (b) a small transfer overhead due to non-overlapping transfers for N VMs. For VMI-SR, a VM that is migrated adds the VM transfer cost to the cost of suspension. We formally express the VM transfer time as

$$t_x = \begin{cases} 0, & \text{VM already present,} \\ t_x^z + t_x^c + t_x^u, & \text{VM zipped, copied, and unzipped,} \\ t_x^c, & \text{VM is copied as is} \end{cases}$$

where $t_x^z = f(\text{size}(\text{VM}_{\text{image}}))$ is the time for zipping a VM, $t_x^c = f_x(\text{size}(\text{VM}_{\text{image}}, |\text{VM}_{\text{instances}}|))$ is the time for transferring the VM, and $t_x^u = f_u(\text{size}(\text{VM}_{\text{image}}))$ is the time for unzipping the image.

For the *VM start*, our model accounts for both the time to boot the VM and the time to locally configure the VM:

$$t_c = \begin{cases} 0, & \text{VM used by the same user with the same configuration,} \\ t_{\text{resume}}, & \text{VM to be resumed (if suspended),} \\ t_{\text{boot}} + t_{\text{cfg}}, & \text{otherwise} \end{cases}$$

where $t_{\text{resume}} = f(\text{size}(\text{VM}_{\text{memory}}))$ and $\text{VM}_{\text{memory}}$ is the size of the instantiated VM's memory (RAM and disk).

Finally, we define the time to remove a VM as follows:

$$t_r = \begin{cases} 0, & \text{VM is used by the same user with the same configuration,} \\ t_{\text{stop}}, & \text{VM stops with no removal necessary,} \\ t_{\text{cleanup}}, & \text{VM removal necessary,} \end{cases}$$

Table 19.1 reports the modeled parameter values under the assumption that at most 10 VMs are started on the same physical machine.

19.5   EXPERIMENTS

19.5.1   Setup

We performed experiments using traces from a real MMOG called Rune-Scape[4], ranked second by number of players in the U.S. and European markets (see Figure 19.1). RuneScape is not a traditional MMORPG, but combines elements of RPG and FPS (and other genres) in specific parts of the game world

---

[4]Jagex, Ltd. *RuneScape. The massive online adventure game.* http://www.runescape.com/

TABLE 19.1. Realistic Parameter Values for the Heavy VM Instantiation Model[a]

VM	Image Creation	Transfer	Start	Removal
Oceano	0 (pre-created)	0 (present)	$t_{boot} + t_{cfg} = 130$	n/a
VMPlants	$t_{image} = 27 + 100 \cdot S$	$t_x + t_s = 90 + 80 \cdot S$		n/a
Kadeploy	0 (pre-created)	$t_x + t_s = 200 + 0.33 \cdot N$		$t_{c/up} = 0.2 \cdot N$
Shirako		$t_{image} + t_x^z = 100s, t_x^{cz} + t_x^u + t_s = 20 + 2 \cdot N$		n/a
VW	0 (pre-created)	$t_x + t_s = 110 + 54 \cdot N$		n/a
XGE	$t_{suspend} = 15 + 22.5 \cdot S$	n/a	$t_{resume} = 20 + 18.3 \cdot S$	n/a
VD caches	$t_c + t_x = 248 + 0.09 \cdot S$		n/a	n/a
VMI-Plain	$t_c = 5$ (config. only)	$t_x = Xfer(S) + 0.09 \cdot N$	$t_{boot} + t_{cfg} = 180$	$t_{stop} = 10$
VMI-SR	$t_{suspend} = 20 + 25 \cdot S$	$t_x = Xfer(S) + 0.09 \cdot N$	$t_{resume} = 20 + 20 \cdot S$	$t_{stop} = 10$

[a] Measured in Seconds, where S is the size of the data to transfer in gigabytes, N is the number of VMs to instantiate, and $Xfer(S)$ is the transfer time for data of size S from the data source to the resource that instantiates the VM (e.g., $Xfer^{ideal}_{1Gbps}(S) = 10s \cdot S$, $Xfer^{ideal}_{100Mbps}(S) = 100 \cdot S$.

called mini-games, where player interaction follows different rules. Thus, various levels of player interactivity coexist, and the game load cannot be trivially computed—for example, using the linear models employed in Meng and Long [23]. We started monitoring and collecting traces from the official RuneScape Web page[4] in August 2007.

We performed experiments in a simulated RuneScape-like environment with the input workload consisting of the first two weeks from the trace data. The traces are sampled every two minutes (called *simulation steps*) and contain the number of players over time for each server group used by the game operators. This gives over 10,000 metric samples for each simulation, ensuring statistical soundness. The data centers are located on four continents and seven countries, as summarized in Table 19.2.

The hosters can use different hosting and lease policies, where each policy describes resources offered in one bulk. The resources considered are CPU, memory, and internal and external (Internet connection) network bandwidth. The policies for virtualized resources also contain a group of parameters describing the performance of the utilized virtualization technique, extracted from the model described in Section 19.4.4. In the simulated environment, game operators make requests to hosters and select resources based on the policies described in Section 19.4.3. All hosters considered provide machines with at least enough resources to handle one game server at full load—for example, 2000 simultaneous clients for RuneScape. For virtualized resources, we used the VMI-Plain instantiation model introduced in Section 19.4.4. We did not use the VMI-SR model because the suspended VM images are stateless in the current implementations and lose game state information upon suspend. Additionally, the MMOG images are large in size and cause a VM start time upon resume as large as the VM creation.

We run a series of experiments using this simulation model to evaluate the impact of virtualized and nonvirtualized resources, either separately or in conjunction, in scenarios involving one or more MMOG providers.

TABLE 19.2. RuneScape Data Centers Physical Characteristics

	Location		
Continent	Country	Hosters	Machines (Total)
Europe	Finland	2	8
	Sweden	2	8
	United Kingdom	2	20
	Netherlands	2	15
North America	United States (West)	2	35
	Canada (West)	1	15
	United States (Central)	1	15
	United States (East)	2	32
	Canada (East)	1	10
Australia	Australia	2	8

We evaluated the quality of the game experience using a *resource under-allocation* metric that characterizes the percentage of resources that have not been allocated from the amount necessary for the seamless execution of the MMOG. We defined resource under-allocation $U(t)$ (in percentage) within one simulation step T as

$$U(t) = \frac{(A - L) \cdot t}{T \cdot L_{max}} \cdot 100$$

where t is the duration of the under-allocation event, A is the amount of allocated resources, L is the amount of needed resources (measured from the traces), and L_{max} is the maximum load determined by game design.

We further evaluated the efficiency of resource allocation using a *resource over-allocation* metric that characterizes the percentage of a resource (i.e., CPU, memory, network) allocated from the used amount for the seamless execution of a MMOG session. We defined the resource over-allocation $O(t)$ within one simulation step T as

$$O(t) = \frac{(L - A) \cdot t}{T \cdot L_{max}} \cdot 100$$

using the same notation defined before.

Finally, we defined the *relative load* of an experiment in a certain machine configuration as the percentage of the maximum theoretical RuneScape load that could be hosted in the given setup. For example, the relative load of a game session consisting of N zones hosted on M machines, where a machine can host exactly one zone, is $(N/M) \cdot 100$.

19.5.2 Impact of Virtualized Hosting on MMOG Hosting

In this experiment we evaluated the effect of utilizing virtualized resources on the game-play quality quantified using the resource under-allocation metric. We used a fixed set of resources distributed around the world (see Table 19.2) and assigned to them five different allocation policies summarized in Table 19.3, ranked from the ideal policy (Policy 0, indicating nonvirtualized resources) to the least favorable policy (Policy 4) from a virtualization standpoint.

Figure 19.3 displays the variation of the average RuneScape under-allocation as a function of different relative load configurations using the five different policies. The results demonstrate that different virtualization policies have an important impact on the quality of the game play indicated by the resource under-allocation. The first two virtualized resource policies (Policy 1 and Policy 2) exhibit very close to ideal behavior. However, this is not the case for the other two policies (Policy 3 and Policy 4), which have a negative effect on the provisioning mechanism. The big difference in average under-allocation between the first two policies and the others is explained by the fact that our resource allocation algorithm uses a prediction service (see Section 19.4.2). If a

TABLE 19.3. Virtualization Section of Allocation Policies

Policy Name	CPU (Units)	Memory (Units)	ExtNet (in/out) (Units)	Time (min)	VM start (sec)	Image Size (GB)	Bandwidth (Mbit)	Virtualization Penalty
Policy 0	0.4	0.25	n/a	360	0	0	0	0
Policy 1	0.4	0.25	n/a	360	30	0.25	500	1%
Policy 2	0.4	0.25	n/a	360	60	0.5	500	3%
Policy 3	0.4	0.25	n/a	360	90	1	500	5%
Policy 4	0.4	0.25	n/a	360	120	2	500	10%

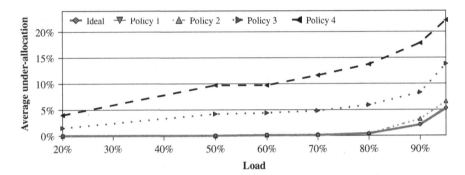

FIGURE 19.3. The impact of using different virtualized resources on quality of the resource provisioning under increasing load.

provisioned resource becomes active (e.g., finishes the initialization process consisting of VM transfer, VM start, and game server start) in a shorter time than predicted, it will not cause any under-allocation events.

We conclude that using virtualized resources directly affects the served MMOG sessions, especially at higher load volumes (which is very often the case in MMOG hosting) to a degree dependent on the data centers' allocation policies. The impact of these policies is quantified in Section 19.5.3. The use of prediction to drive the proactive resource allocation hides the virtualization overheads to a certain degree given by the prediction timestep and accuracy.

19.5.3 Impact of Data Center Policies on MMOG Hosting

In the previous section we showed a significant negative impact on the quality of service delivered by the game operators when using virtualized resources when confronted with high relative loads, however, it is not yet clear which characteristics of the virtualized resources determine this behavior.

In this second batch of experiments, we quantify the impact of the virtualization parameters modeled in Section 19.4.4 on the resource under-allocation. We preserved the same pool of resources as in the previous experiment; we also generated four ranges of hosting policies, each of them sweeping the value ranges of one virtualization parameter while keeping the others fixed (see Table 19.4). The fixed values are selected based on realistic data published by major providers of virtualized resources and other benchmark reports. We set the VM preparation time to zero (since all MMOG images can only be pre-created), the VM start time to 80 seconds as determined in Ostermann et al. [26], the VM size to 0.5 GB (which is average for base images with pre-deployed software), the transfer bandwidth to 100 Mbps, and the performance penalty of the game servers running inside virtualized resources to 5% [1]. We varied the relative load from 70% to 95% using a stride of 10.

Figures 19.4 and 19.5 show that average resource under-allocation grows linearly with the VM size and VM start time. The same growing pattern holds for different degrees of relative load with no artifacts. We conclude that the impact of these parameters on the game play is predictable and that the resource under-allocation is roughly growing by 10% per GB of VM image size and by 1.5% for each additional 10 sec of VM start time.

Figures 19.6 and 19.7 show that the VM transfer bandwidth and virtualization penalty have little or no impact on the resource under-allocation, since

TABLE 19.4. Data Center Resource Allocation Policies Used for the Quantification of the Impact of Each of the Virtualization Parameters

Policy Name	VM Start (sec)	Image Size (GB)	Transfer Bandwidth (Mbit)	Virtualization Penalty
VM start (1−6)	20−170	0.5	100	5%
VM size (1−6)	80	0.25−1.5	100	5%
VM transfer (1−6)	80	0.5	100−100	5%
Virtualization penalty (1−6)	80	0.5	100	2%−12%

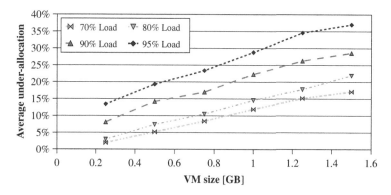

FIGURE 19.4. Variation of under-allocation with image size for different loads.

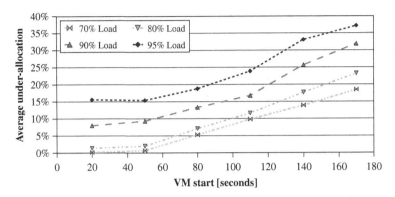

FIGURE 19.5. Variation of under-allocation with image boot time for different loads.

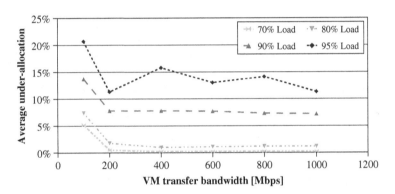

FIGURE 19.6. Variation of under-allocation with image transfer bandwidth for different loads.

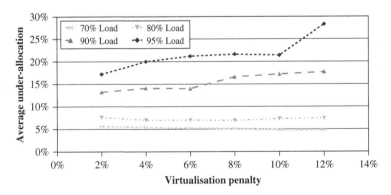

FIGURE 19.7. Variation of under-allocation with virtualization penalty for different loads.

their effect is negligible compared to the other virtualization parameters and can be easily hidden by the proactive (prediction-based) resource allocation. However, at relative load values higher than 90%, they exhibit irregular behavior as a result of less powerful resources being used which introduce significant overheads.

19.6 FUTURE RESEARCH DIRECTIONS

Currently we are conducting more experiments in an environment consisting of multiple game operators competing for resources. We are also studying the impact of resource selection policies on under-allocation, the virtualization impact on resource over-allocation, and different player interaction and complexity models.

19.7 CONCLUSIONS

In this chapter we proposed an enhanced MMOG ecosystem in which a game operator manages a distributed MMOG session by renting on-demand virtualized resources from distributed cloud providers called hosters. We presented a new analytical model for expressing the overheads added by the virtualization software consisting of four components (VM image preparation, VM transfer, VM start, and VM removal) extracted from published benchmarks. Using trace-based simulation, we evaluated the effect of utilizing virtualized resources on the quality of game-play of a highly popular MMOG called RuneScape. We learned that using virtualized resources can negatively affect the MMOG session at high load volumes, which is a common case in MMOG hosting.

We quantified the impact of our virtualization overheads on the quality of game play and found out that resource under-allocation grows linearly with the VM size and VM start time, while the VM transfer bandwidth and virtualization penalty have little impact.

ACKNOWLEDGMENTS

This work was partially funded by the European Union through the IST-034601 edutain@grid project and the Austrian Federal Ministry for Education, Science, and Culture through the GZ BMWF-10.220/0002-II/10/2007 Austrian Grid project.

REFERENCES

1. R. Bartle, *Designing Virtual Worlds*, New Riders, Indianapolis, IN 2003.
2. A. Shaikh, S. Sahu, M.-C. Rosu, M. Shea, D. Saha, On demand platform for online games, *IBM Systems Journal*, **45**(1):7–20, 2006.

3. V. Nae, A. Iosup, S. Podlipnig, R. Prodan, D. Epema, T. Fahringer, Efficient management of data center resources for massively multiplayer online games, in *Proceedings of the International Conference on High Performance Computing, Networking, Storage and Analysis*, November 2008, pp. 1–12.

4. B. Walters, VMware virtual platform, *Linux Journal*, Vol: 1999, Issue: 63es, Article: 6, 1999.

5. P. Barham, B. Dragovic, K. Fraser, S. Hand, T. Harris, A. Ho, R. Neugebauer, I. Pratt, A. Warfield, Xen and the art of virtualization, in *Proceedings of the ACM Symposium on Operating Systems Principles*, 2003, pp. 164–177.

6. Y. Lamia, R. Wolski, and G. Brent, Paravirtualization for HPC Systems, ISPA Workshops, Vol. LNCS 4331, Springer, Berlin, 2006, pp. 474–486.

7. E. Deelman, G. Singh, M. Livny, B. Berriman, J. Good, The cost of doing science on the cloud: The Montage example, in *Proceedings of the IEEE Supercomputing Conference*, 2008, pp. 1–12.

8. M.R. Palankar, A. Onibokun, A. Iamnitchi, and M. Ripeanu, Amazon S3 for science Grids: A viable solution?, in *ACM International Workshop on Data-Aware Distributed Computing*, 2008, pp. 55–64.

9. E. Walker, Benchmarking Amazon EC2 for high-performance scientific computing, *Login*, **33**(5):18–23, 2008.

10. A.B. Nagarajan, F. Mueller, C. Engelmann, and S. L. Scott, Proactive fault tolerance for HPC with Xen virtualization, in *ACM 21st International Conference on Supercomputing*, 2007, pp. 23–32.

11. Y. Lamia, K. Seymour, H. You, J. Dongarra, and R. Wolski, The impact of paravirtualized memory hierarchy on linear algebra computational kernels and software, in *ACM High Performance Distributed Computing*, 2008, pp. 141–152.

12. B. Quetier, V. Neri, and F. Cappello, Scalability comparison of four host virtualization tools, *Journal of Grid Computing*, **5**(1):83–98, 2007.

13. N. Sotomayor, K. Keahey, and I. Foster, Overhead matters: A model for virtual resource management, in *International Workshop on Virtualization Technology in Distributed Computing*, 2006, pp. 4–11.

14. T. Freeman and K. Keahey, Flying low: Simple leases with workspace pilot, in *Proceedings of EuroPar*, Vol. LNCS 5168, Springer, Berlin, 2008, pp. 499–509.

15. C. Xingchen, K. Nadiminti, C. Jin, S. Venugopal, and R. Buyya, Aneka: Next-Generation Enterprise Grid Platform for e-Science and e-Business Applications, in *Proceedings of the 3rd IEEE International Conference on e-Science and Grid Computing*, 2007, pp. 151–159.

16. R. Buyya, C. Shin Yeo, and S. Venugopal, Market-oriented cloud computing: Vision, hype, and reality for delivering IT services as computing utilities, in *IEEE International Conference on High Performance Computing and Communications (HPCC 2008)*, Dalian, China, 2008, pp. 5–13.

17. M. D. de Assuncao, A. di Costanzo, and R. Buyya, Evaluating the cost–benefit of using cloud computing to extend the capacity of clusters, in *ACM International Symposium on High-Performance Distributed Computing*, 2009, pp. 141–150.

18. M.-E. Begin, An EGEE Comparative Study: Grids and Clouds—Evolution or Revolution?, Technical Report, Enabling Grids for E-sciencE Project, 2008.

19. J. Rolia, X. Zhu, M. Arlitt, A. Andrzejak, Statistical service assurances for applications in utility grid environments, *Performance Evaluation*, **58**(2−3):319−339, 2004.

20. B. Urgaonkar, G. Pacifici, P. Shenoy, M. Spreitzer, and. A. Tantawi, An analytical model for multi-tier internet services and its applications, in *Measurement and Modeling of Computer Systems*, ACM SIGMETRICS, 2005, pp. 291−302.

21. B. Urgaonkar, P. Shenoy, and A. C. P. Goyal, Dynamic provisioning of Multi-tier Internet applications, in *2nd International Conference on Autonomic Computing*, IEEE Computer Society, 2005, pp. 217−228.

22. M. Aron, P. Druschel, and W. Zwaenepoel, Cluster reserves: A mechanism for resource management in cluster-based network servers, in *Measurement and Modeling of Computer Systems*, ACM SIGMETRICS, 2000, pp. 90-101.

23. Y. Meng and C. Long, System performance modeling for massively multiplayer online role-playing games, *IBM Systems Journal*, **45**(1):45−58, 2006.

24. V. Nae, R. Prodan, and T. Fahringer, Neural network-based load prediction for highly dynamic distributed online games, in *Proceedings of Euro-Par*, Springer, Vol. LNCS 5168, 2008, pp. 202−211.

25. A. Karve, T. Kimbrel, G. Pacifici, M. Spreitzer, M. Steinder, M. Sviridenko, and A. Tantawi, Dynamic placement for clustered web applications, in *15th International Conference on World Wide Web*, ACM, 2006, pp. 595−604.

26. S. Ostermann, A. Iosup, N. Yigitbasi, R. Prodan, T. Fahringer, and D. Epema, An Early Performance Analysis of Cloud Computing Services for Scientific Computing, Delft University of Technology, *Technical Report*, PDS-2008-006, 2008.

CHAPTER 20

BUILDING CONTENT DELIVERY NETWORKS USING CLOUDS

JAMES BROBERG

20.1 INTRODUCTION

Numerous "storage cloud" providers (or "Storage as a Service") have recently emerged that can provide Internet-enabled content storage and delivery capabilities in several continents, offering service-level agreement (SLA)-backed performance and uptime promises for their services. Customers are charged only for their utilization of storage and transfer of content (i.e., a utility computing [1] model), which is typically on the order of cents per gigabyte. This represents a large paradigm shift away from typical hosting arrangements that were prevalent in the past, where average customers were locked into hosting contracts (with set monthly/yearly fees and excess data charges) on shared hosting services like DreamHost [2]. Larger enterprise customers typically utilized pervasive and high-performing Content Delivery Networks (CDNs) like Akamai [3, 4] and Limelight, who operate extensive networks of "edge" servers that deliver content across the globe. In recent years it has become increasingly difficult for competitors to build and maintain competing CDN infrastructure, and a once healthy landscape of CDN companies has been reduced to a handful via mergers, acquisitions, and failed companies [5]. However, far from democratizing the delivery of content, the most pervasive remaining CDN provider (Akamai) is priced out of the reach of most small to medium-sized enterprises (SMEs), government agencies, universities, and charities [6]. As a result, the idea of utilizing storage clouds as a poor man's CDN is very enticing. At face value, these storage providers promise the ability to rapidly and cheaply "scale-out" to meet both flash crowds (which is the dream and the nightmare of most Web-site operators) and anticipated increases in demand. Economies of scale, in terms of

Cloud Computing: Principles and Paradigms, Edited by Rajkumar Buyya, James Broberg and Andrzej Goscinski   Copyright © 2011 John Wiley & Sons, Inc.

cost effectiveness and performance for both providers and end users, could be achieved by leveraging existing "storage cloud" infrastructure, instead of investing large amounts of money in their own content delivery platform or utilizing one of the incumbent operators like Akamai. In Section 20.2, we analyze the services provided by these storage providers, and well as their respective cost structures, to ascertain if they are a good fit for basic content delivery needs.

These emerging services have reduced the cost of content storage and delivery by several orders of magnitude, but they can be difficult to use for nondevelopers, because each service is best utilized via unique Web services or programmer APIs and have their own unique quirks. Many Web sites have utilized individual storage clouds to deliver some or all of their content [7], most notably the *New York Times* [8] and SmugMug [9]; however, there is no general-purpose, reusable framework to interact with multiple storage cloud providers and leverage their services as a content delivery network. Most "storage cloud" providers are merely basic file storage and delivery services and do not offer the capabilities of a fully featured CDN such as automatic replication, fail-over, geographical load redirection, and load balancing. Furthermore, a customer may need coverage in more locations than offered by a single provider. To address this, in Section 20.3 we introduce MetaCDN, a system that utilizes numerous storage providers in order to create an overlay network that can be used as a high-performance, reliable, and redundant geographically distributed CDN.

However, in order to utilize storage and file delivery from these providers in MetaCDN as a Content Delivery Network, we want to ensure that they provide sufficient performance (i.e., predictable and sufficient response time and throughput) and reliability (i.e., redundancy, file consistency). While individual storage clouds have been trialed successfully for application domains such as science grids [10, 11] and offsite file backup [23], their utility for general-purpose content delivery, which requires low latency and high throughput, has not been evaluated rigorously. In Section 20.4 we summarize the performance findings to date for popular storage clouds as well as for the MetaCDN overlay itself. In Section 20.5 we consider the future directions of MetaCDN and identify potential enhancements for the service. Finally, in Section 20.6 we offer some concluding remarks and summarize our contribution.

20.2 BACKGROUND/RELATED WORK

In order to ascertain the feasibility of building a content delivery network service from storage clouds, it is important to ascertain whether the storage clouds used possess the necessary features, performance, and reliability characteristics to act as CDN replica servers. While performance is crucial for content delivery, we also need to examine the cost structures of the different providers. At face value these services may appear ludicrously cheap; however, they have subtle differences in pricing and the type of services billed to the end user, and as a result a user could get a nasty surprise if they have not understood what they will be charged for.

For the purposes of this chapter, we chose to analyze the four most prominent storage cloud providers: Amazon Simple Storage Service (S3) and CloudFront (CF), Nirvanix Storage Delivery Network (SDN), Rackspace Cloud Files, and Microsoft Azure Storage, described in Sections 20.2.1, 20.2.2, 20.2.3 and 20.2.4, respectively. At the time of writing, Amazon offers storage nodes in the United States and Europe (specifically, Ireland) while Nirvanix has storage nodes in the United States (over three separate sites in California, Texas, and New Jersey), Germany, and Japan. Another storage cloud provider of note is Rackspace Cloud Files, located in Dallas, Texas, which recently launched in late 2008. Microsoft has also announced their cloud storage offering, Azure Storage Service, which has data centers in Asia, Europe, and the United States and formally launched as an SLA-backed commercial service in April 2010. An enterprise class CDN service typically offers audio and video encoding and adaptive delivery, so we will consider cloud-based encoding services such as encoding.com that offer similar capability in Section 20.2.5.

20.2.1 Amazon Simple Storage and CloudFront

Amazon S3 was launched in the United States in March 2006 and in Europe in November 2007, opening up the huge infrastructure that Amazon themselves utilize to run their highly successful e-commerce company, Amazon.com. In November 2008, Amazon launched CloudFront, a content delivery service that added 14 edge locations (8 in the United States, 4 in Europe, and 2 in Asia). However, unlike S3, CloudFront does not offer persistent storage. Rather, it is analogous to a proxy cache, with files deployed to the different CloudFront locations based on demand and removed automatically when no longer required. CloudFront also offers "streaming distributions" that can distribute audio and video content in real time, using the Real-Time Messaging Protocol (RTMP) instead of the HTTP protocol.

Amazon provides REST and SOAP interfaces to its storage resources, allowing users the ability to read, write, or delete an unlimited amount of objects, with sizes ranging from 1 byte to 5 gigabytes each. As noted in Table 20.1, Amazon S3 has a storage cost of $0.15 per GB/month in their standard U.S. and EU data centers, or $0.165 per GB/month in their North California data center. Incoming traffic (i.e., uploads) are charged at $0.10 per GB/month, and outgoing traffic (i.e., downloads) are charged at $0.15 per GB/month, from the U.S. or EU sites. For larger customers, Amazon S3 has a sliding scale pricing scheme, which is depicted in Figure 20.1. Discounts for outgoing data occur after 10TB, 50 TB and 150 TB of data a month has been transferred, resulting in a subtly sublinear pricing response that is depicted in the figure. As a point of comparison, we have included the "average" cost of the top four to five major incumbent CDN providers.[1] An important facet of

---

[1]Information obtained from Rayburn [6] and http://www.cdnpricing.com, part of a popular blog for CDN and streaming media professionals run by StreamingMedia.com. Figures were taken from the latest survey data available (Q4 2009).

TABLE 20.1. Pricing Comparison of Cloud Storage Vendors

Cost Type	Nirvanix SDN[a]	Amazon S3 U.S./EU Standard[b]	Amazon S3 U.S. N. California[b]	Rackspace Cloud Files	Microsoft Azure Storage NA/EU	Microsoft Azure Storage Asia Pacific
Incoming data ($/GB)	0.18	0.10	0.10	0.08	0.10	0.30
Outgoing data ($/GB)	0.18	0.15	0.15	0.22	0.15	0.45
Storage ($/GB)	0.25	0.15	0.165	0.15	0.15	0.15
Requests ($/1000 PUT)	0.00	0.01	0.011	0.02	0.001	0.001
Requests ($/10,000 GET)	0.00	0.01	0.011	0.00	0.01	0.01

[a] Pricing valid for storage, uploads, and download usage under 2 TB/month.
[b] Pricing valid for first 50 TB/month of storage used and first 1 GB/month data transfer out.

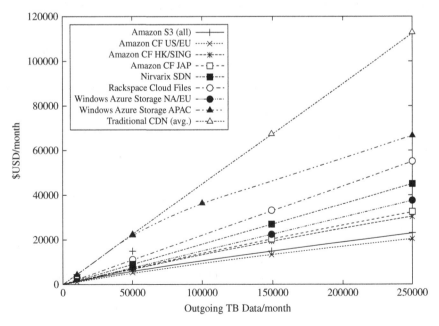

FIGURE 20.1. Pricing comparison of cloud storage vendors based on usage.

Amazon's pricing that should be noted by users (but is not captured by Figure 20.1) is the additional cost per 1000 PUT/POST/LIST or 10,000 GET HTTP requests, which can add up depending on the type of content a user places on Amazon S3. While these costs are negligible if a user is utilizing Amazon S3 to primarily distribute very large files, if they are storing and serving smaller files, a user could see significant extra costs on their bill. For users serving content with a lower average file size (e.g., 100 kB), a larger cost is incurred.

20.2.2 Nirvanix Storage Delivery Network

Nirvanix launched its Amazon S3 competitor, the Nirvanix Storage Delivery Network (SDN), on September 2007. The Nirvanix service was notable in that it had an SLA-backed uptime guarantee at a time when Amazon S3 was simply operated on a best-effort service basis. Unsurprisingly, shortly after Nirvanix launched its SDN, Amazon added their own SLA-backed uptime guarantees. Nirvanix differentiates itself in several ways (depicted in Table 20.2), notably by having coverage in four regions, offering automatic file replication over sites in the SDN for performance and redundancy, and supporting file sizes up to 256 GB. Nirvanix is priced slightly higher than Amazon's service, and they do not publish their pricing rates for larger customers (2 TB/month). Nirvanix provides access to their resources via SOAP or REST interfaces, as well as providing SDK's in Java, PHP Zend, Python, and C#.

20.2.3 Rackspace Cloud Files

Rackspace (formerly Mosso) Cloud Files provides a self-serve storage and delivery service in a fashion similar to that of the Amazon and Nirvanix offerings. The core Cloud Files offering is served from a multizoned, redundant data center in Dallas, Texas. The service is notable in that it also provides CDN integration. Rather than building their own CDN extension to the Cloud Files platform as

TABLE 20.2. Feature Comparison of Cloud Storage Vendors

Feature	Nirvanix SDN	Amazon S3	Amazon Cloud Front	Rackspace Cloud Files	Microsoft Azure Storage
SLA	99.9	99.9	99.9	99.9	99.9
Max. size	256 GB	5 GB	5 Gb	5 GB	50 GB
U.S. PoP	Yes	Yes	Yes	Yes	Yes
EU PoP	Yes	Yes	Yes	Yes	Yes
Asia PoP	Yes	No	Yes	Yes	Yes
Aus PoP	No	No	No	Yes	No
File ACL	Yes	Yes	Yes	Yes	Yes
Replication	Yes	No	Yes	Yes	No
API	Yes	Yes	Yes	Yes	Yes

Amazon has done for S3, Rackspace has partnered with a traditional CDN service, Limelight, to distribute files stored on the Cloud Files platform to edge nodes operated by Limelight. Unlike Amazon CloudFront, Rackspace does not charge for moving data from the core Cloud Files servers to the CDN edge locations. Rackspace provides RESTful APIs as well as API bindings for popular languages such as PHP, Python, Ruby, Java, and .NET.

20.2.4 Azure Storage Service

Microsoft's Windows Azure platform offers a comparable storage and delivery platform called Azure Storage, which provides persistent and redundant storage in the cloud. For delivering files, the Blob service is used to store files up to 50 GB in size. On a per storage account basis, the files can be stored and delivered from data centers in Asia (East and South East), the United States (North Central and South Central), and Europe (North and West). Azure Storage accounts can also be extended by a CDN service that provides an additional 18 locations globally across the United States, Europe, Asia, Australia, and South America. This CDN extension is still under testing and is currently being offered to customers as a Community Technology Preview (CTP) at no charge.

20.2.5 Encoding Services

Video and audio encoding services are also individually available from cloud vendors. Two notable providers are encoding.com and Nirvanix (previously discussed in Section 20.2.2). The endoing.com service is a cloud-based video encoding platform that can take a raw video file and generate an encoded file suitable for streaming. The service supports a number of video output formats that are suitable for smartphones (e.g., iPhone) right up to high-quality H.264 desktop streaming. A variety of integration services are available, allowing the encoded file to be placed on a private server, Amazon S3 bucket, or Rackspace Cloud Files folder. Nirvanix also offers video encoding as a service, offering a limited number of H.263 and H.264 encoding profiles in a Flash (flv) or MPEG-4 (mp4) container. The resulting encodes are stored on the Nirvanix SDN.

20.3 METACDN: HARNESSING STORAGE CLOUDS FOR LOW-COST, HIGH-PERFORMANCE CONTENT DELIVERY

In this section we introduce MetaCDN, a system that leverages the existing storage clouds and encoding services described in Section 20.2, creating an integrated overlay network that aims to provide a low-cost, high-performance, easy-to-use content delivery network for content creators and consumers.

The MetaCDN service (depicted in Figure 20.2) is presented to end users in two ways. First, it can be presented as a Web portal, which was developed using

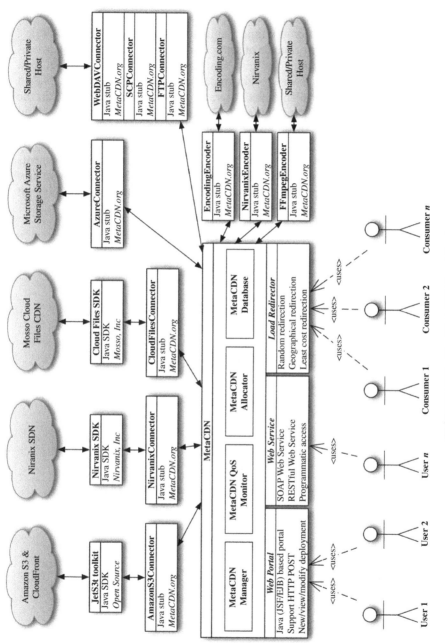

FIGURE 20.2. The MetaCDN architecture.

(a) Java Enterprise and Java Server Faces (JSF) technologies, with a MySQL back-end to store user accounts and deployments, and (b) the capabilities, pricing, and historical performance of service providers. The Web portal acts as the entry point to the system and also functions as an application-level load balancer for end users that wish to download content that has been deployed by MetaCDN. Using the Web portal, users can sign up for an account on the MetaCDN system (depicted in Figure 20.3) and enter credentials for any cloud storage or other provider they have an account with. Once this simple step has been performed, they can utilize the MetaCDN system to intelligently deploy content onto storage providers according to their performance requirements and budget limitations. The Web portal is most suited for small or ad hoc deployments and is especially useful for less technically inclined content creators.

FIGURE 20.3. Registering storage vendors in the MetaCDN GUI.

The second method of accessing the MetaCDN service is via RESTful Web Services. These Web Services expose all of the functionality of the MetaCDN system. This access method is most suited for customers with more complex and frequently changing content delivery needs, allowing them to integrate the MetaCDN service in their own origin Web sites and content creation workflows.

20.3.1 Integrating "Cloud Storage" Providers

The MetaCDN system works by integrating with each storage provider via *connectors* (shown in Figures 20.2 and 20.4) that provides an abstraction to hide the complexity arising from the differences in how each provider allows access to their systems. An abstract class, *DefaultConnector*, prescribes the basic functionality that each provider could be expected to support, and it *must* be implemented for all existing and future connectors. These include basic operations like creation, deletion, and renaming of replicated files and folders. If an operation is not supported on a particular service, then the connector for that service throws a *FeatureNotSupportedException.* This is crucial, because while the providers themselves have very similar functionality, there are some key differences, such as the largest allowable file size or the coverage footprint. Figure 20.4 shows two connectors (for Amazon S3 and Nirvanix SDN, respectively), highlighting one of Amazon's most well-known limitations—that you cannot rename a file, which should result in a *FeatureNotSupported-Exception* if called. Instead, you must delete the file and re-upload it. The Nirvanix connector throws a *FeatureNotSupportedException* when you try and create a Bittorrent deployment, because it does not support this functionality, unlike Amazon S3. Connectors are also available for (a) shared or private hosts via connectors for commonly available FTP-accessible shared Web hosting (shown in Figure 20.4) and (b) privately operated Web hosting that may be available via SSH/SCP or WebDAV protocols.

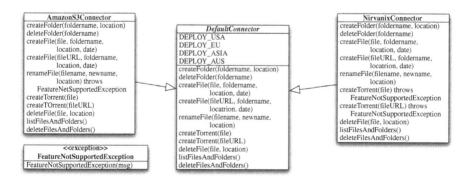

FIGURE 20.4. Design of the MetaCDN connectors.

20.3.2   Overall Design and Architecture of the System

The MetaCDN service has a number of core components that contain the logic and management layers required to encapsulate the functionality of different upstream storage providers and present a consistent, unified view of the services available to end users. These components include the *MetaCDN Allocator*, which (a) selects the optimal providers to deploy content to and (b) performs the actual physical deployment. The *MetaCDN QoS monitor* tracks the current and historical performance of participating storage providers, and the *MetaCDN Manager* tracks each user's current deployment and performs various housekeeping tasks. The *MetaCDN Database* stores crucial information needed by the MetaCDN portal, ensuring reliable and persistent operation of the system. The *MetaCDN Load Redirector* is responsible for directing MetaCDN end users (i.e., content consumers) to the most appropriate file replica, ensuring good performance at all times.

The *MetaCDN Database* stores crucial information needed by the MetaCDN system, such as MetaCDN user details, their credentials for various storage cloud and other providers, and information tracking their (origin) content and any replicas made of such content. Usage information for each replica (e.g., download count and last access) is recorded in order to track the cost incurred for specific content, ensuring that it remains within budget if one has been specified. The database also tracks logistical details regarding the content storage and delivery providers utilized in MetaCDN, such as their pricing, SLA offered, historical performance, and their coverage locations. The MetaCDN Database Entity Relationship is depicted in Figure 20.5, giving a high-level semantic data model of the MetaCDN system.

The *MetaCDN Allocator* allows users to deploy files either directly (*uploading* a file from their local file system) or from an already publicly accessible origin Web site (*sideloading* the file, where the backend storage provider pulls the file). It is important to note that not all back-end providers support

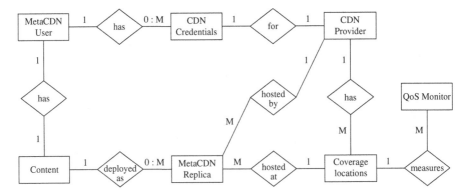

FIGURE 20.5. Entity relationship diagram for the MetaCDN database.

sideloading, and this is naturally indicated to users as appropriate. MetaCDN users are given a number of different deployment options depending on their needs, regardless of whether they access the service via the Web portal or via Web services. It is important to note that the deployment option chosen also dictates the load redirection policy that directs end users (consumers) to a specific replica. The available deployment options include:

- Maximize coverage and performance, where MetaCDN deploys as many replicas as possible to all available locations. The replicas used for the experiments in previous performance studies [12, 13] were deployed by MetaCDN using this option. *The MetaCDN Load Redirector directs end users to the closest physical replica.*

- Deploy content in specific locations, where a user nominates regions and MetaCDN matches the requested regions with providers that service those areas. *The MetaCDN Load Redirector directs end users to the closest physical replica.*

- Cost-optimized deployment, where MetaCDN deploys as many replicas in the locations requested by the user as their storage and transfer budget will allow, keeping them active until that budget is exhausted. *The MetaCDN Load Redirector directs end users to the cheapest replica to minimize cost and maximize the lifetime of the deployment.*

- Quality of service (QoS)-optimized deployment, where MetaCDN deploys to providers that match specific QoS targets that a user specifies, such as average throughput or response time from a particular location, which is tracked by persistent probing from the *MetaCDN QoS monitor. The MetaCDN Load Redirector directs end users to the best-performing replica for their specific region based on historical measurements from the QoS monitor.*

After MetaCDN deploys replicas using one of the above options, it stores pertinent details such as the provider used, the URL of the replica, the desired lifetime of the replica, and the physical location (latitude and longitude) of that deployment in the *MetaCDN Database.* A geolocation service (either free[2] or commercial[3]) is used to find the latitude and longitude of where the file is stored.

The *MetaCDN QoS Monitor* tracks the performance of participating providers (and their available storage and delivery locations) periodically, monitoring and recording performance and reliability metrics from a variety of locations, which is used for QoS-optimized deployment matching. Specifically, this component tracks the historical response time, throughput, hops and HTTP

---

[2]Hostip.info is a community-based project to geolocate IP addresses, and it makes the database freely available.

[3]MaxMind GeoIP is a commercial IP geolocation service that can determine information such as country, region, city, postal code, area code, and longitude/latitude.

response codes (e.g., 2XX, 3XX, 4XX, or 5XX, which denotes success, redirection/proxying, client error, or server error) of replicas located at each coverage location. This information is utilized when performing a QoS-optimized deployment (described previously).

This component also ensures that upstream providers are meeting their service-level agreements (SLAs), and it provides a logging audit trail to allow end users to claim credit in the event that the SLA is broken. This is crucial, because you cannot depend on the back-end service providers themselves to voluntarily provide credit or admit fault in the event of an outage. In effect, this keeps the providers "honest"; and due to the agile and fluid nature of the system, MetaCDN can redeploy content with minimal effort to alternative providers that can satisfy the QoS constraints, if available.

The *MetaCDN Manager* has a number of housekeeping responsibilities. First, it ensures that all current deployments are meeting QoS targets of users that have made QoS optimized deployments. Second, it ensures that replicas are removed when no longer required (i.e., the "deploy until" date set by the user has expired), ensuring that storage costs are minimized at all times. Third, for users that have made cost-optimized deployments, it ensures that a user's budget has not been exceeded, by tracking usage (i.e., storage and downloads) from auditing information provided by upstream providers.

20.3.3 Integration of Geo-IP Services and Google Maps

Cloud storage offerings are already available from providers located across the globe. The principle of cloud computing and storage is that you shouldn't need to care where the processing occurs or where your data are stored—the services are essentially a black box. However, your software and data are subject to the laws of the nations they are executed and stored in. Cloud storage users could find themselves inadvertently running afoul of the Digital Millennium Copyright Act (DMCA)[4] or Cryptography Export laws that may not apply to them in their own home nations. As such, it is important for cloud storage users to know precisely where their data are stored. Furthermore, this information is crucial for MetaCDN load balancing purposes, so end users are redirected to the closest replica, to maximize their download speeds and minimize latency. To address this issue, MetaCDN offers its users the ability to pinpoint exactly where their data are stored via geolocation services and Google Maps integration. When MetaCDN deploys replicas to different cloud storage providers, they each return a URL pointing to the location of the replica. MetaCDN then utilizes a geolocation service to find the latitude and longitude of where the file is stored. This information is stored in the MetaCDN database and can be overlaid onto a Google Maps view (see Figure 20.6) inside the MetaCDN portal, giving users a bird's-eye view of where their data are currently being stored (depicted in Figure 20.6).

---

[4]Available at http://www.copyright.gov/legislation/dmca.pdf.

FIGURE 20.6. Storage providers overlaid onto a Google Map view.

20.3.4 Load Balancing via DNS and HTTP

The *MetaCDN Load Redirector* is responsible for directing MetaCDN end users (i.e., content consumers) to the most appropriate file replica. When a MetaCDN user deploys content, they are given a single URL, in the format http://www. metacdn.org/MetaCDN/FileMapper?itemid = {item_id}, where item_id is a unique key associated with the deployed content. This provides a single name-space, which is more convenient for both MetaCDN users (content deployers) and end users (content consumers), and offers automatic and totally transparent load balancing for the latter.

  Different load balancing and redirection policies can be utilized, including simple random allocation, where end users are redirected to a random replica; geographically aware redirection, where end users are redirected to their physically closest replica; least-cost redirection, where end users are directed to the cheapest replica from the content deployer's perspective; and QoS-aware redirection, where end users are directed to replicas that meet certain perfor-mance criteria, such as response time and throughput.

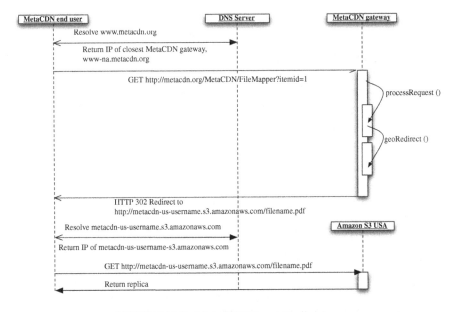

FIGURE 20.7. MetaCDN Load Redirector.

The load balancing and redirection mechanism is depicted in Figure 20.7, for an example scenario where an end user on the East Coast of the United States wishes to download a file. The user requests a *MetaCDN URL* such as http://www.metacdn.org/MetaCDN/FileMapper?itemid = 1, and the browser attempts to resolve the base hostname, www.metacdn.org. The authoritative DNS (A-DNS) server for this domain resolves this request to the IP address of the closest copy of the MetaCDN portal—in this case www-na.metacdn.org. The user (or more typically their Web browser) then makes a HTTP GET request for the desired content on the MetaCDN gateway. In the case of geographically aware redirection, the MetaCDN load redirector is triggered to select the closest replica for the end user, in an effort to maximize performance and minimize latency. MetaCDN utilizes a geolocation service (mentioned previously) to find the geographical location (latitude and longitude) of the end user, and it measures their distance from each matching replica using a simple spherical law of cosines, or a more accurate approach such as the Vincenty formula for distance between two latitude/longitude points [14], in order to find the closest replica. While there is a strong correlation between the performance experienced by the end user and their locality to replicas (which was found in previous work [12, 13] and summarized in Section 20.4), there is no guarantee that the closest replica is always the best choice, due to cyclical and transient fluctuations in load on the network path. As such, we intend to investigate the effectiveness of more sophisticated active measurement approaches such as CDN-based relative network positioning (CRP) [15], IDMaps [16], or OASIS [17] to ensure that end users are always directed to the best-performing replica.

20.4 PERFORMANCE OF THE MᴇᴛᴀCDN OVERLAY

In order to evaluate the potential of using storage cloud providers for content delivery, in prior work [12, 13] we evaluated the major provider nodes currently available to us, in order to test the throughput and response time of these data sources. We also looked at the effectiveness of the MetaCDN overlay in choosing the most appropriate replica. The files in these experiments were deployed by the *MetaCDN Allocator*, which was instructed to maximize coverage and performance, and consequently the test files were deployed on all available nodes. As noted in the previous section, the default MetaCDN load redirection policy for this deployment option is to redirect end users to the physically closest replica. At the time of the first experiment, we could utilize one node in the United States (Seattle, WA) and one node in Ireland (Dublin). Nirvanix provides two nodes in the United States (both in California), one node in Singapore, and one node in Germany. The test files were also cached where possible using Coral CDN [22]. Coral replicates the file to participating Coral proxy nodes on an as-needed basis, depending on where the file is accessed. The second experiment included storage nodes offered by Amazon CloudFront and Rackspace Cloud Files (described in Section 20.2).

For the first experiment, we deployed clients in Australia (Melbourne), France (Sophia Antipolis), Austria (Vienna), the United States (New York and San Diego), and South Korea (Seoul). Each location had a high-speed connection to major Internet backbones to minimize the chance of the client being the bottleneck during this experiment. The experiment was run simultaneously at each client location over a 24-hour period, during the middle of the week. As the test spans 24 hours, it experiences localized peak times in each of the geographical regions. Each hour, the client sequentially downloads each test file from each available node a total of 30 times, for statistical significance. The file is downloaded using the Unix utility, *wget*, with the *no-cache* and *no-dns-cache* options to ensure that for each download a fresh file is always downloaded (and not sourced from any intermediary cache) and that the DNS lookup is not cached either.

In the interests of brevity, we present a summarized set of results. The first set of results (depicted in Table 20.3) shows the transfer speed to download each replicated 10-MB test file from all client locations. The file is large enough to have some confidence that a steady-state transfer rate has been achieved. The second set of results (depicted in Table 20.4) captures the end-to-end response time when downloading each replica of a 1-kB file from all client locations. Due to the size of the file being negligible, the response time is dominated by the time taken to look up the DNS record and establish the HTTP connection.

After performing this experiment, we were confident that cloud storage providers delivered the necessary raw performance to be utilized for reliable content delivery. Performance was especially good when there was a high degree of locality between the client and the replica servers, which was evident from client nodes in Europe, the United States, and Korea. The client in Australia had reasonable throughput and response time but would certainly benefit from more

TABLE 20.3. Average Response Time (seconds) over 24 Hours from Six Client Locations

	S3 US	S3 EU	SDN #1	SDN #2	SDN #3	SDN #4	Coral
Melbourne, Australia	264.3	389.1	30	366.8	408.4	405.5	173.7
Paris, France	703.1	2116	483.8	2948	416.8	1042	530.2
Vienna, Austria	490.7	1347	288.4	2271	211	538.7	453.4
Seoul, South Korea	312.8	376.1	466.5	411.8	2456	588.2	152
San Diego, CA, USA	1234	323.5	5946	380.1	506.1	820.4	338.5
Secaucus, NJ, USA	2381	1949	860.8	967.1	572.8	4230	636.4

TABLE 20.4. Average Throughput (KB/s) over 24 Hours from Six Client Locations

	S3 US	S3 EU	SDN #1	SDN #2	SDN #3	SDN #4	Coral
Melbourne, Australia	1.378	1.458	0.663	0.703	1.195	0.816	5.452
Paris, France	0.533	0.2	0.538	0.099	1.078	0.316	3.11
Vienna, Austria	0.723	0.442	0.585	0.099	1.088	0.406	3.171
Seoul, South Korea	1.135	1.21	0.856	0.896	1	0.848	3.318
San Diego, USA	0.232	0.455	0.23	0.361	0.775	0.319	4.655
Secaucus, NJ, USA	0.532	0.491	0.621	0.475	1.263	0.516	1.916

localized storage resources. In all, we found the results to be consistent (and in some cases better) in terms of response time and throughput with previous studies of dedicated (and costly) content delivery networks [4, 18, 19]. However, further and longer-term evaluation is needed before we can make any categorical claims.

The second experiment (described in Pathan et al. [13]) tested a number of different load redirection policies operating in the MetaCDN overlay. The policies tested were as follows:

- Random **(RAN)**: End users were directed to a random replica.
- Geolocation **(GEO)**: End users were directed to the closest physical replica (as described in 20.3.4).
- Cost **(COST)**: End users were directed to the cheapest replica.
- Utility aware **(UTIL)**: End users were directed to the replica with the highest utility, where utility depends on the weighted throughput for requests, the user-perceived response times from direct replica access and via MetaCDN, the unit replication cost, and the content size. This policy is described in detail in Pathan et al. [13].

TABLE 20.5. Average Throughput (kB/sec) over 48 Hours from Eight Client Locations

	Atlanta, USA	California, USA	Beijing, China	Melbourne, Australia	Rio, Brazil	Vienna, Austria	Poznan, Poland	Paris, France
RAN	6170	4412	281	3594	800	2033	7519	1486
GEO	6448	2757	229	6519	521	2192	9008	2138
COST	3275	471	117	402	1149	523	1740	265
UTIL	3350	505	177	411	1132	519	1809	280

Measurements were from eight clients in five continents: Paris (France), Innsbruck (Austria), and Poznan (Poland) in Europe; Beijing (China) and Melbourne (Australia) in Asia/Australia; Atlanta, GA, Irvine, CA (USA) in North America, and Rio de Janeiro (Brazil) in South America. The testing methodology was identical to the first experiment described in this section, with the exception that the test ran for 48 hours instead of 24. Unsurprisingly in nearly all client locations, the highest throughput was achieved from end users being redirected to the geographically closest replica (depicted in Table 20.5). There were instances where this was not the case, such as for the client in California, suggesting that the closest physical replica did not necessarily have the best network path, performing worse than random redirection.

From an end-user perspective, most clients (with the exception of Rio de Janeiro) perform much worse with a utility policy compared to a geolocation policy. Given that the utility-aware redirection emphasizes maximizing MetaCDN's utility rather than the experience of an individual user, it is understandable that end-user perceived performance has been sacrificed to some extent. For Rio de Janeiro, the geolocation policy leads to the closest Rackspace node in the United States, whereas the utility-aware redirection results in a higher-utility replica, which is Amazon's node in the United States. In this instance, Amazon's node betters the Rackspace node in terms of its service capability, network path, internal overlay routing, and request traffic strain, which are captured by the utility calculation metric used.

20.5 FUTURE DIRECTIONS

MetaCDN is currently under active testing and development and is rapidly evolving. Additional storage cloud resources are rapidly coming online now and in the near future, improving performance and expanding the coverage footprint of MetaCDN further. Rackspace's storage cloud offering, Cloud Files, has recently launched, while Amazon has expanded their content delivery footprint to additional locations in the United States, Europe, and Asia via their CloudFront service. Microsoft has also officially launched their cloud storage offering, Azure Storage Service. MetaCDN was rapidly updated to support each of these new services as they formally launched. Due to the flexible and adaptable nature of MetaCDN, it is well-poised to support any changes in existing storage cloud services as well as incorporating support for new providers as they appear.

However, it is likely that many locations on the so-called "edges" of the Internet may not have local storage cloud facilities available to them for some time, or any time in the foreseeable future. So far, most storage cloud infrastructure has been located in Europe, North America, and Asia. However, MetaCDN users can supplement these "black spots" by adding storage for commercial shared hosting providers (available in most countries) as well as privately run Web hosting facilities thanks to the MetaCDN connectors for FTP, SCP/SSH, and WebDAV accessible Web hosting providers. These non-cloud providers can be seamlessly integrated into a MetaCDN user's resource pool and utilized by the MetaCDN system, increasing the footprint of the MetaCDN service and improving the experience of end users via increased locality of file replicas in these areas.

In future work we intend to better harness the usage and quality of service (QoS) metrics that the system records in order to make the MetaCDN system truly autonomic, improving the utility for content deployers and end users. MetaCDN tracks the usage of content deployed using the service at the content and replica level, tracking the number of times that replicas are downloaded and the last access time of each replica. We intend to harness this information to optimize the management of deployed content, expanding the deployment when and where it is needed to meet increases in demand (which are tracked by MetaCDN). Conversely, we can remove under-utilized replicas during quiet periods in order to minimize cost while still meeting a baseline QoS level. From the end-users (consumers) perspective, we have expanded the QoS tracking to include data gathered from probes or agents deployed across the Internet to improve end-users' experience. These agents operate at a variety of geographically disparate locations, tracking the performance (response time, throughput, reliability) they experienced from their locale when downloading replicas from each available coverage location. This information is reported back to their closest MetaCDN gateway. Such information can assist the MetaCDN load redirector in making QoS-aware redirections, because the client's position can be mapped to that of a nearby agent in order to approximate the performance they will experience when downloading from specific coverage locations. As mentioned in Section 20.3.4, we are also investigating other active measurement approaches for QoS-aware client redirection.

20.6 CONCLUSION

The recent emergence of "storage cloud" providers has tantalized content creators with content storage and delivery capabilities that were previously only obtainable by those who could afford expensive content delivery networks (CDNs), such as Akamai and Mirror Image. However, they can be daunting to use for non-developers, as each service is best utilized via specific web services or programmer APIs, and have their own unique quirks. Furthermore, these "storage cloud" providers are merely basic storage services, and they do not offer the capabilities of a fully featured CDN such as intelligent replica placement, automatic replication, failover, load redirection, and load balancing. In this chapter we presented MetaCDN, a simple, general-purpose, reusable service that allows content creators to leverage the services of multiple "storage cloud" providers as a unified CDN. MetaCDN makes it trivial for content creators and consumers to harness the performance and coverage of such providers by offering a single unified namespace that makes it easy to integrate into origin Web sites, and it is transparent for end users. We have found that the performance of the MetaCDN service (and the "storage clouds" it utilizes) is compelling enough to utilize as a platform for high-performance, low-cost content delivery for content producers and consumers. Up-to-date information on MetaCDN can be found at http://www.metacdn.org.

ACKNOWLEDGMENTS

This work was supported by Australian Research Council (ARC) as part of the Discovery Grant "Coordinated and Cooperative Load Sharing between Content Delivery Networks" (DP0881742, 2008–2010). Thanks go to past and present students who have worked on or with the MetaCDN system; Yudong Li, Mukaddim Pathan, Qiao Zhao, Derick Carvalho, Kushal Thirthappa, Anshul Chopra, Nagendran Mysore Balasubramanya, Ghayathiri Subbramaniam, Jinglian Geng, Wei Qiu, and Joko Parmiyanto. Finally, thanks also go to Professor Zahir Tari and Professor Rajkumar Buyya for their constructive feedback on the project. This chapter is partially derived from earlier publications [12, 13, 20, 21].

REFERENCES

1. J. Broberg, S. Venugopal, and R. Buyya, Market-oriented grids and utility computing: The state-of-the-art and future directions, *Journal of Grid Computing*, **6**(3):255–276, 2008.

2. New Dream Network LLC, Web Hosting by DreamHost, http://www.dreamhost.com, 20/4/2010.

3. B. Maggs and A. Technologies. Global internet content delivery, in *Proceedings of First IEEE/ACM International Symposium on Cluster Computing and the Grid*, Brisbane, Australia, May 15–18, 2001, p. 12.

4. A. Su, D. Choffnes, A. Kuzmanovic, and F. Bustamante, Drafting behind Akamai (travelocity-based detouring), *ACM SIGCOMM Computer Communication Review*, **36**(4):435–446, 2006.

5. M. Pathan and R. Buyya, A taxonomy of CDNs, in *Content Delivery Networks*, Springer, Berlin, 2008, pp. 33–78.

6. D. Rayburn, CDN pricing: Costs for outsourced video delivery, in *Streaming Media West: The Business and Technology of Online Video*, September 2008.

7. J. Elson and J. Howell, Handling flash crowds from your garage, in *Proceedings of the 2008 USENIX Annual Technical Conference*, Boston, Massachusetts, June 22–27, 2008.

8. D. Gottfrid, Self-service, prorated super computing fun! *OPEN: All the code that is fit to printf( )*, http://open.nytimes.com/2007/11/01/self-service-prorated-super-computing-fun/, 1/11/2007.

9. D. MacAskill, Scalability: Set Amazon's Servers on Fire, Not Yours, in *ETech 2007: O'Reilly Emerging Technology Conference*, 2007.

10. M. Palankar, A. Iamnitchi, M. Ripeanu and S. Garfinkel. Amazon S3 for Science grids: a viable solution?, in *Proceedings of the 2008 international workshop on Data-aware distributed computing*, Boston, MA, USA, pp. 55–64, 2008.

11. A. I. Matei Ripeanu. S4: A simple storage service for sciences, in *Proceedings of 16th IEEE International Symposium on High Performance Distributed Computing— Hot Topics Track*, California, USA, June 27–29, 2007.

12. J. Broberg, R. Buyya, and Z. Tari, MetaCDN: Harnessing 'Storage Clouds' for high performance content delivery, *Journal of Network and Computer Applications*, **32**(5):1012–1022, 2009.

13. M. Pathan, J. Broberg, and R. Buyya, Maximizing utility for content delivery clouds, in *Proceedings of 10th International Conference on Web Information Systems Engineering (WISE 2009)*, LNCS 5802, Poznan, Poland, October 5–7, 2009, pp. 13–28.

14. T. Vincenty, Direct and inverse solutions of geodesics on the ellipsoid with application of nested equations, *Survey Review*, **22**(176):88–93, 1975.

15. A.-J. Su, D. Choffnes, F. E. Bustamante, and A. Kuzmanovic, Relative network positioning via CDN redirections, in *Proceedings of International Conference on Distributed Computing Systems (ICDCS 2008)*, Beijing, China, June 17–20, 2008, pp. 377–386.

16. P. Francis, S. Jamin, C. Jin, Y. Jin, D. Raz, Y. Shavitt, and L. Zhang, Idmaps: A global internet host distance estimation service, *IEEE/ACM Transactions on Networking*, **9**(5):525–540, 2001.

17. M. J. Freedman, K. Lakshminarayanan, and D. Mazieres, Oasis: Anycast for any service, in *Proceedings of the 3rd Symposium on Networked Systems Design and Implementation*, San Jose, CA, May 8–10, 2006.

18. K. Johnson, J. Carr, M. Day, and M. Kaashoek, The measured performance of content distribution networks. *Computer Communications*, **24**(2):202–206, 2001.

19. A.-J. Su and A. Kuzmanovic, Thinning Akamai, in *Proceedings of the 8th ACM SIGCOMM conference on Internet measurement*, Vouliagmeni, Greece, 2008, pp. 29–42.

20. J. Broberg and Z. Tari, MetaCDN: Harnessing storage clouds for high performance content delivery, in *Proceedings of The Sixth International Conference on Service-Oriented Computing [Demonstration Paper] (ICSOC 2008)*, LNCS 5364, Sydney, Australia, December, 2008, pp. 730–731.

21. J. Broberg, R. Buyya, and Z. Tari, Creating a 'cloud storage' mashup for high performance, low cost content delivery, in *Proceedings of The Sixth International Conference on Service-Oriented Computing Workshops*, LNCS 5472, Sydney, Australia, December 2009, pp. 178–183.

22. M. Freedman, E. Freudenthal, et al. Democratizing Content Publication with Coral, in *Proceedings of the 1st ACM Symposium on Networked Systems Design and Implementation*, San Francisco, California, March 29–31, 2004.

23. Jungle Disk Inc., Jungle Disk: Reliable Online Storage Powered by Amazon S3, http://www.jungledisk.com, 20/4/2010.

CHAPTER 21

RESOURCE CLOUD MASHUPS

LUTZ SCHUBERT, MATTHIAS ASSEL, ALEXANDER KIPP, and STEFAN
WESNER

21.1 INTRODUCTION

Outsourcing computation and/or storage away from the local infrastructure is
not a new concept itself: Already the grid and Web service domain presented
(and uses) concepts that allow integration of remote resource for seemingly
local usage. Nonetheless, the introduction of the cloud concept via such
providers as Amazon proved to be a much bigger success than, for example,
Platform's Grid Support [1]—or at least a much more *visible* success. However,
the configuration and management overhead of grids greatly exceeds one of the
well-known cloud providers and therefore encourages, in particular, average
users to use the system. Furthermore, clouds address an essential economical
factor, namely, elastic scaling according to need, thereby theoretically reducing
unnecessary resource loads.

Cloud systems are thereby by no means introducing a new technology—just
the opposite in fact, because many of the initial cloud providers simply opened
their existing infrastructure to the customers and thus exploited their respective
proprietary solutions. Implicitly, the offered services and hence the according
API are specific to the service provider and can not be used in other environments. This, however, poses major issues for customers, as well as for future
providers.

Interoperability and Vendor Lock-In. Since most cloud offerings are proprietary, customers adopting the according services or adapting their respective
applications to these environments are implicitly bound to the respective

Cloud Computing: Principles and Paradigms, Edited by Rajkumar Buyya, James Broberg and
Andrzej Goscinski Copyright © 2011 John Wiley & Sons, Inc.

533

provider. Movement between providers is restricted by the effort the user wants to vest into porting the capabilities to another environment, implying in most cases reprogramming of the according applications. This makes the user dependent not only on the provider's decisions, but also on his/her failures: As the example of the Google crash on the May 14, 2009 [2] showed, relying too much on a specific provider can lead to serious problems with service consumption [3].

This example also shows how serious problems can arise for the respective provider regarding his market position, in particular if he/she makes certain quality guarantees with the service provided—that is, is contractually obliged to ensure provisioning. Even the cloud-based Google App Engine experiences recurring downtimes, making the usage of the applications unreliable and thus reducing uptake unnecessarily [4–6].

Since the solutions and systems are proprietary, neither customer *nor* provider can cross the boundary of the infrastructure and can thus not compensate the issues by making use of additional external resources. However, since providers who have already established a (comparatively strong) market position fear competition, the success of standardization attempts, such as the Open Cloud Manifesto [7], is still dubious [8]. On the other hand, new cloud providers too would profit from such standards, because it would allow them to offer competitive products.

In this chapter we will elaborate the means necessary to bring together cloud infrastructures so as to allow customers a transparent usage *across* multiple cloud providers while maintaining the interests of the individual business entities involved. As will be shown, interoperability is only one of the few concerns besides information security, data privacy, and trustworthiness in bridging cloud boundaries, and particular challenges are posed by data management and scheduling. We will thereby focus specifically on storage (data) clouds, because they form the basis for more advanced features related to provisioning of full computational environments, be that as infrastructure, platform, or service.

21.1.1 A Need for Cloud Mashups

Obviously by integrating multiple cloud infrastructures into a single platform, reliability and scalability is extended by the degree of the added system(s). Platform as a Service (PaaS) providers often offer specialized capabilities to their users via a dedicated API, such as Google App Engine providing additional features for handling (Google) documents, and MS Azure is focusing particularly on deployment and provisioning of Web services, and so on. Through aggregation of these special features, additional, extended capabilities can be achieved (given a certain degree of interoperability), ranging from extended storage and computation facilities (IaaS) to combined functions, such as analytics and functionalities. The Cloud Computing Expert Working Group refers to such integrated cloud systems with aggregated capabilities across the individual infrastructures as Meta-Clouds and Meta-Services, respectively [9].

It can be safely assumed that functionalities of cloud systems will specialize even further in the near future, thus exploiting dedicated knowledge and expertise in the target area. This is not only attractive for new clientele of that respective domain, but may also come as a natural evolution from supporting recurring customers better in their day-to-day tasks (e.g., Google's financial services [10]). While there is no "general-purpose platform (as a service)," aggregation could increase the capability scope of individual cloud systems, thus covering a wider range of customers and requirements; this follows the same principle as in service composition [11].

The following two use cases may exemplify this feature and its specific benefit in more detail.

User-Centric Clouds. Most cloud provisioning is user- and context-agnostic; in other words, the user will always get the same type of service, access route, and so on. As clouds develop into application platforms (see, e.g., MS Azure [12] and the Google Chrome OS [13]), context such as user device properties or location becomes more and more relevant: Device types designate the execution capabilities (even if remote), their connectivity requirements and restrictions, and the location [14]. Each of these aspects has a direct impact on how the cloud needs to handle data and application location, communication, and so on. Single cloud providers can typically not handle such a wide scope of requirements, because they are in most cases bound to a specific location and sometimes even to specific application and/or device models. As of the end of 2008, even Amazon did not host data centers all across the world, so that specific local requirements of Spain, for example, could not be explicitly met [15].

By offering such capabilities across cloud infrastructures, the service provider will be able to support, in particular, mobile users in a better way. Similar issues and benefits apply as for roaming. Along the same way, the systems need to be able to communicate content and authentication information to allow users to connect equally from any location. Notably, legislation and contractual restrictions may prevent unlimited data replication, access, and shifting between locations.

Multimedia Streaming. The tighter the coupling between user and the application/service in the cloud, the more complicated the maintenance of the data connectivity—even more so if data are combined from different sources so as to build up new information sets or offer enhanced media experiences. In such cases, not only the location of the user matters in order to ensure availability of data, but also the combination features offered by a third-party aggregator and its relative location.

In order to maintain and provide data as a stream, the platform provider must furthermore ensure that data availability is guaranteed without disruptions. In addition to the previous use case, this implies that not only data location is reallocated dynamically according to the elasticity paradigm [9, 16], but also the data stream—potentially taking the user context into consideration again.

Enhanced media provisioning is a growing field of interest for more and more market players. Recently, Amazon has extended its storage capabilities (Amazon S3) with Wowza Media Systems so as to offer liver streams over the cloud [17], and OnLive is currently launching a service to provide gaming as media streams over the Web by exploiting cloud scalability [18]. While large companies create and aggregate information in-house, in particular new business entries rely on existing data providers so as to compose their new information set(s) [19, 20].

Such business entities must hence not only aggregate information in potentially a user-specific way, but also identify the best sources, handle the streams of these sources, and redirect them according to user context. We can thereby assume that the same strategies as for user-centric clouds are employed.

21.2 CONCEPTS OF A CLOUD MASHUP

Cloud mashups can be realized in many different ways, just as they can cover differing scopes, depending on their actual purpose [21–23]. Most current considerations thereby assume that the definition of standard interfaces and protocols will ensure interoperability between providers, thus allowing consumers to control and use *different* existing cloud systems in a coherent fashion. In theory, this will enable SOA (Service-oriented Architecture)-like composition of capabilities by integrating the respective functions into meta-capabilities that can act across various cloud systems/platforms/infrastructures [9].

21.2.1 The Problem of Interoperability

The Web service domain has already shown that interoperability cannot be readily achieved through the definition of common interfaces or specifications [9]:

- The standardization process is too slow to capture the development in academy and industry.
- Specifications (as predecessors to standards) tend to diverge quickly with the standardization process being too slow.
- "Competing" standardization bodies with different opinions prefer different specifications.
- And so on.

What is more, clouds typically do not expose interfaces in the same way as Web services, so interoperability on this level is not the only obstacle to overcome. With the main focus of cloud-based services being "underneath" the typical Web service level—that is, more related to resources and platforms—key interoperability issues relate to compatible data structures, related programming models, interoperable operating images, and so on. Thus, to realize a mashup requires at least:

- A compatible API/programming model, respectively an engine that can parse the APIs of the cloud platforms to be combined (PaaS).
- A compatible virtual machine, respectively an image format that all according cloud infrastructures can host (IaaS).
- Interoperable or transferrable data structures that can be interpreted by all engines and read by all virtual machines involved. This comes as a side effect to the compatibility aspects mentioned above.

Note that services offered on top of a cloud (SaaS) do indeed pose classical Web-service-related interoperability issues, where the actual interface needs to provide identical or at least similar methods to allow provider swapping on-the-fly [24, 25].

By addressing interoperability from bottom up—that is, from an infra-structure layer first—resources in a PaaS and SaaS cloud mashup could principally shift the whole image rather than the service/module. In other words, the actual programming engine running on the PaaS cloud, respectively the software exposed as services, could be shifted within an IaaS cloud as complete virtual machines (cf. Figure 21.1), given that all resources can read the according image format. In other words, virtualize the data center's resources including the appropriate system (platform or service engine) and thus create a *virtual* cloud environment rather than a real one. Amazon already provides *virtual* rather than true machines, so as to handle the user's environment in a scalable fashion [26].

While this sounds like a simple general-purpose solution, this approach is obviously overly simplified, because actual application will pose a set of obstacles:

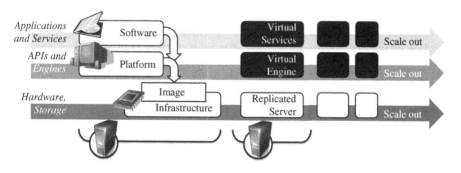

FIGURE 21.1. Encapsulated virtual environments.

- Most platform engines and services currently offered are based on proprietary environments and are constructed so as to shift the status rather than the full software. In other words, not the full software or engine is replicated, but rather only the information relevant to execute the tasks—typically, the engine or the base software will be preinstalled on all servers, thus reducing the scaling overhead.

- Moving/replicating an image including the data takes more bandwidth and time than moving a potentially very small applet.

- The size requirements of an image are less easily adapted than that of an applet/service; in other words, an image occupies more space more statically.

- This is particularly true, if the same engine can be used for multiple applets at the same time, as is generally the case; by default, each image will serve only one customer, thus increasing space requirement exponentially.

- Distributed applications and (data) links between them are more difficult to handle across images than in environments specifically laid out for that.

- The logic for scaling behavior is typically implemented in the engine or service sandbox, rather than in the underlying infrastructure; because not in all cases of service scaling does the image need to be scaled out, the logic differs quite essentially.

As has been noted, to achieve interoperability on the infrastructure layer has completely different implications than trying to realize interoperability on any higher layers. In fact, *interoperability* would imply that all images are identical in structure, which is generally not the case. With different well-established virtualization solutions (Xen, VMWare, HyperV, etc.) there exists a certain degree of defacto standards, yet at the cost of bad convertibility between them. Notably, there *do* exist efforts to standardize the virtual machine image format, too, such as the Open Virtualization Format (OVF) [27] which is supported by most of the virtualization solutions and as of 2009 even by a dedicated cloud computing platform [28]. Nonetheless, in all cases a converter is necessary to actually execute the transformation, and the resulting image may not always work correctly (e.g., [40]).

The main obstacles thus remain in performance issues, resource cost (with a virtual image consuming more resources than a small engine or even applet), and manageability. These are still main reasons why more storage providers than computational providers exist, even though the number of computing IaaS hosts continually grows, as cloud systems reduce the effort for the administration.

However, it may be noted that an image can host the engine, respectively the necessary service environment, thus leaving the cloud to handle the applets and services in a similar fashion to the PaaS and SaaS approach. This requires, however, that data, application, and image are treated in a new fashion.

21.2.2 Intelligent Image Handling

A straightforward cloud environment management system would replicate any hosted system in a different location the moment the resources become insufficient—for example, when too many users access the system concurrently and execute a load balance between the two locations. Similarly, an ideal system would down-scale the replicated units once the resource load is reduced again. However, *what* is being replicated differs between cloud types and as such requires different handling. As noted, in the IaaS clouds, images and datasets are typically replicated as whole, leading to performance issues during replication; what is more, in particular in the case of storage clouds, not the full dataset may be required in all locations (see next section). As opposed to this, applets in a PaaS environment are typically re-instantiated independent of the environment, because it can be safely assumed that the appropriate engine (and so on) is already made available in other locations.

In order to treat *any* cloud type as essentially an infrastructure environment, the system requires additional information about how to segment the exposed service(s) and thus how to replicate it (them). Implicitly, the system needs to be aware of the environment available in other locations. In order to reduce full replication overhead, resources that already host most of the environment should be preferred over "clean slate" ones—which may lead to serious scheduling issues if, for example, a more widely distributed environment occupies the resource where a less frequently accessed service is hosted, but due to recent access rates, the latter gets more attention (and so on). In this chapter, we will assume though that such a scheduling mechanism exists.

Segmenting the Service. Any process exploiting the capabilities of the cloud essentially consists of the following parts: the user-specific data (state), the scalable application logic, the not-scalable underlying engine or supporting logic, the central dataset, and the execution environment (cf. Figure 21.3). Notably there may be overlaps between these elements; for example, the engine and execution environment may be quite identical as is the case with the Internet Information Service and the typical Windows installation.

The general behavior consists in instantiating a new service per requestor, along with the respective state dataset, until the resource exceeds its capabilities (bandwidth, memory, etc.) and a new resource is required to satisfy availability. Note that in the case of *shared* environments, such as Google Documents, the dataset may not be replicated each time. In a PaaS and a SaaS cloud, each resource already hosts the environment necessary to execute the customer's service(s)—for example, in Google Docs, the Google App Engine, and so on—so that they can be instantiated easily on any other machine in the cloud environment. This replication requires not only moving a copy of the customer-specific application logic, but also the base dataset associated with it. New instances can now grow on this machine like on the first resource. In the case of

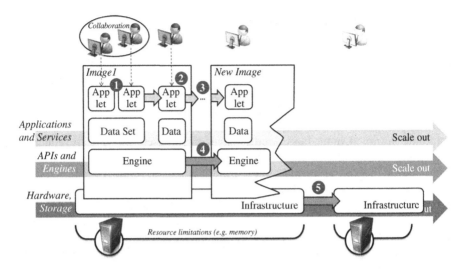

FIGURE 21.2. Hierarchical scale out in an encapsulated, virtual cloud environment.

IaaS platforms, the general scaling behavior tends toward replicating the whole image or consumer-specific dataset in new resources (cf. Figure 21.2).

In order to allow infrastructure clouds to handle (platform) services in a (more) efficient manner, the management system must be able to identify which parts are needed and can be replicated in order to scale out, respectively which ones can and should be destroyed during scale-down; for example, it would not be sensible to destroy the whole image if only one user (of many) logs out from the machine.

Life Cycle of a Segmented Cloud Image. With segmented main services in an IaaS environment, the system can now scale up and down in a (more) efficient manner across several resource providers: Any service requires that its base environment is available on the machines it gets replicated to. In essence, this means the virtual machine image—yet more particularly this involves all "non scalable" parts, such as execution/hosting engine and central dataset. Any services, applications, or applets normally scaled out can essentially be scaled out in the virtual environment just like a real environment. To this end, the virtual machines need to be linked to each other in the same fashion as if the engines would be hosted on physical machines.

As soon as the hosted engine wants to scale beyond the boundaries of the local machine, a new physical machine has to be identified ready to host the new instances—in the simplest case, another machine will already provide the respective hosting image. More likely, however, other machines with the same image will be blocked or will simply not host the image—in these cases, a new resource must be identified to upload the base image to. The base image thereby consists (in particular) of all nonscalable, not user-specific information to allow for new user instances; it must thereby be respected that different scale-outs can occur, depending also on the usage type of the cloud (see below).

21.2.3 Intelligent Data Management

Next to the segmentation of the image, management of the amount of data and thus the distribution in particular during replication (i.e., scale out) is a major challenge for future cloud systems—not alone because the digital contents will exceed the capacity of today's storage capabilities, and data are growing extremely rapidly and even faster than the bandwidth and the processing power of modern computer systems, too [29]. Implicitly and at the same time the size of single datasets increase irresistibly and obviously faster than networks and platforms can deal with. In particular, analysis and search of data is getting more and more time- and power-consuming [30]—as such, applications that require only part of the data typically have to handle the full dataset(s) first.

Much research in the field of efficient data management for large-scale environments has been done recently. The Hadoop Distributed File System (HDFS) [31], the Google File System (GFS) [32], or Microsoft's Dryad/SCOPE [33], for instance, provide highly fault-tolerant virtual file systems on top of the physical one, which enable high-throughput access of large datasets within distributed (cluster) environments. However, with all these efforts, there is still a big gap between the meaningful structure and annotation of file/data contents and the appropriate distribution of particular file/data chunks throughout the environment; that is, files are more or less randomly partitioned into smaller pieces (blocks) and spread across several machines without explicitly considering the context and requirements, respectively, of certain users/applications and thus their interest in different parts of particular datasets only.

To overcome this obstacle, the currently used random segmentation and distribution of data files need to be replaced by a new strategy which takes (1) the semantic contents of the datasets and (2) the requirements of users/applications into account (i.e., data shall be distributed according to the interest in the data/ information). For this reason, users, devices, and applications need to be modeled by capturing relevant context parameters (e.g., the actual position and network properties) as well as analyzing application states with respect to upcoming data retrieval and/or processing needs [34]. In addition, storage resources, platforms, and infrastructures (i.e., entire virtual images) shall also be continuously monitored, so as to react on sudden bottlenecks immediately. While broadcasting such relevant information (actual user and resource needs)—not frequently but in fact as soon as new requirements essentially differ from previous ones—among infrastructure and platform providers, necessary data could be replicated and stored sensibly near to the consumption point, so as to reduce bottlenecks and to overcome latency problems. Apart from distributing entire data records, this concept would also allow for segmenting large amounts of data more accurately by just releasing the relevant portion of the dataset only.

Assuming that certain parts of a database or file are more interesting than others (obtained from access statistics or user preferences), these subsets could be, for instance, extracted and replicated at the most frequently visited site as applied in content delivery networks for quite a long time [35] in order to improve scalability and performance of certain resources, too. Particular mechanisms (as applied in traditional service-oriented architectures) both on user and provider sites need to guarantee that running applications/workflows are still retrieving the correct pieces of data while shifting them among different platforms, infrastructures, and/or locations (e.g., Berbner et al. [36]). This redeployment should be completely transparent for users; they should be unaware if accessing the virtual resource X or Y as long as security, privacy, and legal issues are respected.

Theoretically, two alternatives might be considered to realize the efficient distribution of interesting datasets. First of all, in case of underperforming resources (e.g., due to limited bandwidth) and of course depending on the size of data/contents, providers could think of duplicating the entire virtual resource (image). This concept is similar to known load-balancing strategies [37] being applied if the access load of a single machine exceeds its own capacities and multiple instances of the same source are required to process requests accordingly. However, this only makes sense if local data sizes are larger than the size of the complete virtual image. The second option generally applies for large datasets which are permanently requested and accessed and, thus, exceeding the entire capacity of a single resource. In that case, the datasets might be transferred closer toward the user(s) (insofar as possible) in order to overcome latency problems by replicating the most relevant parts or at least the minimal required ones onto a second instance of the same virtual image (the same type of engine) which not necessarily runs on the same infrastructure as the original one. The latter case could yield to so-called virtual swarms (a cluster of resources of closely related data) among which datasets are actively and continuously exchanged and/or replicated. These swarms could furthermore help to speed up the handling of large files in terms of discovery and processing and might enhance the quality of results, too.

21.3   REALIZING RESOURCE MASHUPS

In order to realize efficient cloud mashups on an infrastructure level, distributed data and segmented image management have to be combined in order to handle the additional size created by virtualizing the machine (i.e., by handling images instead of applets and services). As noted above, we can distinguish between the base image set consisting of (a) the setup environment and any engine (if required), (b) the base dataset that may be customer-specific (but not user-specific), such as general data that are provided to the user, but also and more importantly the applet or service base that is provided to each user equally, and (c) the user-specific information which may differ per access and which may only be available on a single machine.

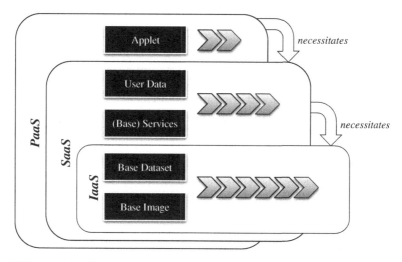

FIGURE 21.3. The relationship between IaaS, SaaS, and PaaS during scaling.

Scale-out behavior now depends on the type of application/cloud service running (Figure 21.3).

IaaS Provisioning. Infrastructures are typically provided in the form of an image containing the full computational environment or consist of a dynamic dataset, which is typically made available to all users equally. Scaling out involves either replication of the image/data set (horizontal scaling) or increasing the available storage size (vertical scale). Horizontal scaling thereby typically implies that the full dataset is replicated, while vertical scaling may lead to data segmentation and distribution.

However, as noted in the preceding section, different users may require different parts of the data, so that replication of the whole dataset every time the machine boundaries become insufficient may not be necessary, thus saving bandwidth and storage.

SaaS Provisioning. Unlike the typical charts related to the complexity of cloud *types*, Software as a Service (SaaS) does pose fewer issues on an infrastructure than does Platform provisioning. This is mostly because provided services scale-out simply by instantiating new services and state data. In most cases, the base environment for SaaS cloud types is fairly simple and can be (re)used for various different processes—for example, a .NET environment with IIS as a hosting engine.

Implicitly, several resources in the cloud environment can host the base image and allow different SaaS customers to make use of these machines. In other words, machines with the respective compatible base image (e.g., hosting a compatible IIS component) can host the replicated service instances, rather than having to duplicate the full image all the time. Notably, when no machine with a compatible base image is available anymore, a new resource has to be loaded with an image that meets the current scale-out requirements best. These may not be defined by a single service alone, but by multiple concurrent processes that have similar and opposing requirements. The same principles as for intelligent data management may be applied here, too. However, the maintenance of replicated datasets in SaaS environments requires more efforts and carefulness because synchronization between multiple instances of the same dataset on the same image might result in inconsistent states, and thus supervision of duplicated data sets is highly recommended. Particular services as applied in Microsoft's Live Mesh [38] could help taking control over this.

PaaS Provisioning. The most complex case with respect to instance management, and hence with respect to elasticity, consists in Platform as a Service provisioning: In this case, multiple different sets have to be managed during scale-out, depending on the original cause to increase the resource load. We can distinguish between the following triggers with this respect: (1) The number of *customers* exceeds the resource limits or (2) the number of *users* leads to resource problems. The actual content being replicated differs between these two cases:

When another customer wants to host more applets than the resource can manage, the additional applet will be instantiated on a new resource that executes the relevant base image (see also SaaS Provisioning above). In case no such machine exists, the backed-up base image can be used to instantiate a new resource or a running image is duplicated *without* customer and user-specific data. This can be effectively considered *horizontal* scalability [39].

In case, however, a customer's applet is taking away more resources than available due to too many users accessing the applet, respectively the appropriate data, a scale-out needs to replicate also the customer-specific data and code. This way, the new machine will have the full environment required from the *user* perspective.

21.3.1 Distributed Decision Making

The main management task for maintaining IaaS platforms for resource mashups hence consists in deciding which parts of image and data to replicate, which ones to duplicate, and which ones to retain. As discussed in the preceding sections, such information must be provided by and with the provisioning type and the appropriate usage of the cloud system.

A particular issue to be addressed in this context consists, however, in the distributed nature of the environment and hence of decision making: In particular, in a cloud mashup, no single instance will control all resources and the corresponding distribution of services, applets, and images across them; instead one will find replications of the same image in various cloud infrastructures (cf. above). Implicitly, during scale-out (and scale-down), only the requirements and restrictions of the local instance can be considered in the classical setup. For example, the original resource leading to scale out may have been freed again, respectively the amount of instances hosted in the appropriate platform environment may have been reduced—with the original contractual bindings and requirements by the according customer, the replicated instances should be reassigned to the original resource or at least the next scale-put should consider the previous hosts in order to reduce the average resource load of a customer and thus the corresponding data consumption, license implications, security relationships, and so on. Obviously, data relationships and access requirements also play a vital role in this decision (see Section 21.2.3).

It is hence difficult to make best use of deployed instances, let alone of shared consumer environments, due to the distributed nature of cloud mashup hosting. Ideally, decisions are hence made from the original instance, or at least informing related instances of the accompanying decisions so as to maintain a resource network that can be used to ensure coherence and consistency (cf. above). In all cases, the mashup should maintain the relationship information between customers, instances, users, and data (according to the differentiation introduced above).

21.4 CONCLUSIONS

We have shown in this chapter that essentially all cloud systems can be reduced to an (enhanced) Infrastructure as a Service environment or resource cloud with additional segmentation capabilities over its contents, respectively the functionalities it provides.

21.4.1 Applying Resource Mashups

Turning back to our previously introduced use cases, one will notice that in particular the overall structure of decision making and data/image distribution takes a user-centric approach whereby relationships between customers and users and their data requirements are respected so as to ensure availability while maintaining scale restrictions. Section 21.2.3 already indicated how data segmentation and distribution strategies are employed to reduce the access delay between user(s) and (common) datasets. As data are replicated according to the scaling behavior, concurrent availability from multiple sites is guaranteed as long as scaling and segmentation do not move a currently accessed dataset—in either case, preemptive caching of data needs to be employed to guarantee handover. In other words, by analyzing user behavior (data consumption) in the same way as for data segmentation, specific requirements can be assessed before the user environment is passed to a new host. Prior to a potential redirecting of the user's access route, the availability of *next required* datasets (and the environment to provide the data) needs to be ensured—only after successful rerouting the initial dataset may be destroyed (i.e., after a move). It is furthermore recommended to cache data at the recipient side, which is common procedure in stream handling these days.

21.4.2 Benefits and Obstacles

It is obvious from what has been described above that the main benefit of a resource mashup consists in an implicit interoperability across infrastructure providers with little additional effort. Nonetheless, the solution is avoiding the actual issue regarding interoperability between providers, as it shifts the problem to a flexible infrastructure management; however, as noted, interoperability through standardization and enforcing commonalities between providers is not a realistic or feasible solution.

The big advantage of a resource mashup as described above consists in respecting the vendors' desires to maintain their individual environments while allowing them to scale beyond the restrictions of their infrastructure and providing enhanced capabilities to customers and users. At the same time, however, such an arrangement implies that the platform owners have to share part of the income, as well as having to rely on other providers while the user would automatically blame the main provider. On the other hand, providers will benefit from the additional capabilities and infrastructure size, as well as from reduced management overhead, in the same way any entity may benefit from exploiting a public cloud, respectively from moving privately hosted services to a cloud.

Not all issues in this context can be solved right away, however; in particular the enhanced requirements toward distributed scheduling where individual customer contracts may be in direct conflict (i.e., the base image and the resource consumption) and need to be aligned for best resource exploitation will pose serious issues. In order to aid resource usage, vertical scalability and segmentation of individual resource to host multiple concurrent environments with little conflicts need to improved, because they do not currently offer the versatility and dynamicity required.

With the growing requirements for resources and the increasing interest in cloud infrastructures, as well as the implicit risk for isolated providers to conflict contracts during provisioning, mashing up cloud environments to provide bigger infrastructures is an implicit next development step. This will also allow providers to extend beyond the *local* restrictions of their resources and pure resource providers to sell their infrastructure everywhere.

REFERENCES

1. Platform Computing. Platform Symphony, http://www.platform.com/workload-management/SOA-grid-computing.
2. S. Shankland, T. Krazit, Widespread Google Outages Rattle Users. http://news.cnet.com/widespread-google-outages-rattle-users/.

3. M. Volpe, Google Crashes the Internet and Frustrates Marketers Everywhere, http://blog.hubspot.com/blog/tabid/6307/bid/4764/Google-Crashes-the-Internet-and-Frustrates-Marketers-Everywhere.aspx.

4. M. Arrington, Google App Engine Goes Down and Stays Down, http://tech crunch.com/2008/06/17/google-app-engine-goes-down-and-stays-down/

5. M. Siegler, Google App Engine Stalled Out For About 6 Hours Today, http://techcrunch.com/2009/07/02/google-app-engine-broken-for-4-hours-and-counting/

6. Google Groups. Google App Engine Downtime Notify, http://groups.google.com/group/google-appengine-downtime-notify.

7. Open Cloud Manifesto, http://www.opencloudmanifesto.org/Open%20 Cloud% 20Manifesto.pdf.

8. W. Vambenepe, Reality Check on Cloud portability, http://stage.vambenepe.com/archives/684.

9. Cloud Computing Expert Working Group, The Future of Cloud Computing Schubert, http://cordis.europa.eu/fp7/ict/ssai/docs/cloud-report-final.pdf.

10. Google Finance, http://www.google.com/finance.

11. W. M. P van der Aalst, M. Dumas, and A. H. M ter Hofstede, Web service composition languages: Old wine in new bottles? in *Proceedings of the 29th EUROMICRO Conference, Track on Software Process and Product Improvement*, 2003, pp. 298–305.

12. MS Azure, http://www.microsoft.com/azure/default.mspx.

13. Google Chrome OS, http://www.google.com/chrome.

14. C. Bolchini, C. A. Curino, E. Quintarelli, F. A. Schreiber and L. Tanca, A data-oriented survey of context models, *SIGMOD Record*, **36**(4):19–26, 2007.

15. R. Miller, Where Amazon's Data Centers Are Located, http://www.datacenter knowledge.com/archives/2008/11/18/where-amazons-data-centers-are-located/.

16. M. Armbrust, A. Fox, R. Griffith, A. Joseph, R. Katz, A. Konwinski, G. Lee, D. Patterson, A. Rabkin, I. Stoica, and M. Zahari, Above the Clouds: A Berkeley View of Cloud Computing, Technical Report, University of California at Berkeley, 2009.

17. Wowza Media Systems, Wowza Pro Unlimited with MPEG-TS for Amazon EC2, http://www.wowzamedia.com/ec2.php.

18. S. Perlman, OnLive: Coming to a Screen Near You, http://blog.onlive.com/2010/03/10/onlive-coming-to-a-screen-near-you/.

19. J. Y Chainon, The End of Non-aggregated News? http://www.editorsweblog.org/newsrooms_and_journalism/2007/09/the_end_of_nonaggregated_news.php.

20. Wikipedia. Aggregator, http://en.wikipedia.org/wiki/Aggregator.

21. M. Klems, Cloud Mashups, http://markusklems.wordpress.com/2009/01/30/cloud-mashups/.

22. A. Irimie, Cloud Mashups—Web 3.0 or Cloud 2.0?, http://www.azurejournal.com/2008/11/cloud-mashups-web-30-or-cloud-20/.

23. N. Singh, What Do You Get When You Cross Salesforce.com and Amazon S3?, http://blog.appirio.com/2008/04/what-do-you-get-when-you-cross.html.

24. Web Service Interoperability Organization, Web Services Interoperability Organization (WS-I) and E-Government, http://www.ws-i.org/Docs/Brochures/Web

%20Services%20Interoperability%20Organization%20(WS-I)%20and%20E-Government.pdf.

25. A. Kipp, L. Schubert, M. Assel, and T. Fernando, Dynamism and data management in distributed, collaborative working environments, in *Proceedings of the 8th International Conference on the Design of Cooperative Systems*, 2008. pp. 16–22.

26. Amazon, 2006. Amazon Elastic Cloud Computing (Amazon EC2), http://aws.amazon.com/ec2/.

27. Distributed Management Task Force, 2009. Open Virtualization Format Specification v1.0, http://www.dmtf.org/standards/published_documents/DSP0243_1.0.0.pdf.

28. AbiCloud, http://abicloud.org/display/abiCloud/AbiCloud + Overview.

29. *The Diverse and Exploding Digital Universe: An Updated Forecast of Worldwide Information Growth Through 2011*, IDC White Paper, (2008).

30. G. Aloisio, S. Fiore, Towards exascale distributed data management, *International Journal of High Performance Computing Applications*, **23**(4):398–340, 2009.

31. D. Borthakur, The Hadoop Distributed file system: Architecture and Design, http://hadoop.apache.org/common/docs/current/hdfs-design.html.

32. S. Ghemawat, H. Gobioff, and S. Leung, The Google file system, *SIGOPS Operating Systems Review*, **37**(5):29–43.

33. R. Chaiken, B. Jenkins, P. Larson, B. Ramsey, D. Shakib, S. Weaver, and J. Zhou, SCOPE: Easy and efficient parallel processing of massive data sets, in *Proceedings of the International Conference on Very Large Databases*, 2009, pp. 1265–1276.

34. D. Yuan, Y. Yang, Y. Liu, and J. Chen, A data placement strategy in scientific cloud workflows, Future Generation Computer Systems, **26**(8):1200–1214, 2010.

35. Y. Chen, R. Katz, and J. Kubiatowicz, Dynamic replica placement for scalable content delivery, *Revised Papers from the First International Workshop on Peer-To-Peer Systems, Lecture Notes In Computer Science*, **2429**:306–318, 2002.

36. R. Berbner, T. Grollius, N. Repp, O. Heckmann, E. Ortner, and R. Steinmetz, An approach for the management of service-oriented architecture (SoA) based application systems, in *Proceedings of Enterprise Modelling and Information Systems Architectures*, 2005, pp. 208–221.

37. C. Hui and S. Chanson, Improved strategies for dynamic load balancing. *IEEE Concurrency*, **7**(3):58–67, 1999.

38. Microsoft Live Mesh, http://www.mesh.com.

39. Horizontal Scalability, http://searchcio.techtarget.com/sDefinition/0,sid182_gci929011,00.html.

40. VMWare Converter, http://www.vmware.com/products/converter/.

41. N. Milanovic and M. Malek, Current solutions for Web service composition, *IEEE Internet Computing* **8**(6):51–59.

PART VI

GOVERNANCE AND CASE STUDIES

CHAPTER 22

ORGANIZATIONAL READINESS AND CHANGE MANAGEMENT IN THE CLOUD AGE

ROBERT LAM

22.1 INTRODUCTION

Studies for Organization for Economic Co-operation and Development (OECD) economies in 2002 demonstrated that there is a strong correlation between changes in organization and workplace practices and investment in information technologies [1]. This finding is also further confirmed in Canadian government studies, which indicate that the frequency and intensity of organizational changes is positively correlated with the amount and extent of information technologies investment. It means that the incidence of organizational change is much higher in the firms that invest in information technologies (IT) than is the case in the firms that do not invest in IT, or those that invest less than the competitors in the respective industry [2].

In another study, Bresnahan, Brynjolfsson, and Hitt [3] found that there is positive correlation between information technology change (investment), organizational change (e.g., process re-engineering, organizational structure), cultural change (e.g., employee empowerment), and the value of the firm as a measure of the stock market share price. This is mostly due to the productivity and profitability gain through technology investment and organizational changes. The research and analysis firm Gartner has released the Hype Cycle report for 2009, which evaluates the maturity of 1650 technologies and trends in 79 technologies. The report, which covers new areas this year, defines cloud computing as the latest growing trend in the IT industry, stating it as "super-hyped." The other new areas include data center power, cooling technologies, and mobile device technologies [4].

Cloud Computing: Principles and Paradigms, Edited by Rajkumar Buyya, James Broberg and Andrzej Goscinski   Copyright © 2011 John Wiley & Sons, Inc.

In order to effectively enable and support enterprise business goals and strategies, information technology (IT) must adapt and continually change. IT must adopt emerging technologies to facilitate business to leverage the new technologies to create new opportunities, or to gain productivity and reduce cost. Sometimes emerging technology (e.g., cloud computing: IaaS, PaaS, SaaS) is quite disruptive to the existing business process, including core IT services—for example, IT service strategy, service design, service transition, service operation, and continual service improvement—and requires fundamental re-thinking of how to minimize the negative impact to the business, particularly the potential impact on morale and productivity of the organization.

22.1.1 The Context

The adaptation of cloud computing has forced many companies to recognize that clarity of ownership of the data is of paramount importance. The protection of intellectual property (IP) and other copyright issues is of big concern and needs to be addressed carefully.

This chapter will help the student to assess the organization readiness to adopt the new/emerging technology. What is the best way to implement and manage change? While this chapter attempts to explain *why* change is important and *why* change is complex, it also raises the question of (a) managing emerging technologies and (b) the framework and approaches to assess the readiness of the organization to adopt. Managing emerging technologies is always a complex issue, and managers must balance the desire to create competiveness through innovation with the need to manage the complex challenges presented by these emerging technologies. Managers need to feel comfortable dealing with the paradox of increasing complexity and uncertainty, and they need balance it with desirable level of commitment and built-in flexibility.

22.1.2 The Take Away

Transition the organization to a desirable level of change management maturity level by enhancing the following key domain of knowledge and competencies:

Domain 1. *Managing the Environment:* Understand the organization (people, process, and culture).

Domain 2. *Recognizing and Analyzing the Trends (Business and Technology):* Observe the key driver for changes.

Domain 3. *Leading for Results:* Assess organizational readiness and architect solution that delivers definite business values.

22.2 BASIC CONCEPT OF ORGANIZATIONAL READINESS

Change can be challenging; it brings out the fear of having to deal with uncertainties. This is the FUD syndrome: Fear, Uncertainty, and Doubt.

Employees understand and get used to their roles and responsibility and are able to leverage their strength. They are familiar with management's expectation of them and don't always see a compelling reason to change. Whenever there are major changes being introduced to the organization, changes that require redesign or re-engineering the business process, change is usually required to the organizational structure and to specific jobs. Corporate leadership must articulate the reasons that change is critical and must help the workers to visualize and buy into the new vision. Corporate leadership also needs to communicate and cultivate the new value and beliefs of the organization that align and support the corporate goals and objectives. The human resources department also needs to communicate the new reward and compensation system that corresponds to the new job description and identify new training and skills requirements that support the new corporate goal and objectives.

It is a common, observable human behavior that people tend to become comfortable in an unchanging and stable environment, and will become uncomfortable and excited when any change occurs, regardless the level and intensity of the change.

A recent study by IBM, "Making Change Work," suggested that some 60% of projects fail to meet objectives; significant expense is incurred in terms of wasted money, lost opportunity, and lack of focus. The respondents from their study identified several of the key barriers to change. The most significant challenges when implementing change projects are people-oriented; topping the list are changing mindsets (58%) and corporate culture (49%). No wonder we keep hearing that the "soft stuff" is the hardest to get right [5].

A survey done by Forrester in June 2009 suggested that large enterprises are going to gravitate toward private clouds. The three reasons most often advanced for this are:

1. Protect Existing Investment: By building a private cloud to leverage existing infrastructure.
2. Manage Security Risk: Placing private cloud computing inside the company reduces some of the fear (e.g., data integrity and privacy issues) usually associated with public cloud.

22.2.1 A Case Study: Waiting in Line for a Special Concert Ticket

It is a Saturday morning in the winter, the temperature is −12°C outside, and you have been waiting in line outside the arena since 5:00 AM this morning for concert tickets to see a performance by *Supertramp*. You have been planning for this with your family for the past 10 months since they announced that Supertramp is coming into town next December. When it is your turn at the counter to order tickets, the sales clerk announces that the concert is all sold out. What is your reaction? What should you do now without the tickets? Do you need to change the plan? Your reaction would most likely be something like this:

- Denial. You are in total disbelief, and the first thing you do is to reject the fact that the concert has been sold out.
- Anger. You probably want to blame the weather; you could have come here 10 minutes earlier.
- Bargaining. You try to convince the clerk to check again for any available seats.
- Depression. You are very disappointed and do not know what to do next.
- Acceptance. Finally accepting the inevitable fate, you go to plan B if you have one.

The five-stage process illustrated above was originally proposed by Dr. Elizabeth Kübler-Ross to deal with catastrophic news. There are times in which people receive news that can seem catastrophic; for example; company merger, right-sizing, and so on. In her book *On Death and Dying*, Elizabeth Kübler-Ross describes what is known as the "Kübler-Ross model" or the "Five Stages of Grief"; this model relates to change management, specifically the emotions felt by those affected by change. The first stage of major change is often the announcement; there are situations when an understanding of the five-stage process will help you move more quickly to deal with the issue.

22.2.2 What Do People Fear?

Let's look at this from a different perspective and try to listen to and understand what people are saying when they first encounter change.

"That is not the way we do things here; or it is different in here. . . ."

People are afraid of change because they feel far more comfortable and safe by not going outside their comfort zone, by not rocking the boat and staying in the unchanged state.

"It is too risky. . ."

People are also afraid of losing their position, power, benefits, or even their jobs in some instances. It is natural for people to try to defend and protect their work and practice.

All these behaviors seem appropriate with respect to cloud computing, companies have historically rewarded people who avoid risks, especially corporations and organizations that have cultivated and tolerated the following philosophy: "No one ever got fired for buying technology from the industry leader measured by market size, and not necessarily decided on the amount of innovation produced."

The more common concerns are related to cloud computing, and some of them are truly legitimate and require further study, including:

- Security and privacy protection
- Loss of control (i.e., paradigm shift)
- New model of vendor relationship management
- More stringent contract negotiation and service-level agreement (SLA)
- Availability of an executable exit strategy

22.3 DRIVERS FOR CHANGES: A FRAMEWORK TO COMPREHEND THE COMPETITIVE ENVIRONMENT

The Framework. The five driving factors for change encapsulated by the framework are:

- Economic (global and local, external and internal)
- Legal, political, and regulatory compliance
- Environmental (industry structure and trends)
- Technology developments and innovation
- Sociocultural (markets and customers)

The five driving factors for change is an approach to investigate, analyze, and forecast the emerging trends of a plausible future, by studying and understanding the five categories of drivers for change. The results will help the business to make better decisions, and it will also help shape the short- and long-term strategies of that business. It is this process that helps reveal the important factors for the organization's desirable future state, and it helps the organization to comprehend which driving forces will change the competitive landscape in the industry the business is in, identify critical uncertainties, and recognize what part of the future is predetermined such that it will happen regardless how the future will play out. This approach also helps seek out those facts and perceptions that challenge one's underlying assumptions, and thus it helps the company make a better decision.

Every organization's decisions are influenced by particular key factors, some of them are within the organization's control, such as (a) internal financial weakness and strength and (b) technology development and innovation, and therefore the organization has more control. The others, such as legal compliance issues, competitor capabilities, and strategies, are all external factors over which the organization has little or no control. There are also many other less obvious external factors that will impact the organization; identifying and assessing these fundamental factors and formulating a course of action proactively is paramount to any business success.

A driving force or factor is a conceptual tool; it guides us to think deeply about the underlying issues that impact our well-being and success. In a business setting, it helps us to visualize and familiarize ourselves with future possibilities (opportunities and threats).

22.3.1 Economic (Global and Local, External and Internal)

Economic factors are usually dealing with the state of economy, both local and global in scale. To be successful, companies have to live with the paradox of having new market and business opportunities globally, and yet no one can be isolated from the 2008 global financial crisis, because we are all interdependent.

Managers are often asked to do more with less, and this phenomenon is especially true during economic downturn. Managers and groups are expected to deal with the unpleasant facts of shrinking market share, declining profit margins, unsatisfactory earnings, new and increasing competition, and decreasing competitiveness.

Following are sample questions that could help to provoke further discussion:

- What is the current economic situation?
- What will the economy looks lik in 1 year, 2 years, 3 years, 5 years, and so on?
- What are some of the factors that will influence the future economic outlook?
- Is capital easy to access?
- How does this technology transcend the existing business model?
- Buy vs. build? Which is the right way?
- What is the total cost of ownership (TCO)?

22.3.2 Legal, Political, and Regulatory Compliance

This section deals with issues of transparency, compliance, and conformity. The objective is to be a good corporate citizen and industry leader and to avoid the potential cost of legal threats from external factors.

The following are sample questions that could help to provoke further discussion:

- What are the regulatory compliance requirements?
- What is the implication of noncompliance?
- What are the global geopolitical issues?

22.3.3 Environmental (Industry Structure and Trends)

Environmental factors usually deal with the quality of the natural environment, human health, and safety. The following are sample questions that could help to provoke further discussion:

- What is the implication of global warming concern?
- Is a green data center over-hyped?

- How can IT initiatives help and support organizational initiatives to reduce carbon footprint?
- Can organizations and corporations leverage information technology, including cloud computing to pursue sustainable development?

22.3.4 Technology Developments and Innovation

Scientific discoveries are seen to be key drivers of economic growth; leading economists have identified technological innovations as the single most important contributing factor in sustained economic growth. There are many fronts of new and emerging technologies that could potentially transform our world. For example, new research and development in important fields such as bioscience, nanotechnology, and information technology could potentially change our lives.

The following are sample questions that could help to provoke further discussion:

- When will the IT industry standards be finalized? By who? Institute of Electrical and Electronics Engineers (IEEE)?
- Who is involved in the standardization process?
- Who is the leader in cloud computing technology?
- What about virtualization of application−operating system (platform) pair (i.e., write once, run anywhere)?
- How does this emerging technology (cloud computing) open up new areas for innovation?
- How can an application be built once so it can configure dynamically in real time to operate most effectively, based on the situational constraint (e.g., out in the cloud somewhere, you might have bandwidth constraint to transfer needed data)?
- What is the guarantee from X Service Providers (XSP) that the existing applications will still be compatible with the future infrastructure (IaaS)? Will the data still be executed correctly?

22.3.5 Sociocultural (Markets and Customers)

Societal factors usually deal with the intimate understanding of the human side of changes and with the quality of life in general. A case in point: The companies that make up the U.S. defense industry have seen more than 50% of their market disappear. When the Berlin Wall tumbled, the U.S. government began chopping major portions out of the defense budget. Few would disagree that the post−Cold War United States could safely shrink its defense industry. Survival of the industry, and therefore of the companies, demands that companies combine with former competitors and transform into new species [6].

The following are sample questions that could help to provoke further discussion:

- What are the shifting societal expectations and trends?
- What are the shifting demographic trends?
- How does this technology change the user experience?
- Is the customer the king?
- Buy vs. build? Which is the right way?
- How does cloud computing change the world?
- Is cloud computing over-hyped?

22.3.6 Creating a Winning Environment

At the cultural level of an organization, change too often requires a lot of planning and resource. This usually stems from one common theme: Senior management and employees have different perspectives and interpretations of what change means, what change is necessary, and even if changes are necessary at all. In order to overcome this, executives must articulate a new vision and must communicate aggressively and extensively to make sure that every employee understands [7]:

1. The new direction of the firm (where we want to go today)
2. The urgency of the change needed
3. What the risks are to
   a. Maintain status quote
   b. Making the change
4. What the new role of the employee will be
5. What the potential rewards are

- Build a business savvy IT organization.
  - Are software and hardware infrastructure an unnecessary burden?
  - What kind of things does IT do that matter most to business?
  - Would the IT professional be better off focusing on highly valued product issues?
- Cultivate an IT savvy business organization.
  - Do users require new skill and expertise?

One of the important value propositions of cloud computing should be to explain to the decision maker and the users the benefits of:

- Buy and not build
- No need for a large amount of up-front capital investment

- Opportunity to relieve your smartest people from costly data-center operational activities; and switch to focus on value-added activities
- Keep integration (technologies) simple

22.4 COMMON CHANGE MANAGEMENT MODELS

There are many different change management approaches and models, and we will discuss two of the more common models and one proposed working model (CROPS) here; the Lewin's Change Management Model, the Deming Cycle (Plan, Do, Study, Act) and the proposed CROPS Change Management Framework.

22.4.1 Lewin's Change Management Model

Kurt Lewin, a psychologist by training, created this change model in the 1950s. Lewin observed that there are three stages of change, which are: *Unfreeze*, *Transition*, and *Refreeze*. It is recognized that people tend to become complacent or comfortable in this "freeze" or "unchanging/stable" environment, and they wish to remain in this "safe/comfort" zone. Any disturbance/disruption to this unchanging state will cause pain and become uncomfortable.

In order to encourage change, it's necessary to unfreeze the environment by motivating people to accept the change. The motivational value has to be greater than the pain in order to entice people to accept the change. Maintaining a high level of motivation is important in all three phases of the change management life cycle, even during the transition period. As Lewin put it, "Motivation for change must be generated before change can occur. One must be helped to reexamine many cherished assumptions about oneself and one's relations to others." This is the unfreezing stage from which change begins.

The transition phase is when the change (plan) is executed and actual change is being implemented. Since these "activities" take time to be completed, the process and organizational structure may also need to change, specific jobs may also change. The most resistance to change may be experienced during this transition period. This is when leadership is critical for the change process to succeed, and motivational factors are paramount to project success.

The last phase is Refreeze; this is the stage when the organization once again becomes unchanging/frozen until the next time a change is initiated [8].

| UNFREEZE | TRANSITION | REFREEZE |

22.4.2 Deming Cycle (Plan, Do, Study, Act)

The Deming cycle is also known as the PDCA cycle; it is a continuous improvement (CI) model comprised of four sequential subprocesses; Plan,

Do, Check, and Act. This framework of process and system improvement was originally conceived by Walter Shewhart in the 1930s and was later adopted by Edward Deming. The PDCA cycle is usually implemented as an evergreen process, which means that the end of one complete pass (cycle) flows into the beginning of the next pass and thus supports the concept of continuous quality improvement.

Edward Deming proposed in the 1950s that business processes and systems should be monitored, measured, and analyzed continuously to identify variations and substandard products and services, so that corrective actions can be taken to improve on the quality of the products or services delivered to the customers.

- **PLAN:** *R*ecognize an opportunity and plan a change.
- **DO:** *E*xecute the plan in a small scale to prove the concept.
- **CHECK:** *E*valuate the performance of the change and report the results to sponsor.
- **ACT:** *D*ecide on accepting the change and standardizing it as part of the process.

Incorporate what has been learned from the previous steps to plan new improvements, and begin a new cycle.

Deming's PDCA cycle is illustrated in Fig 22.1: Deming's PDCA cycle.

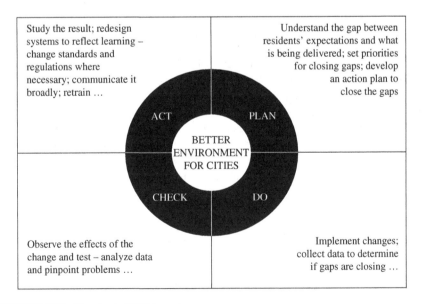

FIGURE 22.1. Deming's PDCA cycle.
Source: http://www.gdrc.org/uem/iso14001/pdca-cycle.gif.

22.4.3 A Proposed Working Model: CROPS Change Management Framework

For many organizations, change management focuses on the project management aspects of change. There are a good number of vendors offering products that are intended to help organizations manage projects and project changes, including the Project Portfolio Management Systems (PPMS). PPMS groups projects so they can be managed as a portfolio, much as an investor would manage his/her stock investment portfolio to reduce risks.

In the IT world, a project portfolio management system gives management timely critical information about projects so they can make better decisions; re-deploy resources due to changing priorities, and keep close tabs on progress.

However, as the modern economy moves from product and manufacturing centric to a more information and knowledge base focus, the change management process needs to reflect that people are truly the most valuable asset of the organization. Usually, an organization experiences strong resistance to change. Employees are afraid of the uncertainty, they feel comfortable with the stable state and do not want to change, and are afraid to lose their power if things change. To them, there is no compelling reason to change, unless the company can articulate a compelling reason and communicate it effectively to convince them and influentially engage them to change.

The best approaches to address resistance are through increased and sustained communications and education. The champion of change, usually the leader— for example, the Chief Information Officer (CIO) of the organization—should communicate the *Why* aggressively and provide a *Vision* of *Where* he wants to go today. There are many writings and models on organization development (i.e., how). A summary of this working model follows: **C**ulture, **R**ewards, **O**rganization and Structures, **P**rocess, **S**kills and Competencies (CROPS) framework.

Culture. Corporate culture is a reflection of organizational (management and employees) values and belief. Edgar Schein, one of the most prominent theorists of organizational culture, gave the following very general definition [9, 10]:

> The culture of a group can now be defined as: A pattern of shared basic assumptions that the group learned as it solved its problems of external adaptation and internal integration, that has worked well enough to be considered valid and, therefore, to be taught to new members as the correct way to perceive, think, and feel in relation to those problems.

Elements of organizational culture may include:

- Stated values and belief
- Expectations for member behavior
- Customs and rituals
- Stories and myths about the history of the organization

FIGURE 22.2. CROPS framework.

- Norms—the feelings evoked by the way members interact with each other, with outsiders, and with their environment
- Metaphors and symbols—found embodied in other cultural elements

Rewards and Management System. This management system focuses on how employees are trained to ensure that they have the right skills and tools to do the job right. It identifies how to measure employee job performance and how the company compensates them based on their performance. Reward is the most important ingredient that shapes employees' value and beliefs.

Organization and Structures. How the organization is structured is largely influenced by what the jobs are and how the jobs are performed. The design of the business processes govern what the jobs are, and when and where they get done. Business processes need to align with organizational vision, mission, and strategies in order to create customer and shareholder values. Therefore, all the components of the CROPS framework are interrelated.

Process. Thomas Davenport [11] defined a **business process** or **business method** as a collection of related, structured activities or tasks that produce a specific service or product (serve a particular goal) for a particular customer or customers.

Hammer and Champy's [12] definition can be considered as a subset of Davenport's. They define a process as "a collection of activities that takes one or more kinds of input and creates an output that is of value to the customer."

A process is where the work gets done, and value creation occurs through transforming input into output.

Skills and Competencies. Specialized skills that become part of the organizational core competency enable innovation and create a competitive edge. Organizations that invest in research and development which emphasize investing in people's training and well-being will shape a winning strategy.

The CROPS model is illustrated in Figure 22.2.

Although each component tackles a different requirement for change, a holistic view of the issue at hand is the best way to pursue a better understanding of the change implications to the organization as a whole. It is almost certain that if one of the specific components is changed, many of the other components will need to be changed as a result.

22.5 CHANGE MANAGEMENT MATURITY MODEL (CMMM)

A Change Management Maturity Model (CMMM) helps organizations to (a) analyze, understand, and visualize the strength and weakness of the firm's change management process and (b) identify opportunities for improvement and building competitiveness. The model should be simple enough to use and flexible to adapt to different situations. The working model in Table 22.1 is based on CMM (Capability Maturity Model), originally developed by American Software Engineering Institute (SEI) in cooperation with Mitre Corporation. CMM is a model of process maturity for software development, but it has since been adapted to different domains. The CMM model describes a five-level process maturity continuum, depicted in Table 22.1.

How does CMMM help organizations to adopt new technology, including cloud computing, successfully? The business value of CMMM can be expressed in terms of improvements in business efficiency and effectiveness. All organizational investments are business investments, including IT investments. The resulting benefits should be measured in terms of business returns. Therefore, CMMM value can be articulated as the ratio of business performance to CMMM investment; for example

$$\text{ROIT(CMMM)} = \frac{\text{Estimated total business performance improvement}}{\text{Total CMMM investment(TCO)}}$$

whereas

- ROIT: Observed business value or total return on investment from IT initiative (CMMM)
- Business performance improvement
  - Reduce error rate

TABLE 22.1. A Working Model: Change Management Maturity Model (CMMM)

	Description	CROPS Practice	Specific to CMMM	Characteristics of Organization	Path to Next Higher Level	Key Results and Benefits (or, the Lack There of)
Level 5	Optimized	P + R	AT this level of process maturity, the focus is on improving process performance.	Operational excellence/organizational competency Change management as part of the core competency. Culturally, employee accepts that change is constant and in a rapid rate.	Achieve strategic/operational excellence. Extensive training exists at all level of organization.	Better business and IT strategic alignment. Enabling innovation. Create competitiveness.
Level 4	Managed	CROPS	Adopted specific change management methodology and process. Centralized and standardized change management control and tracking to manage risks and sustain quality of products and services.	Organization and management can find ways to change, evolve, and adapt the process to particular project needs; with minimal or no impact to quality of products or services being delivered as measured against SLA.	Continuous process improvement. Effective business and IT strategic alignment.	Achieve higher level of quality. Higher degree of customer/user satisfaction. Reduce costs. Higher profitability. Increase revenue and market share.
Level 3	Defined	CROPS	Standardizing change management processes and practices.	Processes at this level are defined and documented. Some process improvement projects initiate overtime.		Better appreciation of value of IT. Better business and IT integration.
Level 2	Repeatable	COPS	Accept the importance of change management process. No standardization/centralization of change management process and practice. Poor change authorization and tracking scheme.	It is characteristic of processes at this level that some processes are repeatable.	Standardize and centralize change management process.	Project failure rate is still too high. Changes are still very disruptive to business operation.
Level 1	Ad hoc (disruptive)	None	No change management processes. No specific or informal change management process and practice exist anywhere. Change can be made with no control at all; there is no approval mechanism, no track record and no single party accountable for the failure.	Chaotic Reactive Disruptive Uncontrolled Unstable Constantly operate in a firefighting mode.	Adopt formal change management practice.	No awareness of the benefits of adopting change management and best practice. Project failures are too often and too costly. No understanding of risk management, and do not have the capacity to manage and minimize disruption to IT and business due to change and/or the failure of the uncontrolled changes.

- Increase customer/user satisfaction
  - Customer retention
  - Employee retention
- Increase market share and revenue
- Increase sales from existing customer
- Improve productivity
- And others
- CMMM investment
  - Initial capital investment
  - Total cost of ownership (TCO) over the life of the investment (solution)

22.5.1 A Case Study: AML Services Inc.

AML (A Medical Laboratory Services Inc.) is one of the medical laboratory service providers for a city with a population of one million, and AML is a technology-driven company with 150 employees serving the city and surrounding municipalities. Although the barrier to entry is high—the field requires a lot of startup investment for equipment and technologies (e.g., laboratory testing, X ray, MRI, and information technologies), as well as highly skilled staff—there is some competition in this segment of the health care industry.

In 2009, AML was experiencing continual growth in demand of service from their patients, partly due to the H1N1 flu phenomenon and partly due to the aging of the population. The company was hampered by outdated IT infrastructure, however; there was urgent need to upgrade the unsupported version of the mail server and to enhance communication between the mobile work force (courier service) and the dispatcher, and it is recommended that courier vehicles be equipped with laptop and Wi-Fi capability. A Web-based reservation application system enabling patients to book their appointment on-line has been approved by the company.

Tom Cusack, the CIO of AML, decides to hire a consulting firm to help him architect the right solution for AML. Potential discussion questions could be as follows:

- Should AML consider cloud computing part of the solution?
- Is AML ready for cloud computing?
- What does "done" look like?
- How can the organization overcome these challenges of change?

22.6 ORGANIZATIONAL READINESS SELF-ASSESSMENT: (WHO, WHEN, WHERE, AND HOW)

An organizational assessment is a process intending to seek a better understanding of the *as-is* (current) state of the organization. It also defines the roadmap (strategies and tactics) required to fill the gap and to get the organization moving toward where it wants to go (future state) from its current state.

The process implies that the organization needs to complete the strategy analysis process first and to formulate the future goals and objectives that support the future direction of the business organization.

The organizational assessment can be conducted by either an internal or external professional, depending on whether the expertise is available. Before the actual assessment begins, the champion of change (perhaps the CEO of the organization) is advised to articulate the vision of the firm, where the organization wants to go tomorrow, and how it intends to get there. This is a critical opportunity for the leader of the firm to influence the crowd and rally the troops to support for the changes the firm desires.

During an effective organization readiness assessment, it is desirable to achieve the following:

- Articulate and reinforce the reason for change.
- Determine the as-is state.
- Identify the gap (between future and current state).
- Anticipate and assess barriers to change.
- Establish action plan to remove barriers.

Involve the right people to enhance buy-in:

- It is critical to involve all the right people (stakeholders) across the organization, and not just management and decision-makers, as participants in any organization assessment. Stakeholders can be interpreted as anyone who may potentially be affected by the changes. A cross-sectional representation from the organization is paramount to success.

Asking the "right questions" is also essential. The assessment should provide insight into your challenges and help determine some of these key questions:

- How big is the gap?
- Does your organization have the capacity to execute and implement changes?
- How will your employees respond to the changes?
- Are all your employees in your organization ready to adopt changes that help realize the vision?
- What are the critical barriers to success?
- Are you business partners ready to support the changes?

Are you ready? Table 22.2 shows a working assessment template.

TABLE 22.2. Working Assessment Template

Nontechnical	Agree	Don't Know	Disagree
Does your organization have a good common understanding of why business objectives have been met or missed in the past?			
Does your organization have a good common understanding of why projects have succeeded or failed in the past?			
Does your organization have a change champion?			
Does your organization perceive change as unnecessary disruption to business?			
Does your organization view changes as the management fad of the day?			
Does your organization adopt an industry standard change management best practice and methodology approach?			
Does your organization adopt and adapt learning organization philosophy and practice?			
How familiar is your organization with service provisioning with an external service provider?			
Technical			
Does your organization implement any industry management standards? • ITIL • COBIT • ITSM • others			
Does your organization have a well-established policy to classify and manage the full lifecycle of all corporate data?			
Can you tell which percentage of your applications is CPU-intensive, and which percentage of your applications is data-intensive?			

22.7 DISCUSSION

Gartner Research has just released the Hype Cycle report for 2009, which evaluates the maturity of over 1500 technologies and 50+ technology trends.

The report suggests that the cloud computing is the latest growing trend in the IT industry. According to Gartner Research, cloud computing is expected to hit the peak of the "inflated expectations" in the next few years. It is expected that cloud computing data security and integrity issues will be refined over time as the technology matured. The pay-as-you-go business model will mature with the technology over time; it will become more transparent and will behave more like a true utility model, such that you can easily work with a service provider without worrying about the security of the data. To summarize what we have learned, one can entertain to leverage the formula developed by management consultant David Gleicher:

$Dissatisfaction \times Vision$ of future possibilities $\times$ Achievable first step)

$\gg$ Resistance to change

This means that any component that is equal to zero or near zero will make the left-hand side of the equation equal to or approaching zero. In order to make the change initiative successful, the product of the left-hand side equation must be a lot greater than that of the right-hand side of the equation (pain or resistance to change).

22.7.1   Case Study: EnCana CORP.

EnCana Corp, Canada's biggest energy company, announced early Sunday afternoon—on Mother's Day—its plans to split into two discrete companies, an oil company and a natural gas company, in an effort to wring out more shareholder value with crude prices at record highs. This has all the DNA of the company's chairman, David O'Brien: In 2001, under O'Brien's visionary leadership, tremendous value was created when CP Limited was split up into five separate companies and one of them was PanCanadian Petroleum. The challenge is to quickly establish a corporate culture that would bridge the somewhat divergent cultures of its two predecessor companies [13, 14].

EnCana is based in Calgary, Alberta, Canada. It is the largest producer of natural gas in North America, producing 3.8 billion cubic feet per day in 2008. EnCana also some conventional oil and shale oil operations, but natural gas production accounts for more than 80% of the total production. According to *CIBC Assessment Management* (May 2008 issue), when EnCana announced its intention to split into two parts, it had a market capitalization of about $65 billion, second only to Research in Motion in companies listed on the Toronto Stock Exchange.

EnCana, a $65 billion energy producer formed in 2002 in a $27 billion merger of PanCanadian Petroleum (which focused on oil) and Alberta Energy Corporation (which focused on gas production), said the move should help investors better gauge and appreciate the real value of the business of the respective products and remove a so-called "holding company discount" it suffers in the stock market.

Over the last few years, EnCana has sold off assets that were deemed non-core to the business, assets that are located in the North Sea, Mexico, and Ecuador in order to focus its operations on North America (i.e., United States and Canada).

EnCana is usually viewed as a major natural gas explorer and producer; the oil sands plays in Alberta were almost treated as after thoughts.

It is expected that the proposed split of EnCana would be similar to the CP Enterprise split in 2001; the reorganization of EnCana should have the same impact on the two new companies being created. It should result in (a) better market valuations because of greater transparency for shareholders and (b) greater clarity when it comes to allocating capital for expenditures within each entity.

2008 Highlights (As Published on Their Web Site): Financial (US$)

- Cash flow increased 13% per share to $12.48, or $9.4 billion.
- Operating earnings were up 9% per share to $5.86, or $4.4 billion.
- Net earnings were up 53% per share to $7.91, or $5.9 billion, primarily due to an after-tax unrealized mark-to-market hedging gain of $1.8 billion in 2008 compared to an after-tax loss of $811 million in 2007.
- Capital investment, excluding acquisitions and divestitures, was up 17% to $7.1 billion.
- Generated $2.3 billion of free cash flow (as defined in Note 1 on page 10), down $112 million from 2007.
- Operating cash flow nearly doubled to $421 million from the company's Foster Creek and Christina Lake upstream projects, whereas lower refining margins and higher purchased product costs resulted in a $241 million loss in operating cash flow for the downstream business. As a result, EnCana's integrated oil business venture with ConocoPhillips generated $180 million of operating cash flow.

In October 2008, EnCana announced that its plan to split into two companies has been put on hold because of the current global financial crisis:

"The unprecedented uncertainty in the debt and credit markets has certainly become more difficult and this kind of extraordinary time we've decided to wait," says Alan Boras, a spokesperson for EnCana.

EnCana officials insisted that the plan hasn't been abandoned and that the reasons for breaking into a pure natural gas producer and an integrated oil firm are still valid, despite the setback.

"We remain committed to creating Cenovus; [then name of the integrated oil company] and we are continuing to work on reorganizing our company's structure so we are ready to move forward with the transaction at the appropriate time," said CEO Randy Eresman.

"However, there is currently too much uncertainty in the global debt and equity markets to proceed ... at this time. We cannot predict when the appropriate financial and market conditions will return, but EnCana will be prepared to advance the proposed transaction when it determines that the market conditions are appropriate," Eresman said.

The discussion questions could be as follows:

1. How would cloud computing be a part of the solution to facilitate the splitting of the company into two effectively and efficiently and with minimal disruption to the business?
2. What would you advise EnCana executives to do at the 2008 worldwide financial market meltdown and the subsequent economic recession?
3. What would your advice be from a business and IT strategic alignment perspective if you were brought in to advise EnCana IT executives?
4. What were the risks if EnCana went ahead with the split?
5. What were the risks if EnCana put the split on hold?
6. If EnCana is successful in its maneuver, could its peers and competitors consider splitting their assets into distinct companies to create greater shareholder value?
7. What IT migration strategy would you recommend EnCana to adopt in order to achieve the highest flexibility and adaptability to changes?
8. Would you recommend that EnCana buy or build a duplicate IT infrastructure for each distinct organization as the most efficient way to align and support the business organization, both the new and the old?
9. Would you recommend cloud computing or utility computing as the solution to EnCana's business problem?
10. How would you assess the organizational readiness for EnCana?
11. Would it make any difference if IT can accommodate all the necessary changes to facilitate the split up of the firm into two distinct entities one-third of the planned required time?

22.8 CONCLUSION

Twenty-first century successful business must be able to cope with the paradox of being an IT-savvy business organization, and it must be able to build a business-savvy IT organization that enables the business to leverage the new infrastructure to prosper.

The design of the IT infrastructure needs to be robust, available, and flexible enough such that it can accommodate all future business requirements, whatever the business processes are going to look like.

In architecting an IT architecture that is future-proof, it needs to include the following capabilities and processes, among others:

- *Full Life-Cycle Management.* Make sure that the solution delivers immediate results and business benefits and yet takes a longer view, and ensure that the data will integrate/migrate with future technology platform easily.

- *Operation Excellence.* Establish and manage the SLA, continuously monitor and control the quality of services proactively, and report and communicate the business values to stakeholders and partners regularly.
- *Strategic Alignment.* Set up and practice an enterprise architecture planning and design process, eliminate building silos and islands of data, and promote standardization and portfolio management principles to manage risks. The objective is to design, integrate, and deploy a resilient IT infrastructure that enables business to deliver value to customers and shareholders.

22.8.1 Going Forward

Business and IT leaders have an unprecedented opportunity today to implement change. Information technology can be used as a catalyst for change, for the right opportunity and relevant solution.

Leadership is crucial to success. Business and IT leaders must first define the vision for change, understand the long-term strategic direction of the business, anticipate the fundamental roadblocks and articulate the potential resistance to successful change, formulate a change in management strategy and plan for actions to overcome those obstacles to successful change, and complete your resource planning to ensure that you have the right resources at the right time to complete the change.

Remember that information technology can be a powerful enabler to business processes, but IT itself is not the panacea to organizational problems. As Harvard Business School professor Rosabeth Moss Kanter said before, develop "a culture that just keep moving all the time."

Is the organization ready for cloud computing? Time is of the essence: Change is the only thing being constant, and if there is one thing technology cannot change, it is *time*. One approach to help business to be more adaptive to change is to architect a flexible and scalable (in both expanding and shrinking) IT infrastructure.

Here are some important pointers that we have discussed earlier:

- Select the right cloud solution that meet the business requirements (e.g., SaaS).
- Build strategic partnership with the right service provider(s).
- Plan, negotiate, execute, monitor, and control your contract and SLA vigorously and proactively.

ACKNOWLEDGMENTS

We would like to thank various people for their comments on this chapter, especially Michael Mohammed and Carol Guay.

REFERENCES

1. M. Murphy, Organizational change and firm performance, in *OECD Science, Technology and Industry Working Papers*, OECD Publishing, Paris, 2002, p. 14.

2. J. R Baldwin and J. Johnson, Business strategies in innovative and non-innovative firms in Canada, in *Analytical Studies Research Paper Series 11F0019MIEI1995073*, Analytical Studies Branch, Canada, 1995.

3. Bresnahan, Brynjolfsson, and Hitt, INFORMATION TECHNOLOGY, WORK-PLACE ORGANIZATION, AND THE DEMAND FOR SKILLED LABOR: FIRM-LEVEL EVIDENCE, 2000.

4. M. Raskino, Gartner's 2009. Hype Cycle Special Report Evaluates Maturity of 1,650 Technologies, http://www.gartner.com/it/page.jsp?id = 1124212, retrieved on March 6, 2010.

5. H. H. Jørgensen, Making change work: IBM continuing, *The Enterprise of The Future Conversation*, 2008, pp. 14–15.

6. N. R. Augustine, Reshaping an industry. Lockheed Martin's survival story. in *Harvard Business Review on Change*, HBS Press, Boston, 1998.

7. J. P. Kotter, Leading change: Why transformation efforts fail, *Harvard Business Review on Change*. HBS Press, Boston, 1998.

8. E. H. Schein, Kurt Lewin's Change Theory in the Field and in the Classroom: Notes Toward a Model of Managed Learning', Edgar H. Schein, Professor of Management Emeritus, MIT Sloan School of Management, http://dspace.mit.edu/bitstream/handle/1721.1/2576/SWP-3821-32871445.pdf;jsessionid = 28CF6FB51B FA9F43A015CE1C5D45C3B2?sequence = 1, retrieved on 8/9/2009.

9. A. Kritsonis, Comparison of change theories, *International Journal of Scholarly Academic Intellectual Diversity*, **8**(1):1–2, 2004–2005.

10. R. H. Rouda and M. E. Kusy, Jr., Organizational culture: Symphony Orchestra Institute, development of human resources—Part 3, Organization development the management of change, *TAPPI Journal, Technical Association of the Pulp and Paper Industry*, 1995.

11. T. Davenport, Process Innovation: Reengineering Work Through Information Technology. Havard Business School Press, 1992.

12. Hammer and Champy Reengineering the Corporation: Manifesto for Business Revolution, Michael Hammer and James Champy. 1993.

13. EnCana follows familiar strategy. http://www.canada.com/calgaryherald/news/story.html?id = e2ce91ee-6c74-4d4d-b3b2-6af0b994c58e, retrieved on 09/12/2008.

14. EnCana revises schedule for creation of Cenovus Energy due to financial markets uncertainty. Reuters, http://www.reuters.com/article/pressRelease/idUS1078211 + 15-Oct-2008 + PRN20081015, retrieved on 09/12/2008.

CHAPTER 23

DATA SECURITY IN THE CLOUD

SUSAN MORROW

23.1 AN INTRODUCTION TO THE IDEA OF DATA SECURITY

Taking information and making it secure, so that only yourself or certain others can see it, is obviously not a new concept. However, it is one that we have struggled with in both the real world and the digital world. In the real world, even information under lock and key, is subject to theft and is certainly open to accidental or malicious misuse. In the digital world, this analogy of lock-and-key protection of information has persisted, most often in the form of container-based encryption. But even our digital attempt at protecting information has proved less than robust, because of the limitations inherent in protecting a container rather than in the content of that container. This limitation has become more evident as we move into the era of cloud computing: Information in a cloud environment has much more dynamism and fluidity than information that is static on a desktop or in a network folder, so we now need to start to think of a new way to protect information.

Before we embark on how to move our data protection methodologies into the era of The cloud, perhaps we should stop, think, and consider the true applicability of information security and its value and scope. Perhaps we should be viewing the application of data security as less of a walled and impassable fortress and more of a sliding series of options that are more appropriately termed "risk mitigation."

The reason that I broach this subject so early on is that I want the reader to start to view data security as a lexicon of choices, as opposed to an on/off technology. In a typical organization, the need for data security has a very wide scope, varying from information that is set as public domain, through to information that needs some protection (perhaps access control), through

---

to data that are highly sensitive, which, if leaked, could cause catastrophic damage, but nevertheless need to be accessed and used by selected users.

One other aspect of data security that I want to draw into this debate is the human variable within the equation. Computer technology is the most modern form of the toolkit that we have developed since human prehistory to help us improve our lifestyle. From a human need perspective, arguably, computing is no better or worse than a simple stone tool, and similarly, it must be built to fit the hand of its user. Technology built without considering the human impact is bound to fail. This is particularly true for security technology, which is renowned for failing at the point of human error.

If we can start off our view of data security as more of a risk mitigation exercise and build systems that will work with humans (i.e., human-centric), then perhaps the software we design for securing data in the cloud will be successful.

23.2   THE CURRENT STATE OF DATA SECURITY IN THE CLOUD

At the time of writing, cloud computing is at a tipping point: It has many arguing for its use because of the improved interoperability and cost savings it offers. On the other side of the argument are those who are saying that cloud computing cannot be used in any type of pervasive manner until we resolve the security issues inherent when we allow a third party to control our information. These security issues began life by focusing on the securing of access to the datacenters that cloud-based information resides in. However, it is quickly becoming apparent in the industry that this does not cover the vast majority of instances of data that are outside of the confines of the data center, bringing us full circle to the problems of having a container-based view of securing data. This is not to say that data-center security is obsolete. Security, after all, must be viewed as a series of concentric circles emanating from a resource and touching the various places that the data go to and reside. However, the very nature of cloud computing dictates that data are fluid objects, accessible from a multitude of nodes and geographic locations and, as such, must have a data security methodology that takes this into account while ensuring that this fluidity is not compromised. This apparent dichotomy—data security with open movement of data—is not as juxtaposed as it first seems. Going back to my previous statement that security is better described as "risk mitigation," we can then begin to look at securing data as a continuum of choice in terms of levels of accessibility and content restrictions: This continuum allows us to choose to apply the right level of protection, ensuring that the flexibility bestowed by cloud computing onto the whole area of data communication is retained.

As I write, the IT industry is beginning to wake up to the idea of content-centric or information-centric protection, being an inherent part of a data object. This new view of data security has not developed out of cloud computing, but instead is a development out of the idea of the "de-perimerization" of the enterprise. This idea was put forward by a group of Chief Information Officers (CIOs) who formed an organization called the Jericho Forum [1]. The Jericho Forum was founded in 2004 because of the increasing need for data exchange between companies and external parties—for example: employees using remote computers; partner companies; customers; and so on. The old way of securing information behind an organization's perimeter wall prevented this type of data exchange in a secure manner. However, the ideas forwarded by the Jericho Forum are also applicable to cloud computing. The idea of creating, essentially, de-centralized perimeters, where the perimeters are created by the data object itself, allows the security to move with the data, as opposed to retaining the data within a secured and static wall. This simple but revolutionary change in mindset of how to secure data is the ground stone of securing information within a cloud and will be the basis of this discussion on securing data in the cloud.

23.3 HOMO SAPIENS AND DIGITAL INFORMATION

Cloud computing offers individuals and organizations a much more fluid and open way of communicating information. This is a very positive move forward in communication technology, because it provides a more accurate mimic of the natural way that information is communicated between individuals and groups of human beings. Human discourse, including the written word, is, by nature, an open transaction: *I have this snippet of information and I will tell you, verbally or in written form, what that information is.* If the information is sensitive, it may be whispered, or, if written on paper, passed only to those allowed to read it. The result is that human-to-human information communication will result in a very fluid discourse. Cloud computing is a platform for creating the digital equivalent of this fluid, human-to-human information flow, which is something that internal computing networks have never quite achieved. In this respect, cloud computing should be seen as a revolutionary move forward in the use of technology to enhance human communications.

Although outside of the remit of this chapter, it is worthwhile for any person looking into developing systems for digital communications to attempt to understand the underlying social evolutionary and anthropological reasons behind the way that human beings communicate This can give some insight into digital versions of communication models, because most fit with the natural way that humans communicate information. Security system design, in particular, can benefit from this underlying knowledge, because this type of system is built both to thwart deceptive attempts to intercept communication and to enhance and enable safe and trusted communications: Bear in mind that both deception and trust are intrinsic evolutionary traits, which human beings have developed to help them to successfully communicate.

23.4   CLOUD COMPUTING AND DATA SECURITY RISK

The cloud computing model opens up old and new data security risks. By its very definition, Cloud computing is a development that is meant to allow more open accessibility and easier and improved data sharing. Data are uploaded into a cloud and stored in a data center, for access by users from that data center; or in a more fully cloud-based model, the data themselves are created in the cloud and stored and accessed from the cloud (again via a data center). The most obvious risk in this scenario is that associated with the storage of that data. A user uploading or creating cloud-based data include those data that are stored and maintained by a third-party cloud provider such as Google, Amazon, Microsoft, and so on. This action has several risks associated with it: Firstly, it is necessary to protect the data during upload into the data center to ensure that the data do not get hijacked on the way into the database. Secondly, it is necessary to the stores the data in the data center to ensure that they are encrypted at all times. Thirdly, and perhaps less obvious, the access to those data need to be controlled; this control should also be applied to the hosting company, including the administrators of the data center. In addition, an area often forgotten in the application of security to a data resource is the protection of that resource during its use—that is, during a collaboration step as part of a document workflow process. Other issues that complicate the area of hosted data include ensuring that the various data security acts and rules are adhered to; this becomes particularly complicated when you consider the cross border implications of cloud computing and the hosting of data in a country other than that originating the data.

Data security risks are compounded by the open nature of cloud computing. Access control becomes a much more fundamental issue in cloud-based systems because of the accessibility of the data therein. If you use a system that provides improved accessibility and opens up the platform to multi-node access, then you need to take into account the risks associated with this improvement. One way this can be done is by adding an element of control, in the form of access control, to afford a degree of risk mitigation. Information-centric access control (as opposed to access control lists) can help to balance improved accessibility with risk, by associating access rules with different data objects within an open and accessible platform, without losing the inherent usability of that platform.

A further area of risk associated not only with cloud computing, but also with traditional network computing, is the use of content after access. The risk is potentially higher in a cloud network, for the simple reason that the information is outside of your corporate walls; for example, a user printing off a sensitive document within an office of a company is more likely to think twice about doing so if her colleagues can see her actions than if she prints out that document in the privacy of her own home or within the anonymity of an Internet cafe.

Recent research by Gartner, on the top 10 "disruptive technologies," outlined these as being key transformation technologies for the industry. The technologies included Cloud and Web ecosystems as well as virtualization and social software [2]. Gartner predict that by 2010, Mashups, used to create composite applications to share and combine internal and external data sources, will be used as the dominant mode of creation for enterprise composite, applications [3]. In addition to this, corporate blogs are being heavily touted as a means of disseminating and collaborating on information: Technorati research for the 2008 State of the Blogosphere report puts corporate blogging at 12% of the total blogs [4],[1] and a Universal McCann study shows that consumers think more positively about companies that have blogs [5]; Statistics suggest that this media will become more heavily used within a corporate context.

A recent survey by Citrix which polled UK IT directors and managers showed that two-thirds of UK companies were computing in the cloud. Of those polled, one-third said they thought there were security risks and 22% said they had concerns over the control of their data in the cloud [6]. However, coupled with these improvements in computing capabilities come new technical challenges and hurdles, in particular in the area of security because of the highly complex manner in which security applications need to operate and inter-operate. The Internet and mobile devices have effectively opened up new points at which data can leak; and as new methods of communicating emerge, they will open up even more potential for information loss.

The development of Web 2.0 technologies has created a new and more dynamic method of communicating information; blogs, social networking sites, Web conferencing, wikis, podcasts and ultimately cloud computing itself offer new and novel methods of getting information from a to b; unfortunately, this can also often be via x, y, and z.

Since cloud computing has come to the fore, there has been a general consensus that data within this domain are more at risk. While on the one hand these new technologies are being met with a degree of enthusiasm, there is also an equal degree of fear in terms of securing data and risk management [7]. Compliance with data security directives and acts still needs to be met, no matter what platform for communication is being used. The lack of security and privacy within a cloud computing environment is hotly debated over whether this problem is perceived or real. However, reports by IT industry analysts suggest that this is a real problem and must be overcome to allow full utilization of cloud computing. A recent report by IDC which surveyed 244 respondents identified security as the main challenge for cloud computing, with 74.6% of the vote stating this as a stumbling block to the uptake of the technology [8]. Reports by Gartner and Gigacom, specifically on cloud security, also confirms this [9, 10].

With new technologies come new exploits; and cloud computing, being by definition a more open way of performing information technology operations, will bring security challenges that will leave Internet-based data vulnerable. As

---

[1]Universal McCann (March 2008) have put the figures for live blogs at 184 million, worldwide.

previously mentioned, mashups have been identified as being a security concern. Data-centric mashups—that is, those that are used to perform business processes around data creation and dissemination—by their very nature, can be used to hijack data, leaking sensitive information and/or affecting integrity of that data. An InfoWorld article summed up this fear: ". . . megabytes of valuable customer or financial data could be compromised in just a few seconds if a rogue data-centric mashup is created" [11].

Cloud computing, more than any other form of digital communication technology, has created a need to ensure that protection is applied at the inception of the information, in a content centric manner, ensuring that a security policy becomes an integral part of that data throughout its life cycle.

Encryption is a vital component of the protection policy, but further controls over the access of that data and on the use of the data must be met. In the case of mashups the controlling of access to data resources, can help alleviate the security concerns by ensuring that mashup access is authenticated. Linking security policies, as applied to the use of content, to the access control method offer a way of continuing protection of data, post access and throughout the life cycle; this type of data security philosophy must be incorporated into the use of cloud computing to alleviate security risks.

We can thus conclude that the risk profile of an organization, or individual, using the cloud to store, manage, distribute, and share its information has several layers. Each layer can be seen as a separate, but tied, level of risk that can be viewed independently, but these risks should be approached as a whole, to make sure that areas constituting a "weakest link" do not end up built into the system.

23.5 CLOUD COMPUTING AND IDENTITY

Digital identity holds the key to flexible data security within a cloud environment. This is a bold statement, but nonetheless appears to be the method of choice by a number of industry leaders. However, as well as being a perceived panacea for the ills of data security, it is also one of the most difficult technological methods to get right. Identity, of all the components of information technology, is perhaps the most closest to the heart of the individual. After all, our identity is our most personal possession and a digital identity represents who we are and how we interact with others on-line. The current state of the art in digital identity, in particular with reference to cloud identities, is a work in progress, which by the time you are reading this should hopefully be entering more maturity. However, going back to my opening statement, digital identity can be used to form the basis of data security, not only in the cloud but also at the local network level too. To expand on this somewhat, we need to look at the link between access, identity, and risk. These three variables can become inherently connected when applied to the security of data, because access and risk are directly proportional: As access increases, so then risk to the security of the data increases. Access controlled by identifying the actor attempting the access is the most logical manner of performing this operation. Ultimately, digital identity holds the key to securing data, if that digital identity can be programmatically linked to security policies controlling the post-access usage of data.

The developments seen in the area of a cloud-based digital identity layer have been focused on creating a "user-centric" identity mechanism. User-centric identity, as opposed to enterprise-centric identity, is a laudable design goal for something that is ultimately owned by the user. However, the Internet tenet of "I am who I say I am" [12] cannot support the security requirements of a data protection methodology based on digital identity, therefore digital identity, in the context of a security system backbone, must be a verified identity by some trusted third party: It is worth noting that even if your identity is verified by a trusted host, it can still be under an individual's management and control.

With this proposed use of identity, on the type of scale and openness as expected in a cloud computing context, we must also consider the privacy implications of that individual's identity. A digital identity can carry with it many identifiers about an individual that make identity theft a problem, but identity should also be kept private for the simple reason of respect. However, privacy is a very personal choice and, as such, the ability to remain private within a cloud, should be, at the very least, an option.

23.5.1 Identity, Reputation, and Trust

One of the other less considered areas of digital identity is the link between the identity and the reputation of the individual identity owner. Reputation is a real-world commodity that is a basic requirement of human-to-human relationships: Our basic societal communication structure is built upon the idea of reputation and trust. Reputation and its counter value, trust, is easily transferable to a digital realm: eBay, for example, having partly built a successful business model on the strength of a ratings system, builds up the reputation of its buyers and sellers through successful (or unsuccessful) transactions. These types of reputation systems can be extremely useful when used with a digital identity. They can be used to associate varying levels of trust with that identity, which in turn can be used to define the level (granular variations) of security policy applied to data resources that the individual wishes to access.

23.5.2 Identity for Identity's Sake

An aspect of identity that again is part of our real world and needs to be mimicked in the digital world is that of "multiple identities," because in the cloud you may find that you need a different "identity" or set of identifiers to access resources or perform different tasks.

If we are to go down the path of using digital identity as the backbone of a cloud-based data security system, then we must make sure that the identity layer of cloud computing is able to handle the very flexible requirements of data security. These include the need for free flow of information, dynamic policies, data-centric security, and privacy. User-centric identity systems, based on dynamic claims (individual identifying artifacts), do seem to have the pre-requisites for this, and the next part of this chapter will look more closely at the currently available cloud-based identities including those based on claims.

23.5.3   Cloud Identity: User-Centric and Open-Identity Systems

As the use of the Internet and cloud computing increases, the risks associated with identifying yourself, via this medium, have also increased. Identity fraud and theft are a real threat to the uptake and acceptance of cloud computing; and as already stated, a robust digital identity can be the backbone of data security in the cloud.

Internet identities such as information cards were originally designed to overcome the problem of "password fatigue," which is an increasing problem for users needing to remember multiple log-on credentials for Web site access. Similarly, OpenID was developed for the purpose of an easier logon into multiple Web sites, negating the need to remember username/logon credentials. Information cards differ from OpenID in a fundamental manner in that information cards have an architecture built on the principle of "claims," claims being pieces of information that can be used to identify the card holder. At this juncture it is worth pointing out that, although OpenID can use claims, the architecture behind OpenID makes this use of claims less flexible—and, more importantly, less dynamic in nature—than those offered by information cards.

One of the most powerful aspects of these Internet identities is the push toward a common framework of operation. This type of framework can make managing such identities simpler and provide more extensible cross-platform and cross-application support, improving scalability and ultimately security. The IT industry is making great strides in this area by coming together in a cooperative way to work toward such a common framework. The work toward this has come about as a result of the large number of prior identity management systems built for purpose, but not for interoperability.

23.5.4   The Philosophy of User-Centric Identity

Digital identities are a still evolving mechanism for identifying an individual, particularly within a cloud environment; and, as such, the philosophy behind the idea is also still being formed. However, one area that is being recognized as a basic component of an identity is that of identity ownership being placed upon the individual (user-centric). Placing ownership with an individual then sets in place a protocol around the use of the identity. The industry is slanting heavily toward allowing users to consent and control how their identity (and the individual identifiers making up the identity, the claims) is used. This reversal of ownership away from centrally managed identity platforms (enterprise-centric) has many advantages. This includes the potential to improve the privacy aspects of a digital identity, by giving an individual the ability to apply permission policies based on their identity and to control which aspects of that identity are divulged. To this end, the term "user-centric" has come to mean that an identity may be controllable by the end user, to the extent that the user can then decide what information is given to the party relying on the identity.

23.5.5 User-Centric but Manageable

One area that often gets confused by the use of the term "user-centric" is the management of users' identities. Although the term "user-centric" implies that the identity is under the control and management of the end user (or that the identity "flows" from the user to the relying application), this is true only within the context of the use of the identity. For example, in the case of many user-centric identities, the user can entirely create and manage them within their own desktop or cloud environment. However, within the context of data security, a personally managed identity may not carry enough assurance or weight of nonrepudiation to be used sensibly. In situations that require a degree of nonrepudiation and verification, where a user is who they say they are—that is, situations that require a digital identity to provide access control and security—user-centric identities can still be under user control and thus user-centric (the user choosing which identity and which identity claims to send across a transaction path) but must be issued and managed by a trusted host able to verify the user (for example, the users bank). This may seem like a security paradox, but it is actually a balanced way of using a digital identity to assign security policies and control while retaining a high measure of privacy and user choice.

23.5.6 What Is an Information Card?

Information cards permit a user to present to a Web site or other service (relying party) one or more claims, in the form of a software token, which may be used to uniquely identify that user. They can be used in place of user name/passwords, digital certificates, and other identification systems, when user identity needs to be established to control access to a Web site or other resource, or to permit digital signing.

Information cards are part of an identity meta-system consisting of:

1. Identity providers (IdP), who provision and manage information cards, with specific claims, to users.
2. Users who own and utilize the cards to gain access to Web sites and other resources that support information cards.

3. An identity selector/service, which is a piece of software on the user's desktop or in the cloud that allows a user to select and manage their cards.

4. Relying parties. These are the applications, services, and so on, that can use an information card to authenticate a person and to then authorize an action such as logging onto a Web site, accessing a document, signing content, and so on.

Each information card is associated with a set of claims which can be used to identify the user. These claims include identifiers such as name, email address, post code, and so on. Almost any information may be used as a claim, if supported by the identity provider/relying party; for example, a security clearance level could be used as a claim, as well as a method of assigning a security policy. Only the claim types are stored in cards issued by an identity provider; the claim values are stored by the provider, creating a more secure and privacy-rich system. One of the strengths of these claims is that they are dynamic and thus can be changed in real time: If linked to a security policy, they can provide a method of dynamic security policy application. As part of the security process inherent in the use of the information card, the cards are backed by an authentication mechanism that the user must satisfy in order to use the card. This could be a password, possession of an X509 certificate, OpenID account, a Kerberos ticket, an out-of-band method, or possession of another information card, and so on.

One of the most positive aspects of an information card is the user-centric nature of the card. An information card IdP can be set up so that the end users themselves can self-issue a card, based on the required claims that they themselves input—the claims being validated if needed. Alternatively, the claims can be programmatically input by the IdP via a Web service or similar, allowing the end user to simply enter the information card site and download the card.

23.5.7 Using Information Cards to Protect Data

Information cards are built around a set of open standards devised by a consortium that includes Microsoft, IBM, Novell, and so on.

The original remit of the cards was to create a type of single sign on system for the Internet, to help users to move away from the need to remember multiple passwords. However, the information card system can be used in many more ways. Because an information card is a type of digital identity, it can be used in the same way that other digital identities can be used. For example, an information card can be used to digitally sign data and content and to control access to data and content. One of the more sophisticated uses of an information card is the advantage given to the cards by way of the claims system. Claims are the building blocks of the card and are dynamic in that they can be changed either manually or programmatically, and this change occurs in real time: As soon as the change is made, it can be reflected when the card is used, for example, by a subsequent change in the access or content usage policy of the resource requiring the information card. This feature can be used by applications that rely on the claims within an information card to perform a task (such as control access to a cloud-based data resource such as a document). A security policy could be applied to a data resource that will be enacted when a specific information card claim is presented to it: If this claim changes, the policy can subsequently change.

For example, a policy could be applied to a Google Apps document specifying that access is allowed for user A when they present their information card with claim "security clearance level = 3" and that post access, this user will be able to view this document for 5 days and be allowed to edit it. The same policy could also reflect a different security setting if the claim changes, say to a security clearance level = 1; in this instance the user could be disallowed access or allowed access with very limited usage rights.

23.5.8 Weakness and Strengths of Information Cards

The dynamic nature of information cards is the strength of the system, but the weakness of information cards lies in the authentication. The current information card identity provisioning services on offer include Microsoft Geneva, Parity, Azigo, Higgins Project, Bandit, and Avoco Secure. Each offers varying levels of card authentication and are chosen from Username and password, Kerberos token, x509 digital certificate, and personal card. Each of these methods has drawbacks. For example, username and password is less secure and also not transparent. X509 digital certificates can be difficult for less technical users to install and use. However, new developments in information card authentication are on the industry roadmap, including Live ID, OpenID, and out-of-band (also referred to as "out-of-wallet"). This latter option offers much higher levels of authentication and thus security, but does have drawbacks in terms of transparency. However, a full gamut of authentication offerings can only improve the security of the information card system. Going forward, it is hoped that GPS location authentication can also be added to the list of authentication choices to control access to resources. Based on geographic location of the person attempting access, this could become a particularly important feature for cloud-based data, which can potentially be accessed anywhere in the world but may be constrained by compliance with industry legal requirements.

23.5.9 Cross-Border Aspects of Information Cards

Cloud computing brings with it certain problems that are specific to a widely distributed computing system. These problems stem from the cross-border nature of cloud computing and the types of compliance issues arising out of such a situation. An identity meta-system based on interoperable standards of issuance and authentication, such as an information card, is an absolute requirement for digital identity to be successfully used across borders. Information cards can potentially provide such a framework, because they are based on the idea of an identity metasystem, the goal of which is to connect individual identity systems resulting in cards issued by a given host being compatible across the entire system. The Oasis Foundation, which is nonprofit organization that is striving to establish open standards for IT, has formed a working committee to "enable the use of information cards to universally manage personal digital identities [13]."

In addition, the Information Card Foundation, headed up by some of the largest IT companies in the world, has a mission statement that includes: to "provide guidance and support for projects advancing information card infrastructure on the widest possible range of platforms, including freely available open source implementations"[2] [14].

The idea of using information cards as a cross-border, interoperable system was presented in March 2009 as an idea at the The European e-ID interoperability Conference: Current Perspective and Initiatives from around Europe in Government and Business [15].

The use of information cards as a method of digitally identifying an individual within the cloud (as well as on the desktop) will gain ground, as its usage model extends with increased support for information cards, from relying parties and as usability through the use of cloud-based selectors becomes more mainstream.

23.6 THE CLOUD, DIGITAL IDENTITY, AND DATA SECURITY

When we look at protecting data, irrespective of whether that protection is achieved on a desktop, on a network drive, on a remote laptop, or in a cloud, we need to remember certain things about data and human beings. Data are most often information that needs to be used; it may be unfinished and require to be passed through several hands for collaboration for completion, or it could be a finished document needing to be sent onto many organizations and then passed through multiple users to inform. It may also be part of an elaborate workflow, across multiple document management systems, working on platforms that cross the desktop and cloud domain. Ultimately, that information may end up in storage in a data center on a third-party server within the cloud, but even then it is likely to be re-used from time to time. This means that the idea of "static" data is not entirely true and it is much better (certainly in terms of securing that data) to think of it as highly fluid, but intermittently static.

[2]Increasingly, government bodies are beginning to see the benefits of user-centric identity systems. For example, the U.S. government has began an initiative to create accessibility through open trust frameworks based on OpenID and information cards: http://openid.net/government/.

What are the implications of this? If we think of data as being an "entity" that is not restricted by network barriers and that is opened by multiple users in a distributed manner, then we should start to envision that a successful protection model will be based on that protection policy being an intrinsic part of that entity. If the protection becomes inherent in the data object, in much the same way that perhaps a font type is inherent in a document (although in the case of security in a much more persistent manner), then it is much less important where that data resides. However, how this is achieved programmatically is a little trickier, particularly in terms of interoperability across hybrid cloud systems.

One of the other aspects of data security we need to assess before embarking on creating a security model for data in the cloud is the *levels of need;* that is, how secure do you want that data to be? The levels of security of any data object should be thought of as concentric layers of increasingly pervasive security, which I have broken down here into their component parts to show the increasing granularity of this pervasiveness:

Level 1: Transmission of the file using encryption protocols

Level 2: Access control to the file itself, but without encryption of the content

Level 3: Access control (including encryption of the *content* of a data object)

Level 4: Access control (including encryption of the *content* of a data object) also including rights management options (for example, no copying content, no printing content, date restrictions, etc.)

Other options that can be included in securing data could also include watermarking or red-acting of content, but these would come under level 4 above as additional options.

You can see from the increasing granularity laid out here that security, especially within highly distributed environments like cloud computing, is not an on/off scenario. This way of thinking about security is crucial to the successful creation of cloud security models. Content level application of data security gives you the opportunity to ensure that all four levels can be met by a single architecture, instead of multiple models of operation which can cause interoperability issues and, as previously mentioned, can add additional elements of human error, leading to loss of security.

The current state of cloud computing provides us with a number of cloud deployment models, namely, public (cloud infrastructure that is open for public use, for example, Google App engine is deployed in a public cloud), private (privately available clouds on a private network used by an individual company; for example, IBM provides private clouds to customers, particularly concerned by the security issues surrounding public cloud deployments), managed (clouds offered by a third-party hosting company who look after the implementation and operational aspects of cloud computing for an organization), and hybrid (a mix of both public and private cloud implementations). It is highly likely, especially in the early years of cloud computing, that organizations will use a mixture of several, if not all, of these different models. With this in mind, to allow an organization to deal with securing data within any of these types of systems means that the issues of interoperability, cross-cloud support, minimisation of human error, and persistence of security are crucial. The fluid movement of data through and between these clouds is an integral part of the cloud philosophy, and any data security added into this mix must not adversely encumber this movement. This requires that you look at that data as a separate entity with respect to the underlying system that it moves through and resides within. If you do not view the data as a free-moving object, you will build a data security model that is not built to suit the data, but instead is built for the specific system surrounding that data. In a cloud-type system, the end result is likely to be only suitable for static data (something that we have already described as not truly existing) which will not be able to transcend that original system without potentially having to be re-engineered to do so, or at the very least having additional features and functions tagged onto the original specification. This type of software engineering results in interoperability issues and an increased chance of bugs occurring, because of feature adjuncts being added as an after thought, as opposed to being built into the original working architecture of the software. In addition, what can occur with security software development, which uses a non-extensible approach to software design, is that security holes end up being inadvertently built into the software, which may be very difficult to test for as the software feature bloat increases. With this in mind, the way forward in creating data security software models for a cloud computing environment must be done from scratch. We must leave the previous world of encrypted containers behind us and open up a new paradigm of fluidic protection mechanisms based on content-centric ideologies. Only through this approach will we hope to achieve transcendence of security across the varying types of cloud architectures.

23.7   CONTENT LEVEL SECURITY—PROS AND CONS

Much of the substance of this chapter has described a new way of thinking about securing data, so that data within a cloud can remain fluid, accessible on multiple nodes and yet remain protected throughout its life cycle. The basis of this new security model has been described as "content or information-centric." What this means in reality is that the content that makes up any given data object (for example, a Word document) is protected, as opposed to the file— that is, the carrier of that information being protected. This subtle difference in approach gives us a major advantage in terms of granularity and choice of protection level, as well as persistence of protection. We will take a Word document as our example here to outline the main pros and cons of this type of security approach.

Imagine that I have just prepared a merger and acquisition (M&A) draft document using an on-line document authoring application, such as Google Apps. I need to share this document with persons within my own company, across several departments, as well as with an external lawyer and with the third-party company to be acquired. In addition, I want to make sure that certain sections are only visible to certain of these parties and that they cannot change any item or copy the content (I don't want some of the sensitive clauses to be placed on an ex-employee's blog page, or leaked to the press to affect share prices). I also want to audit the access and use of the document and to limit the time that these people can read the draft of this document, because I want to close this acquisition within 2 weeks. Thereafter I need to publish the finished M&A document with new access rights and restrictions to reflect its new status. I am also acutely aware that the data center that is holding this sensitive document is being hosted by a cloud vendor, and I definitely do not want the administrator of that data center to see this transaction. How can I achieve this? I could create a shared on-line document portal that controls access to the document using a password login and set up user accounts for those persons I wish to share the document with. The main problem with this type of container-based security is that it relies on the user not sharing their password. In addition, once access is gained, the user can use the document without restriction; for example, copy the document content to their blog page, email the document to others, or download the document to a local computer and share it with anyone they wish to, across their network. In addition, the document is potentially accessible by the cloud vendor themselves. To prevent any of these unauthorized actions, I will need to control the document content itself and improve on the access control measures, because password access is far too insecure. This is where a content-centric approach delivers persistent and pervasive security. Content-centric security, which is also digital identity led (i.e., the identity used to access the content), also dictates the security policy applied to that content and will allow me to control who accesses my M&A draft, because at the time of protecting the draft I will decide who can access it and how access is controlled. This brings us back to the section on information cards. I could protect the draft document by assigning access to persons who hold a managed information card, which contains certain claims—for example, specific email addresses, a security clearance level (set by a specified identity provider), or a specified company number, and so on. Only those persons could then access the document; and because the claims are managed by an identity provider (perhaps my own company), the claims can also be dynamically changed and, as such, if I need to revoke access to the document, I can arrange for the claims to change in line with this, revoke the information card of that user, or alternatively change the security applied to the document. Once access is gained, security policies that control what part of the document can be seen, by which person and what they can do with the content, will be applied; because the access is based on an individual identity, individual content controls can be applied and so some users can be given stronger rights restrictions than others. Importantly, even though the document is held on third-party servers, in the cloud it can't be accessed by even the system administrator of that server, because the access is controlled at the content level and is not dependent on the access to the database holding the data.

You can easily see the advantages that are conferred on data protected at the content level: greater control, more focused access control, increased granular protection over content, and assurance within a cloud-hosted system. But what, if any, disadvantages come with this type of methodology?

Container security is a much simpler way of securing data. Within a cloud computing environment you have the storage and transfer of data, both of which can be easily accommodated in terms of security by using encryption protocols already built for the purpose. It is fairly simple to apply database encryption, because it is applied natively to the data and decrypted, on-the-fly, when there is a query on that data. Similarly, transfer of the data between application and database, or human-to-human transfer, can protect the data as an encrypted package, decrypted when access is granted. Content-centric security measures need to be compatible with both database security and secure transfer of data within a cloud environment. Protecting the content of our Word document needs to be done in such a manner that it does not impact the storage of that data. This may be problematic, especially across different storage types and in use with query engines, which is particularly pertinent with the use of dynamic data updating, as required by modern data storage operations. One of the other aspects of cloud computing data storage that can complicate the area of data security is the use of redundant storage in more than one location [16]. However, at this juncture it is worth noting that this same issue causes more problems for a container approach than for a content-centric approach, in terms of synchronicity between databases. The current state of research, with respect to the protection of data within a cloud computing environment, is focused on the protection of data within the data centers hosting the cloud: The problems therein are compounded by the highly distributed nature of the cloud and the use of multi-center storage and replication of data. Content-centric security needs to overcome these same problems and also needs to retain protection of data within the structure of the database itself; this, however, is a programmatic problem.

23.8   FUTURE RESEARCH DIRECTIONS

This chapter has spent some time discussing digital identity within a cloud framework. The reason for this emphasis was to show the possibilities that can be achieved, in terms of data security, when using digital identity as the backbone for that security. Digital identity is an area that is, as I write, undergoing some revolutionary changes in what an identity stands for and how it can be leveraged. As a means of controlling access to information within a cloud environment, the idea of using a person's digital identity to do this, as opposed to using authentication alone, or some sort of access control list setup, opens up new opportunities, not only from a technological standpoint but also from the viewpoint that ownership of information and privacy of that information are often inherently linked to individuals and groups. And, as such, how they access this information becomes much more natural when that access is by means of truly and digitally identifying themselves.

The idea of using digital identity as a basis for security policy setting and enforcement, by means of inherently associating that policy with a data object, is an area that needs to be researched to offer a much more fluid and all-encompassing approach to cloud-based data security. In particular, the research needs to focus on interoperability across the differing cloud systems. The creation of a seamless security model that can accommodate data while moving through multiple authors and readers, as well as residing within a data center, is a necessary tool to allow cloud computing to fully mature, because this will add the much needed levels of trust currently missing from cloud computing. Without this trust, the communication of information will become naturally stifled and may place a hurdle to the uptake of cloud computing that makes the use of the cloud by users with sensitive information and intellectual property impossible.

Another linked area to the use of digital identity and data security, particularly within the open context that is the basis of cloud computing, is that of privacy: Privacy and security should be viewed as two sides of the same coin. Privacy is a topic that not only has technological implications in how it can be achieved, but also has humanistic concerns that would need to be researched to establish the privacy requirements for digital identity and information used within a cloud domain. This research would potentially take the form of an anthropological study, in the first instance, to determine the attitude and expectations toward privacy that users have and to what extent they need privacy issues addressed by technology. In particular, the association of privacy with the use of a digital identity on-line should be looked into. Currently there are methods of creating more private identity transactions which can hide or obfuscate an identity attribute (a social security number, for example) such as zero-knowledge technology (sometimes called minimal disclosure) or similar Privacy Enhancing Technologies (PETs) [17]; however, these methods are still not used in a pervasive manner, and this may be because of the need to build more user control into the technologies and to add greater granularity into such systems.

The current push by large vendors such as Google and Microsoft, to offer cloud-based authoring tools, only exacerbates the issue of unprotected cloud-based data. Research into integrated forms of encryption and rights management technologies by these types of authoring tools will give the users of such tools a mechanism to protect this intellectual property; however, any data protection technology in this area must ensure that the information protected does not lose its agility in terms of movement within the cloud sphere: Confining the protected data to use within the original authoring application alone may cause the data to lose the benefits of originating in the cloud. It may also be that these data may still require access outside of the cloud domain—that is, on a user's laptop—using traditional authoring tools. This type of cross-application interoperability is likely to be a particularly problematic area of research for applications controlling the use of content, because it will require that the applied protection mechanisms (including potentially support of digital identity methods for access control) are effective in applications that have different approaches to how that content is displayed and used. For example, the control over the use of author applications and menu items, offered to content users using protected data, may be difficult when cross-application support is required.

Another area that warrants research is auditing of the access to and use of information in the cloud. In particular, because of the cross-border nature of cloud computing, there is likely to be a greater need for location-aware security restrictions to be used. The area of jurisdiction is one that is problematic in relation to cloud computing. Often a company will not know the location of the data center that their data are stored within. And because different countries have different laws around the access of data, particularly with respect to governmental access (the USA PATRIOT Act [18], for example), this can be an area of data security that is difficult to tackle. Back doors are never a good idea when creating data security systems, but some type of restricted document access could potentially be built into the system, allowing certain authorities to gain access under certain conditions. However, one area that does need further work is that of locking data access to a geographic location. How that geographic location is assessed is the salient area for research, because currently GPS systems are little used and come with inherent technical difficulties such as the ability to receive GPS coordinates when inside a building[3].

23.9 CONCLUSION

Cloud computing is not just about designing a new type of computing. The nature of such a globalized communication system necessitates that we look at that system from many standpoints: humanistic, legal, business led, philosophical, and so on. With the advent of cloud computing, we have an opportunity to create a more truly robust and usable security system which, arguably, has eluded us in the traditional world of computing—perhaps because in this legacy system, security was never built from the ground up, but instead often as an afterthought: an adjunct to preexisting operating systems and applications.

To create data security that does not affect the free-flowing ethos of cloud-based data, we need to think differently about what security is and how it should work. We need to step outside of the container and make sure that

---

[3]This GPS problem is starting to find a resolution with enhancement of the reception of GPS systems being heavily researched.

security is inherent, as much a part of the data object as the content within that object itself.

Digital identity, based in the cloud or federated via the cloud with network-based identity mechanisms, can be used to give us a starting point to control access to data and also to determine the post-access security policies for that information.

For cloud computing to be ubiquitous and trusted, we need to make data security systems that are not hindered by the application the data originates from, the mode of transport for that data, the place the data is accessed from, or the device it is used upon. The determining factors for successful cloud data security are seamlessness and interoperability built around a core of digital-identity-led security polices.

ACKNOWLEDGMENTS

This chapter is based, in part, on the author's research work for the European Commission Seventh Framework Programme, "Parsifal," as well as on work carried out in designing security solutions for both traditional and cloud computing. I would like to thank Drs. Stephen Hitchen and Paul Battersby as well as Judith Lancet for their comments on this chapter.

FURTHER READING

Open Cloud Manifesto: www.opencloudmanifesto.org.

Laws of Identity: http://www.identityblog.com/?p = 354.

Identity in the Age of Cloud Computing: The Next-Generation Internet's Impact on Business, Governance and Social Interaction http://www.aspeninstitute.org/publications/identity-age-cloud-computing-next-generation-internets-impact-business-governance-socia.

Privacy in the Clouds: A White Paper on Privacy and Digital Identity, http://www.privacybydesign.ca/pbdbook/PrivacybyDesignBook-ch15.pdf.

Human Communication, What Happens? http://www.lucs.lu.se/LUCS/043/LUCS.043.pdf.

REFERENCES

1. J. Forum, The Jericho Forum Commandments, http://www.opengroup.org/jericho, May 2007.
2. P. Kacsuk, Editorial, *Journal of Grid Computing*, **10723**, 2004.
3. C. Claunch, Top 10 Disruptive and Strategic Technologies for Financial Services, *Gartner Research*, http://www.wsta.org/content/download/10004/129714/file/GartnerKeynote.pdf September 2008.

4. Y. Genovese, Session Speech by Gartner Analyst, in Gartner Symposium/ITxpo, October 16, 2008.

5. Technorati, State of the Blogosphere report 2008, http://www.technorati.com/blogging/state-of-the-blogosphere/, June 2008.

6. T. Smith, Wave 3, Universal McCann, http://www.universalmccann.com/Assets/UM%20Wave%203%20final_20080808141650.pdf, March 2008

7. D. Gootzit, G. Phifer, R. Valdes, N. Drakos, A. Bradley, K. Harris, D. Sholler, M. Pezzini, Y. Natis, B. Gassman, D. Mitchell Smith, D. Ceraley, R. Schulte, S. Prentice, S. Gall, W. Clark, and A. Lapkin, Hype Cycle for Web and User Interaction Technologies, 2008: Gartner Research, July 7, 2008, Gartner Inc.

8. D. W. Cearley, T. Austin, |IBM Moves Towards a "Cloud Computing" Infrastructure, *Gartner Research*, http://www.gartner.com/resources/153600/153615/ibm_moves_toward_a_cloud_com_153615.pdf, November 20, 2007.

9. F. Gens, IT Cloud Services User Survey, pt.2: Top Benefits & Challenges, *IDC Research*, http://blogs.idc.com/ie/?p=210, October 2, 2008.

10. J. Heiser and M. Nicolett, Assessing the Security Risks of Cloud Computing, Gartner Research, June 3, 2008, Gartner, Inc.

11. Gigacom Briefing, Cloud Computing, June 2008.

12. C. Hannon, The Video Republic, opendemocracy.net, http://www.opendemocracy.net/blog/yes/celia-hannon/2008/10/06/the-video-republic, October 6, 2008.

13. Oasis Foundation, OASIS Members Form New Committee to Advance Interoperability Standard for Information Cards, http://www.oasis-open.org/news/imi-press-release.pdf, September 2008.

14. Information Card Foundation, http://informationcard.net/about.

15. The European e-ID interoperability Conference Current Perspective and Initiatives from around Europe in Government and Business, http://www.eema.org/downloads/2009/e-ID_interoperability/e-ID_interop_prog_2009_web.pdf, March 2009.

16. C. Wang, Q. Wang, K. Ren and W. Lou, Ensuring Data Storage Security in Cloud Computing, Department of ECE, Illinois Institute of Technology, February 2009.

17. E. Bertino, F. PAci, R. Ferrini, Privacy-preserving Digital Identity Management for Cloud Computing, Bulletin of the IEEE Computer Society Technical Committee on Data Engineering, 2009.

18. 107th United States Congress, Uniting and Strengthening America by Providing Appropriate Tools Required to Intercept and Obstruct Terrorism (USA PATRIOT Act), http://frwebgate.access.gpo.gov/cgi-bin/getdoc.cgi?dbname=107_cong_public_laws&docid=f:publ056.107.pdf, Act of 2001.

CHAPTER 24

LEGAL ISSUES IN CLOUD COMPUTING

JANINE ANTHONY BOWEN

24.1 INTRODUCTION

"Even before the blades in the data center went down, I knew we had a problem. That little warning voice in the back of my head had become an ambulance siren screaming right into my ears. We had all our customers' applications and data in there, everything from the trivial to the mission critical. I mumbled one of those prayers that only God and IT types hear, hoping our decisions on redundancy were the right ones. We had a disaster recovery plan, but it had never really been battle-tested. Now we were in trouble; and the viability of not just our enterprise, but also that of many of our customers, hung in the balance. I can take the hits associated with my own business, but when someone else's business could sink... it's different.

I looked over at Mike and Nihkil, our resident miracle workers. The color had drained from both of their faces. 'I've given you all she's got, Captain,' Nikhil said in his best Scotty from Star Trek voice. Looking over at Mike and sinking even lower into my seat, I knew it was going to be a long and painful day...."

24.1.1 Objective of Chapter

The worst-case scenario hinted at in the vignette above rarely happens. But in a world without cloud computing, in most instances the company whose systems are about to "go down" generally has some measure of control of its fate— either because the IT resources are internal to the company, or the company has reasonably tight reins on the provider, either contractually, through service-level agreements (SLAs) or otherwise. In the world of cloud computing, however, the control points are different. In the cloud computing environment, businesses have essentially outsourced the development, hosting, or running of applications and data to a third party, that part is not entirely new. What is new are the combination of: (a) cloud-based service models, (b) relegation of system control to third parties, (c) use of virtualization, (d) the potential for multi-vendor integration, and (e) the increasingly borderless nature of Internet globalization. Technologically it sounds complicated, and it is. But from a business perspective, cloud computing simply capitalizes on the need of a business to manage costs, stick to its core competencies, and outsource the rest. The business case is easy to grasp, but the technology raises some interesting legal issues that are relevant for both the cloud provider and the cloud customer. This chapter, written primarily from the United States law perspective, is intended to be a survey of those issues.

24.1.2   Definition of Cloud Computing

This chapter assumes that the reader is familiar with the manner in which cloud computing [1] is defined as set forth by the National Institute of Standards and Technology [2], a federal agency of the United States Government.

In brief, cloud computing is a model for enabling convenient, on-demand network access to a shared pool of configurable computing resources (e.g., networks, servers, storage, applications, and services) that can be rapidly provisioned and released. This cloud model is composed of five essential characteristics, three service models, and four deployment models.

24.1.3   Overview of Legal Issues

The legal issues that arise in cloud computing are wide ranging. Significant issues regarding privacy of data and data security exist, specifically as they relate to protecting personally identifiable information of individuals, but also as they relate to protection of sensitive and potentially confidential business information either directly accessible through or gleaned from the cloud systems (e.g., identification of a company's customer by evaluating traffic across the network). Additionally, there are multiple contracting models under which cloud services may be offered to customers (e.g., licensing, service agreements, on-line agreements, etc.). The appropriate model depends on the nature of the services as well as the potential sensitivity of the systems being implemented or data being released into the cloud. In this regard, the risk profile (i.e., which party bears the risk of harm in certain foreseeable and other not-so-foreseeable situations) of the agreement and the cloud provider's limits on its liability also require a careful look when reviewing contracting models.

Additionally, complex jurisdictional issues may arise due to the potential for data to reside in disparate or multiple geographies. This geographical diversity is inherent in cloud service offerings. This means that both virtualization of and physical locations of servers storing and processing data may potentially impact what country's law might govern in the event of a data breach or intrusion into cloud systems. Jurisdictional matters also determine the country's law that is applicable to data and information that may be moved geographically among data centers around the world at any given point in time.

Finally, commercial and business considerations require some attention. What happens to customer information, applications, and data when a cloud provider is acquired? What are the implications for that same set of information, applications, and data when a cloud provider is files bankruptcy or ceases to do business? All of these issues will be explored.

24.1.4 Distinguishing Cloud Computing from Outsourcing and Provision of Application Services

Cloud computing is different from traditional outsourcing and the application service provider (ASP) model in the following ways:

- In general, outsourcers tend to take an entire business or IT process of a customer organization and completely run the business for the benefit of the customer. Though the outsourcer may provide services similar to those by multiple customers, each outsourcing arrangement is highly negotiated, and the contract is typically lengthy and complex. Depending on the nature of the outsourcing, the software belongs to the customer, and software sublicense rights were transferred to the outsourcer as part of the arrangement. The customer's systems are run on the customer's equipment, though it is usually at an offsite location managed by the outsourcer. Pricing is typically negotiated for each outsourced relationship. The outsourcer's ability to scale to meet customer demand is a slow, and also negotiated, process. The location of the data and processing is known, predetermined, and agreed to contractually.

- In the ASP model, the service provided is a software service. The software application may have been used previously in-house by the customer, or it may be a new value-added offering. The ASP offering is a precursor to what is now called "software as a service." The transaction is negotiated, though typically it is not as complex and highly negotiated as a traditional outsourcing arrangement. The provider owns the software and hardware, and the software is accessed over the Internet. The software tends to reside in one physical location or a group of known locations with redundant and disaster recovery backups, if any, being housed with third-party providers. Pricing models vary by service, but tend to be negotiated. The more sophisticated ASPs have realized that the provision of software over the Internet is not the same as licensing of software, and the contracting vehicles for ASP relationships have slowly morphed from typical licensing models into services arrangements. There is no inherent ability to scale the use or availability of ASP services on demand, nor is it required.

Less emphasis is placed on location of data and processing than in outsourcing, though this information was a generally ascertainable.

- Cloud computing covers multiple service models (i.e, software, infrastructure, and platform as a service). As of this writing, access to cloud computing services are (at least in the public cloud computing framework), for the most part, one-size-fits-all 'click here to accept' agreements, not negotiated arrangements. Similarly, pricing tended to be unit-based (hence its comparison to utility computing). In the cloud environment, performance economies are important for the profitability of the cloud provider. Therefore a cloud provider may have multiple data centers geographically dispersed to take advantage of geographic cost differentials. Additionally, the ability of cloud providers to quickly scale up and down to meet customer requirements dictate that secondary and tertiary data centers be available either directly from the cloud provider or through its subcontracted arrangements. The location of data and processing at any given instant in time tends to be less well known to the customer in a cloud environment.

24.2 DATA PRIVACY AND SECURITY ISSUES

24.2.1 U.S. Data Breach Notification Requirements

Generally speaking, data breach is a loss of unencrypted electronically stored personal information. This information is usually some combination of name and financial information (e.g., credit card number, Social Security Number). A breach can occur in many ways—for example, by having a server compromised, loss of a thumb drive, or theft of a laptop or cell phone. Avoidance of a data breach is important to both cloud providers and users of cloud services because of the significant harm, both to the user and to the provider, when a breach occurs. From the user's viewpoint, if personal information is compromised, there is a risk of identity theft and of credit or debit card fraud. From the provider's viewpoint, financial harm, potential for lawsuits, Federal Trade Commission (FTC) investigations, loss of customers, and damage to reputation are all likely results of when a data breach occurs. Data breaches can be expensive. Financial losses from lawsuits, customer claims, protecting reputation, FTC settlements, and other costs for the most serious U.S. data breaches have exceeded US $1 billion.

Almost all 50 states in the United States now require notification of affected persons (i.e., residents of the individual state), upon the occurrence of a data breach. As of this writing, the European Union was considering data breach legislation. Given the breadth of various laws across most of the United States, a breach generally results in a company notification of persons across the country when their information has been compromised. Because of these laws, business customers have attempted to materially expand the contractual obligations of their providers and shift the risk of harm to the provider, the holder of the personal information. Over time, as more mission-critical information migrates into the cloud, cloud providers may have to assume more risk for treatment of personal information in a manner consistent with the obligations of non-cloud providers. For purposes of data breach law, data in the cloud are treated no differently than any other electronically stored information. Cloud providers that have had their systems compromised will be required to notify affected persons and will have to coordinate with the cloud users who provided the data in order to do so.

24.2.2 U.S. Federal Law Compliance

Gramm–Leach–Bliley Act: Financial Privacy Rule. The Gramm–Leach–Bliley Act (GLB) [3] requires, among other things, that financial institutions implement procedures to ensure the confidentiality of personal information and to protect against unauthorized access to the information. Various United States government agencies are charged with enforcing GLB, and those agencies have implemented and currently enforce standards [4]. As part of the requirement to prevent unauthorized access to information, financial institutions must take steps to protect information provided to a service provider. A service provider under GLB may be any number of individuals or companies that provide services to the financial institution and would include a cloud provider handling the personal information of a financial institution's customers.

The implications to the cloud provider that is providing services to financial institutions are that the cloud provider will, to some degree, have to (1) comply with the relevant portions of GLB by demonstrating how it prevents unauthorized access to information, (2) contractually agree to prevent unauthorized access, or (3) both of the above.

The Role of the FTC: Safeguards Rule and Red Flags Rule. At the United States federal level, the Federal Trade Commission (FTC) working under the auspices of the FTC Act has been given authority to protect consumers and their personal information. The Safeguards Rule [5] mandated by GLB and enforced by the FTC requires that all businesses significantly involved in the provision of financial services and products have a written security plan to protect customer information. The plan must include the following elements [6]:

- Designation of one or more employees to coordinate its information security program;
- Identification and assessment of the risks to customer information in each relevant area of the company's operation, and evaluation of the effectiveness of the current safeguards for controlling these risks;
- Designing and implementing a safeguards program, and regularly monitoring and testing it;

- Selection of service providers that can maintain appropriate safeguards; and
- Evaluation and adjustment of the program in light of relevant circumstances, including (a) changes in the firm's business or operations or (b) the results of security testing and monitoring.

In 2007, as part of the Fair and Accurate Credit Transaction Act of 2003 (FACT) [7], the FTC promulgated the Red Flag Rules[1] (these rules were scheduled to go into effect in November 2009, but have been delayed several times). These rules are intended to curb identity theft by having financial institutions identify potential "red flags" for activities conducted through the organization's systems that could lead to identity theft. The rules apply to financial institutions or those that hold credit accounts. Holders of credit accounts include credit issuers, utilities, health-care institutions, auto dealers, and telecommunications companies. The organizations covered by these rules must have a written identity theft program [8] to detect specific activities that could indicate identity theft.

The Red Flag Rules apply to cloud providers to the same degree as they apply to other companies in both the off-line and on-line spaces. The cloud provider must have a written plan and should have monitoring systems to detect unauthorized access and intrusion in the ordinary course of business.

Health Insurance Portability and Accountability Act & HITECH Act. The Health Information Technology for Economic and Clinical Health Act (HITECH ACT) [9] requires notification of a breach of unencrypted health records (similar to that under state data breach notification requirements previously discussed) for all covered entitites that are required to comply with the Health insurance Portability and Accountability Act of 1996 (HIPAA) [10].

USA PATRIOT Act. Shortly after September 11, 2001, the United States Congress passed the "Uniting and Strengthening America by Providing Appropriate Tools Required to Intercept and Obstruct Terrorism Act" (USA PATRIOT Act) of 2001[11]. The USA PATRIOT Act has significant implications for the cloud provider seeking to maintain the privacy of data it holds. For example, the Act allows the installation of devices to record all routing, addressing, and signaling information kept by a computer. This is the rough equivalent of a computer tap. The Act also extends the U.S. government's ability to gain access to personal financial information and student information stored in electronic systems without any suspicion of wrongdoing of the person whose information it seeks. The only requirement is governmental certification that the information obtained would be relevant to an ongoing criminal investigation [12]. A cloud provider may find itself in the awkward position

---

[1]Red Flags Rules, 16 CFR 1681.

of being required to provide information on a cloud user or a cloud user's customers to the U.S. government without providing notice to the cloud user. Neither the cloud user nor its customer likely has much recourse in such an instance.

24.2.3   International Data Privacy Compliance

European Union Data Privacy Directive. In 1995, the European Union (EU) passed the "European Union Directive on the Protection of Individuals with Regard to the Processing of Personal Data and the Movement of Such Data Privacy Directive" (Directive) [13]. The Directive mandated that countries that are part of the EU pass a data protection law covering both government and private entities that process business and consumer data. The Directive covers written, oral, electronic, and Internet-based data that reside in the EU. A key feature of the Directive is its extraterritorial effect. That is, the Directive requires that any geography to which EU personal data is sent must have an adequate level of data protection as measured by EU standards. What does a cloud provider need to understand about the directive?

Article 17 of the Directive requires that a data controller (i.e., the person or organization who determines the purposes and means of processing of the personal data[2]) "implement appropriate technical and organizational controls to protect personal data against accidental or unlawful destruction or accidental loss, alteration, unauthorized disclosure or access...."[3] Article 17 also mandates that there be a written contract between a data controller and a data processor (i.e., anyone who processes data for the controller) that requires, among other things, that the data processor act only on instructions from the data controller. Since a cloud provider will likely be a data processor, Article 17 is particularly important. The language of the cloud provider's contract is also particularly important if the cloud provider resides in the EU.

Many cloud providers are outside of the EU, but wish to conduct business within the EU. The Directive is clear: Data cannot leave the EU unless it goes to a country that ensures an "adequate level of protection[4]." Four methods currently exist to ensure adequate protection. The first, be one of the countries that have laws that EU deems to be adequate protection. At the time of this writing, those countries were Argentina, Canada, Guernsey, Isle of Man, and Switzerland. For the rest of the world adequate protection can be achieved through (1) compliance with safe harbor provisions, (2) use of model contractual clauses prepared by the EU (for which strict conformance to the form language is required), or (3) use of binding corporate rules.

If a cloud provider wishes to conduct business in the EU, place data in its possession in the EU, or otherwise access the personal information of those in

---

[2]Directive, ch. I, art 2(d).

[3]Directive, ch. II, art 17.

[4]Id. At ch. IV, art. 25(1).

the EU, there are compliance obligations under the Directive that must be studied and followed. The cloud user must ask questions regarding geographic placement of data, compliance methods, and so on, and get satisfactory answers prior to placing its personal data (whether through software, platform, or infrastructure as a service) into a cloud that might include data center operations in an EU member country.

A Sampling of Other Jurisdictions: Canada and Australia. Many countries have data protection or data privacy regimes in place, but the coverage and effect of such regimes is varied. For example, Argentina's regime is similar to the EU approach. Brazil, like many countries, has a constitutional right to privacy. But Brazil has no comprehensive data privacy law; instead it relies on a patchwork of sectoral laws. China's constitution refers to privacy indirectly, but the country has very few specific laws. On the other hand, Hong Kong has a Personal Data Ordinance that covers public and private data processors and both electronic and non-electronic records [14]. India, a popular destination for outsourcing, recognizes a right to privacy against entities in the public sector, but has enacted only a limited number of privacy statutes with scant coverage for the private sector.

The protection afforded data in various countries should be a factor in the cloud provider's choice of data-center location since the cloud user's data will be subject to the laws of that country.

Against this backdrop of diverse approaches to privacy around the world, we will look more closely at the laws of two countries, Canada and Australia.

Canada's Personal Information Protection and Electronic Documents Act (PIPEDA). PIPEDA is intended to "support and promote electronic commerce by protecting personal information that is collected, used, or disclosed in certain circumstances..." [15]. Canada, unlike the EU with its state-to-state approach, has taken an organization-to-organization approach to privacy. In essence, organizations are held accountable for the protection of personal information it transfers to third parties, whether such parties are inside or outside of Canada. Since PIPEDA requires that the contractual arrangements provide a "comparable level of protection while the information is being processed by a third-party PIPEDA Principal 4.1.3 [16], the law is enforced through contractual arrangements between entities, regardless of their geographic location. The key to PIPEDA is Principle 1 of CSA Model Code for the Protection of Personal Information [17], which provides that an organization is responsible for information under its control. The CSA principles are in a schedule of PIPEDA.

There are many nuances to PIPEDA; but when transacting in Canadian data or with Canadian companies, cloud providers and users should expect that the contract will expressly handle privacy protection as a matter of Canadian law. Cloud providers should be able to demonstrate methods to protect personal information.

Australia Privacy Act. Australia's Privacy Act [18] is based on (a) 11 "Information Privacy Principles" [19] that apply to the public sector and (b) 10 "National Privacy Principles" [20] that apply to the private sector. These principles address public and private sector use, disclosure, and management of personal data, among other things. Australian entities may send personal data abroad, so long as (1) the entity believes the recipient will uphold the principles, (2) it has consent from the data subject, or (3) the transfer is necessary to comply with contractual obligations.

The Office of the Privacy Commissioner expects that Australian organizations will ensure that cloud providers that collect and handle personal information comply with National Privacy Principles 4 and 9. They require that an organization (1) take steps to ensure that the personal information it holds is accurate, up-to-date, and secure and (2) protect personal information that it transfers outside Australia.

24.3 CLOUD CONTRACTING MODELS

24.3.1 Licensing Agreements Versus Services Agreements

Summary of Terms of a License Agreement. A traditional software license agreement is used when a licensor is providing a copy of software to a licensee for its use (which is usually non-exclusive). This copy is not being sold or transferred to the licensee, but a physical copy is being conveyed to the licensee. The software license is important because it sets forth the terms under which the software may be used by the licensee. The license protects the licensor against the inadvertent transfer of ownership of the software to the person or company that holds the copy. It also provides a mechanism for the licensor of the software to (among other things) retrieve the copy it provided to the licensee in the event that the licensee (a) stops complying with the terms of the license agreement or (b) stops paying the fee the licensee charges for the license.

Additionally, the software license usually offers the licensee protection from the software's violation of the third party's intellectual property rights (i.e., intellectual property infringement). In the case of infringement the license agreement provides a mechanism for the licensor to repair, replace, or remove the software from the licensee's possession.

Summary of Terms of a Service Agreement. A service agreement, on the other hand, is not designed to protect against the perils of providing a copy of software to a user. It is primarily designed to provide the terms under which a service can be accessed or used by a customer. The service agreement may also set forth quality parameters around which the service will be provided to the users. Since there is no transfer of possession of a copy of software and the service is controlled by the company providing it, a service agreement does not necessarily need to cover infringement risk, nor does it need to set forth the scenarios and manner in which a copy of software is to be returned to the vendor when a relationship is terminated. Since the software service is controlled by the provider, the attendant risks and issues associated with transferring possession of software without transferring ownership do not exist.

Value of Using a Service Agreement in Cloud Arrangements. In each of the three permutations of cloud computing (SaaS, PaaS, and IaaS), the access to the cloud-based technology is provided as a service to the cloud user. The control and access points are provided by the cloud provider. There is no conveyance of software to the cloud user. A service agreement covers all the basic terms and conditions that provide adequate protection to the cloud user without committing the cloud provider to risk and liability attendant with the licensing of the software.

24.3.2 On-Line Agreements Versus Standard Contracts

There are two contracting models under which a cloud provider will grant access to its services. The first, the on-line agreement, is a click wrap agreement with which a cloud user will be presented before initially accessing the service. A click wrap is the agreement the user enters into when he/she checks an "I Agree" box, or something similar at the initiation of the service relationship. The agreement is not subject to negotiation and is generally thought to be a contract of adhesion (i.e., a contract that heavily restricts one party while leaving the other relatively free). There is complete inequality in bargaining power in click wrap agreements because there is no ability to negotiate them. The click wrap is currently the most commonly used contracting model. The second model, the standard, negotiated, signature-based contract will have its place as well— over time. As larger companies move to the cloud (especially the public cloud), or more mission-critical applications or data move to the cloud, the cloud user will most likely require the option or a more robust and user-friendly agreement. This will be the case notwithstanding the economies associated with resource pooling, multi-tenancy, and virtualization offered by the cloud (that are maximized when the cloud provider uses a one-size-fits-all approach—even at the contracting level), as increasingly complex or sensitive information begins to be process in the cloud; the cloud user will push for a negotiated agreement.

24.3.3 The Importance of Privacy Policies Terms and Conditions

The privacy policy of a cloud provider is an important contractual document for the cloud user to read and understand. Why? In its privacy policy the cloud provider will discuss, in some detail, what it is doing (or not doing, as the case may be) to protect and secure the personal information of a cloud user and its customers. The cloud user may get a sense of how the cloud provider is complying with various privacy laws by reviewing the privacy policy. Even if the cloud provider is in full compliance with laws, a data compromise could still occur. The privacy policy may be where one finds the limits the cloud provider is placing on its liability in such an event. It is not negotiated, but a potential cloud user should be particularly interested in its terms. If the privacy protections appear inadequate or insufficient, the cloud user may wish to consider other cloud providers with more desirable or robust protections.

The cloud provider should be explicit in its privacy policy and fully describe what privacy security, safety mechanisms, and safety features it is implementing. As further incentive for the cloud provider to employ a "do what we say we do" approach to the privacy policy, the privacy policy is usually where the FTC begins its review of a company's privacy practices as part of its enforcement actions. If the FTC discovers anomalies between a provider's practices and its policies, then sanctions and consent decrees may follow.

Risk Allocation and Limitations of Liability. Simply stated, the limitation of liability in an agreement sets forth the maximum amount the parties will agree to pay one another should there be a reason to bring some sort of legal claim under the agreement. As a practical matter, contractual risk (e.g., provision of warranties, assuming liability for third parties under the provider's control, covenants to implement certain industry standards, service level agreements, etc.) is not distributed evenly between the parties. This is due in part because the performance obligations primarily fall on the provider. This sets up the traditional thinking that the contractual risk should follow the party with the most significant performance obligations. In reality, the cloud provider may have the bulk of the performance obligations, but may seek to take a "we bear no responsibility if something goes wrong" posture in its contracts, especially if those contracts are click wrap agreements. In fact, some cloud providers disclaim all liability in their agreements, even disclaiming liability if they are at fault or negligent in their performance. Over time, cloud services will be provided under both types of contracts. For mission-critical deployments the cloud provider will likely take on much more significant financial liability and contractual risk as part of the deal. This risk and liability will be reflected in the negotiated contract. The cloud user will pay a fee premium for shifting the liability and contractual risk to the cloud provider. The cloud provider's challenge, as it sees the risk and liability profile shift requiring it to assume heightened provider obligations, will be to appropriately mitigate contract risk using technological or other types of solutions where possible. Examples of mitigation could include implementation of robust and demonstrable information security programs, implementing standards or best practices, developing next generation security protocols, and enhancing employee training.

24.4 JURISDICTIONAL ISSUES RAISED BY VIRTUALIZATION AND DATA LOCATION

Jurisdiction is defined as a court's authority to judge acts committed in a certain territory. The geographical location of the data in a cloud computing environment will have a significant impact on the legal requirements for protection and handling of the data. This section highlights those issues.

24.4.1   Virtualization and Multi-tenancy

Virtualization. Computer virtualization in its simplest form is where one physical server simulates being several separate servers. For example, in an enterprise setting, instead of having a single server dedicated to payroll systems, another one dedicated to sales support systems, and still a third dedicated to asset management systems, virtualization allows one server to handle all of these functions. A single server can simulate being all three. Each one of these simulated servers is called a virtual machine.

Some benefits of virtualization are the need for less hardware and consumption of less power across the virtualized enterprise. Virtualization also provides greater utilization and maximization of hardware processing power. Because of these benefits, virtualization should lower expenses associated with operating a data center.

Virtualization across a single or multiple data centers makes it difficult for the cloud user or the cloud provider to know what information is housed on various machines at any given time. The emphasis in the virtualized environment is on maximizing usage of available resources no matter where they reside.

Multi-tenancy. Multi-tenancy refers to the ability of a cloud provider to deliver software as-a-service solutions to multiple client organizations (or tenants) from a single, shared instance of the software. The cloud user's information is virtually, not physically, separated from other users. The major benefit of this model is cost-effectiveness for the cloud provider. Some risks or issues with the model for the cloud user include (a) the potential for one user to be able to access data belonging to another user and (b) difficulty to back up and restore data [21].

24.4.2   The Issues Associated with the Flexibility of Data-Location

One of the benefits of cloud computing from the cloud provider's perspective is the ability of the cloud provider to move data among its available data center resources as necessary to maximize the efficiencies of it overall system. From a technology perspective, this ability to move data is a reasonably good solution to the problem of under utilized machines.

Data Protection. In fact, in the cloud environment it is possible that the same data may be stored in multiple locations at the same time. For example, real time-transaction data may be in one geographic location while the backup or disaster recovery systems may be elsewhere. It is also likely that the agreement governing the services says nothing about data location. There are exceptions, however. In fact, a few cloud providers (of which Amazon.com is one) are allowing cloud customers of certain service offerings to choose whether their data are kept in a U.S. or European data center [22].

Examples of the issues raised by data location are highlighted by Robert Gellman of the World Privacy Forum:

> The European Union's Data Protection Directive offers an example of the importance of location on legal rights and obligations. Under Article 4 ... [O]nce EU law applies to the personal data, the data remains subject to the law, and the export of that data will thereafter be subject to EU rules limiting transfers to a third country. *Once an EU Member State's data protection law attaches to personal information, there is no clear way to remove the applicability of the law to the data* [23].

From a legal perspective, flexibility of data location potentially challenges the governing law provision in the contract. If the law specified in the contract (e.g., the contract says that laws of Thailand will govern this agreement) requires a certain treatment of the data, but the law of the jurisdiction where the data resides (e.g., data center in Poland) requires another treatment, there is an inherent conflict that must be resolved. This conflict exists regardless of whether the storage is temporal, and as part of the processing of the data, or long-term storage that might be a service in itself (i.e., infrastructure as a service), or part of a software or platform as a service offering.

24.4.3 Other Jurisdiction Issues

Confidentiality and Government Access to Data. Each jurisdiction (and perhaps states or provinces within a jurisdiction) has its own regime to protect the confidentiality of information. In the cloud environment, given the potential movement of data among multiple jurisdictions, the data housed in a jurisdiction is subject to the laws of that jurisdiction, even if its owner resides elsewhere. Given the inconsistency of confidentiality protection in various jurisdictions, a cloud user may find that its sensitive data are not entitled to the protection with which the cloud user may be familiar, or that to which it contractually agreed.

A government's ability to access data is also directly connected to the jurisdiction in which the data reside. If the jurisdiction has laws that permit its government to get access to data (with or without notice to the cloud user or the individual or entity that owns the data), that data may be subject to interception by the government. In fact, under the USA PATRIOT Act, law enforcement agencies may gain access to personal financial information, email, and all other forms of electronic communications after certifying (a relatively low standard) that the information is relevant to any ongoing criminal investigation [24].

Subcontracting. A cloud provider's use of a third-party subcontractor to carry out its business may also create jurisdictional issues. The existence or nature of a subcontracting relationship is most likely invisible to the cloud user.

If, in the performance of the services, there was a lapse that was due to the subcontractor's performance, the location of the subcontractor or the data acted on by the subcontractor will be difficult for a cloud user to ascertain. As a result, the risk associated with the acts of or the locations of the subcontractor are difficult to measure by the cloud user.

24.4.4 International Conflicts of Laws

The body of law known as "conflict of laws" acknowledges that the laws of different countries may operate in opposition to each other, even as those laws relate to the same subject matter. In such an event, it is necessary to decide which country's law will be applied. Every nation is sovereign within its own territory. That means that the laws of that nation affect all property and people within it, including all contracts made and actions carried out within its borders. When there is either (1) no statement of the law that governs a contract, (2) no discussion of the rules regarding conflicts of laws in the agreement, or (3) a public policy in the jurisdiction which mandates that the governing law in the agreement will be ignored, the question of which nation's law will apply to the transaction will be decided based on a number of factors and circumstances surrounding the transaction. This cannot be reduced to a simple or easy-to-apply rule.

In a cloud environment, the conflicts of laws issues make the cloud provider's decisions regarding cross-geography virtualization and multi-tenancy, the cloud user's lack of information regarding data location, and the potential issues with geographically diverse subcontractors highly relevant.

24.5 COMMERCIAL AND BUSINESS CONSIDERATIONS—A CLOUD USER'S VIEWPOINT

As potential cloud users assess whether to utilize cloud computing, there are several commercial and business considerations that may influence the decision-making. Many of the considerations presented below may manifest in the contractual arrangements between the cloud provider and cloud user.

24.5.1 Minimizing Risk

Maintaining Data Integrity. Data integrity ensures that data at rest are not subject to corruption. Multi-tenancy is a core technological approach to creating efficiencies in the cloud, but the technology, if implemented or maintained improperly, can put a cloud user's data at risk of corruption, contamination, or unauthorized access. A cloud user should expect contractual provisions obligating a cloud provider to protect its data, and the user ultimately may be entitled to some sort of contract remedy if data integrity is not maintained.

Accessibility and Availability of Data/SLAs. The service-level agreement (SLA) is the cloud provider's contractually agreed-to level of performance for certain aspects of the services. The SLA, specifically as it relates to availability of services and data, should be high (i.e., better than 99.7%), with minimal scheduled downtime (scheduled downtime is outside the SLA). Regardless of the contract terms, the cloud user should get a clear understanding of the cloud provider's performance record regarding accessibility and availability of services and data. A cloud provider's long-term viability will be connected to its ability to provide its customers with almost continual access to their services and data. The SLAs, along with remedies for failure to meet them (e.g., credits against fees), are typically in the agreement between the cloud provider and cloud user.

The cloud user may find that many cloud providers offer relatively low SLAs—that is, SLAs that provide little assurance of quality to the user, as well as little likelihood of SLA default by the provider. The cloud user may also find that it bears the burden of establishing the occurrence of and requesting whatever remedies are available for a default. This approach is allowable (though not desirable) because there is no law, for the most part, requiring or mandating SLAs. The SLA is borne out of a business need that outsourcing service providers faced long before cloud computing. The service providers' customers were asking for certain contractual levels of quality. The response over time was the creation of the SLA to incentivize the provider to perform at high levels and to compensate the user when the service quality did not reach that level. The SLA is a contractual creation and is borne out of contract, not out of the law itself. Because of this reality, cloud providers have no requirement to use SLAs, create robust SLAs, or police them.

Disaster Recovery. For the cloud user that has outsourced the processing of its data to a cloud provider, a relevant question is, What is the cloud provider's disaster recovery plan? What happens when the unanticipated, catastrophic event affects the data center(s) where the cloud services are being provided? It is important for both parties to have an understanding of the cloud provider's disaster recovery plan.

24.5.2 Viability of the Cloud Provider

In light of the wide diversity of companies offering cloud services, from early stage and startup companies to global, publicly traded companies, the cloud provider's ability to survive as business is an important consideration for the cloud user. A potential cloud user should seek to get some understanding about the viability of the cloud provider, particularly early-stage cloud providers.

Why is this important? A cloud user will make an investment in (1) integrating the cloud services into its business processes and (2) migrating the data from its environment into the cloud environment. The lack of standardization among cloud providers will make it difficult and potentially costly for the cloud user to transition from one cloud provider to the other. Because of the costs associated with (1) and (2) above, cloud users will tend to stick with a cloud provider in the same way that it sticks with certain software applications. Therefore the long-term viability of the cloud provider is important.

Does Escrow Help?. Software escrow is the provision of a copy of the source code by the owner or licensor of the source code to a neutral third party (an escrow agent) for safekeeping for the benefit of a licensee or user of the code (the user is a beneficiary). The escrow agent releases the software to the beneficiary upon the occurrence of certain predefined events—for example, bankruptcy of the owner. So, at least for SaaS cloud users, escrow is an option. But escrow is not available to the cloud user unless expressly offered by the cloud provider in its agreement.

Even if the cloud provider offers the cloud user the option of source code escrow, the nature of the code—and even the manner in which it is implemented in a production environment—may prevent effective replication of the cloud service by a cloud user in the event of a release. So, it is an option, but it is an unattractive and potentially unworkable one. For cloud users that use the cloud for platform or infrastructure, escrow arrangements are not an option, since there is no practical way to escrow (or utilize in the event of a release) a platform or infrastructure. However, in the cases of platform and infrastructure, escrow may be a non-issue. The organization utilizing the platform or infrastructure may hold and deploy code in its possession; therefore control of the source in the event of a bankruptcy event may not be problematic.

What is a cloud user to do? Assuming that the cloud user has some flexibility to negotiate contract terms, the reasoned approach is for the cloud user to get contractual assurances that in the event of cessation of business, or some lesser event (e.g., bankruptcy), it will at least have access to its data and information without penalty or without being subject to the bankruptcy laws of a jurisdiction as a prerequisite. If the contract does not provide such a right, a user must determine whether to simply run the risk regarding the provider's viability. Equally as important, the cloud user should consider having a business continuity plan that contemplates a cloud provider no longer being able to provide a service.

24.5.3 Protecting a Cloud User's Access to Its Data

Though the ability for the cloud user to have continual access to the cloud service is a top consideration, a close second, at least from a business continuity standpoint, is keeping access to its data. This section introduces three scenarios that a cloud user should contemplate when placing its data into the cloud. There are no clear answers in any scenario. The most conservative or risk-averse cloud user may consider having a plan to keep a copy of its cloud-stored dataset in a location not affiliated with the cloud provider.

Scenario 1: Cloud Provider Files for Bankruptcy. In a bankruptcy proceeding, data are treated as a non-intellectual asset and under Section 363 of the U.S. Bankruptcy Code, and it is subject to disposition in a manner similar to other non-intellectual assets. Data may be consumer-type data, or it may be the business-level transaction data of the bankrupt cloud provider's business customers. Regardless of the type of data, the interests of the cloud provider and the cloud user with respect to the data will most likely diverge upon the filing of a bankruptcy. The bankrupt cloud provider wants to create as much value in the company as possible to facilitate various exits from the bankruptcy (of which an acquisition may be one). Consumer-level data is a valuable asset that might be transferred in a bankruptcy. Furthermore, the ability to access business-level customer data may be particularly attractive to a potential suitor that is competitive with the bankrupt entity, or even competitive with some of the business customers of the bankrupt entity whose data may be subject to transfer.

The cloud user is probably equally concerned about keeping its data (regardless of type) private and out of third-party hands without its consent. The cloud user's options are closely tied to the language of the privacy policy of the cloud provider. That language, along with an analysis by a "consumer privacy ombudsman,"[5] if one is appointed, will likely determine the fate of personally identifiable information. The ombudsman uses a multi-factor assessment that includes a review of (a) the potential gains or losses to consumers if the sale was approved and (b) potential mitigating alternatives.[6] Any transfer is likely to be under privacy terms similar to those of the cloud provider. There is no equivalent analysis undertaken by the ombudsman for business-level transaction data. Business data are likely to be handled at the will of the bankruptcy court. The good news is that a cloud user probably will not lose access to its data. However, a third-party suitor to the bankrupt cloud provider may gain access to such data in the process.

Scenario 2: Cloud Provider Merges or Is Acquired. Any number of situations could lead to the transfer of the cloud provider's operation and the information associated with it, to a third party. The most likely scenarios include the merger or acquisition of the business, or the sale of a business unit or service line. Since a cloud user is unlikely to be notified prior to the closing of a transaction, once again the privacy policy is the best place to look to determine what would happen to user data in such an event. The click wrap agreement will clarify the termination options available to the cloud user should it be dissatisfied with the new ownership.

Scenario 3: Cloud Provider Ceases to Do Business. As a best case, if there is an orderly shutdown of a cloud provider as part of its cessation

[5]11 U.S.C.A. § 332.
[6]Id.

activities, the cloud user may have the ability to retrieve its data as part of the shut-down activities. In the event that a cloud provider simply walks away and shuts down the business, cloud users are most likely left with only legal remedies, filing suit, for example, to attempt to get access to its data.

24.6   SPECIAL TOPICS

24.6.1   The Cloud Open-Source Movement

In Spring 2009 a group of companies, both technology companies and users of technology, released the Open Cloud Manifesto [25]. The manifesto's basic premise is that cloud computing should be as open like other IT technologies. The manifesto sets forth five challenges that it suggests must be overcome before the value of cloud computing can be maximized in the marketplace. These challenges are (1) security, (2) data and applications interoperability, (3) data and applications portability, (4) governance and management, and (5) metering and monitoring. The manifesto suggests that open standards and transparency are methods to overcome these challenges. It then suggests that openness will benefit business by providing (a) an easier experience transitioning to a new provider, (b) the ability for organizations to work together, (c) speed and ease of integration, and (d) a more available, cloud-savvy talent pool from which to hire.

The open-source movement has, over time, changed the way software is developed and distributed. Though the open-source dialogue surrounding cloud computing is in its early stages, an open source will affect the technological, business, and legal conversation on cloud computing.

24.6.2   Litigation Issues/e-Discovery

From a U.S. law perspective, a significant effort must be made during the course of litigation to produce electronically stored information (ESI). This production of ESI is called "e-discovery." The overall e-discovery process has three basic components: (1) information management, where a company decides where and how its information is processed and retained, (2) identifying, preserving, collecting, and processing ESI once litigation has been threatened or started, and (3) review, processing, analysis, and production of the ESI for opposing counsel [26]. The Federal Rules of Civil Procedure require a party to produce information within its "possession, custody, or control." [7] Courts will likely recognize that the ESI may not be within a cloud user's possession, but courts will suggest, and maybe assume, that ESI is within its control. This means that the cloud user likely has the legal requirement to get access to its ESI upon demand. With this as the foundational principle, a cloud

---

[7]Fed.R. Civ. P. 34(a)(1).

user will have to work closely with a cloud provider, perhaps even entering into a separate agreement at the onset of litigation to facilitate the cloud provider's provision of the cloud user's ESI for e-discovery purposes. The agreement, if it is necessary, should deal with issues surrounding retention and preservation of ESI; identify which party bears the responsibility for lost data; and decide how and on what timeframes disclosure of the ESI must occur.

The most challenging issue in the cloud e-discovery context is that of cross-border discovery. There are significant litigation risks where the information sought by a company for disclosure is located in a foreign country. Countries that take radically different approaches to cross-border information transfers simply raise the risk and expense associated with e-discovery. United States courts have not excused compliance with discovery orders based on arguments that foreign laws prohibit the discovery; any company that attempts to avoid e-discovery by asserting that its cloud provider is outside of the territory and that information is undiscoverable is likely to be accused of avoiding litigation. This can result in the imposition of fines and sanctions.

24.7 CONCLUSION

This chapter was intended to survey the broad set of legal issues that may require consideration in cloud computing. The issues primarily fall into four areas: data privacy and security, contracting issues, issues surrounding location of the data, and business considerations.

The law always lags behind technological innovation, and the complexities of cloud computing will force the law to catch up in order for effective legal remedies to be available to prevent and provide redress for harms that occur.

24.8 EPILOGUE

"After 36 nonstop hours, untold cups of coffee, cans of energy drinks, and slices of pizza, Mike, Nikhil, and I finally headed home. The crisis had been partially averted, but that was the best that we could do. There had been an attack on our systems—malicious in nature. Fortunately, that untested disaster recovery plan worked reasonably well. We didn't lose too much data, or have too much downtime. But the breach caught the eye of U.S. and EU officials— and the lawyers, lots of lawyers from all those customers that we had to call. We'd done reasonably well, had our policies up-to-date, and employed best in breed techniques to protect the data. Our systems management applications allowed us to get a quick handle on where our data really was at the time of the attack. And though we'd failed to meet some of our SLAs (our customers experienced a short window of unavailability), those service credits we would have to pay were a mere pittance compared to the losses we could have incurred.

As we walked to our cars, I noticed the color had returned to Mike and Nikhil's faces. Even through the haze of my fatigue, I could tell they'd further elevated themselves to super-miracle-worker status—not totally because of what they did in those 36 hours, but because of all the work they'd done the months and years before that to keep those 36 hours from turning into Armageddon. They'd worked with our security team, our business team, our legal counsel, and senior management to develop a strategy for running our business and to keep it running in the event of a potential catastrophe. All that effort to make sure we'd gotten it right (and that prayer that only God and IT types hear) paid off. Next time you see those guys walking down the street, be sure to thank them. The data they saved might have just been yours...."

REFERENCES

1. NIST Cloud computing definition, http://csrc.nist.gov/groups/SNS/cloud-compu ting/index.html, 2009.

2. National Institute of Standards and Technology, http://www.nist.gov, 2009.

3. Financial Services Modernization Act (Gramm–Leach–Bliley), Pub. L. No. 106-102, 113 Stat. 1338 (November 12, 1999), codified at 15 U.S.C. §§6801-09.

4. T. L. Forsheit, and K. J. Mathews, Financial Privacy Law, Proskauer on Privacy, §2:4.2, pp. 2–46, Practicing Law Institute, USA, 2006.

5. Gramm–Leach–Bliley Safeguards Rule-Subtitle A, Disclosure of Nonpublic Personal Information, codified at 15 U.S.C. § 6801–6809.

6. FTC guidance on business compliance with Safeguards Rule, http://www.ftc.gov/ bcp/edu/pubs/business/idtheft/bus54.shtm, 2009.

7. The Fair and Accurate Credit Transactions Act of 2003 (FACT), Pub. L. No. 108–159, 117 Stat. 1952 (December 4, 2003).

8. FTC guidance on business compliance with Red Flags Rule, http://ftc.gov/opa/ 2007/10/redflag.shtm, 2009.

9. Health Information Technology for Economic and Clinical Health Act (HI-TECH), *Title XIII of Division A and Title IV of Division B of the American Recovery and Reinvestment Act of 2009 (ARRA)*, Pub. L. No. 111-5, 123 Stat 115, February 17, 2009, 42 USC sec. 17931 et seq.

10. Health Insurance Portability and Accountability Act of 1996 (HIPAA), Pub. L. No. 104–191, 110 Stat. 1936 (August 21, 1996) (codified as amended in scattered sections of 42 U.S.C. and 29 U.S.C.).

11. Uniting and Strengthening America by Providing Appropriate Tools Required to Intercept and Obstruct Terrorism Act of 2001 (USA PATRIOT Act), Pub. L. No. 107-56, 115 Stat. 272, October 26, 2001, codified at various code sections

12. The USA PATRIOT ACT, Electronic Privacy Information Center, http://epic.org/ privacy/terrorism/usapatriot/.

13. EU Directive 95/46/EC of the European Parliament and the Council of 24 October 1995 on the Protection of Individuals with Regard to the Processing of Personal Data and the Free Movement of Such Data, 1995 O.J. (L281) 31.

14. Personal Data (Privacy) Ordinance, http://www.pcpd.org.hk/english/ordinance/ordfull.html, 2009.

15. PIPEDA, http://laws.justice.gc.ca/en/ShowDoc/cs/P-8.6//20090818/en?page=1, 2009.

16. PIPEDA.INFO, http://www.pipeda.info/a/s4−1.html, 2009.

17. CSA Model Code for the Protection of Personal Information, http://www.csa.ca/cm/privacy-code/publications, 2009.

18. Australia Privacy Act of 1988, http://www.privacy.gov.au/law/act, 2009.

19. Australia Information Privacy Principles, http://www.privacy.gov.au/law/act/ipp, 2009.

20. Australia National Privacy Principles, http://www.privacy.gov.au/law/act/npp, 2009.

21. G. Goldszmidt and I. Poddar, Develop and Deploy Multi-tenant Web-Delivered Solutions Using IBM Middleware: Part 1: Challenges and Architectural Patterns, http://www.ibm.com/developersworks/webservices/library/ws-middleware/index.html, 2009.

22. Amazon Web Services Offers European Storage for Amazon S3, http://phx.corporate-ir.net/phoenix.zhtml?c=176060&p=irol-newsArticle&ID=1072982&highlight, 2009.

23. R. Gellman, Privacy in the Clouds: Risks to Privacy and Confidentiality from cloud Computing, February 23, 2009, http://www.worldprivacyforum.org/pdf/WPF_cloud_Privacy_Report.pdf, 2009.

24. The USA PATRIOT Act, Electronic Privacy Information Center, http://epic.org/privacy/terrorism/usapatriot/, 2009.

25. Open Cloud Manifesto, http://www.opencloudmanifesto.org, 2009.

26. M. Austrian and W. Ryan, Cloud computing meets e-discovery, *Cyberspace Lawyer*, 14(6): 7−12, 2009.

CHAPTER 25

ACHIEVING PRODUCTION READINESS FOR CLOUD SERVICES

WAI-KIT CHEAH and HENRY KASIM

25.1 INTRODUCTION

The latest paradigm that has emerged is that of cloud computing where new evolution of operating model enables IT services to be delivered through next-generation data-center infrastructures consisting of compute, storage, applications and databases, built over virtualization technology [1].

Cloud service providers who are planning to build infrastructure to support cloud services should first justify their plans through a strategic and business planning process. Designing, building, implementing, and commissioning an underlying technology infrastructure to offer cloud services to a target market segment is merely a transformation process that the service provider must undertake to prepare for supporting the processes, management tools, technology architectures, and foundation to deliver and support their cloud services. These foundation elements will be used to produce the cloud service that will be ready for consumption.

The question then is, How does a service provider qualify and determine that the service is ready for production? What does production readiness mean? This chapter explores elements that are required to be designed, planned, assessed, evaluated, tested, and accepted prior to classifying their service as production-ready and consumption-ready.

25.2 SERVICE MANAGEMENT

The term *service management* has been defined in many ways by analysts and business practitioners.

Cloud Computing: Principles and Paradigms, Edited by Rajkumar Buyya, James Broberg and Andrzej Goscinski Copyright © 2011 John Wiley & Sons, Inc.

The Stationery Office [2] defines service management as follows:

Service management is more than just a set of capabilities. It is also a professional practice supported by an extensive body of knowledge, experience, and skill.

Van Bon et al. and van der Veen [3] describe service management as:

The capacity of an organization to deliver services to customers.

Based on analysis and research of service management definitions, we define service management as a set of specialized organizational capabilities for providing value to customers in the form of services. The practice of service management have expanded over time, from traditional value-added service such as banks, hotels, and airlines into IT provider model that intends to adopt service-oriented approach in managing and delivering IT services.

This delivery model of IT services to the masses, where assets, resources, and capabilities are pooled together, is what we would term a form of cloud service. The lure of cloud services is its ubiquity, pervasiveness, elasticity, and flexibility of paying only for what you use.

25.3   PRODUCER–CONSUMER RELATIONSHIP

As we contemplate on the new paradigm of delivering services, we can reflect upon the closely knit underlying concept of the classical producer–consumer relationship in the design, implementation, and production of the service as well as in the consumption of the service. The producer–consumer relationship diagram is shown in Figure 25.1.

The producer, also known as cloud service provider, refers to the party who strategizes, designs, invests, implements, transitions, and operates the underlying infrastructure that supplies the assets and resources to be delivered as a cloud service. The objective of the producer is to provide value-add as a cloud service, which will deliver value to their customers by facilitating outcomes customers want to achieve.

The consumer refers to the party who will subscribe, use and pay for what they use from the available resources of the cloud service. Consumers are the cloud service users and typically would financially compensate the provider for the use of cloud service. For example, a consumer may have a need for a terabyte (1 terabyte = 1000 gigabytes) of secured storage to support its private human resource documentation. From a strategic perspective, the consumer would want the equipment, facilities, staff, and infrastructure for a terabyte of storage to (a) remain within its span of control, having the flexibility to pay for what they use, and (b) ramp up capacity quickly if the need arises, or scale down deployment as required. The consumer does not want to be accountable for all associated costs and risks, real or nominal, actual or perceived, such as

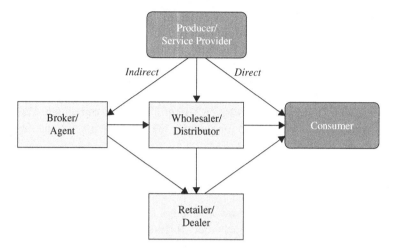

FIGURE 25.1. The producer–consumer relationship diagram.

designing the technology architectures, management tools, processes, and all the resources to manage, deliver, and support the service. This concern is especially amplified when the need for resources is short-term. The design complexity, operational uncertainties, and technical trade-offs associated with maintaining reliable high-performance storage systems lead to costs and risks that the consumer is not willing take.

The law of demand and supply will provide an efficient ecosystem in which the consumer with specific needs will be able to locate and find available service providers in the market that meet the required service demands and at the right price.

25.3.1 Business Mindset

From a producer's perspective, it is critical to understand what would be the right and desired outcome. Rather than focusing on the production of services, it is important to view from the customer's perspective. In order for producers to provide the desired cloud services, some of the questions that the service provider should address are:

- Nature of business (What is the core business?)
- Target consumer segments (Who are the customers?)
- Cloud service value (What does the consumer desire? How is the service valuable to consumer?)
- The service usage and charge-back (How does the consumer use the services? What are the charges?)

Value of service can be added at different levels. Cloud service providers differentiate themselves from equipment vendors through their added value and specialization even while using equipments from those similar hardware vendors as assets. An analogy would be a provider who offers a collaboration service, encompassing presence, conferencing, commuting, and file share, rather than a mere email messaging service. The service provider shifts customer focus from attributes-driven to fulfillment of outcomes. With this business mindset, it is possible to understand the components of value from the customer's perspective.

25.3.2 Direct Versus Indirect Distribution

As shown in Figure 25.1, the arrow lines depict the cloud services that can be offered by the cloud service provider through two different distribution channels: direct or indirect. Channel selection is often a choice and like any other business decisions is highly dependent on the service providers' strategy, targeted consumers of the service (internal or external), and the outlook of the relative profitability of the two distribution channel. Typically, direct channel is more appropriate than indirect channel in the context of a private cloud service and where quality assurance matters.

25.3.3 Quality of Service and Value Composition

One characteristic of services in general is the intangibility of the service. Perception plays a heavier role in assessments of quality in this case than it does with manufactured products. Figure 25.2 shows a diagram of perception of quality. Value perception is typically derived from two components: expected quality and experienced quality. Expected quality refers to level of service that

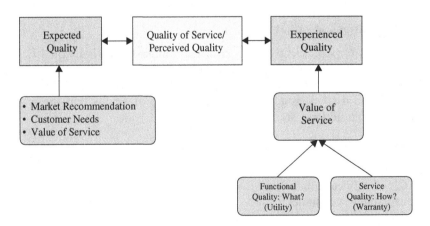

FIGURE 25.2. Perception of quality.

the customer expects when engaging with a service provider (e.g., market communication, customer needs, etc.), whereas, experienced quality refers value of service based on customer's experience.

The value of a service consists of two primary elements [3]: utility (fitness for purpose) and warranty (fitness for use).

- *Utility* (fitness for purpose), or *functional* quality attribute, is perceived by customers from the attributes of the service with positive effect on performance of tasks associated with desired outcomes.
- *Warranty* (fitness for use), or *service* quality attribute, is derived from the positive effect of being available when needed, in sufficient capacity and magnitude, and dependable in terms of continuity and security.

Utility is what the customer gets. Warranty is how the service is delivered. Customers' benefit is derived from a combination of both elements, and it would not be achieved if one element is missing. Thus it is useful to allocate adequate focus on logic for both elements during design, development, and improvement phases. Considering all separate controllable inputs would allow for wider range of solutions to the challenges of creating, maintaining and increasing value.

25.3.4 Charging Model

In the 1990s, value pricing was the key phrase in pricing decisions. It was used widely by many service industries: airlines, supermarkets, car rentals, and other consumer services industry. It started with Taco Bell offering a value menu with several entries, such as tacos, for very low prices. With their successes, other fast-food chains picked up on the concept and started offering their value-priced menu entries. The early 1990s recession caused industries to pick up on the value pricing concept, whose utilization was spread across many service industries. However, we would be careful to distinguish between (a) value pricing and (b) pricing to value. Pricing to value relies on value estimates of the dollar customers associates with the service. When coupled with an estimate of the variable and the fixed costs of producing and delivering a service, this determines ranges of possible price points that can be charged. Deciding on the charging model and pricing strategy is a key business strategy that should not be neglected.

When the term cloud computing was first coined, the general idea was that cloud computing would lower costs [4]. To the consumer, with interim or short-term needs, it is possible that cloud service could provide a lower cost [1]. However, for the producer, with the need to invest in excess capacity and deliver the cloud service, it is an expensive undertaking. Due to this reason, the producer needs to strategically decide the charging model for the service offering.

There are several charging models as describe in Gartner report by Plummer et al. [5], however the below two charging model are the preferred model by the Cloud service provider:

- *Utility Model.* Pay-per-use model where consumer is charged on the quantity of cloud services usage and utilization. This model is similar to traditional electricity charges. For example, a consumer uses secured storage to support its private work documentation. The consumer is charged $0.50 for every 10 gigabytes of storage that is used. This model provides a lower startup cost option for a customer in translating TCO to actual utilization.
- *Subscription Model.* Here the consumer is charged based on time-based cloud services usage. For example, the consumer is charged a yearly fee for a dedicated storage of 10 gigabytes to host the company Web site. This model provides predictable cost outlay and provides a steady stream of revenue for the services provider.

25.4 CLOUD SERVICE LIFE CYCLE

The input to the production of a cloud services are all the resources and assets that will compose the cloud service (i.e., in the form of hardware, software, man power required from developer to the management level and cost). The outcome of the cloud services production is an acceptable and marketable cloud service, which will provide a measurable value to the business objectives and outcomes. The sets of inputs are transformed to derive the outcome by using the cloud service life cycle. The cloud service life cycle consists of five phases as shown in Figure 25.3 and Table 25.1 summarizes each of the phase in cloud service life-cycle.

At the core of the cloud service life cycle is service strategy, which is the fundamental phase in defining the service principles. The main core of the cloud

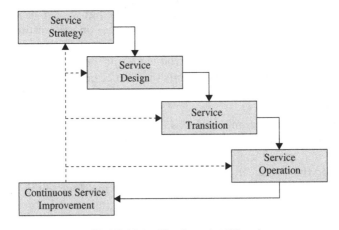

FIGURE 25.3. Cloud service lifecycle.

TABLE 25.1. Cloud Service Life Cycle

Service Phase	Service Strategy	Service Design	Service Transition	Service Operation	Continuous Service Improvement
Description	Defines the business strategies, policies, objectives	Design of the cloud services, processes, and capabilities	Develop the cloud services for the transition of services to production	Production of cloud services and service operational support	Maintain and Improve value of cloud service to consumer
Objectives	Determines the business decision	Design the new/improved cloud service to meet business requirements	Development, deployment and validation to ensure that the cloud service has correct capabilities	Ensure the cloud service value to consumer	Continuously maintain and improve the value of cloud service to meet business needs
Outcome	Business requirements and cloud service descriptions	Cloud service blueprint or Service Design Package (SDP)	Production of the cloud services that is ready to go live	Monitoring report, cloud service feedback	Cloud services improvement

service life cycle is the key principle that all services must provide measurable value to business objectives and outcomes, which is reinforced in ITIL service management as its primary focus [2, 3].

Service design, transition, and operation are the revolving life-cycle stages and are anchored by continual service improvement. This life cycle revolves through the continuous service improvement process to provide performance measurement at each individual phase and a feedback for improvement. This has become crucial as IT organizations are increasingly forced to operate as businesses in order to demonstrate a clear return on investment and equate service performance with business value to the IT's internal customers.

The necessity of specialization and coordination in the life-cycle approach has been made available via feedback and control between the functions and processes across the life-cyle phases.

The cloud service life-cycle approach mimics reality of most organizations where effective management requires uses of multiple control perspectives.

25.4.1 Service Strategy

Service strategy is the core of the service life cycle. It signifies the birth of the service. This is the phase where the business defines the strategies, policies, and objectives and establishes an understanding of the constraints, requirements, and business values. Figure 25.4 illustrates the inputs and outcomes of the service strategy phase.

In the service strategy phase, the cloud service provider would be undertaking strategic planning on various value creation activities, including what services are to be designed, what resources are required to build this cloud services, and what capabilities of the cloud service are to be developed. Typically, the planning includes the detailed description of the cloud services (value to be created), defining the market, service portfolio, project timeline, resources required (number of man-power, budget), risks, and other key factors influencing the cloud service production.

The service strategy phase involves a business decision to determine if the cloud service provider has sufficient resources to develop this type of service

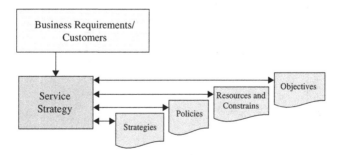

FIGURE 25.4. Service strategy.

and also to determine if production of a cloud service has a business value. The service strategy is comprised of the following key concepts:

- Value creation
- Service provider types
- Defining the service market
- Demand management
- Financial management
- Return of investment
- Service assets, assessment, and portfolios
- Service capabilities and resources
- Service structures and developing service offerings

The outcome of the service strategy phase is service strategy documentation, which includes the following components:

- Business requirements—target consumer market and stakeholders
- Risks involved
- Resources required (man-power and budget)
- Functional service requirements
- Service descriptions
- New/improved service timeline

25.4.2 Service Design

The second phase in the cloud service life cycle is service design. The main purpose of the service design stage of the life cycle is the design of new or improved service for introduction into the live environment. Figure 25.5 shows the input and the outcome of the service design phase. In this phase, the service requirements and specification are translated into a detailed cloud service design including the detailed desired outcome. The main objectives of service design are:

- Aspects of service design
- Service catalogue management
- Service requirements
- Service design models
- Capacity, availability, and service-level management

The key concepts of service design revolve around the five design aspects, the design of services, service processes and service capabilities to meet business demand. The five key aspects of service design are:

- The design of the *services*, including all of the functional requirements, resources, and capabilities needed and agreed.

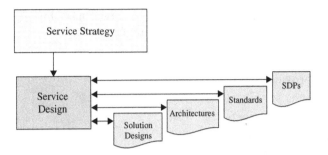

FIGURE 25.5. Service design.

- The design of *service management systems and tools*, for the control and management of sustainable services through the life cycle.
- The design of the *technology architectures*, hardware and software, required to form the underlying technical aspects to provide the services.
- The design of the *policies and processes* needed to design, transition, operate, and improve the services, the architectures and the processes.
- The design of *key measurement methods*, performance metrics for the service, cloud service architectures, and their constituent components and the processes.

The key output of the service design phase is a blueprint of the service solution, architectures, and standards. This output is what ITIL would term the service design package (SDP) [2]. The SDP defines the following with respect to the service:

- Service-level requirements
- Service design and topology
- Service and operational management requirements
- Organizational readiness assessment plan
- Service program
- Service transition plan
- Service operational acceptance plan
- Service acceptance criteria

25.4.3 Service Transition

The service transition phase intends to implement and deploy what has been designed and planned. As shown in Figure 25.6, the service transition phase takes knowledge formulated out of the service design phase, and uses it to plan for the validation, release and deployment of the service to production. Key disciplines in service transition are:

- Service *development* or service change is service built according to service design package (SDP).
- Service *release and deployment* ensures the correct release in live environment.
- Service *validation and test* ensures that the service has validated correct capabilities and functionalities.
- Service *knowledge management* is to share information within the organization to avoid rediscovering of cloud service capabilities.

Service transition provides a consistent and rigorous framework for evaluating the service capability and risk profile before a new or a changed service is released or deployed. The key output of the service transition is production of the services that is ready to go live, which includes:

- Approved service release package and associated deployment packages.
- Updated service package or bundle that defines end-to-end service(s) offered to customers.
- Updated service portfolio and service catalogue.
- Updated contract portfolio.
- Documentation for a transferred service.

25.4.4 Service Operation

Service operation is the stage in the cloud service life cycle to provide the production of the cloud service and the service operational support. Service operation spans the execution and business performance of processes to continually strike the balance between cost optimization and quality of services. It is responsible for effective functioning of components that support services.

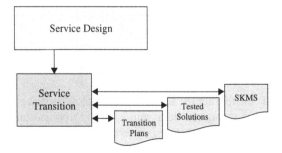

FIGURE 25.6. Service transition.

Effective service operation relies on the ability to know the status of the infrastructure and to detect any deviation from normal or expected operation. This is provided by good monitoring and control systems, which are based on two types of tools:

- *Active monitoring* tools that poll key configuration items (CIs) to determine their status and availability. Any exceptions will generate an alert that needs to be communicated to the appropriate tool or team for action.
- *Passive monitoring* tools that detect and correlate operational alerts or communications generated by CIs.

25.4.5 Continuous Service Improvement

As business demand increases, customer requirement changes, market landscape fluctuates, and the service needs to adapt to these changing conditions to improvise and compete. Buyya et al. [6] mentioned that: *"Quality of service requirements cannot be static and need to be dynamically updated over time due to continuing changes in business operations."* The continuous service improvement phase is to ensure that the service remains appealing to meet the business needs. This is achieved by continuously maintaining and improving the value of service to consumers through better design, transition, and operation.

25.5 PRODUCTION READINESS

An authorization to commence service transition is considered one of the key outputs from service design to initiate the transitioning activities. In the cloud service life-cycle point of view, production readiness refers to the successful conclusion of the service transition phase and the production of the required outputs from service transition to service operation. Reaching the state where a service is ready to be transitioned into service operation is what we term production readiness.

A service is deemed to be implemented and within the service operation stage of its life cycle when its processes, functions, organizational structure, and underlying technology have reached the business operational state.

25.6 ASSESSING PRODUCTION READINESS

The underlying IT infrastructure supporting the cloud service is similar to the ecosystem of compute resources, data, and software applications, which need to be managed, measured, and monitored continuously to ensure that it is functioning as expected. The healthy functioning of this ecosystem is what we would refer to as operational health of the service. Operational health is determined by the execution of this ecosystem in delivery of the services and is dependent on the ability to prevent incidents and problems, achieve availability targets and service-level objectives, and minimize any impact to the value of the service.

Several key criteria that the cloud service provider needs to assess before the service is ready for production is what we term *assessing production readiness*. The main objective in assessing production readiness is to achieve a successful transition from development of cloud service into the service operational phase. The secondary objective is to ensure that the cloud service is healthy functioning. The readiness of a service for operation is to ensure that the following key assessments are in place.

- *Service Facilities Readiness.* Facilities to build and sustain a cloud service have been established.
- *Service Infrastructure Readiness.* Hardware components (servers, storages, and network components) have been delivered and meet the requirements.
- *Service Technology Readiness.* Software components and other necessary components have been installed and deployed on the infrastructure.
- *Monitoring Readiness.* Track the conditions, events, and anomalies on the cloud infrastructure.
- *Service Measurement Readiness.* Evaluate the service utilization and validate that the charge-back amount is accurate.
- *Service Documentation.* Define service procedure, manual, and instruction to ensure that the service is well-defined, structured, maintained, and supported.
- *Communication Readiness.* Identify all activities related to communication issues related to service operation.
- *Service Operational Readiness.* Ready to support operations and maintenance of the services.
- *Key Performance Indicators (KPI).* Effective metric of measurement for the service has been developed.
- *Acceptance Testing.* The service is considered to be ready for production when it has passed an adequate level of measurement set in KPI metrics.

The nature of each production readiness assessment is described in more detail below.

25.6.1 Service Facilities Readiness

At the core of all components required to build and sustain a cloud service is a data-center facility. Facilities refer to the physical real-estate housing infrastructure that is required to host cloud infrastructure for the cloud service. Cloud services boast advantages of elasticity and capabilities to allow consumers to increase or decrease their resource consumption; therefore, it can be implied that there will be a need for constructing excess capacity in terms of the IT infrastructure. This translates to more requirements for hosting space to accommodate more assets, requirement for better facility (i.e., more cooling capacity, power consumption, floor loading).

The facility to host cloud infrastructure plays an important role in cloud service design. Some of the considerations that a cloud service provider should take into account are:

- *Physically Secured Environment.* The cloud infrastructure facility should be reasonably secured and protected. For example, facility space has adequate access controls to permit entry for authorized personnel only.
- Free *or Mitigated from Natural Disaster.* Design of the facility should include mitigation features against common natural disasters known to the area. For example, if the facility is located at an earthquake zone, the data-center facility should be able to withstand a minimum seismic movement without a major outage or to have mitigated such risks to ensure that the service levels are able to be met [7]. An alternative facility should be sourced if no mitigation is possible with regard to infrastructure risk to degree of common natural disasters.
- *Cooling and Power Availability.* The facility design should be at the right size to maintain adequate level of redundancy and availability to meet required service levels for the cloud service. Right-sizing means having a design with adequate tiering (as per Uptime Institute's tier classification) that is sufficient to meet the service levels and not more than required. Cooling and power constraints [7] should be reviewed to ensure that as servicing grows along with the business, there should be sufficient cooling capacity and power capacity to meet the growing physical demand.
- *Network Connectivity Bandwidth.* Cloud services are likely to be delivered to consumers over the network, therefore bandwidth availability and capacity play an important role. There should be capacity planning and accurate forecasting to project the dynamic demands on network bandwidth based on the number of consumers, take-on rates, and usage patterns without direct consequences to the cloud service levels.

Assessing production readiness in terms of service facilities readiness means: Facilities to build and sustain a cloud service have been established.

25.6.2 Service Infrastructure Readiness

Service infrastructure readiness is to ensure that all the hardware components have been delivered and meet the requirements of the service design. Hardware components refer to the physical IT assets of the cloud infrastructure, which will fulfill the compute and storage resources. Hardware components include compute servers, disk storages, network devices, and appliances that are collectively used in the makeup of the technology architecture and configured as the cloud infrastructure. The challenges and considerations for hardware are:

- *Compute Servers.* The following factors influence the decision of compute server selection:
  - Proprietary hardware components and ease of replacement. Because compute resources should be easily provisioned from a collective group of server hardware, proprietary hardware components and ease of replacement or acquisition of the servers should be high in order to easily acquire and grow.
  - Hardware reliability is less of a concern, depending on the ability of the software architecture to automatically re-deploy compute resources whenever there is a fault.
  - Platform or operating systems compatibility. Compute servers should be able to operate on a hypervisor or abstraction layer that can support most of the common platforms or operating systems without compatibility issues.
- *Disks Storages.* The following factors influence the decision of disk storage selection:
  - Virtualization layer that can encapsulate the underlying disk storage arrays. With the design of this layer, it would enable provisioning of lower-cost storage arrays to accommodate storage capacity demands.
  - Proprietary hardware components and ease of replacement. Similar to compute resources, hard disks should be easily provisioned from a collective group of storage pool. Hence, storage architecture should be open and replacement of additional storage should be easily acquired without incurring exorbitant marginal costs.
  - Hardware reliability is less of a concern, depending on the level of data protection in the design.
- *Networking Infrastructure.* Selection and choice of networking devices will be dependent on the topology, architecture design, data flow, and anticipated usage patterns.

The major risks or challenges involved in hardware components is the risk of the hardware failure beyond the tolerance of the acceptable service levels. The design of the cloud service architecture and infrastructure as well as the service strategy is crucial to ensure right-sized infrastructure. To offer a higher-end service level and to prevent the risks of unplanned outages or service-level breaches, some cloud service providers adopts "fail-over" functionality, where it will replace the faulty compute servers or disks storages with the available servers/disks that has similar configuration.

Assessing production readiness in terms of service infrastructure readiness means: Hardware components have been delivered and are right-sized.

25.6.3 Service Technology Readiness

As cloud services are predominantly IT services, the underlying infrastructure are often delivered within the governance of a set of software logic. While the hardware components provide the resources available to the customer, the software components control, manage, and allow the actual usage of these resources by the consumers.

The purpose of service technology readiness is to define the resources required, items of service assets, software components, and other components necessary to build and deploy the services on the cloud infrastructure.

Software components typically cover the operating systems, application technologies, virtualization technologies, and management systems tools to operate and deliver the cloud service. Considerations are what would be the appropriate software technologies to adopt, how these technologies would fit the hardware piece of the equation, licensing considerations, and what are the operational limitations or advantages of the selected software technologies. In terms of software components, the challenges faced by the cloud service providers are:

- *Data Corruption.* Cloud services which host consumers' data are usually burdened with the responsibility of ensuring the integrity and availability of these data, depending on the subscribed service level. In most cases, the bare minimum should be that software applications used are error-free to avoid any major data corruption or outage.
- *Logical Security.* In terms of information security, an appropriate control of logical security should be adopted by the producer to ensure adequate confidentiality (i.e., data and transactions are open only to those who are authorized to view or access them).
- *Data Interoperability.* Producer should follow the interoperability standards in order for the consumers to be able to combine any of the cloud services into their solutions.
- *Software Vulnerability and Breaches.* There are occasions when the public community discovers vulnerabilities of specific software, middleware, Web services, or other network services components in the software components. The producer should ensure that a proper strategy and processes are in place to address such vulnerabilities and fixed to prevent breaches.

Assessing production readiness in term of Service technology readiness means: Software components have been installed, configured, and deployed.

25.6.4 Monitoring Readiness

Monitoring readiness refers to having the ability and functions to monitor and track the conditions, events, and anomalies on the cloud infrastructure during the consumption of the cloud services. In the context of service operation, the measurement and control of services is based on a continual cycle of monitoring, reporting, and subsequently remedial action. While monitoring capability takes place during service operation, it is fundamental to predefine the strategic basis requiring this capability, designing it, and testing this capability to ensure its functional fulfillment. The monitoring readiness should at least include the following features:

- Status tracking on key configuration items (CIs) and key operational activities.
- Detect anomality in the service operations and notify the key personnel in charge.
- Ensure that performance and utilization of key service components are within specified operating condition.
- Ensure compliance with the service provider's policies.

> Assessing production readiness in terms of monitoring readiness means: Capability to track the conditions and anomalities on the Cloud infrastructure.

25.6.5 Service Measurement Readiness

The purpose of the service measurement readiness criteria is to evaluate the service utilization and validate that the service charge-back amount to the consumer is accurate. It becomes necessary for the service provider to monitor, measure, and report on component levels to the point that is granular enough that provides a meaningful view of the service as the consumer experiences the value of service.

> Assessing production readiness in terms of service measurement readiness means:
> Evaluate the service usage and validate that the charge-back amount is accurate.

25.6.6 Service Documentation

Established service portfolio, service catalogue, design blueprints, service-level agreements, operational level agreements, process manuals, technical procedures, work instructions, and other service documentation are necessary to ensure that the service is well-defined, structured, and able to be maintained and supported. When the service undergoes some changes, the service documentation needs to be updated.

> Assessing production readiness in terms of Service documentation means:
> Service documentation (e.g., procedure, manual) are well-defined and maintained.

25.6.7 Communication Readiness

The purpose of communication readiness is to identify all the activities related to communication issues related to the service operation (e.g., identify medium, format, key personnel to be notified for customer support or during critical message). Communication readiness criteria include customer support scenarios, frequently asked questions (FAQs), help-desk personnel, and key personnel when there are abnormalities in the service operations.

> Assessing production readiness in terms of communication readiness means: Identify all the activities related to communication issues related to service operation.

25.6.8 Service Operational Readiness

Being production ready also requires a certain level of maturity in operational processes. Operational processes include the technology and management tools implementation to ensure the smooth running of the cloud infrastructure. These operational processes are broadly categorized into the following:

- *Event management* is a process that monitors all events occurring through the IT infrastructure to allow for normal operation, as well as to detect and escalate exception conditions.
- *Incident management* is a process that focuses on restoring, as quickly as possible, the service to normal operating conditions in the event of an exception, in order to minimize business impact.
- *Problem management* is a process that drives root-cause analysis to determine and resolve the cause of events and incidents (reactive), and activities to determine patterns based on service behavior to prevent future events or incidents (proactive).
- *Request fulfillment* is a process that involves the management of customer or user requests that are not generated as an incident from an unexpected service delay or disruption.
- *Security Management* is a process to allow authorized users to use the service while restricting access to nonauthorized users (access control).
- *Provisioning management* is a process that allows the cloud service provider to configure and maintain the infrastructure remotely. Advantages include ease of use, speed in provisioning, and ease of maintenance of the cloud infrastructure.

> Assessing production readiness in terms of service operational readiness means:
> Ready to support the operations and maintenance of the services.

25.6.9 Key Performance Indicators (KPIs)

KPIs should be set and defined as part of the service design to develop an effective metric of measurement for the service. An effectiveness service metric can be achieved by focusing on a few vital, meaningful indicators that are economical and useful for measuring results of the service performance. Some of the examples of KPIs that can be established are:

- Metrics measuring performance of the service against the strategic business and IT plans
- Metrics on risks and compliance against regulatory, security, and corporate governance requirements for the service
- Metrics measuring financial contributions of the service to the business
- Metrics monitoring the key IT processes supporting the service
- Service-level reporting
- Metrics measuring customer satisfaction

Assessing production readiness in terms of key performance indicators means:
   Effective metric of measurement for the service has been developed.

25.6.10 Acceptance Testing

The last criteria before a cloud service is ready for production is an adequate level of measurement set in the KPI metrics. There are several tests that should be planned and carried out:

- *Load Testing.* Simulating expected and stretched loads for stress testing
- *User Testing.* Simulating user activities, including provisioning, transactional, and other usage patterns.
- *Fault Tolerance Testing.* Fault tolerance testing is to stress test the service architecture in the event of an unexpected fault.
- *Recovery Testing.* Testing of recovery procedures in the event of failure to determine the accuracy of recovery procedures and the effects of failure on the consumers.
- *Network Testing.* Assessment of network readiness and latency requirements to determine if the cloud infrastructure is capable of allowing the maximum number of concurrent consumers (under planned maximum load).
- *Charging and Billing Testing.* Validate charging, billing and invoicing for the use of a cloud services.

Assessing production readiness in terms of acceptance testing means: The service has passed an adequate level of measurement set in KPI metrics.

25.7 SUMMARY

In this chapter we discussed the consideration for cloud service providers to build the cloud service. To the cloud service provider, designing, building, implementing, and commissioning underlying technology infrastructure translates to creating the foundation to produce the service that is ready for consumption. This chapter provides clarity on what are the elements that are required to be assessed, evaluated, tested, and accepted prior to classifying a produced service is ready for consumption. These foundation elements will be used to produce the cloud service that will be ready for consumption.

REFERENCES

1. K. Stanoevska-Slabeva, and T. Wozniak, S. Ristol, *Grid and Cloud Computing: A Business Perspective on Technology and Applications*, Springer, Berlin, 2009.

2. The Stationery Office, *The Official Introduction to the ITIL Service Lifecycle, OGC (Office of Government Commerce)*, United Kingdom, 2007.

3. J. van Bon and A. van der Veen, *Foundations of IT Service Management based on ITIL*, Vol. 3, Van Haren Publishing, Zaltbommel, September 2007.

4. M. Miller, Cloud Computing: Web-based applications that change the way you work and collaborate online, Que, 2008.

5. D. C. Plummer, D. Smith, T. J. Bittman, D. W. Cearley, D. J. Cappuccio, D. Scott, R. Kumar, and B. Robertson, Gartner highlights five attributes of cloud computing, Gartner Report, Vol G00167182, pp. 1–5, May 5, 2009.

6. R. Buyya, C. S. Yeo, and S Venugopal, Market-oriented cloud computing: Vision, hype, and reality for delivering IT services as computing utilities, in *Proceedings of the 10th IEEE International Conference on High Performance Computing and Communications* (HPCC 2008, IEEE CS Press, Los Alamitos, CA, USA), Dalian, China, September 25–27, 2008.

7. D. Alger, Build the Best Data Center Facility for Your Business, Cisco Press, Indianapolis, USA, June 2005.

INDEX

Cloud Computing: Principles and Paradigms, Edited by Rajkumar Buyya, James Broberg and Andrzej Goscinski   Copyright © 2011 John Wiley & Sons, Inc.

Printed in the United States
By Bookmasters